ARAB ATTITUDES TO ISRAEL

Y. HARKABI

ARAB ATTITUDES TO ISRAEL

TRANSLATED BY MISHA LOUVISH

VALLENTINE, MITCHELL–LONDON

First published in Great Britain in 1972 by
VALLENTINE, MITCHELL & CO. LTD.,
67 Great Russell Street, London, WC1 3BT.

First published in Israel by
ISRAEL UNIVERSITIES PRESS
a wholly owned subsidiary of the
ISRAEL PROGRAM FOR SCIENTIFIC TRANSLATIONS LTD.

ISBN 0 853 03157 6

This book has been composed, printed and bound at
Keter Press, Jerusalem, Israel, 1972

To the victims of the conflict—
Jews and Arabs

CONTENTS

INTRODUCTION

CHAPTER 1. THE ARAB OBJECTIVE IN THE CONFLICT   1

INTRODUCTION

This work constitutes a doctoral thesis presented to the Hebrew University of Jerusalem on April 30, 1967, about a month before the outbreak of the Six-Day War. The war intensified public interest in the Arab-Israel conflict and its causes, but I had to delay the (Hebrew) publication of the work to March 1968, since University regulations do not allow a doctoral dissertation to be published before it has been examined and approved.

The Arab attitude to Israel is, of course, affected by the vicissitudes of time, and war can certainly change public attitudes and make descriptions of previous situations out of date. It seems, however, that my description of the attitude is still valid. Hence, I have chosen to publish this work as it was presented to the University, apart from some improvements in the course of revision, the addition of several quotations from books that came to hand after the war, the expansion of several matters dealt with in brief, and a number of omissions, especially in the notes. In the course of translation, too, some of the notes have been incorporated in the text for the reader's convenience. Even when changes take place in the Arab attitude towards Israel, it will have been worthwhile recording the situation as it was, especially as the influence of some elements of the attitude is liable to persist even after it has altered. I have added a postscript to sum up some of the developments since the Six-Day War.

Since many of the opinions and ideas presented in this work were controversial, and were criticized by many people in Israel, I had to support them with evidence and numerous quotations. As a result of the war, and statements by the Arabs before and after, these concepts are now better known, but for the sake of completeness I have kept most of the quotations, even if they may be regarded as proving what is common knowledge. I cannot assess which of the ideas are really generally accepted.

My research was conducted under the guidance of Professor G. Baer and Professor J. Talmon. Without their help, I should have been unable to write this book as a research study, and I am grateful for their assistance. I wish to thank Mr. M. Louvish for his patience and the work he has devoted to the translation. I also wish to acknowledge Mr. Uri Davis' aid in transliterating Arabic names and in compiling the index.

1. AIM AND METHOD

The isolation of the attitude of one party to a conflict is, in a sense, an act of truncation. Nevertheless, it has been possible to make the Arab attitude the subject of a separate study because of the large degree of autonomy that characterizes it, namely, its relative irresponsiveness to the Israeli attitude. Nevertheless, I found it necessary, for my own edification—in the margin of this work, as it were—to survey the Israeli attitude and study the relations between it and that of the Arabs. My conclusions are to be found in my Hebrew booklet: *The Attitude of Israel in the Arab-Israel Dispute* (Devir, 1966/7, to be published shortly in English translation).

Using the terminology of social psychology, I shall distinguish three main components in the "attitude," which is a basic concept in the entire work.[1]

a) THE COGNITIVE-EVALUATIVE COMPONENT: the thinking of the Arabs about the various aspects of the conflict, their view of Israel and their self-images in the framework of the conflict, including their value judgements on these matters.

b) THE EMOTIONAL (AFFECTIVE) COMPONENT: the emotions reflected in the attitude: anger, hostility, affront, hatred and the like.

c) THE ACTION COMPONENT: what they want to do to Israel, their objective in the conflict. This component is also the connective link between the attitude and the reality, the manner in which they want to influence reality, their programme, or the practical and political content of the attitude.

These three components are closely connected and intertwined. From the viewpoint of the Arabs, the explanation of their emotions is to be found in the cognitive-evaluative component; that is, since Israel is described as blameworthy, she deserves their hostility. Conversely, the Arabs are hostile to Israel (the emotional component), and this hostility influences their view of her as vile. The action component, the verdict that is passed against Israel, is the logical outcome of the negative image of Israel and the Arabs' emotional attitude towards her. The cognitive and action components have an ideological and intellectual dimension, which consists of the explanations and reasons used to justify their attitude and policy towards Israel. I have called this intellectual dimension the *Arab ideology* in the conflict.

The usual and accepted methods of research on attitudes, by means of public opinion surveys, questionnaires and interviews, are not available to an Israeli in this case.[2] Even if the road was open, it would be a long one: field studies encompassing the Arab countries would constitute a gigantic operation requiring an enormous team of researchers and involving not only methodological and practical difficulties, but also the problem of obtaining permission from the Arab Governments.

The method I have adopted is to study the Arabs' own statements about the conflict and its various aspects in their press, radio and literature, in which much attention is devoted to the subject. This method raises problems of principle affecting the methodological approach on which this work is based, as well as its spirit and structure.

2. GENERALIZATION, IDENTIFICATION AND SINCERITY

How can the attitude of such a large and variegated population be summed up? We might say that "the Arab attitude" consists of what is common to all the Arabs in connection with the conflict, but such common ground is meagre. Most of the Arabs are not concerned with the conflict, and it has no concrete reality for them. Furthermore, the masses do not usually articulate their opinions: for these, we must turn to the moulders of public opinion: political leaders, journalists and authors, the spiritual mentors of the day. Their statements will serve as the primary source for this study. This procedure has the advantage over the survey method that the research will concentrate on those who develop, mould and articulate the ideology, who establish the link between the political attitude and the public attitude.

It is not enough, however, to record the views of the political and cultural elite. We must enquire to what extent the public identifies with these ideas. Since I cannot examine this question directly by field studies, I shall try to investigate signs that may indicate the extent of identification and factors that may affect it.

There may, it is true, be certain Arab circles whose opinions on the conflict are different from those that are publicly expressed, but so long as these do not voice their views there is no possibility of knowing them, or even of knowing whether they exist at all, and they are not part of the effective public opinion[3] which is expressed in word or deed. Since we are concerned with the public and political attitude, we must pay attention to ideas that have been publicly expressed and are intended to influence the public and stimulate it to action.

Throughout our study, we shall have to be concerned with the question of whether the statements of the Arab spokesmen really express their true attitudes, or are only a facade. Of course, even an ostensible attitude is not devoid of significance, for it reveals the opinions which the spokesmen wish to be given credit for holding, or those they desire to impart to their listeners. From this point of view, considerable importance attaches to the speeches of the leaders and the publications of the propaganda machines, since they indicate the kind of public opinion which the Arab Governments wish to create.

3. PENETRATION IN DEPTH AND PERCEPTION OF SIGNIFICANCE

The Arab attitude in the Arab-Israel conflict is not some metaphysical entity with an independent existence, but a complex of Arab ideas and emotions. We shall examine the structure of this complex and the question of whether it is possible to discover the trends dictated by its specific character.

In order to determine the cognitive element in the attitude, we must identify the themes and ideas which compose it and determine its content; we must then assemble them and try to uncover their implications. To understand the attitude, we must trace the connections between its parts and examine its inner logic. The significance of each item can be understood only in the light of its integration in the fabric of the whole attitude. The quest for the inner logic of the attitude involves the organization of the ideas it contains in a systematic structure, which is the Arab ideology in the conflict. The ideologist tries to present his arguments in systematic form and develops an ideological structure which aims at carrying conviction. In this work, however, the aim is different: a systematic reconstruction of the ideas for purposes of *analysis:* their arrangement in such a way that we can examine them separately and in their mutual inter-relations, paying attention not only to the consistency of the ideas but to the lack of consistency.

In order to discern the significances latent in the ideas and their manifestations, we must use various disciplines and see to what extent the specific viewpoints of each can help to deepen our understanding and insight. An international conflict is a complex phenomenon, which calls for a broad, multi-disciplinary approach drawing illumination from social psychology, sociology, the theory of conflicts, history, political science, the study of international relations, communications theory and semantics, etc. In dealing with the problems which will emerge, a considerable degree of methodological flexibility will be required, sometimes resorting to one method and sometimes to another. The ideal will be to achieve a synthesis of the findings and a comprehensive, generalized view. The effort to assemble and organize the ideas, and lay bare their significance, has been the main concern of this study.

4. IDEOLOGY AND HISTORY

Since the main purpose of this study is the examination of the ideas embodied in the Arab attitude, the discussion follows the content of the ideas and not the chronological order of their development. The aim has been, first and foremost, to describe the attitude, with its various ideas and shades of opinion, and only secondarily its development. Hence the historical events which constituted the background and the conditions for its development do not occupy the place they deserve in this work. However, although it is not a historical study, it is a study in history, in the sense that matters are examined, as far as possible, in connection with the relevant historical situations.

Since the present study does not deal with a chapter from the past, which has come to a final close, but with one which is living and developing, its conclusions are limited in advance from the point of view of time, and they are provisional.

Although the scope of the study is restricted and it does not deal with the relationships between the opponents, but only with the attitude of one side, it is still fairly extensive, and I have been unable to enquire thoroughly into all the subjects involved. Since this is the first research work of its kind on the conflict, I have also regarded it as a kind of field survey. I had to consider what questions should be asked about the various aspects of the conflict and not only to seek for answers. Almost every aspect examined in this work is worthy of detailed historical research and a special monograph. Some aspects appear to me to call for more fundamental enquiry, and occasionally I have noted openings for further research. I have no doubt that detailed studies will correct concepts, limit generalizations, and sharpen distinctions, contained in this study.

5. SELECTIVITY AND THE PSYCHOLOGY OF THE RESEARCHER

I have used many sources from political works, periodical literature and broadcasts, and have had to select what is most important and instructive. Such selection depends on the personal judgement and taste of the selector. I have quoted passages which appear to me to be representative or instructive; since this is a study of ideology, I have had to present an unwieldy mass of quotations from Arab spokesmen in order to illustrate the frequency with which ideas or concepts occur. Of course, I have not read all that has been said or written by Arabs on the conflict, since the flood of material is infinite. There may be important statements that I have not seen, and some that I have ignored because I have not regarded them as important or representative, or because they seem to me to be mere repetitions and variations of themes already mentioned. I have read much of the Arabic material that has come into my hands and I believe that the picture I have painted is fairly complete.*

A fundamental problem in a study of this kind is that of the researcher's own psychology: how can an Israeli be objective, since he is not indifferent to the subject or the results of his research, as he himself is saturated with memories and emotions associated with the conflict? How can he be clear-sighted and avoid a distortion of his judgement by what Professor Rapaport has called the "blindness of involvement" *(Fights, Games and Debates, 1966)*?

* In addition to newspapers and broadcasts, this work is based on an examination of the attitude to Israel in some 120 publications on the subject written by Arabs. Some thirty more have reached me after the Six-Day War. (For a comprehensive list, see the bibliography.) These are actually only a part of the books written by Arabs on various aspects of the dispute—which amount to more than one thousand publications.

It is true that involvement and concern in the subject may also be useful, leading to a more penetrating insight, but I am afraid that this may be an unbalanced insight, springing from "hostile intuition," and liable to uncover the negative aspects and ignore the positive ones which may be revealed by "sympathetic intuition."

There is also an intellectual and moral problem. There are many pitfalls in the way of an analysis of international conflict and an attempt to examine the emotions and behaviour of opponents by psychological means, especially when the scalpel is wielded against one side alone. There is a danger that the act of psychological analysis may imbue the analyst with feelings of superiority, on the ground that he has discovered what an entire people has failed to perceive; and the asymmetrical nature of the study may involve a moral distortion. I had to suspect myself of being alert in criticizing the Arab attitude and eager to discover its faults, hidden motives and weaknesses, while, on the other hand, being insensitive in examining the Zionist and Israeli attitude. I was much troubled by these problems.

I could guard against these pitfalls only by the method of self-criticism. I tried to analyse my own approaches, prejudices and value assumptions in regard to the conflict, in the hope that raising them to the plane of consciousness would help me to arrive at a correct judgement. This analysis is described in the final section, on The Problem of Subjectivity.

Side by side with the collection and analysis of the material, therefore, the work of research was also accompanied by an effort to teach myself empathy and perceive the element of relativity in the justice of the attitudes of the opponents; to understand the Arab attitude, and sometimes to attribute aspects of it to which I am unsympathetic to the tragic historical developments. I believe my account of the Israeli attitude has helped me, for I have discovered to what extent both sides are enmeshed in the net of their conceptions and the web of their destiny.

6. GENERAL REMARKS

In writing this book, including this introduction, I have used more or less the dialectical method; matters first mentioned in passing are later considered in more detail. The reader may, therefore, find replies to his objections at a later stage.

Sources are generally given in parentheses in the text, in an abbreviated form, usually by the surname of the author with the number of the page on which the quotations appear. The full names of the works quoted are given at the end of the book in alphabetical order according to the author's surname. Quotations from the speeches of Gamal Abdel-Nasser are generally identified by the date of the speech, since the texts are to be found in the press and in collections of his speeches. Sometimes the reference is in this form: I.L., XI/2146, which means: Volume XI, p. 2146 of the collection of his speeches in the Ikhtarnā Lak ("Chosen for You") edition. For the sake of brevity, he has been referred to as Nasser, and not by his full name.

Three dots (. . .) in a quotation indicate an omission.

7. TRANSLITERATOR'S NOTES

(a) In the transliteration of Arabic words and names, the spelling and not the pronunciation has been followed; thus, the "l" in the definite article "al" has been retained even when in speech it is assimilated to the following (anteropalatal) letter. Surnames (e.g. Nashāshībī), which are preceded in Arabic by the definite article "al-," will very often appear, for the sake of brevity, without it, but the "al-" will usually appear when they are preceded by the given names. (b) Names of leaders and writers frequently mentioned in the world press, such as King Hussein, Hassanin Haykal and Ahmad Shukairy, have been given in the more commonly known forms; the same will also apply to names (e.g. Ahmad, Muhammad) that are familiar to the English reader. (c) Similarly, names of Arab authors whose books have been published in English have been given in the form in which they appeared in the English versions.

(d) In the transliteration of "Abu," the long vowel and the inflections (Abā, Abī) have been systematically ignored.

(e) The glottal stop (hamza) " ' " is not indicated in transliteration at the beginning of words.

(f) The feminine form ö . . . *(tā'marbūṭa)* is not indicated in transliteration, except when in the construct-state (e.g. Dawla v. Dawlat Isrā'īl).

(g) Nunnation and cases have also been omitted.

(h) Gemination *(tashdīd)* is indicated by doubling of the geminated letter, unless an end vowel, in which case the gemination is dropped.

TABLE OF TRANSLITERATION

ا (ء)	a(')[1]	ض	ḍ
ب	b	ط	ṭ
ت	t	ظ	ẓ
ث	th	ع	'
ج	j	غ	gh
ح	ḥ	ف	f
خ	kh	ق	q
د	d	ك	k
ذ	dh	ل	l
ر	r	م	m
ز	z	ن	n
س	s	ه	h
ش	sh	و	w
ص	ṣ	ي	y

Short Vowels		*Long Vowels*	
ـَ	a	ـَا/ى	ā
ـِ	i	ـِي	ī
ـُ	u	ـُو	ū

Diphthongs

ـَو	aw
ـَي	ay
ـِيّ	iyy[2]
ـُوّ	uww[3]

[1] not indicated when initial

[2] see note (h)

Chapter 1

THE ARAB OBJECTIVE IN THE CONFLICT

The objectives, or the opposition between the objectives, of the rival parties to a conflict are the conscious and quintessential expression of the controversy embodied in it, for the nature of a conflict is a clash between incompatible objectives. The common definition of conflicts is based on this idea.[1] The objective in the conflict is the central axis of the attitude of the party in question and endows it with significance. The present chapter, which deals with the objectives of the Arabs in the conflict, will therefore cover many elements in their attitude which will be explained in detail in later chapters.[2]

Once the conflict has come into being and become institutionalized, it acquires a life and momentum of its own. After the antagonisms have produced a conflict, the conflict arouses further antagonisms. One dispute stimulates further disputes—which lead to the conflict spilling over. Conflict between states as a political phenomenon percolates to the level of the masses and is reflected in attitudes and hostilities, while, on the other hand, popular attitudes and hostilities are liable to influence the political course of the conflict.

The objective of the conflict need not be explicitly declared, but as the leaders wish to mobilize the cooperation and support of their peoples, they must proclaim, explain and justify their policy and aims, for an international conflict is a political and social phenomenon, and a political goal can become common property only if it is publicly proclaimed. Declarations made by the rivals in the conflict about their attitudes, their dedication to the objective and their determination to achieve it, endow the position with an additional dimension, as it becomes a commitment.

The objective which has been proclaimed day and night by the Arab leaders is "the liquidation of the State of Israel."

To what extent does this proclaimed objective indeed represent their thoughts and purposes? What does it signify?

The first phenomenon which leaps to the eye and which, at first sight, seems surprising, is the large number of alternative expressions used by the Arabs to denote their objective. These may be classified in two main groups: (1) express, explicit and undisguised statements calling upon the Arabs to liquidate Israel; (2) ambiguous, oblique expressions, which may be understood in different ways and do not expressly refer to liquidation, but nevertheless imply it.

1. UNDISGUISED EXPRESSIONS OF OBJECTIVE

"Liquidation" or "ending" *(qaḍā' 'alā),* the expression with the highest frequency; "wiping out" *(maḥq, maḥū),* "purification" or "cleansing" *(taṣfiya);* "removal" *(izāla, izāḥa);* "throwing into the sea"; "death sentence"; "throttling"; "crushing" *(saḥq);* "destruction"; "ruination" *(tadmīr);* "pulling up by the root" *(isti'sāl);* "eradication"; "overthrow" *(isqāṭ);* "sweeping out" *(iktisāḥ);* "bringing to an end" *(inhā');* "elimination" *(fanā')* and the like. All these terms emphasize action to implement the liquidation.

Here are a few examples:

> "Arab unity means the liquidation *(al-qaḍā''alā)* of Israel and the expansionist dreams of Zionism." (Nasser at the Festival of Unity, February 22, 1965).

> "The Arab people will pronounce the death sentence against criminal Israel, namely disappearance."
>
> "Israel is the cancer, the malignant wound, in the body of Arabism, for which there is no cure but eradication." "There is no need to emphasize that the liquidation of Israel and the restoration of the plundered Palestine Arab land are at the head of our national objectives." (Commentator on Cairo Radio, April 20, 1963, at 20:55 hrs.).

> "The victory over the power of colonialism in Algeria was a brilliant step for the overthrow of the base in the Maghreb, so that it should be a prelude to the overthrow of another base for colonialism in the East—I refer to Israel." (Nasser, July 3, 1962).

Direct expressions may be divided into two sub-groups: in the first, which covers the majority, the active, liquidating factor is specified, or at least the action necessitates an active factor, and it is clear that it will be the Arabs who will initiate the operation, or at least participate in it.

For instance: "Israel is a plague which must be liquidated" implies that the Arabs must act for the achievement of this goal.

In the second group, the liquidation is presented in somewhat more elegant terms as a process that will take place itself, without the initiating factor being specified.

Such formulae include expressions like: "disappearance," "Israel will disappear" *(takhtafī),* "collapse" *(inhiyār);* "clearing out" *(zawāl),* "downfall" *(suqūṭ);* "Israel will not escape her inevitable fate," "Israel will die" or "the end of Israel" *(nihāyat Isrā'īl);* "non-survival" or "non-existence" *(lā baqā').*

According to *al-Ahrām,* for instance, Ben Bella declared on May 1, 1965:

> "There is a need for Israel to disappear, for it is an artificial creation and it is necessary to put an end to it" *(wa-yanbaghī al-qaḍā' 'alayhā)* (May 2, 1965).
> "No Arab Unity Without the Disappearance of Israel" (name of pamphlet issued by Arab Higher Committee, Cairo, November, 1958).
> "The fate of this State is extinction, for it was born dead" (*al-Maḥlāwī* in *Egyptian Political Science Review*, January–March, 1959, 1. 118).

Even where the process is described as taking place of its own accord, the meaning may be more active, e.g:

> "The collapse of Israel, this is the hope in which we live. The time has come for us to consider it, to discuss and map out the road to this collapse." (Ahmad Sa'īd, the Director of Cairo Radio (Ṣawt al-'Arab), in his introduction to Ṣabrī Abu al-Majd's book, *The End of Israel,* 1960).

2. AMBIGUOUS EXPRESSIONS OF OBJECTIVE

These may be of a positive nature, consisting, not of negative words like "liquidation" or "annihilation," but of terms which have a positive significance, like "liberation," but imply the aim to create a situation which is incompatible with Israel's survival, for so long as Israel exists Palestine is not liberated.

Other such expressions are: "the liberation of the Homeland," "making Palestine Arab," "the return of Palestine to its owners," "the restoration of the stolen rights," "the restoration of the status quo" or "the restoration of the situation to normalcy." In view of the special interest attached to these expressions, we shall analyse some of them in greater detail in the next section: "Terms Used to Express the Objective."

The meaning of these terms is perfectly clear to the Arabs. They emphasize a positive national goal without mentioning subsidiary results or situations which are a condition for its achievement, as if they were saying: "Our goal is the liberation of Palestine and nothing more, and if the liberation of Palestine makes it necessary that Israel should cease to exist, that is not our affair."

a) NEGATIVE EXPRESSIONS

Liquidation is also implied in expressions that deny Israel's right to exist. Examples are: "We shall not agree that the State of Israel should remain in our midst"; "we shall not accept Zionist existence"; "we shall not agree to the *fait accompli*"; "there is no room for Israel in the Arab East"· "Israel will not escape her fate."

Nasser frequently employs such indirect expressions. The following extract from one of his speeches, for example, contains oblique positive and negative expressions side by side:

> "We swear to God that we shall not rest until we restore Arab nationalism to Palestine and Palestine to the Arab nation. There is no room for imperialism and there is no room for Britain in our country, just as there is no room for Israel within the Arab nation." (Speech at Sanʿa, April 23, 1964).
>
> "The Arab people . . . will never allow Israel and those supporting Israel to realize their objectives in keeping Israel in existence in Palestine." (August 17, 1961).

In his speech at the UN Assembly on September 27, 1960, Nasser described the wrong that had been done in the Middle East by the establishment of Israel and added:

> "The only solution to Palestine . . . is that matters should return to the condition prevailing before the error was committed—i.e. the annulment of Israel's existence."

Hāshim Jawād wrote:

> "Israel, being an alien body in the Arab homeland, has no right whatsoever to continue to exist in the territories of the Arab East." (At the UN, October 6, 1960, *Middle East Record*, p. 174a).

The expression "the denunciation of Israel's existence," which also involves opposition to her existence, belongs to this group.

b) FIGURATIVE AND METAPHORICAL EXPRESSIONS

Another group, not so frequently encountered, consists of expressions whose obscurity is due to the fact that the entity to be liquidated is presented in metaphorical terms, or the action to be taken against it is ambiguous and expressed in metaphorical or figurative language.

Such expressions are: "the liquidation of the legend of Israel"—as if Israel's existence is not real, but only legendary; "the obliteration of Zionist existence"—here the intention is not that Israel should cease to be Zionist, but that Israel, as a manifestation of Zionism, should be liquidated; "the light of Israel shall be extinguished"; "the eradication of the root of the evil from our midst"; "the eradication of the root of the disaster."

3. PHRASES COINED TO EXPRESS THE OBJECTIVE

A number of very frequently used conventional formulae have been developed in the language used by the Arabs to express their objective. They are all ambiguous in respect of the direct demand for the liquidation of Israel, and their characteristic feature is that they may be given either of two meanings: moderate or extreme, minimum or maximum.

a) "RESTORATION OF STOLEN RIGHTS"

This is a very widespread expression. On the surface, it might be thought to signify permission to the Arab refugees to return to Israel and have their property restored, but the meaning or the purpose may be more extreme. For instance, in a letter sent by Nasser to King Hussein on March 13, 1961, in which he explained his policy to the Arab world, he wrote:

> "We believe that the evil which has been introduced into the heart of the Arab world must be eradicated *(yogtala*ʿ*)*, and that the rights which have been usurped from the Arabs must be returned to their owners."

That is, the restoration of the rights is connected with or conditional on the liquidation of Israel.

In another statement, Nasser said:

"Arab unity and united action are the way to the liberation of Palestine and the restoration of the rights." (March 8, 1965).

"The liberation of Palestine" means the establishment of an Arab State on the ruins of Israel. Again, the destruction of Israel and restoration of rights are interconnected.

The rights are generally described as applying, not to individuals, but to a "people"; they are not the rights of citizens to their property, but "political" rights or "the right to the national homeland." Thus, Nasser says:

"When we speak of Palestine and say that we want the liberation of the Palestinian people, to which we shall restore its political and social rights . . ." (I.L., X/1903, January 27, 1958).

Nasser thus emphasizes the "rights of the Palestinian people" (a term which he uses repeatedly). Similarly, the decisions of the first Summit Conference on January 16, 1964 refer to "the natural right of this people to return to its homeland" (Shukrī, p. 154).

In the conclusion of his letter of August 18, 1961 to President Kennedy, Nasser wrote:

"My aim was to explain to you that the right of the Arab Palestinian is connected with the right of the Palestinian Motherland, and that the other Arab nations cannot isolate themselves from the aggression launched on one of them." (*al-Ahrām,* September 21, 1962).

It may be assumed that the expression "usurped rights" is not to be understood as referring to the rights of the refugees; for Arab nationalists the exclusion of a territory from Arab rule constitutes "robbery of rights."

Thus, the terms, "the usurped homeland" or "the stolen homeland" (*al-waṭan al-salīb; al-waṭan al-mughtaṣab*) are frequent.

b) "LIBERATION," "RESTORATION" OR "DELIVERANCE" OF PALESTINE, "THE OCCUPIED TERRITORY," "THE MOTHERLAND" OR "THE PLUNDERED LAND"; "RETURN" OR "HOMECOMING" (*TAḤRIR, TAḤARRUR, ISTI'AD, ISTIRDĀD, ISTIRJĀ', ISTINQĀDH, ISTIKHLĀṢ*)

These expressions do not indicate, as might be imagined, the partial return of Israeli territory or the right of the refugees to come and live in

Israel, but that Israel should become entirely Arab. It is not a matter of the return of the refugees to Israeli territory but the return of Israeli territory to the refugees. Thus Nasser said:

> "The people of Palestine will return to be masters in Palestine whether the war criminal Ben-Gurion announces this or not." (Speech in June 1960, quoted in Cremeans: *The Arabs and the World,* p. 189).

The refugees, that is, will return as a nation taking over their country.

Again, Nasser declared:

> "It is not the intention to restore half of our honour or half the homeland, but the whole of our honour and the whole of our homeland." (Quoted by Haykal, *al-Ahrām,* May 18, 1962).

The expression "complete restoration" *(al-'awda al-kāmila)* is frequent.

The preamble to the National Covenant of the Palestine Liberation Organization (May 28, 1964) calls for "the complete restoration of our lost homeland." Article 2 of the Charter states:

> "Palestine with its boundaries at the time of the British Mandate is a regional indivisible unit" *(lā tatajazza').*

and Article 3 adds:

> "The Palestinian Arab people has the legitimate right to its homeland."

Haykal refers to "the restoration of the complete rights of the Palestinian people" (*al-Ahrām,* November 29, 1963).

The return which is involved in the disappearance of Israel is frequently called "an honourable return" *('awda sharīfa).* Nāṣir al-Dīn al-Nashāshībī explains:

> "We do not want to return with the flag of Israel flying on a single square metre of our country, and if indeed we wish to return, this is an honoured and honourable return *(sharīfa, musharrafa)* and not a degrading *(dhalīla)* return, not a return that will make us citizens in the State of Israel." (*al-Jumhūriyya,* May 14, 1961).

These references to "liberation" and "return" have become more frequent and emphatic. The term *al-ʿawda,* return or homecoming, has become a symbol, a central watchword for the activity of the organization of Palestinian refugees (who are, therefore, called "the returners"). The "return" is described as a tremendous historic event in which Israel will be liquidated and the country will become Arab property.

c) "JUST SOLUTION FOR THE PALESTINE PROBLEM," "JUST PEACE," "PEACE ON THE BASIS OF JUSTICE," "NON-ACCEPTANCE OF THE *FAIT ACCOMPLI*," "SETTLEMENT ACCORDING TO LEGAL RIGHTS," "SOLUTION ACCORDING TO UN PRINCIPLES"

The Arabs emphasize that they seek a "just solution" or a "just peace," which constitutes the opposite pole to a peace or solution founded on the *status quo,* on the fact of Israel's existence. The just solution, according to this view, is the annulment of the wrong involved in the very existence of Israel and the restoration of Israel to its legal owners. Justice is a denial of Israel's existence. Thus Nasser says:

> "We talk peace, but we do not accept peace that is based on the usurpation of rights and on the *fait accompli.* That is why we work for peace, but we want peace based on justice." (Speech at Alexandria University, July 28, 1963).

In other words, a just peace, according to this view, means the peace that will reign after the disappearance of Israel.

Joint statements after visits by distinguished personalities and resolutions passed at conferences often include a demand for "a just solution," "a solution according to the UN Charter" or "the principles of the UN," or "a settlement according to natural rights" or "legal rights." The visitor or the delegates to the conference understand this as a "minimal obligation" and it contains no apparent hint that the aim is the destruction of a State. These expressions have quite a different connotation for the Arabs, who are convinced that Israel's existence is an injustice and a violation of the legal rights of the Palestinian Arabs. The National Covenant of the Palestine Liberation Organization refers in the preamble to:

> ". . . the complete restoration of our lost homeland—a right that has been recognized by international covenants and common practices including the Charter of the United Nations . . ."

The Arabs therefore regard the agreement of foreigners to the formula of "a just solution" as support for their rejection of the *"fait accompli"* of Israel's existence.

Nāṣir al-Dīn al-Nashāshībī, the editor of *al-Jumhūriyya,* comments in his paper on a statement by Khrushchev, in a speech at Port Said, supporting "a just solution" of the Palestine problem:

"The people of Port Said listened to the speech of the illustrious visitor from the Soviet Union, in which he said that Russia recognizes the necessity for a logical and just solution to the problem of Palestine. The people of Port Said are well aware that a just solution to the problem of Palestine means the restoration of Palestine to the Arabs and the resettlement of all the refugees in their plundered homeland. The just solution is the liquidation of imperialism represented by Israel, which serves it as a base and bridgehead." (*al-Jumhūriyya,* May 20, 1964).[3]

d) "RECTIFICATION (OR UNDOING) OF THE CRIME (INJUSTICE OR MISTAKE) OF 1948"

On the surface, this expression might be understood as denoting the return of the refugees to Israel and the restriction of Israel to the borders laid down in the UN Resolution of 1947. Again, however, we find that this is not necessarily so and that, in common usage, these are only euphemisms for liquidation. The "crime" or "error" does not consist in Israel's expansion beyond the borders of the UN partition plan, but in the very fact of its establishment.

In the letter to Hussein quoted above, Nasser specifies his goal: "The eradication of the evil that has been introduced into the Arab world" (i.e. Israel), and he goes on to say that forces must be established according to "the extent of the total independent force required to rectify the crime that was committed in 1948"—i.e. a force sufficient to defeat and liquidate Israel.

"The restoration of the situation to normalcy" is also, as we have seen, a euphemism for liquidation.

e) "PURGING (OR LIQUIDATION) OF ZIONIST (OR ISRAELI) AGGRESSION," "LIQUIDATION OF ISRAEL'S AGGRESSIVE EXISTENCE," "LIQUIDATION OF ZIONIST RACISM"

Such terms as these might be understood as expressing an educational purpose: the eradication of aggression and racism in Israel. In the National Charter of the UAR, however, the meaning of these terms is clarified:

> "The insistence of our people on liquidating the Israeli aggression on a part of Palestine is a determination to liquidate one of the most dangerous pockets of imperialist resistance against the struggles of peoples." (Chapter 10).

The parallelism between "liquidating the Israeli aggression" and "to liquidate one of the . . . pockets of Imperialist resistance" shows clearly that the purpose is to destroy and not to change. (Official translation, p. 96).

f) "LIBERATION OF THE MOTHERLAND FROM ZIONISM," "LIBERATION FROM ZIONISM" OR "ZIONIST IMPERIALISM," "THE ENDING OF ZIONIST OCCUPATION," "DELIVERANCE OF THE HOMELAND FROM THE ZIONISTS," "LIBERATION FROM THE DANGER OF ZIONISM"

The overt meaning of "liberation from Zionism" is liberation from the threat of Zionism in general, or from the threat of Zionist expansion—i.e. such an increase in Arab strength that Zionism will cease to be a threat, or a change in the character of Zionism. When used by Nasser, however, the aim appears to be more extreme:

> "We cannot liberate ourselves from imperialism or from Zionism before we liberate ourselves from reaction and exploitation." (January 9, 1963).

Liberation from reaction means putting an end to reaction, and liberation from Zionism, therefore, means, not to exert such an influence on Israel that she will cease to be Zionist, but to put an end to Israel, which is the expression of Zionism. Thus, the decision of the second Summit Conference states:

> "The Conference decided unanimously to define the national goal, which is the liberation of Palestine from Zionist imperialism." (Cairo Radio, September 11, 1964).

The aim is to restore Palestine and make it completely Arab.

In the tripartite treaty of union signed on April 16, 1963 by Egypt, Iraq and Syria, the goal is presented as:

> "The achievement of a military union capable of liberating the homeland from the danger of Zionism and imperialism." (*al-Ahrām,* May 17, 1963).

g) "REPULSION OF THE ZIONIST DANGER" OR "ZIONIST AGGRESSION" OR "ISRAELI AGGRESSION," "DEFENCE OF ARAB NATIONALISM," "PROTECTION OF RIGHTS," "RESISTANCE TO THE ISRAELI DANGER"

The strangest usages, however, are those employing such terms as "repulsion," "defence" and "preservation." These ostensibly describe a defensive situation, but in current usage they may be given an offensive connotation, as if it is argued that because of Israel's essentially "aggressive" nature her liquidation is an act of defence.

Haykal, for example, describes how an Arab leader met the leaders of the Ba'th and asked them

> ". . . what were their plans for repulsing the Israeli danger, adding that without the Egyptian army, especially after the development of its revolutionary armament, there was no prospect of preventing Israeli expansion and restoring Palestine." (*al-Ahrām,* August 9, 1963).

From this wording, it may be understood that "the repulsion of the Israeli danger" had a dual significance: a) defensive: to ward off Israeli expansion; b) offensive: the restoration of Palestine to the Arab world, namely the liquidation of Israel.

Similarly, Nasser said:

> The rights of the Palestinian people must not be lost. We shall claim them, but not with words and talk. We shall claim them with every possible means. We must prepare. It is the army on which we rely in the achievement of our aims and the defence *(ḥimā)* of our hope." (July 22, 1962).

In other words: our right and our hope are the restoration of Palestine, which we shall claim not by words but by force. This task will be carried out by the army, the army is the guarantee for the "defence" of our hope, namely for its implementation. Since the hope is for the restoration of Palestine and the liquidation of Israel, the "defence" of the hope signifies action to carry out the liquidation.

Similarly, Shukairy's introduction to the National Covenant of the Palestine Liberation Organization, which he headed at the time, defines the function of the organization as:

> ". . . a mobilizing leadership of the forces of the Palestine Arab people to wage the battle of liberation, as a shield for the rights and aspirations of the people of Palestine and as a road to victory."

Similar uses of such terms may be seen in the following examples:

After having declared that "Israel will not escape her inevitable fate," Nasser speaks of the time "when we shall decide to enter into the battle in order to face the Israeli danger" (March 27, 1964).

On another occasion he declared:

> "The rights of the people of Palestine must return to this people. Therefore we must prepare to face Israel, Zionism and Imperialism, which supports them." (August 11, 1963).

Facing Israel, which is an ostensibly defensive posture, is presented as involving the restoration of rights, which is an offensive operation.[4] The use of such words as "defence," "facing" or "standing up to" in active senses is not a mere rhetorical device. As we shall see, the conception that the liquidation of Israel is necessary as an act of defence is pretty common among Arab spokesmen.

Nasser uses the widespread concept of "deterrence" in a somewhat unusual manner, for example:

> "We must be capable of deterring *(rad')* Israel in order that the rights of the Palestinian people may be restored." (February 22, 1964).

The deterrence of Israel is, thus, connected with the restoration of the rights of the Palestinians—another use of a term whose basic connotation is defensive and preventive to denote active measures for the restoration of rights.

The expression "defence of our existence" is also used in similar euphemistic senses. For Nasser, it means not only preservation of Egypt's existence, but fulfilment of broader aspirations:

> "When we say that we seek to defend our existence, we mean that we should not fall into the same trap as in 1948." (June 22, 1962).

In 1948, of course, Egypt's existence was not in any danger; "to defend our existence," therefore, is used here to mean fulfilment of the aspiration for victory in war and the defeat of the enemy.

h) "LIQUIDATION OF THE TRACES OF AGGRESSION" *(IZĀLAT ĀTHĀR AL-'UDWĀN)*

This is the Arab aim as defined after the defeat in the Six-Day War. Nasser coined this expression in his resignation speech of June 9, 1967, and it has been given widespread currency since then. It is another example of an ambiguous term which may be given a limited interpretation—bringing about the withdrawal of the Israel Defence Forces to the pre-war lines—or a broader meaning: the liquidation of Israel, for, according to Arab conceptions, Israel is fundamentally aggressive. The advantage of such a formulation is that the goal defined in it may be expanded at a later stage, although the aim may be limited for the time being because of present conditions, and it does not involve abandonment of the old goal.

4. SIGNIFICANCE OF USE OF DIRECT AND INDIRECT FORMULATIONS OF THE OBJECTIVE; CRITERIA OF FREQUENCY

An Arab leader or writer sometimes uses one expression to denote the objective and sometimes another. If we assume that these expressions differ in their meanings and denote various objectives, we must conclude that Arab spokesmen suffer from national schizophrenia, since there is a substantial difference between acceptance of Israel's existence on condition that some change or other is effected and the demand for her liquidation. If we were really confronted with various objectives, the question would arise which of them is the true one and which are only false and unreal. We may spare ourselves, however, the trouble of dealing with this problem; the Arabs are not schizophrenic in their conflict with Israel. The various expressions consistently present a single, though complex objective. The objective is the liquidation of Israel, the rectification of the injustice done to the Arabs, the restoration of the refugees to their possessions, the restoration of the Palestinian people to its land, the removal of the aberrant factor, the restoration of the homeland to Arabism, the restoration of rights, rejection of the fact created by aggression, the implementation of justice, settlement according to legal rights, self-liberation, and so forth—it makes no difference what expression is used.

But what is the meaning of this plethora of expressions and phrases used to denote the objective? Why do the Arabs need such ambiguous and indirect expressions? Is it possible to discern the circumstances in which the Arabs tend to make more use of one class of expressions, and when they use expressions of another type?

First of all, it should be pointed out that such "flexibility" in the definition of the objective is not confined to the Arabs; nor is it merely an expedient for camouflage and concealment. The tendency to define an objective in positive terms by emphasizing the desirable results which the party in question will attain through its achievement, while ignoring the undesirable consequences for the other side, is not unknown in history.

The Germans, for example, emphasized that their aim was the attainment of *"Lebensraum"*—"living space," although more living space for them meant less for their neighbours—as those neighbours realized. The Arabs, too, argue that Zionism also defined its objective in a positive form while ignoring its negative aspects, since it declared that its goal was to solve the Jewish problem, while ignoring the fact that this meant creating an Arab problem. Alternatively, if the positive aim of Zionism was the Judaisation of Palestine, its negative expression was the de-Arabisation of Palestine.[5]

Even if we suspect that the use of ambiguous and indirect expressions involves an attempt at camouflage and deceit, there is nothing new in that either. Euphemism is a common device. Hitler emphasized the injustice of the *"Diktat"* of Versailles and the need to annul its provisions when his intentions were aggressive. It is hardly necessary to recall such a perversion of language as the expression "the Final Solution." The Japanese proclaimed the aim of establishing a "Co-prosperity Sphere" when their actual purpose was the expansion of the territory under their hegemony.

It is noteworthy that the objective which is defined as an "end" may appear to be a "means" to a goal to which it is subservient. The distinction between "end" and "means" is relative. For instance, when a nation sets itself the goal of achieving independence, this is not a final aim, but may be defined as an "intermediate objective" leading to the higher goal of obtaining the benefits to be derived from national independence.

From this viewpoint of a hierarchy in aims and objectives, the Arabs could argue that their objective in the conflict is the rectification of an injustice, the solution of the refugee problem or a national geo-political settlement based on territorial continuity and the eviction of the foreign body from the Arab area, and that the liquidation of Israel is not their objective at all, but only an essential condition for its achievement, or even a subsidiary consequence of its achievement. This concept is basic to the Arab attitude.

From Israel's point of view, however, the Arab objective would be regarded as, specifically, her liquidation, not only because it is that, and not the Arab desires that are to be fulfilled after her existence is brought to an end, which interests her, but also because the liquidation of Israel is the tangible expression of the Arab objective. In this work, however, we shall regard liquidation as the Arab objective in the conflict, without ignoring the fact that from a wider point of view it is part of several objectives organically connected with each other, the results of which would be more or less simultaneous for different aspects of the same event.

It may be that the proclamation of "liquidation" as a political aim and a national ideal arouses some discomfort among the Arabs themselves, for it recalls "genocide" and "the final solution," and may repel world public opinion. A public call for liquidation of a political and national entity may arouse difficulties which, it is thought, can be avoided by the use of ambiguous expressions. Thus, the terms we have reviewed, even if they include the word "liquidation," refer to the liquidation of "aggression" or "Zionism," and not, expressly, of Israel. The ambiguous expression is, therefore, a sublimation of the express goal.

Foreign support for the Arab attitude is recruited by the use of ambiguous expressions such as "restoration of rights," a "just solution," "a peace settlement in accordance with legal rights" or "compliance with UN decisions" (the significance of the last expression will be discussed below). Foreign visitors to Arab countries can testify that they have heard no talk about the liquidation of Israel, for they do not always understand the "liquidationary" significance of the ambiguous expressions. One would hardly suspect, for instance, that liquidation is the aim which hides behind such an innocent expression as "the restoration of the position to one of normalcy"—which Nasser used in his address to the United Nations General Assembly. In a world of tribulations and abnormalities, who would refuse to support the restoration of normalcy?

Express demands for the liquidation of Israel are sometimes to be found in declarations and articles designed for external consumption, but these are in fact very rare.

The overt expressions are more frequent in declarations meant for internal consumption, though ambiguous expressions are often to be found even here. In this sphere, there is room for "ecological" distinctions between the sources of the statements. In most official declarations and statements by leaders, ambiguous, indirect expressions are used. Nasser, for example, generally sticks to such forms of words. On lower levels, especially in commentaries, as on the radio (and particularly in the broadcasts of Sawt al-Arab, which is supposed to be "freer"), the overt expressions are more frequent. This applies especially, of course, to broadcasts meant for refugees.

There may be a valid psychological reason for the use of ambiguous expressions even at home. Direct talk about the liquidation of Israel may make the Arabs themselves feel uncomfortable about the prospects of attaining the goal, for they may feel doubtful whether it is practicable. The presentation of the goal in more indirect and refined, perhaps also more positive terms, increases the likelihood that it can be achieved. The indirect expression, as it were, includes a justification of the goal, and even a guarantee that it can be reached.

Moreover, from the viewpoint of the leaders, the ambiguous and indirect expressions constitute a less binding obligation than the direct ones. "The liquidation of aggression," for instance, is easier to achieve than the liquidation of a State. The direct expression designates a complete and final goal, which has not been achieved, while many of the obscure expressions may be understood to signify a process in which, it may be argued, some advance may be registered—for Israel's failure to expand might be ascribed to the Arabs' success in this aim of "liquidating aggression" (of course before the Six-Day War). The same applies to other indirect expressions. Their very ambiguity facilitates a retreat to a meaning which involves a less far-reaching commitment.

The leaders may also feel that it is easier to get their peoples to support a goal formulated in obscure, indirect and ambiguous terms, since the more ambiguous the formula the more people will agree with it.

If the use of ambiguous expressions is connected with the extent of confidence in the achievement of the goal, it might be assumed that some correlation could be found between the ups and downs in the tide of Arab nationalism, and the proportional distribution of direct and indirect expressions. When Arab self-confidence increases, after what is regarded as an achievement—for instance, the union of Egypt and Syria to form the United Arab Republic in February 1954, which was celebrated as the beginning of Arab unity, the achievement of Algerian independence in 1959, which was regarded as a victory of Arabism over a power like France, or the first Summit Conference in January 1964, which was a symbol of Arab unity in action—there will be a relative increase in the use of direct expressions in the Arab press and radio in comparison with the indirect ones, while the opposite will be the case in times of weakness or depression. (The same trend can be established after the Six-Day War.)

It may, further, be assumed that fluctuations in the confidence of the

Arabs that their national movement is achieving its goals in the conflict will be reflected by an increase in the number of all types of reference to the objective. It appears, for example, that in the first few months after the first and second Summit Conferences there was an increase not only in the proportion of direct to indirect expressions, but also in the frequency with which liquidation was proclaimed as the goal. At these times, all Arab communications media emphasized that inter-Arab cooperation would lead to progress in the Palestine question, which had been in a state of stagnation, with the inception of a new, practical stage in the form of the establishment of a united Arab command, the formation of Shukairy's Palestine Liberation Organization (which was supported at the time by the Arab kings and presidents) and the recruitment of a Palestinian Army as its fighting arm.

These assumptions may be tested by counting the number of references to the objective by Arab communications media. It may be assumed that this technique of "measurement" may be significant in regard to various trends of thought in Arab nationalism,[6] although it cannot be regarded as a simple barometer and its value is no doubt limited. The advantage of such "measurements" is that sometimes, on the one hand, they may draw attention to phenomena which are not generally noticed and, on the other, they may add a measure of objectivity to conclusions that might be regarded as subjective personal impressions.

It may also be assumed that the fluctuations from time to time in the total number of references to the Arab objective in the conflict, or in the distribution of its various forms, are not correlated with any single factor. For example, an increase in the total number of references may be caused by increased preoccupation with the conflict as a result of a development in Israel-Arab relations, such as border incidents or international activity, that brings the conflict to the fore.

Sometimes a rise in the number of references to the objective or anti-Israel statements may have no connection at all with Arab-Israel relations, but be due to an increase in inter-Arab tensions as the result of internal conflicts, failures and frustrations. In such cases, the leadership and the communications media exploit anti-Israel expressions for internal purposes, competing with each other in ostentatious extremism towards Israel. Thus, the numerous declarations about liquidation after the first Summit Conference might be explained by considerations opposite to those already suggested. It might be argued that the sense of impotence was intensified immediately before and after the first Summit Conference, when the

Arabs found that, after repeatedly proclaiming for over three years that they would prevent by force what they called "the diversion of the Jordan," they were unable to do so. From this point of view, the large number of overt and direct expressions used was the outcome of the feeling that Israel was going from strength to strength and that her exploitation of the Jordan waters would increase her economic capability, while the Arabs were doing nothing but talk, and the pugnacious declarations were only a compensation for a sense of weakness.

The Six-Day War, again, provided an example of a rise in the number of declarations giving liquidation as the aim. There was an unprecedented increase in the number of such statements during the two weeks before the war, when they were uttered in the most open and blatant form. The prevailing feeling was that the Arabs had won a great political victory, their self-confidence grew, and it seemed that the day of vengeance against Israel was imminent. After the War, on the other hand, the demand was expressed that "liquidation" should be pigeonholed because it was not practical at that stage and was harmful to the Arabs.

5. THE OBJECTIVE OF COMPLIANCE WITH UN RESOLUTIONS

As well as demanding the liquidation of Israel, Arab spokesmen demand "compliance with UN decisions"—the two demands are sometimes expressed at the same time by the same spokesman. Do these expressions denote two different objectives, one extreme and the other moderate? Or are they merely two formulations of the same aim? What is the relationship between compliance with UN decisions and the call for liquidation?

Ṭībāwī, a Palestinian, who was an education officer under the Mandate and did research on the Middle East at Harvard University, wrote, in an article on the refugee problem in the *Middle East Journal* (Autumn, 1963, p. 510):

> "The majority of Arabs hope to achieve sooner or later the complete destruction of Israel as a sovereign state. Others, less precisely, think of either (a) the reduction of the state to something like the United Nations partition scheme of 1947, or (b) the elimination of the sovereignty in favour of 'Jewish autonomy' within a larger Arab State."

Some Arab circles, no doubt, regard the call for compliance with UN resolutions as a reasonable demand that the Arabs be compensated for what has happened, especially as the claim has received international approval. Others, again, may be dubious of the possibility of liquidating Israel and regard the UN resolutions as the maximum that can be achieved. There are signs that such ideas have been current in certain Lebanese circles, especially as they seem to afford a prospect of getting rid of Muslim refugees.

This approach is apparent, for example, in the statement of Dr. Albert Mukhaybar, then chairman of the Foreign Affairs Committee in the Lebanese Chamber, in a debate held in the committee on January 6, 1964 on the subject of the diversion of the Jordan and the Arab Summit Conference:

> "I propose returning to the partition decisions which the Arab States have demanded in the United Nations, for there are over 150,000 Palestinian refugees in Lebanon, and this is a very heavy burden, especially if we realize that there are only two thousand refugees in Syria. I can see no reason why the problem of Palestine in general should not be raised at the Arab League.
>
> "I want to be frank with the Honourable Minister and ask him: If Israel agrees to pay financial compensation to the refugees and repatriate them, why should the Arab States not accept this solution, so that the Palestine refugees may be resettled in Galilee?" (*al-Ḥayāt,* January 7, 1964).

It should be noted that those who acquiesce in Israel's existence while demanding "compliance with UN resolutions" give the impression that they are not taking into account what the so-called UN resolutions mean for Israel. Others do take this into account, and are aiming at the results that may be expected from the fulfilment of the United Nations resolutions.

Hāshim al-Jisr, the editor of *al-Jarīda,* explains in his paper:

> "If the Western States persuade Israel to comply with the UN decisions, Israel will be transformed from a State based on foundations of racism and religion and aspiring to expand at the expense of the Arab peoples into a minority living amongst the surrounding peoples but not threatening them." (*al-Jarīda,* April 18, 1964).

Compliance, according to this view, will transform an aggressive state into a small Jewish minority, for al-Jisr explains later on that two million of Israel's present Jewish inhabitants would emigrate.

If compliance with UN decisions would undermine the existence of

Israel, this—it is argued—is evidence of the problematical nature of that existence; in these decisions, in other words, the international community has rejected Israel's right to exist. For advocates of this view, the UN decisions do not replace the demand for liquidation but complement and support it. The demand for compliance, as it were, cuts away the ground from under Israel's feet or weakens her as a prologue to her liquidation. Compliance with UN decisions thus becomes an indirect, euphemistic expression for liquidation, as well as a foundation and justification for it.

This viewpoint is very clearly expressed in an interview by a correspondent of the weekly *Rūz al-Yūsuf* with 'Abd al-Khāliq Ḥassūna, the Secretary-General of the Arab League:

> "Q.: A number of foreign journalists have asked me what exactly we want in connection with the Palestine question. The Jerusalem Conference [of Shukairy's organization in May 1964] demanded the whole of Palestine according to its Mandatory frontiers and the disappearance of Israel, but in statements by the Arab League and the Arab States you demand compliance with UN resolutions—first and foremost, as you are aware, the partition resolution. Is this not a contradiction?
>
> "Ḥassūna: No. On the international scene the Arabs must demand compliance with UN resolutions. This shows how unsound are the foundations of Israel's existence. All her values are incompatible with the UN's decisions. Her opposition to the repatriation of the refugees, her thefts of lands, her aggressiveness—all these are violations of UN decisions. The Arab States' demand for the honouring of these decisions means, in practice, cutting away the ground from under the illegal existence of Israel. It is the Palestinian people that is entitled to solve the problem of its country in a revolutionary manner and dictate its future by force of arms, and when it enforces this solution, it will not stand alone." (*Rūz al-Yūsuf,* October 24, 1964).

Nasser, too, sometimes combines the demand for compliance with UN decisions with the demand for the restoration of Palestine to the Palestinian people (e.g. on October 9, 1959), thus, as it were, giving his interpretation of the UN resolutions. Sometimes he emphasizes article II of the General Assembly resolution of December 11, 1949, which is regarded by the Arabs as recognizing the right of the refugees to return. Like other Arab spokesmen, he ignores the fact that it was the refugees wishing to "live at peace with their neighbours" whose return was stipulated by the resolution. Moreover, Nasser declares that the UN recognized the right of the Palestinian people to return to Palestine[7]—which might be taken to imply that Israel's right is no longer valid.

It should be noted that the demand for compliance with UN resolutions is often presented, not as a demand whose fulfilment will necessarily involve the cessation of belligerency and the conclusion of peace, but as merely a first demand (e.g.Nasser on October 6, 1955, I.L., V/1014*; his letter to students September 3, 1957, I.L., IX/1746; on television, CBS, August 26, 1960). The demand is not presented as a substitute for liquidation, but might be interpreted as an intermediate stage towards liquidation. Nasser explains (May 1, 1965) that, like Bourguiba, he called for the implementation of UN decisions,[8] but Bourguiba went too far and also recognized coexistence with Israel. In other words, Nasser's claim for compliance does not include recognition of Israel's existence and coexistence with her.

We thus find that the demand for compliance with UN decisions and the objective of liquidation are presented in turn by the same spokesman. Shukairy, for example, emphasized in the United Nations the right of the refugees to return according to the UN's decisions, while in other speeches he emphasized the idea of liquidation and the return of the Palestinians, as if compliance, the return of the refugees and the liquidation of Israel are only synonymous expressions or denote simultaneous events.

Advocacy of compliance with UN decisions has a number of political and psychological advantages both at home and abroad. On the home front, it helps to convince the doubters and those of little faith: Look, the international community supports our position. On the external front, the demand generates political pressure on Israel and presents her as a violator of UN decisions and an international criminal, while the Arab attitude, which demands the fulfilment of claims bearing the stamp of international approval, is a reasonable one. It also has the advantage of presenting the Arabs' attitude as an expression of a "limited grievance," while their usual declared demand for liquidation expresses an "unlimited grievance," which cannot be satisfied, since no concession by the rival party can meet the case until the rival himself disappears. The Arabs are thus enabled to present a reasonable demand for "some concession" by Israel, which the international community has approved, and if such a concession involves the liquidation of Israel, that is not their fault.

* Nasser's *Speeches and Statements* (in Arabic), published by Ikhtarnā Lak, Vol. V, p. 1014—and similarly in other references of this type.

Bourguiba advises the Arabs to insist on the demand for compliance with UN resolutions and explains that Israel's refusal will strengthen the position of the Arabs when they embark upon a violent solution. In his speech at a students' gathering of his party on April 21, 1965, he said:

> "If Israel refuses to apply the UN decisions, the legality of the UN will be on our side, which will strengthen our position in approaching a solution by force, for there are political situations which support and strengthen the armed struggle." (Agence France Presse, April 22, 1965).

His paper *al-ʿAmal* explains that, since Israel will not accept the UN resolutions, Arab military action will be regarded as justified (April 18, 1965).

At a press conference in Jerusalem on March 6, 1965, Bourguiba explained: "The right that has been stolen can be restored by stages" (*Filasṭīn,* March 7, 1965). And again in Beirut on March 11, 1965, he speaks about the method of stages *(uslūb al-marāḥil).* It may be deduced from all this that he is recommending what is known in American and German strategic terminology as "salami tactics," and by the French as "artichoke tactics"—namely, to slice the sausage, or peel the leaves of the artichoke, until there is nothing left.[9]

There is no doubt political logic in Bourguiba's proposal to use the demand for the return to the partition decision and follow the path of little by little. Nor is there anything novel in this attitude; Arab leaders have often stated in meetings with foreigners that what they demand is the fulfilment of the partition decision. Bourguiba seems to be speaking the truth when he says that other leaders, including Nasser, had agreed with his position. Indeed, Nasser himself prepared the way by emphasizing, after 1962, that he had no plan for solving the problem and that the solution was still far off.

Moreover, the policy of limiting the Arab demand to the fulfilment of the UN decisions—a non-belligerent solution—making it the principal watchword of the Arab side, and concealing the aim of liquidation by violence until a suitable occasion, appears to be an optimal political strategy from the Arab point of view. Israel's refusal to return to the partition decision may be presented, as appears from Bourguiba's statements, as leaving the Arabs with no alternative but to return to the extreme policy of liquidating her by war. Moreover, no political situation is final, and the demands can be subsequently increased. "Take and demand," Bourguiba explained in his Beirut press conference; that is his way in life.

Why had this not been accepted by the Arabs as their general policy in the conflict? I believe that a number of factors militated against it—some of them matters of principle and others connected with temperament and psychology.

Firstly, the demand for a return to the partition decision means recognition of Israel, though with more restricted boundaries. This would undermine the basis of the Arab attitude that the existence of Israel is a matter of principle for Arab nationalism and international morality. The fundamental claim of the Arabs, as we shall see below, is that Jewish settlement in Palestine and the establishment of Israel constituted aggression, that they were incompatible with the right of the majority of the inhabitants to self-determination, and that the existence of Israel is, therefore, an injustice, which cannot be rectified except by its nullification. The central position given to the idea of "justice" in the Arab attitude counteracts any tendency towards compromise and necessitates the approach of *fiat justitia ruat coelum*.

It is not a question of opposing an Israel of twenty thousand square kilometres and accepting an Israel with fifteen thousand square kilometres, or opposing an Israel with a western culture and accepting an Israel whose culture is oriental, but opposition to the existence of Israel in any shape or form and on any territory. There was considerable emphasis in later years on the argument that Israel is a colonialist phenomenon, the liquidation of which is a necessary outcome of the general world tendency towards the liquidation of colonialism; Israel is denounced as a matter of principle.

Secondly, the advice to think about liquidation but never to talk about it—on the lines of Gambetta's counsel to the French after the 1870 war—is not suitable for a national goal and an aspiration for the masses. A national aspiration designed to fan hopes and inspire the masses is difficult to cover up with a tactical attitude. A tactical policy like compliance with UN resolutions cannot be presented as a national goal with the same fervour as the idea of liquidation; it takes the wind out of the sails of belligerency, which Arab propaganda tries to foster. The Arab-Israel conflict has important functions to fulfil in Arab nationalism which cannot be fulfilled by a conflict centred on a watered-down demand.[10]

Thirdly, the very idea of peacefully liquidating a State by forensic tactics is a contradiction in terms. The liquidation of a State is a drastic operation which cannot be carried out by peaceful and pleasant means, but only by force and violence. An admission that there is no intention of going to war, or that war is impossible, may therefore imply acquiescence in coexistence, or at least a shift in the direction of acquiescence.

Fourthly, the allotment of the central role in the conflict to the idea of "liberation," "the liberation of the homeland by a people," or "a war of national liberation," which reflects a tendency toward a radicalization of the Arab attitude, necessitates the rejection of the UN decision and the advocacy of the liberation of the entire homeland. The Palestinian National Covenant proclaims:

> "Palestine with its boundaries at the time of the British Mandate is a regional indivisible unit" (Article 2)

and, in the preamble, proclaims the right to "the complete restoration of our lost homeland."

Fifthly, the present ideology of Egypt, Syria and Iraq emphasizes revolution, forceful, drastic action, and radical change. The presentation of grandiose goals is congenial to such a revolutionary atmosphere. These ambitions are not unbridled, for circumstances impose certain limitations, but there is a tendency to aspire to sublime aims and great deeds. It may be assumed that the radical and drastic aim of liquidation is in keeping with an emotional atmosphere of this kind; it is not the outcome of this mood, but it is presented with greater emphasis, enthusiasm and dedication in a climate of this kind. A moderate attitude is not compatible with revolutionary fervour, while an extreme aim, such as war *à outrance,* is more alluring at the present stage.

Professor Bernard Lewis, head of the Department of History at the School of Oriental and African Studies at the University of London, sums up:

> "They [the Arabs] are agreed that Israel must be destroyed, though not on how this should be accomplished. The official Arab demand is no longer for immediate destruction of Israel, but for its reduction to the frontiers laid down in the 1947 partition proposals—obviously as a first step towards its disappearance." (*The Middle East and the West,* 1964, p. 125).

Compliance with UN decisions becomes a means for the weakening of Israel as a prelude to its destruction; or it may be expected that the weakening will, by itself, result in collapse. The demand is, thus, an intermediate goal, intended to be a step towards a realization of the final aim by installments; as conventional wisdom teaches, if a goal cannot be achieved at one blow, it can sometimes be attained piecemeal.

True, it might be argued that the real aim of the Arabs is to insist on compliance with UN decisions and nothing more, and that as Israel refuses to comply and the UN passively refuses to compel her to do so, the Arabs have no alternative but to undertake the task themselves, on the assumption that forced compliance may bring about—though only as a side-effect—the total ruin of Israel. Liquidation thus becomes a means of compelling Israel to comply with UN decisions by disappearing.

The fact that Bourguiba's proposal aroused a storm of protest in several Arab countries does not necessarily mean that the demand for a return to the partition proposals will not be pressed again at some future date as the principal Arab political demand. Its political advantages may well lead to its being revived at a period of decline in the radical position, as we have seen after the Six-Day War.

6. INADEQUACY OF UN RESOLUTIONS

There is something inherently awkward in the adoption of the liquidation of a State and the national independence of a people as a political programme; in our generation, which is accustomed to the demand for a change of regime as the focus of a conflict, it may be regarded as an incredible exaggeration. I have learned from experience that political scientists who have been brought up on modern theories of international relations and international law, or who have been familiar with other conflicts which serve them as criteria and archetypes, may display an inner resistance to the idea that this is really the goal and objective in the conflict, and cast doubt on the sincerity of Arab declarations that these are really their aims. Some will explain away such statements as exuberant demagogy or the adoption of a bargaining position. Even in Israel, there were widespread tendencies in the past to refuse to believe that the goal was really liquidation, and to put the idea out of one's mind completely.

In recent years, however, this Arab goal had been brought out so clearly and prominently that it can hardly be ignored any longer.

The Arabs are certainly aware of the difficulties involved in presenting liquidation as their aim, and it is significant, therefore, that their spokesmen wonder how Israel can still continue to exist. How, they ask, does she not understand that the Arabs are right and that she must disappear? From this point of view, it is not the demand for liquidation that is strange, but Israel's desire to survive that is unreasonable. Haykal writes in his weekly article:

"There are two facts, as I have said, whose spiritual father is despair: the madness of imperialism in defending the interests stolen from the Arabs, and the madness of Israel defending her existence and her expansion at the Arabs' expense." (*al-Ahrām*, June 12, 1964).

Thus, if Israel acted according to the dictates of reason she would commit suicide. It seems extraordinary that Haykal finds it possible to compare "defending her existence" and the aspiration to "expansion": both, in his view, are manifestations of Israel's madness, and both are reprehensible.

On the same lines, Nasser said:

"Israel's aggression against Arab lands and Arab rights is still in force, and there is no sign that the Israeli leaders regret what they have done or are prepared to retreat." (February 8, 1960).

In other words, not only was the establishment of Israel an act of aggression and injustice, which imposes a heavy burden of guilt on the Israelis, but they are guilty of the further crime of refusing to rectify the injustice by the restoration of Arab rights, which, as we have seen, would mean, in practice, the annulment of Israeli sovereignty. The existence of Israel is, therefore, mere obduracy. The final statement of the second Summit Conference says:

"The Conference emphasizes the need for the total mobilization of potential . . . in order to confront . . . Israel's obstinancy in continuing her aggressive policy and denying the rights of the Palestinian Arabs in their homeland." (Cairo Radio, September 11, 1964, 22:00 hrs.).

Many people may not believe that the Arabs, as represented by their leaders and spokesmen, adhere to the aim of liquidation and reject any settlement based on the partition proposals, that they will not be satisfied by a solution of the refugee problem or by any concession that leaves Israel in existence, and that this is a central feature of the Arab attitude. It is, therefore, necessary to give a number of quotations from Arab declarations in which this is expressly stated.

Here, for example, is an extract from an interview with al-Ḥajj Amīn al-Husseini in the *Middle East Forum*, the organ of the students at the American University in Beirut:

"Q: Do you advocate the implementation of the UN Partition Resolution?

"A: The Palestine Arabs rejected the Partition Resolution and fought against its implementation. They still maintain this position and insist on restoring Palestine as part of the Arab nation.

"Q: In that case where do you think the Jews from Israel could go?
"A: They could go anywhere. There are already 5,000,000 in the United States which has the resources and the space to take more. The Americans like them and they like the Americans, so I don't see why they should not have their own state there." (October 1959, pp. 16–17).

Haykal describes in one of his articles how King Hussein said to him when they met in Paris:

"I have information in my possession that the United States intends to bring all possible pressure to bear in order to get a solution of the refugee problem, imagining that that is all that is left of the problem of Palestine." (*al-Ahrām,* November 27, 1963).

In other words, the refugee problem is only part of the problem and its solution would not mean the settlement of the dispute.

Prof. Walīd al-Khālidī of the American University in Beirut, whose field of research is the Arab-Israel conflict, writes in an article called "Re-appraisal: An Examination of Certain Western Attitudes to the Palestine Problem":

"It is sometimes suggested that the way to solve the Palestine problem is to approach it in a peacemeal fashion. You must nibble at the problem until you end up by swallowing it. Settle the refugees and the biggest obstacle to the solution will be removed. But the Palestine problem will remain as acute as ever with every Palestine refugee settled. The refugees may be outward evidence of the crime which must be tidied out of sight but nothing will remove the scar of Palestine from Arab hearts . . .

"The solution of the Palestine problem cannot be found in the settlement of the refugees nor even in the return to the 1947 partition decision." (*Middle East Forum,* Summer 1958, Vol. 33, No. 8, pp. 22, 29).

Nasser told the UAR National Council:

"Israel and the imperialism around us, which confront us, are not two separate things. There have been attempts to separate them, in order to break up the problems and present them in an imaginary light as if the problem of Israel is the problem of the refugees, by the solution of which the problem of Palestine will also be solved and no residue of the problem will remain. The danger of Israel lies in the very existence of Israel as it is in the present and in what she represents." (March 26, 1964).

Nāṣir al-Dīn al-Nashāshībī wrote in *al-Jumhūriyya*:

"Ḥabīb Bourguiba is a criminal when he says that if Israel complies with UN resolutions there will be room for negotiations with her to achieve an agreement on a basis for the solution of the problem. Never! We are not prepared to negotiate. If we want to return, we shall return with honour and not as citizens of the State of Israel. We shall never agree to negotiations, bargaining or an armistice, nor to declarations to the effect that if Israel makes concessions to the Arabs on her borders or permits the refugees to return, we would be prepared to enter into negotiations with Israel and sign a peace settlement with her. No—a thousand times no." (May 14, 1961).

It should be emphasized that this attitude to UN resolutions is not a new one. Many similar declarations were made in the past. For example, Muḥammad Ṣalāḥ al-Dīn, who was Foreign Minister in the Wafd Government, said:

"It is well known and understood that the Arabs, in demanding the return of the refugees to Palestine, mean their return as masters of the Homeland and not as slaves. With greater clarity, they mean the liquidation of the State of Israel." (*al-Miṣrī*, October 11, 1949).

Similarly, he declared almost five years later:

"The truth of the matter is that we are not all content with the implementation of UN decisions. And if the Arab statesmen have found a diplomatic and tactical way out of their embarrassment at the UN rostrum and at press conferences, the Arab peoples will not be embarrassed to declare: We shall not be satisfied except by the final obliteration of Israel from the map of the Middle East." (*al-Miṣrī,* April 12, 1954).

The sharp reaction of most of the Arab leaders to Bourguiba's proposals shows how unacceptable was his call for a limited aim. Bourguiba's declarations compelled them to adopt a clear and unambiguous stand.

Shukairy declared at a press conference:

"The Palestine Liberation Organization, in its revolutionary will to liberate the lost homeland, rejects President Bourguiba's proposals in general and in detail, and declares that there is only one solution to the Palestine problem: the Arabism of Palestine without partition, without internationalization, and without the settlement of the refugees . . . The first and last goal has been: the liberation of Palestine and its restoration to its legal owners." (Amman Radio, April 23, 1965, 14:00 hrs.).

In later years, the tendency to reject the UN resolutions became more emphatic. The Palestinian National Covenant declared, in Article 17:

"The Partitioning of Palestine in 1947 and the establishment of Israel are illegal and false regardless of the loss of time, because they were contrary to the wish of the Palestine people and its natural right to its homeland, and in violation of the basic principles embodied in the charter of the United Nations, foremost among which is the right to self-determination."

And Article 18 states:

"The Balfour Declaration, the Mandate system and all that had been based upon them are considered fraud" *(sic)*.

7. LIQUIDATION BY PEACEFUL MEANS

The difficulties involved in starting a war in modern days, the world condemnation of any breach of the peace and the fear of Big-Power intervention may lead to the conclusion that war is not the solution. This was the attitude of President Bourguiba, who justified it on the grounds of the impracticability of a solution by force and the inadequacy of Arab strength.

Non-belligerent Arab statements do not necessarily signify acquiescence in Israel's existence; sometimes they indicate the quest for a different road to the liquidation of Israel—by peaceful means.

Some spokesmen explain that the Arab siege will lead to the asphyxiation of the Jewish State. For instance, the veteran Egyptian statesman Muhammad Ali ʿAlūba writes in his book *Palestine and the Conscience of Mankind:*

"It is not an easy thing to destroy by military means. But there is a force which is not stéel and fire, with the aid of which we can win, namely, the economic boycott of Israel." (1964, p. 187).

Another non-belligerent method is the elimination of the State of Israel by the UN and the dispersion of its inhabitants in various countries according to a settlement that will be laid down. There are some who believe that this method will be practical when the nations realize that the Arabs will never acquiesce or give the world any rest so long as Israel exists. ʿAlūba regards the repatriation and dispersion of the Jews on the initiative of international institutions as the only solution, explaining that this was the advice King Ibn Saʿūd gave to President Roosevelt when they met. Accepting the anti-Semitic view that "Zionism aspires to destroy all states and peoples and conspires to dominate the whole world," he believes that the world will one day wake up to the Jewish threat and unite to put an end to the "evils of world Zionism"—only then will it find relief. *(ibid.,* pp. 195-196).

The idea of liquidation with the aid of the big powers and the UN was also put forward by King Hussein at a press conference in 1965. He explained that the solution of the refugee problem did not necessitate war: it could be achieved by recognition of the natural rights of the Palestinians. It was not only the Arabs but the whole world that was responsible for this solution, for the tragedy of Palestine was a human tragedy, and the UN, as the international institution which bore responsibility for the situation, should play a foremost role in the matter (Baghdad Radio, March 16, 1965, 18:00 hrs; see also his autobiographical book *Uneasy Lies the Head,* p. 106).

It is often argued by the Arabs that the liquidation of Israel by the Powers and the UN would not be particularly difficult, for it is what the Israelis themselves really want. Because of the Arab threat which overshadows the Israelis and the loose and ephemeral nature of their attachment to their country, and since Judaism is a religion and not a nationality, it is explained, most of them would prefer to emigrate were they not compelled by the Zionists to stay where they are. Arabs often regarded the need for exit permits at one period and a certain amount of emigration from Israel as evidence of a general desire to leave, while criticism of the Government and the State by Israelis have been interpreted as expressions of hostility to their own country. Zionists are frequently denounced for refusing to enable the Israelis to decide their own destinies and accused of creating an atmosphere of emergency and war in their own interests in order to prevent the Jews leaving Israel. If only this "Zionist terror" could be stopped and the Jews provided with the resources for emigration, the problem would be solved—at least partially—by peaceful means.[11]

This point of view is expressed in the following quotation from an editorial in the *Egyptian Economic and Political Review:*

> "There is however one solution in which the Arabs, and we feel, to a greater extent, the majority of Israeli Jews would agree with enthusiasm, and wealthy Western countries, who are more than able to absorb considerably more people, should make available some 1,000,000 entry visas to their countries. We feel that there are few Jews in Palestine today who would not avail themselves of the opportunity. If necessary, the Arab countries would probably contribute to the cost of settling these unfortunate victims of modern power politics." (October, 1955).

It may be assumed that the drop in emigration from Israel has helped to change this view, but the idea that most Israelis would like to leave is still widespread. Nāṣir al-Dīn al-Nashāshībī writes:

> "If Israel knows that she will be deprived of the water that is not hers, why does she insist on remaining on a land that is not her own? And why does she insist in keeping the migrants who have expressed their desire to return to their homeland in Europe?" (*al-Jumhūriyya,* June 10, 1964).

A call for a "peaceful solution" is often to be found in declarations meant for foreign consumption—it is more fitting. But sometimes it is supplemented by a covert and indirect demand for liquidation. King Hussein declared, for instance, at a banquet in his honour by the President of the German Federal Republic:

> "The Jordanians and the Arab people sincerely hope that a way may be found for a peaceful solution to the problem of Palestine, a solution that will assure the refugees of their right to their homeland." (*Ha'aretz,* November 27, 1964).

Here we have ingredients to suit all tastes: the demand that the refugees should become masters of the country, namely that Israel should be liquidated, on the one hand, and a pacific approach on the other.

It should be noted, however, that such expressions as "a settlement," "the settlement of the problem," "a political settlement," "a constructive solution," or "a positive solution" do not indicate recognition of Israel's existence. The settlement or the solution could be achieved without her. Similarly, the call for "a peaceful solution" may mean a solution not with Israel but without Israel—and could, therefore, be an indirect term for liquidation. This advocacy of the liquidation of Israel by peaceful means is also interesting from another point of view. Logical thinking is liable to lead some Arabs to reject war as a practical solution, but since they are reluctant to abandon the aim of Israel's disappearance, they are attracted by the hope that the same end might be brought about by other means. Thus they pin their hopes on a possibility which is hardly more realistic, but they prefer to ignore the difficulties it involves and refrain from bringing reason to bear upon it, as if it were beyond the range of critical examination.

Between these aims of liquidation by peaceful means and liquidation by force lies a dilemma which is basic to the Arab attitude in the conflict and leads to perplexities which are reflected in the indirect terms used to denote the objective.

Pierre al-Jumayyil (Gemayel), leader of the Lebanese Falangist Party and Minister of Public Works at the time, proposed a solution of a different kind in a talk with Edouard Sa'ab, the *Le Monde* correspondent. Jumayyil suggested that the solution was the repatriation of the refugees, so that the Jewish and Arab populations would be balanced, and the establishment of a State on the pattern of Lebanon, with its mixed population of Christians and Moslems, i.e. "an Arab-Jewish Palestine" with its bi-national character constitutionally guaranteed (*Le Monde,* March 9, 1965). It is noteworthy that, despite the great difference between this proposal and the Arab plans already reviewed, it also means the liquidation of Jewish sovereignty, or the liquidation of Israel as a Jewish State.

A few days later, Jumayyil gave his proposal a more extreme interpretation in an interview with a journalist who quoted him as follows:

> "I never called for peace with Israel or any attempt to conduct negotiations with her. My words may have been distorted or misunderstood. When I talked to the newspapers I only called for a solution to the problem of Israel on a Palestinian basis, namely by the return of the European Jewish migrants to their own countries so that it should be possible to establish a Palestinian State inhabited by the original Jewish and Arab population of Palestine." (*al-Ḥawādith,* March 20, 1965).

Hāshim al-Jisr, editor of *al-Jarīda,* adopts the same attitude and explains in his paper:

> "The establishment of an Arab-Jewish state in Palestine, which will adapt itself from the political and historical points of view to its Arab environment, will influence the two million Jews living in Israel to return to their European countries of origin, and the only Jews that will remain on the soil of Palestine will be those who will regard themselves as belonging to the area and not western imperialists who aspire to establish an Israeli empire with a population of ten million Jews." (April 18, 1965).

In other words, a bi-national state according to this proposal would consist of Muslim Arabs and Jewish Arabs. It need hardly be said that this does not mean recognition of Israel. (The same idea reappears under the slogan of a "Democratic Free Palestine" which the Palestinian organizations have brandished since the Six-Day War.)

8. THE OBJECTIVE IN PROPAGANDA FOR EXTERNAL CONSUMPTION

The embarrassment involved in presenting the liquidation of Israel as a political objective is particularly obvious in Arab publications for external consumption. Not all publications meant for foreign countries are propaganda material in which the Arabs themselves do not believe: at least some of them are analyses of the Palestine problem in what they regard as a scientific form. It is no accident that such literature is composed by academics and part of it published by research institutions. It may also be noted that there is a considerable similarity between the attitude expressed in their statements on the subject in foreign languages and that which is presented in publications for internal consumption. The differences are more in style and emphasis than in substance. In the literature meant for the foreign reader, the objective of liquidation is seldom expressly stated; often it is not even mentioned, but only implied. For example, in Dr. Sayegh's pamphlet *The Arab-Israel Conflict,* which is written in his usually virulently anti-Israel tone, the goal is not mentioned at all. Sayegh enumerates the injustices involved in the establishment of Israel, and his analysis merely implies that such injustices are insufferable.

This applies not only to Arabs, but also to their foreign supporters. Erskine Childers, for example, in his article: "Palestine: the Broken Triangle," in *International Affairs,* does not expressly explain that the Arab aim is the liquidation of Israel's existence as a State or the annulment of her sovereignty, but says that the Arab world will not acquiesce in the situation, that its hatred is deepening, and that if the UN does not act, the united Arab nations will have to act alone. Childers does not expressly say what "action" the Arabs will have to take, but it is clearly implied that their purpose will be the liquidation of Israel, while leaving it to the reader to arrive by himself at the unpleasant but, in his view, unavoidable conclusions:

> "It might be pleasing to hope that the Arabs one day will see the fate of Palestine as Israelis have to, and as Israelis want the West to. But to hold this hope seems to me to postulate that the Arabs are not human beings." (1965, p. 99).

The humanity of the Arabs, it appears, compels them to aspire to the destruction of Israel.

This avoidance of express reference to the goal of liquidation is also to be met with in some of the literature, such as progressive writing, meant for the Arab reader. For example, the leftist journalist Aḥmad Bahā' al-Dīn, the editor of the weekly *al-Muṣawwar,* in his book *Isrā'īliyāt* ("Judaica") (1965), categorically denounces Zionism and all its works and adopts an uncompromising attitude towards Israel, whose existence, he explains, is a challenge to the Arabs which cannot be ignored; he does not expressly call for her liquidation, but his analysis implies that the continued existence of this challenge is intolerable, and that it is a question of "clashing destinies" (p. 257).

As a further illustration, here is another extract from the article by Dr. Walīd al-Khālidī, quoted above, in which the author sums up his attitude to the solution of the Palestine problem:

> "The way I am suggesting is based upon the fact that a terrible injustice has been inflicted, that this injustice carries within it the seeds of still more terrible calamities in the Arab world, that in the Arab world there is no room for two dynamic diametrically opposed nationalisms, and that a choice must be made between them.[12]
>
> "If ever the times demanded an agonizing reappraisal of a policy, they now demand, before it is too late for everybody, an agonizing reappraisal of the whole concept of Israeli sovereignty." (p. 29).

Here, again, the demand for liquidation is concealed behind the elegant phrase about "an agonizing reappraisal."

The difficulty of frankly admitting that the aim is liquidation is particularly obvious when Nasser addresses foreigners. When he is asked whether the Arabs intend to take up arms to destroy Israel, he generally does not answer either yes or no, but describes the birth of the conflict, talks about the injustices done to the Arabs and the right of the refugees to return home, and declares that he rejects the *status quo,* which must be rectified—in brief, he presents the goal of liquidation without actually mentioning it. A correspondent of the London *Observer* asked him:

> "You have said war with Israel is inevitable, but you clearly have not sought war over the Jordan waters. Does this mean you regard attack from Israel as inevitable, but do not intend to attack yourself?"

Nasser:

> "The Arabs will not accept the *status quo* over Palestine at all. We may not be able to do anything to change it today or tomorrow, but the *status quo* is impossible. Palestinians were driven out of their homes, their land and their nation.

The Palestine problem is different from Berlin. Berliners live under different regimes. Some have Russian troops on their soil and some have American and British. But they are all German and one day they will be masters of their own country. But the Palestinians were expelled from their territory and must one day return. United Nations resolutions calling for the return of the refugees have been ignored by Israel." *(Observer,* July 5, 1964).

Not a word about war, only a rejection of the *status quo* (i.e. the existence of Israel) and the necessity for the return of the refugees (so that Palestine should be entirely Arab).

At a press conference in Cairo on October 1, 1963, a journalist from Ceylon asked:

"What solution do you expect in your dispute with Israel? By negotiation, or is war the only solution?"

The British and American delegation asked:

"Why do you want to throw the Jews into the sea?"

Nasser:

"The problem of Israel is without parallel in history. It has to be understood free from deceptive Zionist propaganda. In Palestine there were 90% Arabs and only 10% Jews. Colonization and Zionism combined to dispossess the inhabitants and establish a State founded on religion. How is it possible to accept the *status quo* when the Arabs were expelled, their property plundered and their women and children murdered?... Peace must be based on justice. The problem will not come to an end until justice is done. The Arabs fought the Crusaders, the Arabs have lived in the region for thousands of years ..." *(Egyptian Gazette,* October 10, 1963).

Again, there is no direct reference to the question of war or liquidation, about which he was asked, but only such indirect expressions as the inacceptability of the *fait accompli,* the comparison with the Crusaders, or "a just peace."

The CBS representative asked Nasser in an interview on April 6, 1958:

"You have said recently that the Arabs must unite so that Zionism will have no place amongst you. Does this mean that your policy is the obliteration of Israel?"

The President:

"So that you should understand our feelings it is necessary to go back and survey the events of the past ..." (*Nasser's Speeches,* I.L., XI/2144).

To Frei, the editor of the German Nationalist paper *Nazional und Soldaten Zeitung*, he spoke with complete frankness, according to the account in the newspaper:

"Frei: Your Excellency, permit me to ask with complete brutality: will you crush Israel?

"Nasser: That is what I hope." (May 1, 1964).

It should not be assumed that this reluctance is only a stratagem. If it is, it implies the admission that it is difficult to demand the annulment of Israeli sovereignty when speaking to foreigners, and it is therefore better to use an indirect approach: on the one hand, to justify the liquidation, and, on the other, to present the situation that makes it necessary. However, the need to avoid presenting the demand openly may arouse feelings of disquiet among the Arabs themselves. A national goal which cannot be proclaimed in public may be somewhat problematic even for those who believe in it.

The Arabs are not unaware of the problematical character of the "political" objective, the difficulty of persuading foreigners to accept it as a reasonable goal and the ambiguous attitude to UN resolutions, as may be seen from an article in *al-Ḥayāt* by Jubrān Shāmiya. The article is a criticism of the ambitious inter-Arab plan, adopted at the first Summit Conference, to send Arab foreign ministers all over the world on extensive propaganda campaigns. Shāmiya proposes limiting the effort to a small number of countries which might be influenced. He describes an imaginary interview between a delegation of Arab foreign ministers and a minister from a foreign country:

"The Arab delegation: In the name of the friendship between our countries, we ask you to support our efforts to prevent the diversion of the Jordan by Israel.

"The Minister: Israel only wants to utilize part of the waters which flow uselessly into the Dead Sea. Why do you not cooperate with her to exploit this natural resource?

"Arab delegation: Israel is an aggressive country; she has even refused to carry out UN decisions on the repatriation and compensation of the refugees. We are still in a state of war with her. We refuse to recognize her or cooperate with her.

"The Minister: Will the Arab States agree to comply with all the UN resolutions, or perhaps they only want to implement the article that calls for the repatriation and the compensation of the refugees? . . .

"The delegation: The Arab States do not want to implement the partition resolutions. They rejected them when they were adopted in the UN and fought to prevent their implementation; because of them they are still in a state of war with Israel.

"The Minister: How can you demand the implementation of part of the UN resolutions and reject the other part?

"The delegation: Our demands for the implementation of part of the UN resolutions are meant to clarify Israel's malevolent intentions towards the poor refugees.

"The Minister: If so, why should you not settle these refugees in the Arab countries, where there are extensive areas which can absorb them, while Israel's territory is too small even to accommodate the Jewish immigrants?

"The delegation: The refugees want to return to their homeland instead of the new immigrants who are coming to Israel.

"The Minister: That means the liquidation of Israel, which is a member of the United Nations. We have recognized her and maintained friendly relations with her, so we cannot support your efforts to liquidate Israel."

Jubrān Shāmiya adds:

"I do not know how the discussion would end, unless the Arab ministers refrained from speaking to the foreign representatives as they are accustomed to talk to their compatriots. But if they are bound by the Arab nationalist demands, which call for non-recognition of Israel, opposition to her legal existence and a constant effort to liquidate her, it may be said with certainty that the results of most of the visits will be negative." (*al-Ḥayāt,* March 4, 1964).

9. THE DISTINCTION BETWEEN LIQUIDATING A STATE AND LIQUIDATING ITS POPULATION

In principle, Arab spokesmen demand the "liquidation of Israel" or "the liquidation of Zionist sovereignty," as distinct from the liquidation of the inhabitants. As there is no commonly accepted term for "the liquidation of a State," I have proposed calling it "politicide"—the murder of the *politeia,* the political entity. The aim of the Arabs, thus, is politicidal.

Where the Arab-Israeli conflict is concerned, there may be no absolute distinction between politicide and genocide, at least from the practical point of view. It may be assumed that the Arabs are well aware that the Israelis, who know what would await them if defeated in war, would fight to the death, and that their overthrow and the liquidation of their State would, therefore, involve a massacre. Nasser has declared:

"We shall not enter Palestine with its soil covered in sand. We shall enter it with its soil saturated in blood." (March 8, 1965).

In describing the war that will bring about Israel's liquidation, it is repeatedly emphasized that this will be total war to the death, as stated in the order of the day issued by the Commander of the Egyptian Third Division on February 15, 1956:

"Every commander is to prepare himself and his subordinates for the inevitable campaign with Israel in which we are fully immersed, for the purpose of fulfilling our exalted aim, namely, the annihilation of Israel and her extermination in the shortest possible time, in the most brutal and cruel battles." (A copy of this order was attached to Prime Minister Ben-Gurion's letter of November 14, 1956 to Bulganin—see *Israel Government Year Book,* 1959/60, p. 36.)

The formula "to throw Israel into the sea" certainly does not mean that only the State coat-of-arms will be flung into the water while the Israelis continue to dwell in the land each under his vine and under his fig tree, especially as the less ambiguous term "to throw the Jews into the sea"—which has an undoubted genocidal signficance—is quite frequent.[13] Genocidal motifs may also be seen in the typical caricature which depicts the liquidation of Israel as the killing of a scorpion, or for example the text of a manifesto published in *al-Ahrām* (February 3, 1964) for distribution among the Jews of the world to warn them against migrating to Israel, describing such a move as a "free" one-way road to death, and making the point unmistakably clear with the aid of a drawing showing the Angel of Death with his sickle.

The Arab goal, furthermore, is presented as not only a change in the political status of the country, but also a matter of punishment and revenge. Since the establishment of Israel is denounced as an international crime, her extinction must be carried out as a punitive operation and a massacre. The Israelis, it is explained, had no mercy on the Arabs, and the Arabs should have no mercy on them. The "revenge" theme is quite frequent. For example, the Arab Nationalist Movement *(Ḥarakat al-Qawmiyyīn al-'Arab*), which consists of Palestinian intellectuals, proclaimed in its ideological book *With Arab Nationalism,* published in April 1957, the watchword: "liquidation of Israel with vengeance" *(al-qaḍā' 'al-Isrā'īl bi-al-tha'r).*[14]

Arab intentions in this regard may be understood from their statements as to what will happen to the Israelis after their defeat and the liberation of

Palestine. This question is not, indeed, frequently discussed, for it no doubt appears theoretical; nevertheless, it is not at all exceptional to meet statements that after victory Palestine will be entirely Arab.

A pamphlet called *Ben Gurion . . . the Liar,* by Muhammad Ḥusayn Sha'bān, one of a series of "Books on Nationalism" issued on behalf of the UAR Government Publishing House, stated:

> "The land of Palestine will utterly spew out all that is on it, with the exception of the sons of Palestine, and none will remain except the Arabs, so that they may rebuild the glory of their homeland and cleanse it from the traces of the Jews, and it shall remain a land of the Arabs for the Arabs." (p. 59).

True, the passage does not mean that all Israelis are to be put to the sword, but their number will at least be sufficiently diminished to make it possible to "spew them out" and make the country *judenrein.*[15]

It may be that Haykal's attitude is not very different, if we carefully examine his comments on Bourguiba's statement in East Jerusalem in 1965. Haykal says that Bourguiba's view that a Jewish minority may remain among the Arab peoples after the liquidation of Israel "is at least an outlook about which there is room for discussion" *(al-Ahrām,* March 26, 1965). This passage, which is emphasized by being printed in large letters, implies that even the survival of a Jewish minority is not regarded by the writer as certain.

The existence of Israel depends on the concentration of Jews in it, so its extinction calls for the removal, or at least diminution, of this concentration. Since the Jews will refuse to agree to anything of the kind, however, they will have to be eliminated. The transformation of Palestine into an Arab country, which is the proclaimed goal, means that, at most, only a small Jewish minority will remain. However, since the Jewish population is growing, any dream of making the country Arab inevitably includes a genocidal element. As we have seen, there are those who argue that some of the Jews living in Israel are compelled to stay and will willingly leave, but it is presumably understood that the "spewing out" of the Jews involves a massacre.

According to one version of the argument, the veteran inhabitants ("the Palestine Jews") and their offspring will be permitted to remain and continue to exist as a religious community, which may even enjoy a measure of automony within the framework of the united Arab States. This would be a spiritual centre or a "Jewish Vatican"—to use 'Azzām's phrase. According to Article 7 of the Palestinian National Covenant:

"Jews of Palestinian origin are considered Palestinians if they are willing to live peacefully and loyally in Palestine."

The implication is that there will be no room in the country for Jews who are not of Palestinian origin.

Al-Ṭībāwī, as we have seen, estimates that only a minority of the Arabs would consider Jewish autonomy within the framework of a wider Arab State, which implies that most of them would not be prepared to grant the Jews who will survive even the rights of an autonomous minority.

It is not surprising if Arab spokesmen vigorously deny any genocidal intentions—they can always blame the Israelis, whose obstinate opposition to the liquidation of their State will be the cause of the slaughter. It cannot be crudely asserted that all the Arabs have genocidal intentions, but there is an element of genocide in the political aim and its implications, and it is thoroughly in keeping with the drastic character of that aim. The genocidal objective is liable to be reinforced by the tendency, which I shall survey below, to denounce the Jews on fundamental historical and religious grounds—a tendency which may lead to the implication that the Israelis deserve severe punishment. Descriptions of the abominations perpetrated by Jews and Israelis serve the politicidal-genocidal aim, for they tend to dehumanize them, to exclude them from the pale of humanity and create a callous attitude towards them.

10. SYMBOLS OF LIQUIDATION

The Arabs' refusal to recognize Israel and their demand that she should not continue to exist are also given symbolic expression. In many Arab maps, for instance, the name of Israel does not appear; laws have been promulgated and procedures laid down to ensure that this practice is followed. For example, *al-Difāʿ* (May 18, 1964) reports that, at the demand of the Arab League, the Jordanian Minister of Education had ordered the Inspector of Schools to delete the word Israel from foreign atlases and books used in the schools, "Palestine" or "Occupied Palestine" being substituted.

Sometimes the customs authorities tear out maps or pages bearing the name of Israel from books and other publications, but there is no complete consistency in this respect: the Lebanese authorities, for instance, tore out twelve pages referring to Israel from the Larousse Encyclopedia, but the book seems to have been sold intact in Egypt *(al-ʿAmal,* March 12, 1967). This practice, which may appear strange to an observer, is apparently not only a symbol of non-recognition, but an example of a phenomenon which anthropologists and psychologists call "undoing"—i.e., a symbolic action conceived as magically negating someone's existence, such as the burning of his effigy as a means of bringing about his death.[16]

Arab diplomats, again, are in the habit of ignoring Israeli representatives, and are embarrased if they happen to have shaken an Israeli's hand without knowing his identity. The hostility also extends to individual citizens of Israel as a protest against her existence; Arabs have frequently refused to debate with Israelis publicly, on the radio or television, or even on an academic platform.

This tendency is also expressed in linguistic terms. The Arabs were in the habit of attaching to the word Israel the adjective *al-mazʿūma*—i.e. "so-called," "the alleged," or, in French, "le soi-disant" Israel.[17] It should be noted that the frequency of this expression has declined—the Arabs themselves seem to feel how strange it is to continue describing an existing State as "claiming to exist"; nevertheless the term is still to be met with. The refusal to admit Israel's existence is also expressed in the common custom of avoiding the mention of the name by using an indirect epithet like: "the occupied land" *(al-arḍ al-muḥtalla),* "the usurped land," "the occupation authorities" or "the gangsters' State."

Liquidation is often presented graphically in Arab caricatures, as we have seen, by depicting the trampling on, or destruction of, a creature like a scorpion, which symbolizes Israel.

11. SUMMING-UP OF THE ARAB ATTITUDE

The liquidation of Israel, compliance with UN resolutions, solution by peaceful means—what is the Arab objective in the conflict?

The terms objective, aim, aspiration, purpose are not unambiguous. There is a great difference between vague wishes (e.g.: "May the earth swallow up my enemies!" or "If I were a rich man!") which no action is taken to realize, and a concrete aim, for the achievement of which plans are made and carried into effect. It may be assumed that the abstract wish for the disappearance of Israel is widely cherished among the Arabs, but for many of them it is not only a wish but a practical goal.

The idea that Israel is entitled to exist is not accepted in the Arab world.[18]

The Arabs do not reject the goal of Israel's liquidation for any moral reasons; it is regarded as justified. Ihsān ʿAbd al-Quddūs writes:

> "I do not wish to say that there is any Arab force whatsoever or any factor whatsoever which is liable to oppose the liberation of Palestine, or to support the survival of Israel. That is impossible *(mustaḥīl)*; it does not even occur to me or to any Arab. All Arab forces, progressive and reactionary, are unanimous in regard to the elimination *(izāḥa)* of Israel." (*Rūz al-Yūsuf,* March 8, 1965).

The doubts and questions, therefore, do not apply to the justice of the aim, but to the possibility of its achievement and the methods to be employed. On the subject of methods there is a break in the homogeneity of the Arab attitude. Such doubts are concerned with general world conditions, estimates of Israel's power to resist and the strength of the Arabs themselves. It is because of these doubts and questionings that many Arab leaders have spoken of Israel at least once without using such absolute terms as war, liquidation or destruction, even if this meant a deviation from their usual way of referring to the problem.[19]

If we want to know the basic attitude of such an Arab leader, it seems that we must examine the attitude he adopts in most cases, compare the statements he makes on various occasions, review his actions and the relationship between them and his words, and generalize on the basis of all this evidence. People are not consistent; even when it is a matter of firmly held opinions, they are liable to deviate from their usual way of expressing themselves as a result of a passing mood, a temporary feeling of depression, or the like, but such moments may be outweighed by the attitudes expressed on most occasions. We must not seize on the exceptional statement just because we find it more pleasant, or more reasonable, and assume that it reflects the true attitude of the spokesman; the result may be a distortion of the facts, if not a deliberate deception.

It is not only declarations about the indirect objective, but also outspoken statements about acquiescence in Israel's existence that are sometimes ambiguous. Let us take, for example, the statements by Bourguiba which made such a great impression. His attitude underwent a process of development, and his later statements were considerably clearer than his declarations in Jerusalem and Beirut.

At his press conference in Jerusalem on March 6, 1965 (*Filasṭīn,* March 7, 1965) he spoke of cooperation with the Jews on an honourable basis. He did not expressly refer to recognition of Israel, and he might have been said to have been thinking of tolerance towards "Jews" and "the People of the Book" in general—certainly no novel or revolutionary idea—or the possibility of the Jews living as a community but not as a State.

On the other hand, in his joint statement with King Hussein at the end of his visit to Jordan (Amman Radio, March 7, 1965), they expressed their support for the resolutions and plans adopted at the Summit Conference. In his statements, moreover, Bourguiba continued to advocate "the liberation of Palestine by the people of Palestine," "its restoration to its owners" and "the rectification of the injustice" (in the Turkish Parliament, reported in *Ha'aretz,* March 26, 1965), which amounts to identification with the usual Arab attitude.

Sometimes (as on March 6, 1965), he said that the struggle with Israel involves a process of decolonialization, that the Palestinians must take the initiative in this struggle, and that the Arab countries would help them. He declared that Tunisia was ready to play her part in case of war with Israel (in Beirut, March 11, 1965).

In view of this *embarras de choix,* Bourguiba's listeners, including the Israelis, have a wide range of different possible ways of understanding his attitude. It is noteworthy that even his statement of the need to solve the problem stage by stage is not incompatible with liquidation; Israel could be liquidated by degrees, the demands continuing to grow in accordance with Bourguiba's principle of "take and demand more." "The stolen right can be restored by stages," he says, "and Tunisian experience can help our brethren in the East." (*Filasṭīn,* March 7, 1965).

A Tunisian official in Bourguiba's entourage explained to a journalist in Tehran that the Tunisian President's words had been misinterpreted: the statement that Jews and Arabs could live together on a basis of mutual respect, he explained, did not mean coexistence with Israel as a State but only with the Jews in general (*Ha'aretz,* March 22, 1965).

Haykal took note of this correction and accepted it:

> "His party had issued and repeated this correction, and so had Foreign Minister Mongi Slim in Cairo, explaining that Bourguiba was thinking of the possibility of peaceful coexistence between the Arab peoples and a Jewish minority which would live amongst them after Israel was liquidated.
>
> "I am inclined to accept this correction for two reasons. I do not think that there is any notable Arab who can conceive the possibility of peaceful coexistence between the Arab peoples and Israel. On the other hand, why should I insist on refuting the man's words when he says, 'This was my intention and all

the rest was a matter of unfortunate choice of words or misunderstanding.'?" (*al-Ahrām,* May 26, 1965).

The Tunisian paper *al-ʿAmal* criticized Haykal's article, but wrote in more or less the same vein:

> "We do not hate the Jews because they are Jews, but we are fighting Zionist imperialism, and we have no objection to coexistence of Muslims with Jews in a liberated State." (Quoted in *al-Ḥayāt,* April 1, 1965).

The war against Zionist imperialism means war against Israel, which, according to the Arabs, is imperialist in nature. "A liberated State" does not mean recognition of Israel; on the contrary, it assumes the extinction of Israel's political existence.

This ambiguity enables the Arab leader to express himself in a way which, although in itself it may indicate a very slight possibility of acquiescence in Israel's existence, is liable to be understood by the Arabs in general in its most extreme connotation. The advantage of the ambiguity in indirect statements of the objective is that everyone can understand them as he pleases.

The uncertainty among some of the Arabs as to the possibility of liquidating Israel may also be discerned in the fact that statements recognizing that a war of extermination is not a practicable solution, or indicating even a slight degree of acquiescence in Israel's existence, do not arouse a violent reaction, although they are angrily denounced; it seems that such ideas are no longer regarded as a novel heresy. Perhaps, after all, the Arabs hear them as an echo of their own debates with themselves as to the practicability of the liquidation objectives; even though they have not ventured to express their doubts aloud, there is something familiar in the idea. It is noteworthy that Bourguiba's statements did not arouse a storm at first, but only at a later stage, when his attitude was given publicity and assumed the character of a denunciation of Nasser and the common attitude of the Arabs in the conflict.

It should be pointed out that there is considerable value even in statements which only defer the idea of war as a solution to the problem. They increase doubts as to the possibility of liquidation; they intensify the internal debate and weaken the taboo which Arab public opinion has imposed on all expressions of doubt as to the possibility of achieving the aim.

The aim of liquidating Israel is not, therefore, something fixed and immovable; it fluctuates within a continuum that stretches between the poles of a practical goal and a heartfelt aspiration. People are liable to indulge in dreams, even if they realize that they cannot be translated into reality, in the hope that perhaps, after all, conditions for their realization will be created. The Arab attitude, however, is not merely one of waiting for a miracle, for they adopt practical measures to increase their strength as a preparation for the clash they long for, and in the hope of helping the miracle to take place. With the emergence of the idea of a war of national liberation, which many Arabs regard as the long-sought recipe for the liquidation of Israel, the goal had, as it were, been shifted towards the pole of a practical possibility.

There cannot, therefore, be any categorical reply to the question whether the Arab world (in itself a dangerous generalization) regards the liquidation of Israel as a practical goal or not. Sometimes they think of it as a matter of the distant future and they take no part in the conflict at present. Sometimes they cherish it as an abstract wish.* Sometimes they are convinced devotees of the goal—whether to a greater or lesser extent. The attitude of the Arabs interested in the dispute consists of degrees of non-acquiescence—or of acquiescence—in Israel's existence. It may be summed up by saying that they tell themselves, as it were, that it is still too early to despair of the liquidation of Israel, which may, after all, be possible one day.

12. THE DYNAMICS OF THE OBJECTIVE

Since when has the liquidation of Israel been the objective of the Arabs? Have they also had other aims?

As we have noticed, the Arab attitude in the conflict is not a primary one: their objective had been formulated as a reaction to the activities and achievements of the Jews—first in settling, and then in the establishment of their State. However, it is marked by a considerable degree of consistency. The Arabs opposed Jewish settlement even in the days of Ottoman rule; in its early stages, they expressed their apprehensions that the growth of the Jewish population and the acquisition of lands by Jews might give them a foothold in the country, and that these developments might undermine the rule of the Turks and encroach on the position of the inhabitants.[20] Even in the early stages of Jewish settle-

* It may be assumed that the Six-Day War has shaken the faith of many Arabs in the possibility of liquidating Israel and shifted the objective in the direction of wishful aspirations.

ment, there were some Arabs who attributed to Zionism the goal of establishing a Jewish State. After the Balfour Declaration they were particularly alive to the Zionist danger from their point of view.

There were some indications among the Arabs, especially the non-Palestinians, of a readiness to recognize the special rights of the Jews in Palestine, and even to acquiesce in the establishment of a Jewish National Home.[21] This readiness was at first conditional on Jewish financial aid for the Arabs to facilitate the development of their territories. In one case, there was even a demand that Arabic should become the language of the Jews in Palestine (N. Mandel, in *Middle East Studies,* April 1965, p. 243). Language is a major component of Arab nationalism, so this demand meant the preservation of the Arab character of the country.

Nothing emerged from these few contacts. In his study of the Arab attitude towards Jewish and Zionist settlement, Mandel says that the general feeling in Palestine was already too hostile in 1914 for an Arab-Jewish understanding to remain in force. The motives of the Arab leaders who tried to achieve agreement were tactical and dependent on political aims, which were partially achieved in World War I (*ibid.,* p. 264).

Contacts continued after World War I. There was a readiness to recognize special Jewish rights of immigration and settlement in return for a political *quid pro quo:* Jewish assistance in the achievement of complete Arab independence, which meant the expulsion of the British and, especially, the French, and the unification of the Arab territories: namely, a political sacrifice in Palestine in return for a political gain outside it. This was the point of the reservation that the Emir Fayṣal wrote in the margin of his agreement with Weizmann, making cooperation between the Arabs and the Jewish National Home conditional on the granting of Arab claims.

Zionism was unable to fulfil this function of helping to eliminate the Mandatory Powers, both because its strength was limited and because its continued activities depended on recognition by the British Mandatory, but it was always ready to provide economic compensation, emphasizing the economic advantages derived by the Arabs from Jewish settlement. The dialogue between Arabs and Jew was, thus, conducted on two planes: the Jews stressed the economic aspect and the Arabs the political.

The Arab nationalist movement had not yet taken shape as a mass phenomenon, it is true, and the Arab States were preoccupied with their national problems, but their concern for the Arab character of Palestine emerged at an early stage. They wanted, therefore, to guarantee that Palestine would remain Arab, even if a special status were granted to the

Jews, by ensuring that it would belong to an Arab federation. This would strengthen the Arab character of the country as a counterweight to the Jews.

The main aim of the Jews in any settlement, on the other hand, was to ensure that the country should be open to Jewish immigration. The Arabs, however, could not agree to any such principle. They, especially the Palestinians, understood that continued immigration and Jewish settlement would augment the foreign element in the population and change the character of the country—or, in the terms current among them today, would "liquidate" the Arab national character of Palestine.

This is not the place to discuss whether the way in which the Arab-Israel conflict actually developed—Arab objectives being as they were—was inevitable. It cannot be assumed that, since things developed as they did, they were bound to develop in this way. On the other hand, it cannot reasonably be argued with any confidence that things might have developed differently. Zionism aspired to make the country Jewish and worked to increase the Jewish hold on it. The Arabs, especially the Palestinians, insisted on the preservation of its Arab character; this was their objective in their political struggle, and it was to this end that they tried to frustrate the efforts of the Jews. In such circumstances the antagonism was frontal, and a compromise would, perhaps, have been a miracle. Even if it had been achieved, moreover, it may be questioned whether it could have lasted long, and whether the Arabs of Palestine, in cooperation with the Jews, could have remained outside the tide of Arab nationalism. It is an exaggeration to say that the upsurge of Arab nationalism was due to the stimulus of the conflict; it is a fact that it flared up in other places unconnected with the dispute.

During the period of the Mandate, the constant demands of the Arabs were:

a) The stoppage of immigration, i.e. the prevention of a change in the population balance to the advantage of the Jews, and at the same the prohibition of land sales to the Jews.[22]
b) The immediate establishment of an Arab State in accordance with the right of self-determination, on the grounds that the Balfour Declaration and the recognition of special Jewish rights violated this fundamental principle.

The insistence of the Arabs on the indisputable right to self-determination for the majority of the population involved a danger, from the viewpoint of the Jews, to their existence as a community with a measure of independence and autonomy, for the rights of the majority included the power to oppress the minority. Obviously, an Arab majority would have prevented the absorption of many Jews and the renewal of Jewish sovereignty in an independent State. Arab aims during the Mandatory period may, therefore, be regarded as *preventive action* to frustrate the establishment of the National Home and the Jewish State. It was because the national struggle of the Palestinian Arabs was devoted to these aims that there were uprisings by the Arab national movement and outbreaks of violence. When the possibility of the partition of the country and the establishment of the Jewish State emerged, the efforts of the Palestinian Arabs, supported by the Arab States, were directed to the prevention of such a development. This was the aim of the Arab League's activities from 1946 to the middle of 1948.

When the UN decided on partition, the Palestinian Arabs, again with the help of the Arab States, tried to prevent it by violent means. The direct activities of the Arab States were dedicated to the same end, but at first mainly by political means. When this was unsuccessful, and the British Mandatory authorities evacuated Palestine, the armies of the neighbouring Arab countries invaded, and the struggle changed its character from that of a civil war to a war between States.

After the State of Israel was established, the aim of preventing its establishment gave way to the aim of liquidating the State that had arisen. Although this was the fundamental aim, there were variations from time to time in emphasis and shades of expression. During the early years after the 1948 war, the aim was formulated as "the Second Round"—namely, the quest for an opportunity for a further clash in order to wipe out the disgrace of defeat. Even then, however, there were many declarations about the liquidation which would follow as a result of Arab victory. Particularly prominent was the psychological motivation: the desire for compensation for their injuries and the shock of defeat. The impression may be gained that, with the passage of time, the demand for liquidation had more and more taken on the character of idea and ideology. In general, this development may be regarded as indicating a stiffening and radicalization of the liquidatory objective.

In the early 50's there were widespread hopes in the Arab world that Israel would suffer an economic collapse, so that they would not have to take military action to eliminate her.[23] There was also some talk of limited objectives, such as the severance of the Negev from Israel, which Egypt demanded to prevent her being cut off from the Arab countries in Asia.[24]

This was presented more as a claim than as a condition the fulfilment of which would be followed by a peace settlement.

Let us examine how the development of the objective is reflected in the arguments used to justify it.

Before the establishment of the State of Israel, the central theme in the Arab case was the matter of rights. It was argued that the granting of rights to the Jews was a violation of the natural rights of the Arabs, particularly of the principle of self-determination as the fundamental political right of nations. According to another argument, it was a breach of the undertakings that had been given to the Arabs. The case was simple and, it may be said, natural: opposition to a foreign people gaining control over Arab territory. At that period, the burden of proof lay on Zionism: it had to show why the area should become Jewish. Since the basis of the argument was the right to self-determination, the demands of the Palestinian Arabs were presented as absolute juridical claims (this type of plea may have been to the liking of the Arab leaders, most of whom were lawyers).

Although most of the ideas and arguments which are typical of the period when the demand is the liquidation of Israel were also expressed in previous periods, and the call for liquidation was the outcome of the opposition to the establishment of a Jewish State, the two demands are on different planes. There is no comparison between the harshness of the demand not to establish a State and the call for its destruction. Once the objective had become the liquidation and extinction of an existing entity, the burden of proof was transferred to the Arabs; hence their constant preoccupation with the question, as we shall see below.

Chapter 2

THE ARAB IDEOLOGY OF THE CONFLICT

1. WHY IDEOLOGY?

The rivals in an international dispute find it necessary to explain and justify their aims and methods, as well as to point out the weakness of their opponent's case, in order to secure the support of their peoples in the struggle and imbue them with a fighting spirit. This complex constitutes the ideology of the conflict, which is, as has been noted in the introduction, the intellectual aspect of the "attitude." In the past, kings could lead their peoples to war without taking much trouble to explain their aims, but today much greater attention is paid to propaganda and indoctrination. With the rise of the nation-State, the growth of the democratic idea and the mobilization of the masses, there has been a greater need to substantiate the attitude on ideological lines. In the world of today, rivals tend to ascribe an ideological motivation to a confrontation which would otherwise appear to be a clash of interests, and even to present their hostility to each other as a matter of principle.

There is an obvious contrast between the manner in which the two parties to the Arab-Israel dispute have developed their ideologies of the conflict. While on the Arab side there are a wide variety of ideological activities in connection with the issue, and many books are published on the subject, there has been little ideological treatment of it on the Israeli side. Why do the Arabs devote so much attention to this aspect of the conflict?

First, the development of ideologies plays a particularly prominent role today in societies that aspire to bring about changes in their way of life, whether social and internal or national. In a society which is relatively content with the *status quo,* interest in ideology is less intense. Ideology, and especially the fervor that accompanies it, is mainly characteristic of rebels. Thus, with the progress of industrialization and economic development, with the rise in the standard of living and the achievement of social and national aims, ideological activity may decline. We see this phenomenon in the West, including the Soviet Union, and there are signs of it in Israel as well.

The main foci of ideological fervor in our day, therefore, are societies that feel the need to change their way of life through modernization, industrialization and economic growth, and which aspire to transform their social and moral values and develop their national personalities.

Such ideologies explain the reasons for backwardness and mark out the lines of development to a happier future; they provide a basis for self-respect and help to inspire faith in the change that is required and mobilize support for it; they are presented as a guarantee that the aims will be secured. Ideology is also instrumental in securing popular support for the regime and the ruling group as representing the "true" will of the people. The considerable attention paid in the Arab world to ideology, including that of the Arab-Israel conflict, may therefore be regarded as a case of ideological activity in what are known as the developing countries. Some of its ideas, such as the question of national resurgence and the struggle against imperialism and colonialism (and Israel's association with them) are related to the ideologies current today in these countries.

Secondly, when progress towards the desired aims is delayed, the leaders are liable to resort to exaggerated ideological activity, which serves as a substitute for achievement and a compensation for failure.[1] At such times, the ruling group may make a demogogic use of ideology, by manipulating symbols and slogans to paste over the gap between aims and achievements. There are grounds for the assumption that the growth of Arab ideological activity in connection with the Arab-Israel dispute is also due to the fact that time has passed and Arab aims have not yet been achieved.

Thirdly, such an unusual, radical and grandiose aim as the liquidation of a State calls for, on the one hand, explanation and justification both at home and abroad, and, on the other hand, a political and historical analysis to prove that the goal is indeed feasible. As we shall see, the Arab ideology of the conflict comprises a detailed treatment of these subjects.

a) THE NATURE OF THE IDEOLOGY

In the West, ideologies have been developed by intellectuals, who have given them a historio-philosophical character. In the developing countries, on the other hand, it is the ruling circles that largely give the tone in the development of ideologies, which are more pragmatic, as they are mainly designed to achieve the practical aims of the Government. However, an effort is also made to endow these ideologies with an intellectual approach involving a broad world outlook and historical interpretations. The claim that the ideology reflects great, historical truths helps to secure the support and devotion of the people. This desire to give the ideology a philosophical guise may seem to be aimed at giving it an artificial appearance of depth. Its ideas may be regarded by the foreign observer as eclectic and shallow; he may even deny them the name of ideology and reject them as a mere jumble of rhetorical phrases and slogans—especially as his expectations in this field may be influenced by Marxism as the archetypal ideology. We should beware, however, of measuring ideologies by this criterion, and especially of belittling the importance of other peoples' ideas when they are not to our liking; our reservations should not lead us to conclude that they will not be influential. Israelis should be particularly careful, in examining the Arab ideology, not to be influenced by their own approach to the Arabs, which is an outcome of the antagonism between them.

Another point should be noted. In the Arab countries, ideology today has an intensely nationalist coloration. In most of them, socialism has been adopted not in its universalist, cosmopolitan form, but specifically as "Arab Socialism."

The attempt to achieve completeness and profundity is also to be found in the Arab ideology of the conflict, and much effort has been devoted to the development of its ideas. It is presented as an integral part of the national ideology, which claims to be the result of a historical analysis of the processes which the Arabs have undergone and their place in the world.

b) CRITERIA OF IDEOLOGIES

(i) *The Study of Ideas.* As stated in the introduction, I have tried to collect the ideas which together constitute the attitude of the Arabs and mould their ideology, and have made an effort to detect their significance. Since ideology is not a passionless scientific theory, but fulfils psychological functions and reflects pressures, preoccupations and aspirations, it is not enough to analyse the intellectual content of the ideas. We must examine the roles they play, the emotional charge they carry, and the psychological mechanisms that may have helped to mould them. To clarify the deeper significance of the ideas, we shall also have to enquire into historical and cultural associations, as well as where and under what conditions similar ideas have emerged in the past. Such an ideological analysis may assume the form of a work of comparative cultural and historical research, limited mainly by the author's knowledge and intellectual qualifications. In looking for the psychological significance of the ideas, use has been made of explanations, and even of empirical proofs, of the operation of psychological mechanisms which seem to be relevant and applicable to various ideological phenomena to be found among the Arabs in connection with the conflict. For example, Karl W. Deutsch and Richard L. Merritt state, in their article, "Results of National and International Events and Images" (in Kelman, H. C. [ed.]: *International Behavior,* 1966, p. 167), that in 1933–4 there were signs of opposition in Germany to acts of cruelty against the Jews, but the expulsion of the Jews and their segregation from the population from 1936 onward had a dehumanizing effect, and therefore increased the readiness of the German population to acquiesce in their extermination. The authors reach the conclusion that distance contributes to dehumanization. Although such a conclusion seems self-evident, and even banal, these findings appear to be sufficiently suggestive to justify the speculation that the diminution of contact between Arabs and Jews and the exodus of Jews from the Arab countries may contribute to a measure of dehumanization, which will be reflected in the Arab image of the Jews and of Israel.

Such explanations, it is true, are speculative: there is no certainty that the psychological mechanism described was actually operative in regard to any particular idea. How, for example, can we find out the part played by dehumanization in the Arab expressions which reflect an unfavourable image of Israel and the Jews (especially when we have no opportunity to conduct field researches)? Moreover, there is no guarantee that empirical findings arrived at among other peoples are valid for, or applicable to, the Arabs. However, if we abstain from the use of psychological explanations of this type, or explanations derived from experience and introspection, of whose validity we have no conclusive proof, we shall be abandoning large areas of the field. Every historical work, every social or political analysis, makes copious use of such explanations. Of course, there is a danger of going too far and succumbing to the temptation of speculative psychologizing, and we must be cautious in these matters. Psychological explanations are therefore given as assumptions or speculations, and not as tried and tested conclusions.

(ii) *Coherence.* In examining an ideology it is not enough to examine each idea by itself; we must also pay attention to the connections of the ideas with each other, the extent to which they are compatible or contradictory, and how they are woven into a logical fabric. Ideologies certainly try to reconcile their inner contradictions and minimize their "cognitive dissonances." It may be assumed that the more an ideology is a coherent framework, the more persuasive it will be. An analysis of the ideas from the viewpoint of the gaps in them is also important, because it may shed light on the difficulties that confronted their authors.

(iii) *Repercussions of Influences.* An ideology starts with a description of the situation which it amis to rectify; it is designed to impel men to action. Hence, its main test is the currency of its ideas: the extent to which the public identifies itself with them and is influenced by them. It is not an abstract set of ideas; it carries an emotional charge and involves a commitment to action. It is a social phenomenon—a set of ideas, concepts and beliefs cherished by a community, as distinguished from the ideas of an individual, which, at the most, constitute his personal *Weltanschauung.* Furthermore, since the ideology is meant to influence a community, it must be openly proclaimed; it cannot be an unarticulated "set of beliefs."[2] From this point of view, too, we should pay particular attention to the declarations which are public property and are meant to influence people; opinions that people venture to express only in private are not necessarily part of the ideology.

Such an approach leads to methodological conclusions which are of importance for our study. Only those ideas that exert public influence can be regarded as belonging to the ideology. Ideological research is not concerned with the development of the ideas of authors who have had no influence, no matter how intellectually sublime they may have been. The works of such authors might, it is true, be regarded as ideological, in the sense that they were written in order to influence public opinion and arouse the community to action, without having become a part of its ideology. This does not mean, however, that such books are of no value in ideological research. It is difficult to decide which books may be included in the ideological category as defined here and which may not, since it may sometimes be difficult to foresee the influence—perhaps indirect—of a particular idea, book, or author. Furthermore, a book or an idea, even if it does not have a widespread circulation and influence, may be of symptomatic significance as evidence of the type of ideas that were liable to emerge in a given society under given circumstances. Sometimes it is in books which have not become common property that one can find the more profound dimensions of prevalent ideas and opinions. Such is, for example, the literature on the conflict which was written by Arab professors of the American University in Beirut, and issued by the research centers for the study of Palestine problems in that city. In these books, although they were not read by the masses, the Arab argument in the conflict was elaborated. The attitude they express is no different from that to be found in other publications, but it is better substantiated, especially as some of these books are written in English and are designed to explain the Arab case to foreigners.

Since an ideology relates to ideas with a practical purpose, which are tested by the extent of their influence, it seems advisable to pay special attention to the ideas expressed by political leaders. It is they who determine the political position of their country, which generally influences the public attitude as well. From the propaganda material issued by the leaders we can at least learn what the authorities want the people to believe and what atmosphere they are trying to create. So long as the leaders are popular, it may be assumed that their opinions are accepted. The people look up to them, and in most Arab countries they have exclusive control over the mass communications media (press, radio and television), information and propaganda offices, publicity machinery and the educational system. It is in their power to disseminate their ideas and impress them on the public. It may, therefore, be assumed that statements by leaders exert an influence on the attitudes and opinions prevalent among the Arab public, even if the position of the leaders in several Arab countries is unstable and the ruler who is carried in triumph today may be trampled underfoot tomorrow.

We must take a further step, however, and try to examine to what extent the ideas comprising what we here call the ideology are accepted by the public, digested and made a part of its attitude—to what extent the ideology becomes a personal outlook. It is true that anyone who investigates the "attitudes," "thoughts" and "concepts" of a community or a nation is treading on the shaky ground of generalization and abstraction, for in concrete terms there are only individuals, each with his own thoughts and attitudes, even if these are determined by their membership of the community in question. The statement that a particular attitude is actually to be found in a community is tantamount to confirming that there is a correspondence between the attitudes of the individuals to the issue concerned, and this can be scientifically investigated only by field surveys and polls designed to discover to what extent particular ideas are really public property. Where the Arab-Israel conflict is concerned, it is doubtful whether even non-Israelis would be free to conduct such surveys in the Arab countries. Field studies would reveal the distribution of a particular idea from the point of view of its content, but we are compelled to assume its distribution on the basis of its source, namely who enunciated it and advocates it. This study, therefore, will rely particularly on statements by leaders, ministers, journalists, official publications, propaganda material, press and radio. We shall also try to estimate the frequency with which an idea is expressed: we may assume that the greater the incidence of its advocacy, by many people on various occasions, the more widely it is accepted.

I shall return to this subject, with a more detailed analysis of the factors affecting the identification of the Arabs with their ideology, in Chapter VIII, "From Ideology to Attitude."

(iv) *The Criterion of Sincerity.* We must maintain a very critical attitude in examining the statements of the leaders, in case what they are saying is no more than demagogy, rhetoric or a matter of tactics—although these, too, are of significance, for the question will arise why these specific ideas in particular are susceptible to demagogic and rhetorical exploitation.

(v) *Realism.* The principal test of an ideology is its relevance to the world of action, to reality, and its capacity to influence them. From this point of view, ideology is the intellectual dimension of historical events: it represents people's thinking about the events and the way they try to mould them. We must, therefore, examine the translation of the ideology into a program and into action, and the feedback effect of practical difficulties. Ideology does not always precede action; it may also follow, in order to explain or justify it. Ideology may be the outcome of rationalization, which is the presentation of "respectable" reasons for behaviour without describing its true motives, which may be either interests or impulses. Such rationalizations sometimes give an "ideological" instead of a true and sincere explanation. However, the very fact that acts and tendencies which are not truly ideological in character have to be painted in ideological colours may point to discontent with things as they are.

It is by no means inevitable, therefore, that there should be a simple direct correspondence between ideology and action. There may be gaps and incongruities between action on the one hand, and thoughts and feelings on the other. Ideology represents what is desired and hoped for, rather than what actually exists, though aspirations are also significant.

The evaluation of the realism of an ideology may be problematical and complicated by the prejudices and interests of the evaluator. If the latter, for instance, is hostile to the ideology and interested in it not being realized, he may tend in advance to regard it as unrealistic and conclude that it is the outcome of an "unsound" approach. Realism is also a matter of time. The adherents of an ideology may argue that, while their approach may not be realistic today, the situation will change and their ideas will be realized. Their opponents, too, may expect them to become "realistic" and abandon their ideology in the course of time.

c) SOURCES

The Egyptian Government is outstanding in the Arab world for its activities in the fields of information and propaganda. Not that the ideas expressed are original; many of them have been previously enunciated in various forms in other Arab countries, where authors were more fertile in developing Arab national ideas—and where, even today, some writers go deeper and ask more precise and fundamental questions, which are ignored by the Egyptian ideologists. Egypt, however, has taken up some of these ideas with such force and energy as to make them common property; they are disseminated by the propaganda machine which harps on them repeatedly.

Although much attention is paid to ideology in Egypt, there is not much ideological discussion; there is more repetition than original thinking. Nasser has even complained that, after the regime had laid down the basic lines of the ideology, he expected that the intellectuals would develop these ideas and build them up into an ideological edifice, but they simply went on repeating them by rote instead.

In the study of Egyptian ideology, Nasser's speeches are of particular importance; most of them are of an ideological tenor and they contain the principal themes propagated by Government spokesmen. Furthermore, the status that Nasser has won in the Arab world ensures that his words are listened to, and exert an influence, beyond the frontiers of his country. This does not mean, of course, that everything he says about the conflict is accepted in all Arab countries, and this aspect has to be examined in detail.

The essentials of the UAR's ideology are to be found in the National Charter, presented by Nasser on May 21, 1962 at the National Conference of the Popular Forces and approved June 30.

Ideological activity in Egypt is also expressed in the flood of books, booklets and propaganda pamphlets issued under the direct or indirect patronage of Dr. 'Abd al-Qādir Ḥātim, who was for a long time Deputy Prime Minister and Deputy President for Culture and National Guidance.[3] These publications will be an important source for our study, although we cannot accurately determine their circulation and the extent to which they are read by the people. Nor can we regard every line in this plethora of literature as exactly representing the views of the authorities; we shall therefore have to ascribe importance to the ideas most frequently expressed in it.

These are not only works of information and propaganda, but from the viewpoint of their publishers they are, at least in part, aimed at research, study and the presentation of facts. They contain many historical chapters, describing Jewish history, the development of Zionist settlement, the British Mandate and the history of Zionism. This interest in Zionist history and thought is presented as a pragmatic requirement of the struggle. For example, 'Umar Rushdī, lecturer in National Guidance at the Egyptian Military Academy, writes in the introduction to his book *Zionism and Its Fosterchild Israel* (second edition, 1965), which is described as a textbook used in the Academy:

> "A true conception of Zionism in its factual, living form is a matter that is bound up with the foundation of Arab existence, for the more the Arabs understand this picture the greater will be their faith in their rights and they will risk their lives for its [Palestine's] restoration. Such knowledge is, therefore, armour for the Arabs and a support for their security."

An important source is the books of indoctrination issued by the Supreme Command of the Armed Forces in the UAR, which reached my hands after the Six-Day War. The Egyptian Command also published a series of pamphlets called *Niḍālunā* ("Our Struggle") and *Min Ḥayātinā* ("From Our Lives"). In these publications we find a picture identical with that in the civilian publications.

In reaction to the UAR ideology and the National Charter, Jordan issued its own version of the ideology in 1962 in the form of a "White Paper" officially entitled *Jordan, the Palestine Problem and Inter-Arab Relations,* with an introduction by King Hussein, published by the Jordanian Foreign Ministry. This document was apparently compiled on the initiative of the then Jordanian Foreign Minister, Anwar al-Nusayba, although it deals with subjects beyond the scope of foreign policy. The ideas it contains are repeated in various forms by Jordanian spokesmen, headed by the King. (A statement on the publication of the book was made by Wasfī al-Tall, the Jordanian Prime Minister, at a press conference held on July 2, 1962.)

Another official document is the Palestinian National Covenant of the Palestine Liberation Organization, which was adopted at the first Palestinian Congress in Jerusalem on May 18, 1964.

The rival Palestinian organization, under the Arab Higher Committee led by al-Ḥajj Amīn al-Husseini, the former Mufti of Jerusalem, also published its credo in the form of the Covenant of the Palestinian National Movement.

The Ba'th Party in Syria preceded the rest by publishing, in 1947, the Constitution of the Ba'th, which is supplemented by the resolutions passed at the congresses of this inter-Arab party.

The second source of books on the subject, after the UAR, is Lebanon, in which a large number of books on the conflict have been published. While we may suspect the literature appearing in the UAR as official propaganda material, this suspicion does not apply to the Lebanese literature to the same extent. In Lebanon, there are also two research institutions dealing with the conflict, whose output, which is also published in English, represents an "academic" approach.

Iraq, through the Ministry for Culture and Guidance, has issued a series of information pamphlets in English, which contain references to the conflict.

It is only natural that the bulk of the writers on this subject, not only in Egypt, are Palestinians, who are better versed in the problem and more closely concerned with it. However, they have no monopoly and there are a considerable number of others.

Problems associated with the conflict are prominently featured in Arab newspapers and broadcasts. Of course, I have not been able to scrutinize all the Arab Press (consisting of dozens of daily papers and many weeklies), and the quotations from it are, necessarily, fortuitous.

In this study, the main attention has been paid to the attitude of the UAR, and next to those of Israel's other Arab neighbours. Egypt's status and her close connection with the conflict entitle her to pride of place. This does not mean, however, that the basic attitudes of the other States, apart from programmatic problems, are different from Egypt's. In fundamental matters, there is a large measure of homogeneity in the Arab attitude. As for the North African States, their distance from the focus of the conflict weakens their connections with it.* Generally, apart from Bourguiba's statements, they tend to adhere—if only declaratively—to the accepted Arab attitude. There is a need for a series of research studies and monographs to describe the position of the separate Arab countries in connection with the conflict.

We shall now examine how the Arabs justify the aim of liquidating Israel, and how they define the conflict and what it is about. Next, we shall discuss their idea of the enemy, and what they think about Zionism, the Jews, Israel and themselves in the conflict.

2. JUSTIFICATION FOR LIQUIDATION OF ISRAEL

The objective of liquidation is not expressed merely in the adoption of an attitude; it involves repeated and continuing argumentation to justify it. The various types of justification for liquidation constitute a central chapter in the Arab ideology of the conflict. The discussion of the nature of Israel, the characterization of Israel as an odious State, and the denigration of the Jews are a kind of proof and confirmation that Israel deserves the fate in store for her. The image of Israel is used to support the reasons for her liquidation and is a part of them.

I shall try to take stock, as it were, of the arguments used by Arab spokesmen to justify liquidation. They are not presented in bulk; generally, Arab writers emphasize one idea or another with various nuances, but taken together they may give a picture which is essential for the understanding of the Arab attitude in the conflict.

a) LIQUIDATION AS THE RECTIFICATION OF A HISTORIC INJUSTICE

The Arabs seem to feel that the liquidation of a State is an unusual solution for an international dispute, and they justify it on the grounds that the dispute is also an unusual one, since it is founded on an unusual injustice: the usurpation of a territory and the expulsion of a nation. States and peoples have been defeated on many occasions without the defeat altering the

* The Six-Day War has intensified Algeria's interest in the conflict, at least on the level of political leadership.

nationality of the defeated side's territory; in this case, however, the Arab national character of the territory has been wiped out and a foreign nationalism imposed on it. Israel was created through an appalling crime, and all its history is a chain of actions which are a profanation of the sanctities of international morality. In deliberate disregard for the population's right to self-determination, foreigners were permitted to enter the territory. Gradually and cunningly, they gained a foothold; later, they forcibly expelled the lawful inhabitants from their lands and took over their property. This an act of robbery and theft, the Arab spokesmen argue, to which there is no parallel in the annals of mankind. Here are some examples of such arguments:

al-Jumhūriyya: "It is possible that we may agree to Israel's statement that in the Pact of Unity published by a State-member of the United Nations, attention was drawn to the article dealing with the destruction of another State which is also a member of the UN. But we argue that this is the first time in the history of the UN and of humanity that there has been a case in which a foreign people gained control of the homeland of another people by force and expelled it beyond the borders of its country." (April 30, 1963).

Nasser has often declared that the establishment of Israel was the greatest crime in history:

"To the disaster of Palestine there is no parallel in human history." (December 23, 1953. I.L., I/154, October 1, 1963).

"Israel committed the greatest crime in modern history by liquidating the people of Palestine." (July 9, 1955, I.L., IV/835).

"The mention of Palestine is sufficient to remind every Arab—indeed, every free man—of the greatest international crime that has been committed in the entire history of mankind. History has witnessed from time to time the partition of a territory, or deprivation *(intigāṣ),* but not a criminal attempt like that designed by the Zionists for the obliteration *(maḥū)* of Arab nationality in Palestine." (July 22, 1955, I.L., IV/913).

"There have been wars between States, but the tragedy that has befallen us . . . is not to be compared with any war of aggression, for this tragedy is the expression of the liquidation *(ibāda)* of an Arab people, its expulsion from its homeland and the theft of its soil." (May 15, 1958).

"The episode of the Palestinian refugees is a blot on the record of twentieth-century civilization, since for the first time in history an entire people has been expelled by force from its home." (August 10, 1959).

"Ben-Gurion . . . is the greatest war criminal in this century. Some say that it is Hitler, but did Hitler liquidate the nation of a State *(sha'b dawla)* as Ben-Gurion liquidated an entire nation-state?" (March 4, 1960).

'Abd al-Laṭīf Sharāra called his book: *Zionism the Greatest Crime of the Age* (1964).

Such arguments, besides serving to elucidate ideas, also express a burning sense of wrong and injustice and bear a powerful emotional charge. There are grounds for the belief that the Arabic words for wrong, harm and injustice *(ẓulm, ḍaym, jawr)* have a stronger connotation (or valence) than their equivalents in other languages. It is not only a matter of iniquity, but of personal injury and a sense of disgrace which cries out for vengeance. Moreover, refusal to acquiesce in injustice or robbery is a characteristic that the Arabs ascribe to themselves as part of their self-image; al-Jiyyār describes the Arabs as a people who will not acquiesce in robbery (*lā yaṣburūn 'alā ḍaym,* p. 34).

b) THE AIM: RECTIFICATION OF THE INJUSTICE, NOT LIQUIDATION

This is a basic and recurrent argument, expressed or implied. The rights of the Palestinian Arabs take precedence over those of the Jews, who are recent arrivals. Their right to self-determination has been violated by a series of acts imcompatible with this natural and fundamental right: the Balfour Declaration, the Mandate, the partition decision, and finally, their becoming refugees. "A free and honorable return of the Palestinian Arab people to its homeland is a natural and deeply rooted right," the Council of the Arab League resolved on February 29, 1960 (quoted in Nawfal's article "The Palestinian Entity," p. 35).

First of all, the wrong must be rectified, that is, the refugees must have their property restored and be given the right to decide. If Israel must disappear in order to make this possible, that is only a proof that she should never have come into being. The aim is a positive one: the rectification of the wrong, justice, the liberation of the homeland of a plundered people—and any negative by-product for others would be no fault of the Arabs. This argument, as we have seen, is the basis for the indirect definitions of the objective.

This form of argument constantly recurs in Nasser's interviews with foreigners. When he has been asked if his war aim is the obliteration of

Israel, he has not answered either yes or no, as we have noticed, but has gone on to emphasize the question of right and justice. The extracts given in the previous chapter may be supplemented by the following, from an interview with CBS representatives on August 25, 1961:

Q. "Another question, Mr. President, about Israel. When Mr. Kennedy sent you his letter, one of the Cairo papers said: 'We believe that the only full and dignified solution of the Palestine problem is that Israel be obliterated.' Does this represent the view of the Government also, or do you believe other solutions are possible?"

A. "We believe that the rights of the Arabs of Palestine must be restored. More than a million Arabs have been expelled from their country and must return to their lands. This is our viewpoint, which rests on right and justice. The question which should also be asked is, what is the point of view of the Government of Israel. The reply is that the Government of Israel denies logic which is based on right and justice. They say they will not allow any Arab to return, yet surprisingly they advocate Jewish emigration to Palestine. The contradictory point of view is dangerous. On our part we said at the Bandung Conference and at other conferences that we want the United Nations resolutions on the questions of Palestine implemented. What was the attitude taken by the Israeli Government? They obstinately refused to carry out one resolution."

Q. "It seems that the problems cannot be solved without a struggle, since Israel rejects these conditions while you insist upon them. Is this a correct assessment of the situation?"

A. "There is naturally a problem, there is a continuing danger and an existing threat." (Nasser's Speeches, official English edition, 1961 vol., pp. 213-4).

c) THE UNJUST FACT MUST BE REJECTED

There must be no compromise with Israel merely because she is a fact, for any compromise or settlement which leaves Israel in existence would be an endorsement of aggression. There must be no acquiescence in a historic wrong, even if it has become an accomplished fact. Israel's existence is not legal. Justice must be done before peace is established. This is a matter of moral principle. Justice is indivisible and incompatible with compromise. In Nasser's words:

"We shall not agree to a peace of *fait accompli* no matter what the circumstances may be, for such a peace would not be a true one, but tantamount to aggression." (May 1, 1963).

In an editorial in *Rūz al-Yūsuf,* Iḥsān 'Abd al-Quddūs distinguishes between the balance of power and the balance of justice:

"Those who believe in the balance of power base their policy on enforcing Israel's continued existence and giving her power so that her existence should continue. Those who believe in the balance of justice base their policy on persuasion that it is not justice *('adāla)* that Israel should remain, in the same way as it was not justice for her to be established. Hence the attempt to help her to survive is not just, but an attempt at robbery founded on tyrannical power." (March 1, 1965).

d) THE OBLIGATION TO RESPECT STATE SOVEREIGNTY DOES NOT APPLY TO ISRAEL

Respect for the sovereignty and territorial integrity of States according to the UN Charter does not apply to Israel, for her existence is contrary to the principle of self-determination and incompatible with the foundations of international order and morality. Israel is a case of colonialism, which, like other similar cases, must disappear, even if it is based on international agreements. Even if she was established in accordance with recommendations by international institutions like the League of Nations and the UN, their decisions are not legal; they did not create an international norm, but constitute an aberration. Furthermore, there is no moral sanction behind them, since they were adopted by Europeans alone, and this was a European Zionist imperialist plot against the non-Europeans.

In his booklet *Zionist Colonialism in Palestine*, Prof. F.A. Sayegh writes:

"If the League of Nations was the instrument selected for bestowing upon the Anglo-Zionist partnership a semblance of international respectability, the United Nations was selected for a similar purpose by the American-Zionist entente. Britain had prevailed upon a predominantly European League of Nations to approve a plan of European Zionist colonization in Palestine: the United States led a European-American majority to overrule the opposition of an Afro-Asian minority in the General Assembly, and to endorse the establishment of a colonial Zionist State in the Afro-Asian bridge, the Arab land of Palestine." (1965, p. 16).

The Palestinian National Covenant, in Article 17, declares the UN decision null and void:

> "The partitioning of Palestine and the establishment of Israel are illegal and false regardless of the loss of time, because they were contrary to the wish of the Palestine people and its natural right to its homeland, and in violation of the basic principles embodied in the charter of the United Nations, foremost among which is the right to self-determination."

e) LIQUIDATION ONLY RETRIBUTION FOR PREVIOUS LIQUIDATION

The Arabs are not the first liquidators. Zionism has no consideration for the Arabism of Palestine; from the beginning its aim was to liquidate the Arab character of the country. From this point of view, Zionism is a precedent for liquidation and the Zionists have shown the way. Moreover, this kind of liquidation of peoples is typical of the Jews; it is a continuation of the deeds perpetrated by the Israelites in the conquest of Canaan (according to the Arabs, the Canaanite peoples were tribes of Arab origin). Just as the Jews have liquidated the Arab national character of Palestine, so the Arabs, in retribution, should liquidate the Zionist nationalism of Israel.

This argument also appears to be a reply to the possible claim that the conflict is asymmetrical, as the Arabs want to liquidate the Jews while the Jews have no intention of liquidating the Arabs. The liquidation of Israel is only the completion of the circle by a return to the starting-point.

The Arabs, by the way, tend to use much stronger terms for the liquidation of the Arab nationality of Palestine than they do when speaking of the liquidation of Israel. The direct expression frequently used for the liquidation of Israel is *qaḍā' 'alā,* and, as we have seen, it is often camouflaged by euphemisms. In speaking of Israel's aims, on the other hand, such terms as *ibāda, fanā'* ("destruction," "annihilation") are often used as well. Nasser, for instance, in speeches delivered on August 5 and 8, 1959 and November 1, 1960, refers to *ibādat sha'b filasṭīn*— "the destruction of the people of Palestine." 'Alūba (p. 45) speaks of "the imposition of disintegration and extinction" *(farḍ al-inḥilāl wa-al-fanā').* The intention seems to be to emphasize that Israel's liquidatory aims were more heinous.

f) ISRAEL IS LIABLE TO EXPAND

Zionism has liquidated the Arabism of occupied Palestine but does not intend to be satisfied with that, and threatens further aggression and expansion into additional Arab territories. Israel is, therefore, a danger to the Arab existence of further Arab countries. Constantine Zurayk writes:

> "The forces which the Zionists control in all parts of the world can, if they are permitted to take root in Palestine, threaten the independence of all the Arab lands and form a continuing and frightening danger to their life. The facilities that the Zionist forces have for growth and expansion will place the Arab world forever at their mercy and will paralyze its vitality and deter its progress and evolution in the ladders of advancement and civilization—that is, if this Arab world is permitted to exist at all." (*The Meaning of Disaster,* English edition, p. 69).

The presentation of Israel as a danger to national existence might have been expected to be more widespread among spokesmen of the neighbouring States, Jordan, Syria and Lebanon, since Israeli expansion would presumably be at their expense and into their territories, endangering their existence. This argument, however, is also presented by Egyptian spokesmen, who emphasize the danger of Israeli expansion, even though it may not actually endanger the national survival of Egypt herself. Thus Haykal writes in *al-Ahrām*:

> "The Egyptian people will not permit the danger of expansion to lurk on its borders, a danger that may advance tomorrow towards Sinai, looking out from there to the Suez Canal, and may leap forward the day after tomorrow to drink the waters of the Nile." (June 12, 1964).

Nasser repeatedly emphasizes that Israel is a danger to Arab nationalism, namely, to the Arabs achieving their new place in the world, a danger to their greatness and the realization of their aspirations. According to him, Zionism and Israel were, from the beginning, an expression of this design to liquidate Arab nationalism, and in his speeches he frequently talks of an imperialist Zionist plot to this end:

> "We all know why Israel was established. It was not only for the establishment of a National Home, but she was established in order to be one of the factors for the liquidation *(qaḍā' ʿalā)* of Arab nationalism." (May 14, 1956).

"Imperialism and World Zionism have made an alliance against your nationalism in order to obliterate it and establish a Zionist nationalism in its place." (In Syria, March 11, 1958).

Nasser goes further, apparently in order to emphasize how great is the danger that Israel constitutes for the Arabs, and declares that it is not only their nationality, but their race that is in peril—that it is a question, in fact, of genocide:

"Britain was well aware that inside Palestine [there was] an armed force that was preparing to take over Palestine. Although she knew this, she left Palestine. What was the purpose of Britain and America? They had only one aim! This was the liquidation of our nationality *(qaḍā' 'alā qawmiyyatinā)*. They knew that our nationality unites us from the Atlantic Ocean to the Arab [Persian] Gulf. This is a force which has to be taken into account for the first time in history. Therefore Palestine is completely liquidated *(qaḍā' kāmil)* and the Jews will be brought in to replace its inhabitants. This is the annihilation *(ibāda)* of nationality and race. Its goal is an act of annihilation *('amaliyyat ibāda)* for all Arab nationality. The Zionists used to declare that their sacred homeland would stretch from the Nile to the Euphrates. They used to talk in their parliament about a holy war, the annihilation *(ibāda)* of the Arabs and the liquidation *(qaḍā')* of the race." (July 26, 1956, I.L., X/1399-1400).

Sometimes Nasser says that the aim of Israel and imperialism is to strike a death-blow not only at Arab nationalism but at "the Arab World" *(qaḍā' 'alā al-'ālam al-'arabī)* (August 8, 1959).

g) LIQUIDATION AS A PREVENTIVE AND DEFENSIVE OPERATION

These arguments imply that the liquidation of Israel is basically an act of self-defence, from which there is no escape if the Arabs are not themselves to be liquidated as a result of Israeli expansion, which is an inevitable consequence of her aggressive character and her fundamental nature. Liquidation is presented as a "preventive operation" or an "anticipatory reaction" or "retaliation." It expresses a rejection of coexistence with a rival who, it is feared, may increase his strength and must therefore be got rid of as the only way to achieve security. Thus, the Palestinian National Covenant states:

> "The liberation of Palestine from an international viewpoint is a defensive act necessitated by the demands of self-defence as stated in the charter of the United Nations." (Article 16).

As Israel is described as an aggressor, the Arabs, even if they aim at liquidating her, are not aggressors but defenders.

These ideas also imply an ambivalent approach to the initiation of acts of violence. Not everyone who takes the lead in acts of violence is to be condemned. When committed by the Arabs against Israel, they are not aggression, or a violation of the UN Charter, but a "just war." The liquidation of imperialism or colonialism, which implies the liquidation of Israel as well, is, they argue, a major aim of progressive humanity and the United Nations. Conversely, resistance to the liquidation of colonialism is a reprehensible act of aggression. Thus, for example, *al-Jumhūriyya* writes:

> "When we acquire arms, our aim is to defend peace in this area. But when they [the imperialists] supply arms to their Israel, their aim is to undermine security in the region and to oppose the efforts of the UN to liquidate imperialism. Our arming is designed to preserve the goals of the UN Charter, and the arming of Israel is to violate the Charter." (Editorial on June 20, 1964).

Recently, the connotation of the right to self-defence has been expanded to include national liberation. Thus, Dr. F. Sayegh writes:

> "The right to *national liberation* is an extension of the right to *national self-defence,* which the UN Charter not only supports but declares to be 'inherent' and beyond 'impairment' by the provisions of the Charter itself. If continued acquisition of the fruits of an attack is tantamount to continuation of the attack itself, the liberation of territories seized by aggression is an extension of the inherent right to resist the original aggression." (*Zionist Colonialism in Palestine,* p. 49).

h) ISRAEL IS AGGRESSIVE BY NATURE AND THEREFORE MUST BE LIQUIDATED

Another reason why the Arab States do not regard themselves as aggressive in seeking to liquidate Israel is that Israel is aggressive by the very fact of her existence. Since the inception of Israel was an act of aggression, her continued existence is aggression as well. Israel is organically, by her very nature, aggressive, and is unable to stop being aggressive. It makes no difference what she does and how she behaves—she will remain aggressive, because the aggression by which she was established continues to exist so long as the State of Israel exists. In order to wipe out this aggression, Israel's existence must be annulled.

Thus a sub-committee of the Palestine Conference of 1964 stated in its recommendations:

> "The establishment of Israel in Palestine, which is part of the Arab Homeland, in opposition to the will of its lawful inhabitants, is regarded as a continuous Imperialist-Zionist aggression and contrary to the principle of the right to self-determination established by the United Nations." (Cairo Radio, June 1, 1964, 19:30 hrs.).

History also proves that Israel is aggressive, as is shown by her retaliatory operations and the events of 1956. The Arabs did not launch similar attacks on Israel, it is claimed. In furtherance of this line of argument it is contended that any measures, even if belligerent ones, taken against the aggressor do not constitute aggression, and that the armaments acquired by Egypt are not aggressive. On the other hand, the arms acquired by Israel are always aggressive. Thus, for example, Nasser declared in 1963:

> "Yesterday, Levi Eshkol, Israel's Prime Minister, launched a campaign of lies against Egypt. The campaign is directed against our building missiles and aircraft as well as against our employment of German technicians. He claims that Egypt is a base of aggression and says that Egypt has been manufacturing arms. By saying so, he wishes to deceive the people and make fools of the whole world. Which is the base of aggression and of imperialism in this area? It is Israel, which has always been a base of aggression. In 1948, Israel, backed by imperialism, was the base of aggression. In 1954 and 1955, Israel seeking to expand its territories at the expense of the rights of the Arabs, attacked Gaza and killed peaceful Palestine people residing in the Gaza Strip. In 1956, Israel, in complicity with Britain and France, aggressed against Egypt. Yet Israel's Prime Minister wants to deceive world public opinion and wants to make a fool of it when he claims that Egypt is a base of aggression." (*Egyptian Gazette,* October 23, 1963).

i) ISRAEL IS ESSENTIALLY EVIL AND DESERVES ANNIHILATION

As Israel was born in injustice and crime, these are part of her very existence, and she is therefore an essentially evil State. This is an ineradicable and primordial fault. Israel is a detestable State, which deserves no mercy, a kind of cancer which has infected the Middle East and mankind as a whole, and must be eradicated (see Chapter 6).

j) ISRAEL AS AN IMPERIALIST BASE ENDANGERING THE REGION

Israel is a danger to the neighbouring countries because she is an imperialist base. So long as imperialism exists in or near the Arab countries, they cannot be completely free, develop their personalities and make progress. The liquidation of the imperialist danger entails the liquidation of Israel. Thus Haykal writes:

> "Israel is an aggressive base in the service of imperialism, which the Arab nationalist movements have compelled to evacuate their own countries, following which it stole a territory belonging to the Arab lands and tried to alter its Arab character, so that it should serve as a point of departure from which it could leap whereever it wanted to strike and oppress . . . The Egyptian people will not permit the existence of an imperialist base in its neighbourhood." (*al-Ahrām*, June 12, 1964).

The seventh chapter of the Egyptian National Charter states:

> "Imperialist intrigue went to the extent of seizing a part of the Arab territory of Palestine, in the heart of the Arab Motherland, and usurping it without any justification of right or law, the aim being to establish a military fascist regime, which cannot live except by military threats. The real danger is the tool of imperialism."

k) ISRAEL AS A SOURCE OF INSTABILITY

Israel is a foreign growth in the Middle East and a source of disquiet and trouble. So long as she continues to exist there will be no stability in the

Middle East, and the trouble will spread beyond the region. Israel's existence is, therefore, a danger to the peace of the world. Thus, the Palestinian National Covenant declares (Article 19):

> "Israel in its capacity as the spearhead of this destructive movement [Zionism] and the pillar for colonialism is a permanent source of tension and turmoil in the Middle East in particular, and to the international community in general."

1) LIQUIDATION AS A HISTORIC TASK AND DUTY TO HUMANITY

Liquidation is also presented as a task of universal importance because it will rectify an injustice of general and fundamental historical significance. History cannot rest until the rectification of this injustice, which is presented, as we have seen, as the greatest crime in the annals of mankind. The fate of humanity depends on it. For the sake of progress the world over, this State must be wiped off the face of the globe. This is essential for the benefit of the liberation movements of all peoples. Thus, Chapter 10 of the Egyptian National Charter states:

> "The insistence of our people on liquidating the Israeli aggression on a part of the Palestine land is a determination to liquidate one of the most dangerous pockets of imperialist resistance against the struggle of peoples . . . Our pursuit of the Israeli policy of infiltration in Africa is only an attempt to limit the spread of a destructive imperialist cancer."

In other words, in their struggle against Israel the Arabs are playing a part in the global war between the forces of liberation and the forces of oppression, between good and evil. The liquidation will also be an event of world historic importance because it will mark the beginning of a solution to the other troubles of humanity:

> "The solution of the Palestine problem will pave the way to the solution of the world problems." (*Filasṭīn*, July 26, 1958).

These arguments imply that by liquidating Israel the Arabs will demonstrate that international crime does not pay, thus fortifying international morality and improving the health of the society of nations. All lovers of progress must, therefore, support the Arab campaign against Israel.

m) THE STATE OF ISRAEL IS UNNATURAL

Another reason for the liquidation of Israel is that she had no right to exist from the beginning. Jews are usually defined by the Arabs as a religion and not a people or a nation; therefore, they have no need for a State of their own. The Jews must assimilate in the countries where they live, which will settle the problem. The State of Israel is only an anomaly and an aberration. Hence the frequency with which Israel is dubbed "an artificial state" or "an exceptional situation" *(waḍ' shādhdh).*

n) LIQUIDATION OF ISRAEL WILL SAVE THE HONOUR OF THE ARABS

The defeat of the Arabs in 1948, the establishment of Israel and her continued existence are presented as a blow to the national self-respect, "a stain," "a shame," "a disgrace" or "a bleeding wound." The destruction of Israel will atone for the past and save the honour of the Arabs. Such arguments are not only a justification for liquidation, but also a stimulus to action. Thus, Haykal wrote:

> "May 15, 1948 is a day that will never be forgotten in our history. It is the day of the outbreak of the Palestine war and the establishment of the State of Israel . . . This is the day of the greatest shame in the modern history of the Arabs." (*al-Ahrām,* May 15, 1964).

Nasser declared:

> "The armed forces are getting ready for the restoration of the rights of the Palestine People because the Palestine battle was a smear on the entire Arab Nation. No one can forget the shame brought by the battle of 1948." (Speech on August 11, 1963, reported in *Egyptian Gazette,* August 12, 1963).

Such expressions indicate the role of the psychological factor in the Arab attitude. In her book, *Temperament and Character of the Arabs,* Dr. S. Hamady emphasizes the role of self-respect in Arab society, which she describes as a "shame society."

3. THE EXPANSION OF THE STATE OF ISRAEL

The main justification for the aim of liquidating Israel is the argument that she is not content with the territory in her possession but aims at expanding at the expense of further Arab States. This is not merely a pretext for the Arab attitude in the conflict, but the manifestation of a real fear, arising out of Jewish settlement in Palestine and the defeats suffered by the Arabs, as well as their anxious expectation that, if Israel continues to exist, they have further disappointments and defeats in store. The argument emphasizes the danger to the individual from Israeli expansion and is a stimulus to the war effort against Israel.

This danger, it is argued, has transformed the nature of the problem, which ceases to be only one of Israel as she is, but must be regarded in the light of "Israel *in potentia*," in the territories she is liable to conquer in the future. Nasser said:

> 'Hence the problem of Israel is not the problem of Palestine, but besides Palestine it has dangerous results, for Israel is a real expansionist danger with wide and perilous possibilities, since she plans a larger State than the present one and is working for the day when the Arab peoples between the Nile and the Euphrates will be a horde of refugees." (At the National Council, March 26, 1964).

Naturally, no country's leaders admit that they harbour expansionist ambitions, but even if this is not their purpose, they are liable to exploit opportunities for expansion. It is therefore better not to have a neighbour who, even if he declares that he has no intention to expand, is liable to utilize the opportunity if it arises.

It may be assumed that over-emphasis on the idea of expansionism is also intended to make the conflict more symmetrical by arguing that the aspiration for liquidation is not unilateral, but is paralleled by the aspiration for expansion, which means the liquidation of the Arab character of further Arab territories and their annexation by Israel: there is a Jewish irredentism corresponding with Arab irredentism. Moreover, the extreme nature of the objective of liquidation makes it necessary to present a correspondingly great aspiration for expansion, which will justify the verdict of annihilation.

And where is the proof that Israel aspires to expand?

a) EXPANSION AS ESSENTIAL TO ZIONISM

In regard to Zionism's operations in the future, lessons should be drawn from the way in which it has achieved its aspirations in the past. Israel will expand, if she can. Nasser said, for example:

> "Israel has a certain policy, and it is that she must establish the State of Israel, the Holy State, from the Nile to the Euphrates, and take parts of Lebanon, Syria, Iraq, Jordan and Egypt. We must take this talk seriously and never laugh at it. The Balfour Declaration was issued in 1917 and a National Home was proclaimed in 1917, and they worked from 1917 until 1948 until they succeeded in realizing this promise . . . So, if they talk about an Israeli State and a Kingdom of Israel *(mulk)* from the Nile to the Euphrates, even if they do not expect to realize this talk today or tomorrow, they will persevere on the basis of this hope, until they find the opportunity." (February 21, 1959).

It is frequently stated by Arab spokesmen that the historic tactics of Zionism are to advance by stages: it presents a goal that is less than its true aim and, after achieving one concession, increases its demands. At first the Zionists claimed that they would be content with permission for immigration to Palestine, Jewish agricultural settlement and the establishment of a spiritual centre. Later, in 1917, they said they would be satisfied with a National Home in Palestine. At a later stage they set themselves the goal of Palestine as the National Home and the establishment of the State. Until 1948 they promised that they did not want to dispossess the Arabs; in 1948 they dispossessed them. They accepted the State within the boundaries of the UN decision, but when they were given the opportunity they extended these boundaries. They are liable to go on behaving in this way. The Zionists have constantly expanding horizons. They promised to respect the Armistice Agreements and content themselves with the Demarcation Lines. If they—the Zionists—have no existing plans for expansion, this does not mean that they do not dream of it, and that this is their aim. If they get the opportunity, they will break out beyond their borders.*

Prof. Sayegh writes, in *Zionist Colonialism in Palestine*:

> "No student of the behavioral pattern of the Zionist Movement and the *modus operandi* of the Zionist settler-state can fail to realize that Zionist attainments

* Arabs may regard the results of the Six-Day War as a confirmation of these arguments and their claim that the declarations of Israeli leaders that they would be content with the 1948 boundaries were a deception.

at any given moment, if they fall short of the standing objective constantly aimed at by the Zionist Movement, are only temporary stations along the road to ultimate self-fulfillment and not terminal points of the Zionist journey notwithstanding assurances to the contrary which are solemnly given by Zionist and Israeli leaders . . .

"Territorial extent is a third element of the Zionist plan, regarding which the same strategem of deceptive public disavowal has been utilized."

Therefore, Dr. Sayegh writes,

". . . it would be absurd to believe, ostrich-wise, that Zionism might indefinitely rest content with possessing only a fraction of the territory which, it maintains, is its 'national heritage,' and which in any case it has planned all along to occupy." (pp. 32-3, 38).

The argument that Zionism has aspirations for expansion in the form of "living-space" (Khālidī, 1958, p. 21), serves to create an association with Nazism as a method of transferring opprobrium from one to the other, and is a part of the contention, which will be dealt with in Chapter IV, about the kinship between Nazism and Zionism.

Israel is not the complete and final expression of the Zionist ideal. It is only a means towards, and a part of, the realization of Zionism. Zionism aspires to restore the Biblical promised boundaries. It is a new manifestation of the ancient aspiration for the Land of Israel promised in the Bible. Expansionist aims are thus presented as a religious, mystical, profound and fundamental matter, which is beyond national considerations and therefore immutable.

In the Arab literature dealing with the conflict there are frequent quotations from the Bible referring to the promised borders. 'Alūba writes, for example:

"Their religion urges them to acquire the area from the Euphrates to the Nile." (1964, p. 77).

Na'nā'a, in his book *Zionism in the Sixties, the Vatican and the Jews,* sees a proof of expansionist intentions in the fact that Israel has no Constitution; in other words, the identity of the State has deliberately not been fixed, so that it may be expanded. He quotes the *Encyclopaedia Britannica* and the *Encyclopaedia Hebraica* to show that Zionism aims at rebuilding the Temple and reviving the Kingdom of David, which are expansionistic goals (1964, p. 259).

In using the expression "the Kingdom of Israel" (*mulk Isrā'īl*—e.g., on February 21, 1959, February 21, and 24, 1960) to denote the aim of Zionism, Nasser emphasizes the religious aspect of the expansionist aim.

Boundaries of Expansion

Expansion is presented as a matter so concrete that the boundaries to which Israel aspires can be accurately defined.[4] The expression "from the Nile to the Euphrates" to denote Israel's goal is very common, and is frequently used by Arab spokesmen, as well as in school textbooks and political literature. Nasser describes in detail the territories that, he argues, Israel desires to annex. To a Lebanese delegation in 1958 he explained that Israel wants to annex Jordan, Lebanon, part of Syria and part of Iraq (March 9, 1958). Sometimes, however, he says that a part of Egypt is also to be included (for example, in his speech of February 21, 1959). This argument is not used only for internal consumption. In a talk with American journalists on January 27, 1958, he declared:

> "We are afraid of her [Israel's] aspirations to expand, which Israelis have proclaimed during the 1955 elections. For a number of leaders on that occasion stated that they were planning to realize their goal of achieving a country stretching from the Nile to the Euphrates, and this undoubtedly means that they want to annex Egyptian territories to Israel." (I.L., X/194).

In addressing the National Council, again, Nasser declared:

> "Israel's aspirations regarding Egypt reach as far as the al-Sharqiyya area . . . because the children of Israel lived in the district before their departure from Egypt." (*al-Jumhūriyya,* May 20, 1965).

The purpose here may be to make the danger more concrete when addressing a local audience.

A map showing the detailed boundaries of Israel's aspirations is given by Rushdī on page 35. The territories include Jordan, Syria and Lebanon, Sinai, Iraq, the Delta, and parts of Saudi Arabia including Khaybar and Medina, as "areas which they contend they possessed in the Hedjaz" (p. 37). Such maps are also to be found in other books and publications (on the cover of the Fatah monthly, *Filasṭīnunā*, of September 1964, for example).

The Zionist claim of "historic rights" is, thus, extended to the Land of Goshen in Egypt and the territories inhabited by Jewish tribes in the Arabian Peninsula.

Dr. Sayegh explains in the work quoted above, that Zionism has a minimal conception, consisting of the Jordan Kingdom, South Lebanon, Southwest Syria and the Gaza Strip, and a maximalist conception: from the Nile to the Euphrates (p. 34).

Haykal said that together with the maximalist plans of expansion from the Nile to the Euphrates there was a realistic Israeli plan for the conquest of the West Bank and Sinai. He finds proof of the existence of such a plan at the time of the Sinai Campaign in political declarations and Moshe Dayan's book (*al-Ahrām,* January 7, 1966).

The Map in the Knesset

According to a story constantly repeated in Arab newspapers and books, there is a map hanging in the Knesset which depicts Israel's aspirations for the Biblical borders, flanked by the verse:

> "In the same day the Lord made a Covenant with Abram, saying, "Unto thy seed have I given this land, from the river of Egypt unto the great river the river Euphrates.' " (Genesis 15:18—see: *al-Taḥrīr,* April 12, 1949; *al-Jumhūriyya,* December 31, 1962; 'Alūba, briefly, on p. 175; Ibrāhīm in the *Political Science Review,* January–March 1959, p. 136; Dr. Badūr in the *Egyptian Political Science Review,* September 1963, p. 41—mentioning only the verse without the map; and similarly Rushdī, p. 57; Aḥmad 'Abd al-Karīm, p. 8, and various works used for indoctrinating the Egyptian army).

The idea is that the members of the Knesset receive inspiration in their deliberations, from the map and the verse.

A group of Egyptian officer prisoners of war who were taken to the Knesset after the Sinai Campaign were not convinced that no such map exists, but argued that the Israelis had cunningly removed it before the visit.

b) PROOFS FROM ZIONIST SOURCES

The Arabs find proofs of these expansionist aims in numerous quotations from Zionist literature and statements by Zionist leaders. (A selection of quotations which are repeated in other writings may be found in Ḥasan Ṣabrī al-Khūlī's *The Palestine Problem,* in the Appendix, 1. 58.)

Nasser claimed that the Zionist Congress "demanded the liberation of the Israeli Homeland of which they dream from the Nile to the Euphrates"

(May 13, 1956). He has often repeated the statement that expansionist aims are presented during Israeli election campaigns, e.g.:

> "In every election campaign [in Israel] . . . we can see Israel's intentions from the election speeches. In an article last Friday in a newspaper called *Herut*, which is the organ of one of the parties, it is stated . . . that Ben-Gurion's party has neglected opportunities in the revolutions that have followed each other in Syria for a change in the eastern border of Lake Tiberias and for gaining control over the area where the Syrian army is stationed today and from which Israel, if she wishes, will strike at Syria. They also talked about the Gaza area, declaring that Ben-Gurion's plot in 1956, in cooperating in the threefold aggression, had been frustrated without any result, and they had not succeeded in holding on to the Gaza Strip or carrying out any of their aims. A reading of these articles and a study of election speeches in Israel teaches us about the enemy's aims. The enemy wants to take Jordan, and to get control over the Gaza Strip and the district east of Lake Tiberias." (August 17, 1961).

Similar statements were made by Nasser in a talk with CBS representatives on August 25, 1961 (*Nasser's Speeches,* 1961, official English edition, p. 210).

c) DENIALS OF EXPANSIONIST AIMS ARE FRAUDULENT

The Arabs argue that the Israeli leaders' denials of expansionist aspirations and their readiness to undertake to remain within the 1949 borders and to have the international community guarantee such an undertaking were merely examples of a tactical attitude, which was adopted for external consumption.

Al-Khālidī, in his "Reappraisal," says that the late Moshe Sharett explained that the Arabs suspected that Israel aimed at expansion because they believed in horizontal development, while the Israeli concept of development was that it could be vertical.[5] Al-Khālidī adds mockingly:

> "Sharett ought to explain how Israeli forces were able by a vertical route to reach Yotbat and Sharm el-Sheikh in the far south." (1958, p. 21).

d) ZIONISM AIMS AT INGATHERING THE JEWISH PEOPLE IN THE JEWISH STATE

Zionist Israel adopts a policy of unlimited immigration. It was for this purpose that the Law of the Return was enacted; Zionist leaders call on the Jews of the Diaspora to settle in Israel and bring pressure to bear on them for this purpose. They hope that one day millions of Russian Jews will come to Israel. The resulting overpopulation will make them break out beyond the boundaries. As a deliberate policy, Israel is preparing for herself a pretext and a need for expansion. Israel regards the increase in her population as a security need, but this increase will push her into a war of expansion:

"The Arabs are keenly aware that the inflation of the population in Israel's now narrow territory will undoubtedly lead her to seek ways of expanding her living space. And it is clear that she will not achieve this except at the expense of her neighbors, the Arab States on her borders." (*al-Ḥayāt,* May 5, 1954).

Nasser told the CBS representative on April 2, 1958:

"The problem between the Arabs and Israel was at first the stolen rights of the Palestine people, and Israel added to this her expansionist aspirations. It is sufficient proof of this that in a single year Israel takes in more than a hundred thousand migrants. Can Israel absorb such a number with her present resources? The result will undoubtedly be fresh aggressive operations aimed at expansion." (I.L., XI/2146).

The same statements are repeated in Nasser's letter to President Kennedy on August 18, 1961 (given in *al-Ahrām,* September 21, 1962 and in special pamphlets issued by the Government of the United Arab Republic).

e) EXPANSIONIST ASPIRATIONS PART OF ISRAEL'S NATURE

The Jordanian White Paper states:

"It is the nature of Zionist aggression, being one of the general forms of imperialism, that it will not stop at borders of expansion unless it is confronted by force." (*Jordan, the Palestine Problem and Arab Relations,* Ch. 4, p. 30).

Abdallah al-Tall regards the expansionist aspiration as rooted in the Jewish character:

"The aspiration to expansion is a fact rooted in their corrupt *('afina)* minds and hearts of stone, which will not rest until they conquer Iraq, Syria, Jordan, Lebanon, the coastal strip of the UAR and north Hedjaz, as far as Medina and the Mosque of the Prophet . . . The goal of the criminal State of Israel is that the Arabs should move to the Arabian Penisula, their first homeland 2,000 years ago." (1964, p. 311).

f) ISRAEL NOT CONTENT WITH PRESENT BORDERS WHICH ARE "NOT HISTORIC AND NOT CONVENIENT"

Zionism speaks of "historic" boundaries, which is another proof that Israel is not content with her present borders. When Israelis point out that the frontiers are "not natural," or "anomalous," this is evidence of the desire to change them and establish more convenient borders. Military logic compels Israel to aspire towards better strategic boundaries.

A frequently quoted proof is based on Ben-Gurion's statement in his article "Israel Among the Nations," printed as an introduction to the *Government Year Book,* 1952, where a vital phrase was mistranslated in the English edition (my italics):

> "It must now be said that it [the State of Israel] has been established in only a portion of the Land of Israel. Even those who are dubious as to the restoration of the historic frontiers, as fixed and given and crystallized from the beginning of time, will hardly deny the anomaly of the borders of the new State." (p. 15).

Reference to the Hebrew original (*Government Year Book,* Hebrew, 5713, p. 18) shows that Ben-Gurion referred to ". . . those who are dubious as to the *existence (qiyum) of immutable historic frontiers*"; in the following sentence he points out that Israel is committed to the Armistice demarcation lines, and declares that the real problem is the existence of large unsettled areas within the existing borders:

> "But even within them [the borders of the new State, as delimited by the Armistice Agreements]—and by the Armistice Agreements Israel is committed to them so long as it is not attacked, and it is honouring the commitment—even within these boundaries, State and Land do not coincide. When the State was established only seven per cent of its area was cultivated." (English edition, p. 15).

General Hāmid Aḥmad Ṣāliḥ explained that because the Jews were driven to expand into Sinai because the boundary would be simplified by control over the Suez Canal (*The Battle of Port Said,* 1964, p. 44).

g) ISRAEL MUST EXPAND IN ORDER TO EXIST

Israel's basis for existence, her living space, is too narrow in her present borders. In her present situation, Israel is too small to be viable. The need to exist compels her to expand and to gain control over the resouces of the Arab countries. Thus Zurayk wrote: "Israel covets the natural resources of the Arabs" (1948, p. 20), and Sayegh wrote: "For Israel, to be is to seek expansion" (1956, p. 73).

The National Water Carrier, the pipeline to bring surplus water from north to south, was regarded by the Arabs as symbolizing a desire for expansion, as if it was aimed at creating a basis for expansion and its completion ensured that expansion would indeed take place. Colonel Ḥasan Muṣṭafā wrote:

> "It is a mistake to think that the expansion of Israel is an idea that used to enflame the imagination of the Zionists in the past and nothing more; it was and still is one of their basic goals. They see that its realization is essential to the security and welfare of Israel, to her growth and progress, and hence to her future and life." (*Israel and the Atom Bomb,* Beirut, 1961, p. 116).

h) THE OPPORTUNITY FOR EXPANSION REVEALS THE HIDDEN AIM

Where Israel believed that she had the opportunity to expand, she tried to do so, in the Sinai Campaign. Nasser states that fears of expansion were realized in this operation (January 27, 1958, I.L., X/1904).

Al-Khālidī (1958, pp. 20-21), Haykal (June 12, 1964), and others quote Ben-Gurion's statement in the Knesset on November 7, 1956:

> "Our army did not attack, nor even attempt to attack, the territory of the Land of Egypt . . . Our forces were given strict orders not to cross the Suez Canal or attack the territory of the Land of Egypt, and to remain entirely within the limits of the Sinai Peninsula." (*Jewish Agency Digest,* November 15, 1956).

They regard this as proof that Israel did not recognize Egyptian sovereignty over Sinai and regarded herself as free to behave as she liked in that territory. They also mention Ben-Gurion's statement about Jewish rule 1,400 years ago in the Island of Tiran (Yotbat), "which was liberated . . .

by the Israel Defence Forces," and his reference to "a place called Sharm el-Sheikh until the day before yesterday and now named Solomon's Bay."

i) THE NAME ERETZ ISRAEL (LAND OF ISRAEL)

A frequently cited proof of Israel's expansionist aims is based on the names "Israel" and "Eretz Israel" (Land of Israel). The latter is explained as the land belonging to the State of Israel, namely, the area that Israel regards as her heritage and wants to occupy. For instance, Ben-Gurion's statement, already quoted, that "the State of Israel was founded only in a part of the Land of Israel" is cited as proof that the State intends to expand into the entire Land of Israel (Sayegh, 1956, p. 72; Childers, 1962, p. 176; Nashāshībī, 1962, p. 120; Shukairy at the UN on November 9, 1963, p. 36; Rifā'ī, the Jordanian representative at the UN on December 5, 1962; Abi Mershed, p. 30; Na'nā'a, 1964, p. 261; Sha'bān, p. 40).

Rushdī states that on the official map used in Israeli schools, Transjordan and the Arab parts of Palestine are marked "Israel under Arab Occupation" (1965, p. 38). (This may indicate a tendency to portray the conflict as symmetrical: the Arabs call Israel "the Occupied Area," but Israel, it is alleged, behaves in the same way.)

j) DOMINATING THE WHOLE WORLD

More frequently than might be expected, we find the Arabs arguing that Israel's aim is world domination. This idea is to be found particularly in literature of a religious and anti-Semitic nature, which, like *The Protocols of the Elders of Zion,* sees no bounds to Jewish ambition. "World Zionism" is regarded as only a mask or an instrument for "World Jewry," which aims at world domination on the grounds that such is the will of God. Israel is only a point of concentration and a springboard. Ḥasan Ṣabrī al-Khūlī writes:

> "In Israel there have taken shape the Zionist aspirations for world domination, which are derived from the profound Zionist faith that the Children of Israel are God's chosen people, and that theirs is the sovereignty over the world." (pp. 19 and 24).

Al-Maḥlāwī, in an article in *Political Science Review* (January-March, 1959, p. 115), writes:

"The propagandists of the Zionist movement have arisen in a political movement masked by a religious form, whose watchword is racialism and the establishment of the Jewish State, whose beginnings are in Palestine and which will one day stretch from the Euphrates to the Nile and, moreover, will subdue the entire world to the rule of Israel."

Naʻnāʻa distinguishes between the "actual borders" to which Zionism aspires—the Delta in Egypt, Sinai, Palestine, Tranjordan, Syria, Western Iraq and north Hedjaz—and the spiritual and moral *(al-maʻnawiyya)* boundaries, which comprise the entire globe, as the Jews interpret the visions of their prophets. In support, he cites Isaiah:

"And many people shall go and say, Come, ye, and let us go up to the mountain of the Lord." (2:3) "Lift up thine eyes round about, and behold: All these gather themselves together, and come to thee." (49:18).

4. LIQUIDATION IS FEASIBLE

It is not enough to justify the aim of liquidation; it must be proved to be feasible, especially as the international order is founded on respect for sovereignty of States. The disappointment of the Arabs at the result of their efforts against Israel so far strengthens the need for arguments which will not only be logically convincing but also give hope that they will yet be able to achieve what they have not succeeded in doing so far. Such arguments also serve to strengthen their morale and inoculate them against further disappointments. Israel's victories and achievements, it is argued, are illusory, temporary and transitory, and no deductions should be made from them as to her ultimate survival. The fulfilment of Arab aspirations will surely come, even if it is delayed.

These arguments are of varied types. On the one side there are those founded on a reading of the facts: Israel is small and therefore, in the final analysis, weak in comparison with the Arabs. On the other hand, there are ideological considerations: the injustice involved in the establishment of Israel cannot endure, for justice must win in the end. Sometimes this is presented as faith in some kind of Arab divine right. Liquidation is described as a historical imperative, immune from any moral praise, blame or uncertainty. At the most, history should be helped to realize its goals. The theme of historical necessity *(ḥatmiyya ta' rīkhiyya)* is frequently to be met with in contemporary Arab national ideology; not only the liquidation of Israel, but the achievement of other Arab nationalist aims, is described as the imperative of history. The arguments will be described here briefly, as they will be considered in greater detail in Chapters IV and VI, on Zionism and on Israel in Arab eyes.

a) THE ARTIFICIALITY OF ISRAEL MUST BE FATAL

Israel is an artificial State, and her existence therefore rests on unsound foundations. She is not viable, for the Jews are not a nation and therefore cannot maintain a State. Their State is rent with contradictions, such as the difficulty of defining who is a Jew and determining the relations between State and religion. These contradictions show that Israel is a hybrid organism, which must disintegrate in the end.[6]

Unlike Arab nationalism, which is a natural nationalism expressing the sum-total of the aspirations of a nation dwelling on its soil, Jewish nationalism did not arise in the natural way from below, from a nation living on its own soil. The Zionists developed this artificial nationalism, and then compelled the Jews to accept the idea. Thus Dr. Sayegh writes:

> "Zionism found itself at birth *a nationalism without a nation*—and promptly began to grope for, to find (or else to found) its nation." (1960, p. 76).

But the third factor, a territory, was lacking, so they stole a territory from another nation and settled their people on it. They followed the reverse of the natural trend: instead of progressing from a territory and a nation to an idea, to nationalism, they synthetically fabricated a nation and a State from the idea.

Since this is an artificial nationalism, it cannot be viable; it is an anomaly, which must collapse. Even if the Arabs do not liquidate it, it will liquidate itself through the destiny which is part of its very essence:

> "The truth is that Israel feels herself weak, and realizes that her end is near, not in war or acts of aggression, but as a result of the existing circumstances, which determine that any organism whose body lacks the foundations of life cannot survive." (*al-Akhbār*, editorial, April 30, 1963).

Abu al Majd wrote:

> "It is absolutely impossible that it [this State] should live; it is impossible that it should not collapse with every sunrise, for Israel today lacks the constituents of an existing State: unity of language, culture, tradition, race and feeling. These do not exist today in Israel and that is not what we say, but what is said by the Zionists, their helpers and their allies." (*The End of Israel,* p. 43).

b) THE JEWS ARE QUARRELSOME AND CANNOT MAINTAIN A STATE

Their history shows that the Jews lack unity and the qualities required for life as a State. Since they are not a nation they cannot unite. Their capacity to maintain a State for long is doubtful. They are chronically quarrelsome and divided. They are plagued by communal and fraternal strife. Their history is full of controversies and conflicts. Even Moses complained that they were a stiff-necked and rebellious people. Many quotations (from the Bible and other books) are given to prove this in the Arab literature on the conflict. They asked Samuel to anoint a king over them because of their constant quarrels. Even when they had established a kingdom, in the days of David, it split after seventy years into two "statelets," Judah and Israel. Dr. Naṣr quotes Ibn Khaldūn's dictum that the Jews lack "*'aṣabiyya*"—the spirit of solidarity (pp. 6-7). Dr. Badūr sums up:

> "A State that does not unite the groups of which it is composed, which belong to many different races, languages, cultures and customs, that lives as a minority in a foreign land, surrounded by millions of hostile people, relying on foreign aid . . . , whose economy is not a complete whole and that lives on fanatical and aggressive thinking which is incompatible with the nature of things—cannot be destined to survive and is fated to disintegrate and disappear." (*Egyptian Political Science Review,* September 1963, p. 41).

c) ISRAEL HAS NO BASIS FOR EXISTENCE AS HER TERRITORY AND RESOURCES ARE LIMITED

Haykal writes:

> "Israel's existence lacks the natural factors on which power can be based—her territory is limited . . . , her sources are limited . . . , the numbers of her population are limited." (*al-Ahrām,* June 13, 1963).

Al-Nābulsī writes:

"There is no survival for Israel, since she is an unnatural entity and a State that has no resources, living on aid and charity which she obtains from abroad." (*The Reactionary Alliance and the Return to Palestine,* p. 64).

d) HER EXISTENCE DEPENDS ON TRANSITORY FOREIGN AID

Israel's existence is not natural and autonomous; it is "counterfeit," and therefore she has no independent existence, but depends on foreign aid. Her problems and crises are not temporary, as in other countries, but endemic; they express an essential weakness. Her capacity to resist the Arabs comes from foreign support, whether from imperialists or from the Jews, which will diminish and ultimately disappear. The problem of the Jews in the Diaspora will eventually be solved; they will be assimilated in the countries where they live and their ties with Israel will steadily weaken.

On Prime Minister Eshkol's visit to the United States in 1964 and his statement that America would come to Israel's aid, *al-Akhbār* commented:

"There is no country in the world that seeks guarantees for its survival as Israel does. This very request is evidence that Israel's existence is not natural, and requires artificial and exceptional means to enable it to continue . . . The United States may be able to give Israel a number of soothing declarations, but she certainly will be unable to perpetuate her existence. A State's power to exist does not come from other States, but from itself . . . Israel's problems are not transitory, like those of other States, but problems involved in its very essence." (June 11, 1964).

Hāshim al-Jisr explains that Zionism is condemned to failure, because:

"The disappearance of anti-Semitism in the West deprives Zionism of the excuse of persecution; it will persuade the Jews to remain where they are and to merge with society, and will drive out of their minds the idea of emigration to Israel." (*al-Jarīda,* April 18, 1965).

e) THE ARAB SIEGE AND ARAB HOSTILITY WILL STRANGULATE ISRAEL

The Arab siege of Israel does not permit her to grow, so that she will finally stagnate and disintegrate. (These arguments also express the conviction that Arab hostility is sufficient to bring about Israel's end.)

At the end of his book *The History of the Children of Israel from Their Books,* issued by the official Egyptian publishing house Ikhtarnā Lak (I.L.), Muhammad 'Izzat Darwaza comes to the conclusion that the siege of Israel by the Arabs, whose economic, military, cultural and national strength is growing, will lead to continued Israeli stagnation and ultimately to the "strangulation of the deformed *(al-maskh)* State, its collapse *(inhiyār)* and destruction *(saḥq)* sooner or later" (Part III, p. 579).

The dispute is presented as a categorical conflict: there can be no co-existence between Israel and the Arab countries, and it is easier to liquidate Israel than the Arab States. Al-'Aqqād writes:

> "Either Israel disappears to the place from which it came or the Arab nations will be left as a prey to Israel, which will devour their flesh and blood and stand in the way of their progress, so as to ensure their dispossession today, tomorrow and forever in the spheres of industry, commerce and general progress. Israel's disappearance to the place from which it came is an easier and more reasonable result. Its disappearance to the place from which it came is an inevitable result of the reality of Zion's fate." (1956, p. 155).

Rushdī writes:

> "As we have said and will always say, there is no possibility that Israel shall live in the middle of an environment that loathes *(tamqutu)* and despises her; not only is this the Arab feeling [towards her], but they are profoundly convinced that her existence is a constant danger to the security and integrity of the region, and that Israel does not represent a State but the focus of imperialist plots and intrigues against this region. It is obvious that the absorption of Israel in the Arab homeland is impossible in any shape or form." (1965, p. 61).

The Arabs need only persist in their hostility, and this will bring about the liquidation of Israel. Colonel Muḥammad Ṣafwat writes:

> "Always keep in mind that Israel will disappear entirely out of existence if you do not make peace with her." (*Israel, the Common Enemy,* 1952, p. 233).

f) TIME WORKS AGAINST ISRAEL

Israel cannot long endure the competition with the Arab countries and the strain of the arms race. Time is working against her:

"It is beyond all doubt that if time has up till now worked in Israel's favour in many respects, it has worked much more in favour of the Arabs." (*al-Mawqif al-'Arabī,* January 11, 1964).

"The present and the future do not work in her [Israel's] favour but in favour of the Arabs." (Nasser on December 23, 1962).

The balance of forces on the spot will decide the issue. It is the decree of history that the Arabs will gain the upper hand. The essential greatness of the Arabs is bound to make its mark in the end.

The smallness of Israel's territory imposes limitations on her capacity to increase her strength at the same rate as the Arabs, who are only at the beginning of the road and have unlimited scope for development. Haykal puts it:

"The more the independent strength of the UAR grows, the less will be the proportion that has to be devoted to meeting the Israeli danger. The opposite is the case on the other side of the barricade: the more the power of the UAR grows, the greater is the effort that Israel will have to make [in proportion to her resources]." (*al-Ahrām,* March 16, 1962).

g) THE LESSON OF THE CRUSADES

A comparison between Israel and the Crusader Kingdom is very common in Arab discussions of the problem. This theme is, no doubt, very attractive because it furnishes the argument with an historical and scientific dimension. The past is brought in to testify to the future; history is mobilized in the service of ideology. A book called *The New Crusade in Palestine,* by Wadī' Talḥūq, published in Damascus in 1948, compared the circumstances under which the Middle East was occupied by Britain, France and Zionism with the background to the Crusades. The main idea was that the region has always attracted foreign conquerors, who used spiritual or religious motives as a cloak for materialistic aims, but could not perpetuate their hold and were finally repulsed and "thrown into the sea." This was the fate that awaited Israel, which would ultimately prove to have been no more than an episode in history. Thus, the author wrote:

"If history is repeated, we are not afraid of suffering, for the Arabs, who in the past repulsed all the Western States, cannot fail to be able to repulse gangs of foreigners in the present. True, Zionism is backed by great Governments and powerful States, but that will not frighten us, for we have confronted the like in the past; it is not beyond our strength to confront them and deliver our homeland from their clutches." (p. 50).

Talḥūq explains that his purpose is:

"... to take the past as a mirror of the present in order to benefit from the comparison and draw conclusions in regard to causes and effects." (p. 48).

Nasser has frequently made use of historical proofs based on the Crusades (see, for instance, his speeches on March 20, 1958; November 1, 1960; October 1, 1963 and February 6, 1964) to prove the need for Arab unity as the key to victory and as an argument against what he regards as defeatism and lack of faith. Patience, he claims, is an Arab national characteristic—a point which he has used to justify the postponement of war until all the preparations could be made, though such postponement must not affect the reality of the final aim, namely, liquidation. This argument also has a psychological, consolatory function, presenting patience as a compensation for weakness on the battlefield.

Nashāshībī addressed Israel after a report of Israeli manoeuvres:

"Manoeuvre as much as you like, but remember that greater powers than you, nobler and more honourable peoples than yours, conquered Arab countries before you and afterwards evacuated them never to return, thanks to the Arab will and the Arab struggle." (*al-Jumhūriyya,* June 17, 1964).

The comparison with the Crusades is not only to be found in Arab writings. W. R. Polk, D. M. Stamler and E. Asfour explain, in *Background to Tragedy: The Struggle For Palestine* (Boston, Beacon Press, 1957, pp. 25-26, 371), that the Arabs remember that the Crusaders lived by the sword and believe that Israel, too, was created and survives thanks to her military strength. Both the Latin Kingdom of Jerusalem and the State of Israel were established in war; both of them came into being because the local inhabitants were weak, and both were maintained thanks to their military superiority to the Arabs. Both, too, symbolize Arab dissensions. The authors also point out the following differences: while the Crusaders lived on the labour of Arab peasants, the Jews have established themselves as a self-supporting organism; in those days the right of conquest was sufficient, while today moral legitimacy is also required.

h) THE WILL OF THE ARABS WILL PREVAIL

The liquidation of Israel is guaranteed because it is the national will of the Arab people, which nothing can resist. This will is itself a guarantee of victory. Thus, Nasser says:

> "The Arab will for a change is stronger than Israel and imperialism, and there is no escape from the achievement of the Arab right for the Palestinian people." (July 23, 1964).

The power of the will is frequently emphasized in the ideology of the UAR. The Egyptian National Charter (Chapter I) describes the will for revolutionary change as a mighty power which no force can resist and a guarantee for the achievement of the aims of the national struggle. But the romantic view of the national will is also found in other Arab countries:

> "The people can defeat navies and armies by its will. This is the lesson of history." (*al-Manār,* Jordan, in an article, "How My Land Was Lost"—December 11, 1964).

Difficulties involved in achieving the aim do not discourage the Arabs, but strengthen their determination. Nasser declared:

> "Barriers and obstacles may accumulate, but the free peoples will always find a way to carry out the tasks confronting them. They change their methods and reinforce their determination to overcome the difficulties and obstacles, and then they set forth, realizing themselves and achieving their goal." (April 17, 1965).

This emphasis on the power latent in faith and will implies the primacy of the spiritual factor. Reality must submit to will: "The subjective will mould the objective," as Lio Shao Shi, the former President of China, said. There is much of the heroic and mystic in this approach. Such conceptions appear in various forms in history: for example, Herzl's watchword: "If you will it, it is no legend," or the mystique of the commander's will and daring in the theories of Marshal Foch which had such an influence on the French army and cost it so many casualties in World War I. In our own day, the factor of the human will, "voluntarism" as it is called, is emphasized in the military theories of the Chinese and the Vietnamese. The consciousness and will of man will defeat the machine and the power of technology.

(There are both sublime and foolish elements in these ideas. Sometimes they are the outcome of a situation in which the prospects of achieving the aim seem so discouraging that the will itself is conceived as an independent factor and a guarantee of victory over the obstacles—on the assumption, indeed, that some of the factors in the situation may be exploited.)

The dispute becomes a contest—a trial of endurance—between the determination of both sides. The Arab will, it is believed, must triumph over the Israeli will.

i) ISRAEL'S FATE BOUND UP WITH DECLINING COLONIALISM

The liquidation of Israel is also guaranteed by the fact that the fate of Israel, as an imperialist and colonialist phenomenon, is bound up with the fate of colonialism. The liquidation of colonialism following on the awakening of the subordinated peoples is an irresistible historical trend, which involves the end of Israel. Thus, Abu al-Majd writes:

> "The end of Israel will surely come, for the imperialist regime which created it, built it and protected it has already begun to decline and wither away." (p. 125).

Nasser, too, declared at the opening of the National Assembly on March 26, 1964:

> "... as history and experience have proved, ... it [Israel] cannot survive without imperialism; it is for imperialism, for its service, for its objectives of domination and exploitation.
>
> "Linked with this is the fact that its existence is a continuation of the imperialist existence. It follows that the triumph of freedom and peace in liquidating the imperialist existence cannot pass without affecting the Israeli existence. It is one connected battle however wide its field may expand to embrace whole continents. When freedom has achieved its full victory in Africa—it will reach its goal whatever its difficulties—the sinking sun of imperialism will fall into the ocean, and Israel will not escape the same destiny." (*Egyptian Gazette,* March 27, 1964).

j) THE RELIGIOUS ARGUMENT

Through their contumacy, the violation of their covenant with God, and the killing of the prophets, the Jews aroused the anger of God, who condemned them to "humiliation and wretchedness"—as the Quran twice says

(Sura II: The Cow, v. 61, and Sura III: The Family of 'Imrān, v. 112).* The establishment of Israel as a strong and independent State is, therefore, a violation of this decree. Abdallah al-Tall writes:

> "Despite all their efforts to appear as the possessors of power and the capacity to resist, the word of God is supreme and the Quran records the views of heaven, the will of the heaven and its verdict." (1964, p. 65).

Ahmad Yūsuf Ahmad writes:

> "England and America will help them, France may support them and others may defend them, but they will not on any account be able to exempt them from the divine injunction and decree that they shall have no rest or permanency or tranquility, they will be chastized with degradation and poverty and be visited by the wrath of God." (*Israel—the Misled People,* p. 78).

Muhammad 'Izzat Darwaza, at the end of his book on the History of the Jews (Part III, pp. 580-581), quotes (Sura LIV: Exile, vv. 2-3):

> "He it is Who hath caused those of the People of the Scriptures who disbelieved to go forth from their homes unto the first exile. Ye deemed not that they would go forth, while they deemed that their strongholds would protect them from Allah. But Allah reached them from a place whereof they recked not, and cast terror in their hearts so that they ruined their houses with their own hands and the hands of the believers. So learn a lesson. O ye who have eyes. And if Allah had not decreed migration for them, He verily would have punished them in this world, and theirs in the hereafter is the punishment of the Fire."

The passage has historical associations; it is connected with Muhammad's war against the Jewish tribe of Banū Naḍīr in Medina. (See a similar argument in al-Jiyār, p. 6.)

5. THE NATURE OF THE CONFLICT AS THE ARABS SEE IT

As we have seen, the arguments to justify the aim of liquidation imply adoption of an attitude as to the nature of the conflict. We can see this in another form: the definition of the nature of the conflict, what it is about, and what is at stake in it, constitute the substantiation of the aim.

* Quotations from, and references to, the Quran are from Marmaduke Pickthall's *The Meaning of the Glorious Koran, an explanatory translation* (New American Library).

It is frequently emphasized that the conflict affects all the Arabs: all of them constitute the Arab side. Even at such an early stage as the meeting of the Arab kings and presidents at Inshas in May 1946, it was stated:

> "The problem of Palestine does not concern Palestinian Arabs alone, but it is the problem of all the Arabs." (Nashāshībī, 1962, p. 284).

Nasser said:

> "The action *(al-'amaliyya)* is not the action of Palestine, but the action of all the Arabs, and when Palestine is injured, each of us is injured in his feelings and his homeland." (December 13, 1953, I.L., I/156).

The idea of the unity of the Arab world implies the existence of an organic bond between all its parts and the attitude that whatever affects one part affects the whole. Nasser frequently emphasizes this:

> "A threat to Arab nationalism in any country is a threat to nationalism in all the Arab countries." (March 8, 1959).

The same idea is repeated on, for instance, August 8, 1959 and in a speech in Damascus on March 3, 1961. Leaders of Arab countries, even those distant from Palestine, have repeatedly declared that they regard the problem as of supreme importance for themselves as well.[7]

As a problem affecting all, it is, naturally, of central importance. In his letter to Hussein on March 13, 1961, Nasser wrote that the Palestine problem is "problem number one for the Arabs." It is described as "the Arab problem of problems" (Nashāshībī, 1962, p. 69). "The problem of Palestine is the most Arab of the Arab problems," writes 'Alūsh (1964, p. 61).

Again, Nasser declared:

> "I cannot speak of Arab nationalism without speaking of Israel, for the existence and idea *(fikratuhā)* of Israel are a threat to Arab nationalism in Palestine and the establishment *(iḥlāl)* of Zionist nationalism in its place, followed by expansion and the liquidation of Arab nationalism in the region." (In a speech on the 7th anniversary of the Revolution, July 22, 1959).

The subject is presented as one of historic and decisive importance for the Arabs. Frequent expressions are "a fateful struggle," "a clash of destinies" (Bahā' al-Dīn, 1965, p. 245), or "the battle of Arab destiny." Nasser declares: "The problem of Palestine is a fateful problem for all the Arabs"

(February 23, 1964). It is "a fateful challenge" ('Alūsh, p. 225). As the Palestinian National Covenant puts it:

> "The destiny of the Arab Nation and even the essence of Arab existence are firmly tied *(rahn)* to the destiny of the Palestine question." (Article 13).

According to the Jordanian White Paper (Chapter IV, p. 30): "The Palestinian problem embodies an armed aggression against the Arab existence." In directions to instructors in an indoctrination pamphlet, *"Israel and Its Aims,"* issued by the Supreme Command of the Egyptian Armed Forces, it is stated:

> "The instructor should take note that the question of Israel is regarded as one of the most important questions in our lives, because of the gravity of the aims of Zionist imperialism in regard to us and the entire Arab homeland. The instructor must ensure that the soldiers understand the aims of Zionism and repeat every point on which he feels that the soldiers need additional explanation. He will thus fulfil an important duty which indoctrination *(al-tawjīh al-ma'nawī)* is meant for."

Haykal writes:

> "The dispute [between the Russians and the Americans] . . . is an ideological dispute, over a way of life. On the other hand, in our case, here with Israel, the dispute is life itself; to be or not to be." (*al-Ahrām*, June 12, 1964).

Anīs Qāsim writes:

> "The nature of the battle allows only one of the alternatives, either liquidation of Israel or imperialistic Israeli domination over the Arab fatherland: a third possibility is excluded." (*Revolutionary Preparation for the Battle of Liberation*, p. 37).

Ṣā'ib Salām describes the danger as symmetrical:

> "Two generations are competing with each other: the young Zionist generation in Israel and the young generation in the Arab countries that surround them. If the Zionist generation wins, its prize will be no less than the destruction of the Arabs and of Arabism in most of their countries and the eternal strengthening of the Jewish State. And if the young Arab generation wins, its prize will be the liquidation of Israel and the strengthening of the Arabs in the world." (*al-Nahār*, New Year issue, 1950).

The Arab objective is presented here as absolutely rigid. There are only two possibilities, its complete achievement and the disappearance of Israel, or failure to achieve it, which means the end of Arabism.

There are repeated references to the idea that the realization of Arab aims in the conflict is a pre-condition for the achievement of other Arab nationalist aims—a test of Arab nationalism.[8] Hussein declared in a speech from the throne:

> "Without Palestine the Arabs have no real freedom, sincere unity, or a better life." (Amman Radio, December 1, 1962, 11:00 hrs.).

The objective in the conflict is presented as one of the principal ingredients in the totality of national objectives; without success in this respect, all other national hopes will remain a dead letter. In other words, the existence of Israel is portrayed as creating an alienation of Arab nationalism, for the latent possibilities of the Arab personality and Arab nationalism cannot be fully realized so long as Israel exists. Israel's continued existence is also, therefore, regarded as an obstacle to Arab self-acceptance.

These ideas—that the conflict is an absolute, a war for life and death, that so long as Israel continues to exist Arab nationalism will be incomplete and truncated, and that the danger in store from Israel and Zionism is unlimited—are very common in Arab political literature. On this point there are great similarities between the declarations of the leaders, and such formulations are frequently to be found in the analyses of Arab intellectuals and spiritual guides. The latter, like the former, generally make no attempt to explain why coexistence with Israel is impossible, and confine themselves to abstract statements, denoting a fact which cannot be denied, or they explain it by the danger of expansion which threatens "all" Arab nationalism.*

For example, Constantine Zurayk explains, in his book, *The Meaning of Disaster*:

> ". . . It should be made clear to the Arab mind and the Arab soul that the Zionist danger is the greatest danger to the being of the Arabs. The other dangers either threaten some limited part of their being or else they include both the Arab world and the rest of the world [the reference is to Communism—Y.H.]. This danger threatens the very center of Arab being, its entirety, the foundation of its existence." (English edition, 1956, p. 16).

* The position that Israel's existence is the source of all Arab troubles, and is therefore the central problem in Arab nationalism, reaches its highest point in statements by the Fatah terrorist organization. See my *Fedayeen Action and Arab Strategy*, Adelphi Paper No. 53, The Institute for Strategic Studies, London, December 1968.

Since the conflict is presented as a deadly quarrel and not a coexistence quarrel, the goal of liquidation is justified. The conflict becomes symmetrical: each side equally threatens to liquidate the other. It is presented as a model of a biological war of survival: the liquidation of the rival is a vital necessity in order to ensure one's own survival. In this presentation of the goal of liquidation as reciprocal, we can discern the operation of the psychological mechanism of "projection"—that is, the Arabs ascribe their own goal to Israel.

There are grounds for the assumption that Nasser's outlook on Israel as a danger to Arab nationalism is less abstract and more geopolitical: he regards Israel's existence as the major barrier to unity, which is the Arabs' road to greatness. Nasser has repeatedly claimed that it is Egypt's responsibility and historic mission to unite the Arab world, and he may have reached the conclusion that Israel's existence robs Egypt of the possibility of carrying out this mission. No doubt he reasons that without the Israeli barrier the UAR would not have disintegrated, for he would have been able to crush the Syrian revolt without having to send troops by air to prevent the split.

Nasser also emphasizes that the problem is not only the mere existence of Israel, but also what this existence symbolizes. Here, too, he follows the method of abstract description. The challenge that Israel's existence poses to the Arabs is symbolic and a matter of principle, for it embodies the manifestations which Arab nationalism aspires to overcome. The taking of territory from the Arabs is an insult and a degradation, and it was possible only because of their weakness. Israel's continued existence, moreover, demonstrates their impotence:

> "Israel does not symbolize . . . a warlike or military enemy to us and this region, but she symbolizes something else: the attempt to dominate us . . . , the foreign pressure on the Arabs, the attempt to split them and sow dissension among them and obstruct their unification, in case they should agree between them and benefit from the wealth of their lands and the minerals and other assets in the womb of their soil, and from their geographical position." (July 22, 1955, I.L., IV/914).

Among the intellectuals, there is a tendency to ascribe a spiritual colouration to the dispute, though this conception is also to be found among the politicians, as we have seen in the quotation from Nasser's speech on July 22, 1959. The presentation of the conflict as a profound and fundamental matter, which is not confined to the political aspect, is repeated in various forms.

Aḥmad Bahā' al-Dīn emphasizes, for example, that the clash is not only with Israel as she appears to the naked eye: "Israel is broader than the kilometres which constitute its geographical boundaries" (1965, p. 10). Her existence is "a cultural challenge" *(taḥaddī ḥaḍārī)* in the broadest sense, political, economic, philosophical and human:

> "The clash is not a military struggle or a political struggle but something broader and deeper. This is a clash between civilizations." (p. 9).

This tendency to explain the conflict as a spiritual and ideological clash, and not so much as a quarrel over material things, is very clearly expressed by 'Abd al-Raḥmān al-Bazzāz, Professor of Law at the University of Baghdad, who was Iraqi Ambassador in London and later Prime Minister of his country, and who is regarded as one of the mentors of modern Arab nationalism. In a series of lectures on the subject which he gave in 1961-2 at the Institute of Higher Arab Studies under the auspices of the Arab League in Cairo, and which were later published in book form and have gone into two editions, al-Bazzāz gave this explanation of what the dispute between Israel and Arab nationalism is about:

> "The danger of Zionism is not limited to its taking away a vital and important part of the heart of our Arab homeland, expelling over a million of our people, depriving them of their homes, their homeland and their livelihood, and robbing them of human honour. Nor does the danger consist in the fact that Israel separates our Arab East from our Arab West by a foreign body and a foreign element which is incompatible with the general life of the region. Above all, the danger does not consist in the fact that it is a constant threat to other important parts of our homeland since Israel could one day realize her great dream of a broad Israeli homeland stretching 'from the Nile to the Euphrates!' Nor, pre-eminently and above all, does the danger consist in Israel's establishing a modern industrial society, with skill and ties with the West, with its broad scientific, technical and financial potential and its threat to our economic position in the future, so that the whole of our homeland will remain, ultimately, in a state of poverty, backwardness and ignorance. The great danger of Israel is due to its being an ideological threat to our nationalism which challenges our entire national existence in the entire region. The existence of Israel nullifies the unity of our homeland, the unity of our nation and the unity of our civilization, which embraces the whole of this one region. Moreover, the existence of Israel is a flagrant challenge to our philosophy of life and the ideals for which we live, and a total barrier against the values and aims to which we aspire in the world." (1962, p. 257; 1964, pp. 253-4).

The conflict is, thus, a matter of principle; it is not primarily concerned with concrete subjects of controversy between the parties, or complaints against Israel which might conceivably be settled in a way that would leave Israel in existence. Zionism is a challenge to Arab existence itself, being by its essence a denial of the Arab essence. The antagonism between the Arab countries and Israel is absolute. The clash between the sides assumes the character of an abstract metaphysical polarization—a clash between ideals, values and philosophies, which also, therefore, transcends the boundaries of time.

The non-Arab reader who examines al-Bazzāz's statements might arrive at an opposite conclusion. If the concrete problems (territory, refugees, expansion, the economic aspect, competition) are not of decisive importance, he may find it difficult to appreciate the presentation of the clash as a matter of abstract principle between two ways of life, two entities, which for some reason cannot coexist and arrive at some *modus vivendi.* He is liable to suspect that, in order to dramatize the conflict, Bazzāz takes refuge in abstract metaphors, and that the acute form in which the Arabs describe the nature of the conflict is not a true analysis, but only a device to stimulate themselves to adopt a firm attitude from which there can be no retreat. However, we are mainly concerned here with the question of how the Arabs see the conflict, and it is their views and concepts which determine their behaviour, even if others may find a particular attitude difficult to understand.

A separate aspect is the portrayal of the conflict as a religious, spiritual matter. Abdallah al-Tall, in his book *The Danger of World Jewry to Islam and Christianity,* regards the conflict as based on a religious struggle which has continued throughout the generations:

> "The propagandists of secularism, who leave out of account the religious factor in the Palestine problem, ignore the fact that this is the only bone of contention in the world which has persisted for thirty centuries and is still based on religious and spiritual foundations." (p. 9).

Hence he sees only one solution: the *Jihād,* the religious war.

It should be pointed out that this presentation of the conflict as an absolute spiritual clash is to be found not only in Arab statements to their own people, but also in their foreign propaganda. Dr. Sayegh said, for example, in an address on "The Encounter of Two Ideologies" to a conference of the Middle East Institute in Washington:

> "I hope that the foregoing discussion has demonstrated that, apart from the political conflict, there is a basic philosophical and spiritual incompatibility between the two contending nationalisms. Even if all political disputes were to be resolved, the two movements, Zionism and Arab Nationalism, would remain, spiritually and ideologically, worlds apart—living in separate 'universes of discourse' which are incapable of communication or meaninful dialogue." (1961, p. 90).

Here again, we have the idea that even if a political solution is found and the concrete questions involved in the conflict are settled, the basic ideological conflict will remain.

Bazzāz and Sayegh show a tendency to portray the antagonism between the parties in an ideological guise and present the conflict as an ideological one: even if this is not an ideological controversy in the accepted sense of the term—a controversy between social systems—it is a clash of national ideologies. There are grounds for the assumption that the presentation of the conflict as a spiritual one enhances its importance in the eyes of the Arabs. They are not quarrelling about material assets; this is a highly respectable conflict over principles, which also justifies the adoption of a radical position.[9]

Another possible influence in this presentation of the matter is the general view of the Cold War as an ideological dispute and the wish to have the Arab-Israel conflict regarded as similar in nature. It is a common opinion that coexistence is possible between rival States but is more difficult in the case of rival ideologies. It may be that a further analogy is implied by the comparison; since the Cold War is regarded as a clash between a good ideology and a bad one, so is the Israel-Arab conflict. This attitude fits in with the Arabs' habit of emphasizing that their nationalism is natural and good, while Israeli or Zionist nationalism is artificial, self-contradictory and evil.

Another reason why the conflict is an absolute one is the fact that it is concerned with the principle of justice. It is a confrontation between two opposite poles: the Arabs' right to Palestine, which is the just and natural right of a people dwelling on its land, and the claims of the Jews, which are founded on the fiction of historic rights, and are based on robbery and a *fait accompli* created by force.

The conflict, is thus presented, as it were, on two levels. On the lower level are the concrete problems: claims connected with assets, restitution of property, boundaries, territory, compensation and the like. On this level, the circle is narrow: it contains the Palestinian Arabs and Israel. On the upper level is an ideological conflict, an antagonism between two spiritual entities, good versus evil, justice versus injustice. The scope of the conflict widens: it becomes a comprehensive clash between two national movements.

Thus, Mulḥim 'Ayyāsh writes:

"The problem of the refugees is only the human aspect of the problem, but it is not the source of the problem."

And he goes on to explain that the main point is the fact that Israel constitutes a barrier to unity and a threat to Arab existence (*al-Akhbār,* June 23, 1961).

The solution of the problems on the lower level does not mean an automatic liquidation of the conflict on the upper level. Hadāwī puts it:

"The solution of the Palestine problem does not necessarily mean a settlement of the Arab States-Israeli conflict. While the former may influence the latter . . ." ("Israel's Sham Peace Offers," in *Middle East Forum,* Feb.–Mar., 1964, p. 28).

Nasser has also emphasized that the dispute is not about the refugees and that their repatriation would not be the end of the conflict; the central issue is the existence of Israel:

"Israel thought the ending of the refugee problem would lead to the ending of the Palestine problem, but the danger lies in the very existence of Israel." (At the National Assembly, March 26, 1964).

Dr. Walīd al-Khālidī expressed the same idea very clearly:

"The solution of the Palestine problem cannot be found in the settlement of the refugees nor even in the return to the 1947 partition decision." (*Middle East Forum,* Summer 1958).

Nasser also presents the conflict on two planes, but sometimes in a different, more concrete fashion. He emphasizes that it is a matter of a clash between Israel's aims and those of Arab nationalism— a clash over the existence of Israel, which the Arabs oppose because it means the violation of their rights, and also over the danger of expansion:

"Israel presents two dangers. The first lies in her existence *(wujūd)* in Palestine and her usurpation of the rights of the Palestinian people. The second lies in her tendency to gain territorial expansion at the expense of the Arab people and the extinction *(ibāda)* of the Arab people. The Arab people are not like the Red

> Indians. The Arab people were born here and live in this area. They will never allow Israel and those in the United States, Britain and France supporting Israel to realize their objective of keeping Israel in existence in Palestine *(al-istimrār fī Filastīn)* at the expense of the Arabs." (August 17, 1961; see also April 6, 1958, I.L., XI/2146).

Hence, two types of preparedness are required: the one defensive, to prevent expansion, and the other offensive, to prevent the continued existence of Israel.

In recent years, another approach to the definition of the nature of the conflict has emerged. Although some of the ideas that mark this approach were adumbrated some time ago, they have been emphasized with the increasing involvement of the Arab States, especially Egypt, in the organizations representing former colonial territories, especially the Organization of African Unity, and the refugee organizations. The conflict is portrayed as a struggle against foreign settlement like the European colonization of Africa, and is therefore defined as "a struggle for national liberation." This places it in a historical framework as part of the struggle of peoples for independence against their colonial masters. The advantage of this definition is that it not only provides a conceptual framework and a close tie with national struggles for liberation from the foreign yoke in Africa and Asia, but also attaches the conflict to the Soviet-Chinese concept of "wars of national liberation" against the domination of foreign reactionaries and imperialists. This presentation of the nature of the conflict calls for the maintenance of the Palestinian people as the bearer of the struggle for national liberation. Accordingly, emphasis on this idea is accompanied by efforts to preserve the Palestinian people as an entity, to bring it to the fore and organize it in a militant and military movement.

But why was the conflict not explained in this way from the beginning? It is argued that this aspect was not properly understood previously even by the Arabs, and that the imperialists plotted to disguise and conceal it, as part of their plan to bring about the erosion and "liquidation" of the conflict:

> "The Palestine Liberation Organization believes that the political picture of the Palestine problem in the UN has been distorted according to an imperialistic plan, and it is described as a dispute between the Arab States and Israel, which the UN is in favour of solving by peaceful means. This approach endangers the problem of Palestine. Therefore the Organization started, even at the last session of the UN, to present the Palestine problem as a national problem . . . There is

no political or diplomatic solution for the problem of Palestine—without belittling the importance of political efforts. Like any other imperialist problem, it has to be solved in a war of liberation, in which the Palestinian people will play a decisive part." (*al-Jumhūriyya,* September 27, 1964).

This theme is very common in the statements of Shukairy and others.

Although a general framework has thus been found for the conflict, its uniqueness has not thereby been affected. Struggles for national liberation against foreign oppressors (as in Algeria) or oppressors belonging to the same nation supported by imperialism in Asia, are conducted by peoples living on their own soil, but in the present case it is not a matter of an internal struggle. This difficulty may be overcome by the argument that this is an even more extreme and serious case of colonialism. The white oppressors not only drove the original inhabitants off their lands, but even expelled them from their country. Thus, Shukairy declared:

"In Asia and Africa, imperialism was a foreign domination; it was an alien exploitation. But the peoples, the native peoples, remained in their homes, remained in their farms, remained on their land. No doubt all sorts of hardships, acts of repression and displacement were inflicted upon our brethren in Asia and in Africa, but here the native people in Palestine were uprooted, dispossessed and thrown out of their country by aliens, strangers, just like the *colons* who settled in Asia and in Africa. That is what makes the problem of the Palestine refugees of a unique character, more grievous than all the colonial issues that confronted the United Nations." (In speeches at the U.N. General Assembly, on December 4, 1962 and November 5, 1963).

This phenomenon is referred to as "expulsionist colonialism" *(isti'mār ijlā'i* or *istīṭānī).*

The first Palestinian Congress in Jerusalem resolved:

"The establishment of Israel in Palestine, a part of the Arab homeland against the wish of its legitimate people is viewed as a continuous zionist [*sic*] colonial aggression; it is contrary to the principle of self-determination." (May 28, 1964).

The people of the country now demand the restoration of their rights. The expression "restoration of lands and rights" creates a kind of association with the expulsion of Africans from the fertile lands in Kenya, even if there is a difference in this case, as the "restoration" applies to a people outside the land. The Israelis "enslaved" the Arabs; hence the aim is to put an end to servitude and restore freedom. But in this case the term "servitude" also takes on a different connotation from the usual one (compulsory service and exploitation). The Palestinian people is enslaved by being outside its homeland, and the restoration of its freedom means its becoming once again master in its own country. The servitude is thus expressed in the violation of its right to self-determination, and its struggle for restoration thus becomes a struggle for independence—"a war of national liberation."

The preamble to the Palestine National Covenant, signed by Shukairy, reads, in part:

> "Believing in the right of the Palestine Arab people to its sacred homeland Palestine and affirming the inevitability of the battle to liberate the usurped part from it, and its determination to bring out its effective revolutionary entity, . . . I do hereby proclaim the establishment of the Palestine Liberation Organization . . ."

This way of presenting the conflict is not restricted to the Palestinian Arabs. Nasser, too, has frequently declared that it is a struggle for national liberation from a foreign, "fascist" conqueror, and for the restoration of the freedom and independence of the original people.

> "This is a question of the restoration of the freedom of a people and its right to live honourably on its own soil,"

he wrote in a letter to Arab students in the United States (quoted on Cairo Radio on August 24, 1964).

The list of the main participants in the conflict thus seems to have been cut down, and it has been restored to its original character, with the Palestinian Arabs and Israel as the principal antagonists. Each side, however, has its own hinterland: Israel has world Zionism and imperialism, while the Palestinians have the Arab nation* and world progressive forces. The affiliation of the conflict to a great group of struggles not only makes it more respectable, but also guarantees success as a part of the inevitable success of de-colonialization. The global struggle against oppression has been given the character of a world revolution. Liberation is a revolutionary act. There can be no compromise, no settlement based on coexistence, in a "struggle for national liberation" until the oppressors are completely liquidated.

Although this way of portraying the conflict has become fairly general, it is not so emphatically used in Arab circles favouring the West, like official Jordan and Saudi Arabia. In leftist circles, however, it has become the fo-

* "The supporting front" *(al-jabha al-musānida)* in Fatah parlance.

cus of the ideology. The struggle against Israel is placed in the framework of the internal revolution and the revolutionary struggle against imperialism and colonialism. Home and foreign policy are integrated. Liberation is an internal revolution because it necessitates the liquidation of reactionary circles and liberation from the influence of all foreign factors, and it is a revolutionary struggle against Israel. There is only one road leading to both social and political liberation. These ideas are intertwined in discussions on the programme for the attainment of the goal in the conflict.

This development leads to greater emphasis on the goal of liquidation and, as it were, injects new life into it. The ambiguity in the declarations disappears and the objective of liquidation is proclaimed without disguise.*

6. PACIFISM—EXCEPT FOR ISRAEL

Insisting on the absolute nature of the conflict, many Arab spokesmen repeatedly emphasize that peace with Israel is out of the question. This attitude might appear to be incompatible with the prevailing world atmosphere, in which, owing to the danger of nuclear war, peace is regarded as not only an ideal but an imperative necessity. Many Arabs, too, express their general support for peace.

The tenth chapter of the Egyptian National Charter, which deals with foreign policy, repeatedly expresses devotion to peace:

> "The Egyptian people has spared no effort in the pursuit of peace, and thanks to those efforts the people has won its place in the international arena and has become a force leading the way to peace . . .
>
> "Its sincere call for peace was the outcome of its vital need for peace. Peace is the sure guarantee of its capacity to continue the sacred struggle for development."

In his brochure on Arab nationalism, ʻAbd al-Qādir Ḥātim declares that the quest for peace is one of its essential characteristices (1959, p. 12). Arab spokesmen repeatedly emphasize that the Arab countries are devoted to peace and opposed on principle to the use of force for the solution of disputes. Generally, regarding it as a matter of course, they do not even trouble to add that there is one exception to this pacific attitude. Statements

* As in the Fatah position—see *Fedayeen Action and Arab Strategy,* pp. 11-12.

issued after official visits also speak of a general love of peace, but their ceremonious nature, apparently, makes it inadvisable to spoil the effect by mentioning the exception. For example, at the end of a visit to Moscow by Alī Ṣabrī, a joint statement by Khrushchev and Ṣabrī said:

> "Both parties express their determination to strengthen and consolidate world peace and the security of peoples, as well as to maintain the continued coexistence in peace of various States irrespective of their political and social systems." (Cairo Radio, September 23, 1964, 19:30 hrs.).

A similar statement was issued on September 27, 1964, after Ṣabrī's visit to Czechoslovakia:

> "Both parties believe that States must refrain from using force for the solution of regional disputes and frontier problems, in order to preserve international peace and security." (Cairo Radio, September 27, 1964, 19:30 hrs.).

Nasser explained in the National Assembly that the UAR's foreign policy was guided by one principal aim: to support a world

> "... free from the domination of power politics *(siyāsat al-quwwa),* for in a world where power politics reigns we, as a small country, will suffer and will be exposed to danger." (November 12, 1964).

In the same speech, he said:

> "In our foreign policy we are working for world peace, working for the liquidation of imperialism, and we shall work for the liquidation of power politics"

as if these aims were complementary. The liquidation of Israel is included in the liquidation of imperialism, and even if it is accomplished by violent means such violence is not regarded as power politics, but as a "just war." Israel is beyond the pale within which peace must reign. Its liquidation is an act of peace.

Nashāshībī mentions the contradiction between the love of peace and belligerency against Israel:

> "We seek peace for the whole world. We want the cold war to stop and the whole world to enjoy prosperity and stability, but not at the cost of the continued existence, consolidation and expansion of Israel." (1962, p. 172).[10]

Let us see how Arab spokesmen explain away this contradiction and justify the view that peace with Israel is impossible.

a) JUSTICE BEFORE PEACE

Peace, it is argued, cannot be based on wrong and injustice. Peace can be established only after the wrong is rectified and justice is done by the restoration of the Palestinian people's rights and the disappearance of Israel. Nasser has frequently expressed this idea:

> "Any settlement that ignores the legal rights of peoples is not just, and is therefore incompatible with durable peace." (December 28, 1955, I.L., V/1048).
>
> "There will be no peace so long as the rights of the Palestinian people are neglected." (To American Journalists, January 27, 1958, I.L., X/1903).
>
> "Peace which is not founded on justice is actually no more than an armed truce." (October 12, 1960).
>
> "We talk of peace, but we want peace based on justice." (At Alexandria University, July 28, 1963).

This attitude leads to the paradoxical result that what is meant is not "a just peace with Israel" but "a just peace without Israel." In this case, reconciliation with the rival is predicated on his disappearance.

In reply to Prime Minister Eshkol's statement that Israel wanted peace, *al-Jihād* (Jerusalem) declared:

> "O Eshkol, if you really want to make peace with the Arabs, then take up the staff and go back to the place from which you came, so that the Palestinian Arabs may return to their country without war. Then and only then will there be no hostility between you and us." (July 12, 1963).

Furthermore, it is argued that if an existing peace settlement is not just, it may be violated, even if it is laid down in an international agreement. Nasser dealt with this subject in his speech at the opening of the Conference of Non-aligned Nations, in which he proposed that the principal theme of the Conference's deliberations should be the question of how to turn the truce imposed by the balance of terror into a stable peace. In explaining his proposal he said:

> "The UN ought to include activity for both justice and peace, for peace without justice is not lasting. It would be an illusion to ignore this and be content with a *fait accompli* if it was created on the basis of a usurpation which undermines not only the nature of justice but also the meaning of peace." (October 5, 1964).

Abstention from the use of force in international relations, according to Nasser, is conceivable only through the maintenance of a peace founded on justice. In other words, there is no validity in the call for abstention from the violation of peace unless justice is fully done: Nasser continued:

"Only justice creates permanent peace. Force, even if it can enforce a particular situation for a time, is far from the meaning of peace."

On the same lines, the Palestinian National Covenant expresses support for peace, but only a peace based on justice:

"The Palestine people believe in the principle of justice, freedom, sovereignty, self-determination, human dignity, and the right of peoples to practise these principles. It also supports all international efforts to bring about peace on the basis of justice and free international co-operation." (Article 21).

Nasser defends the violation of agreements (such as the Armistice Agreements, for example) on the basis of Article 103 of the UN Charter (which states that when there is a clash between an obligation derived from the Charter and an obligation under any other international agreement, the provisions of the Charter are binding). Accordingly, a peace settlement which is not based on justice (or as in this case, on the right to self-determination) is not binding even if it is derived from an international pact like the Armistice Agreements, since it is incompatible with the obligations of the Charter. The same applies to colonial rule. Even if the allocation of colonies is based on international treaties, it is not binding, and it is not only permissible but obligatory to oppose and violate it.

Justice is a supreme value, overriding a peace founded on an existing international settlement. This idea is repeatedly expressed and emphasized in various forms and in official resolutions (for example, in the joint statement issued at the end of the second Summit Conference).

b) PEACE CONFIRMING AGGRESSION IS INVALID

Since Israel came into the world as a result of aggression, and embodies aggression by her very existence, peace with her means the recognition of aggression. Such a peace, which gives approval to a state of affairs which is, in principle, aggression, is a contradiction in terms, for peace and aggression cannot coexist. Nasser declared, for example:

"We want the peace that will be established in the Arab world to be an Arab peace, which is not acquiescence in aggression or a violation of the sovereignty of the Arab countries, and which does not mean the establishment of foreign bases. The only peace that will be established in the Arab world will be an expression of the restoration of rights to their owners in Palestine. We will not agree to a peace of *fait accompli,* no matter what the circumstances may be, for such a peace is not a true one, but means aggression." (May 1, 1963).

The Palestine National Covenant declared:

"The people of Palestine believe in peaceful co-existence on the basis of legal existence, for there can be no co-existence with aggression, nor can there be peace with occupation and colonialism." (Article 22).

It follows that any action, no matter by whom it is taken, which is designed to stabilize the situation is aggression or abets aggression. Any confirmation of the *status quo* is, therefore, an aggressive act. Hence, the widespread tendency to describe any aid to Israel as an act of aggression.

The conflict is a categorical one, between a party who is absolutely in the right and a party who is not in the right at all. There is, therefore, no room for a settlement, for any settlement is a compromise and half-justice is a contradiction in terms.

c) NO ACQUIESCENCE IN COLONIALISM

Israel is a case of colonialism, and a war of national liberation against colonial oppression is not a culpable violation of peace.

To Khrushchev's letter of December 31, 1963, calling for the peaceful solution of international disputes, the Arab countries replied that they accepted the general principle, but emphasized their reservations in the case of Israel, which, they said, was a manifestation of colonialism, to which the principle did not apply, as the Russian letter stated:

"The demand of liberated States for the return of territories which are still under colonialist oppression or foreign rule is undoubtedly just." (In the Soviet periodical *International Affairs,* February, 1964).

Resentment was expressed at Israel's audacity in expressing agreement with the letter:

"The Israeli letter to Khrushchev makes a pretence of support for peaceful solutions to regional disputes, as if such solutions meant the stabilization of the usurpation and opportunities for its expansion, and as if Israel were part of the region." (Cairo Radio, February 1, 1964, 20:45 hrs.).

The struggle against colonialism and imperialism is not incompatible with peace. The Egyptian National Charter gives "the war on imperialism," "labouring to consolidate peace" and "international cooperation" as the three principles on which the UAR's foreign policy is founded.

d) THE PSYCHOLOGICAL JUSTIFICATION

Peace with Israel means acquiescence in peace and disgrace, which the Arabs of the world cannot tolerate. There can be no compromise over the dishonour involved in the very fact of the establishment of Israel. Thus, Nasser said, according to Haykal:

"There is no intention of restoring half of our honour or half the Homeland." (*al-Ahrām*, May 1962).

Nasser explained to a *New York Post* correspondent that:

"Arab hatred of the Zionists is very great and it is no use talking about peace with Israel." (October 14, 1955, I.L., V/1022).

e) ANY SETTLEMENT MUST BE FIRST OF ALL WITH THE PALESTINIANS

It is the Palestinians who are the party immediately concerned and it is they, first of all, who must agree to any settlement. This is an argument for pushing peace further into the future and imposing the responsibility on a factor which can hardly be blamed for not acquiescing in the situation.

f) DISTRUST OF ISRAEL AND HER CALLS FOR PEACE

Israel is treacherous and deceitful, and will not keep her word. Experience proves that this is so. Between the Arabs and Israel there exists what the Americans call a credibility gap. Nasser has frequently supported this argument with reference to the Sinai Campaign of 1956: for instance, in his speeches on March 4 and April 25, 1960, or his address at Alexandria University on July 28, 1963:

"In 1956, Israel and the Israeli Prime Minister at that time, Ben-Gurion, declared in parliament that they wanted peace and they were prepared to enter into negotiations with Abdel-Nasser and Arab leaders. After seven days the aggression on Egypt started. Therefore, we must not be deceived nor should we be naive."

(A detailed list of deceitful calls for peace is to be found in the chapter on "Peace Proposals in Israeli Strategy" in Ibrāhīm al-'Ābid's book, *Violence and Peace, a Study of Zionist Strategy,* Beirut, 1966.)

g) THE ARGUMENT FROM UTILITY

The Arab countries will not profit, but can only lose from peace. They have no need of Jewish or Israeli capital, or the technical advice that the Israelis pretend to offer. Nor are the Arabs convinced by the argument that they could save the money that they now spend on armaments. For instance, al-Khālidī wrote:

"The international situation being what it is, it is doubtful whether the level of armaments in the Arab world would in fact be materially affected by peace with Israel." (1958, p. 19).

h) ISRAEL WOULD PROFIT FROM PEACE BY EXPANDING

Peace would strengthen Israel and only she would profit from it. She would be able to absorb immigration on a large scale, extricate herself from the grip of the Arab boycott and strengthen her economy in preparation for expansion. Peace is only a mask for Israeli plots. Thus, Nasser said:

"A settlement would not be the end of the aggression but the beginning of new aggressive measures for the realization of the crazy Israeli dream of a homeland stretching from the Nile to the Euphrates." (February 8, 1960).

In reply to a statement by Prime Minister Eshkol in Paris about Israel's aspiration for peace in the Middle East, the Syrian radio commentator said:

"The history of Israel in the region proves that the peace of which Israel speaks is not a goal in itself, but a means for the attainment of certain goals. When Israel calls for peace, she intends to obtain recognition for her aggressive existence and to carry out mass immigration to Israel. In this way she is also trying to extricate herself from the noose of economic and political strangulation in which she is held as a result of the attitude of the Arab and Muslim world, which isolates her at the conferences of the Asian and African countries and obstructs her purpose of economic expansion." (Damascus Radio, July 11, 1964, 13:30 hrs.).

The point was made clearer in a later broadcast:

"Recently, Israel has taken the trouble to repeat her call for peace. She made such a call during Eshkol's visits to the United States and France, as well as before and after the visit. But this is a lying call, a mask for her aggressive aims. The time has come for world public opinion to realize that these continual attempts at aggression by the Jews are only a result that follows from the Israeli aggressive reality. There is no way to stability in this region except by the liquidation of the causes of the instability, which constitute the cancer—Israel." (Damascus Radio commentator, August 6, 1964, 13:30 hrs.).

i) ISRAEL DOES NOT WANT PEACE EITHER

Sometimes it is argued that it is not only the Arabs who are opposed to peace but that, in her heart, Israel does not want peace either because she might lose the aid she receives. It is noteworthy that by using this argument, the asymmetry of the unilateral Arab opposition to peace is transformed into symmetry. Such, for example, is Ṭībāwī's explanation of the reasons why Israel does not want peace today:

1. Israel would have to compensate the Arabs.
2. Peace would mean demobilization and the weakening of the military machine on which the State of Israel is built.
3. Trade in Arab markets would be difficult, for Israel would meet competition from, for example, West Germany.
4. Financial aid from World Jewry would decline with the disappearance of the Arab danger.

(*Middle East Journal*, 1963, p. 526).

Enforcing Peace

Since peace is defined as an Israeli aim and plot, Israel wants to "enforce" it. "Enforcing peace" is the cornerstone of Israeli policy.

Haykal has explained that this was Ben-Gurion's watchword (*al-Ahrām,* June 12, 1964).[11] The history of the relations between Israel and the Arab countries is seen as a manifestation of the idea of compulsion. Haykal describes how Israel first tried to enforce peace by secret intrigues and indirect subversion in the Arab countries. When these failed to bring peace, she tried to enforce it by border aggression and reprisal operations. This attempt reached its peak in the Sinai Campaign. Next, Israel adopted the method of propaganda and she wants to have peace enforced by the nations of the world (*al-Ahrām,* May 5, 1961).

But the enforcement of peace is a contradiction in terms. As Nasser put it:

> "Their leader Ben-Gurion said that he wanted to enforce peace and compel the Arabs to accept the *status quo.* But the enforcement of peace means aggression. Moreover, the enforcement of peace has only one meaning, namely war on the Arabs." (November 16, 1955, I.L., V/1637).
>
> "What is the meaning of the enforcement of peace? It means war." (June 21, 1960—similarly on February 21, 1959).

The very concept of "enforcing peace," therefore, is an affront, for it implies that someone imagines the Arab countries are so weak that they can be compelled to make peace. A step towards peace, or an effort by neutral parties to bring about a relaxation of the tension, or even talk of peace, may be regarded by the Arabs as designed to enforce peace and, therefore, as an attitude of contempt and a lack of consideration for the Arab standpoint. Nasser declared:

> "No power on earth will be able to compel the Arabs to cooperate with Israel." (April 19, 1954, I.L., II/283).

Chapter 3

HOSTILITY AND THE CONCEPT OF THE ENEMY

Impelled by the danger of nuclear war, psychologists, especially in the United States, have been trying since World War II to make an expert contribution to the healing of international ills. Such a contribution might provide psychological insights into social and political phenomena and enrich our understanding of certain aspects of international life. It will be particularly useful if we realize the limitations of psychological explanation, refrain from going too far in looking at international phenomena from a psychologist's point of view and avoid apolitical explanations which ignore the political aspects of competition between States.

Arab hostility to Israel was not a response to any psychological need to relieve tension or aggressive impulses. In the beginning, it was the outcome of opposition to Jewish settlement, and it reached its peak as a reaction to the establishment of Israel, which Arabs regarded as the usurpation of a homeland. The main cause of the conflict is not psychological, but substantially political: a conflict over territory and a clash over real interests. The conflict that was created is, in Simmel-Coser terms, realistic (as distinct from a non-realistic conflict, which is the result of the need for a discharge of psychological tension—Coser, 1956, Proposition 3). Once the conflict is created, it becomes, indeed, like most conflicts, loaded with "a great amount of excess baggage" (Allport, 1958, p. 226) of prejudices and hostility, and is affected by psychological mechanisms which social psychology can help us to understand.

1. HOSTILITY

How is hostility created, and what is the source of aggression? The superficial explanation given by psychologists is that hostility and aggression arise in A against B if B prevents A from achieving some goal. The obstruction of A by B creates frustration, and frustration is the source of aggression (Dollard, J. et al., *Frustration and Aggression*; Berkowitz, 1962, p. xi, Introduction). Frustration and aggression are coupled in common parlance.

However, it has been realized that the cause of hostility or aggression should be regarded as broader than frustration in the narrow sense of deliberate obstruction. Sometimes, the very existence of an alien factor may be regarded as a provocation and give rise to (or intensify) hostility. It has been found, for example, that the entry of Negroes into a white neighbourhood is a cause of hostility. Sometimes the person who is more succesful may arouse jealousy and hostility. Hostility may be caused by factors which undermine a man's self-respect, or which constitute a threat to his outlook on life, irrespective of whether they are working against him or not; their existence is a hindrance, and suffices to arouse his hostility and his desire to combat them. The existence of countries more developed than the Arab States is itself a cause of discomfort, for it undermines the Arabs' faith in their greatness. On the other hand, hostility itself, the expectation of being able to strike and avenge, is already to some extent sufficient to restore self-respect.

There is great power in hatred. Lenin used to say that class hatred was the first motive for revolution. Hatred between nations is undoubtedly a powerful motive in international affairs. It may be assumed, for instance, that in our day the hatred of the people in the developing countries for those of the developed ones will be an important factor in moulding the shape of the world we live in.

If it were possible to conduct comparative measurements of the quantity or intensity of hostility between various groups, it might be possible to develop an ecology of hostility; perhaps even to colour world maps in accordance with the intensity of the hostility to be found in various areas, or to establish qualitative distinctions in hostility: according to whether, for example, it is hot or cold, more or less fanatical or perhaps even more or less enduring. From this point of view, for example, it may be assumed that the hostility to Israel of the Palestinians who have experienced the 1948 war is "substantial," more spontaneous and founded on immediate experience and knowledge of Israel, while the hostility of the Arabs who do not know us through direct contact is more abstract, and perhaps more demonological and ideological, but not necessarily weaker than the spontaneous hostility.

From the point of view of the Arab attitude to Israel, it would be interesting if we could measure and compare hostility in various Arab countries, or in a cross section of various population strata and classes—to find out, for instance, whether Israel is hated equally by townsfolk and villagers, and so forth.

Once hostility has emerged, it develops self-sustaining impulses, spilling over and creating, as it were, further hostility, so that a process of self-perpetuation is initiated. This type has been called *autistic hostility*.

2. IMAGES IN THE CONFLICT

In studying conflicts, an effort has been made to find out what each side thinks about the other, what characteristics they ascribe to each other, the images of each other that they create, and how these images affect their attitudes and actions in the conflict. The behaviour of human beings is influenced not so much by reality as it is, as by their image of it. It is true that there is a relationship between image and reality, but the image is not a photograph of the reality. The same applies to the self-image: how each side sees itself and interprets its own activity in the conflict.

In cases of conflict, a study is made of the psychological factors and mechanisms which lead to the distortion of the parties' images of each other and of themselves. Disputes between nations are to some extent a war of shadows; each side fights the image of his rival, as he pictures him.

People tend to regard the operation of the mechanism which distorts the image as unilateral and confined to their rivals—as if it is only the rival who distorts *their* image, while they themselves are free from any such tendencies. They may even draw satisfaction from their ability to discover errors in the images cherished by their rival or distortions in his image of himself, and consequently flatter themselves on their moral and intellectual superiority. Since we are dealing with the Arab attitude, I shall restrict myself to such distortions among the Arabs, but it is worth remembering that the Israeli side is not immune from the operation of these mechanisms.

Let us survey several processes or mechanisms operative in disputes which lead to the distortion of the image.

a) PROJECTION

Projection is expressed in the tendency to ascribe undesirable qualities to the rival and to regard him as the source of the evil contained in the situation, as if he alone is to blame for the conflict. Here a defence mechanism enters into operation which enables people to ignore their own deficiencies and their part in the conflict. The rival becomes a scapegoat, a cluster of undesirable characteristics, including their own failings and deficiencies, which, by projection, they ascribe to him. A man is sensitive to his own deficiencies, and therefore discovers them in his rival. Projection weakens self-criticism and, as it were, enables people to derive satisfaction from others' faults. They themselves are purged of faults; in their self-image they become paragons of perfection and arrive at a considerable degree of narcissism.[1]

One example of projection in the Arab-Israeli conflct is the translation of Arab xenophobia into the hatred of the world for the Arabs.

Another example is the habit of both sides to accuse each other of contentiousness and inability to cooperate. Israelis tend to emphasize that the Arabs are quarrelsome and that their aspiration for unity is only demagogy, while the Arabs point to the contentiousness of the Jews and the quarrels between them as a proof that they possess no real national unity and are not a nation, and, therefore, that their State will not endure.

Projection is reinforced by another process, the externalization of guilt, with which I will deal later in this chapter.

b) SELECTIVITY, REJECTION AND REPRESSION

In a state of conflict, people tend to filter information and emotions about the rival, the neighbourhood and themselves, ignoring facts and feelings which contradict the images they have depicted—Erich Fromm calls this "selective inattention." On the other hand, there is a complementary tendency to accept any evidence that the rival is really bad, unjust, weak and the like. In regard to all these qualities, he employs what R.K. White calls "selective attention." Such disregard of part of reality leads to a "slanted interpretation."[2] This also applies not only to data about the environment and factors directly concerned with the dispute, but also to knowledge of oneself. For example, Arabs often tend to ignore positive aspects of Israel and Zionism, disregarding or angrily rejecting praise of Israel by third parties, while seizing on and inflating any criticism of Israel. The Arabs also tended to play down manifestations of conflict between the Jewish population and the British in Palestine, because they were incompatible with their idea of a plot between Britain and the Zionists. Memory is also selective.

Arabs forget that the Arab world was divided for long periods, while remembering and emphasizing the brief periods of unity, which are regarded as typical of their entire history. Rejection, selective attention or selective inattention are accompanied by an active process of repression of inconvenient facts to the subconscious, which becomes a reservoir of information and images that a person wishes to ignore. A double system, as it were, of images—in the conscious and in the subconscious—is created. But repression is not complete. The repressed images still exist in a twilight zone, and sometimes emerge and become conscious. This process, "the return of the repressed," in Freud's term, leads to duality and ambivalence in regard to the enemy: there is a dual image of him: good and evil. For example, the Arabs tend to regard Israel in negative terms, but sometimes they present her as an example to themselves, the good qualities which have been repressed thus rising to the surface.

The effect of these mechanisms of cognitive selectivity is important in situations of conflict, in which they are liable to create distortion and misunderstanding, blocking the channels of communication between the parties. Thought becomes an instrument for justifying the accepted image, rather than for testing and correcting the image in accordance with reality and the messages received from it; it becomes biased and inaccurate, ceasing to be an effective instrument for the discovery of truth. Each rival is blind to other characteristics of the enemy, suffering from the "blindness of involvement," the myopia which is typical of those involved in a conflict. This kind of selectivity also leads to automatic thinking and attachment to a stereotyped image of the rival. A rigidity of conception, a kind of mental cramp, is created, thought and understanding working to sustain and strengthen hostility, as if the entire process of thinking is one of self-persuasion, on the one hand, of one's own righteousness and, on the other, of the rival's wickedness. Distortion becomes a matter of a vested interest. Intermediate shades and uncertainties entirely disappear. The enemy's sins are ugly and odious; he is consumed with complexes, contradictions and psychological problems—a "categorical enemy," in Erikson's term.[3] The aims of our side, on the other hand, are just and sublime; our behaviour is beyond reproach; we have become involved in the conflict through no fault of our own. The image of the rival is confronted with a "counter-image." This polarization is not merely a matter of cognitive concepts; these are always bound up with positive or negative valences and evaluations of good and evil, praise and blame. The polarization between black and white leads to the development of rigid attitudes in the conflict which make compromise and partial solutions more difficult to achieve than when this is not the case.

Selectivity is also liable to narrow the scope of perception and thought. Thinking becomes bound to a particular conception of a single solution, ignoring other possibilities of a way out ("only liquidation"). The tension typical of situations of conflict, which also narrows the range of perception and choice, leads to a primitive understanding of the situation, a fixation on immediate objectives, and a limitation not only in range, but also in depth of perception.[4]

Projection and selectivity may be expressed in what Icheiser called the "mote and beam mechanism," i.e. the tendency to see a characteristic in the other which we do not want to see in ourselves and which we regard as characteristic of him for that reason. This mechanism, therefore, as Morton Deutsch emphasizes, creates a moral evaluation in the form of a tendency to denounce faults instead of trying to understand the circumstances which gave rise to them (see his article "A Psychological Approach to International Conflict," in Sperazzo, G. (ed.): *Psychology and International Relations,* pp. 6-7).

Although these mechanisms of projection and filtration are universal, their operations are not uniform among all people. There are grounds for the assumption that the more open and flexible is a community's system of beliefs, the more it tends to take reality into account; in other words, the more open it is to realistic thinking. The more closed and rigid is the system of beliefs, and the more the image of the rival is involved with, and a cause of, emotional experiences, or the more the community has strong prejudices which the image confirms or promises to realize, the more active are the mechanisms of projection and selectivity, and the more firm the rejection of any ideas incompatible with the goal. On this question, too, there is room for transnational comparative research, especially as regards conflict situations.

Creating the image of the enemy is not only a matter of selection, rejection and repression; the negative image is the outcome of hostile intellectual activity designed to interpret the information and the messages received about the enemy, give them the desired colouration, connect them up, and generalize them within the existing system of images and evaluations. The characteristics ascribed to the enemy are not, therefore, absorbed empirically; they are supplemented by a flavouring of explanation, interpretation and ideology.[5] If he has good qualities, they are interpreted in such a way as to neutralize them. If the enemy is strong, for example, his strength comes from wickedness; it is a satanic strength, which will not endure. Ideology is brought in to interpret the image, and the image to strengthen the ideology, so that the image becomes a part of the ideology.[6] In order to emphasize the ideological element in the image of the enemy, we shall call it "the idea of the enemy." From this point of view, ideology in the conflict is the intellectual formalization of hostility. The "idea of the enemy" is the intellectualized image of the enemy; it is the intellectual dimension of hostility, its interpretation and justification, while hostility, on the other hand, is the emotional dimension of the "idea of the enemy."

How can we study the Arab image or idea of the enemy? Since the usual survey and polling methods are impossible in this case, I shall have to rely on qualitative "contents analysis" of statements by Arab spokesmen, drawing conclusions from an examination of the texts. I must emphasize that since, as stated in the introduction, personal impressions play a prominent role in such analyses, there is a considerable danger of errors and distortions. The aim is to try to evaluate the intensity and distribution of the images and ideas through an estimate of their frequency in printed and broadcast material, and sometimes to consider their importance according to the source. I shall occasionally introduce items that appear to me interesting even if they are neither typical nor frequent, but may be of symptomatic significance. In mentioning the details of a particular image, the implication is that they are to be found among Arabs, without claiming that the same image is to be met with among all of them. Not every stroke in the picture drawn here should be regarded as a tried and tested fact of the collective Arab stereotype, and more attention should be paid to the general tendency than to the details.

This kind of contents analysis research necessarily produces a certain kind of result. The outcome, in fact, is not the stereotyped image that exists in the Arab mind, but that to be found in political literature, declarations and discussions. This image, as has been explained, is an intellectualized, ideological one. It is just because large numbers of Arabs have no knowledge of Israel and no direct experience of "the enemy" that the ideological element in these images is considerable. There are grounds for assuming a reciprocal influence between the idea in the literature and the stereotype to be found among the Arabs. I shall have to examine this problem in evaluating the ideology and the images.

3. THE ENEMY IN ARAB NATIONALISM

The existence of national enemies is a common phenomenon. Peoples and societies are in a state of strife and dispute with other peoples and societies which have become their enemies, with whom they compete and sometimes fight. The idea of the enemy who interferes with the achievement of national aims is usually a component in national ideologies. It has been given particular emphasis and attention in the ideologies of oppressed and colonized peoples, who have denounced the enemy's evil deeds in justifying and glorifying the fight against him. Despite the universal nature of the idea of the enemy, analysis is needed in each case to discern to what extent the idea of the enemy is central to the ideology in question and with what degree of intensity it is endowed. There may also be room for comparative research on the place held by the idea of the enemy in various national movements and their ideologies. Such research may enrich our understanding of the general phenomenon of the idea of the enemy and its various forms; it may deepen our understanding of the specific features of its embodiment in various cases, especially as, in the study of the phenomena of nationalism, there may be a general tendency to pay more attention to the positive aspects than to the hostility involved. There are grounds for the assumption that the idea of the enemy occupies a very important place in Arab nationalism and that this fact has implications for Arab attitudes in the Arab-Israel conflict.[7]

After World War I, the Arab national struggle in the Middle East concentrated on the colonial powers, who constituted "the enemy." This struggle was conducted mainly as a separate struggle within each country, and not on a pan-Arab basis; it was split up according to the different enemies—or powers—in question. The aim was the complete independence of each country (for most of them achieved partial independence almost immediately). The idea of the struggle against the colonial enemy held a prominent place at that time in the Arab national movements. Orientalists, like Gibb, have emphasized that the Arab national movement was more concerned with the denunciation of the oppressor than with the consideration of the problem of what should be done after independence was achieved, and that this gave the movement a negative character.[8] However, this concentration on the struggle without overmuch concern with what would happen after the achievement of independence is not peculiar to the Arabs.

It was hoped that when independence was attained and the Arabs became their own masters, their problems would be solved and they would enter upon a period of progress and national achievement which had been prevented only by the lack of independence. But the problems were not solved after independence was attained; some of them were even aggravated. A feeling was created that the Arab countries were caught in some kind of labyrinth, so that in spite of independence they could not act as they wished and achieve their heart's desire. The Egyptian National Charter says in Chapter 3:

> "Imperialism gave independence only in form, withholding its content; it gave the slogan of freedom while keeping back its reality."

Nasser declared:

> "The Egyptian people discovered immediately, and by means of the general revolution, that raising the banner of national independence could not be the end of the struggle, but, on the contrary, it was the beginning of the true struggle with the aim of restoring social construction." (April 17, 1965).

Once the external struggle against the colonial powers was consummated and the Arab countries achieved their independence, the place of the enemy was not diminished, but, perhaps, even expanded.

Munīf al-Razzāz, one of the Ba'th leaders in Jordan, who was appointed Secretary-General of the movement at the 8th Pan-Arab Conference of the Ba'th in April 1965, wrote in his book *The Evolution of the Meaning of Nationalism:*

> "This new nationalism [that of the Asian and African peoples including the Arabs] began quite differently from the West's. It began as an instinctive xenophobic hatred for imperialism and the imperialists, a hatred of its representatives, its nationals, and anyone affiliated with them."

This stage, however, Razzāz continues, was brief, and nationalism developed further, becoming a positive and dynamic movement (English edition, 1963, pp. 55-9).

There are grounds, however, for the impression that, as far as the Arab countries are concerned, the enemy is still being blamed as much as before, and it does not yet appear possible to confirm Razzāz's analysis of a transition to positive nationalism.

In the early period, the enemy was more concrete: namely, the oppressing powers, Britain, France and Italy; the indictment was also concrete and, no doubt, partially justified. In the following stage, after the achievement of independence, the enemy is "imperialism" and, later, "neo-colonialism." The denunciations become more abstract and indirect: the enemy is accused of harbouring intrigues and trying to maintain indirect domination over the countries where he ruled and prevent their social progress and their economic and political development.

The denunciation of imperialism for real or imaginary reasons is particularly strong in the developing countries. It is terrible to feel that one belongs to a backward segment of humanity; one is liable to writhe in pain, self-denunciation and complaint against destiny. A people and its leaders must possess a considerable degree of maturity if they are to give a realistic explanation of their backwardness and paucity of achievement. It is easier to find a way out of this distress by blaming external factors.

a) EXTERNALIZATION OF GUILT

The externalization of guilt is a universal human characteristic to be found among both individuals and groups. Inadequacy, inferiority, backwardness and faults are blamed, through the operation of this mechanism, on an external factor: the enemy or his agents; they are the residue from the period of his rule. The interpretation of the details of his guilt and the description of the enemy's intrigues produce an ideological image: "the idea of the enemy."

Externalization may be a psychological defence mechanism. Pinning the blame on the external factor brings release from the oppression of guilt and self-denunciation, enabling the subject to become easily and quickly convinced of his own perfection and achieve self-esteem and self-glorification. By purging oneself of guilt one can save the idea of one's greatness. Failures and faults do not affect one's dignity, but are regarded only as temporary setbacks due to foreign intrigues.

Externalization of guilt is also a demagogical political expedient of the rulers. The enemy is blamed for every shortcoming and becomes a focus for resentment, tension and pressure. The idea of the enemy becomes a social safety-valve and thus helps the regime to keep in power.

Emphasis on the idea of the enemy also helps to dramatize the national struggle. An emergency situation, an atmosphere of siege, is created. Since the enemy is incessantly weaving his dark intrigues, constant alertness is called for in order to reveal his activities and track down his penetrations. The idea of the enemy lends dynamism to all national activity, giving it the character of a prolonged campaign. For instance, it helps to maintain the idea of revolution as the central principle of the Ba'th movement and in Egypt today. Revolution is not restricted to the achievement of independence, which may be followed by relaxation; it continues, and calls for further effort and sacrifice. The idea of the enemy becomes both a cause of tension and an outlet for tension.

The explanation of the position as the fault of the enemy is easily absorbed by the common people, and may be particularly favoured by a regime that claims to be of a popular character, regarding itself as a representative of the people, which it aspires to imbue with its own outlook. It leads to a personification of the problems. The question that is posed becomes clearer and more simple: not "What has prevented us from achieving our aims—which historical processes and social forces?" but "Who stands in the way?" By ascribing difficulties to intrigue, the propagandist may also attain a considerable degree of satisfaction, since he has succeeded in exposing the intrigue, and the self-satisfaction is transferred to the hearers who have understood the explanation. Politics becomes the art of mystery.[9] The idea of the plotting enemy arouses curiosity, produces an atmosphere of secrecy, and combines with atavistic fears of the unknown. Stories of plots lead to the search for the hidden hand *(yad khafiyya).*[10] Among the Arabs, the picture may possibly merge with old ideas that there are open *(ẓāhir)* and hidden *(bāṭin)* significances, and that both open and hidden forces are at work.

Hostility is also a unifying factor. The group has not only positive values in common, which make it a "community of consent,"[11] but hatreds too, which make it a community of hatred. Hostility, thus, has a role in the formation of a nation. It is not expressed only in a passive attitude; the community is summoned to activity and battle. At an earlier stage it was oppressed and blamed itself for its submission and acquiescence. Now—as a reaction and compensation for past passivity—hostility and struggle are manifestations of activity and self-respect. It may be assumed that regimes which believe in drastic change and activity will tend to make a particularly widespread use of hatred in their indoctrination and self-justification.

We may assume a correlation between the degree of externalization of guilt and the place held by the idea of the enemy in the society in question.[12] Arab statements and writings give the impression that the idea of the enemy holds a prominent place in Arab nationalism and its ideology, and the externalization of guilt is also very considerable. This leads to a kind of demonological obsession, and creates a collective historical persecution complex. What is the explanation of these phenomena? It can hardly be argued that the Arabs have been more oppressed than other peoples, so that their reaction is correspondingly stronger. Here are a few possible explanations:

Professor W.C. Smith, previously director of the Institute of Islamic Studies at McGill University, Canada, and now Professor of Comparative Religion at Harvard, gives a cultural-psychological explanation. In his book *Islam in Modern History,* he explains that the sense of "greatness" is particularly strong among Arabs. The aspiration or the claim to greatness is not peculiar to them, but among Arabs it is connected with religion and history. Other faiths (like Christianity, for example) won their status and their hold slowly, and their beginnings are associated with persecution, but Islam achieved greatness immediately. A few years after Muhammad, the Arabs burst out of the Arabian Peninsula and established an empire of unparalleled size, larger even than that of the Romans. This they regarded as the work of Providence, which granted them victory in order to demonstrate the truth of their religion. Since then, Smith points out, historical, secular success was regarded as an integral part of Islam; success and Islam were inseparable. The Arabs are more sensitive to this feeling than other Muslims, who adopted Islam as a result of its success.

When Europe showed its superiority and—even more—when the Middle East came under the rule of Christian peoples, the Arabs suffered a great shock. Smith finds proof of this in the flood of apologetic works which try to explain how it is possible that they are neither successful nor "great."

This flood of books has not yet ceased, and some of its themes are prominently and constantly repeated in Arab writings, speeches and newspaper articles. The aim is to explain that it is not the Arabs who are to blame for their backwardness, but malevolent foreign factors: it is the enemy's intrigues, motivated by fear of Arab competition, that have made them backward. We shall see another manifestation of this outlook later in the explanation the Arabs give of the West's motive for supporting the establishment of Israel. The assertion that the big Western Powers are the enemy in itself tends to enhance the Arabs' self-respect.

The apologetic religious and spiritual trend merges with the secularist national trend. The claim to greatness makes the feeling of inferiority and frustration doubly painful. Hostility to the West is the product of the feeling that the Arabs have been robbed of their "greatness," and we can understand their bitterness and humiliation at being "robbed of a country"—which is also evidence of their failure and redoubles the agony and the indignation. The belief in their own greatness limits the capacity of the Arabs to internalize their guilt, and leads to its externalization.

We can find another explanation, in the field of social psychology, in the view that Arab society is marked by its atomization. There is little internal unity and cooperation; every individual is hostile to his neighbour. Such an explanation is to be found in Morroe Berger's *The Arab World* (1962, Chapter 5). Berger explains that the Arabs are quick to break out in vociferous quarrels, which easily go on to the stage of fisticuffs. The extended Arab family is full of strife and tension, and village quarrels are frequent. Berger ascribes these phenomena to the numerous frustrations in Arab society—economic, sexual and political—which create "free floating hostility" that seeks a target.[13] He regards the extensive formulae of courtesy in the Arab language and the procedures of hospitality as defence mechanisms against hostility.

He mentions several empirical studies of the Arabs which confirm the prevalence of hostility. For example, Arab students at the American University in Beirut showed more hostility than American students in a similar survey (Millikan, doctoral dissertation at Columbia, pp. 48-50, quoted in Berger's book, p. 162). A comparative study of students from various countries showed that Egyptian students were more suspicious than others. The subjects were asked to mention three striking incidents that they had experienced. The Egyptian students mentioned more unpleasant incidents, which had caused them to lose faith in their fellow-men, than the others. More than any other national group of students, the Egyptians agreed that "the world is a hazardous place, in which men are basically evil and dangerous" (Gillespie and Allport, p. 23, quoted by Berger, p. 163).

Mutual distrust, suspicion, hostility, exaggerated ego and negative individualism (Berger's terms) are hindrances to cooperation between Arabs themselves.[14] This is a prominent weakness of Arab society, which is manifested in economic activity and is an obvious factor in the internal upsets in Arab political life and in inter-Arab rivalries.

The constant internal bickering is externalized by the frequent ascription of blame to others and a deep consciousness of hostility.

Dr. S. Hamady arrives at a similar conclusion on the
She notes that "in their social relations the Arabs show a great deal of hostility" (p. 39):

> "The Arab is reluctant to assume responsibility for his personal or national misfortunes, and he is inclined to put the entire blame upon the shoulders of others." (p. 43).

This conclusion is supported by Dr. Sayegh in his brochure *Understanding of the Arab Mind* (Washington 1953):

> "The Arab is fascinated with criticism—of foreigners, of fellow countrymen, of leaders, of followers—always of 'the other,' seldom of oneself—which is the product of basic dissatisfaction and general discontent rather than of positive convictions and allegiances and standards, and which accordingly serves to thwart collective personal accomplishment rather than to stimulate creative effort and bold enterprise." (p. 28).

Elsewhere in her book, Dr. Hamady sums up:

> "The Arabs usually look for external causes of their frustrations; they prefer to put the blame on some scapegoat. Similarly, as a rule, their aggressive feelings are not turned inward but are directed towards others. They burst into quarrels and threats; yet these generally remain verbal and often subside easily." (p. 230).

Dr. Hamady explains aggressiveness among the Arabs by their proneness to jealousy (p. 43), and notes that: "Mistrust is another form in which Arab individualism asserts itself" (p. 100).

b) THE ENEMY AS A COALITION

In Arab nationalism, especially in the form current today in Egypt, the enemy is a threefold coalition: imperialism, the main enemy (Y. Oron "The National Myth in Contemporary Egypt," *The New East,* 1960), and Israel and the reactionaries as secondary enemies. In other words, imperialism, the principal enemy, has two arms: one internal—the reactionaries, and one external—Israel. Israel and the reactionaries are described as "agents of imperialism," which implies that they are secondary enemies. Imperialism and Israel are the external enemy with which the national movement must struggle in order to achieve its *national* aims: national liberation and full and complete independence. The reactionaries constitute the internal enemy, who has to be overcome in order to achieve the movement's *social* aims: the transformation and advancement of society. National and social aims are interdependent, for until society has been transformed the external enemy will have a foothold inside the country and independence will not be complete. Reaction is the breach through which foreign influence penetrates, while imperialism and the reactionaries are interested in backwardness, which facilitates exploitation and profit. This trinity of imperialism, Israel and the reactionaries is a coalition of common interest, inter-supporting even without consultation. Even if there is no contact between Israel and the reactionaries, the latter are allies—if only tacit ones—of Israel, as a result of their alliance with imperialism. Nasser has repeatedly emphasized, as evidence of this, not only that Israel refrains from attacking reaction in her broadcasts, but that there is agreement between the statements of the reactionaries and those of Israel:

> "Yesterday those who heard the Saudi broadcasts, the Hussein broadcasts and the Ben-Gurion broadcasts and the BBC found them all saying the same things." (January 9, 1963).

The image of the enemy as a coalition leads to hostility, based on personal experience, against one partner in the alliance spilling to other partners: thus those who feel hostility towards the colonialists learn to hate Israel, even if they know nothing of her. The presentation of the enemy as a coalition and an alliance gives the idea of the enemy the character of a dynamic, continual and ever-renewed plot. The cauldron of intrigue is always boiling. The idea of the coalition extends the scope of externalization and guilt. A charge which is hard to pin on one partner may be pinned on his ally. This trinity holds the central place in the demonological "pantheon" of Arab nationalism.

4. FACTORS IN ARAB HOSTILITY

The Arab-Israel conflict was not created as the result of psychological or sociological factors among the Arabs, or their national or cultural character. It was not created because Arab hostility and aggressive impulses sought a scapegoat and a target for the externalization of guilt, or because of the clash of two different cultures, the social and political processes taking place in the Arab countries, or the difficulties of modernization. Such explanations are, indeed, frequently given; they are founded on the idea that the reason for the conflict lies in some factor to be found among the Arabs themselves, some fault or sickness in the Arab soul and society, and that if there were others in their place there would be no quarrel and no conflict. But this is not so. Israelis should be aware of the temptation to view the conflict in this way, which seems to be in their own interest. Basically, the conflict was created not by subjective causes arising out of the specific Arab character, but by objective circumstances involved in the general human and political situation, expressed in the fact that the same territory cannot be at one and the same time in the possession of two owners. From the very beginning, the threat, seen by the Arabs, that the country might be taken from them was not a subjective nightmare resulting from a persecution complex or a tendency to foresee the worst, but a real threat. The Arabs' opposition to being deprived of a country which they regarded as theirs, their anger at losing it, and their refusal to acquiesce in its loss, should not be ascribed to unique Arab characteristics. It may be assumed that any people would have objected to being deprived of its territory whatever their background or circumstances.

However, once the conflict arose, the specific characteristics of the Arabs influenced their attitude and behaviour. A series of important questions arises: which of the Arabs' characteristics have an influence on their attitude, their hostility and their behaviour? How do factors in their national personality, their national ethos and social character, the modal structure of their personality, their phylogenetic unconscious, prevalent archetypes and spiritual heritage, the social processes to which they are subjected, the historical situation of their development, influence or find expression in their attitude towards Israel?

These factors may have only a vague and general influence, and though it may be conjectured that they constitute part of the factors that mould the Arab attitude or strengthen some of its features, I cannot categorically define the extent of this influence, in what forms it is expressed, and what results follow from it—or, in other words, which manifestations would disappear were this or that factor not operative. Another question will also arise: how does the fact that the conflict is not within one cultural framework, but is between two cultures—even more, between two religions—affect its character?[15] Intensive research would be required to find replies—if any are possible—to these questions. In the present work I will confine myself to mentioning a number of explanations which may have influenced hostility in addition to those already mentioned in connection with the place of the idea of the enemy in Arab nationalism.

a) HOSTILITY AS A CULTURAL MANIFESTATION — LANGUAGE

How do cultural factors affect the attitude of the Arabs in the conflict? This is a difficult and delicate question, and considerable anthropological knowledge, observation and study would be required to answer it. I shall limit myself to one cultural factor: language.

The Arabs are proud of their rich and beautiful language, but its wealth is not confined to positive terms. The literature of the conflict displays a plethora of virulent opprobrious epithets, expressing denunciation, loathing and derision. The last *(hijā')* was a form of poetry in classical Arabic literature. Virulently abusive language is also to be met with in the political controversies between the Arabs themselves, but the expressions used against Israel are usually much stronger. Besides, in the internal debates, the abuse is confined to particular rulers or individuals and is not flung collectively at a people.

It can hardly be assumed that the wealth and virulence of the abusive language we meet in the literature of the conflict are only a matter of flowery language. Nor is it easy to accept the explanation that the language itself inveigles the Arabs into this copious flow of scurrility.[16] The language is a reservoir of such expressions, but it does not compel anyone to make use of them. The Arabs are not merely victims of their beautiful language.

Arab writings and broadcasts contain a rich variety of abuse and scurrility about Israel and the Jews. (For a selection of the most common terms of abuse applied to Israel, see Chapter VI.) Often, defamatory expressions appear one after the other in a string.

For example, Abdallah al-Tall writes:

> "The Bible describes exactly the nature of the Jewish people and clearly brings out the character of the Jewish faith, which is built on treachery *(ghadr)*, baseness *(khissa)*, barbarism *(waḥshiyya)*, hatred *(ḥaqd)*, corruption *(fasād)*, fanaticism *(ta'aṣṣub)*, covetousness *(jasha')*, arrogance *(ghurūr)*, and immorality *(inḥilāl)*" (1964, p. 15).

The aim of this rhythmic chain of epithets is not to present an exhaustive catalogue of the odious qualities of the Jews, but to express his loathing and to transfer the emotional effect to the reader.

Not all the Arabs use such abusive language against Israel. Nasser, for instance, denounces Israel in vehement terms, but does not pour out a stream of abusive language. The tendency to written and oral scurrility is so common, however, that it cannot be ignored. Any Westerner who dismisses it as mere "Oriental exuberance" should bear in mind that this attitude may imply a sense of superiority on his own part. The study of Arabic in Israel and familiarity with the cultural aspects of the conflict may not necessarily endear the Arabs to the Israelis.

The Palestinians are outstandingly prone to the use of defamatory terms about Israel and the Jews, but they are by no means alone. Tall is not a Palestinian (he comes from Irbid in Transjordan). ʽAqqād, who is one of the greatest modern Egyptian authors, and ʽAlūba have nothing to learn in this respect. Nashāshībī describes the Jews whom he saw from the walls whilst on a visit to Jerusalem as:

> "... a collection of the world's hooligans and its garbage ... Dogs, robbers, clear out to your own countries!" (p. 114).

In another passage (p. 164) he describes Israel as:

> "... an international dung-heap in which the squalor *(qādhūra)* of the whole world has been collected."

(This, apparently, is his Arabic version of the term "the ingathering of the exiles.") In a similar style he used to write in his paper, for example:

> "Chicago wanted to recall its notorious criminal past in presenting the key of the city to that hardened criminal Levi Eshkol." (*al-Jumhūriyya*, June 12, 1964).

In an ostensibly academic publication, the *Egyptian Political Science Review*, which is issued by the Egyptian Association for Political Science, we find the following:

> "And thus Britain wanted to exhaust the strength of the Arabs and divide them, and at one and the same time to get rid of the Zionist plague *(wabā')* in her country: she assembled these thousands of vagabonds and aliens *(āfāqiyyūn)*, bloodsuckers *(maṣṣāṣī al-dimā')* and pimps *(tujjār al-aʽrāḍ)*, and said to them: Take for yourselves a national home called Israel. Thus the dregs of the nations *(huthālāt al-shuʽūb)* were collected in the Holy Land." (Fatḥī ʽUthman al-Maḥlāwī, "A Spearhead Against Arab Nationalism," in a special issue of the journal on Arab Nationalism, January-March 1959, p. 117).

The issue carries the usual statement, it is true, that the articles "express the opinions of their authors."

The semanticist Hayakawa distinguishes between informative connotation and affective connotation, which expresses the emotions associated with, and aroused by, a particular term.[17] It may be assumed that the affective aspect of these Arabic terms of abuse is deeper, bitterer, more highly coloured and saturated with hostility than their literal, but sometimes colourless, translation into other languages.

For example, one of the epithets applied to Israel and even to Israeli personalities, is "foundling" *(laqīṭa)*: "the foundling state" or "the foundling Israeli Prime Minister." In translation, the epithet appears, at worst, bizarre, but in Arabic the abusive effect is very strong; it may be a heritage of Beduin society and the period in which the Arabic language took shape. Among the Beduins, a man must belong to a group or a tribe, and "foundling"—one who does not belong—is a term of deep disgrace, meaning a bastard, for only such were abandoned as "foundlings."

Arab representatives also use abusive terms about Israel in European languages and at international forums, but the "affective connotation" cannot always be transferred to a foreign language, and they feel that something of the meaning has been lost on the way.

For example, when the American representative at the UN, Mr. Plimpton, remarked to Shukairy that he was using abusive language, the reply was:

> "I spoke for three hours; was it all abusive? I do not know if in the English dictionary there are so many abusive words that could be related and narrated in three hours before the Committee. I know the English language is very poor indeed, since it is very poor in abusive language." (At the Special Political Committee, 413th sitting, November 19, 1963).

In other words, the stock of abusive epithets in the English language is inadequate, and Shukairy complains, as it were, of the frustration caused by his inability to give full expression to his detestation as felt in his own language, as if the process of translation weakened the strength of the denunciation. Abusive language, as is well known, also has a cathartic function: it substitutes a verbal assault for a real one, abuse being a consolation for impotence and a means of relief. It appears that catharsis is a frequent feature of the Arabic use of words, and more will be said on this subject below.

The terms of abuse may also have a further, symbolic function, that of execration which has an effect on reality. They, as it were, shower disgrace on the object and make him even more loathsome and abhorrent.[18]

A man's words also have an influence on himself, and abuse conveys an instruction to the abuser. If something is described as filth, pollution and excrement, that implies the need for cleansing and sanitary action (*iktisāḥ, taṭhīr* and *taṣfiya* are used to denote the objective of liquidation). If the enemy is described as a cancer or a malignant growth, the implication is that a surgical operation is needed to excise him. It appears, then, that such expression are manifestations of the politicidal and genocidal aim.

A balanced evaluation of Arab vilification cannot be achieved in isolation. It would require comparative research on the expressions used by various peoples to vilify their enemies in times of conflict—"comparative abusive semantics" or "comparative research in scurrility." Such comparisons might shed further light on the linguistic culture of the vilifier and its influence on his attitude in the conflict. It seems, however, if only as a provisional conclusion, that in the field of abuse, Arabs have reached a peak of achievement.

The Arabic language, as a cultural phenomenon, on the one hand, expresses and on the other hand facilitates a considerable intensity of hatred.

b) THE ISLAMIC FACTOR IN HOSTILITY

Islam is basically a combatant, expansionist faith. The world is divided into the "Abode of Islam" *("Dār al-Islām")* and the "Abode of War" *("Dār al-Ḥarb")*—those parts of the world that do not accept the authority of Islam and against which Muslims must wage the Jihād, the Holy War. The Jihād is a collective duty of the community of the faithful *(farḍ 'alā al-kifāya)* until the whole world becomes *"Dār al-Islām."* From a fundamentalist viewpoint, Islam does not recognize coexistence with infidel lands.[19] This phenomenon of basic hostility is not incompatible with tolerance towards alien communities in Islamic countries, which was conditional on their submission to the Islamic authorities.

A verse in the Quran which is basic to the Muslim approach to Christians and Jews reads:

> "Fight against such of those who have been given the Scripture as believe not in Allah nor the Last Day, and forbid not that which Allah has forbidden by His Messenger, and follow not the religion of truth, until they pay the tribute readily, being brought low." (Sura IX, Repentance, v. 29).

So long as Jews and Christians do not submit, the Jihad against them continues.

When Arab spokesmen emphasize that they bear no hostility to the Jews, but are determined to fight their State, they are expressing the spirit of Islam, which recognizes the Jews only as a tolerated minority, while maintaining a state of war against the Jews outside Islamic territory. It is difficult to estimate the force of this Islamic archetype in the attitude to Israel, but it may be assumed that it is a factor, if only a theoretical one, in the popular attitude, which is undoubtedly affected by Islam in the emotional sphere, and that it has a stronger influence in more deeply religious circles.

There are grounds for the belief that we are concerned with a fundamental historical factor which influences the Arab attitude. Islamic consciousness has grown accustomed to Christian independence and the existence of Christian States since the rise of Islam. These are nothing new, although from the viewpoint of basic Islamic principles full recognition of coexistence with them is, as we have seen, problematical. Some Islamic sages have explained the attitude to the infidel States as not peaceful coexistence, but "a truce" or "an armistice" *(hudna),* namely, an arrangement which is only temporary (for ten years). There is also another Islamic concept called *"Dār al-Ṣulḥ"* or *"Dār al-'Ahd"* the "sphere of acquiescence" or "the sphere of the covenant." There are various explanations of this concept, which some theoreticians regard as part of the Dār al-Islām. D.B. McDonald, in *The Encyclopaedia of Islam,* explains:

> "This conception in some vague form was probably also the basis on which treaty relations with Christian states were accepted as possible." *(Dār al-Ṣulḥ).*

This is the position so far as the Christians are concerned. Historically, however, the same does not apply to the Jews. Since Muhammad, Islam has regarded the Jews, basically, as subordinate and inferior, in fulfilment of the Quran's decree that the Jews must be in a lowly position. This concept of the Jews in the Quran will be discussed in the following chapter. An independent Jewish State, is, therefore, a great novelty. Muhammad fought and defeated the Jews, but now the wheel of history has come full turn and the Jews have defeated Muslims. Islam aspires to the expansion of its territory, which makes the establishment of a Jewish State, trespassing on Islamic territory, an intolerable provocation.

If a Holy War is proclaimed to extend the territory of Islam it becomes all the more obligatory if there is danger of a Muslim retreat. The idea of the Jihād is fundamental in Islam.[20] The very word is saturated in the minds of Muslims, and especially Arabs, with emotional memories of the days of heroism and conquest; their present situation is liable to intensify their longings for the glories of the past and stimulate a determination to restore them. The impracticability of the Jihād has led to its withering away as a practical imperative, and attempts have been made in Islam to soften its implications and even to abolish it (see the article on Jihād in *The Encyclopaedia of Islam).*

Arab national ideologists use secular nationalist concepts, rather than religious ones, but when they appeal to the people they frequently employ terms and ideas of Islamic religious significance. The struggle against Israel is often described as a Jihād, with frequent references to its virtues and the religious promises to its fighters, the *mujāhidūn,*[21] with all the traditional and emotional significance of such a call.

Sheikh 'Abd al-Raḥmān al-Ḥajj, the Rector of al-Azhar, the religious university, issued a declaration on May 15, 1958, the tenth anniversary of the establishment of Israel, in which he said:

> "It is now our duty to renew the Jihād in order to restore our usurped country (*al-Ahrām*, May 15, 1958).

Similarly, authorities on Islamic Law issued legal opinions *(fatāwā),* laying down the fight against Israel as a religious obligation for all the faithful (see the collection of *fatāwā* in Īzūlī, *The Warning of the Disaster of Arab Palestine*, pp. 172ff).

The Islamic Factor in the Attachment to Palestine

Islamic motifs also serve to emphasize the sanctity of Palestine for Muslims, who ought to possess it.

1) Muhammad's "Night Journey"—*al-Isrā' wa-al-mi'rāj* from Mecca to Jerusalem, from which he rose to heaven, returned to Jerusalem and thence back to Mecca, is described in the Quran:

> "Glorified be He Who carried His servant by night from the Inviolable Place of Worship [Mecca] to the Far Distant Place of Worship [Jerusalem], the neighbourhood of which We have blessed . . ." (Sura XVII, The Children of Israel, v. 1).

Non-Muslim scholars may explain that "the Far Distant Place of Worship" does not mean Jerusalem, but this makes no difference to the Islamic belief.

Tall explains that Allah's choice of Jerusalem for the Night Journey "was a heavenly strategic plan." The Almighty foresaw that "Palestine would be the first line of defence of Islam and the Muslim countries." He therefore made it sacred to Islam by sending the Prophet there, establishing an eternal bond between the Muslims and Jerusalem (p. 22). Thus the circumstances of the conflict become the framework for a theological doctrine.

2) "The First of the Two Directions of Prayer" *(Ūlā al-Qiblatayn).* At first, Muhammad and his followers turned in prayer *(qibla)* towards Jeru-

salem and continued to do so for 16 to 17 months (this was done to win over the Jews of Yathrib [Medina], but it had no effect). Later he changed the direction of prayer to Mecca. Although Jerusalem is not mentioned in the Quran, it is called "the first of the two directions" and "the third of the sanctities" *(thālith al-ḥaramayn),* namely the third Holy City (after Mecca and Medina).

3) The Blessed and Holy Land. Various proofs are adduced of Muslim and Arab bonds with Palestine, especially the verse in the Quran already quoted, which speaks of "the Far Distant Place of Worship, the neighbourhood of which we have blessed"—namely, God blessed the surrounding land as an expression of its special sanctity. There are also supposed to be references in other Muslim writings, though in almost all of them Palestine is not spoken of as a separate unity, but is included in Syria (al-Sha'm); see, for instance, quotation in al-Dabbāgh, *Our Country Palestine,* pp. 335ff.

These citations are also presented as a counterweight to the Jewish claim of a historic right to Palestine because of a special bond between the country and the Jewish people; it is argued that the Muslims, too, have a special bond of sanctity with the Holy Land.

4) The charge that the Jews intended to demolish the al-Aqṣā Mosque and rebuild Solomon's Temple in its place was revived during the period of the Mandate. Quotations from Jewish and Zionist writings were used to demonstrate the aspirations to rebuild the Temple and revive the sacrifices; attention was drawn to Jewish pictures and tapestry designs showing the Mosque or the "Wailing" Wall. Particular attention was paid to this question around 1929, when the problem of the Wailing Wall was acute.

The World Islamic Conference, which assembled on May 29, 1962 for its fifth session in Baghdad, was presented with a memorandum on the alleged existence of a Jewish plan to demolish the Dome of the Rock and rebuild the Temple on the site. Another memorandum drew the attention of the delegates to a world Zionist plot to liquidate Islam in Palestine and the neighbouring countries (*al-Manār,* May 29, 1962). In its resolutions the Congress expressed its anxiety at the aspirations of the Jews to demolish the al-Aqsā Mosque in order to establish "a Jewish Temple" in its place. The Congress denounced the Jewish aspiration to appropriate the Holy Places of Palestine and the nearby lands in order to establish their great State stretching from the Nile to the Euphrates (Baghdad Radio, June 3, 1962, 21:00 hrs.).

The Islamic theme is not presented with the same emphasis in all the literature of the Arab conflict. The decline in the extent to which it is utilized is no doubt connected with the general tendency to emphasize the secular aspects of Arab nationalism and create a common front against Israel with the Christian Arabs.* For the benefit of the latter, Zionism is accused of intending to attack the Christian Holy Places as well.

In the Palestinian National Covenant and the resolutions of the first Arab Palestine Congress in Jerusalem, the religious aspect is mentioned only in a vague general call in the "Orientation" plan for a proper place to be given to the religious and moral aspect (Resolution 22 on Orientation and Publicity). However, the Arab Higher Committee, the Palestine Liberation Organization's rival, published a manifesto severely criticizing the decision to dissociate the Palestine problem from the Islamic world as being in keeping with the desires of the Zionists, who were making great efforts and were prepared to spend enormous sums in order to divert the attention of the Muslim world from the problem (*al-Kafāḥ,* September 30, 1964).

For Tall, the conflict is basically religious, and he regards religion as pointing the way to a solution. He explains:

> "The problem of Palestine is religious and sacred, and any attempt to deal with it which is not based on a religious Jihād is doomed to failure. There is no alternative; my faith in this is founded on my military experience and historic truths of proven validity . . .
>
> "The leaders of the secular Arab parties ignore the fact that in all the decisive historic battles of Arabism and Islam, from Kedassia, Yarmuk and Ein-Galut to Port Said, the battle-cry was religious and sacred: *Allah Akbar.*" (pp. 8-10).

The slogan *"Allah Akbar"* is often repeated by the Ṣawt al-ʻArab broadcasting station and is included in its station song. (The theme of the Jihād was repeated with great emphasis during the Six-Day War.) In attempts to win the support of the Muslim world outside the Arab countries, there is certainly no hesitation in exploiting religious motifs. Islamic congresses, the first of which was held in Jerusalem in 1931, meet quite frequently and listen to addresses and manifestos about the dangers of Zionism to Islam. Resolutions are adopted against Israel, emphasizing the supreme importance of the Palestine problem for all Muslims. The occasion is used to appeal to Muslim countries not to establish relations with Israel, or to sever

* There has been an increase in the use of Islamic themes after the Six-Day War. See articles in *Majallat al Azhar,* October 1968.

them where they exist. The Islamic Congress at Bandung decided that it was forbidden for all Muslim countries to recognize Israel, and called upon them to recognize the Palestine Liberation Organization on May 15, 1965, as well as to observe the 15th of May every year as Palestine Day. The Muslim States were adjured to concentrate their efforts in support of Palestine in the international arena in order to restore Palestine to Arabism and Islam (*al-Akhbār,* April 4, 1965).

I shall return to the question of Islam in Chapter 5, in dealing with the Islamization of anti-Semitism.

c) SOCIOLOGICAL FACTORS IN HOSTILITY

Sociologists and psychologists point to the unifying effects of conflicts and hostility (see, for example, Simmel, Coser, Proposition 11; Brown, 1964, p. 71; Freud, *Civilization and its Discontents,*[22] summary in Angel's article in the McNeil volume). The tensions involved in conflicts, the need for a united front and the mobilization of resources for the struggle with the rival, the possibility of externalizing feelings of dissatisfaction and hatred, reduce the influence of divisive factors. Perhaps we may take a further step and assume that a society which is lacking in integration needs some such factor as a conflict in order to unite it. These considerations are doubly valid in regard to new States. In his article, "Building the Newest Nations, Short-term Strategy and Long-run Problems," Foltz writes:

> 'The new state may try to unite its people by focusing animosities and frustrations on some external enemy, just as the nationalist movement focused its resentment upon the colonial power or previous ruling class." (Deutsch, K.W. and Foltz, W.J. (eds.), *Nation Building,* 1963, p. 122).

The conflict can, therefore, serve as a positive factor in the process of unification. As Nasser put it:

> "It is the common struggle that unites us and strengthens Arab nationalism." (Quoted in Ḥātim's article on Arab nationalism in the *Egyptian Political Science Review,* January-March, 1959, p. 7).

For Egypt, whose internal national integration is more complete, hostility helps to achieve integration on a second, inter-Arab, level, and the conflict is dealt with mainly on the political plane, while it commands little attention among the common people and what the psychologists call its saliency is low, though there has been a change as a result of the Six-Day War. (I shall have more to say on this point in discussing popular identification with the Arab attitude in the conflict, in Chapter XIII.) This is shown by the fact that in Nasser's speeches to the Egyptian people, before June 1967, the conflict was generally mentioned only in a few sentences, while in Jordan, which has not yet taken firm shape as a political and national unit, the conflict was utilized as a means of national unification. Jordanian spokesmen emphasized the country's special role in the struggle against Israel, and the conflict played a more prominent part in public life. The same applied to Syria.

A possible explanation in the field of social psychology for the function of the conflict in Arab society, and perhaps also for the intensity of the hostility which characterizes it, may be seen in the difficulties encountered by Arab ideologists in defining the content of Arab national identity— a problem to which they devote a great deal of attention.

The definition of identity, according to psychologists, is not only positive, but also negative: it involves differentiation from aliens, or self-identification in respect to a negative reference group.[23] Hostility can help to create the national identity by negating the characteristics ascribed to foreign nations. Thus, Dr. Sayegh writes to explain the Arab approach to neutralism:

> "What is rejected as not-I is a coefficient, a function of what is determined as I." (*Understanding of the Arab Mind,* 1953, p. 31).

There are many examples in Arab national literature of comparisons between the Arabs and other peoples, of self-glorification by denigration of others. Dr. S. Shamir writes:

> "Definition by negation is characteristic of this thinking. Apparently, the authors feel the difficulty of attaching the totality of humanistic ideas to the Arabs, and they strengthen their arguments by presenting contrasts: humanistic Arab nationalism, on the one hand, and non-Arab movements, which are anti-humanist, on the other. Western nationalism is placed at the opposite pole: its two characteristic manifestations are imperialism, with its exploitation, and racialist fascism and nazism." ("The Question of National Philosophy in Modern Arab Thought," in *Hamizraḥ Heḥadash,* Vol. XIV, 1964, No. 6, pp. 22-23).

The same phenomenon is to be seen in the images adopted: the self-image as a negative of the image of the rival.

Modernization and Westernization

We shall not enter here into a discussion of the extent to which modernization and westernization are synonymous today; in any case, modernization means at least partial westernization. The combined process is liable to give rise to impulses of hostility. The internal reorganization which is involved in a change from the traditional socity, the undermining of accepted values, the reaction against tradition, all these are liable to upset self-confidence and lead to hostility. It is humiliating to have to turn one's back on one's own culture and tradition and adopt foreign patterns of life. The idea of the enemy may be particularly useful to societies in which, as a result of sudden changes, values and outlooks have been undermined, and which suffer from feelings of spiritual instability and insecurity. This insecurity may be externalized and ascribed to the work of the enemy. It may be assumed that such phenomena are a factor in the hatred of the West in the Middle East, as a love-hate complex in relation to Western culture. This factor may also intensify hostility to Israel, which is regarded as a representative of the West, and which, in its achievements and way of life, stands for the westernization which is so much desired. It may be no accident that hostility to Israel and activity in matters connected with the conflict are particularly prominent in those societies or sections of the population which are experiencing the process of modernization. In traditional Arab societies and those in which the tribal structure has been preserved, there is much less activity over the conflict.

d) PSYCHOLOGICAL EXPLANATIONS

The Authoritarian Personality

Research has shown that there is a tendency among anti-Semites towards a considerable degree of correlation between certain traits of character making up together a syndrome or complex of characteristics which has been given the name of "the authoritarian personality": ethnocentricity, prejudice, suspicion, conformism, a view of the world as threatening, externalization of guilt, a tendency to categorical judgements and polarization of praise and blame, an ambivalent attitude to parents (acceptance of their authority combined with a veiled hostility towards them), and so forth. There are grounds for the conjecture that this complex of characteristics may be common among the Arabs.[24] It may be assumed that the tendency to authoritarianism in Arab culture and the acceptance of superior authority may contribute towards the creation of this psychological type. Morroe Berger writes:

"There is a high degree of authoritarianism in the personal make-up of Arabs, doubtless the result of centuries of life under authoritarian political and family life."

Berger reports that two studies on Arab students showed a high degree of authoritarianism (p. 177).[25] On the other hand, it should be noted that the authoritarian personality expresses itself in intolerance, while among the Arabs in particular there have been laudable manifestations of tolerance.

This theory of the authoritarian personality has met with some objections and criticisms. Prof. Jessie Bernard (in her article in Singer's *Human Behavior and International Politics*) argues that though the concept may shed light on the psychology and behaviour of the individual, it is of dubious value in regard to the group, since it is a moot question how the attitude of the individual is expressed in behaviour in an inter-group conflict.

For the study of the Arab attitude in the conflict with Israel, Faris' criticism, in his article "Interaction Levels and Intergroup Relations," is more important. He criticizes the theory of the authoritarian personality because it depends on an individualistic interpretation of the attitudes in a conflict and tries to find the reasons for them in the character of the individual, especially in manifestations of abnormality and psychological sickness. Attitudes are created, however, Faris emphasizes, in the course of a social process and are instilled in the individual as a result of his membership in the group in question. It is social organizations that create the human and social characters of their members by educational and other influences. Hostility as a relationship between groups and images does not come from the individual, but emanates from society.

Hence, the hostility to Israel and the images of her that are to be found among the Arabs are not the outcome of the psychological makeup of those Arabs as individuals, but are to be found among them as a result of their membership in the group. A change of attitude, moreover, will not be a matter of some process of healing the individual, but would be the result of a change in the attitude of the group.

Liquidation

The aspiration to liquidate Israel is a political aim, but it is possible that the idea of liquidation, as a drastic, radical and brutal goal, is also the expression of psychological mechanisms. Again, these explanations are suggested as possible, but not necessary.

It may be assumed that groups of people whose self-respect has been injured will seek to inflict severe punishment and vengeance to atone for the injury they have suffered. They may regard the injury as a heinous crime, for which only the severest penalty can be an adequate retribution. It may also be assumed that sensitivity to one's own honour depends upon the degree of development. As Steven Withey and Daniel Katz remark, in a technological bureaucratic society the factor of personal self-respect is weakened (McNeil, E.B. [ed.], *op. cit.,* p. 75). In less developed societies, self-respect and national honour may have greater weight.

The demand for the achievement of a goal which by its nature calls for absolute, indivisible fulfilment may be more characteristic of groups of people who regard themselves as injured. Only the absolute goal provides compensation for injury. For example, Colin McInnes writes that the Negro and coloured movement in the United States and Britain "is insatiable in its demand and won't settle for anything less than absolutes" ("Michael's The Cloak of Colour," *Encounter,* December 1965, p. 161).

The demand for extreme penalties may be connected with the self-image. Self-esteem may be particularly prone to find expression in resentment and vengefulness, leading to the demand that the injury be not forgotten and the full penalty be exacted of the culprit. Thus, Nasser said:

> "We are a people that never forgets if it has been injured, but the injury to us increases our determination and stubborness." (March 3, 1955, I.L., III/667).

The implication seems to be that the Arabs are not worthy of their Arabism if they acquiesce in an injury. The establishment of the liquidation of the rival as the goal also tends to strengthen the ethos of one's own greatness, by insisting that the culprit receive the severest possible punishment. Sometimes, a person may strive for an extreme goal, which does not permit partial retreat or settlement by compromise, because at heart he doubts his own firmness. By adopting the absolute aim, he binds himself and intensifies the loss of self-respect that would result if, after all, he had to retreat. The emphasis, which is so common among Arabs, on a strong and stubborn stand may indicate lack of self-confidence rather than the reverse.

The more radical and rigid the aim, the more despicable must be the image of the rival. Corresponding with the aim of liquidation there must be an absolutely negative image, a severe dehumanization of the rival, and this, in its turn, affects the action to be taken against him. As Stegner says in his article "Psychology of Conflict of Human Beings":

"If we can perceive the opponent as less than human, superego controls do not operate and no guilt is felt over a resort to violence." (McNeil, *op. cit.*, p. 51).

It may be that liquidation represents a judgement resulting from a totalistic approach. This "totalism" is expressed in the polarized view of Israel as evil and despicable in an extreme and absolute degree, which leaves no room for any gradation. Erikson writes about

". . . solutions which betray their totalistic nature in that the totally good may learn to be cruelly stern *ad majorem Dei gloriam*." (In his article in the Bramson and Goethals volume, p. 128).

5. IMPERIALISM AND COLONIALISM

Arabs repeatedly argue that Israel is an imperialist phenomenon. What do they mean by imperialism?

Basically, the idea of imperialism is influenced by the experience of subordination and by the ideas of Hobson and Lenin about imperialism as an advanced phase of capitalism which seeks markets for its surpluses and exploits foreign countries.

For Europeans, imperialism and colonialism are not entirely reprehensible concepts; they involve at least a modicum of esteem, as implying recognition of the capacity to govern distant lands and maintain law and order. The Arabic term *isti'mār,* however, is entirely negative. Its root literal meaning is "to settle," but today it has come to denote exploitation, enslavement and establishing oneself at the expense of others. "Imperialism is Theft and Robbery" is the name of a chapter in Niqūlā al-Durr's *Thus Lost and Thus Redeemed* (p. 153). Arabs are not prone to make a balanced analysis of the factors that led the European peoples to cross the seas, discover new routes and lands, settle and dominate, build and trade. Nor do they wonder whether their ancestors, when they sallied forth from the Arabian Peninsula and conquered a kingdom with the sword, were not also imperialists. In *The New Crusade in Palestine,* Talḥūq explains that the Arabs were not imperialistic in their conquests: on the contrary they brought about an upsurge of culture:

"They did not draw benefit from their conquests as did the conquered countries . . . They disseminated their superior culture and the lights of science wherever they went . . . They did not oppose the renaissance of these countries as the imperialist States do." (1948, p. 12).

In Arabic, colonialism and imperialism have been usually designated by the one term *isti'mār,* and, indeed the distinction is not particularly important today. Imperialism in Arab eyes is not only direct rule over other countries but any manifestation of privilege, advantage or influence. Since, however, influence and advantage are enjoyed by some countries not only as the result of a deliberate policy of domination and rule over other peoples, but as the outcome of basic inequalities between the few wealthy and progressive countries and the poor and backward majority, the inhabitants of the backward countries are liable to regard imperialism as not only the embodiment of inequality, but as its cause: the direct reason for their backwardness and poverty. This is an inequality created and organized by its beneficiaries, the imperialist States, which do what they can to maintain it. It makes a mockery of the independence of States and of democratic relations between them. Sometimes this outlook involves the superficial view that, but for imperialism, equality would reign the world over, and that its abolition would usher in a golden age.

Since inequality and the existence of wealth and poverty constitute an injustice and a chronic disease of the international system, the connotation of *isti'mār* is expanded, and it becomes a symbol of everything that is evil in international relations today, of aggression and covetousness. From the viewpoint of the undeveloped countries, admission of inequality and acquiescence in continued backwardness mean national bankruptcy, and it is therefore convenient to ascribe backwardness to imperialism. Colonialist powers undoubtedly exploited their colonies, but European domination was not the only cause of backwardness. The developed States certainly continue to exploit their advanced economies and their technological and scientific power, and the very fact of their existence makes it more difficult for the backward countries to develop in competition with the advanced ones. Imperialism has become a comprehensive term of protest against past subordination and present inferiority. It is an anachronism, "an affront to the age in which we live" (Nasser, October 5, 1964). In its broader sense, it has become a criminal phenomenon.

War against imperialism is a universal human duty and an Arab national duty. In the third principle of the Constitution of the Ba'th (1947), this war is presented as the outcome of the Arab nation's mission to renew human values: "Imperialism and everything connected with it is a crime, and the Arabs will fight it by all possible means." The war for the liquidation of imperialism was one of the six principles of the Egyptian officers' revolt in 1952, also incorporated in the UAR constitution of January 16, 1965.

In his letter to Hussein of March 13, 1961, in which he explained his principles and policies, Nasser declared:

> "We believe that imperialism in all its forms is a calamity and a disaster, and that it means the decline of the people that are in its clutches. We believe that acquiescence in imperialism is a danger to the peoples that make peace with it, and that negotiations with it or peaceful coexistence with it destroy the strength of these peoples."

The National Charter (Chapter 3) declares that in the struggle with imperialism there is no room for reconciliation or bargaining.

The struggle against imperialism is a global one; through it, the Arabs join up with a large group of States, with whom they can cooperate, if only on a negative basis. The struggle transcends the exclusively national effort, and a transnational solidarity is created. The tendency is to regard imperialism as a single front. Lenin regarded it as a clash between imperialistic States, which would ultimately go to war with each other, but Arabs (as well as others) emphasize the unity of imperialism:

> "As imperialism is united and indivisible, and its aims, plans and aspirations are the same, so the struggle of humanity against it is a single whole." (Shukairy, *Palestine and the Arab Summit Conference*, p. 72).

This emphasis on the unity of imperialism is based both on the tendency to regard the enemy as the centre of a cosmopolitan plot and on the identification of imperialism with the West.

a) IDENTIFICATION OF IMPERIALISM

Imperialism is generally defined as identical with the West. Despite the claim of positive neutralism and non-alignment with either East or West, there is an obvious asymmetry in the attitude of the so-called progressive Arab States to both. A Western action is more likely to be condemned, even if the Soviet Union is responsible for an identical action. For example, the USSR's support for the UN partition resolution and its recognition of Israel upon its establishment are not mentioned with the same indignation as the US's recognition. Attempts are made to find excuses for the Soviet Union's active support of the partition resolution. Nashāshībī, for instance, blames the Arab rulers and kings who provoked the Soviets and aroused their antagonism to the Arabs (1962, p. 176).[26]

The Arabs occasionally mention the fact that the Jews received arms from Czechoslovakia during the War of Independence, but mainly to show the West that the Arabs were not the first to establish ties with the Eastern bloc.

The West is denounced mainly on the grounds that it was the Western countries that were the colonialist rulers. Another reason is the identification of modernization with westernization. Despite the Arabs' pride in their culture, they realize, as Professor Bernard Lewis pointed out in *The Middle East and the West* (1964, p. 135), that they imitate the West in every sphere: in the army, government, construction, industry, economic affairs, educational methods, dress, social customs, and even literature. The conditions of political and social life compel them to abandon traditional ways and adopt those of the foreigner. It is no wonder that they find this humiliating, regarding the very existence of the West, which they imitate, as the source of their sufferings and the target for a profound hatred. As Professor Smith wrote:

> "Most Westerners have simply no inkling of how deep and fierce is the hate, especially of the West, that has gripped the modernizing Arab." (W.C. Smith: *Islam in Modern History*, p. 159).

It should be noted that this was not the attitude to the West from the beginning. The imitation of the West started as far back as the Ottoman period. At first it was mainly concerned with military technique. In the early period of Arab awakening, "the liberal hour," as it is described by Albert Hourani, who places its close at 1939, the attitude to the West was one of sympathetic imitation. The ruling classes saw in it a source of cultural inspiration; then they tried to imitate its administrative and organizational institutions. The virulent hatred of today is typical of the present period in the Arab world, which is know as the popular period, in which representatives of the lower classes and army officers have risen to power in many Arab countries. The imitation of the West did not produce the expected results. When Western democratic methods failed, the blame was laid on the West, and not on the conditions of Arab society, which were not suitable for such systems of government. The West is presented as a historic enemy, whose hostility to the Arabs is a continuation of the rivalry between Christendom and Islam, especially since the Crusades.

b) INVASIONS IN THE ARAB PHILOSOPHY OF HISTORY

In the light of the struggle against imperialism, the history of the Arabs is regarded as a prolonged resistance to imperialist aspirations and invasions. A description along these lines is to be found in an introduction entitled "Imperialism," bearing Nasser's autograph signature, to a book published in April 1954 as No. 2 in the Ikhtarnā Lak ("Chosen For You") series and called *Leaders of the Imperialist Gangs*:

> "Our Arab countries have not ceased for centuries to be the goal of the imperialists' attacks and enmity, as if imperialism wanted to avenge an ancient wrong on the nation that brought civilization to their countries with the conquests of the Caliphate after Mohammad."

Nasser goes on to explain that imperialism has assumed many guises. When the Crusades were exposed in their true colours, another open campaign started, without any attempt to conceal their aims. This was open *(sāfir)* imperialism, which tried to impose its rule in order

> "... to degrade us and acquire what was in our hands and under our feet, to exploit our wealth and our markets for its own benefit, to take our lands as a base for its armies, so that they should consume the fruits of our land in peace and destroy our buildings with their own hands or by the hands of their enemies in war, after which they would sow the seeds of corruption and dissension among us, liquidate the foundations of our nationality and muzzle us to prevent our recalling the grandeur of our past, deaden our hearts to make us insensible of our glorious achievements, and steal away our minds and this world of ours."

Imperialism appears in various disguises in order to conceal its aims—sometimes as working "for the sake of civilization," sometimes as a "humanitarian struggle for the liberation of the slaves," sometimes using economic means to lay the ground for political domination and expropriation, sometimes as a "police operation" to safeguard security in troubled areas, when it appears as "offering" to defend the country and sometimes as "cultural assistance," when the purpose is to undermine morality, manners and faith.

This historical description of imperialism occurs repeatedly in Nasser's writings and speeches. In the introduction to Karanjia's *The Arab Dawn,* Nasser wrote:

> "Imperialism always coveted the Middle East. Sometimes they used violence and sometimes cunning intrigues. But the people always behaved cautiously. It was

always the rulers who surrendered. They were puppets of the imperialists, and served as a means by which imperialism overcame the people. The imperialists erected artificial barriers and unnatural frontiers. They fomented discord whenever unity arose and cunningly sowed dissension. But the people was always one." (1958, pp. 11-19).

Speaking of the Crusades, Nasser said on one occasion:

> "It was England and France that attacked this region under the name of the Crusades, and the Crusades were nothing else but British-French imperialism . . . it was no accident at all that General Allenby, commander of the British forces, said on arriving in Jerusalem: 'Today the wars of the Crusaders are completed.' Nor is it in any way an accident that when General Gouraud arrived in Damascus, he visited the tomb of Saladin and said: 'Behold we have returned, Saladin.' " (On his return from a tour of Syria, March 20, 1958, I.L., XI/2098-9).

The same description is given in an article by 'Abd al-Mun'im Khilāf in a brochure *Arab Nationalism and Imperialim* (p. 131), and is repeated in many other places.

The Egyptian National Charter, in Chapter 10, describes the struggle against imperialism as a historic struggle of the Egyptian people and a "legendary example" in the struggles of the nations. First it was waged against Ottoman imperialism, despite its guise of an Islamic Caliphate; then against the French invasion, compelling "the adventurer who shook the whole of Europe" (Napoleon) to retreat; then against the intrigues of world imperialism and international monopolism. The Egyptian people thus stood firm against the assaults of three empires: the Ottoman, the French and the British. In the same vein, projecting the struggle against imperialism back to the days of the Pharoahs, Iḥsān 'Abd al-Quddūs writes:

> 'If we believed in the 'balance of power' we would have surrendered to imperialism ever since the era of the Hyksos." (*Rūz al-Yūsuf,* March 8, 1956).

c) THE INDICTMENT AGAINST IMPERIALISM

Imperialism is the historic enemy of the Arabs and Arab nationalism. In the light of the present day, Nasser regards the historic aim of imperialism as "the liquidation of Arab nationalism":

"The European armies united in Syria and Palestine under the name of the Crusades for the purpose of liquidating *(qaḍā' 'alā)* Arab nationalism. These armies conquered Palestine and Jerusalem and established fortresses in Syria, and thought that they had thus liquidated our nationalism and established a permanent base for imperialism. But what was the result?" (November 11, 1960).

"Imperialism always wanted the liquidation *(taṣfiya)* of the Arab people and of Arab nationalism which confronted it." (November 16, 1960).

Imperialism is afraid the Arabs may unite, advance and restore their greatness, so it is interested in dividing them. The artificial fragmentation of the Arab world is the work of imperialism. Present dissensions are the effects of the residue of imperialism, which "imposed the difference" between the Arab countries that obstructs their unification. It was imperialism that established local, particularistic nationalistic movements as a counter to the movement for unity (Ḥātim in the *Political Science Review,* January-March, 1959, p. 16).

It foments disputes between the Arabs and prevents cooperation and coordination between them. Thus, Haykal writes:

"What prevents coordination? . . . The intrigues of imperialism, which are meant to sow fear among the Arab world, especially in the circumstances of social antagonisms under which it exists." (*al-Ahrām,* July 19, 1964).

Bazzāz gives a more historical explanation (1962, pp. 254-5). Imperialism brought about the unification of India and Indonesia, but in the Arab countries, which were under the rule of several imperialisms (French, British and Italian), it left a heritage of discord. It split up basic Arab unity into a variety of shades, until the Arabs themselves begin to ignore their own unity and are aware only of their differences.

The fact that Egypt, in the past, stood outside the scope of the Arab struggle is also ascribed to imperialism, which tried to deflect her from her Arab character. It was the British, according to Bazzāz, who prevented the Egyptians understanding that they are a part of Arab nationalism as a whole (p. 417). Nasser also put the same idea:

"Imperialism and its helpers . . . used to say here in Egypt: What have you to do with the Arabs? And in the other countries they used to say: What have you to do with the Egyptians?" (January 16, 1965).

It is interesting to note that it was the Egyptians who accused the British of inventing the idea of Arab unity and the Arab League, which they regarded as a devilish plot to separate the Arabs from the Muslim world. Today, the opposite accusation is made.

The competition between Iraq and Egypt is also regarded as a result of imperialist intrigues. Haykal wrote:

"A basic element in imperialist strategy in the Arab region was the aim of sowing dissension between Cairo and Baghdad . . . It was imperialism which implanted the idea that there is a traditional competition between Iraq and Egypt." (*al-Ahrām,* February 15, 1963).

Imperialism is interested in preventing the economic progress of the Arabs so that they should be unable to compete with it, while it can continue to exploit them. The backwardness of the Middle East is of foreign origin and is the fault of imperialism. During its rule in the Middle East, imperialism made no contribution to the progress of the area. Nasser said, for instance:

"The English were here for 80 years. Did they change us? Have they made us smoke the pipe and do as they do?" (January 9, 1963).

The poverty of the Arab countries is also a heritage of imperialism. Nasser declared that Egypt must bridge the gap between the clay hovels "bequeathed to us by imperialism" and the sublime achievements of the generation symbolized by atomic laboratories (at Port Said, December 23, 1962).

Imperialism tries to undermine the national spirit and to corrupt manners. It introduces materialistic trends and tries to upset the confidence of the Arabs in their tradition and culture. The aim of the European orientalists was to corrupt and degrade Arab culture. According to Dr. Nāṣir al-Dīn al-Asad (in an article "The Philosophy of Imperialism" in *Arab Nationalism and Imperialism,* Ikhtarnā Lak edition, 1957, pp. 96-7), Bernard Lewis, in his book *The Arabs in History,* "sows poison disguised in a scientific style." The West's principal achievement lies in the field of material civilization, and this is sometimes portrayed as being at the cost of moral and spiritual degeneration (Zurayk, *The Meaning of Disaster,* p. 14), as if the Arabs are superior to the West, or at least capable of superiority, in basic spiritual values.

The imperialists are unscrupulous. Their operations are characterized by cunning, persuasion, plotting and intrigue. They exploit cracks in Arab society, which exist so long as complete freedom has not been achieved, unity established and the face of society transformed; they infiltrate through these cracks to work in cooperation with their allies, the reactionaries. According to the Egyptian National Charter (Chapter 9), their activities may be divided into two stages:

Stage I: Direct confrontation with the people. This has ceased since the national revolution.

Stage II: Indirect activities through capitalist factors—"Its national hide-out was within the palaces of reaction." This is one of the reasons why there is a need for a social revolution, which will liquidate reaction and close the cracks:

> "The people understands that the imperialist presence on its soil is not only the open military bases but also the concealed *(khāfiya)* bases, which are more dangerous and more harmful." (Nasser, March 26, 1964).

Haykal explains:

> "Imperialism has not disappeared, but it has changed its form, the indirect method replacing the direct one . . . In the past, its power took the form of invading armies. Today the method has changed. Power is expressed by the signing of unequal agreements between the minority ruling in that State and the [foreign] State for the purposes of exploitation." (*al-Ahrām,* August 13, 1965).

Thus imperialism assumes a new, indirect form: neo-colonialism.[27]

There is a widespread desire in the Arab countries to denounce the West and to attack it if only by verbal means. Nasser's great prestige in the Arab world may be explained by the fact that he has come out openly against the West and thus given the Arab masses the satisfaction of seeing it pilloried. Haykal writes:

> "At the beginning of 1958, the masses uttered their historic acclamation, which was imbued with the tempestuous emotions kindled by the appearance of the hero."

And he adds immediately:

> "O Nasser, the giant, O shatterer of imperialism!" (*yā jabbār, yā muhattim al-isti'mār—al-Ahrām,* October 17, 1961).

The acclamation for Nasser is bound up with his role as the "shatterer of imperialism."

There is some convenience in abstract denunciation of imperialism, for it enables a particular State or States to be denounced without mentioning names in such a way that everyone understands who is meant, which has the advantage of defiance without constituting a diplomatic affront. This style is common in speeches and formal resolutions passed at international conferences and its clamorous dissemination by mass communications media is one of the factors that characterize the atmosphere of international life. Despite the hatred for imperialism, however, there is a need for its favours, especially those of the leading imperialist power, the United States. This produces a feeling of discomfort and ambivalence, and sometimes a lowering of the tone of the denunciations uttered against imperialism. The *politique de grandeur,* founded on principles, gives way to the expediencies of the *politique des intérêts;* sometimes this has been reflected in more moderate action, though not in a more moderate attitude, even against Israel.

6. SELF-CRITICISM FOR EXTERNALIZATION OF GUILT

Some Arabs, however, have criticized the exaggerated tendency to blame external factors. Those who are connected with, and dependent on, the West, such as the leaders of Jordan, are particularly sensitive to denunciation of Western imperialism. Thus, for example, the Jordanian White Paper states:

> "This problem is the scurrilous and irresponsible attitude of some of the Arab propaganda machines and leaders who stigmatize with expressions like 'imperialism,' 'servitude' and 'dependence' *(tab'iyya)* anyone who advocates an outlook or a policy different from theirs. The Government of Jordan looks forward with sorrow and concern to the future of the Arab nation because of the change in the meaning and signficance of these concepts, such as 'imperialism' and 'dependence,' from expressions symbolizing a real political situation and social condition to a weapon of meaningless talk which corrupts the atmosphere of balanced political discussion and gradually leads to the loss of Arab self-confidence. Imperialism, as we have noted, is a real political emotion and spiritual fact, and it is a disease that must be uprooted from the soul before it is expelled from the country. After it has been expelled from the country, imperialism does not remain in the soul, while leaders in one country continue to ascribe every political event or change to the hidden hand of imperialism and plots manufactured in darkness. This political style, expecially in the manner into which several of the propaganda machines have sunk, can only lead to a decline of self-confidence in the ranks of

the Arab people, the destruction of all standards in the style of political activity, and bringing it into contempt." (Chapter II, pp. 18-19).

Haykal, too, has felt that there has been some exaggeration in the externalization of guilt. In an article in *al-Ahrām* in 1962 he asked whether the blaming of Britain for everything was not merely a smoke-screen. To illustrate the question he told a story about a lion who used to terrify a Kikuyu tribe in Kenya. The tribesmen could neither capture or kill it, and their chief reached the conclusion that the tribe had no alternative but to arrange its way of life on the assumption that the "danger" would continue to exist. The existence of the danger was of advantage in the life of the tribe. One day, however, one of them succeeded in killing the lion and told the chief of his success. The old chief was deeply concerned in case the tribesmen heard that the danger had gone and returned to their former lackadaisical ways; so he agreed with the huntsman to keep the death of the lion a secret. Every morning they used to bang a drum made of the skin of the beast, which sounded like a lion's roar, so that the tribesmen should imagine that the lion was still prowling about the neighbourhood. And Haykal asked:

> "Are we in the Arab region not acting in the same way from the political point of view with the British lion?"

However, he answered in the negative, giving as proof Britain's action in Yemen. (December 28, 1962).

Haykal also had similar doubts in regard to Israel:

> "I wish to state that I detest attempts to involve Israel in matters in which she plays no part, only because of the desire to brandish her name in front of the masses as a scarecrow." (*al-Ahrām,* December 21, 1962).

The latter passage shows that Haykal was aware of the habit of blaming Israel for things which had nothing to do with her, though, of course, he ascribed it to others and not to himself.

Self-criticism over the use of the idea of the enemy is fairly rare, but it exists (more so after the Six-Day War). It is more common in criticism of the Arab States by each other, but it may be assumed that this also leads to self-examination, even if it is not expressly admitted. There is a kind of twilight realm of self-doubt, of rejected and repressed ideas which rise to the surface again from time to time, of ambivalent attitudes. The same phenomenon also occurs in other aspects of the Arab attitude to the conflict.

At times, Arab spokesmen may recognize the distortions in their viewpoint, and then close their eyes to them again; they may feel that they are trying to escape from reality and take refuge in these distortions, and the result is, though only to a certain extent, doubt, uncertainty and discomfort.

7. IMPERIALISM AND ISRAEL

The bond between imperialism and Israel is presented as essential and historic, as a political community of interests.

From the general historical point of view, the Israelis are the modern Crusaders, a link in the chain of imperialist invasions of the Middle East. The fact that the early Jewish settlements were called "colonies" *(musta'marāt)* creates a semantic link with colonialism.

The bond is regarded as part of the nature of the Jew and his history. Dr. Muhammad 'Abd al-Mu'izz Naṣr explains, in his book, *Zionism in International Affairs,* 1957, that the Jews never stood on their own feet, but always relied upon the neighbouring empires, Egypt or Persia, and therefore developed the art of flattery to the full (pp. 27-8). No wonder Israel can never free herself from this ancestral tradition of dependence on a great power (p. 33). It is also a matter of spiritual affinity, according to Abdallah al-Tall. He declares (1964, p. 20) that the Bible permitted "collective punishment" and the killing of the sons for the sins of the fathers (as an example he gives Joshua's punishment of Achan). The British, French and Italians took this custom from the Jews. The British, he declares, used to destroy a house, together with the women and children in it, if the owner was accused of cutting the telephone lines.

Sharāra says that fifty Jews accompanied a Roman expedition that left Aqaba in 27 B.C.E. to occupy Yemen and Saba:

> "It is characteristic of the Jews that they are agents of invaders and conquerors and sanctify the money in their money boxes," he declares (*On Arab Nationalism,* p. 68).

The tie between Israel and imperialism has continued: Israel is described as an advance base for imperialism, a starting-point for the conquest of the region. Her existence, therefore, is a danger to the independence of the Middle East States. Thus, Nasser wrote in his letter to Kennedy on August 18, 1961:

"Since her establishment, Israel has not deviated from the imperialist path, and she obviously feels the bond of interests between herself and imperialism. Imperialism on its part has used Israel as an instrument for the geographical fragmentation of the Arab world and a base from which to threaten any movement working for liberation from its rule. I have no need to give proofs of this, for it is sufficient to recall the circumstances that led to the tripartite aggression against us and the plot that preceeded this in 1956." (Published in *al-Ahrām*, September 21, 1962).

The tie between Zionism and imperialism is also expressed in the doctrine that "Zionism is the most advanced phase of imperialism," as in the title of Fatḥī al-Ramlī's book (1956). This is, as it were, a revised version of Lenin's maxim that imperialism is the advanced stage of capitalism. Al-Ramlī explains that imperialism aspires to dominate other countries, while Zionism is an effort to concentrate economic influence with a view to world Jewish domination—hence the danger it involves for all peoples. This watchword is repeated in other books published in the non-socialist States; for instance, in the text-book, *The Palestine Problem,* by the Jordanian Minister of Education, al-Hindāwī, p. 147.

a) THE ESTABLISHMENT OF ISRAEL

When Arab authors and statesmen use the expression "the establishment of Israel" they are not necessarily referring to the proclamation of the State on May 15, 1948, but to a prolonged process which started with the Balfour Declaration.

The existence of Israel, they emphasize, is due not so much to herself as to colonialism. Thus, Dr. Sayegh writes:

"Whereas unilateral Zionist colonization failed, in the thirty years preceding the First World War, to make much headway, the alliance of Zionist Colonialism and British Imperialism succeeded." (1965, p. 9).

In his *Philosophy of the Revolution* (Chap. 3), Nasser adopts a similar attitude:

"Even Israel itself was but one of the outcomes of imperialism. If it had not fallen under British mandate, Zionism could not have found a necessary support to realize the idea of a national home in Palestine." (Arabic edition, p. 69).

The establishment of Israel is often ascribed to imperialism, which is regarded as the father of Zionism, because it facilitated the creation of the Jewish State:

"It was imperialism that established Zionist nationalism." (Nasser, at an officers' meeting, March 11, 1958).

"And who is responsible? Who pushed the Jews and aroused them to seize Palestine and put an end to the Arab people? It was England." (Nasser, December 14, 1953, I.L., I/154).

The Zionist settlement programme is described by Dr. Sayegh as a colonialist operation, part of the scramble for Africa:

"The frenzied scramble for Africa of the 1880's stimulated the beginnings of Zionist colonialization in Palestine. As European fortune hunters, prospective settlers and empire-builders raced for Africa, Zionist settlers and would-be state-builders rushed for Palestine." (*Zionist Colonialism in Palestine,* p. 1).

Arab spokesmen quote statements by Zionist leaders who tried to convince British statesmen that the establishment of a Jewish National Home would be advantageous for Britain as a guardian of imperial communications, especially through the Suez Canal. They also quote British statements about the imperial interest in the Jewish enterprise in Palestine. Shukairy frequently repeated this argument in the United Nations: in his speech on November 19, 1963, for example, he quoted Churchill, Lloyd George, Amery, Herzl and Weizmann.

b) THE BALFOUR DECLARATION

November 2, the anniversary of the issue of the Balfour Declaration, is observed as a day of mourning every year in the Arab countries. The word "ill-omened" *(mash'ūm)* is always attached to the name of the declaration. The Arabs are well aware that the Balfour Declaration contains the seed from which the Jewish State grew:

"We must take the Balfour Declaration as the first report on the Palestine refugees." (Shukairy at the UN on November 19, 1963).

"The Balfour Declaration is the beginning of the road to the end of Palestine." (Nasser, on December 13, 1953, I.L., I/154).

The Declaration is felt as an unbearable affront, for it implies that the Arabs were so weak that Arab territory could be taken away and given to others:

> "We thought that the danger of Israel was mainly the weakness of the Arabs. But for this weakness, she could not have stolen one of the most sacred and purest territories from the Arab homeland." (Nasser on July 22, 1957, I.L., XI/1672).
>
> "When the United States agreed to the Balfour Declaration, she did so on the assumption that we did not exist as a people . . . , as if Palestine were an island in a no-man's-land." (Shukairy at the UN, November 19, 1963).

The Declaration is portrayed as an international crime, for it contradicted the primary and basic principle of international order: self-determination. Shukrī denounces it as incomparably the greatest crime in history (p. 21). Nasser wrote in the letter to President Kennedy already referred to:

> "The one who had no ownership gave the promise to the one who had no right, and both together succeeded by force and cunning in dispossessing the owner of the legal right and depriving him of his ownership and his right This is the meaning of the Balfour Declaration, which Britain undertook, in giving a land which did not belong to her but to the Palestinian Arab people for the establishment of the National Home. Even on the human plane, Mr. President, and all the more on the international plane, this is a matter of open robbery, and any ordinary court could have condemned those responsible. Unfortunately, Mr. President, the United States threw its weight into the balance, not on the side of right and justice in this problem, ignoring all the American principles of freedom and democracy."

The Balfour Declaration is described as the outcome of "bargaining between a Jewish merchant and an English merchant," without taking human or moral considerations into account (Dr. Muhammad Naṣr, p. 21).

c) WHY IMPERIALISM "CREATED" ISRAEL

Much attention has been devoted by Arabs to the motives of the British in issuing the Balfour Declaration. Sometimes it has been said that they needed the aid and influence of American Jewry because of their difficult military situation, but this explanation is felt to be inconvenient, as it seems to magnify the importance of the Jews and it is therefore rejected by some writers. Bahā' al-Dīn believes that the Declaration was motivated not by the strength of the Jews but by a Christian guilt complex vis-à-vis the Jews. Another motive he gives is the imperialist tendency to find support among a minority and afterwards to disguise this as a humanitarian act (1964, pp. 22–23). A prominent feature of these explanations is the tendency to ignore spiritual motives, such as support for the Zionist ideal, and, on the other hand, to emphasize selfish imperialist interests.

The main British motive is generally given as, not the desire to protect imperial communications, but the creation of a provocative factor which would distract the attention of the Arabs and prevent the rebuilding of their strength and the restoration of their glories, of which the imperialists were afraid. Israel was established to perpetuate Arab backwardness and prevent the emergence of a rival to imperialist supremacy.[28]

In an article "Arab Nationalism and Israel," in *Arab Nationalism and Imperialism* (1957, see p. 149), Anwar al-Jamal explains that as early as 1914 Lord Kitchener pointed out the importance of Palestine for the protection of the Suez Canal and proposed including it in the British sphere of influence. When the British realized that the rising tide of nationalism would sweep them out of the Middle East, they tried to stake a claim in the area by creating Israel in the heart of Arab nationalism, in order to

> ". . . use it as an instrument of pressure on Arab policy with a view to realizing the aims of imperialism in that region and obstructing the advance of its peoples to national liberation, thus leading to the liquidation of nascent Arab nationalism." (p. 152).
>
> "The existence of the National Home in Palestine would distract the Arabs from their national problems and they would be unable to find time for their internal or external problems." (p. 154).

The question of protecting lines of communication is also mentioned, however, for instance in Dr. Sayegh's *Zionist Colonialism in Palestine*. The Turco-German campaign through Sinai in the direction of the Canal showed the British that the Peninsula could be crossed, he explains. In order to protect it, therefore, it became necessary to ensure control of Palestine and get rid of the previous agreement with France to internationalize it. This was the origin of the alliance between British imperialism and Zionist colonialism, Zionism acting as a catalyst in the process of establishing British rule in Palestine (p. 12).

The idea of Israel as a diversionary factor is regarded as so important that it is included in the Egyptian National Charter (Chapter 4):

"Part of the Arab territory in Palestine was handed to an aggressive racial movement *(ḥaraka 'unṣūriyya 'udwaniyya)* with neither historical nor natural justification, to be used by the imperialists as a whip in their hands to fight the struggling Arabs if one day they were able to overcome their humiliation and survive the crisis. The imperialists intended this territory to be a barrier dividing the Arab East from the Arab West, and a constant drain of energy of the Arab Nation diverting it from the positive construction. All this was carried out in a provocative manner disregarding the existence of the Arab Nation and its dignity."

In the tenth chapter of the Charter the same idea is repeated in other words:

". . . Israel is the base of imperialism, which was brought into existence by means of plots with the object of intimidating the Arab Nation and tearing it apart."

Sometimes it is explained that the British goal was to prevent the Arabs becoming leaders of the world and that they were afraid of economic injury resulting from the loss of colonies and markets. For instance, in the final chapter of the pamphlet *This Is Zionism* (beginning of 1954, the first in the Ikhtarnā Lak series which appeared with an introduction by Nasser), it is explained that the British aim in establishing Israel was:

". . . the breaking of the Arabs' vigour, the rending of their unity and their infection with the Jewish cancer in a sensitive spot in the body of their nation. Britain preceded others in understanding that the Arabs were on the brink of a renaissance which would soon unite their ranks and their aims, and restore them to the first place among the nations of the world. Britain realized the harm this would do her, for it would lead to the loss of what she exploited in her Asian and African colonies, and, as a result, her Empire would collapse." (pp. 147-8).

Nasser has sometimes declared that the main initiative in the establishment of Israel came from the imperialists, and not from the Jews. It was imperialism which tried to make a nationality out of the Jews, who only constituted a religion.

In his introduction to *The Arab Dawn,* he wrote:

"When imperialism felt that its end was near, it tried to perpetuate its hold . . . Then it presented a racialist idea which transformed religion into race and Judaism into Zionism, and Israel was established as an imperialist bridgehead against the Arab States." (Karanjia, 1958).

In this way, Zionist achievements are credited to Britain and there is less self-reproach. The Arabs' opposition to Jewish colonization did not bear fruit because they were confronted by world powers. As we shall see, the victory of 1948 was also ascribed to imperialism. As the allegation of a bond between imperialism and Israel fulfils the psychological function of protecting the self-respect of the Arabs, any attempt to convince them that this is not exactly the case is liable to meet with resistance.

Nasser very frequently uses the argument that the establishment of Israel is an imperialist design to liquidate Arab nationalism. He refers to:

> "... Israel, which is supported by imperialism which does not want liberty in this area, which regards us as a chattel for its own advantage, as it is always the imperialist plan to put an end to all the Arab nations, and this is not a short-term but a long-term plan, whose aim is to put an end to the whole of Arabism. . ." (December 13, 1953, I.L., I/155-6).

Similar formulations are to be found in his speeches of May 14, 1956, I.L., V/1140, February 11, 1957, I.L., VIII/1560, and also on March 11, 1958, May 14, 1957 and August 8, 1959. He sounded the same note in his speech on the tenth anniversary of the Revolution:

> "Israel, which imperialism established in the heart of the Arab world to give a death-blow to Arab nationalism, to strike at the Arab nation in order to prevent the Arab nation awakening and building itself from the social, economic and political points of view. . . " (July 22, 1961).

In another article in the booklet *Arab Nationalism and Imperialism* (1957), entitled "Arab Nationalism in the Balance," Dr. 'Abd al-Qādir Ḥatim describes the efforts of imperialism to preserve its interests in the region as a matter of life or death for the imperialists. After various attempts to stake a claim in the area and crush the spiritual personality of its peoples, imperialism

> "... crowned all this by establishing a State in the middle with Zionist gangs and a number of displaced persons from here and there, and breathed the breath of life into this statelet. It thought that if it called the gangs a State, it would finally liquidate Arab nationalism, and that through this State it would place a dagger at the throat of the Arabs, so that whenever they should feel inclined to oppose its rule, it would stab them in the back, strike their movement with paralysis and subject them to constant threat and terror." (p. 143).

It is also frequently stated that imperialism wanted to protect its oil interests by installing Israel as a divisive factor to safeguard its rule. Haykal writes, for instance:

> "The flow of Arab oil is one of the important factors in the establishment of Israel on the soil of the Arabs in order to threaten them and prevent their unity." (*al-Ahrām*, June 19, 1964).

Sometimes the establishment of Israel is presented as inspired by anti-Semitism: the West was interested in getting rid of its Jews. The postcript to *This is Zionism* declares:

> "What interested them [the British and others] was first and foremost to break the vigour of the Arabs and get rid of the Jewish boils *(awrām)* on the body of their peoples, and thus they worked for the realization of these two aims by helping the Jews to establish a state that would give them shelter in Palestine." (p. 147).

Sometimes the establishment of the Jewish National Home is presented as a deliberately hostile act inspired by Christian hatred for the Muslims. 'Aqqād, for instance, declares that imperialism established Israel not for love of Zionism but because of anti-Islamic fanaticism (pp. 36-7).

Haykal sums up a number of themes:

> "Imperialism's drive to establish Israel came from the aspiration: 1. That it should serve as a geographical barrier to the spread of Arab unity. 2. To establish among the severed parts of the Arab world a base from which there would be a constant threat [to the Arabs]. 3. To serve as a leech which would suck the marrow and exhaust the efforts of the Arab revolutionary force." (*al-Ahrām*, May 12, 1961, and in similar terms on September 4, 1964).

The theme of the diversionary stratagem is also repeated in regard to the continued existence of Israel, in which imperialism is interested in order to prevent the economic and social progress of the Arab world by compelling it to devote resources to rearmament, thus ensuring the survival of the reactionary regimes (Resolutions of the Ninth Ba'th Conference, August 1966).

d) THE MANDATE PERIOD

Since it was imperialism that created Israel, it continues to support and cooperate with her. The British extended their patronage to the Jewish community in the period of the Mandate and discriminated in its favour. They prevented the Arabs organizing and arming, but protected the organization of the Jewish underground armed bands:

"It [Britain] trained the mobile Zionist striking forces [the Palmach] and condoned the existence of 'underground' terrorist organizations [the Stern group and the Irgun Zva'i Le'umi]." (Sayegh, 1965, p. 14).

"The British officers supervised the training and arming of the Jews on the pretext of protecting their colonies. They treated them as a father treats his spoiled child." (Tall, 1964, p. 275).

"When the Jews persecuted the Arabs, the Arabs replied to Jewish aggression, but the British perverted justice, found in favour only of the Jews and avenged them on the proud *(abī)* Arabs who replied to aggression. Whenever a quarrel broke out between Arabs and Jews the British hastened with their tanks and guns to kill the Arabs and defend the Jews. The British used to blow up an Arab house if they thought firing had taken place from it."

The British saw to it that the Jews should increase their strength in preparation for the expected clash with the Arabs. For instance, they allowed Jews demobilized from the Jewish Brigade to keep their weapons as a gift from the British army (*ibid.*, p. 284). The British official was a slave to the Jews (*ibid.*, pp. 54 and 163) and was afraid they might complain against him in London and get him dismissed.

The struggle between the Jewish community and the Mandatory Government is explained as the result of differences of opinion in regard to the pace of achieving the goal, especially as the British were afraid that an increase in Jewish power might make them too independent. Dr. Sayegh explains:

"But Britain had not entered into the partnership with Zionism in Palestine solely in order to serve the purposes of Zionist Colonialism; it had expected the partnership to serve, equally, the purposes of British imperialism as well. Whenever Zionism sought to accelerate the processes of state building (which would eventually render the British continued presence in Palestine neither necessary nor desired in the Zionists' eyes), Britain pulled in the opposite direction to slow them down." (1965, p. 15).

In some cases, it is true, especially in 1950–1951, admiration was expressed for the struggle of the Jews and the activities of the anti-British terrorists. Passages from Begin's book *The Revolt* were published at the time in *Rūz al-Yūsuf,* as if there was an area of common interest between Jews and Arabs. Since then, the approach has changed, and descriptions of terrorist activity against the British are used to demonstrate the aggressiveness of the Jews. Examples are to be found in 'Awwīs's *Israel and the Great Powers* (Ikhtarnā Lak series No. 23, 1956) and 'Alūsh's *The Jour-*

ney to Palestine, 1964, where a chapter is devoted to "Menahem Begin's Zionism."'Alūsh's extreme anti-imperialist approach should have led to some measure of approval for Jewish resistance to British rule, but he finds more blame than praise for them, and declares that no moral considerations were involved in their activities. (Similar ideas are expressed in Ahmad's *Israel—the Misled People,* 1962, p. 18, and in Ali and Ḥamṣānī's *Israel, a Base for Aggression,* 1964, p. 35. A pamphlet of over a hundred pages, *The Terrorist Origins of the Israeli Herut Party,* by Bassām Abu Ghazāla, was published by the Research Centre of the Palestine Liberation Organization.)

e) THE ENDING OF THE MANDATE

The ending of the Mandate is often portrayed as an Anglo-Jewish plot.

Anwār al-Jamal explains, in the article quoted above, that Britain suddenly abolished the Mandate without prior warning after agreeing with the Jews that they should seize the main cities with British aid. The clashes between the British and the Jewish "gangs" were nothing but a sham. The British supplied the Jews with arms and deceived the Arabs with promises so as to involve them in a war the results of which the British knew in advance. (Hence the responsibility for the opening of hostilities by the Arab armies rests with the British, who laid a trap for them.) When the Arabs were at the gates of Tel Aviv, the British intervened again and stopped the war by a truce. The same happened when the second truce was imposed, the purpose being to supply the Jews with arms and withold them from the Arabs.

Ḥasan Ṣabrī al-Khūlī explains that the British first evacuated the towns, so as to enable the Jews to seize them, and then left Palestine after they were sure of the Zionists' military strength and America's readiness to help them (p. 16).

Nasser also repeats the idea that the ending of the Mandate constituted the abandonment of Palestine to the Jews, for the British knew in advance what the result would be (e.g. his speech of February 22, 1964).

The handing back of the British Mandate to the United Nations is also depicted as an "imperialist trick" aimed at transforming Palestine into a Jewish State. Britain wanted to achieve this through the UN, so as to get international approval for her final abandonment of her promises to the Arabs, since she did not want to be blamed for the Palestine catastrophe.

It was also a precautionary measure to prevent damage to her interests in the Arab Muslim countries, so that she could argue that the disaster was not her fault (see Shukrī, p. 40).

When the tie with Britain was broken, Israel attached herself to the United States, since her bond with imperialism is a part of her nature. Dr. Sayegh writes:

> "The alliance of Zionist Colonialism with one Western Imperialist Power was momentarily dissolved after it had served its purpose; but it was simultaneously reincarnated in a new form, to suit the new world circumstances and the new stage of Zionist Colonialism. As one Western sponsor retreated to the background, other Western sponsors rushed to the foreground. Zionist Colonialism made a tactical change of allies but did not abandon the strategy of imperialist alliances as such. For, without the umbilical cord linking the Zionist settlers' community with the extra-regional sources of supply and power it has and can have little ability of its own renewal." (1956, pp. 17-18).

Imperialism continues to support Israel, supplies her with arms and grants her economic and political aid. As the fosterchild *(rabība)* of imperialism, she receives unlimited subventions and preferential treatment. Imperialism ignores the rights of the Arabs and turns a blind eye to Israel's continued refusal to carry out UN resolutions. Whenever Israel is in danger, imperialism rushes to her aid.

Ḥatim describes this process in picturesque language:

> "Imperialism has found in the Israeli gangs its 'cat's claw' *(mikhlab al-qiṭṭ)*, a hook to hang on, or a point of support [an epithet which is repeatedly used for Israel by other writers]. When it was weakened by the burning Arab coals *(al-jamraw al-muta ahhija)* and its foot trembled and a tiger almost tore it to pieces, imperialism came forward to protect it, thus removing the veil from its face." (In his article, already quoted from *Arab Nationalism and Imperialism*, p. 147).

Imperialism strengthened Israel so that the Arabs should have no choice but to accept its defence and join its network of alliances (Nasser, April 30 and May 15, 1958).

Imperialism imposed on Israel a long list of functions: "a spearhead," "a bridgehead," "a base" and "a support" in the Middle East. Her functions go beyond the limits of the area, however. In developing countries a new field of cooperation between Israel and imperialism has been created, for the main purpose of breaking Afro-Asian solidarity (declaration by

Cloduis Maqṣūd, Arab League representative at New Delhi, according to *al-Ḥayāt*, September 24, 1964).

First imperialism weakens the African countries by sucking their marrow; then it sends Israel for the ostensible purpose of helping them. Israel presents herself as a small country with no political interests, intent only on cooperation, but her real purpose is to erect obstacles to the liberation and progress of the African countries. Israel is the Trojan horse of Western interests; Zionism was colonialist as far back as the 4th Zionist Congress.

Israel's activities are carefully followed, especially in Egypt. In a book called *Zionist Imperialism in Asia and Africa* (which is a mixture of information and nonsense), published as No. 331 in the series of Political Books, a detailed account is given of Israel's mission in these countries, the mode of operations of Israeli companies, the Histadrut (General Federation of Labour), shipping agencies, the Gadna Youth Corps, the Afro-Asian Institute, etc., as well as the story of Israel's "failures" all along the line.

Writers and spokesmen often wonder how Israel, which lives on aid and support, can help Africa. Rushdī, for instance, asks how Israel can assist farmers when the well-known Israeli leader Avraham Harzfeld speaks in the Knesset of hardship and bankruptcy in Israeli agriculture (p. 249).

Israel's assistance to African and Asian countries is certainly very annoying to the Arabs—hence the great attention they devote to it—for it contradicts the idea that Israel has nothing to contribute to the world and that its only friends are the imperialistic countries. If African and Asian countries welcome her aid, she cannot be loathsome, after all. However, it can be argued that Israel is leading these countries astray with her cunning.

Dr. Sayegh wrote a detailed pamphlet, *The Afro-Asian Institute in Tel Aviv*, published by the Research Centre of the Palestine Liberation Organization, explaining that the Institute is part of an extensive plan of infiltration into Asia and Africa. Arabs have repeatedly emphasized that all these efforts are bound to fail, since Israel's colonialist character must lead to a clash with the developing world. Thus, Naʿnāʿa writes:

> "It is inevitable that [Israel] should reach a blind alley and suffer the logical consequences, as an agent of neo-colonialism." (*Zionism in the Sixties, The Vatican and the Jews*, 1964, p. 5).

The author goes on to explain that South Africa understood the situation correctly when she warned Israel that the latter would be next in line for expulsion from the UN at the demand of the Afro-Asian nations.

In addition to the role imposed on her by imperialism, Israel has far-reaching aims of her own. Haykal writes:

"True, Israel was established by imperialism, which created her and guarantees her existence in accordance with her plans . . . but Israel herself has aims of her own, more far-reaching than the goals for which she was established by imperialism . . .

"Israel is an instrument but not an instrument without a will of its own. She is not merely a puppet activated by those who pull the strings . . . Israel as an instrument may be compared with a hired murderer who receives money and arms from his employer in order to murder, but is not a mechanical murderer and has his own aspirations, opinions and dreams. Moreover, when he carries out the functions imposed on him to serve his master, he is liable to go beyond the aims defined, especially under pressure of danger and pursuit, and in a moment of despair—in the hope of saving himself from destruction—to do things that no one dreamed of, not even his master, who supplied him with money and weapons." (*al-Ahrām,* January 14, 1963).

Haykal returns to this idea in his article of January 7, 1966, in which he declares that Israel has dreams unconnected with imperialist plans, resulting from her racial character and expressed in the aspiration for expansion from the Nile to the Euphrates. On September 15, 1967, he comes back to the idea again and visualizes the possibility of exploiting the contradictions between the "root"—imperialism—and the "branch"—Israel.

Imperialism, however, will not always support Israel. It will defend her so long as the situation does not become more serious, but when this happens, imperialism will betray Israel and leave her to her fate:

"When the army and the people of the UAR decide to restore Palestine, the West will leave Israel to herself, and the struggle will lead to her defeat." (Nāfūrī, August 31, 1962).

The relation between the West and Israel is neither simple nor symmetrical. Bahā' al-Dīn develops a psychological explanation of the complex relations between Israel and the West, which leads to ambivalence on both sides—rejection and attraction at the same time:

"Israel is a daughter of Europe, it is true, but she is an illegitimate daughter. The persecution of the Jews in Europe is a historical fact, and this persecution was carried out by European civilization, which is what impelled hundreds of thousands of them to flee [to Palestine], in small numbers before Nazism and in large numbers afterwards. These migrants are all undoubtedly Europeans.

> Hence their complex-ridden bond with Europe—the bond between a bastard son and his father. The father is ashamed of his son, whom he begot as a bastard, and does not want to have him laid at his door. He cannot permit him to live with his legitimate sons under the same roof, but he does not forget that this is his son and his own flesh and blood."

Bahā' al-Dīn explains that Europe is ashamed of the slaughter of the Jews, but at the same time does not want them to stay on its territory. On the other hand, Zionism, despite European persecution, has not established a society hostile to Europe, for despite his experiences the bastard wants to remain bound to his father and his family (1965, pp. 250-1 and a similar passage in *al-Muṣawar,* August 13, 1965).

The family tie between Israel and imperialism is emphasized by the frequent reference to her as the "fosterchild" *(rabība)* of imperialism. Nasser dubs Israel "the spoiled child" of the great powers (July 9, 1955, I.L., IV/835).

Since Israel's survival depends on imperialism and colonialism, the fate of both will be sealed when the oppressed peoples achieve liberation and independence. The downfall of colonialism is bound to lead to the collapse of Israel. Conversely, the downfall of Israel is a stage in the defeat of imperialism. The disappearance of Israel, therefore, has a significance which transcends the bounds of the Middle East.

f) APPENDIX

Epithets Denoting Israel's Ties with Imperialism

The following is a selection: Israel is a "bridgehead" *(ra's jisr),* a "camp" *(mu'asker isti'mārī),* a "base" *(qā'ida),* a "forward base," a "support" *(rakīza),* a "fixed centre," a "tail," a "scourge," an "arrowhead," "a spearhead," a "willing tool" *(sanī'a),* a "fosterchild" *(rabība),* an "instrument" *(adāt),* a "military arsenal," an "agent" *('amīla),* a "lair" or "den" *(wakr),* and even a "fortress" *(qal'a),* a "nail" or "peg" *(mismār),* etc., of imperialism.

There are also such expressions as "a destructive imperialist cancer," (UAR National Charter, Chapter 10); "the parasites of imperialism," "the spider of imperialism," "the pandars of imperialism," "an imperialistic plague" *(wabā' isti'marī*—Maḥlāwī in the *Egyptian Political Science Review,* January-March 1959, p. 115), the "lean hunting dog of imperialism," "the cat's claw," and so forth.

8. HIERARCHY OF ENEMIES AND DANGERS

As the enemies form a coalition, which is the principal enemy and which the secondary one? Which presents the greater danger? Nations engaged in a conflict cannot be expected to be consistent in the designation of the major enemy: the emphasis on one or the other as the more dangerous may fluctuate in accordance with changing circumstances. Nevertheless, it is worth examining how the problem is considered, especially since the Arabs themselves pose the question.

a) IMPERIALISM THE PRINCIPAL ENEMY

Fundamentally, as we have already seen, imperialism is regarded as the principal enemy, with Israel and reaction as its agents. "Imperialism is the source and Israel the shadow," declares Brigadier-General Maḥfūẓ (*Our Armed Forces Facing the Challenges of the Next Stage,* p. 126).

Imperialism is the principal enemy because it represents not only the world powers which have ruled or exercised influence in the area, but also the world phenomenon of backwardness and inequality—the major malady of the era. Imperialism or colonialism is also the factor of which all the Arabs have had experience, whether through the memory of colonialist servitude or through dependence and the need for economic assistance. For many Arabs, imperialism is bound up with personal experience of the need to serve foreigners or the envy of foreigners. As a result of "the revolution of rising expectations," the desire for the advantages of Western civilization becomes common to all. Moreover, the designation of such a great and notable enemy as imperialism has a reciprocal influence on the Arabs' self-image: they may feel honoured by their enemy, and their importance is increased thereby.

The postcript to *This is Zionism* states:

> "We must realize that our first enemy in this struggle [against Israel] is not the Jews alone, but first and foremost the English and their American allies, and afterwards the Jews, and so on with other enemies in Eastern and Western Europe." (1954, p. 146).

Niqūlā al-Durr, at one time one of Shukairy's assistants in the Palestine Liberation Organization, asks in the opening sentence of his book *Thus Lost and Thus Redeemed* (1963):

"Who is the first enemy of the Arabs: imperialism or Zionism? Which of the two is the master and which the servant?"

On the next page he replies:

"Our true enemy is not Israel, but our enemy is the one that created Israel and still nourishes and fosters Israel . . . In his hands are the factors of her life or death . . . By creating Israel, this enemy had the general purpose of diverting our attention from him, from his crimes and evil deeds, so that he might suck our blood by inducing us to fight the tail and not the head."

The emphasis on imperialism as the principal enemy is particularly strong in leftist literature and among the radical Ba'th. For them, the liquidation of imperialism in the Arab world—of Western influence—and of reaction takes priority over the campaign against Israel, not only in theory, but also in the programme of action in connection with the conflict. Thus, 'Alūsh writes:

'Those who demand concrete action over the problem of Palestine ought to understand first and foremost that the liquidation of reaction is the first step towards the liberation of Palestine." (1964, p. 184).

In the section on "Enemies of Arab Nationalism as an Ideological Trend" in his article on Arab Nationalism in the *Political Science Review* (January–March 1959), Dr. Ḥātim does not mention Israel expressly at all among the enemies. For him, the enemy is a trinity: imperialism, reaction and opportunism. The article was written in the thick of the struggle against Qassem, who is regarded as representing opportunism, or anti-unity local nationalism. Since the brunt of the attack is directed against him, the question of Israel as the enemy becomes of lesser importance, and she is included under the head of imperialism.

It is not easy to say what is the general opinion among the masses on these matters. It is stated, for instance, that during the Suez war of 1956 the Department for Technical Studies in the Egyptian Ministry of Education and Culture investigated morale in Egypt in a poll of 1,350 secondary-school pupils and students. When asked which was the enemy of Egypt, they arranged the enemies in the following order: 1. Britain, 2. Israel, 3. France, 4. the United States, 5. Belgium, 6. Turkey (*al-Ahrām,* December 12, 1958).

As we have seen, there is a lack of consistency in these matters. In a single speech, for instance, Nasser declared:

"Who are our enemies today? Israel, imperialism and reaction."

and also:

"Our enemies are imperialism, Israel and reaction, which are in alliance." (March 8, 1965).

No profound significance should be ascribed to this order of importance. The emphasis is more on a cluster of enemies than on their relative importance.

b) ISRAEL AS THE MOST DANGEROUS ENEMY

Closely allied to the question of who is the enemy is the question: Which is the most dangerous? Sometimes it is argued that, even if the greater enemy from the point of view of size is imperialism, Israel is more dangerous, since, while colonialism is on the retreat in the Middle East and its hold is temporary, Israel is young and active, close to the Arab countries and actually present in the Middle East. Moreover, while there is something abstract about imperialism, though its identity is clear, Israel is the actual enemy.

In a text-book for secondary schools in Syria, Dr. Muhammad writes:

"Zionist colonialism is the greatest danger threatening the Arab world." (1966, p. 81).

The Crusaders, the Turks, the French under Napoleon, the British and the French in modern times—all held only superficial, and therefore temporary, sway. Israel, however, is a more dangerous form of imperialism, since it marks the introduction of another nation which has been settled in place of the Arabs. This is frequently emphasized by Nasser. Haykal calls Israel the "peak of danger" *(dhurwat al-khaṭr)* (*al-Ahrām,* April 16, 1965).

Professor Zurayk also emphasizes the Zionist danger as greater than that of imperialism. He explains that the latter, even if its roots are deep, is a temporary danger, but Zionism seeks to liquidate a nation and settle in its place (English edition, p. 15). He goes on to declare that only the Zionist danger threatens the existence of Arabism and that, unlike the ties of Zionism with Israel, the connection of imperialism with the Middle East is superficial.

Nasser sometimes emphasizes that Zionism, or World Zionism, is a more dangerous enemy than Israel or imperialism, for it is the source of Israel's strength (June 22, 1957, I.L., IX/1672).

c) DISPLACEMENT OF HOSTILITY

Psychologists note the possibility that the transference of hostility and aggression may be focussed on the weakest element (Berkowitz, 1962, Chapter 5; Brown, 1964, p. 70). The displacement of hostility does not mean, as Faris emphasizes, that there is a certain quantity of hostility which has to find an outlet, so that if it cannot be directed against one factor it is vented on another. The displacement is shown by emphasis.

Since the enemies are described as a coalition, an injury to a weak link is harmful to the entire system. The Western countries are proof against injury by the Arabs, so they may divert their hostility and concentrate it on Israel. Indeed, one of the derogatory epithets against Israel is "the focus of the evil" *(bu'rat al-sharr)*. With the decline of colonialism, moreover, there may be a diminution in the scope of the confrontation and antagonism between the Arab States and the West, with a resulting concentration of hostility against Israel, which would become a main goal for all the feelings of frustration and hatred. Psychologists also point out that aggression against the powerful factors may assume an indirect, symbolic and verbal form, the weaker link becoming the target of direct aggressiveness and the desire for actual attack and injury.

Chapter 4
ZIONISM

1. THE VILENESS OF ZIONISM

a) THE SOURCE OF THE VILENESS OF ZIONISM LIES IN ITS AIM

"Zionism" is the root of all evil: it is the cause of the conflict; it is the evil spirit of Israel.

The fundamental wickedness of Zionism is the outcome of its aspirations, which took the form of a deliberate plot to steal a territory that belonged to another nation. This is the original sin of the Zionists. Although the Zionist leaders often denied that it was their aim to make Palestine a Jewish State, this was an attempt to mislead. Zionism assumed a philanthropic cloak, as if its only aim was to deliver persecuted people, but its true goal was political (Sa'ab, *Zionism and Racism*, 1965, p. 1). If the aim had only been the solution of the Jewish problem, other places to which they might have migrated could have been found. Zionism spoke in respectable, positive terms: "the solution of the Jewish problem," "a home secured by public law," or "a National Home," but it ignored the negative implications of these terms, for the Judaization of Palestine meant its de-Arabization, and the solution of the problem of the Jews meant the creation of a problem for the Arabs.

In *Zionist Colonialism in Palestine,* Dr. Sayegh writes:

> 'From the Basle Program of 1897 until the Biltmore Program of 1942, Zionists preferred the euphemism a 'home' to the clear term 'state' which would have been certain to arouse opposition in many quarters. But, in spite of public assurances to the contrary, Zionists were aiming from the outset at the creation of a settler-state in Palestine." (1965, p. 3).

The establishment of the Jewish State was not possible without the displacement of the Arabs and injury to Arab nationalism. All the suffering and injustice caused to the Arabs were implicit from the beginning in the Zionist programme; in other words, they were potentially present in Zionist aims.

Dr. Sayegh declares that Weizmann's call in 1919 for a Palestine as Jewish as England is English implied the intention to get rid of the Arabs. In a UN address, Shukairy described Zionism as "a movement of genocide" (December 3, 1962). In *Zionism and Racism,* Dr. Sa'ab writes:

> "This Palestinian exodus came as the logical result of the Zionist determination to conquer Palestine. The atrocities committed by the Israelis in 1948 were only an episode in the systematic Zionist program aimed at the dispossession of the Palestinian Arabs." (p. 15).
>
> "The Zionists' real objective was irreconcilable with the reservations and safeguards which were incorporated into the Balfour Declaration." (p. 27).

When Zionism set itself the aim of Judaizing Palestine it took no account of the Arab character of the country, nor was it deterred by the unfortunate consequences of its programme for the Arab people. Zionism did not seem to regard the Arabs as human beings, assuming that their welfare and rights could be sacrificed if only its goal was attained, and that the achievement of its aims was a supreme value which could justify depriving others of their rights. Zionism is, therefore, a reactionary movement, for it is founded not on the fraternity of peoples but on preference for one people over another. It did not follow the Jewish principle: "Whatever is hateful to thee do not do to thy neighbour"; it violated the basic principle of international life, which underlies international democracy: respect for the right of the local inhabitants to self-determination. This is its mark of Cain, which will always stamp it as a criminal movement. Because of its aggressive character, it suffers from an aggression complex, from which it cannot liberate itself.

Al-Khālidī wrote:

> 'At the centre of Zionist philosophy is the premise of Arab expendability. If the Arab in Zionist eyes had been held to be of equal dignity with the Zionist the whole structure of Zionism, at least of military and political Zionism, would have tumbled to the ground. Zionism could be maintained only by affirming for the Zionists what was denied for the Arabs; indeed the very affirmation for

the Zionist was in itself a denial for the Arab. It was this Zionist attitude which was at the basis of the 'National Home' concept and its climax was the Arab exodus of 1948. It was this attitude which ultimately perpetrated the pogroms of Deir Yasin, Sha'afat, Qibya, Nahaleen, Wadi Fukin, Kafr Kassem and Khan Yunis, in all of which a sickening disregard for the dignity of the human Arab body was carried to its logical conclusion." (1958, p. 20).

Zionism continues this policy of discrimination by opening the gates of the country to Jews from distant lands who have never lived in it before, while preventing the repatriation of Arab refugees, who have a direct bond with it. Dr. Tannous writes:

"It is indeed beyond comprehension how a Zionist Jew can come from every country to occupy the home of the Arab and the Arab is shot at if he tries to approach his home on the Israeli side." (1957, p. 34).

Again, Dr. Sa'ab writes:

"This disregard for the rights of others is a characteristic of national movements which are totally absorbed in their own emotions, prejudices, drives, and objectives. It is a symptom of totalitarian nationalism. Zionism grew in the 19th and 20th centuries in the midst of such nationalisms." (p. 18).

The portrayal of Zionism as coveting territory is more fully expressed in the idea, which we shall examine below, that Zionism represents a permanent characteristic of Judaism: the "selfishness" symbolized by the concept of the "chosen people," which the Jews regard as a licence to injure their neighbour and steal his property. This interpretation reaches a climax in the frequent insistence that Zionism seeks to dominate not only Palestine and, with that as a starting point, the region between the Nile and the Euphrates, but the whole world. (See, for example, Rushdi, pp. 39ff, Wākid, *Israel in the Balance,* p. 30, and Ahmad, p. 3.) These ideas merge, as we shall see, with those connected with *The Protocols of the Elders of Zion.*[1]

As a result of the aim of removing the Arabs and seizing their country, Ibrahim al-'Ābid explains, Zionism has developed an ingrained inclination to violence. Nietzschean tendencies to admire physical strength are to be found in the writings of Zionist authors like Micah Yosef Berdichevsky and Shaul Tchernikhovsky. Expressions indicating the intention to use force in order to achieve the aim are to be found in the words of Zionist leaders quoted by al-'Ābid. Even those who opposed Jabotinsky, the

Zionist Revisionist leader, carried out his principles in the end. Al-'Abd also cites criticisms of these tendencies in Zionism by such Jewish writers as Ahad Ha'am, Moshe Smilansky, Rabbi Benjamin, Hans Kohn and Ben Halpern. The violence which is ingrained in Zionism has produced a spirit of militarism and brutality which finds expression in terrorism and attacks on the neighbours of the Jews, and is today characteristic of the atmosphere in Israel (*Violence and Peace, a Study of Zionist Strategy,* Beirut, 1967).

b) ZIONISM, COLONIALIST AND RACIST

The Zionist aim of establishing a homeland for one human group at the expense of another is a manifestation of colonialism, racism and discrimination against the local inhabitants in favour of a foreign race. The Jews who settled in Palestine insisted on their superiority to the Arabs, and, like the Europeans who settled in Africa, treated the Arab peasant as a member of an inferior race. The watchword of Jewish labour was a racist principle by which work was allotted according to national origin, and wage-rates, too, were determined by race. The Jews insisted on the racist principle of buying agricultural produce from Jews and boycotting Arab produce. They also practiced racism in the social sphere by isolating themselves in a closed Jewish society. The idea that Zionism is racist is very frequently emphasized, with indignation, bitterness and a sense of injustice, in Arab political literature. Dr. Sayegh writes, for example:

> "Zionist racial identification produced three corollaries: racial self-segregation, racial exclusiveness, and racial supremacy. These principles constitute the core of the Zionist ideology." (1965, p. 22).

He goes on to explain that Jewish opposition to integration and assimilation in itself amounts to racist isolationism. Zionist colonialism would not agree to coexistence with the inhabitants of Palestine, but expelled them. From the point of view of exclusiveness and isolationism, it is, therefore, worse than South African and Rhodesian colonialism, which was content to take over the country and reduce its population to servitude:

> "Race-supremacist European settlers elsewhere in Asia and Africa have, by and large, found it possible to express their 'supremacy' over the other strands of 'lesser people' and 'inferior races' within the framework of 'hierarchical racial coexistence.' Separate and unequal, the European colonists and the 'natives'

> have on the whole coexisted in the same colony or protectorate . . . Race-supremacist settlers in Palestine have found it necessary to follow a different course, more in harmony with their ideological system. They have expressed their fancied 'supremacy' over the Arab 'natives' first, by isolating themselves from the Arabs in Palestine and, later on, by evicting the Arabs from their homeland." (p.224).

What is more, Zionism is hypocritical, for, while the Afrikaners in South Africa "brazenly proclaim their sin, the Zionist practitioners of apartheid in Palestine beguilingly protest their innocence" (p. 27).

Sayegh explains that by defining the Jew on a racial basis, Zionism *ipso facto* becomes a racist movement. Its racialism also takes the form of opposing mixed marriages, not on religious but on Zionist grounds. This is an example of the tendency to blur the distinction between Judaism and Zionism, which seems to be frequent among Arab spokesmen (see pp. 21-22 in Sayegh's book).

Zionist racism is also presented as connected with its associations with imperialism:

> "The Zionist movement is, from a scientific point of view, an integral part of world imperialism." (*al-Manār,* March 9, 1965).

This point has been particularly stressed in recent years, with the growing tendency to trace parallels between the circumstances of African liberation and those of the Arab-Israeli conflict, and to present the conflict as a "war of national liberation." This argument has become a central one in the organization of the Palestinians and symbolizes what is described in Chapter 8 of this work as a "radicalization" of the Arab attitude in the conflict. The portrayal of Zionism as an embodiment of foreign colonialism and racial supremacy is also designed to arouse antagonism against Israel among the Afro-Asians. Even more significant is its influence upon the Arabs themselves, in whom it arouses humiliation and indignation. In the cognitive component of the Arab attitude, this argument constitutes an incitement and an ideological justification for politicide, while in the emotional component it serves to fan the flames of hatred and the desire for revenge.

c) ZIONISM AND NAZISM

Zionism is depicted as the spiritual sister of Nazism, like which it has caused great human suffering. Although it preceded Nazism it is presented as its spiritual heir. Dr. Sa'ab writes, for example:

"The concept of a 'chosen race' in Zionism differs from the concept of a 'chosen race' in Nazism, only in the identity of that race—the Zionists speaking of a 'Jewish race,' and the Nazis of an 'Aryan race.' But anti-Semitism, Nazism and Zionism are different manifestations of a racism and nationalism which grew up in the same area and in the same intellectual climate." (1965, p. 9).

And Dr. Sayegh writes:

"The Zionist concept of the 'final solution' to the 'Arab problem' in Palestine and the Nazi concept of the 'final solution to the Jewish Problem' in Germany, consisted essentially of the same basic ingredient: the elimination of the unwanted human element in question. The creation of a 'Jew-free Germany' was indeed sought by Nazism through more ruthless and more inhuman methods than was the creation of an 'Arab-free Palestine' accomplished by the Zionists: but behind the difference in techniques lay an identity of goals." (1955, pp. 26-7).

Nasser used the expression "Zionist Nazism" (February 22, 1962). Bahā' al-Dīn describes Zionism as "a school for racist fanaticism *(ta'aṣṣub)* which is not inferior to Hitlerism" (p. 25) and declares that the Nazis were partners with the Zionists in the establishment of Israel. To prove the latter point, he cites statements in Jon and David Kimche's *The Secret Roads* that there were negotiations between the Jews and the Nazis, who agreed to set up training camps for Jews and permit clandestine emigration to Palestine, but Eichmann demanded a great deal of money. At the beginning the Nazis supported the emigration of Jews to Palestine and the establishment of a Jewish State.

"Eichmann, as the two authors say, participated in laying the foundation stone on which the State of Israel later rose," Bahā' al-Dīn writes (p. 219).

The author's explanation of the persecution and extermination of Jews in Germany is simple:

"It is natural and logical that a racist movement should inevitably clash with another racist movement. And if there was a people which claimed to be better and purer than any other people, it was obvious that it would clash with another

> people which claimed that it was better and purer than any other people." (p. 196).
>
> "Zionism and Nazism stand on the same foundation and therefore they struggle with each other and interchange the most repulsive hostility. History says that Zionism appeared before the appearance of Nazism. The Nazis slaughtered Jews and it was not the Jews who slaughtered Nazis, but this is not because the Jews were good and the Nazis bad, but because the Nazis were stronger and more numerous than the Jews. And if the proportions had been reversed, then the Zionists would have inflicted the same slaughter on the Nazis." (p. 199).

Here Bahā' al-Dīn, who was known as a leftist, uses Zionist and Jew as synonymous terms, and presents the relationship between the Nazis and the Jews as symmetrical, both parties having identical purposes. In other words, it was only in self-defence that the Nazis got their blow in first and sent the Jews to the gas chambers. Realizing, apparently, the implications of his statement, Bahā' al-Dīn immediately adds:

> "Is this a defence of Nazism? Certainly not, or course. Nazism is a black page in the annals of world thought and civilization, but Zionism is also a black page. Both of them are founded on the same logic and the same loathsome racist philosophy which has to be wiped off the face of the earth. This is a most important point, which we must clarify thoroughly to ourselves and the world, so that Israel should not derive benefit from the world's condemnation of Nazism and hostility to it, and so that Zionism should not appear to the world as the opposite of Nazism. The truth is that the latter fought the former because the two were similar and competitors with one another." (1965, p. 199).

The horrors of the Holocaust, according to the author, are only a result of competition, a kind of Darwinian struggle for survival, and nothing more. It cannot be assumed that he was merely swept away by the momentum of his own rhetoric and the desire to condemn Zionism.

d) ZIONISM AND ANTI-SEMITISM

Zionism is not interested in the establishment of a liberal atmosphere in the countries where the Jews live and conditions that will lead to the solution of the Jewish problem by the absorption and assimilation of the Jews; it is interested in the maintenance of anti-Semitism; it thrives on the persecution of the Jews. Zionism and anti-Semitism are, therefore, close to each other in spirit and outlook. Thus Dr. Sa'ab writes:

"Anti-Semites and Zionists drew from the irrational sources of modern nationalism much more than they drew from the rational. They both doubted the possibility of the assimilation of the Jew even in Western liberal societies . . . Similarly, the anti-Semite believes that Jewish exclusiveness will not change, with emancipation or without it. The Zionist maintains that the anti-Semitic prejudices of the Gentiles will never disappear. Their common ground is a profound distrust of human nature and human reason." (p.10).

Dr. Sayegh writes:

"From Herzl to Weizmann, from Ben-Gurion to Goldmann, the leaders of Zionism have all believed and preached that the chief enemy of Zionism is not Gentile 'anti-Semitism' but Jewish 'assimilation.' 'Anti-Semitism' and Zionism thus agree on the basic premise: that all Jews are one nation, with common national characteristics and a common national destiny. The difference between them is that, whereas 'anti-Semitism' disdains the alleged 'national characteristics' of Jews and delights in Jewish suffering, Zionism idealizes those fancied characteristics and strives to bring all Jews together into a single Jewish State, to which even moderate Zionists attribute a 'special mission.' " (p. 22).

Both movements thus arrive at an identical policy. As Dr. Sa'ab puts it:

'Anti-Semites confined the Jews to separate areas; Zionists have sought to confine them to Palestine." (p. 22)

It is often stated that Zionism was built up by anti-Semitism. Nasser put it this way in a letter to Prof. Erhard, then Chancellor of the German Federal Republic:

"Zionist racism exploited the sufferings of the Jews under the Hitlerite regime in order to execute a terrible plot against the Arab nation and tear off part of their territory in order to establish a national home in Palestine . . . Through the disaster inflicted on it, the Arab nation served as a scapegoat for the German conscience." (*al-Ahrām,* May 16, 1965).

Bahā' al-Dīn says that Zionism threatens the Jews with anti-Semitism, spreading tales of persecution in order to pressure them into emigrating. Israeli agents, "as has been publicly stated," draw swastikas on synagogues:

"In Israel there is a powerful view that there is no escape from the disruption of Jewish life in a number of countries in order to compel the Jews to migrate to Israel."

If this weapon does not succeed, it will be necessary to undermine the loyalty of the Jews to the countries where they live, to foment fanatical racist trends, and thus to create problems for them and the majority of the population, so that the Jews will be compelled to leave (pp. 57-8).

Shukairy declared at the United Nations:

"The tactics of Zionism and Israel are to align themselves with anti-Semitism and with all the evils of anti-Semitism. The most important utilization of the anti-Semitic outbreaks as a device to achieve Zionist ends is clearly revealed in an article in *Davar,* the official organ of the Socialist Labour [Mapai] Party in Tel-Aviv . . . The article says: 'I would select a score of efficient young men—intelligent, decent, devoted to our ideal and burning with desire to help redeem Jews, and I would send them to the countries where Jews are absorbed in sinful self-satisfaction . . . The task of these young men would be to disguise themselves as non-Jews, and, acting upon the brutal Zionism, plague these Jews with anti-Semitic slogans, such as "Bloody Jew," "Jew go to Palestine" and similar intimacies [*sic*]. I can vouch that the results, in terms of considerable immigration to Israel from these countries, would be ten thousand times larger than the results brought by thousands of emissaries!" (November 19, 1963).

Some of the phrases in this alleged quotation, for which no date is given, are clearly Shukairy's own glosses.

e) THE HIERARCHY OF SCURRILITY

There are grounds for the assumption that the term Zionism arouses among the Arabs greater resentment and disgust than the term Israel, having a very strong "affective connotation" as a term of abuse. This was also the conclusion of a study of the Egyptian prisoners who fell into Israel's hands during the Sinai Campaign:

"Many of them refused to reply when asked for the meaning of the term Zionism, and it could be seen from their reactions that the word was known to them but its meaning was so terrible that they preferred not to touch it. There were cases of physical revultion at the sound of the word, and even a kind of fear of some unknown evil." (See Oron's article "The Nationalist Myth in Contemporary Egypt," in *Hamizraḥ Heḥadash,* Vol. 10, p. 157).

Hatred of Zionism arouses the desire to denounce it with every possible term of abuse, and even these are not enough. There are many examples in Shukairy's speeches in the United Nations. For example:

"Zionism was nastier than Fascism, uglier than Nazism, more hateful than imperialism, more dangerous than colonialism. Zionism was a combination of all these evils. Its motive power was aggression and expansion." (At the Special Political Committee, December 4, 1961).

The condemnation of Zionism is not merely a matter of passion; it is to be found in official documents of national importance, like the Palestinian National Covenant:

"Zionism is a colonialist movement in its inception, aggressive and expansionist in its goals, racist and segregationist in its configurations and fascist in its means and aims." (Article 19).

The UAR National Charter is more restrained. In Chapter IV it states: "Palestine was handed to an aggressive racial movement."

'Aqqād describes Zionism as a "hellish movement" (1965, p. 15). It is described as brazenly "criminal" *(bāghiya)*, "vile" *(khabītha),* or as "the Zionist viper" *(al-of'a al-Ṣahyūniyya)* (Niqūlā al-Durr, p. 143).

The word "Zionist" is often used to intensify a term of abuse; it often has a demonological connotation, and is used to denounce the activities of the dark forces in the world. The noun "plots" is generally accompanied by "Zionist" and not "Israeli." Israel is described as "the Zionist State" or "the State of the Zionists" to emphasize its vileness. A similar purpose underlies the description of the Israelis as "a Zionist nation." Although "Israeli," "Jew" and "Zionist" are often used indiscriminately as synonyms, there seems to be a "hierarchy of obloquy," a distinction in the degrees of condemnation attached to these names. Zionism is the worst of all; Israel is only second. An undesirable phenomenon will be called "Zionist" even when it would be absurd to ascribe it to Israel as a State, for it can still be attached to Zionism as a satanic power and a world conspiracy. The dispute between Iraq under Qassem and Kuwait was described by someone as "a Zionist plot," and the same term was applied by Damascus Radio on December 7, 1962 to calls for birth control in Egypt. Zionism is also presented as a greater and more dangerous enemy than Israel (as in Zurayk, p. 22).

Nasser declared that the attack on Gaza disclosed the truth that

"Israel is the centre of an assembly of power which is more dangerous than Israel and imperialism, namely, World Zionism." (At the opening of the National Council on July 22, 1957, I.L., IX/1672).

2. ACTIVITIES AND INTRIGUES OF "WORLD ZIONISM"

a) WORLDWIDE ORGANIZATION

Zionism has an organization extending over the entire globe. Its tentacles are worldwide—hence it is referred to as "World Zionism." It is described as a satanically efficient body, which exploits the weaknesses of nations and controls enormous financial resources—"the kingdom of gold." Its influence is everywhere; it stops at nothing. These images, apparently, fit in with the descriptions given in *The Protocols of the Elders of Zion*, as well as with the traditional Islamic ascription of treachery to the Jews.

Particularly strong emphasis is laid on Zionist control of mass communications media. The Zionists are pictured as masters of public relations: they control press, radio, television and cinema. The Arabs are unable to state their case in the world and win support for their attitude despite its obvious justice (Rousan, Introduction, p. xii). These arguments, of course, also serve as an excuse for failure.

The power of Zionism, it is explained, does not testify to inner strength and soundness; it is a satanic power derived from the exploitation of weakness by means of various machinations. It has been supported by individuals, groups and States not out of conviction of its moral validity, which does not exist, but because it was able to exercise pressure, seduction and deceit. Support of Zionism is due to ignorance: the fact that it has been backed by various nations, by the League of Nations and the UN is not evidence of the justice of its cause, but a result of intrigue and pressure:

> "A study of the problem of Zionism indicates the tragedy of international morality and not only the tragedy of Palestine, for the Jews negotiated in their traditional style with most of the world's countries for their support of the deal they made with England and the United States." (Dr. Naṣr, p. 27).

Zionism has always been alert to world developments; it is opportunistic and was always able to exploit the international situation. The Jews found their talent in levying interest useful in external relations (Dr. Badūr in the *Political Science Review*, p. 25). On the eve of World War I the Zionists tried to convince the Turks, the Germans and the British at one and the same time that each of them would benefit by agreeing to Jewish settlement. They always wooed the strongest power, and after taking advantage of it, turned to another without the slightest compunction. Thus they turned their backs on the Germans and the Turks and concentrated on the British, but later, when they realized that the British had grown weaker, they turned to the Americans. The treacherousness *(ghadr)* of Zionism is a part of its nature ('Alūba, pp. 160, 172; Sayegh, 1965, pp. 17, 18). In Mandatory Palestine the Zionists were skilful in applying to the political leadership in London over the heads of the local British officials, who were familiar with the situation (Bahā' al-Dīn, p. 38). They succeeded with the British and the Americans because they harped on the "mixed Machiavellian" tendencies of the Anglo-Saxons, who combined interests with humanitarian and spiritual watchwords (Bahā' al-Dīn, p. 22).

Zionism has succeeded in creating the impression that no one can call himself liberal unless he supports it. It has persuaded liberal circles which believe in the assimilation of the Jews that the emigration of part of them will help to strengthen liberalism (Bahā' al-Dīn, p. 41).

It has traded in Jewish suffering, which it has exploited for its own ends. It casts the stigma of anti-Semitism on anyone who opposes it. It has exploited the guilt feeling of the Europeans towards the Jews:

> "... a feeling that Zionism deliberately fosters and exploits. There is no doubt that the horrors of Nazism have enabled the Zionists to bring pressure to bear on the European conscience, and that this pressure had a direct influence in the establishment of Israel." (Khālidī's address on "Israel's Strategy," in *al-Anwār,* May 21, 1963).
>
> "[Zionism] is based on the exploitation of feelings of compassion towards the Jews, although they [the Zionists] were the pioneers of racist, religious persecution." (Dr. Badūr, p. 20).

Zionism has cunningly pretended that it was bestowing benefits on the Palestinian Arabs by improving their material conditions, an argument which influenced the West, with its materialist approach (Dr. Naṣr, p. 20). The Arabs frequently emphasize that their nature is "spiritual."

Zionism is often described as having had a carefully worked-out, detailed plan from the beginning:

> "They prepared a practical, systematic plan, like the plans which were characteristic of modern revolutionary movements like Communism, Fascism and Nazism." (Dr. Naṣr, p. 14).

These references to the prepared plan underlying Zionist activity also imply the self-criticism that Arab activities are improvised.

Zionism is an ambitious movement. For tactical reasons it concealed its aims and revealed them step by step, pretending that each stage was the final aim, while the goal was extended with the movement's progress:

> "We have seen how Zionism makes its way gradually from aim to aim, whenever it perceives encouragement or acquiescence on the part of the imperialist States." ('Aqqād, 1956, p. 30).

There is no limit to Zionist aspirations: the goal, it is often stated, is not only Israel, but world domination. This theme, it is true, is not always present; it is typical of that part of the literature of the conflict which is imbued with hostility to the Jews, where Israel is depicted as only a base for domination over the Arab countries and, from that starting point, over the whole world. Ḥarb, for instance, describes Zionism as a plot against the human race (*The Conspiracy of the Jews Against Christianity,* p. 82). The term "world" applied to Zionism indicates not only worldwide organization but worldwide aspirations. Zionism aspires "to be one large State, the only one that God will bless" (Ṭahir al-Ṭanāḥī, in the introduction to 'Alūba's book, p. 33).

Maḥlāwī writes:

> "It is easy to perceive clearly the aims and methods of Zionism if we consult *The Protocols of the Elders of Zion,* which contain twenty-four chapters and are regarded by the Jews as sacred enactments. They call for the imposition of a Pax Judaica, like the ancient Pax Romana, but in the form of a dictatorial world Jewish Government which will arise on the ruins of the present international society of mankind." (*Political Science Review,* January-March 1959, p. 116).

Zionism has various disguises and front organizations (again we have the idea of the "hidden hand," perhaps influenced by the notion of Communist front bodies). The First Arab Palestine Congress resolved in 1964 on the need to "uncover and combat the Zionist societies which hide under glittering humanitarian names *(asmā' insāniyya barrāqa).*"

Zionism is the source of ideas hostile to Arab nationalism and draws the West in its wake:

> "The Zionists invented the idea of the Baghdad Pact as a resuscitation of the old intrigues between the Abbasids and Ummayyads, and passed on the idea to England and America [arguing] that this Pact meant joint defence of the Middle East." (Luṭfī, *We and Israel,* p. 21).

Zionism exploits every opportunity:

> "If it happens that an Arab and a Jew are studying in some academic institution, they are immediately photographed, ostensibly by chance, and exploited. Israeli beauty queens stand beside Arab beauty queens and they are photographed, so that Zionism can pretend that Jews and Arabs are on the way to reconciliation with each other." (Na'nā'a, 1964, pp. 291-2).

b) ZIONIST INTRIGUES

If Zionism is regarded as a satanic power, it is natural to believe, or to cite proofs, that it is involved in all kinds of troubles and credit it with cunning intrigues.

It is described as a murderous movement:

> "The history of the Zionist Movement proves that it has put political assassination at the head of the list of the means for the achievement of its aims. For this purpose there is a special organization in Israel headed by Ben-Gurion, whether he is inside the Government or not." (Na'nā'a, 1964, p. 254).

The Zionists are accused, for instance, of murdering James Forrestal, the US Secretary of Defence who committed suicide in 1949. They engineered his dismissal because he defended American interests; then Jewish terrorists threw him out of a window in his house and announced that he had committed suicide as the result of a nervous breakdown. Then he was "treated" by a Jewish doctor called Menninger, who concealed the true reason for his death (Tall, 1964, p. 294).

The Arab press repeatedly accused the Zionists and the Jews of murdering John F. Kennedy (*al-Manār,* November 26, 1963; *al-Jumhūriyya,* November 24 and 25, 1963; *al-Difā',* November 26, 1963; *al-Jihād,* November 26 and 27, 1963). The papers did not confine themselves to mere statements. Kennedy was on the side of the Arabs, they explained: he resisted pressure to cut aid to Egypt, demanded the repatriation of the refugees, was against the French over the question of Algeria, and brought pressure to bear on Israel over the atomic reactor at Dimona. For all these reasons, the Jews wanted to get rid of him. True, Oswald was not a Jew, but this only proved the cunning of the Zionists and their success in diverting attention to others. It was a Jew who murdered Oswald, and this showed that the Jews were afraid Oswald might talk and reveal their secrets. A report of the Norwegian Peace Research Institute says that the belief that Kennedy was murdered by the Zionists was current in the Gaza Strip (Galtung, I. & J., "Some Factors Affecting Local Acceptance of a UN Force, A Pilot Project from Gaza," *International Problems,* Vol. IV, Nos. 1-2 [Jan.-June, 1966], Tel Aviv, pp. 16-17; p. 21 in the original edition published in Oslo).

An entire chapter is devoted to this subject in Na'nā'a's *Zionism in the Sixties, the Vatican and the Jews,* which was published by the official national publishing house in Cairo in 1964 (pp. 249-258). The author explains that much effort was devoted to covering up the truth by pretending that Kennedy was murdered by conservatives opposed to equal rights. Later, Oswald was alleged to have been involved in a Communist plot. But Kennedy had improved relations with the USSR and it is unlikely that the Soviets wanted his death. At the time there were reports in all parts of the world of secret threats to assassinate various heads of Government—the prime ministers of Australia and Sweden, de Gaulle, Harold Wilson, and national leaders who took part in Kennedy's funeral, including Eshkol. The aim of all these reports was to deceive and confuse public opinion. Rubinstein (Ruby) himself admitted that he had tried to assassinate Kennedy. In Israel there was "satisfaction" at the murder, which Na'nā'a tries to "prove" by quotations from the Hebrew press, showing the "obvious" possibility that Zionism was behind the assassination.

This idea is supported by the belief of the Zionists that Kennedy's successor would not resist extreme Zionist aspirations, as well as by the possibility that the "Jewish" candidate Goldwater might win the presidency, and the confidence of the Zionists that their control of mass communications media would enable them to conceal the traces of the crime.

The finishing touch in the plot was the appointment of Earl Warren, who visited Israel with his wife and lectured there in 1957, to head the enquiry committee. His visit was organized by Ben Swig, a Jewish hotel owner from San Francisco. Warren studied Talmud with Rabbi Finkelstein, who took part in Kennedy's inauguration and was the first rabbi to do so. It was Warren, too, who ruled that Christian religious instruction in American schools was illegal; moreover, it was the Jewish justices Frankfurter and Brandeis who had secured his appointment to the Supreme Court. It was the Jewish Senator Jacob Javits who demanded that there should be no hurry in investigating the murder of Kennedy, and—a final proof—Johnson offered to cooperate with Israel in establishing an atomic desalting plant.

On the same lines, *al-Kifāḥ* (June 6, 1968) explained that the murder of Robert Kennedy was also a Zionist plot to prevent the revelation of the true story behind the assassination of his brother.

It should be noted that the idea of assassination as a regular Zionist method links up with the ascription of this expedient to the "Elders of Zion" and with the Protocols (Quṣrī, *The Palestine War, 1948,* p. 37). Furthermore, since Zionism is depicted as a murderous movement, killing and murder are legitimate means of defence against it—so that these ideas buttress the politicidal and genocidal elements in the Arab attitude to Israel.

3. ZIONISM AND THE JEWS

a) ZIONISM AS A POLITICAL MOVEMENT DOMINATING JEWRY

Arab writers repeatedly emphasize that Zionism is not a spiritual or religious movement, but a crude secular political movement, since the epithets "spiritual" and "religious" have a favourable connotation for the Arabs (especially for 'Aqqād and al-Tall). The description of Zionism as political, in contrast to Arab nationalism, which is glorified by its spiritual characteristics, has a pejorative effect, as well as helping to counteract the claim that the special ties and longings of the Jews for Palestine constitute a justification of the Zionist enterprise.

Zionism, it is argued, aspired mainly towards Jewish sovereignty, and not specifically towards Palestine. The choice of Palestine as the objective is very frequently described as a cold and practical political stratagem. Zionism exploited the special position held by Palestine in the religious emotions of the Jews in order to recruit their support for its effort to establish a State. This argument fits in with the general view of Zionism among the Arabs as a tyrannical and conscienceless movement.

In Chapter I of his book, Bahā' al-Dīn, following in the footsteps of Taylor's *Prelude to Israel,* emphasizes that the political success of Zionism shows that it is a practical political movement and not a spiritual one. It emerged as a reaction to anti-Semitism, and not as the realization of religious prophecy; it even described itself as "political." Another indication of the absence of the religious element is the fact that Herzl regarded the establishment of a State anywhere in the world as the main thing. The idea of "return" was only introduced later in order to exploit the romantic religious tie. It is a practical, and not an ideological or religious movement, and the religious aspirations of the Jews should be distinguished from Zionism (pp. 16-17). Bahā' al-Dīn regards the fact that many of the pioneers who settled in Palestine were atheists as conclusive proof that Zionism is not religious.

Dr. Naṣr writes:

> "Zionist propagandists in the nineteenth and twentieth centuries did not express their attachment to Palestine by tears and yearnings . . . When they chose Palestine as the place for the new State, they appreciated the collective emotional factor . . . They used these emotions which are aroused in the heart of the ordinary Jew, as the motive force with the aid of which they would fanatically achieve their aims, which they had fixed with a coldness and callousness which knows no spirituality or compassion in religion." (pp. 14-15).

'Aqqād pours scorn on any idea that Palestine is sacred to Jewry. The use of the element "Zion" in the term Zionism is itself part of the plot.[2] At first the tribe of Benjamin lived with the Jebusites and claimed no special rights in Jerusalem, he says. Then the tribe of Judah conquered and destroyed the city, to which they ascribed no particualr sanctity, and the Jebusites rebuilt it. Even after Solomon's Temple was erected, its sanctity and that of Jerusalem were not recognized by all Jews. Jehoash, King of Israel, occupied it, defiled the Temple and plundered its treasures. This was not regarded as a crime, for the Bible says of him that he was "gathered to his fathers," namely, that he died by natural means and was not subjected to the divine wrath (1956, pp. 10-13).

Dr. Badūr, in his article in *The Egyptian Political Science Review*, explains the success of Zionism in winning support among the Jews by its claim to save them from persecution and

> ". . . the exploitation of some of the things said of them in the Talmud, for instance: O Jew: separate thyself from the nations and continue to preserve thy identity among them; know that thou art the only one with God, believe in victory over the entire world, and that everything will surrender to thee, and therefore exploit and live, see and hope." (September 1963, p. 22).

Zionism used all kinds of machinations to compel the Jews to go to Israel even if their situation was good and they had no reason to leave the places where they lived. Shukairy declared:

"They were whipped by Zionism, whipped by Israel to migrate—there was no persecution. There was no reason for the Jews in Iraq or for the Jews in Syria—and for that matter in the United Arab Republic or in Tunisia, or in Morocco or anywhere else in the Arab world—to leave. They were treated with chivalry and with benevolence." (Statement to Special Political Committee of the UN General Assembly, November 5, 1963).

Zionism imposes dual loyalties on the Jews of the world, or, rather, disloyalty to their homeland and loyalty to Israel alone. Rushdī writes, for instance:

"Zionism calls on every Jew in the world to merge himself with it and believe in its aims. According to it, Zionists alone among all citizens should have, side by side with their political homeland, which is common to them and the other citizens, a symbolic spiritual homeland to which all the Jews of the world can emigrate." (1965, p. 26).

Dr. Sayegh writes that, according to Ben-Gurion, when Jews in the United States and South Africa say "our Government" they mean Israel. Such expressions are "too far-reaching and too frequently uttered to be ignored as irrelevant or dismissed as expressions of irresponsible zeal" (1961, p. 86). This implies a warning to the nations of the dangers involved in dual loyalty.

Others, in a less elegant and more outspoken fashion, describe Zionism as a subversive movement undermining the accepted structure of States and nations, and demand, therefore, that it be outlawed. Arab representatives (e.g. Shukairy on December 5, 1962) have made this demand at the United Nations. The Palestine National Covenant declares in Article 20:

"The causes of peace and security and the needs of right and justice demand from all nations, in order to safeguard true relationships among peoples, and to maintain the loyalty of citizens to their homeland, to consider Zionism an illegal movement and to outlaw its presence and activities."

b) ZIONISM INTERESTED IN CREATING A JEWISH NATION

According to Zionist concepts, the Jews are a nation; but, the Arabs argue, this is a distortion of the nature of Judaism, which is a spiritual and religious entity. Zionism is afraid the Jews may regard themselves as only a religion (Bahā' al-Dīn, p. 75) and it therefore tries to transform Judaism into a secular nationalism. The Arabs are defending Judaism from Zionism. Al-Khālidī declares, at the beginning of his article, "The Arab Exodus from Palestine":

> "In many respects, Zionism is a betrayal and perversion of the universal values of Judaism."

Judaism as a world religion, it is argued, cannot attach itself to one particular place. (Rushdī presents this as a criticism of Ben-Gurion's speech at the 25th Zionist Congress, in *Zionism and Its Fosterchild Israel,* p. 55.)

An argument repeatedly used by Arab ideologists and political writers is that the Jews are a religion, and not a people or a nation. Sometimes proof is adduced from Jewish writings; scholarly or scientific works may be quoted for this purpose. For instance, Shukairy quoted the opinion of Prof. Harry Shapira, in *The Jewish People,* that the Jews are not a race or a nation in the exact meaning of the word (at the Special Political Committee, November 19, 1963). Since the book was published by UNESCO, Shukairy declared that this was the verdict of UNESCO.

Arab nationalist ideologists declare that the Jews lack the constituents of a nation. They mention Renan's definition of nationality as based on the will, as a daily plebiscite, but they do not regard this concept as applying to the Jews. Rousan writes:

> "Jewish so-called nationalism is sterile, a complex fiasco, which lacks historic characteristics of the demands of nationalism." (1965, Introduction).

Rushdī explains that the idea that the Jews are a people is the result of their segregation in ghettos during the period of religious fanaticism in Europe (p. 31).

The principle that the Jews are not a nation is projected backwards into the past; it is argued that they were never a nation, but only some kind of mixed multitude, and this approach is displayed in Arab accounts of Jewish history. It is also denied that the Jews have a common national origin. Wākid says that the Jews were not all descended from Abraham, who was accompanied on his wanderings from Ur of the Chaldees by another "four thousand people." Throughout the generations, people of various races adhered to Judaism; they had nothing in common but religion. Wākid sums up:

> "Even in their most ancient period the Jews were never a nation, but a religious group united only by the religious tie."(1959, p. 5).[3]

Arab leftists find support for this contention in the fact, mentioned by 'Alūsh, that at the Second Congress of the Russian Social-Democratic Party in 1903, Lenin refused to allow the Bund, the Jewish Socialist Party, national representation (the same argument is repeated by al-Ramlī, p. 154, and Adīb Dimitrī, in "The Jewish Question and Scientific Socialism," *al-Kātib,* August 1967). 'Alūsh quotes from the Arabic translation of Lenin's *On the National Problem,* to point to Lenin's opposition to Zionism as a reactionary movement, the Comintern's ruling in 1920 that the Jews are not a nation, and its opposition to the Jewish National Home (pp. 130-1).

An empirical proof that the Jews are not a nation is the fact that they are always quarrelling and have no national solidarity. (Statements to this effect are quoted in the next chapter.)

The principle is regarded as so important that it features in the Palestine National Covenant (Chapter 18):

> " . . . Judaism because it is a divine religion is not a nationality with independent existence. Furthermore the Jews are not one people with an independent personality because they are citizens of the countries to which they belong."

This insistence that the Jews are not a nation is not, of course, a matter of theory, but is meant to prove that the Jews do not need a State at all; in fact, that their State is incompatible with their own nature. The sentence before the one quoted in the last paragraph reads:

> "The claims of historic and spiritual ties between Jews and Palestine are not in agreement with the facts of history or with the true basis of sound statehood."

From the viewpoint of the modern principle of separation of religion and the State, a Jewish State is a regressive phenomenon. The definition of the Jews as a nation also arouses difficulties for Jewish citizens of other countries. In his address in Washington in 1960, Dr. Sayegh explained that the Zionist ideologists are confronted with difficulties and dilemmas in defining a Jew, if the definition is to be based on Jewish national allegiance and a desire to belong to such a nation or the consciousness of belonging to it, but since Zionism aims at arousing such a desire and consciousness, they obviously do not exist. The usual components of nationality—consciousness, will, a common territory or language—are absent. There remains the possibility of defining Jewish nationality by race or creed. If it is defined as a race, Zionism, like anti-Semitism, arrives at a biological theory of blood. If, on the other hand, it is defined as a religion, that cuts away the ground from under the existence of Israel, for a modern nationalism cannot be founded on a creed, especially as the reigning tendency in the world today is to separate religion from the State, and the establishment of a State on a religious basis is an anachronism. To appeal to the Jews to settle in Israel is the same as appealing to all Muslims to live in Mecca or all Christians in the Holy Land. Besides, not all those who belong to the Jewish faith will be included in Israel, and if Judaism is defined as a nation, that means that Jews belonging to this nation will also belong at the same time to other nations as citizens of the countries where they live, which creates a contradiction in terms. The Zionists escape from these dilemmas by arguing that there is no need for a definition and transferring the task of defining a Jew to others. These dilemmas are presented as conclusive proof that a Zionist State like Israel has no right to exist (Sayegh, 1961).

The Zionists regard the concentration of the Jews in an independent country and the renewal of their sovereignty as a normalization of their position, but the Arab contention is diametrically opposite: namely, that it is a distortion of Judaism. Hence the establishment of a Jewish State should be opposed, and since it is founded on an anomaly its fate is sealed.

The close attention paid by the Arabs to this problem of the relation between nationality and religion in Zionism may also imply, apart from the ideological aim of denouncing Zionism, a projection of their own difficulties in defining their nationalism. Even if Arab nationalism is described as secular, it is closely associated with Islam, which in the popular consciousness is one of its major factors. Familiarity with their own difficulties arising out of the religious element in nationalism probably makes them sensitive to a similar difficulty among others.

This Arab view that the Jews are not a nation gives rise to a further conclusion: namely, that any effort of the Jews to preserve their identity is a Zionist measure.

Na'nā'a, for example, discusses the efforts of the Zionists to maintain contact between various Jewish communities and the congresses that discussed the question, and adds:

> "It is not far from the truth what we hear these days in the cries of warning that issue from the lips of the leaders of World Jewry about the signs of disintegration which have begun to be clearly seen in that artificial mixture *(al-khalīṭ)* which the Zionist leaders have been pleased *(ḥalā)* to refer to as the Jewish people *(Sha'b)* when what they mean is the Jewish communities *(ṭawā'if)* scattered all over the world." (1964, p. 6).

Thus the Arabs themselves unintentionally appoint the Zionists as trustees for Judaism.

4. REFUTING THE HISTORIC RIGHT

The Arabs have a number of arguments to refute the Zionist claim that the Jews have a right to Palestine because of their prolonged ties with it.

a) REFUTATION ON PRINCIPLE

The historic right is a fiction, for if such claims were approved, the result would be universal chaos, since many peoples would come forward to present claims based on the fact that their ancestors lived in some territory or other (see Dr. Sayegh's address "The Encounter of Two Ideologies—Zionism and Arabism," 1961, p. 81; Rushdī, p. 30; Sha'bān, p. 8). Luṭfī explains that if the Jews have a historic right to Palestine the Arabs are entitled to lay claim to Spain (p. 32). Tarabīn emphasizes that the Arabs lived in Spain for 800 years, and therefore their rights are sounder than those of the Jews to Palestine. The Turks, similarly, could demand the Balkans. Moreover, how could 15 million Jews take over a country which is sacred to a thousand million Muslims and Christians (p. 6)? Ahmad raises the question of why the Jews do not demand the Land of Goshen, where they lived for 210 years (p. 38).

By using the historic rights argument, Zionism claims to be regarded as a special case, thus violating the categorical demands of morality. On the one hand they argue that the Jews are a nation like all the rest, but on the other hand they claim exceptional status, on the grounds that the Jews are different from all other nations (Sayegh, *op. cit.*, p. 82). The claim of the Jewish right in Palestine is based on the Israelite conquest after the Exodus from Egypt, but the same argument would justify claims by other nations, including the Arabs, who conquered the country at a later date (Basīsū, *Zionism,* 1945, pp. 44-5). Sha'bān quotes Ben-Gurion as stating that the Arab refugees cannot be repatriated since the clock cannot be turned back to 1948; nevertheless, he argues, Ben-Gurion does not hesitate to turn the clock back 2,280 years (*Ben-Gurion the Liar,* p. 8).

b) HISTORICAL ARGUMENTS

The ancient Hebrews, it is argued, ruled in Palestine only a short time; their control was never complete, but was limited to a part of the country, and other nationalities shared it with them (Ahmad, p. 59; Wākid, *Israel in the Balance,* p. 12; Rushdī, p. 29; Darwaza, 1960; Bayhūm in Sylvia Haim's anthology, pp. 54-5; 'Alūba, pp. 54-5; Tall, p. 23; Nashāshībī, p. 39; Ṣafūt, p. 26). Abraham was a refugee, a stranger in the land, as is proved by the fact that he did not even have a grave-plot and had to purchase the Cave of Machpelah from the Sheikh of Hebron (Bayhūm, *op. cit.,* p. 130). The description of the period of Jewish rule as a Golden Age is a distortion of the facts. Even during the reigns of David and Solomon, their kingdoms were limited. Their history is packed with persecution and war against their neighbours; they were always a cause of instability. The absence of a real tie with the Holy Land is also shown by the fact that only a minority—principally the poor—returned after permission had been given by Cyrus (Bayhūm; Darwaza). The Hebrew were strangers, "passers-by," as their name testifies (Ṭarabīn, p. 2).

Furthermore, it is claimed, the Hebrews conquered the country from the Arabs, who had lived there before them. Arab tribes inhabited Palestine since pre-historic days, for the Arabs very frequently trace their pedigree to the Canaanites, Edomites, Arameans, Jebusites, Phoenicians, Hittites and Assyrians (Zurayk, 1956, p. 72; Rushdī, p. 9; Rousan, p. 3; 'Alūba, pp. 54–5; Ṣafwat, p. 20; Ṭarabīn, p. 2; Shukrī, p. 18; al-Jiyār, p. 3; Hasan Ṣabrī al-Khūlī, p. 4), and even to the Hyksos and the Philistines (Wākid, *op. cit.,* pp. 6-7). The Canaanites and the other nationalities referred to in the Bible are often spoken of with sympathy, as partners with the Arabs in resistance to "Zionist" pressure (Tall, p. 17; Dabbāgh, pp. 553-4). Nashāshībī claims that the Palestine Arabs are their offsprings (p. 193). The Arabs conquered the country from the Byzantines and not from the Jews, so the Jews cannot demand its restoration from the Arabs ('Alūba, p. 56).

The Hebrews left no lasting cultural and historical traces (Barghūthī, p. 230; Tall, p. 23; Wākid, *op. cit.,* pp. 9, 14-15). While the Zionists claims that the Western (Wailing) Wall is a relic of Solomon's Temple, Rousan declares that it was really built by the Phoenicians (1965, p. 7). Darwaza writes:

> "Their history is devoid of any colonizatory, political or military glory, and after they were finally uprooted from Palestine they hardly left any traces there." (p. 7).

"Scientific" proofs of this argument are sometimes adduced from Gustav Le Bon's book on early civilizations, which was translated into Arabic. For the building of the Temple, Solomon had to bring in Phoenician craftsmen (Darwaza, pp. 186-7, 210). Not only history but archaeology is cited to prove the early existence of Arab tribes in Palestine (Wākid, *op. cit.,* p. 9). Such arguments are, no doubt, also meant to counteract the publicity given to the discovery of Jewish archaelogical remains, especially the Dead Sea Scrolls.

Arithmetical calculations are given to show that the Arabs have lived in Palestine longer than the Jews, taking into account the period before the coming of the Hebrews and the centuries since the Muslim conquest in 636, so that their rights are better (Rushdī, p. 29, Rousan, p. 23; 'Alūba, pp. 54-5; Wākid, p. 7; Tall, p. 23; Sha'bān, p. 13).

c) THE QUESTION OF RACE

Another argument, also very frequently used, is that there is no racial continuity between the ancient Hebrews and the modern Jews, who cannot, therefore, be regarded as their heirs or lay claim to any historic rights (Ṣafwat, pp. 52-3, and others). Thus, Darwaza writes:

> "The argument of a Jewish tie today with the Children of Israel and their history . . . is a complete forgery." (Part I, p. 7).
>
> "The majority of the small and unimportant group of Jews who remained in Palestine after the decisive blow by the Romans in the first and second centuries converted to Christianity, joined the rest of the population, and afterwards joined Islam and Arabism." (Part III, p. 572).

In all generations a mixed multitude was converted to Judaism. For instance, the peoples who were exiled to Palestine from Iraq by Esarhadon became Jews (Darwaza, Part III, p. 573). Even Moses was, according to Freud, of Egyptian origin (Muhammad Zakī 'Abd al-Qādir, in *al-Akhbār,* March 19, 1964). Adhesion to Judaism, therefore, is not a matter of origin but of obedience to the Jewish Holy Scriptures. Much emphasis is laid on the case of the Khazars, in the Crimea, who embraced Judaism in the 8th century. Very high estimates are given of their numbers (which makes it easier to claim that a large part of the modern Jews are of Khazar origin). 'Alūsh, (p. 65), citing Hānī Hindī and Muḥsin Ibrāhīm, *Israel: Idea, Movement and State,* declares that there were ten million Jewish Khazars. The

Jews of Eastern Europe, who were "the most Zionist Jews," therefore did not belong to the Kingdom of Judah and were not even Semites (see also Zurayk, p. 72). Wākid, in *Israel in the Balance,* says that over ten million Khazars became converted to Judaism (pp. 16-21), while Rushdī estimates the number at eight to ten million. Nashāshībī says that the Jews of Eastern Europe, including such leaders as Dizengoff, Ben-Gurion, Ben-Zvi and Sharret, were Khazars (p. 193), and Bayhūm declares that the majority of the Zionists are Khazars (in Sylvia Haim's anthology, p. 145). Darwaza says that the Khazars were the largest group to join Jewry, and it is they who are known as Ashkenazim (Vol. III, p. 573), while Wākid declares that at least half the Israelis are of Khazar origin (*op. cit.,* p. 21).[4]

Rushdī explains that the physiognomies of the Jews shows that they are a mixed breed, containing elements from every race. He says that Professor Gurewitch, "Lecturer on races at the Hebrew University and Rector of the Medical School," proves on the basis of a study of the composition of the blood among the Jews that they are not one people, and only a very small part of them, from the Arab countries, are the children of Issac and Jacob (similar statements are made by Rousan, p. 24).*

d) THE DIVINE PROMISE

The Promise Already Fulfilled. Dr. Tannous, writing in English for Christian readers, cites Professor Alfred Guillaume's argument that the divine promise of the Return to Zion was fulfilled by the return of the Babylonian exiles, and does not foreshadow a further return (1957, p. 5), and that the heritage of Israel has been transferred, according to the Epistle to the Galatians (3: 25-29), to the Christians, who are the seed of Abraham (p. 6). A similar argument is put forward by ʿĪsā al-Safarī, who explains that since the canon of the Hebrew Scriptures was completed during the exile in Babylon, the prophecy of the return to Zion was fulfilled in the time of Cyrus (*Arab Palestine between the Mandate and Zionism,* 1937, p. 67; see also al-Jiyār, p. 3).

* The late Professor Joseph Gurewitch was not a "lecturer on race" or Rector of the Medical School; he was head of the Department of Clinical Microbiology.

The Promise Not Only For the Jews. Ahmad deals with the divine promises at length and in great detail (pp. 41-56). According to him, if God indeed promised the Holy Land to the seed of Abraham, the intention was not to single out the Jews, as is proved by the fact that the promise states that Abraham's seed will be as numerous as the sand or the stars. This cannot apply to the Jews, whose numbers are small, but only to Jews, Christians, and Muslims together, who are all of the seed of Abraham. Hence, one group alone cannot monopolize the Land as its heritage (p. 36).

The Validity of the Promise Has Expired. Moreover, the argument continues, the divine promises were given to the Children of Israel on condition they remained faithful to their Covenant with God, but the Jews, despite the numerous and repeated warnings of the prophets, violated the Covenant, worshipped idols and did evil in God's sight. Hence, the validity of the promises has expired, as is shown by many verses from the Quran and the Bible. The former, for instance, speaking of the Children of Israel says, "And because of their breaking the Covenant, We have cursed them and hardened their hearts" (Sura V, The Table Spread, v. 13). The Almighty tried and tested them but they turned their backs on him; therefore he cursed them. While Isaiah declares, "If ye be willing and obedient, ye shall eat the good of the Land. But if ye refuse and rebel, ye shall be devoured with the sword" (i:19-20); and Moses told them, "But it shall come to pass, if thou wilt not hearken unto the voice of the Lord thy God, . . . that all these curses shall come upon thee, and overtake thee" (Deuteronomy 28:15).

Denial of the Promises. According to the Muslim religious approach of 'Aqqād, Tall and Darwaza, the Jewish Scriptures are a forgery perpetrated by the Jews to suit themselves, in order to justify their actions and claim divine sanction for their undesirable tendencies. It is inconceivable that God should order one group of people to destroy another group, including men, women and children, not even sparing the cattle, but the Jews blamed the Deity for their crimes, pretending they had acted at His behest.

Thus, Darwaza writes in the introduction to his *History*:

> "The text of the Holy Scriptures reveals signs of strong fanaticism, great selfishness and narrow-mindedness, which govern their [the Jews'] ways and their behaviour to others, or their character and the qualities they claim for themselves.

This is manifested by their ascribing to God the transfer of the inheritance and the blessing from Abraham to Issac, with the disinheritance of Ishmael, his first-born, and his other sons, and then the transfer of Isaac's inheritance and blessing to Jacob their great father, with the disinheritance of Esau, his first-born. It is also shown in their claim that all the nations should be their servants, whom God has destined to serve them, and that they are a people holy to God, whom God has distinguished by his interest in them and his aid to them, and that they alone out of all the nations will serve him and that he appointed them to have the eternal absolute right over the Land of Canaan, whose boundaries changed in accordance with their circumstances: sometimes it lay west of the Jordan, or part of it; sometimes it stretched both east and west at the same time, and sometimes from the Nile to the Euphrates. Also in the claim that God—may he be exalted and sanctified—placed at their mercy, or rather ordered and commanded them to destory, all the inhabitants of the Land of Canaan, men and women, young and old, sometimes even cattle and beasts, and burn their dwellings. And also in that he strictly forbade them to enter into any agreement to spare the life of a single inhabitant of the Land of Canaan, or to leave him amongst them, to the extent that they even recorded the anger of God against them because on a few occasions they did not carry out the work of destruction; and also the anger of Moses against them for this reason (Exodus, 34; Deuteronomy, 7 and 20; Numbers, 31). "They recorded such words from the mouth of God, and believed that he would forgive them their sins and religious and moral aberrations (Numbers, 14), and that if He was angry at them and allowed them to suffer for these aberrations, this would be for the sake of punishment, but immediately afterwards he would relent without delay and save them again. In this there are shocking extremes which contradict the sublimity, justice and mercy of God. These are proofs of the sources of the books and their flaws and defects: they almost certainly originate in the discrimination and persecution they suffered in Egypt, the traces of which remained imbedded in them and created among them a psychological complex, which made them write as they did in such texts, or led to the crimes of brutal extermination which they committed against the people of the East and the West of the Jordan whom they defeated." (1960, pp. 8-9).

e) SIGNIFICANCE OF THESE ARGUMENTS

These arguments imply a number of significant trends:

i. The Zionist claim to a historic right is presented as not only baseless but also deliberately deceitful. This fits in with the ascription of treachery and trickery *(ghadr, makr)* to the Jews, which is frequently found in Muslim writing and is repeatedly emphasized in the literature of the conflict. The claim of historic right is odious in itself and is evidence of the odiousness of Zionism.

ii. The Israelis and the Jews are denigrated on the ground that they have not preserved the purity of their race. Ahmad writes:

> "There is not one of them who can truly claim a pure lineage from Israel or of whom it can be justifiably said that he belongs to the Children of Israel." (p. 39).

In the introduction to *This is Zionism* (1954), Nasser explains that the reader will see:

> ". . . how a religious faith evolved into a political orientation of people who have a religion but are not united by either race or paternity." (p. 10).

As noted in the previous chapter, the Arabs sometimes affix the epithet "foundling" to the name of Israel and its leaders. For themselves they claim purity of race and use the adjective "noble" *(karīm)* or "pure" *(aṣīl)*.

iii. The emphasis on the racial impurity of the Jews may also imply the rejection of the claim that they have a common Semitic origin with the Arabs. The process of dehumanizing the rival may produce a tendency to narrow the common ground between the two parties: consanguinity between Israelis and Arabs is denied, so that the Israelis need not be treated as relatives, but must be subjected to the severest punishment.

S. Rosenblatt explains in his article "The Jews in Islam" (p. 119) that the belief in consanguinity was one of the factors that led to a liberal attitude to the Jews in the Muslim countries. It would not be surprising if an attempt were made today to deny this relationship.

5. IDENTIFICATION OF ZIONISM AND JUDAISM

Arab writers and leaders repeatedly emphasize that they bear no hostility to the Jews but only oppose the Zionists. However, this distinction is not maintained, and Zionism and Judaism are often used as synonyms, a denunciation of Zionism leading naturally to a denunciation of the Jews. It is not a matter of confusing "Jew," "Zionist" and "Israeli" in the flow of speech or writing, in the same way as even Israelis do not always preserve the distinction; the identification is deliberate.

One expression of this tendency is the identification of Israeli and Jew as a figure in Arab caricatures. The Arabs draw the Israeli like a Jew in the anti-Semitic caricatures—a bearded figure with a large hooked nose. This image was already in existence before World War II and was not created merely under Nazi influence.

a) FACTORS AND SIGNIFICANCES

Let us examine the factors that led to this identification, the attitudes it implies, and its significance.

i. *The Pragmatic Approach.* The Jews abroad supported the Jews of Palestine and now support Israel, and the supporter of a rival arouses anger and hostility. Al-Khālidī writes:

> "However thin may be the line distinguishing Judaism from Zionism, in any case it is not to the advantage of the Arabs to preserve the distinction between the two. The first basic factor is that the source of Israel's strength lies in Jewry, which gives her direct material support through the annual appeals." ("Israel's Strategy," in *al-Anwār,* May 21, 1963).

Na'nā'a, who devotes a chapter (1964, pp. 295-301) to the relationship between Judaism and Zionism, expresses a somewhat similar attitude. He argues that, even if Zionist and Jew are not synonymous terms, the fact is that Zionism dominates Jewry, exploiting the profoundest Jewish emotions, and he asks:

> "Where are the Jews who are not Zionists and who are not loyal to Zionism? Where is their voice?"

He notes that Dr. Nahum Goldmann was at the same time President of the World Jewish Congress and of the Zionist Organization, and that Israeli leaders, like Ben-Gurion and Golda Meir, claimed the right to speak in the name of the entire Jewish people. Zionism regards the Jews as a people with national characteristics scattered all over the world, with a part of it in Israel—and this implies the identity of Zionism and Jewry.

ii. *Judaism Was Always Zionist.* The prolonged ties of Jews with Palestine and the place of that country in the Jewish faith show that there is an organic bond between Zionism and Judaism.

Rushdī explains that Judaism is not only a faith like others, but "also a political movement":

> "The bond between Judaism and Zionism is primordial, ever since Judaism and Zionism became coupled in the sense that one cannot be separated from the other, representing two sides of the one coin." (1965, p. 19).

He accuses the Jews of having concealed their true aims and tried to cover the plans and purposes of Zionism with a humanitarian mask, as a movement for the salvation of persecuted Jews, being afraid that Zionist publicity might affect their status in the countries where they lived. But the connection between Judaism and Zionism

> ". . . is clearly expressed in many provisions of Jewish law. In the Talmud it is stated that a Jew who leaves the Land of Israel cannot compel his wife to accompany him, and one who emigrates to the Land is entitled to divorce his wife if she refuses to come with him.[5] There is also a similar doctrine in the Jewish faith which says that he who lives in the Land of Israel is forgiven by God for all his sins." (p. 20).

Zionism is, therefore,

> ". . . a political movement whose source is in Zionist thought, which is derived from the beliefs of the Bible and the laws of the Talmud, which draws its vitality from the intellectual attachment to religious and racial faiths that have gained a foothold in their thinking." (p. 22).

The author also supports this view by quotations from Solomon Schechter and Theodor Herzl's famous saying, "The return to Zion must be preceded by the return to Judaism" (p. 20).

Tall shows that Zionism is an essential part of Judaism by citing historical precedents from ancient and modern times, from the Maccabees and Bar Kochba to Moses Montefiore and Baron Edmond de Rothschild (1964, pp. 157-9). Na'nā'a says that World Zionism holds special prayers in synagogues throughout the world on Israel's Independence Day (p. 299), and quotes the Israeli paper *Al Hamishmar* to show that Hatikvah, the anthem of Zionism and the State of Israel, is sung in Jewish schools throughout the world (p. 301).

Similar ideas are widely expressed. Dr. Naṣr sums up:

> "Zionism is really nothing but the national behaviour of the Jew in his reaction to the nations throughout history as it has taken shape under the pressure of modern Western civilization." (1957, p. 95).

iii. *Deeper Sources of Odiousness of Zionism.* Zionism is presented as such an odious phenomenon that only an odious community could believe in it. Consequently, Arab writers try to find the deeper sources of Zionism in a basic fault of the people from whom it sprang, namely, the Jews. Israel is a young State, so that it is difficult to claim that the odious characteristics of its people are a manifestation of the Jewish character. Thus the effort to find an ostensibly scientific basis under the guise of historical research leads to the discovery of deep roots for their obnoxiousness as a culturally, religiously and historically organic feature of the Jewish character. The odium attached to the Jews gives a dimension of depth to the vileness of Israel. This is the genetics of the evil of Israel: Zionism is not a group among the Jews but a fundamental trait in their character. 'Aqqād thus defines Zionism as

> "... the odious character which, in ancient times, struck root among a group of Hebrews and made them hated and despised in every place in which they lived or to which they came. We refer to the character of aggressiveness, unjust demands and selfishness. This is an ancient disease of this people, which has never left them." (1956, p. 40).

Sayegh, Sa'ab and al-Khālidī, who are intellectuals with a Western education, declare that Zionism is odious because it coveted the property of others. By regarding Zionism as only a manifestation of Judaism, they add a dimension of historical and cultural depth to their analysis. It is not merely a matter of a specific aspiration or series of acts: Zionist settlement and Zionist belligerence in 1948 are only links in a long chain of trespasses and insatiable lust for the property of others. Fundamental Zionism is manifested in the claim that God is the God of Israel, and other nations have no part in him (Rushdī, p. 41); Zionism's aspiration for Palestine is not something spiritual, but an evil and insatiable ambition. Hence, Zionism will not be content to dominate Palestine, but will aspire to bring the whole world under its rule. This explanation also gives greater cohesion and depth to the portrayal of Zionism as an imperialist phenomenon, for imperialism is the aspiration for mastery and exploitation. The same idea is expressed in the Jordanian White Paper (Ch. II, 3e).

iv. *Identification as Implying Israel's Weakness.* Another psychological mechanism may be operative in the identification of Judaism with Zionism. The politicidal aim may lead to Israel being regarded as something superficial, adventitious, a thin cloak for the basic reality of Judaism. In other words, the denial that Israel is essentially Israeli or Zionist is required to strengthen the belief that she has not struck root as an autonomous entity and is a transitory phenomenon.

v. *Continuity of Guilt.* The identification of Zionism with the Jews may have a further function: to create continuity of guilt. At first glance, only the veteran Zionists who founded Israel can be blamed for robbing the Arabs of their country, while the Zionism of their children is a matter of birth and not of choice. However, by making Zionism a permanent racial characteristic of the Jews, the guilt is transferred from fathers to sons. Thus, Rushdī declares that Zionism is a deep-rooted basic characteristic:

> "The Zionist is first and last a Zionist, in his flesh and blood, in his thought and belief. It makes no difference what form his ideology takes and how it alters, whether he clings to Communism or fights it, opposes democracy or supports it, believes in Messianism or proclaims atheism, the Zionist is a Zionist first and foremost; whatever his nationality, whether his citizenship is British or American, he nevertheless supports his Zionism. And if a contradiction arises between the two, he becomes a Zionist and only a Zionist." (p. 41).

b) ZIONISM AS THE EMISSARY OF JEWRY

The distinction between "World Jewry" and "World Zionism" becomes blurred in Arab writing. The character of the former as an organized conspiracy, as depicted in anti-Semitic literature, is ascribed by the Arabs to the latter, which is described as an instrument in the hands of Jewry.

Tall, for instance, explains:

> "Many believe that Zionism is very different from Jewry, but in fact they are one and the same thing, for Zionism is the executive machinery *(al-jihāz al-tanfīdhī)* of World Jewry, which tries to work for the ruin of the world and the control of its destiny. There is not a single Jew who opposes Zionism and its aims ... Those Jews who pretend to oppose Zionism do so according to a plan which has been laid down, and there are few of them today, not more than a few thousand among the 15 million Jews. They are exceptional, and no conclusion should be drawn from exceptions. Zionism, in my opinion, is Jewry, violent *('anīfa)*, deep-rooted *('arīqa)* and tyrannical from the time of Moses to our own day." (1964, p. 171).

Bahā' al-Dīn, the Socialist (1965, p. 52), displays a similar attitude to that of the fanatically religious Tall, using the same epithet, "violent." While trying to oppose anti-Semitism he is not aware, apparently, that by identifying Jewry with Zionism, which he describes as an odious enemy, he is also making the Jews an object of hostility.

Many Arabs emphasize the need, in their own interests, to maintain the distinction between Jews in general and Zionists and Israelis; they want to deter the Jews from supporting Israel, so as to narrow the front. In their discussions of the subject, however, they are drawn to the opposite extreme of identifying Zionism with Judaism, thus broadening the front. The Jews become the enemy, the source of strength for Israel, which is the centre of Jewry. Thus 'Alūba declares:

> "Every Jew in every country in the world believes that his homeland is Zionism and its centre in Palestine." (1964, p. 184).

And on the next page:

> "The Government of Israel is all the Jews in the whole world."

Na'nā'a writes on similar lines (p. 300).

Others blame Zionism, which claims to be the centre for all Jews and demands their allegiance, for the identification of the two concepts. This is given as the reason for the refusal of some Arab countries to give visas to even non-Israeli Jews, and for Saudi Arabia's ban on the service of Jews in Aramco or in the American bases in that country. Dr. Sayegh explains that this is

> ". . . a political reaction of the Arab States against the fundamental ideological basis of the Zionist claim." (1961, p. 90).

c) RELIGIOUS, CULTURAL AND HISTORIC VILENESS OF ZIONISM

It is frequently alleged that the source of the vileness of Zionism lies in the faith and laws of Judaism. Dr. Naṣr explains that, since Zionism is only a continuation of Judaism, it should be studied historically, in the light of both the distant and the recent past:[6]

> "For no movement has been enabled to maintain such continuity of development, unity of thought and identity of expression as Zionism. This is because it

has been associated with a people of which conservatism is one of the outstanding characteristics, so that you can see in the slaughter at Deir Yasin behaviour in keeping with the Biblical description of the Israelites' war of annihilation against Jericho." (p. 33).[7]

(President Nasser's recent statement, in an interview with *Time* (May 16, 1969), that he is reading the Bible in order to understand the behaviour of Israel probably implies a similar line of thought.)

Rushdī says that the foundations of Zionism were laid by the rabbis, and that the Talmud is its holy book (p. 55). Zionism believes in the Talmud as a source of law and faith, and behaves in accordance with its terroristic instructions *(ta'līmihi al-irhābī*—p. 50). He professes to "quote" the Talmud to prove his point:

> "When the Jews are victorious in battle, they must utterly destroy *('an bakrat abīhim)* their enemies. Anyone who disobeys this rule disobeys the instructions of the Bible and rebels against God. This is what the Jews did to the Canaanites when they entered Palestine after Moses for the first time, and this is what they did recently to the Arabs of Palestine in the slaughter at Deir Yasin and in other places." (p. 51).

The conquest of Jericho under Joshua is frequently linked with the taking of Deir Yasin (Shukrī, p. 19; Dabbāgh, p. 554).

Deir Yasin, it is argued, was not an isolated case, but a manifestation of the Jewish character as expressed in their creed. This argument helps to explain away the Arab defeat, for the struggle was against a vile enemy with inhuman, satanic ways—thus, to some extent, alleviating the sense of failure and defeat.

For Abdallah Tall, the Exodus from Egypt and the Israelite conquest of Palestine were "the first aggression." The Canaanites, according to his view, were Arabs and the country was the centre of a flourishing culture. The Quran says that God gave the Jews the opportunity to win their freedom from the Pharaonic yoke so that they should live in peace and harmony with the other nations—

> "But the nature of this people and the characteristics and customs rooted in its soul made it miss this precious opportunity presented by divine Providence, and instead of trying to achieve a peaceful and stable life with their fellow creatures of God, they made the Exodus from Egypt and their conquest of Palestine the beginning of that barbarity *(hamajiyya)* which is manifested in their history, their book, their scholars and their philosophy." (p. 14).

Elsewhere, Tall expresses his feelings of sympathy and identification with the Ammonites, Moabites and Canaanites of Biblical days:

> "When I read today what is written in the Bible about the Jews under Joshua's leadership against the places known to me in Jordan and Palestine, I compare the first savagery of the Jews with their latest savagery three thousand years later, when the Arabs of Palestine did not go out to welcome the immigrants and therefore they were punished with destruction at Deir Yasin and other towns and villages." (p. 17).

By identifying Jewry and Zionism, each is stained with the iniquities of the other. Jewry is vile because it produced Zionism, or because Zionism exists in it, while Zionism is vile as the concentrated embodiment of the odious characteristics of the Jews.

The identification gives the dispute a profound and historic character and necessitates considerable research into the nature, history and religion of the Jews. It would not be far from the truth to say that the study of Judaism and Jewish history in Arab universities is largely tendentious and designed to serve the needs of the conflict. When, for example, *Filastin* reported on November 29, 1964 that an institute for the study of Zionism and Jewish history was to be set up in Egypt, the combination of the two subjects was no doubt significant.

d) THE ANTI-ZIONIST JEWS

The identification of Zionism with Jewry raises a problem: the attitude to be adopted by the Arabs towards anti-Zionist Jews, especially the American Council for Judaism, which the Arabs support and praise, and which has been a valuable ally in their anti-Zionist propaganda in the United States. The existence of such Jews is frequently mentioned as a proof of the vileness of Zionism, and books by such leaders of the A.C.J. as Elmer Berger and Alfred Lilienthal have been translated into Arabic and are frequently quoted.

Nevertheless, the attitude towards them is ambivalent. On the one hand, their activities are interpreted as deliberate deceit (as in the above quotations from Shukrī and Tall—as we shall see in Chapter VI there was a similar attitude to the "Semitic Movement" in Israel). Abū al-Rūs savagely attacks Alfred Lilienthal, of the A.C.J., for hypocrisy and deceit (*World Judaism and its Continuous War against Christianity,* 1964, p. 132). Jews and Jewry are denounced with such vehemence that the idea of "good Jews" is regarded as a contradiction in terms. Some authors recognize the existence of anti-Zionist Jews, but belittle their importance (see above, Tall, 1964, p. 171). Na'nā'a, who deals specifically with the American Council for Judaism, describes its activities, but discounts its prospects of growth because of the Zionists' success in finding a way to the Jewish heart and their skill in playing on the feelings of the Jews and dominating all means of publicity (pp. 295-6). The demonological view of Zionism leads the Arabs to regard the opposition to it as of minor importance.

6. CONTRADICTIONS OF ZIONISM

The Arabs find a number of contradictions in Zionism, which are a proof of its vileness and give it no rest, since these are antagonistic and incompatible tendencies which will consume it from within.

a) The fundamental weakness of Zionism, as a movement which plotted to steal the territory of another nation, not only makes it an odious phenomenon, but afflicts it with a disease which is manifested in a lack of inner consistency, internecine strife and perplexity. This is the "original sin" of Zionism, which makes it impossible for it to justify itself and will continue to plague it. This is a fundamental problem which Zionism will strive in vain to solve.

In an article "The Jewish Personality in the Zionist Story of Our Time" (*al-Ādāb,* March 1963), Kanafānī explains that there is a fundamental and insuperable difficulty in every Zionist work of fiction, namely the need to explain what led the hero to settle in Palestine. The usual reason, that his ancestors ruled the country for a short period thousands of years ago, cannot be convincing. Zionist literature, therefore, is compelled to find a justification for the hero coming to Palestine by glorifying him and describing him as a physical and spiritual superman in comparison with the Arabs, as if these heroic qualities give him a right to regard the country as his (as in the case of Ari Ben Canaan in *Exodus*). On the other hand, Zionist writers tend to depict the Arabs as inferior and degenerate. Nevertheless, this does not solve the problem or provide an answer to the troublesome question that afflicts the writer, for no heroism can justify the uprooting of the Palestinian Arab people and its expulsion from Palestine.

Bahā' al-Dīn finds a similar difficulty in Yael Dayan's book *Envy the Frightened,* in which the hero is described as a fearless superman, a man of iron. Zionist education, says Bahā' al-Dīn, is designed to this end: the usurpation of the Land, disregard for Arab rights and the need to live by the sword produce a special type of Israeli, who admires and lives by violence. Nimrod, the hero of the book, did not play with toys in his childhood; he was given a pistol at an early age. He admires courage and violence, and all his emotions and spiritual propensities are suppressed. This upbringing endows him with endurance and the fighting spirit, but from the emotional point of view he is an invalid, an animal rather than a man, "a hundred-per-cent Nazi type" (p. 92). This hero is typical of the new generation among the Jews of Palestine. His character is destructive: he destroys not only his environment but also himself.

In turning its back on religion and spirituality, Zionism fosters the animal qualities, Bahā' al-Dīn says in summing up the lesson of the book. The claim that it is creating a new type of man is a typical manifestation of racism. Furthermore, since the Zionist man is unnatural, he will ultimately be torn by emotional crises and can never attain inner peace. He regards the establishment of the State of Israel as the solution to all problems, but the younger generation of Israelis will find out one day that the problem of "Whither?" still remains unanswered.

Kanafānī analyses "Zionist literature" in his book *The Literature of the Resistance in Occupied Palestine 1948-1966* (Beirut 1966), which is designed to glorify the national achievements of Arab poets and authors in Israel and their resistance to Zionist pressure and official restrictions. Throughout history, he says, Jewish and Zionist literature has glorified the Jewish hero on the basis of a combination of religion and race, which he regards as the root of all evil. In the Bible, the hero is portrayed as possessing superhuman powers bestowed by God, who intervenes on his behalf, and the same theme is found in the stories of the Talmud. Hence, the traditional self-glorification of the Jew. Judah Halevi, in his *Ha-Kuzari* ("The Khazar"), depicts the Jewish hero as an intellectual superman. The same motif is to be found in Jewish and Zionist literature, from Jacques Halevy's opera *The Jewess,* Disraeli's *David Alroy,* George Elliot's *Daniel Deronda* and Herzl's *Altneuland* to Uris' *Exodus* (which Kanafānī regards as a major example of Zionist literature, which has had a decisive influence on other Zionist books), Robert Nathan's *Star in the Wind* and the novels of Yael Dayan. The author explains that the main feature of Zionist literature is the need to serve propaganda ends. This produces artistic and—even worse—moral faults, for the combination of race and creed demands self-glorification and the denigration of others. The self-praise in Zionist works written since 1948, which reaches extraordinary heights, unparalleled in all the stories about heroism in World War II, is required in order to justify violence against the Arabs and the establishment of Israel at their expense.

Kanafānī vehemently attacks Professor S. D. Goitein for his book *Jews and Arabs,* accusing him of an "extreme racist outlook" (p. 59), an unnatural confusion of creed and race, and a misrepresentation of the ties between the Arabs and Islam. When Professor Goitein portrays the Jews as a nation, he is ignoring a serious lacuna in the argument, for the Jews have not been a single nation for thousands of years. Moreover, Goitein describes the Jews as superior to the Arabs, alleging that their mentality is founded on principles while that of the Arabs is commercial, and arguing that the priority in time of Judaism over other religions means that it is superior to them.

It is worth noting that Professor Goitein's purpose and the spirit of his book are the opposite of those ascribed to him by Kanafānī. His aim is to demonstrate the historical and cultural affinity between the Jews and the Arabs. It is not surprising that Arabs like Kanafānī should be infuriated by such an attempt, for it contradicts the basic aim of describing the conflict as insoluble and the gap between Israel and the Arab countries as unbridgeable. Professor Goitein does not chauvinistically exalt the Jews above the Arabs, as Kanafānī says he does; the latter's criticism of the comparison between the mentalities between the two races, for instance, is a distortion of a passage in Professor Goitein's book (pp. 30-39), which describes the differences between the conditions under which Judaism and Islam developed. However, since the Arabs describe Zionism, Israel and the Jews as the lowest of the low, Goitein's comparison of them with the Arabs is regarded as intolerable arrogance.

Kanafānī devotes a great deal of attention to the degrading attitude to the Arab in Zionist literature (such as books by Uris, Nathan and others). It is fairly clear from his writing that he does not know Hebrew, for he makes some absurd mistakes in translating Hebrew names. (The same applies to most other Arab authors who write on Jewish subjects.) Most of the "Zionist books" which he mentions were not written in Hebrew, but this does not prevent him claiming to be an expert on "Zionist literature." In *al-Hilāl,* January 1967, he denounces the award of the Nobel Prize for Literature to the Hebrew writer, S. Y. Agnon, whom he regards as a mouthpiece for Zionist expansionist aims. (The article was quoted in *Ha'aretz* of February 24, 1967.)

In contrast to the numerous books in English which he mentions, he deals with only three short stories in Hebrew, although if there is any tendency in "Zionist literature" to approve the "suppression" of the Arab minority, it should find expression in Hebrew works and not in such works as *Daniel Deronda,* the author of which was not even a Jewess. The three stories are well chosen for this purpose. They are: "The Story of an Olive Tree" by Benjamin Tammuz, which describes the dislike of a Jewish family for an olive tree left behind by the Arabs whose house the Jews now occupy; "The Swimming Competition," by the same author, about an Arab and a Jew who used to swim together as boys and compete again when the Arab is taken prisoner during the war; and "The Prisoner," by S. Izhar, which describes the perplexities of a young Israeli soldier who is put in charge of an Arab shepherd taken prisoner during the War of Independence.

Kanafānī says that these stories show some advance in objectivity of approach, as the authors lived in Palestine before 1948 and were more familiar with the true conditions. Accordingly, they do not go so far in self-glorification and contempt for the Arabs as their predecessors. However, he continues, they are unable to find a natural conclusion for their stories. Tammuz's olive tree, whose branches he describes as "yearning for the daughter of Maḥmūd" (Kanafānī calls him Ali), symbolizes their "expectation of the return of the absentees" (i.e., the restoration of the Palestinians), but since the author does not have the courage to admit this, he resorts to a trick and has the tree cut down. Izhar knows that it is wrong to be brutal to the elderly shepherd and that he ought to be restored to his family, but the end of the story is obscure and it is not clear what his ultimate fate will be. The same thing applies to the Swimming Competition, in which Kanafānī sees a symbol of the unadmitted knowledge that the struggle with the Arabs is not over and the victory of the Jews is not final. In order to evade the issue, the author adopts the artificial expedient of a shot in the middle of the competition, which kills the Arab. All three stories, he argues, have been given artificial endings, because the writers were unable to complete them. This symbolizes the unnatural nature of Israel's existence. He sums up:

> "No doubt they feel that the theoretical description of the life and future of this State is not practically compatible with the reality, and in their new State they have realized the traditional contradictions which Zionism has been unable to evade, but to which it has frequently added." (p. 75).

Apparently, Kanafānī is trying to find in these stories indications that the authors feel grave anxiety as to the future of Israel because of the contradictions inherent in her existence. This may be due, on the one hand, to his conviction that the wrong done to the Arabs is so terrible that those responsible for it are bound to feel grave misgivings, and, on the other hand, to his own lack of confidence in future developments, so that he tries to draw reassurance from the belief in Israeli perplexities.

b) Another contradiction is involved in the inability of Zionism to define the term "Jew": the dilemma as to whether the definition should be based on nationality or religion. If a Jew is defined as someone whose mother is Jewish, the criterion is racial, for the mother must also be the daughter of a Jewess, and so on. The Zionists arrive at the strange position of transferring the responsibility to the anti-Semites:

> "These Zionists . . . resort to the dialectics of self-consciousness—through other-consciousness." (Sayegh, 1961, p. 80).

This incapacity to define their own nature shows how basically unsound and artificial it is. Hence the complex of problems associated with the relations between religion and State in Israel.

Nashāshībī also deals with the nature of Judaism and the reasons for its persistence. He says that Hegel was correct in saying that historical units constitute specific historical "unities" only in so far as they remember their past, but Jewish unity, historically speaking, is the poorest of human unities, for of all its history it remembers only persecution and sufferings: namely, only a prolonged misfortune. What unites the Jews throughout their history is neither history, territory nor past. In so far as Jews exist, therefore, what distinguishes their character is the capacity of the Jew to live in a society that regards him as a Jew:

> "The Jew could assimilate in the society of any of the modern nations, if it wanted him. In other words, the Jew owes his existence not to history which moulded him, but to the society that rejected him. The Jew is the result of an aberration *(bid'a)* of Christian society." (pp. 53-54).

c) The sickness of Zionism is also expressed in the peculiar predicament that in order to bring Jews to Israel it is interested in the position of the Jews in the world being unsatisfactory, in failure to solve the Jewish problem, in anti-Semitism. Bahā' al-Dīn writes:

> "Salo Baron [the Jewish historian] admits that Zionist thought has led in the course of time to an attitude opposed to the movement for liberation, equality

and tolerance, feeling that world liberation deprives it of its assets among the Jews, whom it regards as destined to form part of its flock and, in the end to settle in Israel." (1965, p. 62).

d) Another contradiction lies in the doubts about the relationship between the Diaspora and Israel and about the loyalty of the Jews in the country where they live. How can the Jews continue to be loyal both to their homeland and to Israel? As ʻAqqād puts it, in a rhetorical question:

"Can the Jews live in a state of national fanaticism between the two homelands to whom they owe loyalty?" (p. 118).

a) ZIONISM DOOMED TO FAILURE

These difficulties are only symptoms of the basic weakness of Zionism and its State. Zionism is an artificial nationalism. Here again we find the extreme contrast, as between black and white. The "evil" in Zionism is, as it were, magnified in comparison with the "good" in Arab nationalism. Dr. Sayegh puts it:

"By contrast with Zionism, Arabism has been spared such dilemmas, by virtue of the fact that it sprang spontaneously within a concrete national society." (1961, p. 80).

The entire development of Zionism demonstrates this sickness. It is not the normal nationalism of a nation dwelling on the soil and developing its national aspirations. On the contrary, it started with an idea, and then looked for a bearer of the idea. The Jews were persuaded and compelled to settle in Palestine, and thus a synthetic, artificial and unnatural nationalism was created. Since the third element—a territory—was lacking, they stole the territory of another nation. Arab nationalism, on the other hand, is spontaneous, springing from a nation dwelling on its land; it means simply "the task of reorganization and re-vitalizing an already existing national society" (Dr. Sayegh, *op. cit.,* p. 80). It is virtuous and believes in human values, which are an essential part of its nature. It is democratic and liberating, it is not involved in internal contradictions like Zionism. Arab nationalism is not built on Islam; it is secular and is founded on language as its central component, while Zionism, because of its artificiality, is consumed with contradictions, which the Zionists insincerely try to conceal. It is narrow, egoistic, nationalist, imperialist and covetous, since it is founded on the original sin of the usurpation of a territory; it is the embodiment of tyranny. Zionism is reactionary, for it aspired to establish a State founded on religious and racialist principles opposed to the spirit of the age. It is, therefore, characterized not only by internal contradictions, but also by the external contradiction between itself and the age and the world.

Since Zionism is unnatural, it cannot succeed. It owes its persistence more to inertia and bureaucratization than to a natural inner vitality. Darwaza writes:

"The aim of Zionism has not been achieved in its national, religious and historical significance and scope, despite the tremendous endeavours of Zionism over eighty years and its extraordinary propaganda, despite the extensive intrigues it undertook and the measures it adopted. Sometimes, it is true, the vital results seem to be tremendous—as expressed in the influx of many Jews . . . and the agricultural, industrial, commercial, cultural and settlement undertakings established with the great assistance they have received. For the Jews who have so far reached Palestine are only twelve per cent of the Jews of the world. Ninety per cent of them did not come as a result of a Zionist national, religious and historic impulse, or of their own free will, but under the pressure of poverty, unemployment, fear of persecution and the attraction of a safer and more satisfying life. Of the Jews whose material position is good and who live in peace and security in Western Europe and North America, only a very small number have come . . . , because the aim of Zionism is incompatible with the nature of things, with historical evidence and the facts of reality. All the signs show that the Zionist movement is now in a position of stagnation or retreat . . . This movement continues its activity, its propaganda and its persuasion, for it has become bureaucratized, supplying a livelihood to tens of thousands of officials." (Part III, pp. 577-8).

Owing to the impression of Zionism's successes and the demonological view of the movement, less emphasis is laid on its weaknesses as a movement than on its achievements and activities, but it is still hoped and believed that these achievements will not save it.

Rushī writes, for example:

"World Zionism is doomed, and the international situation which reigns today dictates its inevitable fate, towards which it will advance willy-nilly, for its character and the nature of its activities and its aims are incompatible with the spirit of the age in which we live. World Zionism is a transitory force, for the factors working for its elimination are stronger than those working for its stability and survival." (p. 42).

7. PRAISES OF ZIONISM

Underlying the contempt and denunciation, there is also some laudatory evaluation. Nashāshībī, whose *Return Ticket* (1962) is packed with hostility to Israel and Zionism, gives extensive descriptions of its activities and capacities, often expressing envy, if not admiration. He describes how it has succeeded in influencing world leaders and inducing them to support it, how it has mobilized strength—though some of its methods have been unsavoury—and, through persuasion and pressure, has established the State of Israel, whose rise is due, not to the rise of the Jewish population of the country, but to Zionist activity. He has certainly no intention of praising Zionism, but he does not object to the unsavoury methods which he ascribes to it, and presents them to the Arabs as an example. In spite of himself, he describes the work of Zionism as a great, though satanic, epic (pp. 124-129).

At the end of the book *This is Zionism,* which is an abbreviated translation of Israel Cohen's *The Zionist Movement,* the editor added the following note:

> "We have described how Zionism was realized. This is not a divine miracle beyond the capacity of man. The Jews had no power or factors for victory not at the disposal of others. Nor are they favoured by men and God, so that they found it easy to do what was difficult for others. But they were men who believed in themselves and what they thought was their right, so they united and were skilful in planning and execution."

The implied praise of Zionism is seldom an independent evaluation, or a recognition of good qualities; it is purposeful, the aim being to stimulate and arouse the Arabs. Generally, therefore, it is confined to those subjects in regard to which the Arabs criticize themselves: disunity, the absence of a "scientific approach," lack of planning, improvization, indifference to the general good and preference for private interests, lack of devotion to the goal, emotionalism, unfamiliarity with the world's ways and the inability to exploit them, lack of skill in propaganda. (The latter point implies a certain degree of self-praise; i.e., the Arab cause is just, but the Jews control the communications media and distort the picture.) The success of Zionism in all these fields is presented as an outstanding talent for action. It should be noted that not all those who deal with the conflict present such an evaluation of Zionism.

As we have seen, there is frequent emphasis on the need to study Zionism and Judaism, on which research institutions have been set up and so many books published. In addition to the need to know the enemy in order to frustrate his efforts, there is the aim of studying the factors that have produced the Zionists' success in order to adapt them for Arab purposes. Among the Zionist works translated are Weizmann's *Trial and Error* Eban's *The Voice of Israel* and Begin's *The Revolt*.

The successes of Zionism have undoubtedly made a great impression on the Arabs. In a few decades it succeeded in creating a "nationalism," mobilizing a people and "usurping a homeland." Its methods appear to constitute a tried formula for success; hence, it appears, it should be imitated and the goals will surely be attained.[8] Thus, for example, Nashāshībī proposes the establishment of a "World Arabism," parallel to World Zionism (1962, p. 129). He even suggests building the central Arab organization on the lines of the departments of the Jewish Agency.

Situations of conflict, which find expression in hostility and tension between rivals, lead to reciprocal influences. Since the conflict is basically a competition, each side tries to learn from the other. The competition takes the form of an effort to frustrate the endeavours of the rival and defeat him, but this aim is partially achieved by imitation. The competition leads, on the one hand, to emphasis on the difference between each party and the other and, on the other hand, to an increased resemblance between them.

The Zionist example of devotion to the Holy Land, unweakened by the vicissitudes of generations, has undoubtedly helped to produce a profound emotional attachment to it by the Palestinian refugees, which has found expression in their literature and poetry, as if to say, "You Jews had a profound devotion to this land, but we are not inferior to you." Some of them even call their aspiration "New Zionism."

The influence of Zionism also extends to elements in the Arab programme. Zionism was an expression of hope. It established an organization and created facts without having a clear picture of how it would advance from the gradual acquisition of land to a Jewish State. We Arabs must follow its example, it is argued. True, we have no clear plan for liquidating Israel, but we must create factors of strength and hope that we shall achieve our aim with their aid.

It cannot be demonstrated that the following passage from an article by Haykal was really influenced by Zionism, but in the closing phrases, at least, it recalls the style of the practical Zionists:

"The armed battle is the last chapter in every international struggle, but it is preceded by prolonged developments which prepare the ground for this last chapter and determine its results. Our independent strength grows from day to day. Every new enterprise is like an effective bullet in the true war between ourselves and Israel, the war which exists now, in practice, without the echo of the shots and the shedding of blood. Every new field, every civilian job, every hospital, every school, all these are noiseless shots in the true battle for independent strength." (*al-Ahrām,* May 12, 1961).

Praise of Zionism might appear to be a breach in the consistency of the negative attitude towards it, but this point should not be exaggerated. Firstly, it should be noted that the praises are only an insignificant proportion of the denunciations. The denunciation is direct, brutal; the praise is indirect and implied. Secondly, we should not exaggerate the significance of the inconsistency or the dissonance created by the presence of both praise and denunciation. The praise is expressed by emulation, but it leads to a greater flexibility in the attitude of the Arabs, enabling them to refrain from closing their eyes to facts which it is difficult to ignore. The praises are, as it were, an insignificant payment for the much larger distortions contained in the image of Zionism and Israel, a safety valve to protect the image as a whole. This is especially so because the praise can be explained away and is mainly confined to Zionist efficiency; it does not apply to the sphere of spiritual values.

8. COMPLEXITIES

The Arab ideas described in this chapter involve a number of complications, inconsistencies and dilemmas. Firstly, there are difficulties in defining the relationship between Zionism and Jewry. It should be noted that the difficulty is not specific to the Arab outlook; it is due to the problematical nature of the definition of Jewishness within the accepted categories which distinguish nationality from religion.

As we have seen, Arabs need the definition of Judaism as only a religion and not a nation, in order to refute Zionism and prove that the Jews do not need a land of their own at all, and that Zionism, therefore, distorts their character by compelling them to live as a nation in a territorial framework, and is a perversion of Judaism. On the other hand, when they examine Judaism as a religious and historical phenomenon, they find that it always had an attachment to the Land of Israel. This means that it is "Zionist" in essence and history, so that Judaism and Zionism are one and the same. At one time they oppose Zionism and defend Judaism against it; on other occasions they denounce Judaism because of its Zionist nature, or identify the two; sometimes Zionism is only a new embodiment of a quality or characteristic which has deep roots in the Jews.

Secondly, while it is argued that the Jews are not a nation, their attachment to each other is, nevertheless, so strong that it is explained as an international plot. This contradiction is outstanding, for example, in Na'nā'a's arguments. On the one hand the Jews are "an artificial mixture which the Zionist leaders have made up their minds to call the Jewish people" (p. 3); on the other hand, when he examines the bonds between Zionism and the Jews and the ties between Jews and each other, he realizes that they are so profound that even Jewish Communists from various countries maintain ties with each other and confer together:

> "The Jews insist on believing that their condition constitutes a people which contains national elements, and even the [Jewish] Communists do not deny this." (p. 300).

Moreover, all the Arab anti-Semitic literature assumes that Jews have a special, stable and profound character which is the source of their wickedness.

Thirdly, if the Jews are neither a race nor a nation, and are not the offspring of the ancient Hebrews, how is it possible to explain their devotion to the Holy Land throughout the generations? Ahmad recognizes this devotion:

> "In their hearts the Jews believed that they would remain wandering, uprooted and scattered, even if they lived in affluence among the nations, so long as they were far from Palestine; they therefore took no pleasure in life, and could not rest until after they had seized Palestine." (p. 30).

Rushdī vehemently denounces Zionism and the idea of the historic tie with Palestine, which he describes as "a fabrication" (p. 27), but when he discusses the diversion of Jordan waters to the Negev he explains:

> "Historical motives played an important part in Israel's interest in the Negev, for the Jews, as the Bible says, lived in the Negev and they have eternal *(khālida)* memories and great glory *(amjād 'idda).*" (p. 302).

Moreover, how can it be explained that so many of those who are Israelis today chose to settle in Palestine although they were not all compelled to do so? How did they decide to defy danger and discomfort, and were not even deterred by the Arab threat (which, for their own self-respect, the Arabs tend to regard as terrifying)? It is difficult to believe that they themselves are completely convinced by the answer that this is the work of Zionist cunning, which drove into the heads of the settlers "the superstitious belief in the bond between the Jews and Palestine" and led them astray.

Fourthly, if the Jews have settled in Palestine as a result of the pressure of World Zionism, who are this group which constitutes "World Zionism"? Who are these plotting and intriguing leaders, and what is their motive? Why should these men, who are depicted as cold-blooded and lacking in ideals, have an attachment to this particular country? Why did they take so much trouble? The explanation that they exploited an attachment which was the result of religious emotions is not convincing, for it means that the Jews possess special, namely national, religious emotions. This problem is ultimately solved by the allegation of a plot, a cabal, a historical design on the pattern of *The Protocols of the Elders of Zion.* Again the question arises, however: if all that these leaders wanted was a fulcrum for the achievement of world power, why did they choose Palestine?

Fifthly, if Zionism is a deceit and an odious, unhealthy phenomenon, how has it succeeded? The success can be ascribed, it is true, to the satanic skill of the powers of darkenss, but the internal antagonisms in Zionism ought to have undermined it from within, and since the first Zionist Congress over seventy years have elapsed, which should have been a long enough period for the contradictions to take effect.

Chapter 5
THE JEWS

1. ISLAM AND THE JEWS

The Arabs frequently emphasize that the Muslim countries, unlike the Christian ones, have never persecuted the Jews, that Arabs and Jews have lived together in peace and mutual respect, and that whenever the Jews were compelled to leave Europe they found refuge in the Arab world. Anti-Semitism was born in the West; Zionism, which was a reaction to it, also originated in Europe (Bahā' al-Dīn, p. 196).

It is true that the position of the Jews was much better in the Arab countries. Although there were outbreaks and restrictions there, too, they were not so severe, or on the same scale, as in Europe.[1] The Muslims did not impose their creed on the Jews by force, or expel them, as the Christians did.

The modern emphasis on equality of civil rights may lead us to equate toleration with lack of discrimination and civil equality. This is the impression that Arab spokesmen like Shukairy try to create. Aḥmad writes, for example:

> "Since God decreed their dispersion in the countries of the world, we have never heard that they were saved from harm and found a good life and security for themselves and their property anywhere except in the Islamic countries . . . In every Muslim country, they enjoyed the protection of Islam and lived under its wing, safe, peaceful, free to trade, enjoying equality in all civil rights and not suffering from any oppression whatsoever." (1962, p. 75).

The atmosphere of the conflict leads to some expressions of compunction over the tolerance extended to the Jews, which Sharāra says, they exploited in order to bring about the corruption and disintegration of Islam (1964, p. 23). He sums up:

> "The liberation of the Jews in the framework of Arab civilization paved the way to its destruction." (p. 24).

Jews in the Arab countries, it is sometimes stated, were Arabs of the Mosaic faith until Zionism came along and spoiled it all. Dr. Sayegh writes, for example:

"There were in Palestine at the end of World War I no more than 57,000 Jews. Many of these Jews were *Arabs of Jewish faith,* who, throughout Arab history, had lived in friendship and harmony with *Arabs of Christian or Muslim faith.*" (*The Arab-Israel Conflict,* 1956, pp. 5-6).

The truth is that this tolerance of Islam toward the Jews was founded on discrimination: it was a tolerance towards inferiors. Morroe Berger, in *The Arab World,* sums up the position: "Tolerance was not equality" (p. 259). According to the basic Islamic approach, there was no room for pagans, who must be destroyed, but the Jewish and Christian "People of the Scripture" were recognized as inferior groups. Professor Von Grunebaum says:

"Their personal safety and their personal property are guaranteed them at the price of permanent inequality."

"The minority situation within the world of Islam is, however, most clearly portrayed by saying that the minorities bought their safety at the price of *Geschichtslosigkeit,* at the price of having more or less the status of crown colonies in our day." (*Medieval Islam,* University of Chicago, Phoenix edition, 1961, pp. 178-81).

He adds that non-Muslims, indeed, sometimes rose to high positions in the State, but this was illegal, and was opposed by religious circles.

Professor Bernard Lewis describes their position as follows:

"The Dhimmis were second-class citizens, paying a high rate of taxation, suffering from certain social disabilities, and on a few rare occasions subjected to open persecution. But by and large their position was infinitely superior to that of those communities who differed from the established church in Europe." (*The Arabs in History,* p. 94, cited by Berger, p. 259).[2]

The position of the Jews in the Arab countries was not so idyllic as it is portrayed today by Arab spokesmen. They were liable to degrading restrictions—though these were not always enforced. It is typical, perhaps, that they suffered particularly from discrimination, pressure and insult in the

Yemen, which Professor Goitein has called "the most Arab of all the Arab countries" (*Jews and Arabs,* 1964, p. 73); Jewish orphans were regarded as State property and forcibly converted to Islam (p. 77); Jews were set apart by their dress, and frequently stoned (p. 76).

It may be assumed that the attitude of the Quran, which contains numerous anti-Jewish expressions, especially from the Medina period, had a major influence on the image of the Jews in the eyes of the Arab populace. Special importance may be attributed to sayings that are repeated twice with slight differences in wording: for instance, that

> ". . . humiliation and wretchedness were stamped upon them and they were visited with wrath from Allah." (Sura II, The Cow, v. 61; Sura III, The Family of 'Imrān, v. 112).

These passages were understood, not as referring to the punishment of the Jews in the time of Moses, but as of wide historical significance: a divine decree, which, as the Arabs understood it, was fulfilled under historical, political and cultural conditions by lack of political independence and a position of inferiority. Bayḍāwī, one of the greatest commentators on the Quran, who lived in the 13th century, gives this interpretation of the verse in the first place where it appears:

> "The Jews are, in most cases, inferior and wretched, whether in truth or as a pretence in order to reduce the *jizya*" (the "part" or tax which was imposed on the tolerated infidels).

On the second passage he comments:

> "The Jews were in most cases poor and wretched."[3]

The Quranic phrase *"al-dhilla wa-al-maskana"* ("humiliation and wretchedness") is very frequently used in Islamic reference to the Jews. It is also to be found in Judah Halevi's philosophical work *The Khazar*:

> "The Scholar said: I see that you denounce us for poverty and wretchedness." (Part I: 113; in Hirschfeld's Arabic version, p. 62).

The "humiliation and wretchedness" of the Jews were presented by the Muslims as a proof of the falsity of the Jewish faith, while the righteousness of Islam was demonstrated by its worldly success (see Professor W.C. Smith's explanation of the Islamic attitude to success in Chapter 3).

The Opening to the Quran, which every Muslim repeats in every prayer, reads:

'Show us the straight path, the path of those whom Thou has favoured; not (the path) of those who earn Thine anger nor of those who go astray."

According to a common interpretation, though almost certainly not the original intention, it is the Jews who are meant, for they are rebuked by God. Al-Jiyār, whose approach is a Muslim one, emphasizes that the dispersion of the Jews and their continued exile is the will of God, who never wants them to have a Government (p. 4); in another passage, he says that their dispersion is an expression of the doom of wretchedness and humiliation (p. 33).

The divine verdict is described as a punishment for the evil character of the Jews. Aḥmad writes:

"This group *(fi'a)* was the lowest *(dhalīla)*, most despicable *(khasīsa)* and degraded *(mahīna)*."

He goes on to explain that this verdict was carried out in the history of the Jews, as described in the Holy Scriptures, as a long chain of tribulations and invasions by Shishak, Tiglath-Pileser, Sennacherib, Pharoah Necho, and so forth (1962, pp. 51-2).

The *jizya* tax was not only a source of income but a mark of subordination and humiliation, and payment was often accompanied with humiliating gestures, in keeping with the interpretation of the words of the Quran:

"Fight against such of those who have been given the Scripture as believe not in Allah nor the Last Day, . . . until they pay the tribute readily, being brought low." (Sura IX, Repentance, v. 29).[4]

Muhammad hoped that the Jews would accept his mission, and was ready to make gestures of goodwill towards them, but when they refused, he was furious and denounced them vehemently. The existence of the Jews did not in itself constitute a provocation and an affront to Islam, as it did to Christendom, particularly as they were recognized as subordinate and degraded. Since the image of the Jews in Islam was connected with wretchedness and humiliation, however, the establishment of the State of Israel as the result of a military victory appeared to be incompatible with the traditional view. Thus the Quranic image became a matter of importance.

The inconsistency between the political reality of sovereign independence today and the divine decree of wretchedness seemed to call for some explanation. Tabbāra explains, on the basis of another part of Sura III, The Family of 'Imrān, v. 112

"Ignominy shall be their portion wheresoever they are found save (where they grasp) a rope from Allah and a rope from men,"

that "a rope from men" means that the assistance the Jews receive from the Western countries, as a result of which the divine verdict has not been realized, and that "a rope from Allah" means that God wished the Jews to win their victory so as to draw the attention of the Arab peoples to the corruption that had spread amongst them, so that they should rectify the situation (1966, pp. 45-6).

Another element in the image of the Jews is, no doubt, connected with the attribution to them of deceit, cunning and treachery *(ghadr)*. This is associated with Muhammad's dispute with the Jewish tribes in Arabia, who, according to Muslim tradition, violated their agreements and tried to seduce the believers, as well as to deceive him. I will return to these points later.

Ancient Arabic literature, including the Quran, contains not only expressions of opprobrium and contempt for the Jews, but also laudatory passages.[5] Within the framework of the present work, it is impossible to make any scientific estimate of the relative influence of the various factors in creating the image of the Jew. Thorough and comprehensive literary and historical research would be required for the purpose.[6] Generally, however, the impression is that the image is a negative one, emphasizing their disloyalty, treachery and cunning. This is the conclusion of the orientalist Vajda, who writes that in the Ḥadīth, the traditional lore about the life of the Prophet, which was of major importance in Islamic religious consciousness, the Jews are presented "in very dark colours" ("Juifs et Musulmans selon le Hadith," in *Journal Asiatique,* II, 1937, p. 124). Among the vices ascribed to them are treachery, religious particularism, forgery of the Holy Scriptures and incitement; they are accused of cursing the Prophet by saying *"samm 'alayka"* ("Poison upon you") instead of *"Salām 'alayka"* ("Peace be upon you").

Anti-Jewish motifs are to be found in medieval Islamic religious polemics. For example, there are criticisms of the "chosen people" idea, which became of topical significance in the circumstances of the conflict, supporting the denunciations of Zionism, of Jewish separatism and of preferential treatment for the Jews. It may be assumed that, even if the conflict exists mainly on the secular, political plane, it reinforces religious antagonisms, as we have already seen in the writings of Tall and 'Alūba. But it is no accident that a 12th-century anti-Jewish book, *Ifḥām al-Yahūd* ("Silencing the Jew") was reprinted in Egypt in 1961 in the Library of the Great Jihad.[7]

The Arab-Israel conflict and Arab hostility to Israel were not the result of Islam's attitude to Judaism and its unfavourable image of the Jews, but once the conflict arose the antagonism to Israel was liable to derive ideas and emotions from these attitudes. The Islamic factor is neither a primary nor a principal one in the Arab attitude, but it is one of those that affect its character.

Since it is the conflict that has brought to the fore the anti-Jewish elements in Islam, such anti-Jewish expressions are rare in those parts of the non-Arab Muslim world where it does not exist, and insofar as they do appear, they may be assumed to be due to Arab influence. There is little feeling of involvement in the conflict in the non-Arab Muslim world, for which the rise of Israel does not constitute a provocation. Muslim anti-Jewish feeling, therefore, is particularly prominent in Arab Islam.

2. THE STUDY AND SOURCES OF ARAB ANTI-SEMITISM

It is somewhat inappropriate to use the term "anti-Semitism" for Arab hatred of the Jews. Arabs themselves find it difficult to translate, and often use such terms as *"muḍāddat al-yahūd"* ("opposition to the Jews") or *"al-haraka al-mu'adiyya lilyahūd"* ("the movement hostile to the Jews") instead. However, the word has been specifically applied to Jew-hatred, and the argument that Arab anti-Semitism is a contradiction in terms is only a play upon words. If the publication of *The Protocols of the Elders of Zion* is an anti-Semitic act in Sweden, why should the issue of an Arabic translation be regarded in any other light?

Books written in an anti-Semitic spirit by Christian (especially Catholic) Arabs appeared in the Middle East in the second half of the 19th century under French influence. Brief surveys of this phenomenon may be found in articles by Eliahu Sapir, Joshua Ben-Hanina and Sylvia Haim.[8] As is explained by Sylvia Haim and Professor Perlman, who added a brief footnote to her article, these publications were at first sporadic and did not indicate any social or national trend. The suspicion aroused by Jewish settlement in Palestine led to Arab denunciation and the resort to ideas drawn from the stock of anti-Semitic arguments. Thus a number of books displaying anti-Semitic tendencies appeared in the twenties, thirties and forties, and anti-

Semitic ideas made their appearance in the Arabic press. As Sylvia Haim states, *The Protocols of the Elders of Zion* was translated as far back as the twenties. In the thirties the German factor joined in as collaborator and supplier of ideas. The sharpening of the conflict since 1948 has been accompanied by an increase in manifestations of anti-Semitism in literature and press.

Isolated Arabic works of this type need not have caused any particular concern. Anti-Semitic books, pamphlets and manifestoes are published by individuals in many countries of the world and the Arab world cannot be expected to remain immune. It might even be argued that the Egyptian propaganda machine is so extensive and ramified that some subordinate may have interpreted the order to issue anti-Israel books as meaning that he should publish an anti-Semitic work as well. After all, we cannot assume such strict control that every word printed exactly represents the will of the authorities and is issued with their specific blessing.

The picture is changed, however, by the multiplicity of such publications in Arabic, as well as anti-Jewish statements in newspapers and broadcasts. Several of the anti-Semitic publications have the official stamp of approval, which makes them particularly important. Several official Egyptian series of books for national guidance and training include a number of anti-Semitic works. Others have been translated into Arabic from various European languages and published under official auspices. Well-known Arab leaders use anti-Semitic themes and give their patronage to anti-Semitic publications by signed introductions. For example, 'Alūba's anti-Semitic book *Palestine and the Conscience of Mankind* is prefaced by a letter from Nasser describing it as "a historic treasure" and "a political document," which "reveals truths." All this can hardly be mere chance; it appears to be a matter of deliberate policy. Arab anti-Semitism, by all indications, is a part of the official ideology; it stems not from the fringes of Arab society but from its centre. (For a list of anti-Jewish books translated into Arabic, see Bibliographical Appendix.)

Arab anti-Semitism, as we shall review it here, is of a literary character and, especially in the UAR, it appears to be guided by the Government. It can therefore be controlled, directed and halted if the authorities so desire, especially if it proves to lead to criticism abroad. The study of these manifestations and the publication of the results may perhaps have an influence on them; indeed, publicity and criticism in various foreign circles may already have had some moderating influence.

Arab anti-Semitism is the outcome of political circumstances. As has been emphasized in connection with the psychological and sociological factors involved, it is not a cause of the conflict but a product of it. The Arabs did not oppose Jewish settlement for anti-Semitic motives; their opposition aroused anti-Semitic emotions among them. However, once the conflict exists and anti-Semitism has been created, it becomes one of the factors that give the conflict its character, and it must therefore be included in a study of this nature.

a) STUDY OF ARAB ANTI-SEMITISM

The phenomenon has been little studied in Israel. Possibly Israelis were not particularly sensitive to it, perhaps owing to some slight feeling that it might be condoned, as the Arabs have some reason to hate us. The linguistic difficulty certainly presented an obstacle, for some experts in the study of anti-Semitism do not know Arabic, and those who know Arabic may have felt reluctant to admit its existence. There may also have been a psychological difficulty. A study in depth of Arab anti-Semitism might have revealed the profundity and gravity of the conflict, which Israelis prefer to regard as superficial and transitory. Apparently, a defence mechanism of selective perception was operative; it was more comfortable to paint idyllic pictures of the Golden Age of Jewry in Spain, or to regard the Arabs as merely wayward disciples of Europeans in general and the Germans in particular, laying all the blame on their teachers. Anyone who is anxious for peace of mind tends to repress factors which are liable to cause concern.

Since Arab anti-Semitism exists at this stage mainly on the literary and political plane, and not as a matter of popular sentiment, its study is relatively simple. In the study of anti-Semitism as a social phenomenon, it is not sufficient to rely on the publication of some article or pamphlet, but it has to be demonstrated that the publication represents opinions current among the people or has had an influence on them. The importance of Arab anti-Semitism, however, lies not in the claim that it represents popular tendencies, but in the fact that it reflects views and tendencies among the political and cultural leadership. It is designed to influence the populace, but it is not derived directly from their concepts, although it exploits images and fears that are to be found among them. On this assumption, the study of Arab anti-Semitism is concerned with mass communications media. We cannot conduct scientific research, through field surveys and questionnaires, on the extent to which these opinions are absorbed by the people, but their importance is not affected even if we adopt the optimistic view that they are not accepted. They are evidence of the Arabs' antagonism to Israel and their readiness to resort to any defamatory arguments, even anti-Semitic ones, against their rival.

b) ORIGINALITY AND ORIGINS

The ideas contained in Arab anti-Semitic literature are not new, and most of them are, no doubt, a repetition, a kind of delayed echo, of ideas expressed years ago in Europe, America and even the Middle East. Such ideas have been expressed in many parts of the world in various forms and with endless repetitions, so that it is difficult to determine whether any particular anti-Semitic idea to be found among the Arabs is derived from any specific author or group. So long as direct influence has not been demonstrated, it is always possible that other influences have been active. Even the quotation of the source is not always conclusive proof of the origin of the idea; it might have come from elsewhere and the citation of the source in question be merely a matter of convenience and opportunity. It is also to be remembered that anti-Semitic doctrines are easily absorbed even by the self-taught, and the art of anti-Semitic commentary can easily be developed on a do-it-yourself basis. On the other hand, although it is difficult to evolve original ideas in this field, it should not be assumed that the Arabs are only copyists. Ideas that have appeared long ago may be new to those who express them now, and what others may regard as a repetition of the familiar may be novel and original to the Arabs themselves.

I suspect that the Israeli habit of emphasizing foreign influences as responsible for Arab anti-Semitism, as if the Arabs are unable to be original, underestimates them. There is no reason to think that this is so. Apparently, Professor Berger was right when he wrote:

> "Since the creation of the State of Israel, anti-Semitic propaganda has not needed to be imported from Europe; 'Westernization' has made the Near East self-sufficient in this as in some other kinds of production." (*The Arab World*, p. 262).

The Arabs have no doubt been influenced by ready-made ideas of this type from abroad and utilized them, but the Islamic colouration which they have given their anti-Semitism by associating it with the dispute between

Muhammad and the Jews, and the introduction of elements connected with the Arab-Israeli conflict, constitute a local addition.

Furthermore, the perusal of Arab denunciations of the Jews and the opprobrious epithets they shower on them is bound to arouse echoes from ancient Arabic literature. The characteristics ascribed to the Jews recall numerous terms from the Quran, even from Jahilite poetry. The flood of abuse we find in works by Abdallah Tall, Darwaza, 'Alūba, al-Ramādī and Aḥmad is one of Islamic origin; they employ linguistic formulae which embody concepts, ideas and stereotypes drawn from that culture.

In addition, because Arab anti-Semitism, as we shall see below, declares that what is evil in the Jews is their character as moulded by their Holy Scriptures, considerable attention is paid to Islamic Bible criticism, which regards the Scriptures in their present form as fabricated by the Jews. Denunciations of the Jews drawn from the interpretation of the Bible become of topical significance. In order to bespatter the Jews and their Scriptures, the Arabs have no need to draw on foreign sources.

I have been unable to determine how many of the writers who denounce the Jews have read or been influenced by a medieval work: *Kitāb al-Fasl fī al-Milal wa-al-Ahwā' wa-al Niḥal,* by Ibn Ḥazm (994-1064).[9] The author describes the Bible as full of falsehoods, inconsistencies and deplorable anthropomorphisms; in particular, he condemns it as a shocking collection of immoral acts, such as the story of Lot's daughters; Sarah lying to God; Abraham refusing to believe God's word, feeding the angels as if they were flesh and blood, and marrying his sister; Issac stealing; Jacob marrying Leah by mistake; Reuben lying with his father's wife and Judah with his son's wife; Moses born of a marriage between Amram and his aunt; David and the wife of Uriah, Absalom lying with his father's wives, and so on. He accuses the Jews of odious qualities which are frequently brought out in the modern literature of the conflict. There is no other people as despicable as the Jews; they are cunning, cowardly, deceitful, quarrelsome and the like. (See, for instance, pp. 138 and 202, Vol. I, Cairo edition, A.H. 1317.)

While the Arabs can boast of their own contribution to the defamation of the Jews, it may appear that the idea of a world Jewish conspiracy is derived from late foreign influence. According to the Islamic image, the Jews are religiously and morally degraded, and wretched in status; the idea that they have a secret organization, which endows them with threatening power, seems to be drawn from foreign sources, while the readiness to accept it is due to Jewish achievements during the Mandatory period and Israel's military exploits. The despicable has become dangerous. The idea of the secret organization is the central theme of *The Protocols of the Elders of Zion,* which is, no doubt, the reason for the acceptance of the book and its dissemination in Arabic.

The Arabs do not deny the foreign influences in anti-Semitism. On the contrary, they are generous with citations from authorities, implying that the evil in the Jews has been revealed not only to them but also to others. The temptation to try to conceal influences in order to appear original is weaker than the desire to reinforce the argument, as is shown by the use of quotations from Alfred Rosenberg and Hitler.

Quotations and references from English and French are much more numerous than those from German[10]—mainly, it appears, simply because the Arabs are more familiar with the first two languages. It would seem far-fetched to argue that they do not want to disclose Nazi influence, for German sources are referred to without concealment. If the destruction of the Jews by the Nazis is sometimes described with understanding and sympathy, there seems no reason why they should hesitate to mention German sources. It might be noted, for example, that Dr. Naṣr, in his book *Zionism in International Affairs,* cites Hitler's *Mein Kampf* as incontrovertible evidence of the authenticity of *The Protocols of the Elders of Zion* (pp. 88-95). Nor is this an isolated example: there are quotations from Hitler, for instance, in Ṭabbāra's *The Jews in the Quran,* 1966, pp. 35, 39 50, etc. There is an extensive anti-Semitic literature in English and French, and anyone who is looking for such ideas can find enough in these languages, without taking the trouble to learn German.

In regard to the "ecology" of Arab anti-Semitism it should be noted that anti-Jewish themes are generally more frequent the further down we go on the scale of political respectability. In the UAR, for example, there are many anti-Israel and anti-Zionist motifs, but few anti-Jewish expressions are to be found in Nasser's speeches (though he did use the phrase "commercial methods of a Cohen," May 7, 1969). In the leading Egyptian newspaper *al-Ahrām,* anti-Jewish motifs have been very rare in recent years, but they did appear in *al-Jumhūriyya,* which was the organ of the officers' junta after the 1952 revolution, while it was edited by Nāṣir al-Dīn al-Nashāshībī.

I believe that there are more anti-Semitic references in the UAR's weeklies than in the dailies, while in Jordan they are also to be found in the daily press. As for the radio, there is more crude anti-Semitism in the Voice of the Arabs and less in the Cairo stations. For example, the director of the Voice of the Arabs, Ahmad Sa'īd, made the following points in the programme called "Ḥattā Lā Nansa" ("Lest We Forget") on March 9 and 10, 1961: the Talmud permits the Jews to commit crimes against non-Jews; the Jews will collect so much treasure in preparation for the coming of the Messiah that they will need three hundred asses to carry the keys. The song *"Yā Filasṭīn Ji'nāki"* ("O Palestine, We have Come to Thee"), which was frequently broadcast over this station, contained the refrain: "Jesus revealed to us who they are, Muhammad warned us against them, God cursed them and destroyed their land." (Sa'id was dismissed after the Six-Day War.) Such references are heard with considerable, though fluctuating, frequency. (There was a great increase in the number of anti-Semitic statements immediately before and after the Six-Day War.)

3. THE PROTOCOLS OF THE ELDERS OF ZION

In Arab anti-Israel literature, wide use is made of *The Protocols of the Elders of Zion,* which played an important part in the creation of Nazi anti-Semitism and has been of equal significance in Arab anti-Semitism. The book has been translated a number of times into Arabic, from English, French and perhaps also from German. Nine complete translations are listed in Bibliographical Appendix 2. Numerous Arabic books quote or summarize the Protocols, or use them as authorities.

The Protocols of the Elders of Zion is an anti-Semitic fabrication first circulated in Western Europe in 1919 by Russian emigrés. It purported to consist of the minutes of secret deliberations by "the leaders of World Jewry" on a plan to undermine all existing regimes, corrupt Christian civilization and establish a world Jewish empire which would exploit and enslave the whole of mankind. The work was first published by a Russian priest called Sergei Nulus in 1903.

The Protocols were translated into numerous languages and published in many editions, but in 1921 Philip Graves, Constantinople correspondent of the London *Times,* proved that they were a plagiary from a book called *Dialogue aux enfers entre Machiavel et Montesquieu,* published in Brussels in 1865 by a non-Jewish journalist, Maurice Joly, as a satire on Napoleon III.

Despite this demonstration that they were a clumsy forgery, they were widely exploited by anti-Semites, particularly in Germany. In fact, they have exercised a tragic influence on the destiny of the Jews in Europe, perhaps more than any other work. In his book, *Warrant for Genocide, The Myth of the Jewish World Conspiracy and the Protocols of Zion* (London, Eyre and Spottiswoode, 1967), Professor Norman Cohn explains that the belief in the genuineness of the Protocols was one of the main factors in the Nazi attitude to the Jews and the decision to exterminate them: if the Jews were really planning the establishment of a world tyranny and their secret powers were so enormous, the only solution was their destruction.

For the Arabs, the Protocols have been a veritable treasure. They contain, in a concise, tangible and allegedly documented form, a comprehensive account of all the despicable qualities ascribed to the Jews by the anti-Semites, and confirmation of the existence of a world Jewish conspiracy which constitutes a pseudo-historical explanation of world events. Its tales of plots and stratagems are piquant and thrilling. The story fits in with the idea of a "hidden hand," which is frequently developed in part of the Arab literature about the conflict, as well as with the traditional Arab conception of the cunning, treachery and deviousness of the Jews. It is also convenient that the description comes from an allegedly Jewish source.

The Arabs found the Protocols a useful support for their denunciation of Zionism. In Palestine they quoted them in their arguments against Jewish settlement. They provided them with an explanation, and some consolation, for their defeats: they need not feel humiliated, because they had to confront, not only the Jews of Palestine, but a satanic organization of worldwide scope: "Israel and all that stands behind her"—a phrase very commonly used. The war against Zionism becomes a more momentous matter; it is not a narrow nationalistic struggle, but part of the eternal clash between good and evil. The importance of the struggle is also enhanced by the fact that Israel is regarded as the rallying point of the "Elders of Zion," the "focus of evil" *(bu'rat al-sharr)* and the base from which the Jews will continue their subversive efforts to win world domination. The explanation of the development of the conflict is also simplified by the personification of the factors operating in history. The Protocols are both an explanation and an illustration of the way "World Zionism" operates, closing the circle between "World Zionism" and "World Jewry." In *The Danger of World Jewry to Islam and Christianity,* Tall presents the Protocols as having the same authority for the Jews as their religious books, like the Bible and the Talmud, making up one complete whole which has moulded the Jewish character (p. 171—the same idea is repeated by, for example, Quṣrī, p. 34, and others). Nuwayhiḍ explains certain features of the Bible as an expression of the spirit of the Protocols, although the latter were written at the end of the 19th century. When, for instance, Esther did not reveal her Jewish origins, she was following the instructions of the Protocols, which thus become a criterion for the interpretation of the Jewish Scriptures.

A complete edition, entitled *The Protocol* (sic) *of the Elders of Zion,* was officially issued on April 13, 1956, in Cairo in the "Political Books" series published by the UAR Information Services. No translator's name is given. The series is described on the cover as "a hundred-per-cent Egyptian series, which examines the international, political, social and economic problems of the hour from an Egyptian point of view." In the introduction, signed "The Committee on Policy Books," the work is presented to the Arab public as a "most important secret Zionist document." In a later passage, the Committee says:

> "We believe that the Arab reader should examine the Zionist Protocol and read it attentively, so that he should know the scope of the purposes of World Zionism, whose accursed spore Israeli imperialism has sown in our country Palestine."

In a concise list of literature published on behalf of the Ministry of Education between 1955 and 1960 (No. 5, 844 in the list), it is expressly stated that the book has been published by the Ministry of National Guidance.

The text is preceded by an ostensibly scientific introduction with quotations and proofs, dealing with the source of the documents and the question of their authenticity. It contains a detailed account of their history, declaring:

> "Latest investigations show that this plan was not framed, as many believe, at the Zionist Congress which assembled at Basle in 1897, and also that it was not written by Zionists and has no connection with Zionists."

Citing the 1934 Berne Trial, at which Swiss Nazis who had disseminated the Protocols were sued by a group of Swiss Jews for libel, the introduction rejects allegations that the Protocols were stolen from the records of the Basle Congress. It also quotes an article by Theodor Fritz, whom it describes as "the great teacher of anti-Semitism," from the Nazi periodical *Der Hammer,* of April 1925, declaring that they had no connection with the Zionist Organization and that the expression "Elders of Zion" should be understood as referring to the spiritual leaders of the Jews.

The introduction admits that Philip Graves, who proved that the Protocols were a plagiary from a dialogue written as a satire on Napoleon III, may have been right. Nevertheless, it continues, this does not show that they were not a true Jewish document:

"What is important, as the *Times* wrote, is to know whether a Jew wrote the Protocols for Jews. It is of no importance whether the author copied them from another book in deciding the question of whether this is really a Jewish plan, or on the contrary, an anti-Jewish invention, for the Jews have not proved this assumption at all, and all the efforts to blame Rashkovsky or the Russian Police have been a dismal failure." (p. 15—the reference is to statements made at the Berne Trial).

A detailed account is given of the Berne Trial, the subsequent appeal, the "intrigues" of the Jews to "twist" the trial to their own ends, and the conclusive evidence of the book's authenticity given by Fleischhauer, a Nazi Colonel described as an "expert" on Jewish affairs, leading to the conclusion that the Jews failed to disprove the authenticity of the documents. The final proof is a pragmatic one, namely, that the actions of the Jews are in accordance with the statements made in the Protocols. As "conclusive evidence" that this is the case, the introduction quotes from the summing up of Alfred Rosenberg, the Nazi race expert, at the end of his book on the subject (the quotation is re-translated here from the Arabic):

"The researches and documents mentioned leave no room for the slightest doubt as to the conformance of the ideas of the Protocols with those of other Jewish books and their present policy, which is completely identical in its details with the lines laid down in the Protocols."

It is also stated that the Protocols are consonant with the words of the Prophets and the principles of the Talmud and the Cabbalists (similar statements are made by Darwaza, p. 559). The introduction concludes:

"In these circumstances, an investigation of the identity of the author of the Protocols is of secondary importance, for the text of the documents is sufficient to prove that it is beyond the power of *any Aryan mind* in the world to draw up such a programme" (my italics).

The numerous quotations from German, the references to Nazis, especially Alfred Rosenberg, and to the Nazi news agency Welt Dienst, of

Erfurt, and the final reference to an "Aryan mind" indicate that this introduction was written by a German or was translated from the German—which is perhaps the reason why it was not signed.

The argument that the Protocols are the product not of Zionism but of Jewry as a whole also represents a Nazi line, for the Arabs' tendency to concentrate the attack on Zionism, as the source of the evil, would lead them to insist on their Zionist provenance. In most Arab books, indeed, it is emphasized that they are minutes of secret deliberations at the Zionist Congress, and even of a secret speech by Herzl. (See 'Alūba, pp. 85ff; Tall, p. 164; Rushdī, p. 43; Tūnisī, p. 32; Ibrāhīm al-Ḥilū, p. 16; Ḥarb, 1947, p. 45; Wākid, pp. 17-18; Shamīs, 1957, p. 31; 'Iṣmat, p. 69, Yamīn, p. 3; Aḥmad, p. 4; Quṣrī, who says that they were published in 1897, p. 38; al-Hindāwī, p. 35.)

Nuwayhiḍ is an exception: he ascribes them to the Zionist philosopher Ahad Ha'am, whose post with the Wissotzsky tea firm, he says, was only a cover (Part I, pp. 37-54). Dr. Naṣr, in *Zionism in International Affairs,* 1956, bases the authenticity of the Protocols on their agreement with world political conditions. Quoting an article in the London *Morning Post,* published in February 1920, he writes:

> "Anyone who reads the Protocols and compares them with the events of modern history will realize that the verdict of the *Morning Post,* that the contents of the Protocols are drawn from the true influence of Jews upon European policy, is a correct one. Their essence is that the Jews of the world made up their minds long ago to establish their rule above any other, and that they do not consist of minorities scattered in various countries in East and West, but a single whole, despite the geographical distances, for there are ties between their communities founded on cunning organization and planning. Furthermore, their dispersal is a source of power which assures them of the aid of the various Governments." (p. 82).

As conclusive proof, he goes on to give extensive quotations from Hitler's *Mein Kampf,* which confirm the extent of Jewish influence in the world and show how closely they have approached the achievement of their aims (pp. 89-95).

Quṣrī, on the other hand, presents evidence similar to that mentioned in the introduction to the Arabic edition of the Protocols, including the Berne Trial, the "expertise" of Fleischhauer and the quotation from Rosenberg (*The Palestine War,* Part I, p. 39).

Another proof of the genuineness of the Protocols is the alleged fact that every time they are printed all copies immediately disappear from the market ('Aqqād, 1956, p. 34; Aḥmad, p. 4); World Zionism immediately buys them up to prevent their being read, because it regards them as a dangerous revelation of its plots.[12] 'Aqqād, indeed, discusses the difficulty involved in the belief that the Elders of Zion have been holding secret meetings for many years without the truth being disclosed. This implies strict discipline among the Jews, which contradicts his fundamental conception, which he expounds at great length, that the Jews are a quarrelsome people, constantly squabbling with each other and their leaders. He therefore leaves the question of the authenticity of the book open.

Arab writers frequently refer to a deliberate effort to suppress the Protocols, 'Alūba and 'Iṣmat, for instance, say that Herzl issued a special order on the subject, especially after it was known that they had been stolen by a woman (p. 69). Rushdī quotes a statement by Douglas Reed that Zionist influence has prevented the Protocols being republished since 1921 (p. 43). Tūnisī (p. 44) believes that anyone who translates or publishes the Protocols will be murdered, or at least die by unnatural means (which, of course, explains his boasting of his courage in defying this danger). 'Aqqād and Tūnisī emphasize how difficult it is to get a copy, the latter adding that *Rūz al-Yūsuf* (according to No. 1211, August 28, 1961) paid 500 Egyptian pounds for one.

It is difficult to estimate to what extent the slanders contained in the Protocols have been absorbed by Arab public opinion, and whether the authors who use them believe their own statements. The frequency with which the Protocols are mentioned is not conclusive proof, but the instinctive feeling of Jews that their absurdity would prevent any sensible man taking them seriously is no doubt over-optimistic. It is true that the traditional Islamic and Arabic image of the Jews as a weak, degraded group, which cannot be dangerous, is incompatible with the Protocols, but the image has certainly been altered by the establisment of independent Israel and the struggle against it. Moreover, the idea of Jewish cunning and the quest for a "hidden hand" are liable to reinforce the credibility of the Protocols. In any case, even if we assume that the story does not win much credence in the Arab world, the importance of the Protocols in the context of Arab anti-Semitism lies in the fact that governmental authorities make use of them and back their dissemination, whether they believe them or not.

According to *al-Jumhūriyya* (Iraq) of April 18, 1967, President Aref expressed his appreciation to the historian 'Ajjāj Nuwayhiḍ for his book on the Protocols (Beirut 1967) in a letter signed by Dr. Badī' Sharīf, head of the Presidential Bureau. It was also stated that the Palestine Liberation Organization had decided to buy a thousand copies—and the book was indeed found in its offices in Gaza and Jerusalem.

Nasser himself had no compunction about using the Protocols in an interview with R.K. Karanjia, editor of the Indian English-Language paper *Blitz,* to whom he said:

> "I wonder if you have read a book 'Protocols of the Learned Elders of Zion.' It is very important that you should read it. I will give you a copy. It proves beyond the shadow of a doubt that three hundred Zionists, each of whom knows all the others, govern the fate of the European Continent . . . and that they elect their successors from their entourage." (Karanjia, *Arab Dawn,* 1958, Bombay edition).

It is noteworthy that the appendix containing this interview was omitted in the edition of the book printed in England, but a report of the talk, mentioning the Protocols, was printed in *al-Ahrām,* September 29, 1958, and broadcast on the same day by Cairo Radio. The passage is also given in the Egyptian official edition, in English, of *President Gamāl 'Abd al-Nasser's Speeches and Press-Interviews during the Year 1958,* Part II, p. 30.

Nasser's statement is an echo of the words of the German statesman Walter Rathenau, who once wrote: "Three hundred men, each of them knowing the others, direct the economy of the Continent and select their successors from among themselves." This denunciation of the controllers of the capitalist economy was twisted into a reference to the Elders of Zion, of whom Rathenau was alleged to be one; German anti-Semites (including Ludendorff and Rosenberg) often quoted it as proof of the existence of the conspiracy. Professor Norman Cohn, who gives these details (*Warrant for Genocide,* pp. 144ff), quotes from the proceedings at the trial of Rathenau's murderer to show that belief in the Protocols was one of the factors that led to his assassination. In this quotation, therefore, Nasser reveals the influence of German anti-Semitism. Nasser's brother, by the way, published a new edition of the Protocols in 1967.

While I have no evidence that Nasser himself continued to exploit the Protocols in official publications, the Government of the UAR used and quoted them, not only in Arabic, but also in other languages. An extract from the Protocols is given in a propaganda pamphlet in English, *Israel, the Enemy of Africa,* which was distributed in Africa at the beginning of 1965 on behalf of the UAR Information Department.

Arabs regard them as an instrument of political propaganda, and it has been expressly stated that the Arab League was taking steps to have them published in several languages. The Jordanian paper *al-Jihād* reported that the Arab League Committee for the Palestine Organizations would consider the publication of the Protocols in all languages in order to inform world public opinion of the truth about world Zionist intrigues and aims (December 10, 1963 and January 23, 1964). *Al-Akhbār* stated on August 23, 1967 that the Supreme Council for Islamic Affairs had decided to publish a book containing the Protocols in English and French translation.

Ḥasan Ṣabrī al-Khūlī, Nasser's personal representative, said in a lecture published by the Supreme Command of the UAR Armed Forces:

> "One of the most outstanding Zionist works on general political planning is *The Protocols of the Elders of Zion,* which clearly lays down the way to the achievement of their aim, Jewish domination of the world, by the corruption of virtue, economic profiteering, the dissemination of vice, the destruction of religion and, finally, the use of murder as a means of reaching their destination." (*The Palestine Problem,* pp. 5-6).

The Protocols have also been introduced into the school curriculum. For example, a book called *The Palestine Problem,* by the Jordanian Minister of Education, Dhūqān al-Hindāwī, published in 1964 by his ministry for pupils of the third form in the literary trend of the secondary schools, contains eight pages (pp. 35ff) of quotations from the Protocols. These are given as evidence of the vileness of Zionism and are linked with the Bible. It is explained that these things actually took place. For instance, the Protocols call for the use of espionage, and Moses sent spies into Canaan, while the imperialistic espionage services use Jewish spies, like Beria (head of the Soviet secret police under Stalin), who is described as a "Zionist Intelligence octopus" *(akhṭabūṭ).* The Protocols call for the use of corruption and immorality to achieve the aim, and the Jewish connection with immorality is proved by history, for the spies sent by Joshua "slept" with Rahab the harlot.

Another Biblical association is to be found in Nuwayhiḍ's book *The Protocols of the Elders of Zion,* 1967. At the beginning of the second volume, he discusses the story of Haman, who, according to the Book of Esther, planned to exterminate the Jews. Following ancient commentators, he traces Haman's descent to Agag, the Amalekite king who was slain by the prophet Samuel, and explains that the Amalekites were Arabs, thus giving the Arab-Israel dispute a dimension of great historical depth. Nuwayhiḍ says that Haman's actions were a reaction against the Jewish aim of liquidating Amalek, and regards his plan as right and praiseworthy.

In the light of the history of the Protocols, the connection between them and the attempt to annihilate the Jews,[13] as pointed out by Professor Cohn in the work cited above, and the extraordinary array of Arab publications on the subject, the question arises: Did the Arabs simply seize on the Protocols as a valuable asset in their propaganda against Israel, or did they, perhaps, feel in their heart of hearts that the Protocols fitted in with the Arab objective of liquidating and destroying the Jewish State?

4. ZIONISM, JEWISH COMMUNISTS AND FREEMASONS

a) ZIONISM AND COMMUNISM

As far back as the Mandatory period, the Palestinian Arabs declared that the Jews, through their licentious way of life and socialist sympathies, were allied with Communism and might introduce Communist and atheist ideas to the Middle East. At the time, the Arabs still regarded Socialism and Communism as terms of abuse.

Allegations of ties between Communism and the Jews and Zionists in Egypt may be found in Nasser's speeches during the early days of his rule. In the middle of 1954, for example, there was labour unrest in the country (several workers were hanged in Kafr al-Dawar). Nasser accused the Communists of organizing the disturbances and denounced Communism for its ties with Zionism. In his speech to the workers (on April 19, 1954, I.L., II/297), he declared that Zionism was working for the Communist organizations, which, he alleged, were financed by the Zionist Kūriyāl (a wealthy Egyptian Jew with Communist sympathies). It is true that Jews played some part in the Communist movement in Egypt at the time.

Nasser returned to the idea after the spy trials of 1954, declaring that Communism had proved to be working together with Zionism in Egypt with the common aim of producing anarchy (on August 21, 1954, I.L., III/482), or that the two movements were trying to prevent agreement with the British over the Suez Canal (press interview on September 13, 1954, I.L., III/552).

A different type of allegation is the identification of Jews and Zionism with Communism under the influence of anti-Semitic literature, like *The Protocols of the Elders of Zion.* Al-Tūnisī gives long accounts of these ties. At the beginning of his book he copies from the English version of the Protocols the "coat-of-arms" of Bolshevik Jewry, surrounded by the "symbolic serpent" according to the European anti-Semitic tradition.

The same approach may be found in two anti-Semitic works, one Christian and one Muslim. Ḥarb deals at length in *The Conspiracy of the Jews Against Christianity* (Beirut, 1947) with the Jewish-Communist plot, citing Heine, Marx, Hess, Lassalle, Leon Blum and Disraeli as evidence of the Jewish spirit among the revolutionaries (p. 26). He devotes much space to alleged atrocities in Russia, for which he blames Jewish women. 'Iṣmat, who deals with this subject in *Zionism and Masonry* (Alexandria, 1950), regards the Bolshevik revolution as the work of Zionism (p. 76).

It is no accident that several books abusing Communism for its closeness to Zionism and *vice-versa* appeared in 1959, a year in which UAR-USSR relations deteriorated. Some of the authors harp on the idea that the difference between Communism and Zionism lies in the fact that Zionism is founded on the Jewish faith while Communism wants to be a religion on its own. The affinity between the two movements is explained on the grounds that both are subversive and corrupt in their methods and aspirations. Communism is said to have been influenced by the Jews, who played an important part in its leadership and bequeathed to it the odious traits inherent in the Jewish character. The allegation that the Protocols are both a Jewish and a Zionist document is repeated by several authors.

In Māhir Nasīm's *Communism and Zionism,* No. 8 in the Kutub Dawliyya ("State Books") series, the author explains that there is a great similarity between Communism and the ideas outlined in the Protocols (in his verbatim quotations the translation is identical with that of the Political Books edition). They are described as both a Zionist document and a blueprint for Communist operations.

The author declares that he has no intention, of course, of attacking the Jewish religion; he only wants to draw attention to the dangers inherent in Communism and Zionism.

The same ideas are repeated in Ibrāhīm al-Ḥilū's *Communism and Zionism are Twins* (published in Damascus), which says that the bond between the two is an ancient one, since both Karl Marx and Herzl were influenced by Moses Hess. The author regards the two movements as similar in their aspiration to world domination and their belief that the end justifies the means: both aim at controlling public opinion, destroying liberty and undermining the economy; both are destructive movements, employing techniques of deceit, corruption and infiltration.

Wākid's *Israel, the Den of Imperialism,* published in 1959 in the Political Books series, describes how Palestine fell into the hands of the "destructive trinity" (*al-thālūth al-haddām*): imperialism, Zionism and Communism. Communist thought, the author says, "was crystallized in the Jewish crucible" (p. 19). Like other works of the kind, it lists Jewish "communists" like Brandeis, Laski, Disraeli and Frankfurter (p. 19). A chapter entitled "Communist Principles = Zionist Principles" aims at demonstrating the identity of the ideologies: both are atheistic, preach immorality and chaos, and aim at world domination (pp. 22ff).

The newspapers repeatedly cited Soviet support for the UN partition plan and the establishment of Israel, and the supply of arms to Israel by Czechoslovakia in the 1948 war, as evidence of the historic ties between Israel and the Soviet Union. For example:

> "What is the role of international Communism in the disaster of the establishment of Israel? Karl Marx was a Jew. This is a fact. The day will come when historians will prove that Communism is nothing but a Zionist plot which aims at unifying the world in order to dominate it. It is sufficient to point out that it was the Jews who financed the Communist movements in all the countries of the Middle East. Russia and her satellites worked against the rights of the Arabs all along the line during the deliberations at the UN. When a truce was declared in 1948, it was Czechoslovakia that supplied the Jews with heavy arms and planes. The aim of international Communism in this plot was to compete with Western capitalism in the new State and to create a base for Communism in the Middle East." (*al-Taḥrīr,* Egypt, April 12, 1959).

Since the improvement in relations between the UAR and the Soviet Union, references to the Communist-Zionist plot have been rare. The images of the USSR and of Communism in the Arab world have been improved, and it is unlikely that Arab public opinion still suspects the existence of ties between Communism and Zionism, although the idea recurs from time to time. It is particularly emphasized in works of a religious Islamic character, like 'Alūba's *Palestine and the Conscience of Mankind* (Cairo, 1964). The author's bitter antagonism to Communism is inspired by his Islamic creed and recalls the trends that were current in the twenties and thirties. (These views do not prevent Nasser praising the book in a letter to the author.) 'Alūba harps on the following ideas: Jews and Zionism had a major influence on the 1917 revolution (p. 78); Lenin's wife was a Jewess, and Kerensky was a Jew (p. 111); the Soviet Union supported the establishment of Israel, to the advantage of Communism; in the end, the true character of Israel will be revealed, and it will become a Communist State, a part of the Soviet Union, a focal point for the Communist struggle against the West (p. 173).

Somewhat similar arguments are advanced by Tall, Tūnisī, 'Aqqād and Darwaza.

b) FREEMASONRY

Allegations that the Freemasons have ties with secret subversive movements and the Jews are made in several books. The idea, which is also to be found in the Protocols, was, apparently, introduced by Arabic-writing Catholics, but orthodox Muslim authors have also found it useful and made extensive use of it. An article by Joshua Ben Hanina in *Ha'aretz,* Tel Aviv, described a book called *History of the Secret Associations and Subversive Movements,* by Abdallah 'Inan, editor of the Egyptian paper *al-Siyāsa,* published in the twenties by al-Hilāl, which states, on the basis of French writings, that it was the Jews who stood behind the movement of secret associations against Islam and Christianity, and that Freemasonry is founded on the Cabbala (*Ha'aretz,* December 19, 1926).

Books devoted specifically to this subject include: Yūsuf al-Ḥājj, *For the Sake of the Truth, Solomon's Temple or the Jewish National Home* (Beirut, 1934); 'Iṣmāt, *Zionism and Freemasonry* (Beirut, 1949, Alexandria, 1950).[14]

'Alūba deals with the subject at length. Masonry, which he connects with Communism, and the Rotary movement are Jewish organizations which aim at maintaining the domination of the Jews and undermining the religious faith of all the nations. Only Jews, he says, can rise to the highest degree of Masonry. The aim of these organizations is to infiltrate various bodies for purposes of espionage. The Vatican realized the danger and banned them (pp. 77ff). It was Masonry and Jewry that disseminated Communism. The Jews have two faces: capitalist in the West and Communist in the East. This duplicity (another example of Jewish cunning) was prescribed by the decisions of the Elders of Zion (p. 111). 'Alūba calls for the prohibition of Masonry and Rotary in Arab countries (p. 189). Tall, who devotes a complete chapter to the subject (p. 143ff), using the writings of Arnold Leese, the English author, as his authority, also brings in other "subversive" movements like the B'nai B'rith.

The belief in these satanic secret organizations gains topical significance from the special role attributed by the Arabs to the Jewish underground fighting movements in the establishment of Israel, which is often referred to as "the gangster State" or "the gangster Government." Wākid's *Israel in the Balance* has a chapter on this subject, explaining, as a matter of social psychology, that the Jews have a tendency towards secret organizations—which is the reason why they immured themselves in ghettos. This was not a response to the pressure of the environment, but a voluntary expression of deep-lying Jewish tendencies. The ghetto was fertile soil for the growth of underground terrorist organizations and the study of secret mystic lore ("secret hellish studies," as he puts it). Zionism, too, was born in this atmosphere of secrecy; hence the underground movements that preceded the State and the use of codes and enigmatic terms. Apparently, the author found a satanic significance in the Israeli habit of using initials as words, e.g. *Tzahal* for *Tzeva Hagana Le-Yisrael, Palmach* for *Plugot Mahatz* or *Etzel* for *Irgun Tzevai'i Leumi.* It seems that Arabs at first found it difficult to decipher such words, which seemed to them to be wrapped in mystery. Wākid explains that even though Israel has a State and a Government today, each party maintains its own secret organization. On the establishment of the State, an order was given for the abolition of these movements, but Israel still swarms with them, and they number no less than thirty-three (*Israel in the Balance,* pp. 29-34).

5. THE VILENESS OF THE JEWS

a) THE FUNDAMENTAL EVIL

Arab writers try to answer two basic questions: What is the source of the vile and evil characteristics of the Jews? How has this evil been preserved?

The evil nature of the Jews is portrayed as something profound and basic. Since the Arabs are also regarded as Semites, they can hardly ascribe the root of the evil to the Semitic origin of the Jews, especially since some Arabs (as noted in the previous chapter) deny that the Jews are Semites. The evil in the Jews is ascribed, not to race or blood, but to their spiritual character and their religion. This is the commonest explanation in Arab anti-Semitic literature. The evil existed even before the composition of the Jewish Scriptures; the evil Jews created in their own image a faith and a collection of sacred writings which have preserved and enhanced their evil characteristics. Thus there is at least a racialist kernel in the idea that the culture of the Jews is the root of the trouble. A kind of vicious circle is created: the evil Jews created an evil religion, and so long as they remain devoted to it they will continue to be evil.

Despite the Arabs' repeated insistence that they respect religion and have nothing against Judaism, but are only fighting Zionism, their anti-Semitism traduces the spirit of the Jews as embodied in their religion. The Jews, they insist, are not a nation; their nature is expressed by their religion, which is also the source of their vileness because they have deliberately distorted the word of God that was revealed to them. This denunciation of Judaism is tied up with the tension between Muhammad and the Jews of Arabia and the Islamic denigration of the Jewish faith. Darwaza declares:

> "The Jewish religion is the distinctive characteristic of the groups which adhere to this religion and which, from the point of view of blood, belong to various races, like other religions which contain groups of various origins and races. The books of the Old Testament—which the Jews study together with the Talmud and regard as the source of religious, juridical and historical authority—have influenced them and moulded their abnormal *(shādhdh)* nature, for which the Children of Israel have been distinguished." (Vol. III, p. 574).

Tall explains the ties between Zionism and Judaism as a religion:

> "I connect Zionism as a political movement with the Jewish religion, which is based on two permanent foundations: the Bible and the Talmud. I regard *The Protocols of the Elders of Zion* as the third element in the foundations of the Jewish faith, to which the Jews are devoted. This [faith] is not [expressed] in the words of the heavenly mission which came down to Moses, may he rest in peace, [because] afterwards the Jews distorted them, remoulded them according to their own desires, and wrote them down ten centuries after the mission of Moses. A critical and honest examination of the provisions of this faith will show that the criminal character of the Jews is not accidental or due to the persecutions that were their lot for many centuries, but is the outcome of the Jewish faith itself . . . —this religion that sowed in their souls the seeds of crime, hostility *(ḥaqd),* corruption *(fasād),* vileness *(radhīla),* barbarity *(waḥshiyya),* immorality *(inḥilāl),* fanaticism *(ta'aṣṣub),* arrogance *(ghurūr)* and insolence *(waqāḥa).*" (pp. 170-1).

Hence, they acquired the barbaric and savage *(hamajiyya)* character which is the fundamental nature of the Jews. (Tall also gives a similar list on pp. 274-5.)

To demonstrate the vileness of Judaism, many alleged quotations are given from the Talmud, exemplifying anthropomorphisms and moral degradation. Al-Khūlī, for instance, adds an appendix consisting of quotations from the Talmud, including repulsive descriptions of Jewish sexual customs. The Political Books series included one with the title *The Talmud, the Law of Israel,* which may have been influenced by such anti-Semitic publications as Rohling's work on the subject, which was translated into Arabic as far back as 1899 and was one of the sources used by Tall. It serves as the source in Shawqī 'Abd al-Nāṣir's edition of the Protocols and al-Khūlī gives many quotations from the Talmud, which he regards as a manifestation of the same spirit that reached maturity with the Protocols. His source is a 115-page book which I have not seen, by Būlus Hannā Mas'ad (apparently, by his name, a Christian), *The Barbarity of the Zionist Regulations,* published in 1938.

Despite the different approach of the Arab Left to this question, they share the idea of the essential vileness of the Jews, though as a social group, rather than a religious community. An example may be found in 'Alūsh's *The Journey to Palestine,* Beirut, 1964. In analysing the Communist approach to Israel, he quotes Marx's ossay, "The Jewish Question," which appeared in Arabic translation in Beirut in 1957. ('Alūsh's book was the first of the Selections from World Policy series. It is noteworthy that the Egyptian Chosen for You and Political Books series started with *This is Zionism* and *Secrets of Zionism*; it is by no means accidental that books connected with the Arab-Israel conflict were the first in each series.) The Leftist 'Alūsh, who does not write like an anti-Semite and uses hardly any opprobrious epithets about Jews and Zionism, accepts Marx's view that the Jew represents the capitalist spirit and carries the seeds of capitalism, which moulded his character. Adīb Dimitrī, in an article "The Jewish Question and Scientific Socialism," *al-Kātib,* August 1967, presents a similar analysis, also citing Marx's *The Holy Family,* which he wrote in collaboration with Engels. 'Alūsh writes:

> "It is true that the Jews are leading the United States on to treacherous ground *(mazāliq)* and spread disintegration and mockery *(inḥilāl wa-'abath),* but they are not a separate phenomenon from the life of the United States, for the Jews are the active element in its capitalism." (p. 76).

The faults of the Jews are, therefore, those of a particular social system and not a matter of race.

'Alūsh, Dimitrī and al-Ramlī combine the denigration of the Jews as a capitalist phenomenon with the denunciation of Israel as an imperialist phenomenon, thus intensifying the antagonism to the Jewish State. The salvation of the world from capitalism will undermine the basis of the undesirable qualities of the Jews, while the liquidation of Israel is involved in the liquidation of imperialism, of which it is a part. Neither the Jews nor Israel have a place in the world of tomorrow. Zionism is vile since it is opposed to the trend of historical progress (in other words, because it is a counter-revolutionary moverment), and therefore its doom is sealed.

b) QUARRELSOMENESS AND HATRED

It is very frequently and emphatically alleged that the Jews are quarrelsome by nature. To prove this, 'Aqqād quotes a long list of verses from the Pentateuch, the Prophets and the New Testament, which show that the Jews were a stiff-necked people, often denounced by Moses and the other prophets (pp. 15ff, 35). They rebelled against their leaders, were unstable in their loyalties and displayed a tendency to fraternal strife:

> "It is exaggerated, in our opinion, to ascribe to Zionism [meaning the Jewish character—Y.H.] the traits of discipline and loyalty . . . The history of this group does not show that they obeyed the discipline of any framework, secular or religious. In the whole of their annals, there are not ten continuous years without controversy, revolt and rebellion against their leadership, whether of their own kin or others. As far as this chronic disability among these people is concerned, it makes no difference whether the leadership was religious or secular. Furthermore, they were never loyal to even a single prophet, from the time of Abraham to that of Moses, and then until the end of the period of Israelite prophecy and the appearance of the Lord Messiah. The Quran described them most fittingly in the saying of God: 'They have great strength among them, you will think them united, but their hearts are divided, for they are people who do not understand.' This is an accurate divine description of them in all eras, only we do not want to condemn them according to a book in which their Western helpers do not believe.[15] In their own books there is enough and to spare to demonstrate this trait of character which we call their chronic disability, which has never left them and never will." (p. 35).

This internecine quarrelsomeness, when projected onto the outside world, makes them hate others because they hate themselves, and the others return their hatred. Thus, 'Aqqād writes:

> "They are never tired of repeating that persecution is the primary cause of Zionism and that Zionism will put an end to this cause or prevent its renewal. But the truth we wish to emphasize is that the persecutions are the results of the chronic disability of the Jews, which will remain with them in the new State as it was in their old State. What persecutions did the Jews experience in the time of Solomon's kingdom, which led to its division into two by its inhabitants?" (p. 15).

When the Israelites split up into two kingdoms,

> ". . . what the Northerners said about the Southerners and what the Southerners said about the Northeners was much worse than what was said by all the anti-Semites put together, old and new." (p. 41).

Aḥmad describes the quarrels and dissensions among the Israelites from the period of the tribes until the times of the Maccabees and of Herod the Great (pp. 58ff). To sum up:

> "They were never free from disputes, treachery, and the love of libel and slander, in any time past or in the future. There is no city or country that has been invaded by a foreign State without the Jews being an instrument for the purpose." (p. 68).

Dr. Naṣr regards the abnormal *(shudhūdh)* history of the Jews as the main reason for their abnormal character:

> "The truth about them may be summarized by saying that they are not civilized *(ghayr mutaḥaḍḍirīn)* in the political sense of civilization." (p. 34).

He also draws psychological conclusions from his political analysis. It is true that the Jews have produced individuals distinguished for their understanding of man and nature,

> "but they did not understand political civilization, and Aristotle's definition of man as a 'political animal' cannot be applied to them. This is the source of the

accursed disease which is associated with the Children of Israel. Wherever they turn, they are unable to submit to the limitations of peaceful civic life: they do not understand the ordinary needs of the ordinary citizen who follows the principle of give and take or 'Obey today and rule some other day'; they do not understand that civic rights depend on civic duties and responsibilities. This is what drives them to extremes in their behaviour: they display pitiful weakness and, when they get the opportunity, resort to unrestrained violence and bloodshed." (pp. 34-5).

This lack of social discipline destroys the inner balance of the Jews and leads them to take up extreme positions. According to Aḥmad:

"The Jews are a fundamentally alien element, different from the other races of humanity in their restlessness and movement, in their comings and goings. From ancient days until the end of time, the personality of the Jewish individual has been marked by a combination of qualities each of which is connected with its opposite. For observers see the Jew in every place as strong and weak, respected and despised, speedy and slow, economical and spendthrift, moderate and extravagant, clever and foolish, enjoying life and oppressed, popular and boycotted—and with all these qualities he is hated, for everyone dislikes him and he is despised by all the nations." (p. 20).[16]

'Aqqād goes further, using scientific terminology:

"They suffer from every symptom of paranoia enumerated by the psychiatrists. The symptoms of paranoia are arrogance, selfishness and self-isolation from the environment in which the patient lives, a dominant imagination, consciousness of persecution and constant fear of enemies. Which of these symptoms is not to be found clearly among the Zionists (i.e. the Jews—Y.H.)? They call God the God of Israel, who created them alone to serve him and created the other nations to serve them until the end of time. They practise isolationism and separatism everywhere; they allege the existence of persecutions and provoke them by their own obdurate attitude, whether they oppose them or cause them by isolationism, intrigue and exploitation of others." (p. 46).

The internal strife among the Jews and their lack of stability and inner integrity are externalized and affect their relations with their environment. Numerous examples are given with great emphasis by Arab writers to show that the Jews have always quarrelled with those around them, and that the whole of their history is one of strife with their neighbours ('Aqqād, Aḥmad, Tall, Bayhūm, Rushdī and 'Alūba).

If the Jews are so quarrelsome and factious, what, after all, unites them? 'Aqqād replies:

"They are fanatical, splitting up into factions everywhere. They are not united by love of each other, but by hatred of others and hostility to the whole world, for in all countries and at all times they have provoked evil thoughts about themselves and repelled their neighbours. They hate every country and know that they are hated." (p. 36).

Stubbornness and obduracy as basic characteristics of the Jews have also been emphasized by Christians in past centuries, but then the aim was mainly to explain why the Jews refused to accept Christianity. Among the Arabs, these characteristics are adduced to show that the Jews are not a nation and, therefore, that their State is artificial, unnatural and ephemeral. The factiousness and obduracy of the Jews will lead Israel to her doom. 'Aqqād writes:

"There is general agreement *(ijmā')* on their obduracy, coarseness and quarrelsomeness. This is a disability which their State will never get rid of, as it did not get rid of it in the past, until they [themselves] put an end to it before their enemies put an end to it." (p. 16).

c) "THE CHOSEN PEOPLE" AND ITS ATTITUDE TO THE GENTILES

The concept of the "chosen people" is frequently attacked. By assuming this title, the Jews reject the principle of the equality of man and do not disseminate their faith so as to deprive others of a share in its glory. Their religion is, therefore, racist ('Alūba p. 57). The idea that the Jews claim a monopoly of religion and of God is repeated with various degrees of disapproval (Rushdī, p. 41; Tall, p. 18). The chosen people concept is presented as narrow fanaticism, in contrast with the universalist and tolerant attitude of Islam, as expressed in the verse:

"O mankind: Lo: We have created you male and female, and have made you nations and tribes that ye may know one another. Lo: the noblest of you, in the sight of Allah, is the best in conduct." (Sura XLIX, The Private Apartments, v. 13).

'Alūba writes:

> "The Muslims recognize the faith of Jesus and the faith of Moses and regard their devotees as People of the Scriptures. But the Jews recognize neither the faith of Jesus nor the faith of Muhammad and regard their devotees as infidels and enemies of God." (p. 65).

The Jews are very frequently denounced as "selfish," interested only in their own benefit. This "selfishness" is the basis of Zionism, which was prepared to sacrifice the welfare of the Arabs to that of the Jews. This anti-Semitic argument fits in with the ideas of Arab modernists like Sayegh, Sa'ab and al-Khālidī, which have been described at the beginning of the chapter on Zionism. Zionist colonialism is another expression of Jewish selfishness; Jewish exclusiveness is exemplified in Zionist colonization. Here, again, Zionism is regarded not as a foreign growth in Judaism but as deriving its selfish, colonialist, racialist and exclusive character from the selfishness which is basic to Judaism as faith and civilization.

As a chosen people, the Jews believe that the rest of the world was created only to serve them ('Alūba, pp. 176-7; 'Aqqād, p. 42). They therefore consider themselves entitled to perpetrate atrocities against the "Gentiles," allowing themselves what they forbid to others. The brochure *Israel, the Enemy of Africa,* published on behalf of the Egyptian Ministry of Information, declares:

> "The Talmud considers the Jews equal to God, and as such everything on earth should by right be theirs. For instance, the Talmud says, that if an ox owned by a Jew kills an ox owned by a non-Jew the Jew need not pay compensation, whereas if an ox owned by a non-Jew kills an ox owned by a Jew the Jew received ample compensation. The Talmud also says: If a non-Jew steals from a Jew, he must be put to death whereas if a Jew lays his hand on the property of a non-Jew he is not liable to punishment. The Jews base this on the commandment that one must not rob a relation. And as they do not consider non-Jews to be related to them then they may rob them as they please.
>
> "The Talmud also allows the Jew to cheat the non-Jew and charge him high interest on loans, but he must not cheat a Jew like himself.
>
> "The Talmud condones the murder of the non-Jew. It says: 'The killing of a non-Jew is not a crime. On the contrary, it pleases God!' The Talmud adds that it is forbidden for a Jew to help a non-Jew get out of a hole. It decrees that the Jew must cover the hole with a stone and bury the non-Jew alive." (p. 3).

Similar statements are repeatedly made in various forms by different writers (e.g., Rushdī, p. 50; Aqqād, p. 44; Wākid, p. 55; Ṣabrī Abu al-Majd, pp. 7, 12-13; Ali and Ḥamṣānī, 1964, p. 3; Darwaza, p. 559; Muqammad al-Zu'bī, *Israel, Britain's Firstborn Daughter,* p. 57; al-Quṣrī, Appendix I; al-Khūlī, p. 32; Sharāra, p. 37; Shawqī 'Abd al-Nāṣir, pp. 31-2).

Wākid explains the attitude of the Jew to the non-Jew as a result, not only of the laws of Judaism, but also of historical development:

"Some scholars argue that the main reason for the Jew's vengeance against the world is the spiritual isolation in which he has lived for generations, which has created in him a cruel mentality, disposed to evil, destructiveness and bloodshed." (p. 57).

Nashāshībī offers a psycho-historical explanation: namely, that the Jews were impressed by the sufferings of Jesus and therefore tried to depict themselves as a people suffering for humanity, like him:

"They tried to transform their degradation into glory, and the hostility of humanity into martyrdom, thus lying to the world and themselves, and assuming the haloes of the apostles and prophets." (pp. 40-1).

The Jews, therefore, are not really persecuted, but only cunningly pretend to be so.

The chosen people idea has led to the historical isolation of the Jews. They live in a particular area, but are never a part of it. Even when they migrated to Egypt they lived apart in the land of Goshen (Dr. Naṣr, pp. 9-10). 'Aqqād sums up:

"Zionism is to blame for the differentiation between them and the other nations, for since days of old the world has been divided into two parallel parts: one part was Israel, the elect of mankind, favoured by God for no other reason except their being the Children of Israel, and the other part, which they call the nations or the Gentiles, includes the rest of humanity." (p. 43).

It may be suspected that this analysis is partly influenced by the Islamic division of the world into *Dār al-Islām* and *Dār al-Ḥarb.*

Dr. Naṣr declares:

"Every nation which has been kind to them has suffered before long from their evil activities as a foreign minority which preserves its alienness and egoism and does not share the feelings of the other sons of the homeland." (p. 8).

Pharaoh, he explains, gave them shelter when there was famine in the land of Canaan, but they repaid good with evil, spoiling the Egyptians and leaving with great wealth in their possession. He adds:

> "The feelings of the Jews are summed up in the saying: 'He that gave you life, give him death.' " (p. 29).

Ṣafwat supports this interpretation of the Exodus:

> "It appears that odiousness, cunning *(dahā')* and ingratitude had struck deep roots among the Jews in ancient times. Pharaoh demanded nothing of them but participation in the services for the general good in the region where they lived, but they rebelled against him and left Egypt under the banner of the prophet Moses." (p. 22).

This harking back to the Exodus is probably also a reminder that Egypt has a long account to settle with the Jews.

The Arab interest in the chosen people concept is no doubt influenced by similar claims on their own behalf. Dr. al-Faruki, with whose outlook I shall deal later, declares:

> "That the Arabs are the best people is for all of us a point of faith: the Quranic judgement, 'Ye are the best people brought forth unto mankind,' is a statement of this faith. Those who do not believe this on the authority of the Quran believe in it as a judgement by the Arab spirit pronounced at its highest moment of self-consciousness." (p. 3).

a) JUDAISM AS CONSPIRACY FOR WORLD DOMINATION

In accordance with *The Protocols of the Elders of Zion,* the Jews are portrayed as an underground of world scope aiming at universal corruption, the enemy of the human race.

It is emphasized that they are hostile to the world's religions. Tall's *The Danger of World Jewry to Islam and Christianity* and Ḥarb's *The Conspiracy of the Jews Against Christianity* are founded on this idea, and it is a central theme for 'Alūba, who says that when the Jews realized that Christendom and Islam were spreading, their sages worked out a plan to corrupt the Christian and Muslim States and plunge them into chaos (p. 173). He sums up:

> "The aim of the Jews is to undermine the existing order and establish a world Jewish dictatorship."

The official UAR pamphlet already mentioned, *Israel the Enemy of Africa,* says that according to No. 14 of the Protocols, the Elders of Zion resolved that, when all power was concentrated in their hands, all other religions except Judaism would have to be destroyed (p. 24).

The Jews dedicate their efforts to the corruption of morality the world over in order to undermine any possibility of resistance. For this purpose they deliberately develop subversive theories. 'Aqqād has a complete chapter (Chapter 10, pp. 90-104) on the efforts of Zionism (meaning Judaism) to corrupt cultural life. He quotes an article of his own on existentialism, in which he wrote:

> "It is quite impossible to understand the new schools of thought in Europe without recognizing the undoubted truth that one of the fingers of the Jews is hidden behind every trend that belittles moral values and aims at undermining the foundations on which all society has been based in all ages. For the Jew Karl Marx is behind Communism, which destroys the foundations of virtue and religion. The Jew Durkheim is behind sociology, which subordinates the institution of the family to artificial conditions and tries to deny its influence on the development of virtue and culture, and the Jew or half-Jew Sartre is behind existentialism."

'Aqqād says that in the study of these theories, or of any new theory that appears in Europe, attention should be paid to the underlying aims. The same applies to Freud, who ascribes trends in culture, religion, ethics, art, mysticism and family life to the sexual instinct in order to defile them, make men ashamed of them and undermine belief in their sublimity, degrading them to the level of their own lowest instincts, thus severing their bonds with the family and society. Freud pretended to be a freethinker, but he used only Jewish assistants in his clinic. He was in love with complexes, and full of complexes himself, as his disciple Dr. Ernest Jones testifies. In the end, when Freud himself was analysed after his death, it was realized that his contribution was nugatory. Another example is Albert Einstein. In him, too, the Jew played a prominent part, although many thought that he was concerned only with science, for in his letters he showed himself a fanatical supporter of Zionism and accused the "Gentiles" of persecution.

The Jews are frequently accused of spreading immorality and sexual degeneration, of running brothels all over the world, and the like (Tall, p. 64; Hindāwī, pp. 335 ff; *Ākhir Sā'a,* March 3, 1965, p. 8). Wākid alleged that the Jewish secret societies are engaged in the White Slave trade (*Israel in the Balance,* p. 32).

In the Mandatory period, Jewish immigrants were already accused of corrupting the purity of Arab life in Palestine. In February 1923, the editor of the Egyptian newspaper *al-Maḥrūsa* published a 36-page pamphlet *Zionist Aspirations in Palestine in Past, Present and Future,* vilifying the Jewish people, its prophets and sages, and alleging that the number of brothels in Palestine had increased as a result of Jewish immigration (reviewed in *Ha'aretz,* December 19, 1926, by J. Ben-Hanina).

Allegations of Jewish immorality started with comparisons between the dress and behaviour of the Jewish immigrants in Palestine and those of the Arabs, but the main aim was to create a "counter-image" to the chastity and modesty which the Arabs were in the habit of claiming (as expressly stated by Tall, p. 68).

While the German anti-Semites, in harping on the sexual theme, accused the Jews of corrupting the race, the tendency among the Arabs is to emphasize that they use sex to corrupt the morals of their enemies in order to weaken them. (Anthropologists may regard this attitude as revealing a suppressed fear of impotence.)

It should be noted that the idea of the Jews as corrupters, seducers and fermenters of factionalism and controversy is to be found in the teachings of Islam. They are associated with the concept of *fitna* (seduction of the faithful to heresy, scission, sectarianism and revolt). They tried to seduce the followers of Muhammad, and they plot to subvert accepted and official religious doctrines. (al-Jiyār, for example, refers to the connection between the Jews and Zionism and the *fitna.*)

The Jews are also accused of having brought about the world wars. 'Alūba takes it as a fact that only the Jews profited from them; after the First World War they got the Balfour Declaration, and after the Second they established their State. A third would give them world domination (p. 162). The Versailles settlement was preceded by a world Jewish masonic assembly (p. 127).

The Committee on Political Books writes in an introduction bearing its signature:

> "Zionism is not a danger to the Arabs alone, but to the whole of humanity, which it has pushed into two world wars to weaken the rival States and destroy their economy, so that Zionism should appear in monkish *(ruhbān)* garb to offer loans to countries that were being strangled by crises, and then Zionism gained control of them and forced them to do its will in order to achieve its aim, the

ruin of the world, so that Israel should arise upon the ruins." (Introduction to a translation of a book by Jerome and Jean Tharaud, *Quand Israel est Roi,* which deals mainly with the Hungarian revolution, Political Books, 1957).

'Alūba declares that the Jews have been responsible for a long line of coups and revolutions: in France, 1848 and 1871; Portugal, 1905; Turkey, 1805; China, 1911; Russia, 1917; Hungary and Germany, 1918; Spain, 1936—as well as the two world wars. They aimed at plunging the world into chaos with their hellish plots, and afterwards to establish "a World Zionist Government, revolution and riot" (p. 82).

The idea that Zionism and Jewry aim at world domination is also to be found in the indoctrination material issued to the Egyptian army. Ḥasan Ṣabrī al-Khūlī declares in a pamphlet, *The Palestine Problem,* published on behalf of the General Staff of the Egyptian Armed Forces:

"Zionism, in its new political sense, aims in the long run at world domination, claiming that God has appointed them to rule the world and that they are the chosen people of God. It is thus regarded as the most ancient racialist and imperialist approach in the world. Zionism in this sense is the national philosophy of most of the Jews in the world. Palestine is the immediate aim of Zionism, after which they will strive to achieve their more distant goal." (p. 7).

e) JEWISH DISTINCTION IN THE CULTURAL FIELD

How is it possible to explain the distinction of the Jews in the intellectual and cultural spheres? Dr. Naṣr, as we have seen, admits that there have been distinguished individual Jews, but he finds fault with them, too, denying them the right to claim the Aristotelian title of "political animal." 'Aqqād says that they achieve distinction thanks, not to their own culture but to that of the land where they live. The achievements of outstanding individual Jews are part of the world Jewish plot:

"The Zionist author [whom 'Aqqād describes as "the fifth column of Zionism"] gets more publicity than he deserves. This is clearly seen in the fame of such men as Ludwig, Maurois, Zweig, Kafka, Rilke, Proust, Sartre and others. In their own countries, they are of less importance than other authors, but they achieve a reputation because of the propaganda that they are Zionists and the sons of Zionist fathers or mothers." (p. 51—"Zionist" here, obviously, means "Jew"—Y.H.).

But the true test of the Jews is what happens when they no longer feed in foreign fields. In their library at Alexandria, which contained spiritual treasures from all spheres, there was not a single Jewish work, as Appion charged in his controversy with Josephus Flavius, whose only excuse was that the Jews were a small and isolated people. But Voltaire drew the correct conclusion that the Jews wrote little and were ignorant of all the sciences, and that the Bible is, after all, a modest contribution, consisting of only twenty-two books.

If the Jews are so odious, where does their power and influence come from?

'Aqqād sees a fifth column of World Jewry everywhere; his book is divided into chapters on the fifth column in political and economic life, the fifth column in the legislature, and so forth. Jewish position and influence are the tragedy of international morality. The main means by which they have achieved their power is their financial talent. Hindāwī says that Judaism is the only religion that has made espionage a religious duty (p. 40). Dr. Naṣr writes:

> "The Jewish talent in political affairs, as it has also been revealed in financial matters, is derived from one talent, or rather, from one secret and one activity; the exploitation of the distress of individuals or States, for they are expert at exploiting the crises of individuals or peoples, and they do not care whether they achieve their ends by voluntary means or by coercion. They exploit the distress of anyone who is in financial distress by exorbitant interest, and if anyone is in distress owing to a military or electoral struggle, they help him on condition that he pays them the political interest." (p. 26—Tall also pays special attention to interest as a Jewish characteristic, p. 64).

Their financial skill is an essential part of their character, and it is manifested in many ways in their history. For instance, they succeeded in spoiling the Egyptians and leaving "with great substance" ('Alūba, p. 69). Their love for gold was demonstrated when they set up the golden calf in the wilderness. The Jews of Yathrib [Medina] and Khaybar in the Arabian Peninsula were financiers and goldsmiths. The Jews do not like agriculture, because it calls for effort and toil ('Alūba, pp. 69-70).

Dr. Naṣr explains their influence as due to the fact that "the holder of money can exploit the holder of power"; as Marx taught, economics is the foundation of politics. The Jews have become powerful in the shelter of Western civilization, which has cast off all moral shackles:

"Anyone who read Hitler's *Mein Kampf* will be convinced that through their domination of the national economy in Austria, the Jews were able to control policy in its wider sense, and even its cultural aspects: education, theatre, cinema, press and so forth. There is no doubt that if an American or English patriot had written a book like Hitler's, he would not have confined himself to these spheres. But the English and Americans prefer a whisper to an open statement." (pp. 28-29).[17]

6. THE HISTORY OF THE JEWS

Jewish history is presented by Arab writers in order to: a) counter the Zionist claim of a historic right to Palestine, b) to find historical justification for the denunciation of the Jews by showing that they preserve their odious characteristics, which are passed on from father to son, and even infect converts when they accept the Jewish Scriptures. In view of the historical continuity of Jewish life, anyone who wishes to understand them must seek the roots of their character in the past. Arab accounts of Jewish history are generally written with an eye on the present day: the past is compared with the present in order to draw conclusions for the future. There is also a theological tinge in these historical studies, which are a kind of modern continuation of the religious polemics of the Middle Ages.

Unlike Christianity, Islam, while adopting many of the Biblical heroes and tales, did not adopt the Bible as a whole. Muslims can therefore deny its sanctity and accuracy. There are many differences between the accounts of the same events in the Bible and in the Quran (according to Orientalists, Muhammad received many Jewish traditions by word of mouth), thus implying—from a Muslim point of view—a slur on the authority of the Quran as a divinely inspired work. Muslims, therefore, may be impelled to claim the superiority of the Quran's versions to those found in the Bible and to look for contradictions between the two. The argument that the Jews forged, distorted or altered *(tazyīf, taḥrīf, tabdīl, naskh)* the text of the Holy Scriptures is often met with, and it derives from the Quran itself:

"And because of their breaking their Covenant, we have cursed them and made hard their hearts. They change words from their context and forget a part of that whereof they were admonished." (Sura V, The Table Spread, v. 13, and other passages).

This accusation, too, links up with the image of Jewish treachery and deceit. Arab writers explain that the Jewish Scriptures were written centuries after the events they describe, from the viewpoint of a later period, in a spirit of tendentiousness and self-justification. Tall declares, for example:

> "Their religion is not what God handed down to Moses, but what was invented by the Jewish religious leaders to adapt it to their evil and barbarous character. Is it conceivable that God should permit one people to attack a peaceful and tranquil people and kill men, women and children?" (p. 15).

Muhammad Darwaza's *The History of the Children of Israel from Their Books,* in three parts, in the Chosen For You series, is entirely devoted to Jewish history, from the days of Abraham to the destruction of the Second Temple, with further material relating to the time of Muhammad. His main source, apart from the Bible itself, is Muṭrān (Archbishop) Yūsuf al-Dabas' *Maqāla fī al-'Ibrāniyyīn* ("A Treatise on the Hebrews"). Darwaza also used the Apocrypha and the Arabic translation of the works of Josephus.

In his introduction, Darwaza explains that the Bible itself shows how Jewish history was lacking in beauty and grandeur, for it is packed with descriptions of degrading vice, immorality, bloodshed, aggression and robbery, religious, moral and social failings, quarrelsomeness, factionalism and so forth. The stories of the Jews about the conquest of the Holy Land are full of exaggerations and inconsistencies. The country was conquered not through their valour but through the miraculous intervention of Providence (i.e. the Almighty in those days fulfilled the function of modern imperialism), because they were cowardly and mutinous and lost their nerve at the approach of danger. They were always an undisciplined band, and were even unfaithful to their only good quality—their belief in one God. The Bible shows that they were thoroughly selfish, always interested only in their own good without considering the rights of others (another hint at the basic evil in Zionism). By selfishly claiming the status of the chosen people, they tried to get a monopoly of God, as a private concession of their own. The claim is a false one, for their history, replete with scandals, idolatry and violence, shows how inferior they actually are. Their accounts of arguments with God show their disrespect for Him. They always quarrelled with their neighbours. (The implication is that, since they cannot live at peace with other peoples, any peace settlement with them is out of the question, as Aḥmad declares, p. 60.) Whether in Palestine or outside it, they were always alien to the peoples among whom they lived. Anyone who reads the Bible will, therefore, realize how great is the arrogance of the Jews when they boast of it, and, furthermore how they have succeeded in using it to deceive the whole world. This is the reason, Darwaza explains, why he undertook to write his book: so that the Arabs, especially the younger generation, should understand the history of the Jews and the true worth of these gangsters' claims to a homeland and to kinship with the Arabs.

Darwaza's book follows the chapters of the Bible, pointing out the special characteristics of the Jews, the faults "that existed and still exist." He repeatedly says that, although the stories in the Bible are full of exaggerations and inconsistencies, they also contain a grain of truth. The approach is analytical and rationalist; the author exposes illogicalities and contradictions, ignoring the relativity of historical circumstances and the background of developments, and taking it for granted that there is an immutable Jewish character. Since the Bible is full of self-denunciations, that is further evidence of the odiousness of the Jews. History becomes a continuous series of scandals. As Tall puts it:

> "In the written history that has come to the notice of mankind no one has matched them in recording savagery and barbarity." (p. 14).

Here are a few points from Darwaza's account. The Jews were steeped in cruelty, malice, treachery and selfishness. This is repeatedly stressed in connection with the behaviour of the Israelites to the peoples of Canaan (p. 84). They exterminated the inhabitants without warning them or calling on them to make peace, killing women, old people and children without mercy. Their aggressiveness reached such heights that they describe the inhabitants of Canaan as their enemies although the latter had done no wrong, and their ancestors had lived in peace together, as the book of Genesis tells. (See pp. 120ff and many other places.) This charge of cruelty to peoples who had done them no wrong links up with the accusation that the Jews did evil to the Arabs, who had never persecuted them. These hatreds and complexes developed among the Jews as a result of the persecution they suffered in Egypt (p. 123). It is repeatedly stated that their experiences there moulded their character for generations.

They wreaked vengeance on the Midianites, although Moses had found shelter among them and his first wife was one. The attribution to God of the order to kill the Midianites, and Moses' anger at the Children of Israel for sparing the lives of women and children, influenced the character of the Jews by intensifying their cruelty and treachery (p. 114). Other examples are the prophet Samuel's brutality to Agag the Amalekite (p. 176) and Saul's treachery to the Gibeonites, despite his promise to them (p. 185). A typical example of treachery is the killing of the people of Shechem after they had been circumcised, in connection with the story of Dina (p. 64). The depth of iniquity is exemplified in the episode of David and Uriah the Hittite (p. 191) and the spirit of cruelty is evident in the prophet's rebuke to Ahab for sparing the life of Ben Hadad (p. 240).

Other examples are given from later periods. In the days of the Emperor Trajan, for instance, the Jews are said to have attacked and slaughtered the pagans in Cyprus, Kairwan and Egypt:

> "They destroyed them with indescribable brutality and barbarity, for they ate the flesh of their victims and drank their blood, girded their loins with their entrails and covered themselves with their skins." (p. 554).

The source is Muṭrān Dabas. (In referring to the story of Jephthah's daughter, on the other hand, Darwaza notes that human sacrifices were not allowed by the Jews.)

The source of this brutality to others is their claim to uniqueness *(ikhtiṣāṣ)* and the idea of the "chosen people" (a charge also made by Toynbee). Even the tribes of Reuben, Gad and half of Manasseh, who were allocated territories in Transjordan, were afraid the rest of the Israelites might one day reject them, saying, "What have ye to do with the God of Israel?" (Joshua, ch. 22), so they built an altar as a witness to their unity (p. 145). The claim to uniqueness creates complexes, which find expression in isolationism and hatred of others, as is shown by numerous passages in the books of the Jews (pp. 92-3). Examples of their selfishness are Jacob's theft of the birthright from Esau (p. 57) and the refusal of Zerubbabel and the returning exiles from Babylon to allow the inhabitants of Palestine to join them in building the Temple, although they had accepted the Jewish faith (pp. 376-7).

Their control over the Holy Land was never complete. There were always other tribes who lived in it. There are also contradictions: the book of Joshua tells of the conquest of cities in which, according to Judges, other peoples continued to live (p. 139). The weakness of the Jews' devotion to the Land is shown by the fact that the majority did not return from exile in Assyria and Babylonia, while those who did lived in Jerusalem and the Philistines, as well as other peoples, remained in the South (p. 409). The Book of Esther shows that the Jews were scattered in a hundred and twenty provinces under Persian rule (p. 399). Moreover, the Jews who came to Palestine in modern times were only 12% of world Jewry, and they came under pressure of persecution, not under the impulse of national, religious and historic attachment. Despite the propaganda, those who lived comfortably in the West did not come to settle in Israel (p. 577).

Despite their claim to a monopoly over God, they are not devoted to Him and are easily induced to follow other gods. As far back as in the time of Moses, they worshipped the golden calf, and in the days of the Judges they frequently bowed down to idols. Solomon was influenced by his wives. The Israelites are frequently rebuked by the prophets; their numerous lapses from the right way show their instability (p. 149). Their repeated complaints to Moses show that they have no power of endurance. They grumble when they meet opposition and difficulty—so it was in the past and so it will always be (p. 93). (The aim may be to assure the Arabs that Israel will never be able to endure a long conflict, or it may be a case of a "counter-image," implying that the Arabs are blessed with endurance and patience.)

The Jews are not a pure race. David was descended from Ruth the Moabitess (p. 178). In the 12th-century anti-Jewish tract *Ifḥām al-Yahūd* (see note 7), it is explained that King David, who is such a pre-eminent figure among the Jews, was the product of Lot's incestuous union with his daughters, the elder of whom was the ancestress of the Moabites (p. 59 in Perlman's edition).

The two stories about Abraham concealing the fact that Sarah is his wife, even being ready to give her up to Pharoah and Abimelech, show how prone the Jews are to intrigue and how they stop at nothing to save their skins (p. 53)—this may be an echo of the Quranic Sura II, The Cow (v. 96): "And thou wilt find them the greediest of mankind for life."

The uprising of the Maccabees, of which the Jews are justly proud, was marred by their characteristic failings. The Jews quarrelled with each other and co-operated with the Seleucid and Roman authorities against their brethren. They were riddled with controversy, strife and bloodshed, and plagued by religious and moral perversions. The result was that the period of complete independence under the Hasmonean dynasty was brief and ended with subjection to foreign rule (pp. 420-1).

Darwaza sums up:

> "It may be said that they have no human mission and their only interest is an aggressive, callous and most brutal selfishness, as is shown by the account in their books." (p. 127).

The books about the conflict (such as those by Tall, ʻAlūba, Aḥmad and Shaʻbān) contain many scattered references to events in Jewish history and attempts to trace their significance. A complete chapter in the Lebanese writer Muhammad Jamīl Bayhūm's *Arabism and Its New Enemies,* Beirut, 1957, deals with the subject in very much the same spirit as Darwaza. This chapter has been reproduced in English in Sylvia Haim's anthology *Arab Nationalism.* According to Bayhūm the Jews were always a treacherous and subversive element in the Middle East. He even denies their claim to be the originators of monotheism, alleging that Moses learned to worship the one God from his Arab (according to the Bible: Midianite) wife.

In the schools, ancient Jewish history is taught according to Islamic tradition, ascribing to the Jews basically undesirable characteristics. Even in recounting past events, there is a general tendency to depict Jewish traits as permanent features of their character. The following, for instance, is a translation of the chapter on "The Children of Israel" in Saʻīd al-ʻAryān and Hasan ʻAlwān's book *Religious Education,* part II, for the fourth form of the primary school, published on behalf of the UAR Ministry of Education (7th edition, 1965):

"Moses, on whom be peace, was a prophet to the Children of Israel, sent by God to deliver them from punishment, lead them to truth and goodness, teach them righteousness and fidelity, and accustom them to be pure of heart and merciful. But the Children of Israel did not keep the Law of Moses; they denied God and followed vanities, gave in to their lusts and were overcome by the love of gain, which they accumulate by every possible means without heeding honour and virtue. If they promised anything to anyone, they betrayed him; if anyone trusted them, they deceived him; when they saw anyone with money, they resorted to every kind of trick to rob him; they cheated in selling or buying. Their hearts were hard; they permitted themselves to shed blood, which they did with or without reason, until people hated them and feared them. God wanted to extricate them from their errors, restore them to truth and goodness, and teach them to love and mercy, and then He sent one of them as a prophet, namely Jesus, on whom be peace: perhaps he would restore them to the Law, teach them to respect the divine yoke and prevent them shedding blood. But the Children of Israel did not turn to the right way and repent of their forbidden deeds, and our Lord Jesus himself was a target for their infidelity and treachery, but God saved him from their wickedness." (p. 98).

There is a chapter on Judaism and the Jews in Dr. al-Faruki's *On Arabism, Urubah and Religion* (Amsterdam, 1962), which was written at the famous Institute of Islamic Studies at McGill University, Montreal. Although al-Faruki admits that some Jews were devoted to the basic monotheistic faith, he says that the religion of the Israelites contradicts monotheism by "nationalizing" the Deity, thus denying the fundamental idea of universal justice and the divine fatherhood of all men. The Jewish religion as it took shape is "the Hebrew transvaluation of Judaic values" (p. 18). The nationalization of God is reflected in Jewish isolationism; Judaism is not a monotheistic religion but a tribal creed. Even the "Hear O Israel" implies the idea of God as a private possession of the Jews.

Although the Arab-Israel conflict is not Dr. al-Faruki's subject, it is interesting to note that his analysis endows the themes we meet in the literature of the conflict with an additional dimension of historical and religious depth, and helps us to understand the atmosphere and modes of thought that produced them. For example, al-Bazzāz's conception of an irreconcilable ideological antagonism as fundamental to the conflict (chapters 3, 5) fits in with al-Faruki's explanation of the categorical opposition between Arabism as nationalism, which he defines as open—and especially Islam, which is a universal religion—and Judaism, which is a closed and isolationist creed. The exclusivity and isolationism of Zionism, which are emphasized by Sayegh and Sa'ab (chapter 4), also gain in depth in the light of the argument that these characteristics are fundamental to the Jewish religion; the same applies to the charge that the Jews themselves were the cause of anti-Semitism.

Dr. al-Faruki insists that the faults of the Jews are basic: they existed before their historical experiences and influenced them. He criticizes Dr. Muhammad Kāmil Hussein's essay on "The Exodus from Egypt and the Jewish Spirit," in his book *Mutanawwi'ā* ("Miscellany"). Hussein says in this essay that the separatism of the Jews was the outcome of their persecution in Egypt, and that the Exodus, as an abrupt transition from profound despair to hope, was the origin of their cruelty and callousness. Al-Faruki argues that, although this explanation is better than Freud's in *Moses and Monotheism,* it confuses the effect with the cause. Separatism, shown by their segregation in the Land of Goshen, existed prior to their persecution, but Pharaoh's oppression imbedded it in the Jewish character:

> "To say that their persecution was the cause of their Jewishness is to put the cart before the horse." (p. 19).

The author believes that the fundamental characteristics of the Jews are isolationism and a tenacious devotion to life (which is also expressed in their hopes for redemption—again, apparently under the influence of a verse in the Quran which ascribes this quality to the Jews). In the final analysis, the evil features of the Jewish character have a racial basis.

The analysis of the Jewish claim to "uniqueness" becomes a condemnation of their religion as an embodiment of their character, echoing the traditional charges levelled at the Jews in Europe:

> "The kind of relationship which obtained between the Hebrews and their Egyptian hosts after four hundred years of residence in their midst, namely, economic exploitation, political infiltration, social snobbery, racial separatism, cultural and spiritual isolationism, is deducible from the account given of them in the first chapter of Exodus . . .
>
> "The Hebrews had never allowed themselves to be absorbed into Egyptian society; while they worked themselves into a position of political and financial might in Egypt, they gave no evidence of ever identifying their interests and survival with those of the Egyptians." (p. 20).

Why did God choose Abraham and his seed? Dr. al-Faruki objects to the idea of an arbitrary divine choice as an affront to morality. The Bible does not explain God's attitude to Abraham and his departure from Ur of the Chaldees. Only the Quran, the author says, has explained the choice as a reward for Abraham's revolt against idolatry in his father's house; there is no explanation, al-Faruki says, in the Talmud, or the *Midrash Rabba,* and only traces of an explanation in the *Midrash Hagadol* and in the story told about Abraham by Rabbi Nissim of Kairwan, both of whom are influenced by the Quranic story. The "Covenant between the Pieces" was not arbitrary: God's choice of Abraham was the result of Abraham's choice of God. The Covenant was neither absolute nor eternal; the Jews were not assured that they would always remain sons of God even if they sinned (Faruki quotes Rabbi Meir), as they pretended in order to quiet their consciences when they deviated from the moral law. They built their separatism and exclusivity on the foundation of this theory of an eternal bond between God and Israel, but the Covenant was conditional upon their behaviour, otherwise it would have no moral significance. (This is also one of the basic concepts of Islam, according to which the Jews were denounced because they violated their Covenant with God.) The Jewish attitude to circumcision as a symbol of their bond with the Almighty which is intrinsically valid can only be understood as a method of preserving their separateness.

Al-Faruki also analyses the development of the idea of God among the prophets. Even they regard Him as private Jewish property, for they depict His arbitrary preference for the Hebrews. The Jews portray God as if His attention is concentrated on their own history. With undisguised sarcasm he writes:

> "The 'God of Israel' . . . is obsessed with his people, with the nethermost details of their daily chores. He watches their daily obscenities and their sins without moving a hair. After a few pretentious overtures in the first pages of Genesis, he has spent all his time, energy and intelligence, while the rest of the cosmos rotted, to dispossess a wretched little people of their land, put them to the sword and enter 'his people' into possession of land and whatever tree, beast or child who escaped his 'wrath.' The truth is that this god has never travelled, has never seen the world, nor to speak of making it. He is a 'country' man whose world ended with his tribe, beyond which everything and everybody is equally foreign and equally an enemy. In short, he is a regional, tribal, separatist god, with whom monotheism has absolutely nothing to do." (p. 47).

7. "ISLAMIZATION" OF JEW-HATRED

While much is being done in the Western world for the deliberate purpose of neutralizing the religious aspect of anti-Semitism, we find that opposite tendencies prevail among the Arabs as a result of the conflict with Israel. Religious motives are exploited to strengthen and deepen the hatred of Israel and the Jews, and establish it on a religious basis.

The traditions of Islam include a number of aspersions against the Jews in connection with the conflict between Muhammad and the Jewish tribes in the Arabian Peninsula. They are accused of treachery, breach of agreements, incitement, attempts to seduce the Prophet's followers from their allegiance, falsification, attempts to deceive Muhammad and introduce heresy into the Quran, and preference for pagans over Muslims despite the monotheism which is common to Judaism and Islam. There is also some criticism of Judaism as a religion in the Quran. However, although Islam, unlike Christianity, could not accuse the Jews of murdering the central figure of its faith, various ancient traditions about Jewish attempts to assassinate Muhammad are being revived today. According to one story,

Muhammad went to negotiate with the Jews and sat down beside a wall. The Jews plotted to drop a rock on his head, but God warned him and he changed his position. On another occasion, after the exile of the Jewish tribe of the Banu Naḍīr and the defeat of their counter-attack, they told a Jewess to poison him, but he was miraculously saved. (See *The Jews and Islam in Ancient and Modern Times,* a pamphlet issued by the Palestine Committee in Egypt, 1937; Tall, about the attempt to assassinate the Prophet, p. 36; al-Jiyār, p. 39.)

The use of such themes is not new: it goes back to the period of the Mandate and is particularly typical of those works that emphasize the religious aspect. Aqqād and 'Alūba make much use of these arguments. Tall goes into the matter in detail, citing authorities from the Quran and Ibn Hisham. References to the infamous attitude of the Jews to Muhammad are also to be found in the works of Darwaza, p. 569; Ṭabbāra, pp. 25ff; and al-Ramādī.

Sometimes new life is injected into these anti-Jewish traditions, which were almost certainly dormant, by connecting them with topical events and presenting the Jews not as a new enemy but as a historic foe. Thus, Tall writes:

> "The propagandists of secularism, who leave the religious factor out of account in the problem of Palestine, ignore the fact that this is the only conflict in the world which has lasted for thirty centuries, and still rests on religious and spiritual foundations." (p. 9).

It is frequently emphasized that the Jews cherish a historic hatred for Islam and its Prophet, as if this implies that the Muslims, in return, should hate the Jews. Tall quotes the verse from the Quran which charges the Jews with being the greatest enemies of the Muslims:

> "Thou wilt find the most vehement of mankind in hostility to those who believe (to be) the Jews and the idolaters. And thou wilt find the nearest of them in affection to those who believe (to be) those who say: Lo: We are Christians." (Sura V, The Table Spread, v. 82).

This verse is repeatedly quoted in the literature of the conflict and is given as a motto at the head of a chapter in Nashāshībī's book (p. 191).

There is a parallel in ancient Islamic literature to the medieval charge of a bond between the Jews and the powers of darkness. It is foretold that the Jews will follow the *Dajjāl*—a satanic eschatological manifestation which arouses disbelief and controversy, a kind of Muslim Antichrist or enemy of Allah. This idea is a central theme in 'Abd al-Ghaffār al-Jiyār's *Palestine for the Arabs* (Cairo, 1947), which explains that, while Muslims and Christians know that the Messiah has already come, the Jews still await his coming, and their Messiah is none other than the *Dajjāl.* Hence al-Jiyār identifies Zionism and Jewish Messianism with *"fitnat al-Dajjāl"*— "the rebellion of the *Dajjāl.*" The idea of the Jewish association with witchcraft and satanic powers is also developed in Ṭabbāra's *The Jews in the Quran,* pp. 51-2.

The modern outlook may make it somewhat difficult for Arab anti-Semitic publicists to exploit such ideas, but literature is somewhat freer from these limitations. Ali Muhammad Bākathīr's play *The God of Israel* (Dār al-Qalam, Egypt) describes the Jews as demons, devils and enemies of the human race born of unions betweens demons and women.

Dabbāgh draws topical conclusions from the treacherous attitude of the Jews to Muhammad and the Prophet's success in repulsing them:

> "The Arabs today made friends with the Jews and arrived at the same result as the Messenger of Allah over 1,300 years ago. We will continue to preserve the teaching of the mighty Arab Prophet." (1965, p. 138).

The struggle against Israel thus becomes part of the heritage of the Prophet (see al-Ramādī's *The Israelis and the Great Conspiracy*).

A common theme is that the Quran gave an accurate description of the Jews. Darwaza writes:

> "How extraordinary it is that we realize that their characteristics today, although they live in various places, are exactly as they were described by the Quran and the preceding books. Time does not add to their qualities, but makes them more deeply rooted . . . The vices pass on from fathers to sons." (p. 571).

He gives a catalogue of the evil characteristics ascribed to the Jews by the Quran:

> "Unbelief, denial, quarrelsomeness *(ḥijāj),* provocative behaviour *(lajāj),* selfishness, hardheartedness, arrogance, boastfulness, self-aggrandisement and assumption of superiority to other men, lack of sincere devotion and stable loyalty to anything, deception, machination *(dass),* fraud *(tadlīs),* intrigue, lust for the possessions of others, deep envy even when they enjoy much greater com-

fort, efforts to dominate everything, efforts to influence everyone, contempt for all restrictions, assumption of the right to take over the property of others, denial of responsibility towards others, miserliness, lack of reciprocity in friendship and in assurance of loyalty, involvement in every base and immoral situation, . . ."

and so on, and so on—the list extending to double the length of the items translated here (pp. 570-1).

.Tall has a chapter called "The Quran and the Jews" (pp. 53-68), in which he analyses the characteristics of the Jews on the basis of verses from the Quran. He declares that the accuracy of the description, which he confirms from his own experience in fighting the Jews in 1948, fortifies his faith in the truth of the Islam, the greatness of its sacred book, and its divine inspiration. His conclusion is that there has been no change in the odious *(qabīḥa)* characteristics of the Jews, and he goes on to list them:

Cowardice (jaban)—this is a permanent instinctive characteristic of the Jews, even if they try to make the opposite impression. "Even if they assume the garb of lions, they hide within them the fear of dogs and jackals," the author writes. The Quran says of the Jews:

"They will not fight against you in a body save in fortified villages or from behind walls." (Sura LIX, Exile, v. 14).

They are also afraid of death: ". . . and thou wilt find them greediest of mankind for life" (Sura of the Cow, v. 96). Tall says that this was confirmed in the Palestine war; the Israeli method of the "indirect approach" in battle, which has been praised by Liddell Hart, is ascribed by Tall to cowardice. (Ṭabbāra explains that this quality is due to the Jews' love for the delights of this world, because they do not believe in a hereafter [p. 44].)

They are always looking for someone to do their work for them. When Moses sent them to fight the people of Palestine, they refused, saying:

"O Moses: We will never enter (the Land) while they are in it, so go thou and thy Lord and fight: We will sit here." (Sura V, The Table Spread, v. 24).

Similarly, they said to their English henchmen: "You take Palestine and give it to us."

(The charge of Jewish cowardice is very common in the Arab literature of the conflict. This may be due to a combination of factors: a kind of verbal retribution for the victories of the Jews, a compensation for Arab self-criticism for their own defeat and fear, and the attribution to the rival of the opposite qualities to those contained in the self-image, for the claim to valour is frequently found in the Arabs' descriptions of themselves. It may also be a form of virulent abuse, as Arabic linguistic culture was moulded on the Bedouin society, which glories in courage and heroism.)

Callousness and brutality—there is no parallel in history to Jewish callousness (in contrast to the Jews' description of themselves as merciful and compassionate). The Quran describes the cruelty of Joseph's brethren, whose hearts were hard as stone. The Jews behaved in the same way to the Canaanite tribes. Tall adds that the cruelty of the Jews was notorious—in Cyrenaica against the Greeks, in the Spanish Civil War (quoting Arnold Leese), and going on to Deir Yāsīn.

The killing of the prophets—the Quran repeats in a number of places that the Jews killed the prophets who were sent by God; they held nothing sacred.

Falsification and the undermining of faith—in their fight against Islam, they adopted despicable methods, lies, falsification, deception, distortion of the word of God, the use of money for their ends, and the seduction of Muslims from their faith. This is repeated in many verses of the Quran.

Dishonesty and intrigue (al-makr wa-al-kayd)—the early Muslims suffered severely from Jewish deceit and treachery, according to a number of passages in the Quran. Tall offers thanks to the Almighty for having drawn attention to these characteristics. The Jews pretend to adhere to another faith in order to injure it. In the twentieth century they assumed the guise of Muslims in order to play a part in the abolition of the Caliphate, helping Ataturk to abolish the Arabic alphabet, combat religion and make Turkey a Jewish-American base. (On p. 231 this is described as the vengeance of world Jewry on Turkey for the Sultan's rejection of Herzl's approaches, while on p. 233 Ataturk is alleged to have been a Jew of the Dönme sect.)

The worship of gold and the misuse of money—the Jews worship and sanctify gold. At first they save and accumulate money, then they use it to serve their aims of world domination, corruption of morals and the liquidation of religion. Their love of gold is brought out in the Quran in connection with their worship of the golden calf.

Violation of agreements—frequently denounced by the prophets.

Arrogance (mukābara)—they behaved arrogantly to God himself and rejected him. They pretend to be united, but they are riddled with mutual hatred and strife. They have been disunited ever since Moses and Jesus. In moden Israel, for instance, there are more than ten parties, which despise each other and are always engaged in furious quarrels. The victories of the Jews in the world are due not to their own strength, but to the weakness and folly of others. As the Quran said:

> "We have cast among them enmity and hatred till the Day of Ressurection. As often as they light a fire for War, Allah extinguisheth it." (Sura V, The Table Spread, v. 64).

This is a very frequent charge; possibly, since the Quran condemned them to degradation, every sign of self-respect on their part is regarded as insufferable arrogance.

Vice and immorality—they try to undermine virtue and disseminate vice, own brothels everywhere, and are a focus of corruption and sexual immorality.

Usury—they rob others of their money by degrading them, thus ruining individuals and States. The instrument they use for this purpose is interest on loans; therefore the Quran fights them through the most precious thing in their lives: their covetousness and usury.

Degradation, wretchedness and disgrace—God, who knows their nature in past, present and future, has condemned them to degradation, wretchedness and shame. Even if they try to appear strong, the word of God will prevail. Degradation and wretchedness are characteristics implanted in them by God, and they cannot get rid of them.

Summing up, Tall declares that the clash between Jews and Muslims is inevitable because the gulf between them is unbridgeable:

> "It is natural that there should be a clash between Jews and Muslims, once it has become clear that Islam proclaims supreme values which contradict everything proclaimed by the Jews." (p.66).

In three pages he enumerates, in parallel, the virtues of Islam and the vices of the Jews (the image of the enemy as a negative of the self-image), winding up:

> "Islam forbids uprightful bloodshed, robbery and immorality. The Jews permit the shedding of a non-Jew's blood and allow him to be robbed and his honour desecrated. It is true that the Ten Commandments forbid killing, robbery and adultery, but the Jews have interpreted them in their own favour to suit them-

selves. The meaning of the command 'Thou shalt not kill' is: Thou shalt not kill a Jew; 'Thou shalt not steal' means: Thou shalt not steal from a Jew; 'Thou shalt not commit adultery' means: Thou shalt not commit adultery with a Jewess." (pp. 66-68).

Anyone who looks for Islamic anti-Jewish pronouncements can even find a tradition according to which the Resurrection will be preceded by a massacre of the Jews by the Muslims—an eschatological "final solution." The following, for example, is quoted in the brochure *The Jews and Islam,* mentioned above:

> "A tradition from Abu Hurayra (in another collection of *ḥadīths,* by Abdallah Ibn 'Amr): Said the Prophet, on whom be peace: the hour of the Resurrection will not come until the Muslims fight the Jews and the Muslims kill them, until the Jews hide behind the stones and trees, and then the trees and stones will say: O Muslim! O Abdallah! Here is a Jew behind me, come and kill him! Apart from the *gharqad,* for it is one of the Jews' trees. Said the Imam al-Ṭabarī: The *gharqad* is a well known tree, with thorns, which is to be found in Jerusalem, where the killing of the *Dajjāl* and the Jews will take place." (p. 13).

The same tradition is partially quoted in al-Jiyār's book, p. 6.

Denunciations of adherents of other religions are to be found in the literature of every creed, including the Jewish, but such traditions as this are generally abnormal phenomena—excrescences of a kind to be met with in every extensive literature. Such expressions cannot be said to be an essential part of Islam; they are dormant, even unknown to its adherents, and have no influence or significance. Even if they are brought to the surface in certain pamphlets or books, it should not be assumed that they are therefore capable of influencing public opinion. So long as they are not repeated with some frequency, they can only be testimony to the outlook of those who write and issue such publications.

The Six-Day War has led to increased emphasis on the Islamic aspects of the hostility against Israel and the Jews. This trend is exemplified by the frequency and tenor of anti-Jewish articles in the monthly of the oldest and principal Muslim religious university, al-Azhar. In the October 1968 issue of the periodical, an article called "The Prophecies *(Bashā'ir)* About the Battle of Destiny Between the Muslims and Israel" by Nadīm al-Bishr is devoted to the *ḥadith* about the killing of the Jews. The author explains that this tradition is of major importance in Islam. For thirteen centuries its meaning was hidden, for it was not fitting to kill the impotent Jewish minorities. Now the meaning of the tradition has been unfolded, for in order to enable it to be realized, God has ordained that the Jews should attain power and establish a State, which would become aggressive and justify the killing of the Jews.

8. THE BLOOD LIBEL

So powerful is the hostility of some Arab authors that it has led to the revival of the charge that the Jews use the blood of Gentile children for ritual purposes. According to Professor Yosef Yoel Rivlin, the medieval "blood libel" in its accepted form was not known in the Muslim countries until the middle of the nineteenth century. The first allegations of this kind in the Islamic world were made in Damascus in 1840 and Deir al-Qamar in 1847, in both cases by Christians ("The Damascus Libel," in *Mahanayim,* No. 111, Part II). As early as the fifteenth century, anti-Jewish slanders were disseminated in the Ottoman Empire, but the Sultans defended the Jews. (See Professor H.Z. Hirshberg's article, "Turkey and Religious Slanders, the Attitude of the Authorities of the Ottoman Empire to Blood Libels," *Mahanayim,* No. 110. Professor Hirshberg mentions further libels, in Jerusalem in 1849, in Istanbul in 1866 and in Jerusalem in 1870.)

Charges that Jews killed Muslim children, though without the additional element of the use of the blood for ritual purposes, were made centuries ago. Such a libel in Jerusalem and Hebron is described by Bezalel Landau ("The Blood Libel in Jewish History," *Mahanayim,* No. 80). Dr. Jacob M. Landau notes six blood libels in Egypt during the period 1870-1892, though they were initiated by Christians ("Blood Libels and the Persecution of the Jews in Egypt at the End of the 19th Century," *Sefunot,* Book V, Ben Zvi Institute, 1960-61). The concentration of such cases in the Middle East in the 19th century, especially towards the end of it, undermined the confidence of the Egyptian Jews, as Dr. Landau explains in his article.

A book entirely devoted to this question has been published in Egypt, and it might be regarded as a curiosity if it were the only one of its kind and were it not for the auspices under which it was published. It was issued in a series of information pamphlets, "National Books" No. 184, 1962, 164 pp. In the list of books published by the UAR Ministry of Education, *al-Nashra al-Miṣriyya lil-Maṭbū'āt,* it is given the number 3931. On its cover, the book bears the symbol of the Egyptian Institute for Publications, with a line above: "Selections from Radio and Television." The book, which is called *Human Sacrifices in the Talmud (al-Dhabā'iḥ al-Bashariyya al-Talmūdiya),* is a reprint of an old work issued by Ḥabīb Fāris in Cairo in 1890. The fact that such a book should be found suitable for "national guidance" is shocking. It was seen through the press by 'Abd al-'Ātī Jalāl, who checked the text and added linguistic notes on the differences between Arabic idiom in 1890 and today.

In his introduction, dated June 16, 1962 (p. 4), the editor explains how, while writing a play called *The Tragedy of Jerusalem* and studying the relations between the Jews and the Romans, he came across an old, tattered book:

> "I found before me an important document, which it is fitting that we should publish at a time when the Jews constantly boast that they are a civilized people, guides of humanity and the people of God, who exist on this earth in order to lead mankind from darkness into light. This is a clear indictment, resting on conclusive evidence, which history has preserved for us as proof that this people permits bloodshed and makes it a religious obligation laid down by the Talmud. This is a people which does not recoil from resorting to the vilest methods in order to achieve its aims, irrespective of whether it involves killing, money or debauchery."

He describes how the author, Ḥabīb Fāris, began to publish the book in the paper *al-Maḥrūsa,* which appeared at the time in Alexandria and later in Cairo, under the name of "The Cry of the Innocent with the Trumpet of Freedom" *(Ṣurākh al-Barī' fī Būq al-Ḥurriyya)*:

> "The innocent one was a boy called Henry 'Abd al-Nūr, who had not yet passed his sixth year, whom the Jews slaughtered in Damascus and sucked his blood to mix it with the dough from which they prepared *matzah* for the Festival of Passover. The affair did not end with the condemnation of a single one of the Jews, despite the conclusive proof of the extraction of the boy's blood." (p.5).

This account refers to the Damascus blood libel of 1890; according to Jalāl, the Jews were acquitted owing to bribery and the weakness of the authorities. Fāris, he adds, wrote another book giving details of similar cases in East and West, but no copy of it survived because the Jews quickly buy up and destroy any books that describe their crimes (a repetition of the allegations made in connection with the Protocols)—even copies of the paper *al-Maḥrūsa* disappeared. The surviving copy of the book was found in the possession of a descendant of the author. (According to an article by E. Sapir, "Hatred of the Jews in Arab Literature" (*Hashiloah,* Vol. VI, 1899), a book on the blood libel *Ṣawt al-Bari',* translated from the French, and containing numerous slanders against the Jews, was published in Egypt, and "the Government ordered it to be destroyed" [p. 231].)

Jalāl goes on to explain:

> "The Talmud believes that the Jews were made out of a different material from the rest of humanity, for those who do not believe in the Jewish faith are senseless beasts, or servants and chattels of the Jews. They said that heaven and earth were created only for them and they are gods on earth. God multiplied their errors and they believe that God, may He be praised and exalted, when He condemned them to degradation and wretchedness, wept and lamented when He ordered the destruction of the Temple. The sages went further; they had not law but their will, no rule but their lust, and they ordered (the Jews) to do evil to the other nations, to kill their children, suck their blood and take possession of their wealth." (p. 7).

In this connection, the editor mentions a pamphlet *al-Talmud Sharī'at Isrā'īl* ("The Talmud, the Law of Israel"), which was published in the Policy Books series, No. 18, 1957. The work is not in my possession, but according to the vilification of the Talmud quoted here, it may also refer to the blood libel. It may be based on Rohling's book.

In addition to the 1890 affair, the paper deals with the notorious Damascus blood libel case of 1840, from which he quotes parts of the interrogations including confessions extorted from the Jews. He also surveys other blood libel cases in the Middle East: at Aleppo, 1810; Beirut, 1824; Antakia, 1826; Homs, 1829; Tripoli (Lebanon), 1834; and Alexandria (undated, apparently 1881), with contemporary press references.

This is not the only, or the last, revival of the blood libel by the Arabs. 'Abd al-Mun'im Shamīs, in pp. 96-103 of his book *Secrets of Zionism,* published in Cairo in 1957 as No. 1 of the Policy Books, deals with the subject, going into greater detail on the two Damascus cases, quoting Jewish confessions and so forth. He regards the use of blood for ritual purposes as part of the crimes of Zionism.

In a book called *The End of Israel,* published in 1960 in Cairo by the Arab Printing and Publicity Company, affiliated to the Voice of the Arabs (the director of which, Aḥmad Sa'īd, wrote an introduction to the book), Abu al-Majd quotes the alleged evidence of a "Rabbi Taunitus," a convert to Christianity, who testified:

"The Zionists believe that Christian blood is essential for the performance of several religious rites."

He goes on to give details. At weddings for instance, bride and groom are given an egg stained with Christian blood. At a circumcision ceremony, the Rabbi puts a drop of Christian blood into a glass of wine, stirs it, puts a drop into the child's mouth and says, "Thy life is in thy blood" (perhaps an echo of Ezekiel, 16:6: "I said unto thee when thou wast in thy blood, Live.") On the 9th of Tammuz (an obvious mistake for the 9th of Av) the Zionists lament the destruction of the Temple and smear their foreheads with ashes of flax stained with Christian blood. When Christian blood cannot be obtained, they make do with Muslim blood, as many Christians have embraced Islam, and Muslim blood therefore contains some Christian blood.

Apparently, Taunitus is a corruption for Neophytus—which is very similar in Arabic script—the name of the reputed author, said to have been a converted Moldavian rabbi, of a pamphlet published in "Moldavian" in 1803, translated into Greek and Italian, published in Naples and, in Arabic translation, in Beirut, 1869. It is referred to by Giacomo Castro in an Arabic pamphlet defending the Jews published in 1872 in Alexandria, and in Henri Desportes, *Le Mystère du Sang, chez les juifs de tous les temps,* Paris, Albert Savine, 1890. Nuwayhiḍ, in his book *The Protocols of the Elders of Zion* (1967), mentions the book on pp. 224-9 and says he had a copy in his hands in Damascus in 1952.

Abu al-Majd declares that the Zionists tried to get Gentile blood in Alexandria and Port Said in 1881. He gives a detailed account of the blood libel case at Trent in 1840 as an undoubted matter of fact, and even ascribes to "Rabbi Theonitus" a confession that it was Zionism which fomented the First and Second World Wars.

Surprising statements are made by Tall in his book *The Danger of World Jewry to Islam and Christianity,* published by Dār al-Qalam, an affiliate of the National Publishing Institute. He returns to the blood libel repeatedly, devoting a 28-page chapter (pp. 77-105) to the subject. In the introduction he explains:

"The God of the Jews is not content with animal sacrifices; he must be appeased with human sacrifices. Hence the Jewish custom of slaughtering children and extracting their blood to mix it with their *matzot* on Passover." (p. 20).

He regards the use of human blood as belonging to the esoteric aspect of Judaism, connected with witchcraft, to which, he says, the Talmud devotes much attention. (His main source is A. Leese's *Jewish Ritual Murder,* London, 1938.)

On two of the Jewish festivals, Tall goes on, the Jews mix human blood with their food; using the blood of adults at Purim and that of children at Passover. On page 80 he quotes, as evidence, Sir Richard Burton's *The Jews, the Gypsies and Islam,* 1898, p. 81, according to which Jews use blood on Passover and at the circumcision ceremony. From Leese's book he quotes a statement by a Dr. Eric Bishop that the sacrifice of non-Jews, who are regarded as animals, not human beings, is mentioned in the Cabalistic work *Tikunei Hazohar.* Tall gives a long and detailed list of Jewish ritual murders from the 12th century until modern times, drawn from Leese. When he reaches the Damascus libel of 1840, he gives an account covering several pages, with the details of the case and the Jewish "confessions," relying on an Arabic translation of Rohling's *The Jew of the Talmud.* As a source for the Middle East blood libels he mentions Ḥabīb Fāris' book.

Tall gives details of how the Jews kill their victims, taking as his authority a book by the Turkish general Jawād Rif'at Atīl Khān, Istanbul, 1958 called *The Barrel with Needles.* According to this book, the child is placed in a barrel equipped with numerous hollow neddles, which pierce his body and through which the blood flows into drainage pipes. This kind of killing is extremely painful, to the satisfaction of the Jews, who believe that the suffering purifies the blood which they collect (p. 78).

Summing up this chapter, Tall says that relatively few cases of ritual murder have been discovered, but the Jewish crimes that have been revealed are only a minute proportion of those that have remained undisclosed, for thousands of children and others disappear every year:

> "These are mostly the victims of Jewish religious rites and their blood sinks into the bellies of the Jews together with the *matzot* of their four festivals." (p. 104).

Few of these crimes are discovered, for the nations are foolish and the police are weak.

The Jews are pleased if the victim is one of their friends, and particularly if he is an innocent man, for they believe that by killing they are fulfiling a sacred religious duty, which will win them a special blessing. It is true that they deny the use of human blood, but the charge has been confirmed by investigation, as well as by the confessions of converted Jews, like the Jewish sage Abulafia, who adopted Islam during the investigation of the death of Father Thomas in Damascus. Despite the passage of time, punishment and the danger of vengeance, the Jews do not abandon these crimes. As evidence he quotes a story from the newspaper *Akhbār Filasṭīn* on May 21, 1963 about the killing of a Russian boy and the use of his blood by the Jews for religious purposes, and another from *al-Muṣawwar,* February 14, 1964, about a scandal in Colombia over the killing of children, the extraction of their blood and its sale to hospitals. Tall remarks that the latter newspaper did not realize that the criminals were Jews.

Mahmoud Rousan, in *Palestine and the Internationalization of Jerusalem* (English), published by the Iraqi Ministry of Culture and Guidance, Baghdad, 1965, follows in Tall's footsteps, giving the same quotations from Burton (p. 25) and *Tikunei Hazohar* (p. 102).

Na'nā'a also uses the blood libel in his *Zionism in the Sixties, the Vatican and the Jews,* published by the official Egyptian Institute for Publications and bearing its symbol. After discussing the prohibition of the baking of *matzot* in the Soviet Union, he continues:

> "The kneading of Passover *matzot* with Gentile blood is not a groundless charge against the Jews. We have in our possession hundreds of proofs *(shawāhid),* from East and West, in ancient history and modern times, of this barbaric traditional Jewish custom. The subject of this book does not permit me to expatiate on this matter, therefore I shall be content with the confirmation *(ithbāt)* of the case published by the news agencies and referred to in *The Jewish Chronicle* of May 17, 1963." (p. 113).

The Jewish Chronicle indeed refers to a Russian case in which a Jew was accused of sucking the blood of a child, but Na'nā'ā, despite his enthusiasm for facts, deliberately ignores the continuation of the episode and actions taken by the Soviet Government to counter the blood libel, including the allegations in the case in question.

The list of Arab books dealing with this charge has not been closed. Nuwayhiḍ devotes a section of his book *The Protocols of the Elders of Zion,* Beirut, 1967, to the Rabbi Neophytos mentioned above, affirming that this is indeed a custom among the Jews.

Another book dealing with the blood libel is Iliyā Abu al-Rus: *World Judaism and its Continuous War Against Christianity,* Beirut, 1964.

The blood libel, as presented in these eight books, is a shocking thing, but it is not frequently met with in the literature of the conflict, and it does not seem to have been adopted by Arab public opinion. It may also be foreign to the basic attitude of the Arabs to the Jews, for in the Muslim countries, unlike Christian Europe, the Jews have not been accused of such atrocities as the use of human blood, the poisoning of the wells and the dissemination of plague. It may, perhaps, be hoped therefore that these ideas will not take root. The matter is significant as a symptom showing to what lengths hatred of Israel may drive Arab publicists.

9. JUSTIFICATION OF NAZI CRIMES

It is repeatedly argued in Arab writings that Germany's actions were justified because of the evil the Jews did her and the danger they constituted for the country. These actions, it is explained, were necessary for self-defence.

According to Shukrī, the Jews engaged in large-scale subversion in Germany; it was they who led to her defeat in World War I. This was the reason for Hitler's attitude to them (p. 23).

Tall denounces the Jewish slander *(firya)* against the Nazis. Realizing that the Jews were the cause of their defeat in World War I, the Germans, he says, were afraid they might bring about a second defeat in World War II—"and this is what happened." Hitler has been "wronged and slandered," for he did no more to the Jews than Pharaoh, Nebuchadnezzar, the Romans, the Byzantines, Titus, Muhammad and the European peoples who slaughtered the Jews before him. The crimes and barbarities of the Jews, founded on the Talmud and the Protocols, the sucking of human blood, poisoning of the wells and Freemasonry, have not changed. Hitler appointed a committee of scholars, who reached the conclusion that the Jews must be liquidated or expelled:

> "Hitler carried out the decision of his scholars, and did to the Jews as has been done unto them throughout the generations—killing, burning and expulsion from the countries which they betrayed and whose peoples they deceived." (pp. 115-117).

Tall adds, indeed (pp. 119-120), that he does not want the reader to think that he agrees with the slaughter of the Jews, for nothing could be further from the minds of the Arabs than the idea of massacre. He recalls the events of the past only because they confirm the evil character of the Jews and their foul customs, and he regrets that the Arabs have had to suffer for the sufferings of the Jews at the hands of the Germans. In another passage, he explains:

> "The blame [for the massacre of the Jews] applies first and foremost to the Jews themselves and their characteristics of treachery *(ghadr),* deceitfulness *(makr),* crime and treason, and in the second place to European civilization, which apparently could not long suffer the vile *(maqīt)* Jewish character, and in the course of time hatred of the Jews and loathing for their vices led to a movement of collective killing." (p. 283).

'Alūba's attitude is similar. After enumerating the evil deeds of the Jews, he continues:

> "This is what led Hitler to alarm the world against them, not because he was a believer and feared God, but because he wanted to save his nation and the world from this malignant evil that had permeated the Christian peoples, and the poison that flowed in the bodies of the non-Jews. It is well known that the German people is one of the most progressive in the world in science, technology and nationalism, and it has an immunity which can defend it against the activities of Zionism. Nevertheless, Hitler realized what was weakening his people to the extent that it almost brought about its end. The same applies with greater force to other nations, which are not so immune." (p. 176).

Na'nā'ā puts forward similar ideas (p. 10).

These arguments imply not only an attempt to explain, understand and justify the acts of the Germans against the Jews, but also, it seems, a readiness to learn from the Nazis. Dr. Naṣr writes:

> "The truth is that the study of what Hitler wrote on World Zionism has become a vital matter for anyone who lives in the Arab countries after the year 1948." (p. 87).

It is repeatedly argued that the Germans did not really exterminate six million Jews, and the Jews and Israel exaggerate the dimensions of the holocaust in order to derive political advantages from it. They pretend to be persecuted for the purpose of extorting compassion; other peoples were also injured by the Nazis, but only the Jews trade in their sufferings. In a talk with Dr. Frei, editor of the *Deutsche Soldaten und Nazional Zeitung,* President Nasser is quoted as saying:

> "No one, even the simplest of men, takes seriously the lie about six million Jews who were murdered. How is it with you?"

Dr. Frei replied:

"No one denies the fact of the murder of the Jews as such, and every man of feeling deplores it deeply." (May 1, 1964).

In a speech on March 8, 1965, Nasser declared:

"They say that in World War II the Jews suffered from Germany. Was it only the Jews who suffered from Germany? The Czechs suffered from her, the Yugoslavs suffered, the French suffered."

Bahā' al-Dīn explains the Jewish technique:

"The Hitlerite regime destroyed more Soviet atheists, Polish Catholics and Orthodox members of the Balkan peoples than it did Jews. But all the accounts of these massacres have been closed and settled, except for the account of the Jews, which has remained open, for there is someone who keeps up its continuous exploitation and its transformation into a complex which must be atoned for with reparations and aid." (p. 226).[18]

Such arguments are repeated by, for instance, Dr. Sīdham (p. 22, Tall, p. 200) and Dr. Dhū al-Faqār Ṣabrī, Nasser's political advisor, according to the French News Agency, May 4, 1961.

The sufferings of the Jews at the hands of the Nazis are presented as slight in comparison with what the Arabs suffered at Israel's hands. The former, which were exaggerated, were those of individuals, but the Arabs really suffered as a people.

a) REACTIONS TO THE EICHMANN TRIAL

Israel was condemned repeatedly in the Arab press for violating international law by abducting Eichmann. Still more frequent were expressions of sympathy with him, and even statements that his example should be followed. There were, indeed, some condemnations of Eichmann, but they cannot outweigh these expressions of sympathy.

In the Lebanese paper *al-Anwār* of June 9, 1960, there was a caricature showing Ben-Gurion and Eichmann shouting at each other. The text below the drawing is as follows:

Ben-Gurion: "You deserve the death penalty for killing six million Jews."

Eichmann: "There are many who argue that I deserve the death penalty for not finishing the job."

The Jordanian English language daily, *Jerusalem Times*, published the following "Open Letter to Eichmann" on April 24, 1961:

"Dear Eichmann,

"I address you in your glass cell to extend a word of sympathy in your present plight. German genius that has invented sputniks and missiles and all sorts of things has failed to inspire you to avert the disaster that has befallen you.

"What a pity Eichmann that you allowed those swine to arrest you and stage their drama. But don't worry Eichmann it will in the end fall on their heads.

"Listen Eichmann you are accused of dissimating *(sic)* six million of this breed. Whether this is correct or not it is not our object to debate this issue but what we like to say is this if you actually managed to liquidate six million of them and if the remaining six million have been instrumental in inflicting so much havoc and suffering on the Arabs and disgorging them from their homes we wonder what would have been the result if the dissimated *(sic)* six million would have been allowed to survive.

"It is likely that a similar drama would have been staged in another part of the Arab countries. So that by liquidating six millions you have minimized the extent of the calamity and conferred a real blessing on humanity you can imagine dear Eichmann the feelings of the million or so of Arab refugees at this drama. . .

"The object of this trial is simply to attract more tourists to the occupied section and to exploit it for fund raising and for skinning the rest of mankind.

"But be brave Eichmann find solace in the fact that this trial will one day culminate in the liquidation of the remaining six million to avenge your blood and the manner in which you have been kidnapped and brought to trial by the very same people who tortured and ejected a million or so from their homes."

Tall writes of Eichmann as one "who fell in the Holy War" *(shahıd)*:

"We have not forgotten the abduction of the martyr Eichmann, whom the Jewish gangs brought over from Argentina to the gangster Government in Palestine and put him to death in order to make of his fate a terrorist sword to be brandished over the head of anyone in the West who might dare to deviate from the line laid down by criminal World Jewry." (p. 282).

Ali Muhammed Ali, in his book *Inside Israel* (Policy Books series), describes the Eichmann trial as a show:

> "In outward appearance it was a tragedy, but in its essence it was a vile comedy . . . , because both the accused and the judge were criminals. Eichmann was accused of liquidating a number of Jews, but Israel, which judges him, is accused of liquidating the people of Palestine, with this difference: that the charge against Eichmann was spun by the Zionists out of their imagination and exaggerated, for historical facts have confirmed that it is really exaggerated, but the charge against Israel is an undoubted fact."

Let us examine the psychological motives that might have stimulated this sympathy for Eichmann, and these shocking attempts to justify the massacre of the Jews and slur over the dimensions of the holocaust.

Firstly, the Arabs' hatred of Israel and sense of injustice impel them to equate the catastrophe involved in the loss of Palestine and the creation of the refugee problem with the Jewish catastrophe in Europe, and to regard the Nazi holocaust as a kind of "advance retribution" for the crimes of Zionism. The Arabs go further: in their view, Israel's guilt is even more heinous, for it meant the liquidation of a nation, whilst the Germans "only" liquidated individuals.

The Arabs are not alone in making this analogy between the two cases and emphasizing the gravity of what Zionism has done, for Toynbee repeats it several times, and the Arabs quote him as an authority (for example, in the numerous pamphlets they have issued about the debate in Montreal between him and the Israeli Ambassador, Yaakov Herzog, which they use to support their arguments).

Secondly, if the Arabs join the ranks of the anti-Semites, it is in their interest to prove that they are not in disreputable company, and that the guilt is on the other side.

Thirdly, since some of the support for Israel has been motivated by an admission of the world's share in the responsibility for the extermination of European Jewry, or, at least, by serious disquiet on the subject, it becomes an Arab interest to minimize the dimensions of the holocaust, with the implication that the world owes nothing to Jews.

Fourthly, the Arabs wish to use the holocaust to condemn the Jews for allegedly trying to collect humanity's debt to them "with interest"—which would be a characteristically Jewish thing to do.

Fifthly, since the memory of the holocaust produces a repulsion against anti-Semitism, the Arab view of the conflict as a global one makes it their interest to strengthen the anti-Jewish and anti-Israeli camp.

Lastly, the argument on this question may also constitute a kind of "preliminary plea" to justify their own objective of liquidating Israel, on the grounds that the idea of liquidating Jews is not something exceptional; it is a normal and accepted part of history. This objective may be perceived in the case presented by Tall, at least.

10. ARAB EXPLANATIONS OF ANTI-SEMITISM

The Arabs repeatedly emphasize that they cannot be anti-Semites because they themselves are Semites, and they do not hate the Jews at all; they only oppose Zionism. Anti-Semitism is a European product and never existed in the Arab countries. We sometimes even find severe denunciations of anti-Semitism, as in Bahā' al-Dīn's statement that "Anti-Semitism is oppressive reactionary propaganda" (p. 94). It is argued, too, that the Arabs cannot be anti-Semites because they themselves have suffered from imperialism and racial discrimination. Nasser also declares that he is no anti-Semite, but how else is it possible to explain his advice to Karanjia to read *The Protocols of the Elders of Zion,* or the flood of defamatory literature that has appeared in Egypt under official auspices?

Tall argues (see pp.173 ff) that anti-Semitism is simply a fiction, invented by the Jews in order to achieve their aims; there has never been a greater falsehood in history. The term itself is tendentious, for the real meaning is anti-Judaism, while most of the Semites are Arabs. The intention is to create the impression that the Jews are hated because they are Semites and not because they are Jews, while the term was invented and is being exploited by the Jews, who are of Khazar origin. The charge of anti-Semitism is an expedient for attacking anyone who stands in their way. The Jews cry "anti-Semitism" whenever anyone reveals their intrigues in the organization of wars, including the wars of religion in Europe, when the Sassoon family in China is discovered to be trading in opium, when the Soviet people groans under Jewish tyranny and millions of Orthodox Christians are liquidated after the Revolution, when the Jews are found to control the gold and diamond mines in South Africa and foment the Boer War, when the peoples reveal their plots to rob various countries of their wealth, when the Jewish doctors' plot to poison innocent people in Russia is discovered in 1953, when Jews are found using children's blood, infecting patients with cancer, and so on and so forth.

'Aqqād, as we have seen, describes anti-Semitism as a natural reaction to the Jewish character. He explains:

> "Hatred of the Semites is not, therefore, a sickness of all the nations with the exception of the Zionists; it is a sickness of the Zionists, which is always and everywhere to be found among them and arouses the natural reaction in every sane man." (p. 42).

Since he defines the evil qualities of the Jewish character as Zionism he calls anti-Semitism "hatred of Zionism" (p. 39). (This conception is shared by Na'nā'a.) 'Aqqād goes on to explain:

> "The persecutions are the outcome of a chronic disease in the Jews which will remain with them in their new State as it was with them in their old State." (p. 15).

Zionism, therefore, will not prevent anti-Semitism:

> "They have attracted persecution in every country, at every time and in every community, and therefore it is not reasonable that the cause should reside in others." (p. 16).

Similar arguments are presented by Dr. Naṣr (p. 33), Basīsū (p. 3) and Darwaza (1960, p. 571).

We can better understand the basic problem of the Arab attitude, even among the more moderate and progressive writers, from Bahā' al-Dīn's attack on Sartre's book on the Jewish problem (*Isrā'īliyāt* ["Judaica"], pp. 93ff). He severely criticizes Sartre for overstepping the mark in his opposition to anti-Semitism and going over to the opposite extreme of giving a blanket justification to everything that is Jewish, putting all the blame on the Gentile world. He charges him with writing like an advocate defending a client, denying all guilt. It is not reasonable to blame only the non-Jews for a problem that has existed for three thousand years and affected so many peoples. Sartre ignores the fact that the nations tried to absorb the Jews and did not always persecute them. The problem of the Jews has persisted, and they have maintained their separateness, even in the Communist countries, where Christianity is no longer the State religion and there are so many atheists, and where it should not have been difficult for the Jews to be absorbed in society. Sartre's argument that the Jews participated in the French resistance organizations is unsound. This was not a sign of a desire to be absorbed in French society. They fought Hitler as Jews fighting for survival, and not as Frenchmen fighting for the glory of France. The Jews reserve the right to choose whether or not to belong to the country in which they live. In Algeria, for example, where they were among the original inhabitants, they chose to receive French citizenship after the French occupation and constitute a section of the European foreigners. Bahā' al-Dīn's purpose is to emphasize that the separatism of the Jews is voluntary and a part of their nature, and not a result of external pressure.

He does not deal with the main subject discussed by Sartre, namely, the psychological effect of the minority's "situation," from which it cannot escape. He criticizes Sartre for not analysing Zionism: if he had done so, he would have found that it possesses all the features of racial fanaticism. A study of the Jewish problem without Zionism, he continues, is intellectually, politically and historically inadequate. The implication is that the faults Bahā' al-Dīn finds in Zionism are evidence of the odiousness of the Jews. Despite the aim of objectivity, his arguments exemplify the difficulty involved in anti-Semitism: that anyone who tries to defend it, even along moderate lines, is liable to be entangled in it himself.

It is not surprising, therefore, that even Bahā' al-Dīn becomes involved in anti-Semitism when he tries to defend it "somewhat." True, he tries to counter the charge of anti-Semitism against the Arabs, explaining that they are anxious for the welfare of the Jews in their own countries and, moreover, that it is in their interest that racial fanaticism should vanish from the earth, since it was basically responsible for the establishment of Israel. The Arabs have no objection to the advocacy of a favourable attitude to the Jews in the countries where they live, but they allege that the defence of the Jews is exploited by Israel against the Arabs and used as a smokescreen to conceal its crimes. Israel is interested in bringing pressure to bear on the conscience of the world by means of a variegated all-round propaganda offensive; she tries to make the whole world feel guilty in order to extort guarantees for her safety and obtain funds, to arouse hostility against the Arabs and present them as the new enemy of the Jews. She tries to induce the world to forgive her for her crimes and regard the expulsion of a million Arabs as reasonable compensation for the sufferings of the Jews. Sartre, the author declares, has been deceived by Israeli propaganda.

Behind Bahā' al-Dīn's arguments we can perceive the suspicion that any favourable statement about the Jews strengthens Israel. This is an indication of the conclusion drawn by the Arabs from the basic conception of the dispute, in terms of games theory, as a "zero-sum game," i.e., a game in which any advantage to one side is automatically an injury to the other. It is also clearly expressed in the attitude that there can be no coexistence for the two rivals, and that whatever strengthens the one weakens the other. If, therefore, a decline in anti-Semitism means improvement in the position of the Jews—and hence a profit to Israel—such a decline must inevitably be counteracted.

11. THE WORLD MISSION OF ARAB ANTI-SEMITISM

The anti-Semitism of the Arabs has Messianic overtones. In their fight against Israel and the Jews, they claim that they are fighting a defensive battle on behalf of all mankind. This is not merely a conflict between themselves and Israel, for the Jews are the enemies of the whole world, and especially of the monotheistic faiths, Christianity and Islam. Their struggle thus becomes more dignified, and their extremism more justified.

'Alūba emphasizes that the Jews regard Christendom as their principal enemy, Islam being only second (p. 69), but the focus of their offensive against the rest of the world passes from Christians to Muslims and back again. He presents this historical analysis:

> "When imperialism [the reference is in this case to the Mongols—Y.H.] ravaged the Muslim countries and put an end to their culture, progress and independence, and the well-known Renaissance took place in the western Christian world, the greatest force of Jewish fanaticism was directed against their first enemy, Christianity. The Christians suffered in the economy of their countries, in their tranquility and political life. As a result, the Christians struck at the Jews, expelled them from their society and banished most of them. Then the Jews had no choice but to decide that their first aim would be self-defence: by closing their ranks, accumulating gold and silver, and avenging themselves against Christianity by dangerous secret means. When they had settled accounts with their first enemy, it would be easier for them to dominate the Muslims." (p. 76).

This was the order of priorities in the Jewish plan. The world must, therefore, be warned of the danger, which is being neglected by the Muslims and, even more, the Christians.

'Alūba denounces the world's leadership for its blindness to the Jewish danger. He declaims against the growing number of Jewish scholars in the universities and their participation in the production of the nuclear bomb, for the fate of mankind depends on its secrets and many of the Jews have been accused of espionage. The Jews, indeed, have destructive intentions against the whole world (p. 136). The attention of the Christian nations must be drawn to the fact that the Jews are not loyal citizens, but first and foremost Jews in the religious and racial sense (p. 137).

In his introduction to his translation of the Protocols, Tūnisī writes:

"This warning of mine against the Zionist danger is not a call to a merely temporary war because of the existing struggle between ourselves and Zionism today, nor is it a call in continuation of a previous struggle and its traces in the struggle of today, but my purpose is to issue a humanitarian warning about the continuing danger that there will never be peace or quiet for the world unless or until this people changes the effects of its barbarous studies on its soul." (p. 9).

a) FROM IDEOLOGY TO ACTION

The struggle against Israel assumes global significance: it is an effort to strike at the sources of Israel's strength—the Jews of the world. The tendency to identify Zionism with the Jews impels the Arabs to expand their activity to embrace the globe. So far, we have dealt with anti-Semitism as an ideology, but ideology is meant to lead to action. Since this study is concerned with principles and is not an historical survey, I shall restrict myself to "chapter headings" on Arab activities in this sphere.

Regarding them as their allies, the Arabs have established contacts with the anti-Semitic movements. In a number of cases it has transpired that there are operative ties between such movements and the diplomatic missions of Arab countries, especially those of Egypt and the Arab League, which have given them financial support. (e.g., there was the case of the association between Col. al-Shazalī, the Egyptian Military Attaché in London, and Tyndall, one of the assistants of the British Nazi leader Jordan, which came into court in 1962 and was reported in the press.)

The offices of the Arab League are used as a centre for the dissemination of anti-Jewish material.

Arab publications issued abroad, especially in South America, contain incitement against the Jews. For example, virulent anti-Jewish material, including extracts from *The Protocols of the Elders of Zion,* has been published in *Nacion Arabe,* a periodical published in Argentina. Jose Baxter, leader of the Tacuara in Argentina, has visited Egypt as a guest of the League (*Background Material on Jewish Activity in Latin America,* World Jewish Congress, July 1962).

Shukairy defended the Tacuara at the UN, expressing the hope that it would spread to other Latin-American countries and that the UN would adopt its principles (speech in the Assembly's Special Committee, December 4, 1962).

The Arabs disseminate anti-Jewish material in Africa and Asia, where anti-Semitism was previously unknown. An example is the pamphlet, already mentioned, published by the Egyptian Ministry of Information. Their support of anti-Semitism and their activities against the Jews face the Arabs with a dilemma of which they are quite conscious. On the one hand, their incitement is meant to injure the Jews so as to reduce their capacity to help Israel: a deterioration in the Jewish position would be a direct blow at Israel and would be reflected in her standing. On the other hand, anti-Jewish activity is incompatible with the aim that the Jews should be absorbed in the countries where they live, for anti-Semitism would impel them to leave and settle in Israel. In Africa, no such possibility exists, and therefore there is no such restraint on anti-Semitic incitement, but it certainly exists in South America, where Arab anti-Semitic activity is widespread. In an article on the Vatican's "Jewish Schema," Bahā' al-Dīn indeed emphasizes that it is in the Arab interest that the Jews should not be persecuted in the countries where they live in case the result should be pressure on them to migrate to Israel; what the Arabs want is

> ". . . that the Jews should find their natural place in their own countries and not in Israel." (*al-Muṣawwar,* December 11, 1964, and also in *Isrā'īliyāt,* p. 225).

The Arabs might well have been expected to give priority to their interest in avoiding pressure on the Jews to emigrate, but their hatred and their desire to injure Israel, if only indirectly, have generally been stronger in the end. Thus the Arab countries opposed an express condemnation of anti-Semitism when the Human Rights Commission discussed a general convention for the abolition of all forms of intolerance; Iraq opposed the amendment in this sense proposed by Chile during the deliberations on March 14-16, 1966.

b) INFLUENCE OF ARAB ANTI-SEMITISM ON WORLD ANTI-SEMITISM

Arab anti-Semitism, in its governmental form, has official and political facilities at its disposal; it therefore has organizational, financial and operational advantages which cannot be enjoyed by non-governmental anti-Semitic bodies. Not only, therefore, has it the means to help the anti-Semitic movements with money, cover and shelter, but the fact that it has State backing gives it influence, leadership and patronage. It is also liable to be more fervent and determined than Western anti-Semitism. Even if we assume that the latter has more veteran leaders, better equipped to develop their ideology, nevertheless the more determined element, which also has stronger motives, is likely to take up a leading position, especially as modern Western anti-Semitism is not distinguished for originality or intellectual fertility, while the younger Arab anti-Semitism may be more dynamic. Its ardour and energy may also be reflected in its ideological activity, and even in this sphere it may become a leading factor and a source of inspiration. Actually, Arab influence on Western anti-Semitic publications may be seen in their adoption of ideas that express Arab interests, e.g. the argument that the Jews in the Diaspora embroil their Governments in the Middle East against the interests of their countries, or that, by supporting Israel, Governments act against their own national interest, which is to win the friendship of the Arabs. Anti-Semites have, thus, demanded cuts in support for Israel and opposed measures harmful to the Arabs like the reduction of American economic support for Nasser. In South America, the anti-Semites emphasize—also under the influence of Arab interests—that Jews, as citizens of the State, cannot be Zionists.

Pro-Arab organizations may be drawn into anti-Jewish tendencies through adopting the Arab nationalist attitude even if anti-Semitism was not at first a prominent element in their policy. Anti-Jewish themes may be found in denunciations of Israel and her actions. Pro-Arab tendencies become anti-Israel, and then anti-Semitic. In so far as there were anti-Jewish elements in pro-Arab circles at the beginning, cooperation with the Arabs is liable to strengthen them.

Today, there are no Western Governments that support anti-Semitism, which is rejected by the developed countries, but the fact that a considerable bloc of States, aided by Egypt, which plays an important role among the new States, have adopted anti-Semitic attitudes, which have sometimes been expressed by their representatives, may have given the anti-Semites the feeling that their movement was respectable. In this way, Arab anti-Semitism may have been a source of encouragement and legitimation for the anti-Semitic groups.

There are also grounds for the assumption that the Arabs represent a prevalent trend in world anti-Semitism. In the past, Western anti-Semites sometimes tended to distinguish between the Jews and Israel, and there were even some who supported Zionism as a way to get rid of the Jews. This attitude, of course, was inconsistent, for if the Jews are evil, the State they establish must inevitably be an obnoxious one, for it will represent their faults in concentrated form. Indeed, there was a tendency towards hostility to the National Home and the State of Israel among the more extreme and bellicose anti-Semites. Arab anti-Semitism moved in the opposite direction: from the denunciation of Zionism and Israel to the condemnation of the Jews. In their emphasis on hostility to the State of Israel, the Arabs may be exemplifying a trend in world anti-Semitism—or at least its active elements—to complete the circle in the opposite direction: from hatred of the Jews to hatred of their State. There is a further motive for the organized anti-Semites to hate Israel: the fact that she plays an active part in the struggle against anti-Semitism. It is only natural, moreover, that they should regard the Jewish State as a symbol and a centre for "World Jewry."

In short, anti-Semitic organizations have become supporters and allies of the Arabs in their struggle with Israel, and even serve them in their anti-Israel propaganda. Even if Arab anti-Semitism is the disciple of the Western variety, the latter is today a branch of the former, rather than the opposite. In the West, it is true, Arab activity helps to sustain anti-Semitism rather than to create it, but in other parts of the world, such as Africa and Asia, where it was not previously known, such beginnings of Jew-hatred as exist are due first and foremost to Arab influence. The struggle against Israel has assumed worldwide scope.

c) THE CATHOLIC "SCHEMA" ON THE JEWS

The struggle against Israel leads the Arabs not only to disseminate anti-Semitism as an anti-Jewish activity, but also to undertake active measures against the Jews. They were infuriated, for example, when the Catholic Church was considering the exoneration of the Jews from collective guilt for the crucifixion of Jesus. Many furious protests against the proposal appeared in the Arab press. It was explained that this was not merely a religious issue, but mainly a political one: it was the result of a World Zionist plot to compel the Vatican to take this step, exploiting the Zionist power of intrigue and making capital out of Pope Pius XII's failure to denounce the destruction of the Jews by the Nazis. Israel would be strengthened if the Vatican Council confirmed the "Jewish Schema," "which will arouse the Zionists to further crimes against the Palestinian peoples" (the Syrian Minister of Religious Trusts in *al-Jihād,* November 22, 1964). The suspicion was expressed that the Schema was a step towards Vatican recognition of Israel and the establishment of diplomatic relations. Its adoption was repeatedly represented as an anti-Arab measure and an act of hostility to Arab nationalism. Although the main argument was that it was not really a religious and theological, but a political question, the Arabs, both Christians and Muslims, presented religious arguments to prove that Jewish guilt for the death of Jesus is still valid, and that any change must be opposed even for purely religious reasons. It was emphasized that the change would lead to controversy and dissension in the Church, and there were forecasts, or threats, that Christianity might suffer as a result in the Middle East countries.

It was even suggested that the adoption of the Schema would be harmful to the Jews and to Zionism:

> 'There is even a danger to the future of World Zionism—for the Jewish philosopher Spinoza said that it was the historical persecution of the Jews, which followed from the crucifixion of Jesus, that led to the unification of the Jews as a people . . . But for it, they would have assimilated and disappeared among other peoples." (Salīm Najjār, in *al-Ṣafā',* Lebanon, November 10, 1963).

It would be no exaggeration to say that no other group or body in the world brought direct public, political or diplomatic pressure to bear to prevent the adoption of the Schema. No other organized Christian community protested, as those in the Arab countries did, sending cables and memoranda which were published in the Arabic press (e.g. *al-Manār,* November 23, 1964; *al-Jumhūriyya,* October 27, 1964). It is not surprising that Lebanon was particularly active. Its President and diplomatic representatives made direct and urgent representations against the adoption of the Schema. Even if we assume, which seems likely, that the activities of the Arab Christian representatives in the institutions of the Church, and even the diplomatic missions, were less virulent and aggressive than their public statements, it is significant that the matter should have had to be presented to the Arab public in the way it was.

The Government of the UAR conducted an international propaganda campaign. It was decided to issue a book called *The Spurious Israel,* by Farīd Abdallah Jūrjī, to denounce the manoeuvres by which World Zionism was trying to persuade the Vatican to exonerate the Jews and prove that the Schema was a purely political affair. Dr. 'Abd al-Qādir Ḥātim, the Minister of Culture and National Guidance, ordered the book to be translated into foreign languages and given worldwide distribution *(al-Idhā'a wa-al-Tilifizyūn)* (November 21, 1964). He also gave instructions for the preparation of a film, "The Jews and Jesus," based on a book called *The Trial of Jesus* (not identified in the report) to counter the proposal to exonerate the Jews (*al-Jumhūrriyya,* April 7, 1965).

There would be material for an instructive monograph dealing solely with this episode and the feverish activity of the Arab world in connection with it, but I shall have to be content with a brief survey of several outstanding aspects.

The question of the Jewish Schema is the central subject of Na'nā'a's *Zionism in the Sixties, the Vatican and the Jews,* which has already been mentioned several times. The author explains the historical framework of the document:

> "The Jews saw that Israel does not solve their problems, but its existence intensifies the complications of the problem, and imposes on them material and spiritual difficulties from which they were free before the Zionist movement . . .
> "The Jews realized that instead of Israel solving their problem, it is still incapable of solving its own problem." (pp. 4-5).

Zionism has lost its prestige, but its organizational capacity and activity are still great. Therefore it tried to achieve a new victory, which would strengthen the movement and weaken the Arabs. For this reason, it approached the Vatican. Zionism began to spin its intrigues. The Jews organized Protestant-Christian friendship leagues all over the world. Then they turned to the Catholics and organized similar associations with them. Zionism infiltrated converted Jews, like Monsignor Oesterreicher, into Catholic posts, with the function of serving Judaism as Christians (p. 59). The plot began to thicken. For the first time a Jewish representative was present at the inauguration of a Pope—John XXIII—as well as at his funeral. When Paul VI was consecrated, a Rabbi was appointed as member of the American delegation—again for the first time at such a ceremony. For the first time the Jews succeeded in preventing Christian prayers in American State schools (p. 26). The author goes on to survey the various attitudes, deliberations and publications connected with the Schema.

The Quran accuses the Jews, not of crucifying Jesus, but of hanging a man who resembled him, but Na'nā'a takes a great deal of trouble to prove that the guilt was not confined to the Jewish leaders; according to his account, the entire people forced the crucifixion on Pontius Pilate, who was afraid of the harm the Jews threatened to do him if he refused to do their will. In support of this charge, Na'nā'a presents "archaeological evidence" dating back 15 centuries, which was found in England, proving that Pilate made desperate efforts to save Jesus (p. 44). Na'nā'a goes on to demonstrate the continuity of Jewish collective guilt up to modern times. Since, he argues, the Jews have not repented of their crime or done anything to atone for it, all Jews throughout history identify themselves with the murderers of Jesus and share their guilt. The author goes on to describe how the Jews show disrespect for Christianity and the Virgin Mary, while Islam pays them honour.

Abdallah Tall adopts a similar line of argument. He bases his allegations of Jewish hatred to Christianity on the Arabic translation of Rohling's book and the latter's quotations from the Jewish *Book of the Generations* and *Book of Genealogies.* He accuses the Jews of responsibility for the persecution and killing of the Christians in Rome, Libya and Cyprus, of charging the Virgin Mary with immorality and shamefully blackening the name of Jesus. He reproduces from the Lebanese paper *al-Ṣayyād,* November 19, 1963, quotations from inferior "Jewish" books about Jesus and allegations of his immorality published by the "Jewish" publishing house of Simon and Schuster, which are disseminated among young people in order to corrupt them (pp. 28-37).

Bahā' al-Dīn, who devotes to the episode a chapter in *Isrā'iliyāt* (pp. 222-32—also printed as an article in *al-Muṣawwar,* December 11, 1964), has a different approach. He starts with a fair and balanced account of the Christian aspect of the religious persecutions of the Jews in Europe, which were based on the crucifixion charge, while Islam "declares that the crime itself did not exist, and therefore there was no responsibility and no one responsible." He goes on to say that Zionist policy follows three parallel lines of action. First it is interested in arousing fear of persecution so as to stimulate the Jews to settle in Israel (in a previous chapter we have noted the author's view that the Zionists regard anti-Semitism as an ally). At the same time, Zionism establishes contacts with liberal circles to get their support for its work. When neither of these two methods, "fanaticism or liberalism," produces results, it turns to "the dangerous wonder-weapon, the weapon of the guilt complex" (p. 226). Here he is not far removed from Na'nā'a's tale of intrigue, though he uses more elegant language. (Another writer on the same lines is Anīs Qāsim, in *We, the Vatican and Israel,* Research Centre, Palestine Liberation Organization, Beirut, June 1966.)

Zionism conducted a ramified campaign with the aid of Hochhuth's play *The Vicar,* exploiting the dilemma of Pope Pius XII, who was afraid to come out against Nazism in case Europe should be submerged by Soviet Communism. Revelations on this subject from the Vatican archives, Bahā' al-Dīn suggests,

> "... are not unknown to Israel and World Zionism, and by exploiting this opening, it [Zionism] can, of course, terrorize the Vatican in the same way as it publicly terrorizes Western Germany by threatening to blacken the name and destroy the future of any politician or senior official by revealing his former ties with the Nazis. At the same time, it conducts a campaign on another plane, to tie up 'liberalism' in a general form with Israel, the State, and Zionism as a movement, and not with Judaism purely as a religion." (p. 232).

Bahā' al-Dīn agrees with the general Arab approach in regarding Jewish activity in the Vatican, in so far as it existed, as part of the intrigues of the powers of darkness and an example of the hypocrisy and cunning of World Zionism: terror on the one hand and liberalism on the other.

He calls upon the Arabs to avoid a hasty and nervous reaction and goes on to describe the Arab attitude in terms which are not at all in keeping with reality, for even a somewhat moderate attitude, like that of Bahā' al-Dīn, is far outweighed by the prevalent extremism. He writes:

> "The principles of liberation, toleration and avoidance of racialism are our principles, for Israel is the manifestation of a racialist reactionary movement, namely Zionism, which is the heritage of European and not Arab persecution, for the true meaning of liberation and equality are on the side of the Arabs and not against them, and the Arabs should take the initiative in this matter. We are always ready to expose every Israeli attempt to exploit religion and religious bodies for political purposes, and we shall not agree that Europe should settle its grave racial and political heritage at our expense." (p. 232).

If Bahā' al-Dīn makes any reservations, they are only in regard to extremist activities against the Schema, which make him feel somewhat uncomfortable and adopt an apologetic tone. However, even his arguments ultimately imply approval on principle for the campaign, on the grounds that the Schema was designed to serve political interests under the cloak of religion.

12. ANTI-SEMITISM IN THE ARAB COUNTRIES

To what extent is anti-Semitic propaganda liable to influence the Arab public and the position of the Jews in Arab countries?

As has already been emphasized, Arab anti-Semitism has not, on the whole, been deeply rooted among the people; it has been mainly propagated by leaders, authors and journalists. But the constant emphasis on the vileness of all the Jews leads to the same qualities being ascribed to those in the Arab countries as well. Furthermore, there are factors in the circumstances of the conflict which are liable to arouse and foster hatred of the Jews.

Since the Jews were not previously regarded as a threat, they were not hated; at most, they were despised; but the trumpeting of the Jewish threat was bound to arouse hatred.

It is only natural that the circumstances of the conflict have placed the Jews who remained in the Arab countries in a difficult position. Their relationship with Israel as a Jewish State and the relatives they have there are regarded as ties with the enemy and proof of national disloyalty. If they favour Israel, they are traitors to the declared national objective of its liquidation, especially when underground Zionist organizations and ties with Israel are discovered among them. The emigration of Jews from the Arab countries to Israel and their attempts to take out or transfer their property are also suspected as anti-national activities designed to strengthen the enemy, and cast doubts on the national loyalty of other Jews to the Arab countries in which they live.

'Iṣmat wrote in *Zionism and Freemasonry* (1950), citing Israel Abrahams' *Jewish Thought*, that it is Zionism which strengthens the spirit of Jewish solidarity, and goes on to say:

> "Let no one advise us to exonerate from Zionism the Jews in the Arab countries who pretend to be innocent, no matter how wretched and degraded they appear to be, for they are Zionists like the rest of the Jews in the world. If they conceal their Zionism for a while, they will reveal it at a suitable opportunity, like the other Jews in the other countries. They will reveal it openly and in public, for they are none other than Zionist vipers as 'Antara [the poet] said: 'Even though the viper is smooth to the touch, the venom flows in its teeth.' They are nothing but a fifth column in every country." (pp. 49-50).

The same image is used by Bayhūm, quoted in Sylvia Haim's anthology, *Arab Nationalism*.

Ṣafwat wrote along the same lines in 1952 about the Jews in the Arab countries:

> "They are an extremely great fifth column, which willingly supports Israel, and helps it by information and ties with prominent men to collect information and pass it on regularly." (1952, p. 198).

On the eve of the Jewish New Year, Nasser was in the habit of sending greetings to the Egyptian Chief Rabbi, and the occasion was fairly reported in the Egyptian press. However, when Muhammad Najīb visited the synagogue to greet the Jews on the occasion of the festival, the Damascus paper, representing the extremist attitude of the Syrians, wrote:

> "It is a common mistake in the Arab countries that the law regards alien Jews as citizens equal in rights and duties to the other members of the nation. The Jews have a different creed and nationality than the Arabs, and they are aliens in every country. The Jew lives only for his profit; he has one aim: to accumulate capital by all possible means in order to restore the glory of Israel. Many peoples in the world have realized that the Jews are a growth which must be eradicated from the body of the homeland. Hitler found that his country's defeat in World War I was due to the Jews, who gained control over the country, exploited the people's resentment at the horrors of war, created anarchy, and compelled the German army to agree to the armistice and to defeat. Hitler's luck failed him, and the Jews returned to corrupt the country and subordinate the defeated Germans and their victorious rivals to their own ends. They established the State of Israel on Arab territory, sacred to millions of Muslims and Christians, and exiled its inhabitants in defiance of the United Nations and its sublime principles." (*al-Liwā',* October 30, 1952).

Specific cases sometimes arise which are liable to stimulate anti-Semitic feelings among the Arabs and lead to discrimination and other measures against the Jews. For example, a debate about the Jews was aroused in the Lebanese press when Dā'ūd Mizrahi, a wealthy Jewish merchant of Tripoli, closed down his business and disappeared from the country under suspicious circumstances. Similar cases occur from time to time.

Al-Muḥarrir wrote in an editorial on January 25, 1966:

> "We all know that Zionist influence—through western influence—brought about the transfer to Israel, with the agreement of the reactionary regime of the

time, of thousands of Jews from Yemen who had been settled in that country for centuries. We all know that up to a short time ago the reactionary regime in Morocco allowed thousands of Moroccan Jews to go to Israel through Spain. We also know that the same thing was done in Tunisia, and that the separatist regime in Syria also tried to follow the same policy. As a result of all this, Israel today presents proposals of a grave character. She argues that tens of thousands of Jews who previously lived in the Arab countries have settled in the country in recent years. If so, Israel asks, why should the Arab refugees not be settled in their stead?

"It is obvious that this foolish and opportunistic logic cannot solve the problem and is not even worthy of consideration. At the same time, this proposal—and that is what Israel wants—can serve as a propaganda card to arouse the interest of world public opinion. In any case, Jewish emigration to Israel from the Arab countries, whatever its scope, shows clearly that the Arabs have not understood this matter properly and have not perceived the true nature of this emigration: that a large part of the Jews, who lived here for centuries in a freedom the like of which they did not know anywhere else in the world, and which they still enjoy, are loyal first and foremost to our enemies and await a suitable opportunity to accumulate great wealth by unsavoury means and escape to the occupied territory, where they will serve, at best, as a propaganda weapon and, at worst, for espionage and sabotage . . .

"It has taken us a long time to understand that the enemy regards our tolerance of the Jewish religion as unmitigated political folly. Palestine fell because of this folly, and a number of things have been done by espionage networks to exploit this tolerance. Nevertheless, most of the Jews whom we call 'Arab Jews' have remained loyal to our enemies and await the opportunity to spy on us in order to injure our people and then to emigrate to Israel and escape punishment, so that the enemy should begin to talk about them as a substitute for the return of the Palestinian people to its soil . . .

"It is perfectly obvious to all our citizens that we have gone to the limit in our chivalrous efforts and that there is no longer any possibility to stab us in the back or carry out any new plot, and that those responsible in all the Arab States must arise and stand guard against this danger, and adopt a series of measures to put an end to these hostile activities."[19]

The incitement continued after the Six-Day War, and the maltreatment of Jews in the Arab countries was justified in the resolutions of the Islamic Congress, which met in Amman in September 1967:

"The Jews in the Arab countries have not respected the defence that Islam has given them for generations. They have encouraged World Zionism and Israel in every way in its aggression against the Arabs, in its usurpation of the Land and the Muslim Holy Places in Palestine. The Congress hereby declares that the Jews in the Muslim countries whose ties with Zionism and Israel are proved shall be regarded as fighters against the Muslims, unfit for the patronage and protection which the Muslim faith prescribes for adherents of peaceful protected faiths, and it will be the duty of the Muslim Governments to treat them as aggressive fighters." (Amman Radio, September 22, 1967, 14:15 hrs.).

The development of an anti-Semitic attitude to Jews in the Arab countries is liable to be influenced by a number of psychological and social factors. Anti-Jewish prejudice in the West was often particularly rife among the middle class. Social stratification in the Arab countries is producing an Arab middle class, which may become fertile ground for such ideas, especially as economic hardship, internal malaise and unemployment among intellectuals add to the temptation to blame the Jews for the difficulties. The rise of a fervent Arab nationalism, which has become the central theme of public life, intensifies the consciousness of national identity and, at the same time, of the "mark-off" and "social distance" towards those who have come to be regarded as belonging to an "out-group."

It may also be necessary to take into account the fact that in the past, when Jews and Arabs lived as close neighbours, direct contact to some extent counteracted the attribution of vile and satanic qualities to the Jews, even if they were a competitive factor. So long as Jews were constantly being met in daily life, it was obvious that they were human beings like any others, but their departure was liable to contribute to the process of dehumanization. (It should be noted that there are hardly any Jews left in the Arab countries of the Middle East. In Egypt, for example, there are only some 2,000 in a population of 31 million, i.e. less than one for every 10,000.) This is supported by evidence—though only empirical—from Germany. Deutsch and Merritt, in their article, "Effect of Events on National and International Images" (Kelman, H. C., ed., *International Behavior*, p. 166), explain that distance is liable to lead to dehumanization. In Germany, in 1933-4, there was at first some resistance to brutal measures against the Jews, but after they had been expelled and were no longer to be seen in public, distance deprived them of their human character and contributed to the readiness of the Germans to acquiesce in their liquidation. To hate the Jews it is not necessary to know them personally.

13. SUMMARY

The theories commonly advanced to explain the rise of anti-Semitism in the West during the past two centuries, on the basis of social, economic and psychological factors, are not applicable to the phenomenon in the Arab countries. Anti-Semitism in the West is connected with the rise of the Jews in European society after emancipation and their achievement of positions in the economic and cultural spheres. Ambition was the main feature of the Jewish stereotype. Among the Arabs, however, there was no emancipation to raise the status of the Jews to a level that aroused the envy of the population; they did not symbolize the development of capitalism or occupy such an important place in life as in the West; they were not prominent in political or party activities; they never became prime ministers. The Arab could always regard the Quran's decree on Jewish degradation and wretchedness as vindicated, generally, by the absence of a Jewish political centre, and, more literally, in respect of at least part of the Jewish community. Some authorities have ascribed the rise of anti-Semitism in the West to various upsets and crises, but Arab anti-Semitism has nothing to do with internal crises or the processes of modernization. For others, the Jews symbolize the discomforts of urbanization (Allport, 1958, p. 242), but this is not applicable to the Arab world. In Europe the Jews occupied an irritatingly central place in the self-image of the population, but again this did not apply to the Arabs, among whom they were not outstanding in literature, the theatre or the press, as in the West. In the United States, an elaborate theoretical structure has been erected on the basis of a tendency to anti-Semitism which was attributed to certain particular types, such as the "prejudiced personality." It cannot be denied that such types exist in the Arab countries; perhaps, as we have noted, they may even be common, but Arab anti-Semitism cannot be founded mainly on psychological reasons. In the West there was an element, noted by the pioneer Zionist thinker Pinsker, of fear of the Jew as an unnatural element, but no such fear existed in the Arab world; on the contrary, the Arabs were confident of their own superiority. For the Christians, the very existence of the Jews, who refused to accept the Gospel, was a provocation, while Islam accepted their presence in its midst, though under conditions of subordination.

While the Jews may be hated because they are regarded as different and alien, Islamic society was founded on the recognition of religious groups existing side by side, with power and superiority reserved for the Muslim faith. The Ottoman Empire did not resent the foreignness of the Jews, for it was based on the existence of distinct religious groups, which it accepted as a matter of course. It is true that the rise of Arab nationalism, which inevitably creates a consciousness of national uniqueness and an aspiration for inner homogeneity, intensifies sensitivity towards aliens, but even this cannot be regarded as a primary cause of anti-Semitism.

Western anti-Semitism contained a popular element, which started from the Jewish stereotype and the prejudices current among the people, and was nourished by the charge that the Jews killed God. Arab anti-Semitism, on the other hand, is not basically popular, nor is it founded on the stereotype of the Jew that has been current in the Arab world. On the contrary, it tries to contradict the stereotype, which is based on weakness, and replace it by the image of a powerful, dangerous and threatening enemy. People are inclined to despise the weak, and to fear and hate the strong. Arab anti-Semitism is not based on stereotypes and prejudices, but tries to implant them in the popular imagination. If the Arab-Israel conflict was settled, anti-Semitic manifestations would die out, but the continuation of the conflict is liable to deepen the anti-Semitic elements in the popular consciousness.

The distinctive feature of Arab anti-Semitism is that from the beginning it was not directed against Jews as a minority, whether as individuals or as a group living in the Arab countries, but against Israel and the Jews living outside the Arab world. When the authorities fomented anti-Semitism in Europe, it was part of their internal policies and strategies, or, at most, a means of subversion abroad, as it was used by Hitler. Arab anti-Semitism, however, is a part of the Arab countries' struggle against Israel and their strategy in foreign policy; its main stress is on the Jews as a political organism. It is rooted in external political motives.

To sum up, it should be stated with the utmost emphasis that Arab anti-Semitism is not the cause of the conflict but one of its results; it is not the reason for the hostile Arab attitude towards Israel and the Jews, but a means of deepening, justifying and institutionalizing that hostility. Its rise is connected with the tension created as a result of Zionist activity, and especially of the traumatic experience of defeat, the establishment of independent Israel and the struggle against her. Anti-Semitism is a weapon in this struggle. It is functional and political, not social: it presents the Jews mainly as a political, not a social threat, and it is partially directed by the administration which conducts the political struggle, or at least gives it its blessing. Hence, it describes the Jews, not as passive, shrinking parasites, but as aggressors. Unlike Western Christian anti-Semitism, it is not the result of generations of incitement which have created an archetype in the popular consciousness, although there are elements in Islam on which anti-Semitism could build.

It does not follow, however, from the difference between Arab and Western anti-Semitism that the numerous anti-Jewish books do not deserve to be called "anti-Semitic," or that there is no "Arab anti-Semitism." Western anti-Semitism contains a Christian religious element, but it does not follow that there cannot be another type, in which such a factor is not present. The limitation of anti-Semitism to the type that involves a Christian element and a popular emotion is purely arbitrary.

The difference between the hatred of the Jews in the West and in the Islamic world was defined by Sapir in his article "Hatred of the Jews in Arab Literature" (1899), in these terms:

> "The Muhammadan Arabs' hatred of the Jews was only an external hatred, or an external war which was necessary at the time: when the Jews were powerful they regarded them as a barrier to their victory and glory, but when the Jews were submissive and did not interfere with their positions, the hatred disappeared. On the other hand, we can see in the hatred of the other nations towards the Jews an inner hatred, a profound and ineradicable natural emotion, which appeared also—or particularly—at a time when the Jews were trampled upon and anyone could strike at them with impunity." (*Hashiloah*, Vol. VI, p. 223).

On the establishment of the State of Israel, the Jews again became "a barrier to their victory and glory," and Jew-hatred came to life, with the old and new elements inextricably intermingled.

Despite the superficiality of Arab anti-Semitism and its shallow roots in popular feeling, there are a number of factors that are liable to make it particularly fervent and powerful. In the West there was something artificial and abstract in the presentation of the Jews as a danger; it could be done only by weaving ingenious tales of plots and stratagems. The Arabs, on the other hand, regard Israel as a real danger; they have experienced several defeats and fear more. Neither the Russians nor the Germans burned their fingers in their relations with the Jews as the Arabs did. The Germans accused them of responsibility for the "stab in the back," but for the Arabs the blow was direct, they were defeated by the Jews in face-to-face confrontation. Western anti-Semitism denounced the Jews as a secret enemy; for the Arabs, Israel is an enemy without pretence or concealment.

Anti-Semitism among the Arabs is, therefore, vigorous and aggressive; it is so ardent that it overcomes even the restraints created by the memory of the Nazi holocaust. Their motivation is so strong that they are not inhibited even by the example of the moral, human and national havoc that anti-Semitism wrought in Germany. Their anti-Semitism is fervent and vengeful; its very existence is cathartic and helps to restore their wounded self-respect.

The starting point of Arab anti-Semitism is the culpability of the State of Israel; next it goes on to attribute odium to the Jews, which is then passed back to their State. In Europe the Jews were an evil in themselves; the Arabs regard them as partners with imperialism, the major satanic power in the world today. The kingdom of darkness, in the Arab version, is ruled by a trinity: imperialism, Israel (and the Jews), and reaction. The fundamental Arab conception was that imperialism, as an embodiment of aggression against the peoples, was the root of the evil, which "created" Israel and from which the evil of Israel emanated as a manifestation and a product of aggression, but Arab anti-Semitism has been developing the idea that Israel's Jewishness produces a further evil. Its bond with imperialism is not accidental; it is a result of its Jewishness.

Arab anti-Semitism might have been expected to be free from the idea of racial odium, since Jews and Arabs are both regarded by race theory as Semites, but the odium is directed, not against the Semitic race, but against the Jews as a historical group. The main idea is that the Jews, racially, are a mongrel community, most of them being not Semites, but of Khazar and European origin. Their despicable qualities are transmitted not by biological inheritance, but through cultural and religious channels. The Jewish creed and spirit are emphasized as the root of the evil. However, since the Jewish religion is described as the creation of the Jews, who distorted the element of truth it contained, the origin of the evil goes back to the ancient Jews—which means that it is racial after all.

The first anti-Semitic books in Arabic were written by Christian Arabs under French influence, but Arab anti-Semitism today is of an Islamic religious character. It is no accident that this is emphasized in such books as those of 'Aqqād, 'Alūba, Tall, al-Jiyār, Ṭabbāra and Rousan, or in articles in the *al-Azhar* monthly. This religious character, however, prevents the struggle against Jewry being conceived as a confrontation between the slave mentality and morality and that of the master race, as it was presented by the Nazis. Nor, of course, does Arab anti-Semitism involve a war against religion, as in the Soviet Union, for example.

A question of principle arises: Was the adoption of anti-Semitic ideas the inevitable outcome of the refusal to acquiesce in the existence of the

State of Israel? It seems natural that a prolonged and virulent quarrel with Israel was liable to lead to a tendency to denigrate its people. Once an international conflict breaks out, it is not restricted to the political level; it spills over into the rival peoples. The denial of Israel's right to exist leads to the attribution of odious characteristics to the Israelis, and the odium is extended to their Jewishness, especially as most of the Israelis are recent settlers: the fact that they are in Israel and not in the Diaspora is often accidental; it does not reflect any inherent difference between them and their brethren living abroad, and an Israeli identity, distinct from the Jewish identity, has not yet taken shape. The fundamental characteristic of the Israelis is that they are Jews, and their Israeli identity is only a shallow surface layer—especially as the Diaspora Jews assist Israel and are connected with them by bonds of kinship and aid.

Furthermore, Israel as the Arabs see her is so vile that she deserves no lesser penalty than extinction. It is not only a question of antagonism to some policy she adopts or some action she has perpetrated, or a quarrel over some limited subject, but a denunciation of the very existence of her political personality. Since this is a State doomed to death, it must be evil, and since it is the incarnation of evil, its odiousness is not limited merely to its political superstructure, but pervades all the strata of its population. Good men could not establish and maintain such a monstrosity. The evil in the State reflects the character of its inhabitants—and is reflected in them. Besides, in order to prepare for the brutality of liquidating Israel by violence, the Arabs must harden their hearts against her inhabitants and dehumanize them.[20] Anti-Semitism becomes an educational necessity in furtherance of the politicidal aim.

Thus, Professor Fāris wrote:

> "If we have to kill, the task is made less painful to the extent that we can define the victim as nonhuman. The soldier has to think of the enemy as subhuman, if he is to bring himself willingly to use the dagger against him." (From his article "Interaction Levels and Inter-group Relations," p. 37).

It may, therefore, be assumed that the advocacy of the liquidation of Israel creates an inclination to develop anti-Semitic concepts. This is not a matter of logical determinism. Anti-Semitism is not a necessary condition for the advocacy of liquidation, but it helps. It closes the circle and makes the attitude more complete and consistent.

Even Nājī Alūsh, who does not resort to anti-Semitism, is not entirely free from it; citing Marx's analysis, he denounces the Jews as the embodiment of capitalism and Israel as the outcome of colonialism. The implication is that Israel cannot possibly be immune from some kind of odium, whether through capitalism, or colonialism, or both.

Although the abuse of Israel, Zionism and the Jews is a secondary phenomenon, motivated by the existence of the conflict, it serves to support and justify the aim of liquidating Israel. The hostility against the State overflows onto the Israelis and the Jews. Not only the State, but the Jew who lives in it and his brethren, wherever they may be, are also odious. Moreover, if the State deserves to be liquidated, the same applies to the odious Israeli. The growth of anti-Semitic ideas reflects a highly significant development in the Arab attitude in the conflict. In the name of the idea of justice for the Palestinians, which may arouse understanding and sympathy, the Arabs are summoned to perpetrate an act of politicide—the destruction of a State—and the ideology which defames Israel and the Israelis impels them to complete the circle by fostering genocidal tendencies. The existence of Israel involves the concentration of the Jews in it, and its liquidation, therefore, inevitably depends on the ending of this concentration, either by bloodshed or by some miraculous kind of bloodless "evaporation."

Anti-Semitism widens the scope of this conception. If the Jews aim at world destruction, the world is faced with the alternative of either submitting to them and accepting their rule or, on the contrary, subduing them and destroying the threat by abolishing their existence. If Judaism is loathsome, and so are the Jews who profess it, there must be an end to Judaism and the Jews. "A final solution"—no matter in what style, whether by violence or by gentler means—is an integral part of anti-Semitism. Since anti-Semitism regards the Jews as a pathological phenomenon, a cancer in the flesh of humanity, it rejects their right to a future and cherishes the ideal of a world without Jews. 'Aqqād says that, against the Jews,

> "...the nations have no expedient except, ultimately, to subdue them or surrender to them completely. But this is a sheer absurdity on any assumption. The malady which is innate in this group is that they constitute a socially degenerate entity, for they are a group which can neither become a nation nor return to the Bedouin [tribal] organization. This group has become entangled with the world; it is in a stage of stagnation, unfit for growth. Any cure will be useless, so long as the world does not make it overcome its own nature, and absorb it compulsorily among its nations; this is what will inevitably happen, for nothing else will come to pass." (pp. 16-17).

Aḥmad sums up:

> "The day will soon come when this gang will be wiped out of existence and disappear from off the face of the earth, and then, with its obliteration, an era of robbery, treachery and crime will come to an end." (pp. 77-8).

The redemption of the world, in other words, will come with the disappearance of the Jews.

The demand that the Jews must assimilate is also repeated in Arab works which lay the emphasis on anti-Zionism rather than anti-Semitism, and it is thus a general one. Since the Jews are denied any unique character which would entitle them to a national life of their own, their failure to assimilate is denounced as racialism. Thus, for example, Darwaza condemns Moses Hess' statement that the Jews have survived because of their racial instinct, the theories of Pinsker and Herzl, and Ahad Ha'am's call for the preservation of Jewish distinctiveness, which reveal a tendency to racial superiority on the part of the chosen people (*A Short Survey of the Palestine Problem* (in English), pp. 15-16). A similar point of view is expressed by Dr. Sayegh. Bahā' al-Dīn also regards the continued survival of the Jews as deplorable; as we have seen, he identifies assimilation with liberalism and Zionism with anti-liberalism. The difference between the anti-Zionist approach and the anti-Semitic one is that the former sees no place in the world for Jewish distinctiveness, while the latter can find no room for Jews at all.

Chapter 6
ISRAEL

1. ORGANIC ODIOUSNESS

The odious characteristics attributed to Israel are described as an instrinsic part of her nature, as if a good Israel would be a contradiction in terms. All the odiousness of Zionism, as a movement aiming at stealing a territory, is focused in the State which it has established. If Zionism is odious because of its aspirations, Israel is odious as their embodiment. Moreover, Israel stubbornly continues to exist, repeating each day, as it were, the crime involved in her establishment, thus intensifying her fundamental odiousness. Israel's odiousness is organic: ideological, historical, cultural and political—a comprehensive combination of the odiousness implicit in her forebears, Zionism and Judaism, with the addition of a further odium specific to herself.

An example of a mélange of denunciation, containing a wide variety of ingredients—historical, anti-Semitic, anti-Zionist and anti-Israel—may be found in an article by Sayyid Nawfal, Assistant Secretary-General of the Arab League, "The Struggle of Arab Nationalism Against Imperialism and Zionism," in the *Egyptian Political Science Review* (April, 1962):

> "The Israelis and afterwards Zionism, in both ancient and modern times, are characterized by blind fanaticism, a bond between race and religion, the exploitation for their private benefit and their covetous desires of the peoples among whom they live, disloyalty to the homeland where they live, the fanning of the flames of hostility and war as a means of profit and exploitation, the violation of every alliance and agreement, lamentation for the State they have lost, the utilization of an extraordinary mixture *(al-khalīṭ al-shādhdh)* of despicable qualities *(mathālib)* and human failings as a stratagem to establish a State for themselves, which deprives the lawful inhabitants of their rights and carves out a political path of expansion and aggression, relying upon power and the accomplished fact." (p. 89).

According to Arabs, the "uniqueness" claimed by Jewry (the "Chosen People") is reflected in Israel, which is an abnormal, unnatural entity, and therefore odious; hence the repeated and emphatic use of the adjective *shādhdh,* abnormal, in connection with it.

Descriptions of Israel's odiousness are meant to justify and prepare the way for her liquidation. She is described as a satanic, vile entity, quite unlike any other State ('Alūba, p. 183). The denunciation has a pre-emptive purpose: to forestall any possible pangs of conscience on account of hostility to Israel and the aspiration to liquidate her. The politicidal ideology and the negative image of Israel are complementary.

It may be assumed that a politicidal aim—even if based on political arguments like the denunciation of the usurpation of Arab territory and the demand for its return, and not so much on the portrayal of the culprit as vile in himself—will ultimately lead to a tendency to find fault with him. Apparently, the trend is, in the main, from the solution to the description of the situation: i.e., from the doom of death pronounced on Israel to the attribution of vile qualities to her, rather than the opposite: from denunciation to the doom of destruction.

The denunciation also contains an element of competition and fear. Zionism is an abstract enemy, but Israel is a concrete factor, a State with resources, achievements and power. For the Arabs, Israel's achievements arouse irritation and self-deprecation; they need to denounce Israel in order to console themselves. Israel's strength gives rise to anxiety and fear; hence the tendency to belittle her achievements, or to recognize them but attribute them to external aid, or to admit her strength but explain it away as satanic and ephemeral.

The denunciation is also required in order to prove that Israel can actually be liquidated, on the grounds that her organic vileness creates organic weakness. As an odious State, Israel is not a healthy State; her fate is sealed because she is an aberration.

The outcome of all these ideas is the creation of a selective mechanism for the absorption of Israel's dark side and negative aspects. The Arabs grasp every unfavourable manifestation with joy and enthusiasm, building on it lofty edifices of interpretation and regarding it as confirmation of their beliefs. From the psychological point of view, moreover, there are grounds for the assumption that in creating images of Israel they tend to ascribe to the enemy opposite characteristics to those they attribute to themselves or would like to possess. Israel is the negative of the self-image. Israel is bad, they are good; Israel is divided against herself, their unity is the decree of history; Israel lives in panic, they live in tranquility and confidence; Israel is aggressive, they are the victims of aggression; Israel is on the downgrade, they are making constant progress; and so on, and so forth.

Israel is denounced in greater detail than Zionism and Jewry. The confrontation of the Arabs with Zionism is connected with a matter of principle, while their confrontation with Israel is rich in events and clashes in many fields—military, political and economic. The Arab States have hardly had to compete with Zionism, while competition is an outstanding feature of their relations with Israel. Hence, their indictment of Zionism is concerned with principles; the charges against Judaism are matters of history and culture; but the denunciation of Israel constitutes a long and detailed account of actual events.

As against these factors, which intensify the denunciation of Israel, there is one main factor which tends towards mitigation. Israel is a more concrete entity than, on the one hand, Zionism as a world movement or a characteristic of the Jews, or, on the other hand, than Judaism, the investigation of which requires a journey into the depths of history. As we have noted, this concreteness limits the possibility of developing a demonological interpretation of Israel and makes it more difficult to attribute to her an abstract and theoretical vileness. In the literature of the conflict, therefore, there are many accurate facts about Israel, whether statistical, descriptive or analytical. For example, Muhammad Ali's *Inside Israel* (367 pp.), which was published, it appears, in 1963 in the National Books series, is full of data on parties, names of personalities, the composition of the Knesset, tables and statistics. A collection of many facts is to be found in an 890-page volume published by the Syrian Intelligence: *Israel, Political, Social and Economic Information, 1964–1965,* which reached me after the Six-Day War. In Rushdī's *Zionism and Its Fosterchild Israel,* the section that describes the actual situation in the country is more factual than the demonological description of Zionism following the Protocols.

The factual nature of the image of Israel presented by Arab communications media makes it necessary to go into considerable length if it is to be described in detail, especially if quotations of statements by Arabs themselves are to be given. For brevity's sake, therefore, I shall try rather to summarize than to cite details and examples, especially as some of the aspects of Israel have already been described in previous chapters—for instance, the odium that is derived from ties with imperialism, or from Zionism and the Jews.

2. THE EXTERNAL ASPECT: AGGRESSION, INTRIGUES, EXPLOITATION

A major characteristic which is very frequently attributed to Israel, with much repetitious emphasis, is aggressiveness. She is said to be the meeting-point of several components, each of which would be enough to make her aggressive. First, there are her roots in Zionism, which is described as basically aggressive, and of which Israel is the realization; her history since her establishment by an act of aggression, usurpation of Arab territory and war, stamps her as aggressive by nature. Then she is a manifestation of colonialism and imperialism, which are also essentially aggressive. Lastly, there is her Jewishness, which necessarily imbues her with the qualities of covetousness and selfishness; all she is interested in is her own advantage, for she regards herself as a continuation of the "Chosen People," which can do as it likes.[1] Israel is, therefore, a brutal and aggressive State, which lives by violence and encroaches on the territory of others, always waiting for the moment when she can strike out at her neighbours and rob them unscrupulously of their lands.

Ali and Ḥamṣānī explain that since Israel is founded on the ideas of Zionism, which aims at realizing the plans of the Protocols, she will be

> ". . . a brazenly oppressive and aggressive *(bāghiya)* State, a Government that recognizes neither right nor law, regarding right as what it has stolen, and law what it has seized for itself." (*Israel, Base for Aggression,* 1964, From East and West series, 1964, p. 4).
>
> "Israel has been helped to be what imperialism meant her to be, an instrument of evil, by the fact that she rose on a foundation of evil." (*Ibid,* p. 3).

The aspiration to enslave the whole world, which is ascribed to the Jews and to Zionism, finds expression in Israel. Ibrahim 'Izzat explains that, while Israel is divided on many things,

> ". . . All the inhabitants of Israel are united in their envy of all mankind, of all faiths and races, and one lust unites them, the lust to rule the world." (*I Have Returned from Israel,* p. 69).

Israel is described as not only threatening, but committing aggression daily; she may always be expected to act suddenly. This is partly a reaction to the element of surprise in Israel's military operations. Thus Nasser said:

> "Israel means the possibility of aggression at any moment. Foreign journalists have asked me if I expect war in the Middle East, and I always used to reply that

experience has taught me to expect it at any moment. In 1956 Ben-Gurion talked of peace, when the Israeli-French-British plan of aggression was already in existence. The upshot is that Israel will strike at us when she finds the opportunity." (March 9, 1965).

The underground organizations which helped to establish Israel have bequeathed to her their gangsterlike characteristics. The Arabs frequently describe Israel as the "gangster State"; Nashāshībī calls her national anthem, *Hatikvah,* "The Hymn of the Gangs" (1965, p. 24).

Like the Zionists before them, it is explained, the Israelis do not boggle at personal terrorism and political assassination. Many proofs are adduced to support this charge: terrorist acts against British soldiers in Mandatory times; the murder of Lord Moyne; the blowing up of the King David Hotel; the assassination of Count Bernadotte; shots fired at UN Observers; the persecution of German experts in Egypt; the violation of Argentinian sovereignty by the abduction of Eichmann; the massacre at Deir Yāsīn, the attacks on Qibyā, Naḥḥālīn, and so forth. Details of these episodes are given by Ali and Ḥamṣānī in a chapter entitled "Zionist Butcheries" (pp. 297 ff).

Israel is also accused of violating international law. The Mixed Armistice Commissions often ruled against her and the UN Observers found her guilty of aggression. She put an end to the activities of the MACs, took over demilitarized zones and expelled Arabs. She does not comply with UN decisions; she does not deserve to be a member of the family of nations and should be expelled from the UN. Since her existence was incompatible with international norms from the beginning, she has never tended to comply with them. This is a criminal State:

"It drew the violation of the law from its very existence, for it was created by gangsters." (Cairo Radio, September 17, 1962, 19:15 hrs.).

Arabs often enumerate Israel's offences against international law and the United Nations. Shukairy gave details in an address to the Special Committee of the Assembly: the Assembly, he said, had adopted 25 resolutions on Palestine and Israel had violated them all; the Security Council had called for a just solution on 55 occasions, in four resolutions it had censured Israel for lawlessness and aggression, which no other member-State had committed; the Trusteeship Council had adopted five decisions on the internationalization of Jerusalem, all of which Israel had rejected (December 5, 1962).

Ali and Ḥamṣānī list Israel's acts of aggression by types and categories, covering more than two hundred pages. Al-Khuli gives statistics on 1,700 acts of aggression during the years 1948-63 (p. 55), but Ibrahim al-Abid, in his book *Violence and Peace, Study of Zionist Strategy,* arrives, on the basis of Arab League figures, at a total of 63,121 Israeli violations of the armistice agreements in 1949-64.

In Arab terminology, aggression is not merely a matter of the intention to inflict injury. For instance, Israelis would certainly not imagine that the establishment of the Knesset building was "an act of aggression," but on September 2, 1966, the office of the Palestine Liberation Organization in Beirut published a statement, quoting Shukairy, describing the erection of the Knesset building as:

> ". . . aggression reinforcing the previous aggression committed in Palestine in 1948, and a part of the plan to make Jerusalem the capital of Israel." (*al-Anwār,* September 3, 1966).

Such statements are not indications of a paranoic tendency to see hostility and aggressive intentions in places where they do not exist; they are expressions of a basic conception. Since the establishment of Israel is regarded as aggression, any attempt to strengthen her must be a continuation of the aggression. The Arabs are therefore prone to describe any gesture of friendliness by a Western power towards Israel, or any agreement or contact with her, as aggression against them, even if there is no intention to harm them. "A hostile act" is sometimes translated in Arabic, not "*'idā'ī*" but "*'udwānī*"—i.e., aggressive, as if any act hostile to the Arabs is necessarily aggressive. There is, indeed, a close connection between hostility and aggression. The source of the Arabic word for the latter implies encroachment or transgression. The aggression of the Jews lies in the fact that they crossed or transgressed the border and encroached on Arab property, so that so long as they hold on to their gains they are aggressors. Israel's very existence is often described as "the aggressive existence of Israel" *(kiyān Isrā'īl al-'udwānī),* e.g., in As'ad Razūq's *A Glance at the Israeli Parties,* p. 102. On these principles, the diversion of the Jordan, i.e., the drawing of water from Lake Kinneret (the Sea of Galilee) was an outstandingly "aggressive act." A chapter in Ali and Ḥamṣānī's book, which contains a detailed survey of the question, is called "The Zionist Attack on the River Jordan." It is noteworthy, by the way, that many books have been devoted to "the diversion of the Jordan"—which may, perhaps, indicate the magnitude of the provocation entailed in the execution of Israel's national water plan.

a) TREACHERY AND INTRIGUE

In keeping with the description of the Jews as basically treacherous and cunning, and the attribution of treachery to imperialism, Israel, too, is described as a State of intrigue; hypocritical, scheming, and prone to plots and stratagems. Her outward appearance is not the reality.

Ibrāhīm 'Izzat, who was perhaps the only Arab journalist (before the Six-Day War) who visited Israel and described his impressions in a book, says, for example, that he did not believe Alexander Dotan, the Foreign Ministry official, who accompanied him, when he said that they would not go to a children's performance by Danny Kaye in Haifa so that they should be able to drive up the Carmel and see the city at night from above. 'Izzat remarks:

> "I did not find it easy to accept these excuses, for I had learned from my stay in Israel that there is something behind every smile, every apology, every word." (p. 77).

'Izzat later explains that Danny Kaye was sent by UNICEF to perform for the children, but their parents had stolen most of the tickets and gone to see the show themselves, and it was this scandal which the Israelis wanted to conceal from him. Here we have a double exhibition of cunning, that of the parents and that of the Foreign Ministry.

There is a widespread tendency to explain Israel's acts as stratagems and believe in "revelations" of deep and devious underlying reasons for them. When, for example, demonstrations were held against the visit of Franz Josef Strauss, the West German statesman, it was explained that these were engineered with the connivance of Ben-Gurion, who wanted to show that Israel had not forgiven the Germans, in order to create pressure to extort further financial concessions (Nashāshībī in *al-Jumhūriyya,* May 27, 1963).

This view of Israel as a cunning enemy, from whom anything can be expected, was also influenced by the war of 1948, which made a deep impression on the Arabs. It was a "spectacular event," in the terminology of Deutsch and Merritt, who distinguish between the effect of cumulative events and of spectacular events on the image (see their article, "Effects of

Events on National and International Images," in *International Behavior,* ed. H. C. Kelman, 1965).

When the Israelis achieve unexpected victories in war, the Arabs accuse them of cunning, obduracy and readiness to use any means to achieve their aims. Thus, 'Ārif al-'Ārif, in his book on the 1948 war, *The Disaster,* enumerates the following qualities of the Israelis, which may be connected with the traditional Arab image of the Jews:

> "Baseness, cunning *(makr),* stratagems *(dahā'),* deceitfulness *(ghashsh),* iron determination, skill in propaganda and war of nerves, the exploitation of all their strength and of all kinds of methods in order to arrive at the goal, for in their eyes the end justifies the means. In character they are hard, because they are stubborn and obdurate. They avenge themselves on people, for people have always taken vengeance on them. They are callous and barbarous without considering what people will say of them, for they suffered in the past from callousness and persecution." (Vol. IV, p. 860).

Since Israel is treacherous and cunning, any conciliatory attitude towards the Arabs or a call for concessions to them is only a trick. Even criticism of Israel's official policy is described as part of Zionist trickery. Part of a chapter in Rushdī's *Zionism and Its Fosterchild Israel* gives an account of the Semitic Movement in Israel, which, as the author explains, advocated a relaxation of the tension between Israel and the Arab States, believed that Israel should cease to be a foreign body in the Middle East, criticized the "Zionist gangs" and Israel's ties with the West, and worked for greater equality and a share in the administration for the Arabs in Israel, cooperation with the Arab States, the establishment of a Semitic bloc, and so forth. However, Rushdī declares, the movement had one basic fault: it wanted to ensure Israel's survival and change the Arab determination to liquidate her; it was, therefore, only another form of the plot against the Arabs, designed to prepare the way for further expansion once Israel had achieved tranquility:

> "The attractive garb of principles with which this movement covers itself is only a mask to hide Israel's aggressive aims and prepare the way for further advance and attack, as it conceals the basic aim of preserving Israel's existence until the realization of the watchword which hangs on the frontage of the Jewish parliament: 'From the Nile to the Euphrates.' " (p. 57).
>
> ". . . It hides in the folds of this beautiful garment the qualities of treachery *(ghadr)* and readiness to attack when the time comes, and this is what we have known of the Jews and their race in their history and through their books

throughout their lives, which are full of this treachery, and these purposes cannot be hidden even if they are smeared with the choicest honey." (p. 61).

Israeli Arab support for the Communist Party may also be presented as a plot. Ali writes:

"There is a phenomenon which is both strange and important, namely, that the Communist Party has succeeded in attracting many votes from the Arabs of Israel, for it masquerades as the defender of their rights and duties. The importance of this is that Israel, in her propaganda to the Western world, says that Communism is attractive not to the Jews but to the Arabs, as is proved by the fact that the Communist Party in Israel relies on the support of the Arabs in Israel, and thus Israel refutes the charge that she is the only country in the Middle East in which a Communist Party exists. The strangeness of this situation underlies the fact that the leader of the Communist Party, Moshe Sneh, who for the reasons described defends the Arabs today in Israel, was in 1948 and previously one of the most determined leaders of the Zionist gangs, one of the most brutal and strong in hostility to the Arabs. But praise to God who brings about changes." (*Inside Israel,* p. 159).

Israel's quest for peace with the Arabs, even if it is recognized, may be interpreted as concealing hidden purposes. 'Izzat repeatedly emphasizes Israel's aspirations for peace and the fact that this aspiration is general and widespread:

"Israel lives in hope of peace with the Arabs. This hope is the aim and dream of every Israeli, from Ben-Gurion to Eli Hadawi ['Izzat's Israeli driver on his tour of the country]. Everyone I talked to in Israel always repeated this hope, which is Israel's dream. They all know that its realization may be delayed for a long time, perhaps ten years, but they believe it is not impossible, for if they lose this hope, they will lose what they call the National Home." (p. 22, and again on p. 63).

Nevertheless, on the next page after this quotation, he attributes aggressive purposes to Israel. When Abba Khoushy, the Mayor of Haifa, told him of the aspiration for peace, he comments:

"This does not express the reality, but hides terrible aims which are revealed in everything that Israel does." (p. 65).

This approach is very common.

b) BORDER INCIDENTS AND REPRISAL OPERATIONS

A subject of great instructive interest, and perhaps even of practical political importance, is the way in which Israel's retaliatory operations were understood by the Arabs and the purposes they attributed to them. In recent years, research has been done in the United States, particularly by Professor Schelling, on the "bargaining" process which may underlie the behaviour of States towards each other. The activities of States not only create facts, but also have "symbolic" value as indicating policies and intentions, and as signals of what each side is prepared to do in particular circumstances. It may be assumed that Israel's purposes in her retaliatory operations, namely, to induce the Arab States to prevent infiltration and attacks against her, were better understood in official circles than appeared from the way they were interpreted in the Arab communications media, which generally tended to regard them as the expression of much broader, more "serious" tendencies, to connect them with inter-Arab and world events, and explain them as the results of hidden plots and stratagems and malicious intentions.

It would have been worth while surveying each of these operations separately and examining the interpretation that was given to them, but that would call for long and detailed research. I will only indicate briefly some of the main themes in Arab comments before the Six-Day War, rather as examples than as a complete account.

a) Border incidents and acts of retaliation were described as if they had no connection with local events but involved deeper aims than were visible to the naked eye and were the outcome of plots with Western countries, imperialist elements and even other Arab States. The idea that Israel is a creature and an instrument of imperialism implies that her actions are designed for its benefit. Western countries were repeatedly accused of encouraging Israel in her acts of retaliation.

Thus, for example, the attack on Gaza on February 28, 1955, was described as connected with the Baghdad Pact. Sāliḥ associated it with Nasser's statement of opposition to the Pact (*The Battle of Port Said,* p. 45), while al-Rāfi'ī believed that it was meant to impel Egypt to join the Pact (*The Revolution of July 26*, p. 141).

Reacting to incidents on Israel's border with Syria towards the end of 1964, a Syrian radio commentator explained that the latest Israeli "aggression" was timed to fit in with the declaration by the Iraqi Kurdish leader, Mullā Muṣṭafā Barzānī, of his intention to establish an independent Kurdish State. He added that it was meant not only for provocation, or to display Israel's "muscles" after the recent frightening Syrian army manoeuvres, but to show Israel's support for "the second, Barzanite Israel" (Damascus Radio, November 4, 1964, 14:44 hrs.).

Ākhir Sā'a, the Cairo weekly, connected the shooting down of six Migs on the Syrian border in April 1967 with events in Aden, since it took place 24 hours after the departure of a UN mission from the colony (April 12, 1967).

Incidents were sometimes said to be designed to serve the interests of the oil companies by exercising pressure for the acceptance of their conditions.

b) Against the background of inter-Arab rivalries, border incidents were sometimes alleged to be planned by Israel in order to benefit some particular Arab regime. Thus, incidents on the Syrian border in 1962 were ascribed by a UAR broadcast to an Israeli plan to save the Syrian regime from the masses (Cairo Radio, December 12, 1962, 20:44 hrs.).

The shooting down of two Syrian Migs in August 1966 was attributed by the Syrian and later the Egyptian Radio to a plot between Britain and the "reactionary" Arab States, Saudi Arabia, Tunisia and Jordan, in order to create pressure on the other Arab countries (Damascus Radio, August 17, 1966).

c) Sometimes border incidents were said to have been initiated by a rival Arab State to save its regime and divert the wrath of its people, thus admitting that Arab countries might be interested in hotting up the border for reasons of internal policy. For instance, the incidents on the Syrian border at the beginning of 1967 were alleged to have been designed to divert the pressure of the Arab people on the monarchical regimes, especially Hussein's, and to hamper the forces which aimed at liquidating them (Cairo Radio, January 14, 1967, 14:45 hrs.).

d) Conversely, incidents were sometimes presented as initiated by Israel in order to distract her own public opinion from her internal problems: economic difficulties, internecine strife, low morale, and even the difficulty of defining a Jew.

e) The aim was sometimes alleged to be to impress the Jewish world with the seriousness of Israel's security problems and so extort donations:

> "The truth is that Israel does not want peace to reign on the borders, for if it did, she would lose her excuse to pass the hat round on the pretext that she is a country which is being attacked and living in fear, threatened with destruction by seven Arab countries." (Abu al-Naṣr, *The End of Israel,* 1955, p. 194).

f) Border incidents and reprisal operations were alleged to be designed to bring pressure to bear on the Arab countries and show them that they would have no rest until they made peace with Israel (e.g. Abu al-Naṣr, p. 193). Ḥasan Muṣṭafā wrote:

"Israel has resorted to violence and force in order to compel the Arabs to accept her and recognize her existence. Thus, from her establishment until 1956, she carried out a series of attacks on neighbouring Arab States, thinking she could terrify them and compel them to submit to her will." (*Israel and the Atomic Bomb,* p. 122).

g) Sometimes they were said to be aimed at achieving military victories in order to undermine the confidence of the Arab countries in their capacity to liquidate Israel and to lower the morale of their armies by proving that their Governments could not block Israeli aggression.

h) Another purpose was to convince the world of the need to intervene, to impose a peace settlement, and to portray the Arab States as aggressive and obdurate. Here, for example, is a report in *al-Akhbār:*

"Sayyid Nawfal, Assistant Secretary-General of the Arab League, explained the hidden aim of Israel's aggression and said that Israel was making another attempt to raise in the UN the question of direct talks with the Arabs and to hold up the process of Arab unification. Through her acts of provocation, Israel is trying to give the members of the UN the impression that the Middle East endangers world peace. Afterwards, her propagandists will spread the tale that the reason is the reluctance of the Arabs to make peace with Israel." (August 23, 1963).

i) On similar lines, the incidents were alleged to be designed to extort Western guarantees for Israel's security.

j) They were sometimes said to be a nervous and emotional reaction to some Arab achievement, such as the development of rockets by Egypt.

k) Reprisals were sometimes described as arbitrary acts by Israel, not preceded by any Arab provocation. The tendency was to ignore Arab initiatives or to argue that there was no connection between them and the act of retaliation.

l) The reprisal operations were taken to be an indication of Israel's desire for expansion and her aggressive character (Sha'bān, p. 20).

m) Alternatively, they were described as a sign of Israeli cowardice, thus taking verbal revenge for Arab impotence and restoring self-respect.

n) Occasionally, an act of retaliation was described as a diversionary act, in the expectation that Israel was about to mount a surprise attack in some other place. Thus, 'Amīd (Brig. Gen.) al-Imām commented on a warning by the Israel Government to Syria:

"This aggression will not be against Syria, as is imagined, but it will take place on some other front, to which Israel is trying to avoid to draw attention, for what prevents Israel repeating the same tactics she adopted in 1956 for the sake of camouflage and deception?" (*al-Jumhūriyya,* September 29, 1966).

As far as results were concerned, Israel's retaliation was described as increasing the hostility of the Arabs. Ḥasan Muṣṭafā wrote:

"These acts of aggression have only increased obstinacy, hatred of Israel, and the desire to take revenge on her. They have had a powerful effect in the Arab countries, leading to a clearer recognition of the Zionist danger and the need for increased strength to resist it. They have also brought about a growth in nationalist awakening in the entire Arab world and a greater need for Arab cooperation and unity so that they may stand as one man to confront the grave danger which surrounds them." (1961, pp. 122-3).

There was also a tendency to find ingenious explanations for Israeli successes. For instance, the appearance of Israeli fighting planes in the neighbourhood of Damascus was explained in the Egyptian press *(al-Muṣawwar,* April 14, 1967) as due to the planes approaching from the direction of Jordan, where Syrian preparedness was weak.

c) ISRAEL'S FOREIGN RELATIONS

References to the relations between Israel and other countries vary, of course, in accordance with the changing political circumstance, but, without going into considerable detail, several tendencies may be noted. These are clearly expressed in a special chapter on the subject in Rushdī's *Zionism and Its Fosterchild Israel*:

"Israel's political and economic character, the circumstances of her life and growth, the imperialist and exploitationist nature of Zionism, and the interests of the Western States in the Arab world and its oil—all these factors have made Israel a natural and permanent ally of the West." (p. 199).

Israel always votes with the West and the imperialists in the UN. She receives unlimited economic aid, which enables her to survive. This is assured by World Zionism and Judaism, which have a great influence in the West:

> "The domination of American policy by World Zionism and the dominant Jewish financial and political influence on American circles, on statesmen, press and publicity, and the various manifestations of American society, have led to the subordination of the [US] Administration to Zionist aims and have made it impossible for responsible American factors to liberate themselves from the yoke of World Zionism, which has a decisive influence on every vital aspect in their country. Thus the United States has given extensive monetary aid, which has helped her [Israel] to survive until this day." (p. 199).

Rushdī believed that the Soviet Union was opposed to Israel's inclinations towards the West, but not to her existence as a State (p. 203). Russia was often said to have reservations about the Arab attitude in regard to the liquidation of Israel.

Israel's ties with external factors are also said to be guided by internal considerations. Israel cannot survive alone. She depends on donations and has developed appeals for aid to the level of a fine art. She lives on contributions from the Zionists, and extorts money from Germany by appealing to her feelings. Israel is a "parasitic State," whose existence is "false" (epithets which are frequently repeated). Abu al-Naṣr alleges that there is an Israeli "Ministry for Collection of Donations" (*wizārat al-istijdā'*, p. 192). 'Izzat declares:

> "If financial aid is withheld or halted, Israel's heartbeats will immediately come to a stop, for it is a State that cannot live on its inner resources despite its greatest efforts." (p. 22).

Israel, on the other hand, is sometimes said to make a hypocritical pretence of weakness, claiming to need and deserve assistance, and complaining of Arab aggressive intentions, while in fact, she is the aggressor; and at the same time she spreads rumours that she is strong, for she needs the prestige of strength in order to deter the Arabs. This paradoxical pretence of weakness and strength at the same time is another example of Jewish duplicity:

> "Ben-Gurion presents Israel as a little country in need of pity, but at one and the same time he portrays it as strong and determined, without realizing the dilemma or having any shame because of this contradiction." (Sh'bān, p. 49).

3. INTERNAL ASPECTS

In describing Israel's internal affairs, there is a common tendency to give prominence to her vileness and weakness, the latter being a result of the former.

In the conflict between the United States and the Soviet Union, both sides tend to distinguish between the people, who are "good"—American or Russian, as the case may be—and the "bad rulers": the Wall Street plutocracy or the Communist leadership (see Ralph White's article, "Images in the Context of International Conflict: Soviet Perceptions of the US and the USSR" in *International Behavior,* ed. by Kelman, p. 249). Such distinctions are not met with to the same extent in Arab statements about Israel. The Arab tendency is to generalize the evil: everything about Israel is bad. The reason, no doubt, is that in the conflict between the US and the USSR the goal is limited, while the aim in regard to Israel is politicide.

The nature of the Jews is regarded as having moulded the character of Israel. The former lived in isolation in the ghettos, and Israel is a continuation of this phenomenon: one large ghetto, isolated from its environment:

> "Israel will live in the ghetto which she has imposed on herself within the Arab world, as she lived in the countries to which they [the Jews] belonged, until history condemns her to a new Babylonian exile." (Rushdī, p. 61).

The historical circumstances of her establishment, the nature of the Jews as a religious body, and their unfitness for life in a State of their own, make Israel an artificial, abnormal State—a diseased organism. Rifā'ī, the Jordanian representative, argued at the UN:

> "The sovereignty of Israel was in any case questionable because Israel's statehood itself had not been defined. Israel was a State which did not own the territory it occupied, a State whose people had no definite criteria of nationalism. It was a State which had no boundaries, for the line of partition was one thing, the armistice line was another and the line which Israel envisaged as including all of Palestine, Jordan and the territory beyond as far as the Euphrates was still another." (December 5, 1962).

Al-Jumhūriyya characterizes Israel as:

> ". . . a State without a Government; a country without frontiers, a people without unity; a bankrupt treasury; quarrelling parties; a people whose Eastern section curses the Western section, whose subjects curse its rulers and whose leaders

shed tears to collect donations in order to live; its trials are like Hitchcock Sherlock Holmes plots; lachrymose speeches to collect money; a gang surrounded by 90 million Arabs who would rejoice to trample on and destroy it; a black colonialist colony; a crowd of displaced persons from all parts of the world and the dregs of the human race, who lived by meeting oppression with oppression and hatred with hatred; the world is hostile to them and they hate the world—the appropriate moment will surely come when they can be wiped off the map of the world and the Arab East." (April 20, 1961).

a) THE SYSTEM OF GOVERNMENT

Israel's friends and other observers describe her as a bastion of democracy in the Middle East, but the Arabs frequently insist that she is a militaristic State, a "garrison State" to use Harold Lasswell's term. The importance of security problems and the special place held by the Army are interpreted as meaning that the Army is the true ruler.

"Israel is a mobilization *(ta'bi'a)*, namely totalitarian, State, which devotes all its resources to warlike preparations." (*Egyptian Political Science Review*, September 1963, p. 41).

If the Army has such an important position and such ample resources are placed at its disposal, Israel must, on the face of it, be strong; so it must be explained that her militarism is not a source of durable strength. Thus Haykal writes:

"In order to implant confidence in the heart of the population, who are encircled within the present framework of their existence, the political leadership in Israel has found it necessary to exaggerate the strength of the Israeli Army and create a fantastic legend around it."(*al-Ahrām*, March 16, 1962).

The "gangster mentality" also leaves its mark on the system of government:

"The Governmnet of Israel is a gang which has become a Government, but we shall yet see a terrorist Government which, with the lapse of time, will become a gang." (Nashāshībī, 1962, p. 38—a similar statement has been made by Nasser).

Wākid, quoting the Israeli weekly *Ha-olam Hazeh*, described the regime as a Ben-Gurionist dictatorship (*Israel in the Balance*, p. 45).

The Israeli parties are described at great length, with particular emphasis on their multiplicity. The Arabs' approach to this subject is influenced by the nature of political life in their own countries. Since parties and parliamentary rule have been suppressed in most of them, a derogatory explanation has to be found for the maintenance of parliamentary life in Israel. The existence of so many parties is presented as a phenomenon without parallel anywhere else in the world, an expression of widespread factionalism, communal and social tensions, and the quarrelsomeness of the Jews. It is portrayed as a sign of political instability, on the one hand, and corruption on the other, Israeli democracy is a mere sham (Razūq, *A Glance at the Israeli Parties,* p. 102).

Numerous books have been written on this subject. The Arabs, naturally, find it difficult to understand the character of the Israeli parties and the distinctions between them. The nationalist Herut Movement has come in for special treatment, as an expression of expansionism and "terrorism." My impression is that its leader, Menahem Begin, was the most frequently mentioned Israeli after Ben-Gurion before the Six-Day War. His book, *The Revolt,* which has appeared in Arabic translation, was quoted to exemplify terrorist methods and prove Israel's malignant intentions towards the Arabs (see, frequently, in Nashāshībī's book; Ali and Ḥamṣānī, p. 40; 'Alūsh, p. 21ff; Rushdī, p. 259; Tall, p. 275, and so forth). Deep hatred was frequently expressed against Ben-Gurion, whom the Arabs regarded as a symbol of uncompromising Israeli nationalism. They found it difficult to distinguish his attitude from Begin's, for they attributed to him equally far-reaching expansionist aspirations. Sayegh, therefore, writes of his "selective activism" (1964, p. 188).

Finding it hard to define the differences between the parties, Razūq defines them as "artificial controversies" *(khilāfāt muṣṭana'a).* They are all Zionist, he says, and so long as that is the case he regards all other questions as marginal. Here, it seems, is another example of Jewish cunning: party activities are believed to be only a matter of show. Ibrahim al-'Ābid explained:

"The Eshkol group does not reject the idea of war and expansion; it differs from the Ben-Gurion group in regard to tactics, and the time and place of the blow. The Rafi Party has been trying lately to appear more extreme than Eshkol, and it calls for powerful and vindictive attacks on the Arab States. But both are more or less identical in their aggressive intentions against the Arabs." (*Mapai, the Ruling Party in Israel,* p. 128).

The difficulties which have prevented Israel from enacting a Constitution are explained as proof that this is an abnormal State (Rhushdī, p. 184). Institutions which seem to be specific to Israel, or which have attracted attention abroad, such as the Histradrut, the General Federation of Labour, are frequently discussed. 'Izzat, for example, devotes a good deal of space to it (pp. 28ff). He describes it as a dictatorship; its very existence is incompatible with democracy (p. 57). It owns all the kibbutzim, whose members receive only their elementary necessities, while all the profits are grabbed by the Histadrut. The moshavim (smallholders' villages) are in its grip, too, and their members cannot do as they like with their property (p. 37).[2]

The kibbutzim also receive special attention. They are described as disguised military posts and extremely leftist; 'Izzat alleges that he saw portraits of Stalin and Trotsky displayed in the dining hall of every kibbutz he visited (p. 31). They are centres of immorality (this point is also made by Wākid, *Israel in the Balance,* p. 63). They are confronted with the problem of continuity, because they were established for purposes of settlement and defence, which are the main concern of their ideology, while today the situation has altered (*ibid.,* p. 64).

The research centre of the National Liberation Organization published a booklet on the subject, *The Kibbutz, or The Collective Settlements in Israel,* by 'Abd al-Wahhāb Kiyālī (September 1966, 130 pp.). This is a detailed study, covering many aspects of kibbutz life and quoting numerous sources, such as the writings of Darin-Drabkin, Spiro, Ben-Gurion, Moshe Pearlman on Ben-Gurion, Ben Halpern, Moshe Kerem, etc. It discusses the history of the kibbutz, the position of women, education, social questions, the kibbutz as a military factor, and so forth, but there is an obvious effort to emphasize the derogatory aspects. The kibbutz, the author insists, is not a form of socialism. It was difficult to make propaganda among the Jews in Eastern Europe, who were attracted by revolutionary movements, so it was necessary to give them something that looked like socialism (another example of cunning). The kibbutz is an example of the arrogance contained in the idea of the Chosen People (p. 105), since it boasts of being better than other forms of organization. It is "an instrument of settlement and a means of aggression and robbery which maintains racial discrimination and believes in racial superiority" (p. 108). The members are very self-contained (another Jewish characteristic) and hate others. Women are wretched in the kibbutz. Egalitarianism is only formal: it is a caricature of equality, and is limited to consumption. Oriental Jews are oppressed and discriminated against. The youth growing up in the kibbutz are fascists (p. 111). Martin Buber is denounced for writing that the kibbutz is an experiment which will not fail and claiming that it is creating a new type of man (pp. 105 ff). The ideological collectivism of some kibbutzim is a manifestation of their military character (p. 116). To sum up, the kibbutz is doomed because of its failings and contradicitions.

There is a tendency to seize at irregularities and indications of corruption in order to portray Israel as corrupt. One reason, no doubt, is the consciousness of corruption in the Arab countries and the desire to show that Israel is no better. Wākid goes to great lengths in this direction:

> "The maladies that consume the body of the governmental administration of Israel are six in number: favouritism, bribery, collusion between officials and offenders against the law, embezzlement, forgery and waste." (*Israel in the Balance,* 1959, pp. 35ff).

There is corruption everywhere, in the Cabinet, the Army and the Police, among ambassadors, managers of government companies and the Jewish Agency. A contributory factor is the party quota in the distribution of posts. According to Wākid, the State Comptroller found over 4,831 cases of bribery in the year 1956/57. The Government, the Army and the Police, cooperate with smugglers, thieves, and traders in women and drugs.

A similarly black picture of corruption in the Civil Service and the defence establishment, with bribery, embezzlement and immorality as a deliberate policy, is painted by Anīs Qāsim in his proposals for exploiting Israel's weakness and "contradictions" for a comprehensive campaign of psychological warfare in his *Revolutionary Preparation for the Battle of Liberation,* 1967, pp. 194ff.

b) NATIONAL DISUNITY

The age-old factionalism of the Jews is clearly manifested in their State. Furthermore, since the Jews are not a nation, and the only bond between them is religion, which is not a sufficient basis for the establishment of a State, it is not natural for them to have a State of their own. The people of Israel are, therefore, an artificial conglomeration, with a morbid nationalism, rent by dissension and conflicting internal pressures. The unity and cohesion which the Israelis claim is spurious; deep down they are consumed by social decay:

"Israel is a collection of the dwellers in the world's Jewish quarters *(ḥārat al-yahūd)*... It is therefore a ghetto State, whose inhabitants are concentrated in three cities." (Dr. Jamāl Ḥamdān in *al-Ahrām*, September 13, 1964).

"Israel is a patched-up State containing various races speaking various different languages and representing various continents." (July 22, 1955, I.L., IV/913).

Wākid deals with dissensions at great length. Zionism has succeeded in transporting Jews to Israel, he says, but not in making a society out of them, and this failure will be fatal to the State, which he describes as "a society faulty in all respects" (p. 19). He enumerates the various types of discord: in colour, blood, character (tradition, customs and nature), origin (the *Landsmannschaften* preserve the ties of the Jews with the countries they came from), religion, outlook (religious and freethinking), ideology (progressives, conservatives, Communists, fascists, Zionists and anti-Zionists), party, class and economic status (pp. 20-1).

Reviewing a book called *The System of Government in Israel*, by Dr. 'Abd al-Ḥamīd al-Mutawallī, containing his lectures at the Arab League's Institute for Higher Arab Studies, Muhammad 'Abd al-Qadir says that the only thing that unites the Israelis is the external danger, but for which Israel would split like the Jewish kingdom after the death of Solomon (*al-Akhbār*, March 19, 1964).

The Jews of European origin are frequently accused of discriminating against those from the Arab countries by Arab writers expressing their sympathy for the Oriental Jews. This kind of discrimination is innate in Israel as a Zionist State; which was based from the beginning on the racial principle: it is the internalization of her racial attitude towards the world outside.[3] In *Zionism and Racism*, Dr. Sa'ab writes:

"The State of Israel has emerged, not as a humanitarian refuge, but as the incarnation of neo-racism, which discriminates between Jews and Arabs, Zionist and anti-Zionist Jews, and even between Western and Eastern Israeli citizens" (p. 16).

Arab broadcasts often appeal to the Oriental Jews as the "Arab Jews" and call upon them to rise against the domination of the Ashkenazim (e.g. Cairo Radio, August 25, 17:45 hrs.).

One of the leaders of the Palestine guerrilla organization al-'Asifa (the military force of al-Fatah) explained to a *Jeune Afrique* correspondent:

> "We hope to create political problems in Israel and call the Arab minority to revolt. And why should we not arouse this vast proletariat, consisting of the Sephardi Jews from the Arab countries, who are the Arabs of the Jews, against the Jews of Europe, the Ashkenazim?" ("Palestine—is it in War in 1967?", December 18, 1966, p. 38).

The Arabs may feel some kinship with the Jews from the Arab countries, but this does not alter their general attitude towards Israel, which includes these Jews. Anti-Semites have a tendency to make an exception in favour of some particular Jew, whom they may describe as "one of their best friends," thus defending themselves against self-criticism on the grounds of generalized prejudice and racial hatred, and showing their objectivity. Allport called this "defence by bifurcation" (*The Nature of Prejudice,* p. 318). Psychologists have noted, however, that the knowledge that good Jews exist does not necessarily affect the idea that Jews as a group are all bad. The exception is taken as proving the rule, and even if that implies a dissonance, the human mind can contain it without serious pangs of conscience. It may be assumed that a similar process is involved when Arabs distinguish between Oriental and Western Jews. This show of sympathy for Jews from the East actually facilitates inveterate hostility to all the Jews put together, including the Oriental ones.

Attitude researches in Israel have shown that Jews from Oriental countries are much more anti-Arab than those from the West. A memorandum to the heads of the Arab States by the Arab Higher Committee states that the Oriental Jewish soldiers were the most cruel in the Six-Day War (*al-Kifah,* May 29, 1969). However, Arabs outside Israel frequently show a complete misunderstanding of the attitude of the Oriental Jews, failing to realize that it is precisely they who bear a grudge against the Arabs.

c) THE ISRAELIS

The denunciation of Israel leads the Arabs to find fault with its inhabitants. It is not surprising that we find them criticizing those very aspects that others have praised as Israeli achievements. Sha'bān, for example, objects to the settlers being called pioneers. This is false, he declares: there may be room for pioneering in the discovery of a neglected or abandoned territory, but this cannot apply to Palestine (p. 16).

The Israelis' victories, which have won them a widespread reputation for military capacity, give rise to an impulse to accuse them of cowardice. On the one hand, this is a projection of the traditional image of the Jews; on the other hand, it is necessary to assure the Arabs of success in the clashes to come. Thus, Nashāshībī writes:

"We know our enemy. Despite his power, he is no stronger than we, and he will never be stronger than we. We know better than anyone else the cowardice, the weakness, the fear and the submission which have struck root in the souls of the Jews." (p. 237).

Elsewhere he describes them as "a criminal and cowardly people" (p. 155).

Nasser describes his experiences in the battle of ʻIrāq al-Manshiyya (in Southern Palestine) in 1948:

"I saw the Jewish soldier and he fled in fear at the mere sight of us. I saw them running away, despite their tanks and armoured cars, which they left behind on the battlefield." (March 3, 1955, I.L., III/667).

As a result of the artificiality of the Jewish State and the ring of hostility around them, there can be no tranquility for the Israelis. They are afraid of the future, and their basic approach is: "Eat and drink, for tomorrow we die." Hence, as Ṣawt al-ʻArab explained on May 31, 1963, the prevailing corruption. Wakīd gives a similar explanation: the Israeli intellectuals are corrupt because they have lost faith in the future of the State; they grasp at every opportunity to make money and leave the country (*Israel in the Balance,* p. 44).

It is not surprising that much is made of the problem of emigration from Israel, its scope, motives and significance, with quotations from statements by Jewish leaders and Israeli newspapers (Naʻnāʻa has a sub-section on "Immigration in Reverse," pp. 182ff; Wākid, *Israel, the Den of Imperialism,* p. 40; *Israel in the Balance,* p. 75; Rushdī, p. 171). The Arabs regarded this phenomenon as a practical demonstration of their main arguments: that Israel is an artificial State and, as such, cannot survive; that the Jews are not a nation and the State cannot make them one; that their odiousness overflows into their own lives, which become so unbearable that the people run away.

As for the youth of Israel, Haykal writes:

"The Israeli press is full of discussions on this problem, the main tenor of which is that Israeli youth today, under the influence of its school education, are full of arrogance because they have been told so often that they symbolized the fortunate Jewish generation which has returned to the Promised Land after thousands of years of exile. This generation is not prepared today to toil in isolated Negev settlements, as the previous generation did. This is a generation which is strongly attracted to life in Tel Aviv that Carl Levin described it in an article in the *New Leader* as 'the Expresso Generation.' . . . In justifying the abduction and trial of Eichmann, it was said that Ben-Gurion wanted to shock this new, empty generation by means of the trial, to remind them of the fate of the Jews in the Diaspora, and to arouse in their hearts the spirit of the generation of 'adventurers' who worked for the establishment of Israel." (*al-Ahrām,* May 5, 1961).

d) CONFUSION AND FEAR IN ISRAEL

It is alleged with very great frequency that Israel is gripped by panic. This is an expression of a number of tendencies. It is a projection on the national level of the attribution of fear and cowardice to the Israeli, and also, perhaps, of a lack of self-confidence. This may be a logical conclusion from Arab intentions vis-à-vis Israel, for a country threatened with liquidation could not be peaceful and tranquil. It may even indicate a degree of self-importance: in view of the hostility of the Arabs, with their vast potential, the Israelites could not possibly enjoy a sense of security. Rushdī writes, for example, that Israel

". . . cannot free herself from the fear that is the necessary consequence of this situation and the fear of the inexorable doom that will come in due time." (p. 61; similarly, Abu al-Naṣr, p. 188).

Israel's alleged fears are often used as proof of substantial progress in Arab measures and preparations for action against her:

"The existence of the Palestinian Entity shocks Israel so profoundly that she sees in it a storm which is blowing against her artificial and spurious existence and is almost destroying her." (Sayyid Nawfal in *Egyptian Political Science Review,* November 1965, p. 27).

Haykal wrote on the Egyptian intervention in the Yemeni Civil War:

"These proofs that I have given of Israel's attitude to Egypt's support for the Yemeni Revolution speak for themselves, and are sufficient to show that Israel feels concern, that she is reconsidering the question of her security, and that she has arrived at the conclusion, or is close to the conclusion, that she must embark on a military adventure before 1964." (*al-Ahrām,* December 7, 1962).

Cairo Radio announced, almost three years later, that panic reigned in Israel as a result of the Jeddah agreement between Nasser and Fayṣal for the ending of the Yemeni war (August 26, 1965, 07:00 hrs.).

Haykal frequently comes back to Israel's "state of mind":

"The critical point in Israel's state of mind today is that up to less than a year ago she believed that time was working on her side and that she would win in the future, but later she discovered that the positions were reversed, and that circumstances were working to her disadvantage." (*al-Ahrām*, April 26, 1963).

He was attributing the change to the development of Egyptian missiles (which were fired on June 21, 1962) and to the revolutions in Yemen, Iraq and Syria.

(In situations of conflict, both parties are apparently drawn to engage in psychological analysis of their rivals.)

e) ATTITUDE TO THE ARAB MINORITY (BEFORE THE SIX-DAY WAR)

The way in which the Arabs described the position of the Arab minority in Israel and her Government's attitude towards them is another subject which deserves a monograph on its own. I shall have to be content to note a few examples of the common trends and attitudes before the Six-Day War. The major theme was that the Israeli Arabs were brutally oppressed by the authorities: their situation was wretched; they were second-class citizens, without civil rights even in regard to getting jobs and earning a livelihood (the over-emphatic allegations that their economic position was bad might have been partly due to the knowledge that it was actually much better than it was said to be). Nashāshībī wrote, for example:

"Those who lived all their lives as a despised minority in the countries where they dwelt come along today, after they have become a majority, and domineeringly victimize the first minority with which they have come in contact throughout their history. They apply to it the same restrictions as Hitler imposed on them." (p. 195).

The Arabs in Israel behaved like heroes. They were tried only by military courts. Their lands were confiscated. The authorities cut off their irrigation water. They received half the pay of a Jew. There was not a single Arab clerk among the 35,000 Jewish civil servants (p. 145). The Jews oppressed them, treated them as hostages, and prevented them setting up schools in which they could teach their children the language of their fathers (p. 195). They were forbidden to observe Arab festivals and were heavily taxed in order to compel them to emigrate (p. 161).

Rushdī writes:

> "The Arab minority in Israel is subject to comprehensive racial persecution." (p. 293).
>
> "There is no limit to Israel's assaults against the sanctities of Islam and Christendom." (p. 294).

A flagrant example of the discrimination against the Arab minority, Rushdī explains, is the Law of Return , which grants Jews automatic citizenship (p. 295).

'Izzat declared that in Israel only the Arabs were liable to military jurisdiction. The Government controlled the most trivial details of their lives: a law was even passed forbidding polygamy among Muslims on the pretext of imposing civilized practices, but the Muslims said that the real aim of the law was to cut down their natural increase, so that Israel should find it easier to liquidate them (p. 24—another example of Jewish cunning).

> "The Military Government sentenced one of the Arab inhabitants to death because he left his town on account of a sick daughter after the Governor had refused to give him a permit." (p. 109).

As far as the internal position is concerned, Ali says that the Israeli Arabs are producing a leadership which is not attracted by the blandishments of the Zionist parties,

> ". . . because the Arabs who remained in Israel lacked any political or cultural leadership . . . The Arabs, in turn, observe how the Israeli parties haggle over them [compete with each other for their votes], but they are not interested in a debate about the difference in ideological trends between the parties, and most of them regard the election period as a suitable time for extracting promises from the parties to improve their position." (p. 162).

There are repeated statements that some of the Israeli Arabs are traitors who collaborate with the "Zionist occupation authorities," but in recent years, after the return of the Palestinians to the stage, there is a strong tendency to emphasize that the Israeli Arabs are also a part of this Palestinian people's movement, but are unable to demonstrate their allegiance. Thus

Shukairy declared, in the opening address to the Palestinian Conference in Jerusalem on May 28, 1964:

> "We represent one people, all the Palestinians, and all those who are unable to come, even the Palestinians in the occupied territory. They are for us and we are for them. We send them our blessing to the occupied area, to men, women and children, and we look forward to meeting them soon again." (Amman Radio, May 28, 1964).

There is a strong tendency to praise the Israeli Arabs while expressing sympathy for their sufferings, since they stand face to face with the enemy and endure his pressures. For Palestinian spokesmen, such glorification is also required by the place they reserve for the Israeli Arabs in the "War of National Liberation." Another reason may be that the Palestinian refugees feel some guilt because of their flight, mingled with envy of those who remained and whose position has been much better than theirs.

Kanafānī, in his book *The Literature of the Resistance in Occupied Palestine,* 1948–1966 (Beirut, 1966), praises their literary achievements. He explains that it was mainly the rural population that were left in Israel after the city Arabs, including the cultural leaders, had gone. Those who remained were subjected to a "cultural siege" (p. 11) owing to suppression by the Jewish authorities, restrictions on their spiritual activity and the severance of their ties with the Arab world. The Egyptian Revolution of 1952, however, brought about a change, and the Arab poets, who had previously concentrated on the subject of love, began to write nationalist poems of struggle and defiance. According to Kanafānī, while the "exile literature" *(adab al-manfā)* of the refugees living in the Arab countries is characterized by bitterness and lamentation, the poetry of struggle is full of ardent faith in victory and redemption. It breathes confidence into the hearts of the Israeli Arabs and is recited at meetings, weddings and the like. Popular verse, which is also marked by an attitude of revolt against the enemy, has also developed. Another characteristic of this poetry of revolt is its sympathy with the Left, owing to the rural origin of the poets and the oppression by the authorities. The poets watch what is going on in the Arab countries from "a position of hope and capacity to endure," and feel that they are partners in their development and their national achievements.

The Jewish authorities put obstacles in the way of Arabic culture, prevent the publication of works of literary value, and deliberately keep down the level of Arab schools. Arab students admitted to the universities come up against a series of limitations which prevent them registering in certain departments, and "the special departments for the study of Oriental literature suffer from an outstanding lack of professional qualifications, which is a deliberate lack" (p. 19). In other words, the authorities (in their cunning) prevent Arabs developing their own literature, and even take the trouble to see to it that they should not be able to derive advantage from their university studies.

The literature of the struggle, Kanafānī sums up, fulfils three functions:

a) "When the enemy tries to draw the Arabs into some kind of dialogue, he is met with a burning irony, which reveals that the Arabs regard him as a passing phase." (p. 50).

This irony is also a reply to the enemy's attempts to suppress the Arab personality.

b) The poetry of the Arabs is a fortress in their distress.

c) When the confrontation reaches a climax and the clash is near, the literature of the struggle becomes a frontal attack.

f) BELITTLEMENT OF ISRAELI ACHIEVEMENTS

There is a strong tendency to belittle Israel's achievements, either by categorically denying their existence, or by an interpretation which deprives them of any real significance, or by attributing them to foreign factors.

Israel's social and cultural achievements are a thorn in the flesh of the Arabs, so that they want to deny them. Nashāshībī writes:

"Let us put it like this: After the passage of 14 years since its establishment, the State is quite incapable of being the source of any values in the world, either Jewish or non-Jewish! It has taken everything, material and spiritual, and cannot give anything except trouble, attacks, hostility, bloodshed, racial discrimination and perseverance in a policy of arrogance, insolence and intrigue." (p. 49).

Sha'bān does not regard the revival of the Hebrew language as an achievement:

"The revival of ancient languages is an easy thing anywhere, but progress demands a living language and not the revival of an ancient language which is out of date and which cannot meet the demands of modern civilization, modern thought and world culture. It is not surprising if some of the pioneers feel disappointment, as Ben-Gurion says, and abandon the Promised Land." (p. 17).

On the other hand, the revival of the Arabic language was highly praised in Muhammad 'Aṭiyya al-Abrūshī's book, *The Semitic Cultures,* Egypt, 1936, p. 33.

Israel's military successes are belittled, denied, or attributed to foreigners (the same trend continued even after the Six-Day War). The Arabs' image of the Jews as far removed from heroism or military pursuits leads them to interpret these achievements as due to foreign intervention. The literature is full of stories about foreign military experts who served or still serve in the Israel Defence Forces. Nashāshībī says, for instance, that experts from East Germany served in Israel during the first and second truces in 1948 (p. 177).

Israel's economic and industrial progress is attributed entirely to an endless inflow of foreign money, while the Arab countries received comparatively small sums, especially when calculated per head (Sha'bān, p. 51). 'Izzat describes, for example, a visit to a factory for the processing of citrus fruit in Gan-Shmuel, which, he notes, utilizes all the fruit, even the peel and the seeds. However, he explains:

"These industrial enterprises cannot be regarded as Israeli, for they are really American industries." (p. 21).

Again, when he writes about the skill of the industrial workers, he adds that all this industry is meant to facilitate domination over the Arab world (p. 25).

Even the modernity of the country becomes a reason for reproach:

"Everything in Tel Aviv is a primitive imitation of everything in America." ('Izzat, p. 31).

"If they have achieved anything, it is through external aid, and therefore they will inevitably lose it, and the scandal, deceit and swindle will be revealed." (Aḥmad, p. 78).

Sha'bān declares that if Israel has achieved anything, it is thanks to the land she has stolen without paying for it:

"What she has erected stands over the palace built by millions of Palestinian Arabs with their toil and effort during thousands of years in which they planted their vineyards and tended their olives and oranges since days of old." (p. 49).

Much is written about Israel's economic difficulties, such as the foreign trade deficit, and her resources are analysed to prove the unsoundness of her economy.

Wākid sums up the targets Israel failed to achieve during her first decade: economic and political independence; the creation of a closely-knit society; a sense of confidence and stability; an adequate response to the call for immigration. In the same way as the Jews were wanderers among the peoples, so Israel "wandered" between the blocs; she did not solve the psychological problem of the Jews; and so on, and so forth (*Israel in the Balance*, pp. 59ff).

4. ISRAEL'S ANTI-ARAB ACTIVITIES

a) GENERAL

Since the Arabs aspire to liquidate Israel, it must be her aim to prevent their doing so. This means that she has a substantial interest in their weakness and backwardness, and this must be apparent in her behaviour towards them. It follows that Israel must be trying to make difficulties for every Arab country; her agents are active in sowing dissension among them; she tries to frighten the Arabs and undermine their self-confidence, to divide them and put obstacles in the way of their nationalism. Thus, according to Haykal, Israel

> ". . . wages incessant war to sap his [the Arab enemy's] strength and undermine his self-confidence. She is interested in raising doubts in the UAR of its capacity, and therefore she spreads stories about her victory in Sinai. Her aim is to sow defeatism among the Palestinian Arab themselves, so that they may lose all hope of victory or return." (*al-Ahrām,* February 23, 1962).

Her policy is

> ". . . threats, terrorism and the paralysis of the Arab will by fear." (*al-Ahrām,* February 12, 1965).

Nasser stated:

> "We have succeeded in overcoming many of the difficulties which faced the Arab nation and which Israel and our enemies have always nourished." (November 12, 1964).

b) ISRAEL AS THE ENEMY OF ARAB NATIONALISM

Israel, the Arabs repeatedly declare, knows that unity will make the Arabs strong, thus enabling them to liquidate her, so she is interested in their disunity. She is always worried by any apparent progress towards unity, and wages ramified psychological warfare in order to arouse disputes and dissensions among them. Nasser said, for example:

> "I read what Israel broadcasts and I have found that all her efforts and aims are to arouse local nationalism. Why? Because Israel thinks that unity is a danger to her, for the meaning of unity is her doom *(fanā'uhā),* since she will continue to survive so long as controversy continues within the Arab nation." (April 17, 1961).
>
> "Israel tries by her broadcasts to divide the Arabs, because their division strengthens her." (June 26, 1962).

The assumption that Israel opposes Arab unity leads to a tendency to see her influence behind every dissension. Some declare that Israel had a hand in the break-up of the UAR. Haykal said that in 1958-61

> ". . . the Egyptian forces covered a considerable distance in order to reach a position that would put them on a level with the forces of the enemy . . . The achievement of this stage—and history will prove this one day—was the first hidden reason for the plot to split Egypt from Syria in 1961." (*al-Ahrām,* September 25, 1964).

Arab national victories are necessarily failures for Israel, even if she has no direct connection with them. The replacement of a reactionary regime in an Arab country by a revolutionary popular regime is an occasion for mourning in Israel. That was why she bewailed the 1958 revolution in Iraq, the fall of the Qassem regime, the revolution in Yemen and the national victory in Algeria. Conversely, Israel rejoices at any setback to Arab nationalism:

> "Israel sees in the Yemeni revolt a continuation of the Arab revolutionary tide which she thought had been halted by the break-up of the UAR. Israel knows that this tide will create new situations in the Arab East, which will affect the balance of forces between the Arab national movement and the Zionist movement." (*al-Ahrām,* December 21, 1962).

c) ISRAEL AS AN ENEMY OF SOCIAL PROGRESS

Since the development of the Arab countries will strengthen them, it is in Israel's interest that they should not develop or progress. She is the enemy of resurgence, liberation, independence, inner renewal and progress. Nasser coined the slogan: "It is backwardness that ensures the survival of Israel" (February 22, 1962). Similarly, Haykal said: "Arab progress is death to Israel and backwardness is her ally" (*al-Ahrām,* February 12, 1965). Nasser comes back to the idea: "Israel has a deadly hatred for everything we do for our progress, since our progress means death to Israel" (March 9, 1965). Thus Israel is presented as not only a national, but also a social enemy. Israel is afraid of social resurgence, which may strengthen the Arab countries. Another reason for her interest in their backwardness is her ties with imperialism, which wants the backward peoples not to advance so that it may continue to exploit them. Imperialism is interested in backwardness for the sake of exploitation and profit, but for Israel it is a condition of her survival, so her interest in it is stronger. That is why she uses her influence to prevent development in the Arab countries, interfering and employing pressure to make it harder for them to get loans and aid.

Such an argument may have important psychological consequences. From the distant and abstract plane of nationalism, the hostility may overflow onto the personal plane, making Israel a barrier to the progress of the individual and his efforts to improve his way of life.

This argument is typical of the popular-Socialist period of Arab nationalism. In the early period, during the twenties and thirties, Arab leaders denounced the Jewish community as a disturbing factor and a source of harmful ideas of hasty progress, undermining tradition and social and spiritual stability. Today, on the contrary, Israel is stigmatized as the ally of conservatism and reaction, so that political antagonism to the existence of Israel is reinforced by social motives. Thus, Erskine Childers writes:

> "The existence of the Israeli state was regarded by *ancien régime* Arab politicians primarily as a diplomatic affront, a political injustice and a military danger. But for the new, revolutionary generation there is an added dimension of grievance and revolution—the social dimension." ("Palestine: the broken triangle," p. 87).

This tendency to regard Israel as a social enemy, which also takes the form of emphasizing her colonialist character, is one of the explanations of the fact that the transition of Arab countries to progressive Socialist regimes does not lessen the hostility towards Israel, as was hoped by many Israeli circles which regarded Arab antagonism as a result of Arab social and political weakness, but—on the contrary—intensifies it.

d) ZIONIST ANTI-ARAB PROPAGANDA

Israel presents herself as an island of progress and democracy in the Middle East and is interested in lowering the prestige of the Arabs and belittling their achievements, depicting them as impotent talkers in order to lower their status and bring herself into greater prominence. Nasser complained, for example:

> "The Zionists distort the Arab image in the United States, Canada and Europe." (July 27, 1961).
>
> "We have all seen how Israel disparages the Arabs and says: 'Let the Arabs talk. They talk and do nothing.' " (February 21, 1965).

Israel exploits the Arab boycott by portraying it as an illegal weapon and describing the Arab States as aggressors. She accuses them of anti-Semitism, alleging that their antagonism to her is due to anti-Jewish feelings and religious and racial hostility, and that they do not distinguish between Jews and Zionists (e.g. Rushdī, p. 235).

Israel is also accused of damaging the position of the Arabs in the cultural field. In his article "The Struggle of Arab Nationalism against Imperialism and Zionism," Dr. Nawfal says that Zionism tries to disparage Arab achievements in the scientific as well as other spheres. He furiously attacks Professor Hans Kohn, who gave the ancient Hebrews credit for being the first to give expression to nationalism, thus putting them on the same level as the Greeks, whereas, in Nawfal's view, nationalism began in ancient Egypt (of which the modern Egyptians often regard themselves as the heirs, the Pharaonic civilization being described as Arab). In this he sees a deliberate Zionist attempt to belittle the significance of the role played by the Arab world and its culture, and an example of the Zionist practice of distorting the truth behind a mask of scientific objectivity (*Egyptian Political Science Review,* April 1962). It is an irony of history that a man like Kohn, who left Palestine because he believed that Arab national aspirations were incompatible with Zionism, should be criticized with such vehemence and his extensive studies on the question of nationalism be presented as a Zionist plot.

Israeli and Zionist activities in American universities are regarded as damaging to the status of Arabic culture, as in this report:

> "The Supreme Council for Arabic Culture, which convened for its first meeting in Baghdad, considered an important report on the danger of Zionist penetration into the American universities, and the distortion of Islamic values and the misrepresentation of Arabic literature by Israeli lecturers teaching in the universities according to a prearranged plan. According to the said report, Zionism has prepared a plan to gain control over the study of the Arabic language and Islamic faith and culture in American universities and institutes through Jewish lecturers trained for the purpose. These lecturers, in effect, completely dominate these subjects." (*al-Akhbār,* March 22, 1965).

Al-Ramādī goes to the length of accusing Israel of disseminating spurious copies of the Quran in Africa (p. 73), while Qāsim adds the Christian Scriptures to the indictment (1966, p. 135).

Israel is interested in isolating the Arabs and disrupting their foreign relations; she portrays them as aggressors and quarrelmongers, while presenting herself as peace-loving; she describes their armaments as aggressive and her own as defensive. Nasser, for example, once described a visit he made to New York:

> "World Zionism always tries to explain that the Arab people is quarrelsome and recalcitrant, that Israel is the victim and the Arabs aggressors . . . Zionism tries to describe us as barbarians, and the people of New York, for example, expected to see Jamāl 'Abd al-Nāṣir thrashing about like a madman and screaming." (October 10, 1960).

Ṣafwat declared that Israel

> ". . . disseminates destructive principles in the Middle East countries with the aim of damaging the regimes so as to subordinate them to the Communist camp, so that in the eyes of the West she would appear to be the only democratic State in the Middle East." (p. 200).

In her propaganda in the West, Israel ignores the anti-Communist activities of the Arab countries, and emphasizes their ties with the Soviet bloc and China, describing the policy of positive neutralism as hostile to the United States.

5. FAVOURABLE AND AMBIVALENT REFERENCES

The Arab image of Israel as reflected in the references given so far is entirely negative and pejorative, but this is not the whole story. Side by side with denunciation we often find commendation, either explicit or implicit. The praises generally present Israel as an example to be imitated, as we have seen in connection with Zionism. Sometimes, Zionism and Israel converge and both are presented as an example to learn from and a demonstration that certain methods have been tried and been found useful. The aim in presenting Israel as a model, is therefore, practical: to stimulate the Arabs to action. In a visit to the Gaza Strip in 1955, Nasser said:

> "All I ask of you is to persevere, and unite, and act, and be patient, and take an example and a lesson *('ibara wa-durūs)* from the Jews." (March 29, 1955, I.L., III/687).

a) MODERNITY AND EFFICIENCY

In such praises of Israel, major prominence is given to her efficiency and modernity, her achievements in technology and science, her thorough planning instead of improvisation. Israel stands for dynamic enterprise and achievement. Indeed, the implication of these references is that Israel is strong and healthy, instead of weak and unstable.

Hottinger explains that the Palestinian Arabs are convinced that Israel won because of her modernity, a quality which they regard as an ideal (p. 247). Hence, they regard Israel as the embodiment of this ideal and an example of the goal which they would like to attain.

In a speech to Syrian students on December 29, 1962, Prime Minister Nāẓim al-Qudsī referred to the high percentage of engineers and physicians in Israel, emphasizing that Syria and the other Arab countries must also produce large numbers of them. He was severely criticized for this statement by Cairo Radio and the Egyptian press, but a Damascus Radio commentator retorted:

> "Qudsī drew the attention of the Arab nation to the truth: Israel our enemy is not—as Nasserist propaganda describes her—weak and unstable in her social structure; she is a State with various possibilities and human potential. By revealing this truth, Qudsī is stimulating the Arabs to comprehensive action and progress in all fields." (Damascus Radio, January 9, 1962, 19:30 hrs.).

'Ārif al-'Ārif notes the Jewish tendency to study and go into matters deeply (*The Disaster,* Vol. IV, p. 859), while Israel is praised in many places in Qamḥāwī's *Disaster and Reconstruction.* There are many laudatory references to Israel's army and military preparedness, especially in the course of appeals to the Arabs to strengthen their own military forces (e.g. Ṣafwat, *Israel, the Common Enemy*).

Israel's achievements help to reinforce appeals to the Arabs to surpass her. Ṣā'ib Salām calls upon Arab youth to prepare for a long and difficult struggle:

> "We must tell the younger generation openly the facts as they are: Israel is not a 'so-called State' and never was even in the past. Israel has become a real and legal State, living the life of an independent State. She has a powerful, trained and equipped army to defend her. She has an efficient and modern administration. She has extensive sources of income at home and abroad. She is growing and her inhabitants are multiplying in an unnatural manner. She acts at every suitable opportunity to expand her borders. We deceive ourselves if we imagine that Israel is doomed and that we shall surprise her one day and wipe her off the face of the earth." (*al-Nahār,* New Year issue, 1950).

b) UNITY

Arab writers often describe their own divisions, dissensions and backbitings in contrast to Israel's hard work and practical approach, drawing the conclusion that they must stop their quarrels and learn from Israel's unity. This, of course, is in contradiction to the repeated allegations of Israel's factiousness.

Thus, for instance, the Damascus paper *al-Naṣr* writes that, while the Arab broadcasting stations are engrossed in an internecine war of scurrility and slander, and Nasser squanders millions on propaganda in order to sow dissension and confusion in their ranks, dozens of delegations from Asia, Africa and all over the world come to Israel to make a close study of her development and progress, while she sends many missions to various countries in order to explain her point of view and establish friendly relations (August 14, 1962).

We find the same tendency with regard to the Jews. Despite Dr. Naṣr's theory about the Jews' factiousness and lack of "*'aṣabiyya*" (unity or solidarity—see Chapter V, 5, above), he emphasizes that they have a strong spirit of patriotism:

"The Jews, truth to tell, have succeeded under the pressure of modern European persecution in creating among themselves a deep and stubborn patriotism *(waṭaniyya),* which embraces all their communities the world over . . . They have thus supplemented the Jewish brain and the Jewish faith, which have enabled them to preserve their will to live for generations despite recurrent persecutions." (p. 30).

c) SPIRITUAL VALUES

References to spiritual values and achievements are rarer, but they are to be found, even in the writings of Nashāshībī, who knows no bounds in the virulence of his denunciations. He describes how in his visits to Europe he found that when the French press discussed the dissemination of French culture Israel was mentioned at the head of the list of its consumers. Israel was also active in the cultural sphere:

"Israel, little more than ten years old, could send to Paris a Jewish ballet company to sing and perform in the ancient Hebrew language on a distinguished French stage. I mean the Opera. Indeed, time will pass and the Arabs may increase their strength and achieve superiority over Israel in the military sphere; years will pass and the Arabs may avenge their defiled honour and liquidate Israel in Palestine, but it will be quite impossible to liquidate Israel in the eyes of the world and demonstrate to mankind our right that Israel should die so that we should live, unless we can approach the world in the language in which Israel has spoken to them and touched their hearts: the language of art, culture and music." (*Return Ticket,* 1962, pp. 135-6).

Despite all his hostility, his antagonism to Israel and his denunciation of her people as "garbage collected from all over the world," he cannot help recognizing that she enjoys spiritual superiority.

Many Arabs appear to listen to Israel's Arabic broadcasts, as may be seen from the frequent public reactions of their leaders, including Nasser. This seems to indicate curiosity and interest, and perhaps even belief in their accuracy. Possibly, too, since there is a widespread distrust among the Arabs of their leaders' statements, they want to hear the other side, and they may have learned by experience that the Israeli station is to be trusted. When they listen, however, they cannot help hearing the story of Israel's constructive and progressive activities, and it may be assumed that some of these things sink in.

d) AMBIVALENCE

The duality arising out of this combination of praise and censure creates a mixture of ambivalent feelings: hatred and loathing, appreciation and admiration, envy mingled with hostility, and envy mingled with the desire to imitate. Ambivalence is inherent in the circumstances of conflict. Rivals not only hate and despise each other; the very existence of the conflict implies that the other side is important enough to be a rival. The opposing parties compare themselves with each other, but this involves the recognition that the rival is worth the comparison—if he were trivial and impotent, there would be no point in it. The conflict is an arena of competition, which involves a considerable measure of recognition that the rival, whether qualitatively or quantitatively, is worth competing with. Moreover, since Israel and Zionism have been successful in the struggle against the Arabs, it is in the latter's interest, for the sake of their own self-respect, to exaggerate the the power and influence of the former, to avoid the implication that they have been defeated by an insignificant force.

There are grounds for the assumption that the ambivalence in the Arab image of Israel is manifested on two layers or planes of consciousness. There is the upper, official and open layer of denunciation of the Jews, Zionism and Israel, and a suppressed lower layer of recognition of their positive qualities. The second image is not so complete or detailed as the official one; it is a combination of impressions and evaluations in regard to Israel on various subjects. The effort of self-persuasion that the Israelis are indeed despicable entails repression and suppression by setting aside or submerging any favourable information from without. The virulent criticism of anyone who brings the repressed image to the fore, as in the case of Nāẓim al-Qudsī above, shows that there is a strong interest in repression. Nevertheless, despite the power of inclination and emotion, something of the positive aspect strikes root. The repressed image exists, as it were, in a twilight world.

The repressed image rises to the surface when the Arabs find that they have a pragmatic need to utilize it, either for self-reproach, or as a weapon in inter-Arab rivalries, when the Israeli example is used to prove that a rival Arab country is not acting properly.

However, this pragmatic and tendentious use of the repressed image reduces its value as a portrayal of the truth. These references to the positive aspect are not an admission of truth for its own sake, but a means to an end. It is also noteworthy that such characteristics as "efficiency," "technology" and "scientific achievement" are emphasized mainly as secrets of success, and not as basic features of intrinsic value. Arab recognition of the positive aspects of Israel is, therefore, truncated and distorted.

Ambivalence is no doubt a universal phenomenon, but it would be interesting, if possible, to measure differences in its incidence among individuals and groups, classifying groups in respect of the types and relative frequencies of ambivalent manifestations among them.

It may be assumed that there will be many ambivalences in a society which is in process of cultural transition and change, desiring the new while still attached to the old. The same will apply to a "closed" society, committed to rigid conceptions and ideologies. Ambivalence in such cases may facilitate the admission of facts which contradict the ideological orthodoxy. It constitutes a kind of correction to the ideological falsehood, offering a way out from ideological consistency, a kind of lip-service to the Freudian "reality principle," creating a degree of flexibility and thus facilitating continued devotion to the ideology. Ambivalence provides the human spirit with a defence mechanism against itself, even if it introduces an element of dissonance, and it may be beneficial. Deutsch and Merritt note that "a moderate level of inconsistency may be conducive to better reality orientation, and more receptivity to new information and to greater combinatorial resourcefulness" ("Effects of Events on National and International Images," Kelman volume, p. 159).

It appears that manifestations of ambivalence are particularly prevalent among the Arabs, for their yearning to believe in their own greatness is not supported by the reality.[4] Hence, on the one hand, addiction to illusions of grandeur, a wide variety of apologetics to explain away their distress and the development of an ideology to demonstrate their greatness, and, on the other hand, the creation of escape hatches and safety valves by fragments of correct conceptions and glimpses of reality.

So far as the attitude to Israel is concerned, the ambivalence is expressed in the contempt and admiration which are reflected in conflicting attitudes towards her: on the one hand, the official image describes her as weak, her position as unstable and her doom as certain; on the other hand, there is a recognition of her strength, dynamism and superiority, and a fear of defeat at her hands. It might be imagined that this is also a question of different phases: the belief that, while today, before the Arabs have accumulated strength, they are weak, they will ultimately become stronger and then they will overcome. There is no doubt that such a conception does exist among them; basically, however, ambivalence is not a question of a time table but of a dual outlook, in which, according to the changing times, sometimes one pole (Israel's weakness and Arab self-confidence) and sometimes the other (Israel's strength and Arab apprehension) is emphasized. From this point of view, we could examine the "balance of ambivalence" from time to time. Immediately after Sinai, for example, it appears, there was a shift towards the pole of fear and the leadership had to make an effort to redress the balance by persuasion and propaganda. In the course of time, it seems, the fear weakened, but did not disappear. (A similar fluctuation took place after the Six-Day War.)

Ambivalence is also required in order to explain the postponement of the confrontation with the enemy. Haykal notes that the exaggeration by propagandists of Israel's weakness raises the question why the Arabs do not attack her:

> "The attitude of disparagement and the oversimplified picture of the enemy expressed by many of us have gone so far that the question arises . . . Why are we waiting? Why do we not attack Tel Aviv and finish it?" (*al-Ahrām,* January 24, 1964).

On the other hand, the descriptions of Israel's weakness, which are to be found in Haykal's own articles, are required to nourish the hope that she can be defeated one day. Ambivalence therefore makes it possible simultaneously to admit the strength of the enemy, who poses a threat that must be taken into account, and to cherish the belief that one day he can be overcome.

Fluctuations in descriptions of weakness and strength may be seen in the following example. Over the years Arab spokesmen made extravagant predictions of the importance of Israel's National Water scheme and the advantages it would offer: it could enable the Israelis to settle the Negev and add five million to their population, it would guarantee the basis for Israel's survival and serve as a springboard for expansion. The purpose of all this was to stimulate themselves to action in order to frustrate the plan. But when they proved unable to prevent the completion of the plan and the drawing of the water from Lake Kinneret, Arab spokesmen had to change gear. Thus, Haykal wrote:

> "There is no need or justification for the inflation of the Israeli scheme. Inflation is liable to have a deleterious effect on Arab public opinion. It portrays the enemy as all-powerful, and unjustifiably creates fertile soil for feelings of fear, impotence and complexes among the Arabs."

On the contrary, he continues, it is the Arabs who have worked wonders, for the cultivated area in the "Liberation Province" is many times greater than that which will become available for cultivation in the Negev (*al-Ahrām,* January 24, 1964).

Praise breaks the "inner consistency" of the image and creates dissonances, which, according to Professor Festinger's theory, produces an inner impulse to narrow the gap. This does not mean that the negative image of Israel will be changed owing to the positive concepts, and the effect of the dissonance in changing the image should not be exaggerated. Kurt Lewin explains that the influence on a person's general attitude of true perceptions of a particular object is limited if they are not consistent with the emotional attitude of the individual towards it. The individual's sentiment towards a particular group is determined less by his information about the group than by the social atmosphere of his environment (*Resolving Social Conflict,* p. 63). As Lewin puts it:

> "As a rule the possession of correct knowledge does not suffice to rectify false perception." (p. 61).

On the assumption that many Arabs have a negative emotional attitude towards Israel, correct information about her does not tangibly alter their basic attitude. The contradiction which is expressed in ambivalence may also express different mental "layers." The admission of the positive aspects of Israel may sometimes come from a level of logical thinking, as when Nashāshībī reflects on Israel's capacity to speak to Europe in the language of culture, while the same author's denial that Israel could ever be the source of any values comes from the emotional layer of hate (see above).

Furthermore, even if this kind of ambivalence shows that the Arabs are dubious about the complete accuracy of their hateful image of Israel, dubiety does not mean disbelief.

6. SCURRILITY, ABSURDITY AND FALSEHOOD IN ARAB STATEMENTS

Arab statements about the conflict are liberally scattered with scurrility, absurdity and falsehood. This phenomenon is so frequent and prominent that we would be false to ourselves if we ignored or condoned it. Indeed, we would be committing a double fault: giving way, on the one hand, to arrogance, by implying that we are too superior to be affected by such things, and, on the other hand, to contempt, as if implying that such manifestations are to be expected of the Arabs. The converse danger, of course, also exists: we may be tempted to grasp at the uglier aspects of the Arab attitude and even seize on them joyfully in order to ignore their valid and sensible arguments, which we may find convenient. The effort to see the truth must embrace all aspects, positive and negative, and aim at a balanced view in accordance with their relative weight.

It might be argued that since we are dealing with such a vast number of statements by numerous writers in so many volumes, we might expect a certain number of unconsidered expressions and some percentage of nonsense. But is it not true to say that the Arabs have exceeded the "margin of tolerance" where nonsense is concerned? Furthermore, the frequency, repitition, emphasis and virulence of such statements are incompatible with the argument that they are only a matter of chance. It is true that some of these utterances are expressions of anger and indignation, but it is not a case of passing temper, to which we might apply the Talmudic saying "Never blame a man for what he says in a moment of distress"; this is an enduring and intransigent wrath. We might well remember another Talmudic saying: "By three things may a man be known: his pocket, his cups and his anger"—i.e. by his behaviour in business affairs, in his amusements and under conditions of conflict. The language and the images a person adopts in his quarrels are certainly of significance; his language is a part of him, influenced by his thinking and influencing it in turn.

a) SCURRILITY

In Chapter III, we discussed the Arab use of scurrilous language. We may well regard it as common practice for rivals to use coarse language against each other in order to find an outlet for their hatred, anger and contempt. The Arab attitude to Israel is expressed in concentrated form by the epithets they use about her. The following collection does not claim to be complete. Epithets connected with imperialism have been surveyed in Chapter III. Here is a further series, classified into groups:

Transitoriness and Weakness. The pseudo-State or the so-called State *(al-maz'ūma);* the artificial State *(al-muṣṭana'a);* the statelet *(al-duwayla);* the nugatory statelet; the cardboard or paper State; the impotent State; the pampered State; the State of donations.

Contempt and Loathing. The foundling *(laqīṭa)* State (implying bastardy); deformed *(mamsūkha)*; brazenly exploiting *(al-bāghiya)*; base *(khabītha)*; parasite; aggressive invader *(al-ghāziya)*; criminal *(al-jāniya)*; the State of tyranny *(istibdād)*; chaotic; the State of crime *(ijrām)*, or evil; the gangs of the gangster Government; oppressive *(ẓulm)*; the robber *(luṣūṣ)*; the hunters' State *(al-qunnāṣ)*; Satan; irreligion: prostitution; provocation *(istifzāz)*, etc.

Other Epithets. The Zionist monster; the pollution of Zionism, the Zionist plague *(wabā')*; the enemy of the peoples; the ally of the murderers; the occupation authorities; the purulent abscess; the illegitimate daughter of Europe; a cancer in the heart of the Arab nation, or in the Middle East; the Zionist cancer; the imperialist cancer (see below); Israel the bleeding thorn *(shawka dāmiya)*; the gang of hypocrites and criminals; the focus of evil *(bu'rat al-sharr)*; dirt, filth, sewage *(ḥuthāla, qādhūra)*; the Zionist gangs *(shirdhima ṣahyūniyya)*. The comparison with cancer implies the danger of expansion. Ali Muhammad Ali, in the introduction to his book *Inside Israel*, criticizes this term as inaccurate, since cancer comes from inside the body, while Israel is a foreign element; besides, there is no cure for cancer, which puts an end to the sufferer, while in Israel's case "the effective treatment is known."

Biological Epithets. The viper State; the adder; the Zionist adders; the octopus *(akhṭabūṭ)*; the spider; the bacillus of evil *(jurthūmat al-sharr)*; the claws of the cat *(makhālib al-qiṭṭ)*; the parasites; the claws *(barāthin)* of Zionism.

Jews and Zionists. Aliens, riffraff *(shudhdhādh al-āfāq, āfāqiyyūn, dakhīl, dukhalā')*—expressions frequently applied to the Jews even in Mandatory times, the Jews being regarded as aliens always and everywhere; Shukairy told a *Jeune Afrique* correspondent that "Hebrew" means a transient, an alien—December 18, 1966, p. 37; foundlings; criminals; heads of criminal gangs; terrorists; demons; despicable; beggars (*shaḥḥādḥūn*—referring to fund-collecting); wanderers; liars; master butchers *(saffāḥūn, saffākūn)*; bloodsuckers; white slavers. Nashāshībī described the Prime Minister of Israel as "a consummate criminal and a great robber" (*mujrim aṣīl wa-liṣṣ kabīr*—in *al-Jumhūriyya*, June 12, 1964).

b) MEASUREMENT

The frequency of these epithets and terms can be measured, and may be assumed to be of some significance. It is also possible to compare the frequency of use of a particular term in various countries, to examine fluctuations in frequency, and enquire into the factors which produced such fluctuations and their significance. It is my impression, for instance, as I have already noted, that the use of the term "imaginary" or "alleged", or "so-called" *(al-maz'uma)* in regard to Israel has declined, since her survival for over twenty years has shown that she is not merely "alleged" to exist. At the same time, there has been a rise in the use of "artificiality," "cancer" and, particularly, epithets implying ties with imperialism and colonialism. The latter are connected with the prominent tendency in recent years to regard the conflict as part of the struggle for liberation.

c) ABSURDITIES

Arab arguments and allegations contain quite a number of obvious absurdities. These include all the demonological features of Arab anti-Semitism, many of the historical comparisons and conclusions, the talk of Zionist plots, and many other indications of a mental balance upset by hatred. Whether a particular argument or interpretation is regarded as an absurdity or a cock and bull story is, often, no doubt, a matter of opinion, but it is sometimes quite clear and unmistakable where known facts are concerned.

Thus, for example, Justice Brandeis, Disraeli and Frankfurter are described as Communist leaders. The first two names in a list of Zionist terrorists given by Nashāshībī are those of Max Nordau, the author, who was Herzl's colleague, and Joseph Trumpeldor, the Jewish labour pioneer, who was killed in 1920 (p. 155). Tawfīq Luṭfī declares that at Yalta "Stalin, Churchill and Roosevelt each declared that he was the first Zionist in the world" (p. 25).

Under the heading, "Israeli Blood Bank Equipped with Arab Blood," Na'nā'a tells a story of a young Arab who reached a certain Arab country from Israel and collapsed in a faint as soon as he arrived. The youth told how he had been held in an Israeli prison and compelled to give frequent blood donations in larger quantities than those medically permissible. This, he said, was a regular routine in the Israeli prisons for Arab offenders, for Israel did not care if they died or fell dangerously ill when they left prison as a result of loss of blood. Na'nā'a appealed to Bishop Ḥakīm, head of the Greek Catholic Church in Israel, to investigate and to submit his conclusions to the Vatican (pp. 282-3).

The sexual aspect usually arises in racial conflicts, such as that between black and white. Where the Arab-Israel conflict is concerned, the customs of Arab society, with its restrictions and frustrations, may have some effect in this sphere (Berger, p. 161). In Nazi Germany, the Jewish men were denounced as rapists and defilers of race purity; among the Arabs, the main targets for attack are the Jewish women, who are described as seductive and provocative (see Bashir Ka'dān and Shafīq Shālātī, *These Zionists,* Damascus). It is sometimes alleged that beautiful Jewesses were sent to influence UN delegates before the partition decision. Sha'bān says that they persuaded Christian Arab boys in Israel to convert to Judaism (p. 59).

The allegation that Jews are engaged in the white slave traffic is frequently repeated. A chapter in 'Izzat's book, entitled "The Oldest Profession Comes from There" (Israel), describes the growth of prostitution:

> "The Israeli Government indirectly encourages prostitution and the disruption of the family." (p. 88-9).

Sexual licence in the *ma'barot,* the immigrants' temporary quarters, he continues, went so far that the Government had to liquidate them (p. 91). Wākid says that in Israel there are hundreds of existentialist colonies, in which people live licentious bohemian lives—

> ". . . and if anyone is in need of sexual activity, he can do it straight away." (p. 63).

There are also a considerable number of scholarly absurdities, which are marked by a pretence of scientific objectivity which covers up superficiality and Levantinism. Examples are Kanafānī's generalizations about Zionist literature, such as that the heroes of Zionist stories always come from Germany and know the Bible by heart (p. 66), or that Zionist books describe all nations except the Americans and the Danes as persecutors of the Jews (1966, p. 72). Nawfal's attack on Hans Kohn for an alleged attempt to denigrate Arabism is another instance.

d) FALSEHOOD AND DISTORTIONS

Another phenomenon, the use of falsehoods in connection with the conflict, is actually part of a wider one: distortions of the truth and misleading slogans in Arab political life. Political scientists, sociologists and historians seem to feel reluctant to mention this aspect in their analysis of the Arab world. Hottinger, who is undoubtedly a balanced observer, does not refrain from speaking openly. He refers to achievements in "the reinterpretation of the truth" and their shocking influence on Arab public opinion. Defeats become victories, history is rewritten, conditions which have in fact remained unaltered are made to appear as if they have been magically transformed by the announcement of development plans, and slogans for the future are endowed with hypnotic power, as if they are guarantees that the aims will be achieved. Hottinger explains that propaganda succeeds in misleading the people because it fulfils the latent aspirations of the Arabs. If there are difficulties because of a chasm between the slogan and the reality, it is always possible to bring the facts into line by brandishing some other watchword which will be greeted with enthusiasm, such as talk of anti-colonialism, anti-Zionism, anti-feudalism and anti-regionalism. Ideas like these can compensate for anything (*The Arabs,* 1963, pp. 291-4).

It might be argued that the presentation of the unvarnished truth, the honest description of the difficulties involved in the quest for the modernization of Arab society, and the admission that progress must be gradual and will take a long time, will weaken morale, and that propaganda, even if it involves deviations from the truth, is required in order to give the people hope that change is really possible and secure their support for the effort to bring it about. Without such distortions, it may be suggested, there is no possibility of overcoming indifference and fatalism; in other words, for the sake of progress towards modernization there is no alternative to the use of these tactical falsehoods or the manipulation of misleading slogans; falsehood, it may be argued, is only a temporary expedient which will ultimately be forgotten, while the desirable results will be permanent. Even if we agree that moral idealism is not always compatible with political realism, and that political affairs cannot be conducted on a purely ethical basis, one cannot help wondering whether lies may not become second nature.

S. Hamad goes further than Hottinger and regards falsehood as an expression of national character:

> "Lying is a widespread habit among the Arabs, and they have a low idea of truth . . . The Arab has no scruples about lying if by it he obtains his objective. His conscience possesses an interesting elasticity." (*Temperament and Character of the Arabs,* 1960, p. 36).

If an "elastic" attitude to truth and falsehoods is adopted in internal affairs, how much easier it is to resort to lies and distortions about the external enemy, especially as the Arab authorities can utilize their control of mass communications media, for their society is not particularly open to information from the outside world, especially from the enemy. In previous chapters, we have given examples of exaggerations and the development of a demonology of Zionism, the Jews and Israel, which contains many elements of distortion and falsehood. It is only natural that the disseminator of lies may unwittingly come to believe in his own statements, but it may be reasonably assumed that Arab spokesmen also make use of deliberate misstatements and falsehoods.

No society anywhere can claim to be entirely free of falsehood. Statesmen and leaders do not restrict themselves to the truth; no doubt they use lies, half truths, rhetoric, demagogy and ambiguity. There can hardly be any society which is entirely free from conventional lies and the distortion of facts. But this does not mean that lies are current and accepted in all countries to the same degree. A judgement which insists that, as a matter of principle, if falsehood exists at all quantitative differences do not matter, is in itself a moral falsehood and distortion, undermining the foundations of morality by the adoption of an absolute criterion, which is not met by any human society. There is a difference between a lack of moral consistency, occasional lying, and frequent lying. Even without a comparative study of the place of truth and falsehood in various societies and the use of lies as between rivals in situations of conflict, there are reasonable grounds for the impression that the Arabs make a widespread, obvious and emphatic use of lies in their quarrel with Israel. Here is a brief selection:

The Arab authorities have often issued false statements about the results of border disputes and reprisal operations—in particular, exaggerating the number of Jewish casualties. After the Israeli reprisal operation at Sabkha (November 2, 1955), for instance, the Egyptians announced 200 Israeli dead. Journalists who visited the scene of operations were told that the reason why there were no Jewish bodies to be found was that the Israeli soldiers had a special appliance as part of their equipment in order to carry the bodies, and that they had taken them all away when they retreated (see press of the time and Rāfi'ī, p. 185). Mr. and Mrs. La Couture comment on this incident:

> "This technique of phoney casualties might appear contemptible, but it is better than if there had been real ones." (*Egypt in Transition,* 1958, p. 237).

At Nuqayb, Nāfūrī said that 480 Israelis were killed (Damascus Radio, August 27, 1962).

Statements about fedayeen operations have often included boasts of deeds that were never done. The announcements of the Fatah organization for example, are outstanding for their boastfulness and the extraordinary differences between the achievements of its men and the stories published about them. There were repeated statements about "daring military operations" which sowed fear and terror into the hearts of the Zionists and caused heavy casualties and losses of ammunition and equipment (as in *al-Ba'th,* February 6, 1966) in connection with operations which either did not take place at all or were of trivial importance.

There are indications that false reports by Arab military units have given the authorities a false picture of what actually happened. Egyptian bombers who were sent to bombard Tel Aviv during the Sinai Campaign dropped their bombs in an uninhabited area near Gezer, about 15 miles away, and, it seems, announced the completion of their mission. As a result, a history of the war declares:

> "Our bombers carried out continuous attacks during the 30th and the 31st [of October 1956] on Israel's airfields and destroyed them." (Fahmī, *The Threefold Aggression and the World Conscience,* 1964, p. 73).

Decorations have even been awarded for acts of heroism that never took place. According to an order published in Damascus on December 8, 1964, Syrian pilots were decorated for, according to the Syrian authorities, shooting down an Israeli Mirage fighter on November 14, 1964 (*al-Manār,* December 9, 1964). Nasser decorated pilots who were supposed to have shot down an Israeli plane in July 1963 (Cairo Radio, July 23, 1963, 22:00 hrs.). Cairo Radio reported a statement by a Yemeni delegation that a brigade of Yemeni Jews, sent by request of the Jordanians, was fighting in Yemen. Later, Major-General Fatḥī 'Abd al-Ghanī, Commander of the Egyptian forces in Yemen, announced that Israel had sent hundreds of volunteers and dozens of experts to fight in Yemen (*al-Muṣawwar,* June 12, 1965, p. 28).

Ben Bella declared that 1,500 Israelis were fighting for Tchombe in Katanga (U.P., according to *Ha'aretz,* November 2, 1964). Shukairy told the United Nations General Assembly that Israel was supplying arms and men to the Katanga army (November 6, 1961).

The story of the alleged map in the Knesset indicating Israel's expansionist ambitions has already been mentioned. In the Jordanian parliament a tale went the rounds that Jordanian territorial concessions in the "Triangle" area were due to the deceitful use of maps by the Israelis (also mentioned by Nashāshībī, p. 141).

Fahd al-Marik, in his book *How We Shall Overcome Israel* (1966, pp. 361-371), alleges that in 1948 the Jews filled the al-Jazzār Mosque in Acre with Arab girls whose husbands they had killed so that the Israeli soldiers might enjoy them.

Many of the quotations attributed to Zionist leaders are forgeries. In the *Egyptian Political Science Review,* which is ostensibly an academic publication, an article called "Britain Was the First to Call for the Existence of Israel," by al-Sayyid Muhammad Ibrāhīm, contains a fabricated quotation from a speech alleged to have been made by Ben-Gurion "in the year 1949," which was full of belligerent fury and vowed to fight until the entire Israeli homeland was liberated. According to the article, Ben-Gurion declared:

> "We have restored our swords to their scabbards only as a temporary measure. We shall draw them when freedom in this land is in danger and when the vision of the prophets and the Bible is realized; then the entire Jewish people will settle again in the lands of our fathers, which stretch from the Euphrates in the East to the Nile in the West." (January-March, 1959, p. 136).

Arab States have frequently been falsely accused by their rivals of negotiations, secret collaboration and intrigue with Israel and imperialism. For example, Cairo Radio alleged on July 19, 1962 that an Israeli delegation was visiting Jordan to assist in irrigation plans. To make the story realistic, it was stated that the delegation was being accompanied by a Jordanian sergeant-major, whose name was given (BBC, ME/1001/A/2-3, July 19, 1962).

Akram Ḥawrānī accused Nasser of being the initiator of the idea of drawing water from Lake Kinneret instead of diverting the Jordan, and passing the suggestion on to Ben-Gurion through Eisenhower (*al-Ayyām,* June 13, 1962).

Haykal makes a habit of presenting piquant secrets in the form of alleged intelligence reports and documentary evidence from closed sessions. For instance, in 1961 he described an incident that was supposed to have taken place over six years before, in February 1955, when Israeli army officers were said to have tried during the night to expel Pinhas Lavon, then Minister of Defence, from the Ministry, threatening to take over power in the country (*al-Ahrām,* May 5, 1961).

A year later he came back to the subject in greater detail:

> "On the evening of 5 February 1955, over 400 officers assembled in the building of the Israeli Defence Ministry in Tel Aviv, and sent [Prime Minister] Moshe

Sharett an ultimatum demanding the dismissal of Lavon from the Ministry of Defence before dawn and the appointment of Ben-Gurion in his stead."

Sharett, according to the story, had no alternative but to submit (*al-Ahrām*, March 16, 1962).

Later in the same year, in an article on the reasons for changes in Israel's security policies, he wrote:

"Immediately after the break-up of the UAR, Ben-Gurion called a meeting of the Israel Defence Forces General Staff with the participation of Chief of Staff Zvi Zur and Deputy Defence Minister Shimon Peres. At this meeting Ben-Gurion said: 'The position of the enemy surrounding Israel has been completely transformed. The Arab nationalist movement has been exploded from within and torn into pieces. I am convinced—from information at my disposal—that Nasser will again try to impose unity with Syria by force. This is liable to open the way to many interventions. This morning I received from Hussein, King of Jordan—through a mutual friend—a letter saying that he intends to give military support to the revolt that has taken place in Syria. King Hussein has asked me to permit his aircraft—which are likely to take part in air operations, especially in Northern Syria—to land on Israeli airfields if they have to do so for lack of fuel in view of the great distance between northern Syria and the Jordanian airfields, on condition that this should remain a secret between us. I immediately agreed to his request." (*al-Ahrām*, December 14, 1962).

On another occasion, he alleged that Israel was about to attack the Egyptian missile base from the air, but gave up the idea when the Egyptians forestalled them by building a number of bases.

The revelation of closely guarded secrets and the utilization of special channels of information are recognized journalistic expedients. Possibly, the Egyptian Intelligence sometimes helped Haykal to deceive himself and others. He may sometimes have been aware that his statements were not accurate, but perhaps thought that they were correct on the whole, or portrayed a true situation. He may not have regarded it as particulary important whether Ben-Gurion actually said the things which he attributed to him, or which, in his opinion, he was capable of saying, and therefore took it upon himself, as a matter of poetic licence, to present them as facts.

Chapter 7

THE ARABS' SELF-IMAGE IN THE CONFLICT

To understand the attitude of a party to a conflict, we must examine not only how he sees his rival, but also how he understands his own role in the conflict. His self-image affects, not only his view of the reality and the external circumstances which are a background to the conflict, but also his ideology. As Morroe Berger puts it, ideology "provides an interpretation of reality that is consonant with the holder's self-image" (*The Arab World*, p. 322). There is a reciprocal relationship between the self-image and the image of the opponent. As a competitive situation, the conflict involves a comparison between each party and his opponent. Some aspects of the Arabs' conception of themselves have, therefore, been discussed in previous chapters, and the present one may be brief.

1. THE SELF-IMAGE

Although nations tend to be satisfied with themselves, their virtues and what they regard as their mission to mankind, they differ in the strength and nature of this tendency. Side by side with a comparative study of the terms of condemnation and abuse used in conditions of conflict, there is room for a study of self-praise and self-glorification: the virtues claimed by various nations. Such a study would facilitate a better understanding of a particular case of conflict.

The epithets applied by the Arabs to themselves are marked by conspicuous self-glorification. Arab spokesmen address their hearers as members of a proud and noble people *(nabīl, karīm, abī).* Na'nā'a speaks of

> ". . . the battle for life through which our glorious *(majīda)* Arab nation is living with heroism *(basāla),* manliness *(rujūla),* and endurance *(jalad).*" (1964, p. 3).

Even in official announcements, which in most countries are couched in unemotional terms, we find, for example: "our valiant armies and our valiant pilots" (Damascus Radio, August 25, 1966, 08:59 hrs.).

Al-Quṣrī, in a play called *Palestine, the Tragedy of the Arab World*, characterizes the Arabs as follows:

> "There is none among the nations of the entire world so good as the Arabs, and they are a noble people." (p. 109).

In another place, explaining why the Arabs cannot acquiesce in Israel's existence, he defines them as

> ". . . a proud *(abī)* people which injustice *(ḍaym)* does not allow to sleep, which speedily takes vengeance and regards hatred for its enemies as a duty rather than a necessity." (p. 108).[1]

This self-glorification may also be a compensation for the dissatisfaction and frustration caused by the position of the Arabs in the world today—a matter of what Daniel Katz calls "compensatory identification" (McNeil volume, p. 75), i.e. the achievement of satisfaction by the enhancement of one's own value through images and daydreams of grandeur.

Arab writers often emphasize their contribution to culture, especially in reaction to Western criticism. Sharāra declares, for instance, in reply to Bertrand Russell's slighting view of the original Arab contribution to philosophy:

> "'Man' is the greatest invention in the world, which was discovered by Arab culture." (p. 91).

Hence:

> "The Arabs are more interested than any other people in humanist studies, especially history, geography, legislation, language, ethics and medicine." (p. 92).

Many peoples claim that they were the first to make important discoveries and inventions. Thus, Rousan declares:

> "The Arab invented the wheel, on which modern civilization is built, and is now supplying the oil to keep that wheel turning." (*Palestine and the Internationalization of Jerusalem,* English edition, p. 2).

Arab writers frequently sing the praises of Arab Nationalism: unlike other nationalisms, which are merely a transitional stage, it is "eternal," as the Ba'th constitution declares, and "has an eternal mission to mankind."

Bazzāz, like other ideologists, enumerates its essential qualities: it is universal, democratic, Arab-Socialist, progressive, revolutionary, positive and active. All these characteristics are inseparable parts of its very being (1964, Chapter 3). Arabs often contrast their spiritual qualities with the materialism of the West.

The concept of *'Urūba* (Arabism) is so heavily loaded with adoration, that they appear to distinguish between it as an abstract entity, which exists apart from its bearers, and the Arabs themselves. Arabism is greater and more sublime than its embodiment in the Arabs, but, on the other hand, the sublimity of Arabism is believed to be a guarantee that the Arabs will be deserving of it. We may find a similar approach in De Gaulle's statement:

> "France is not herself except when she is in the front rank . . . France cannot be France without her grandeur." (*War Memoirs,* French Edition, Part I, p. 1).

In other words, grandeur is an integral part of France, without which she would not be France.

The ideal image which people see in their mind's eye, or which they aspire to translate into reality, may come to be regarded as their actual image. Communities may come to see themselves not as they are, but as they think they could be, or ought to be capable of being—as if some potential or hidden greatness, on the brink of realization, were latent within them. Similarly, they may ascribe a hidden vileness to their opponents: the positive characteristics of the latter are deceptive and the basic reality is vile. Where they themselves are concerned, on the other hand, negative manifestations are superficial and transitory, while the basic reality is glorious. This latent greatness may influence their evaluation of their capacities and bridge the gap between present impotence and future omnipotence, as well as inducing them to cling to objectives which appear unpractical today. Thus the self-image of grandeur may be of great importance for the course of the conflict, leading to the rejection, as irrelevant, of the criticism that the liquidation of Israel is unattainable in the light of reality.

This tendency to self-glorification finds emphatic expression in situations of conflict, as a means of self-justification and self-comparison with the opponent. A psychological mechanism is liable to operate which distorts both the self-portrait and the portrait of the enemy, leading to polarization: exaggerated contempt for the enemy, who is all black, all guilt and the personification of evil, contrasted with the portrayal of oneself in the most glorious and attractive colours.[2]

Since the Jews are frequently described as treacherous and deceitful, the Arabs are characterized by integrity and fidelity. Tūnisī explains that the characteristics of the Jews are the opposite of those of the Arabs, as shown by the *Jāhilī* (pre-Islamic) poem which says that

> ". . . the Jews lack the generosity of the Arabs, their valour and their fidelity to their promises." (p. 63).

Against the background of the conflict, and in comparison with the Jews, we frequently find descriptions of Arab glory which may echo the poetic style used in the classic period of Arabic literature. Nashāshībī's book (1962) is full of self-glorification, contrasted with denunciation and mockery of the Jews. The Palestinians are fearless:

> "We reek not *(la yuhimmunā)* of death . . . We know better than anyone else the cowardice, weakness, fear and submissiveness that are stamped on the soui of the Jews."

In Gaza the Jews were gripped by fear and terror when they heard the very word *fedayeen* (p. 237).

Nashāshībī also exemplifies the tendency to define the self-image in sublime terms, with the implication that these characteristics are the opposite of those to be found in Israel. Explaining why the Palestinians are Arabs, he writes:

> "Why are we Arabs? Because we believe in God and not matter; we sanctify the prophets, and not the cannon; our strength is the basis of our existence, and if we forget this we shall be like our enemies. There is no reason in us for their hostility towards us, nor is any advantage to be gained from their friendship. We are Arabs because we have a universal mission, which calls for the good of all, social justice and mutual aid between classes. We are Arabs because we love the indedence of our countries and the independence of all peoples together with ourselves. For that reason we attack no one, and we rob no man of his right to life. We are advancing, and we shall grasp the hand of anyone who wishes to advance with us. We are Arabs because we maintain ties with our past, are proud of our traditions, and glory in the heritage of our fathers. Our generation guards this heritage so as to pass it on, pure and complete, to our children and grandchildren. We believe in eternity, the eternity of the spirit and the eternity of the Homeland. We are Arabs because we cherish spiritual values; we shall neither renounce them

nor exchange them for others, for the foundations of these values are the true, the beautiful and the good. In these values there is something of God; in them are the attributes of God. We are Arabs because we do not cling to a social philosophical outlook which is taken from beyond our horizons, beyond our borders, beyond our great Homeland, for such outlooks would shatter our existence and strike a blow at all that is sacred to us. We are Arabs because we adhere to Arab Nationalism and are built by it. It belongs to us and we belong to it. We are part of it and it is part of us. In it are our common tongue, united history and united sentiments; in it is the permanent definition of the truth of our past and our present; in it is the clear manifestation of our roots, which go far back to far generations; in it are the strong bonds and true ethnological and anthropological meanings that confirm our adhesion to the Arab race, of which we embody all the special characteristics, culture and intellectual standards." (*Return Ticket*, pp. 117-8; *The Arab Union and the Palestine Problem*, pp. 28-29).

And this is how Abdallah Tall concludes his chapter on "The Quran and the Jews":

"Islam calls for adhesion to the chivalry of generosity, courage, pride, zeal and energy for the defence of the weak, the stranger and the convert, and the Jews have nothing of all these qualities. Islam calls for faith in another world, paradise and hell, while the Jews do not believe in another world and all their aim in life is materialist effort which will give them complete enjoyment and fulfil their degraded aspirations and their vile purposes in this world. Islam honours woman and protects her honour and nobility; the Jews despise woman, employ her as a servant and as cheap merchandise with which to earn money to achieve their aims and reach their goals. Islam forbids the shedding of blood except by law, forbids robbery and immorality, while the Jews permit the shedding of the blood of a non-Jew, the stealing of his money and the defilement of his wife's honour." (pp. 67-8).

Hence, the clash between the Jews and Islam is, according to Tall, as inevitable as the clash between good and evil.

Since this superiority in values has not been realized, as it should have been, in the actual world, the self-glorification is translated, against the background of failure, into self-pity. History and destiny have been cruel to the Arabs, who have been unjustly and unfairly treated. The world does not behave properly to them, it is hostile (an "unsupportive environment," in the term used by Holsti and North in their study of the outbreak of World War I in the McNeil volume, p. 163).

The injustice continues. For instance, the West discriminates in favour of Israel, turning a blind eye to her misdeeds. Nasser complained, for example:

"The West forgives Israel for any act. They kidnapped innocent people. Every month there were kidnappings and bomb-throwings. They killed people and sent explosives to scientists to liquidate them. For all those things, Israel is forgiven. The West made a great fuss about the charge that we kidnapped a single Israeli spy from Rome, in connexion with the well-known story of the crate incident." (March 3, 1965).

He was referring to the story of the Israeli spy employed by the Egyptians who was found shut up in a crate at Rome Airport ready for transportation to Egypt. Earlier, Nasser complained:

"When Israel talks about a National Home for the Jews and of the Holy Land that will stretch from the Nile to the Euphrates, nobody is shocked. But when we talk about Palestine and the Arabs' rights in their country, that is shocking talk, which threatens the peace of the world." (May 14, 1956, I. L., V/1143).

"I have noticed that whenever you want to talk about this subject you confine yourself to questions about Israel and forget the rights of the Palestinian people." (In a talk to American journalists, January 27, 1958, I.L., X/1903).

The fundamental injustice lies in the fact that the Arabs, who never persecuted the Jews, have paid for the crime of the West. 'Alūsh writes:

"The Arabs are the innocent victim with which the West has atoned for its sins against the Jews." (p. 64).

The West has no compunctions in helping Israel, although its assistance encourages her to persevere in her aggression. Along these lines, Ḥasan Ṣabrī al-Khūlī, Nasser's special representative and advisor on Arab affairs in the Presidential Office, explained that the crisis began with the signature in 1952 of the Reparations Agreement, through which Germany paid for her persecution of the Jews:

"This assistance was one of the important factors that impelled Israel to commit the aggression of 1956, so that the Arabs, as it were, had to pay the price for the Nazi persecution of the Jews." (*Ākhir Sā'a,* March 24, 1965).

In contrast to this self-commiseration, the Arabs are presented as mighty and powerful, not only vis-à-vis Israel, but also on an international scale.

Thus, a Cairo Radio commentator declared, reacting to Eshkol's visit to the United States:

> "It is obvious that in this struggle no force will be able to withstand the Arab people. We say this because we know that the West's balance of economic forces in our region depend on us, and we can teach any factor that tries to plot against us a lesson that will not be forgotten, so that anyone who assists Israel will ultimately forfeit all his interests in our region." (June 2, 19:45 hrs.).

Having this good opinion of themselves, it is only natural that the Arabs externalize any feelings of guilt and put all the blame on Israel and imperialism. It is all the fault of the Jews, and the Arabs are guilty, at most, of failure to succeed. To back up this claim, a simple historical argument may be used: since the conflict started with the coming of the Jews, they are its cause. It was not the Arabs who invaded Jewish territory, but the Jews who invaded and usurped Arab territory. Hence, since the Arabs were not the cause of the conflict, it is repeatedly emphasized that they are not the aggressors, but always only the defenders. This line of thinking makes it possible to utilize the conflict to inflate feelings of moral superiority. The Arabs tend to regard themselves as a "target of hostility" and not an "agent of hostility," in Holsti and North's terms. These scholars have found a way of measuring the conceptions of the major countries on the eve of World War I by comparing the degree in which they regarded themselves as targets or agents of hostility, the ratio between these two values being called the "index of persecution." We may assume that the "index of persecution" among the Arabs is high (McNeil volume, p. 161).

Hence the failure to understand, or to show any sign of understanding, that the Israelis, too, may regard themselves as persecuted and the objective of liquidating Israel as aggression. In the light of this way of thinking, Israel's defensive operations are regarded as aggression and Arab acts of aggression as self-defence. This is not hypocrisy, but an inference from the basic assumption that the Arabs are not aggressors. Where they are concerned, they tend to emphasize their non-aggressive *actions* and ignore their aggressive *purposes*. Thus, Nasser said:

> "We have always said that we have never started aggression. We were always in a position of defending our lives." (May 1, 1965).

Israel, on the other hand, is aggressive for completely selfish reasons:

> "Israel wants to get everything for herself and deny everything to the Arabs." (February 26, 1960).

It is frequently argued that the Arabs cannot be aggressors, because it is they who were attacked. Munīf al-Razzāz, who was the Secretary-General of the Ba'th, extends this argument to all the nations that have recently achieved their independence:

> "The new nationalism rejects and could never contemplate aggression, because it is itself the product of rebellion against aggression and injustice." (*The Evolution of the Meaning of Nationalism,* 1963, p. 61).

In his article, "Images in the Context of International Conflict: Soviet Perceptions of the U.S. and the U.S.S.R." (Kelman volume), White explains that a psychological mechanism which he calls the "slanted interpretation" operates in such cases. The attention of the Arabs is concentrated on the arrival of the Jews, which they regard as an act of aggression, as well as on Zionism and Israeli reprisal operations, while they ignore their own purposes, as well as their acts of infiltration and attacks on Israel, which were the causes of the reprisals. A similar mechanism may be operative when they claim that all they want is justice and the complete restoration of the rights of the refugees, while ignoring the practical consequences for Israel.

a) SELF-CRITICISM

A compensatory mechanism also operates to prevent, as it were, an exaggerated departure from reality. Side by side with boastful manifestations of an inflated self-image, there are indications of mordant and melancholy self-criticism. The portrayal of Israel as a model for emulation, of which instances were given in the previous chapter, involves self-rebuke and admission of faults.

Even Nashāshībī, whose hostility to Israel is inordinate, occasionally directs severe criticism at the Arabs. He asks, for example, why the Jews had movements like Hibbat Zion ("Love of Zion," the precursor of Herzlian Zionism), using the Hebrew name, and why the Arab refugees do not display the same love of their country and organize in similar movements (p. 19). In times of crisis, he points out, the French, British and Yugoslavs produced men like De Gaulle, Churchill and Tito, who called upon their peoples not to submit, but to gird up all their energies to change the situation, and the Jews did likewise. (The same examples were given by Nasser after the Six-Day War.) The implied question is why there was not a similar phenomenon among the Arabs (pp. 215-219). A few lines further on, however, Nashāshībī goes back to extravagant self-glorification.

Since this kind of self-criticism usually has practical aims, it is generally directed against the manner in which the Arabs have acted in the course of the conflict, and not to the basic attitude. The paucity of criticism of the attitude itself is highly significant, and indicates that it is widely accepted. A typical example of this kind of self-criticism is an article called "The Arabs, Their Own Enemies," in the Beirut daily *al-Ḥayāt*:

> "We have said that the Arab States are in need of a special policy on the Palestine question. The entire Arab mentality is in need of a fundamental transformation in this matter. Since the grim struggle between Arabs and Jews in Palestine began, in the second decade of this century, the Arabs have known nothing but negation, concentrated in the word 'No,' without connecting it with a practical policy. We demand what we want, but we do not think about what we are capable of doing, and thus we have achieved nothing since we rejected the White Paper of 1947.
>
> "Events in Palestine have developed in opposition to our aspirations. We did not demand or act in accordance with our capacity and we were not content with the possible. Thus we have been living for over a third of a century in illusionary hopes, hopes devoid of logic and practicability, will and loyalty, entranced by the deceptive spell of falsehood and ignorance.
>
> "Our enemies are well aware of this failing; that is why they built their State on it, and now they rely on us in order to expand it . . .
>
> "When will we have a practical policy, based on Arab, regional and international facts? . . .
>
> "The whole world laughs at the Arabs when they talk of Palestine.
>
> "And what will history say? In the problem of Palestine the Arabs were victims of themselves, their ignorance, their blindness and their arrogance.
>
> "O God, be lenient to us and pardon us! O God, give us wisdom, even before nobility, honour, exaltation, glory and the righteous road.
>
> "O God, shorten our tongues and broaden our logic." (June 24, 1959).

Despite its limitations, however, this self-criticism produces cracks in the edifice of self-satisfaction and ambivalences in the self-image. It reflects and also creates disquiet, lack of confidence and gloom.

2. HISTORY IN THE LIGHT OF THE SELF-IMAGE

a) GENERAL

Studies of Arab history which are being written today in the Arab countries are seriously criticized by Orientalists. Von Grunebaum notes the influence of the Arabs' self-image on the writing of their history.[3] Because of their dissatisfaction with the position in the present, the Arabs seek encouragement in the past, where they find the glory which they lack today. In this quest they are selective. They tend to choose a number of episodes in the past which show success, and use them to cover up manifestations of which they are not particularly proud. History assumes an apologetic character. Professor Cantwell Smith wrote:

> "The Arab writing of history has been functioning, then, less as a genuine inquiry than as a psychological defense. Most of it is to be explained primarily in terms of the emotional needs that it fulfills (and is designed to fulfill)." (*Islam in Modern History*, p. 120).

Such tendencies are not exclusive to any people, but there are grounds for the conjecture that they are particularly strong among the Arabs, among whom recollection of the past serves as a consolation for the present and a guarantee for the future. They criticize Israel for this very fault. Sha'bān severely denounces Ben-Gurion, for instance, for his use of history to glorify the endurance of the Jews despite hardships and the power of empires. He explains it as

> ". . . the reaction of the diseased spirit, which, confronting the challenges of the times, finds refuge in fantasies of past glory and its utilization as a basic factor in the effort to develop the future." (p. 23).

There are grounds for the assumption that the gloom caused by the circumstances of the conflict, the defeat, and the chain of failures and frustrations, enhances the need to adapt history to emotional and political needs. History becomes a part of the ideology and an instrument for its consolidation.

In previous chapters, we have mentioned Arab accounts of their own history in the distant past and in the period of the establishment of the Jewish national home. In the present chapter I shall confine myself to surveying several aspects of their description of the Palestine struggle, and especially of the 1948 war.

b) THE NATIONAL STRUGGLE IN PALESTINE

There is a common tendency among the Jews to belittle the importance of the national struggle of the Palestine Arabs; for example, to describe what the Arabs call the Rebellion of 1936 as mere "riots." The Arabs, on the other hand, err in the opposite direction. Their struggle in the Mandatory period is presented as a tale of heroism and grandeur. The Jews, it is true, won, but not because of the weakness and factiousness of the Arabs; it was because the conditions of the confrontation were unfair from the beginning, since the Palestinians had to face not only the Jews but the British.

When the Palestine Liberation Organization, headed by Ahmad Shukairy, was established, efforts to represent the "Palestine Entity" as a reality made it necessary to depict the history of the struggle in such a way as to make it a source of inspiration and faith. The Organization's radio repeatedly broadcasts feature programmes about sublime acts of heroism in the war of the Palestinians against the Jews and the British.

The Palestine National Covenant opens:

> "We, the Palestinian Arab People, who waged fierce and continual battles to safeguard its homeland, to defend its dignity and honour, and who offered all through the years continuous caravans of immortal martyrs, and who wrote the noblest pages of sacrifice, offering and giving . . . "

Nashāshībī says of the Palestinian people:

> 'We, who fought as no other people did, and who sacrificed as no other people sacrificed, and the people opened its heart and its mind to science and knowledge . . . " (1962, p. 250).
>
> "For six months we abstained from work and from life, we retired to the mountaintops, we endured a prolonged struggle for forty years, we fought the English, the Americans and the Jews, we imperilled our lives and sacrificed ourselves to poverty and want, but we did not weaken or submit." (p. 156).

There is an obvious tendency to ignore the sale of lands to the Jews, the absence of national determination, the fratricidal strife which went to extremes in bloodshed, the collaboration with the Jews, and the like. Today, even non-Palestinians are prone, in keeping with the general Arab self-image and the requirements of solidarity, to praise the activities of the Palestinians, although in the past they often criticized their weaknesses. (It seems only natural that, in the confrontation between a primitive and loosely integrated society and the Zionist organizations, who were fired and stimulated to determined action by Jewish needs and sufferings, the Arabs should have been on the losing side.)

The struggle in Palestine is presented as not only an event of local significance, but an example of heroism which astonished the world. Tall declares that the forces of ʻAbd al-Qādir al-Husseini (Arab guerrilla leader in the Jerusalem area) carried out "operations full of heroism which astonished the world and shocked the Jewish entity in Palestine" (p. 299).

On the other hand, Riyād al-Ṣulḥ, then Prime Minister of Lebanon, wrote to Muzāḥim al-Bājjy, after the agreement on the second truce on August 14, 1948:

> "I am disturbed lest the spirit of impotence, defeatism and self-distrust which has gripped the Palestinians should take hold of the Arab nation, if its rulers discourage it by failure to renew the fighting." (Quoted by Niqūlā al-Durr, p. 137; *al-Qaṣrī,* p. 202, and Ta'iʻ, p. 131, and published in *al-Nidā'* and *al-Ḥayāt*).

Self-criticism over the activities of the Palestinian Arabs, thought not common, is expressed by Dr. Walīd al-Qamḥāwī, a Palestinian member of the Executive of the Palestine Liberation Organization. His historical survey is more balanced; he sees the main weakness of the Arabs as a lack of constructive approach. He sums up the opposition to the Jewish National Home as follows:

> "Riots lasting a few days, and then the eruption of emotion subsides, things go back to the status quo, the Zionists build and the Arabs do everything else except building." (1962, Part I, pp. 55-6).

Qamḥāwī also gives a good description of the social disintegration that brought about the great Arab exodus, when the wealthy families were the first to run away and left the fighting to the workers and villagers:

> "It was collective fear, moral disintegration and chaos in every field that exiled the Arabs from Tiberias, Haifa and dozens of towns and villages." (*Ibid,* p. 70).

There is bitter criticism by some of the younger generation, who describe themselves as "revolutionary," of what they call the "generation of catastrophe," as in Niqūlā al-Durr's open letter at the beginning of his book:

> "Most of our statesmen and leaders, leaders of the 1948 catastrophe, have conducted a policy of charlatanism, falsehood, boasting and hypocrisy; pre-

tending to be brethren though they are enemies, pretending to be heads, though they are tails, to be lions though they are flies, to be a unity though they are families, factions, tribes and dynasties. In that black year they made their people a byword to the world, captive to the Jews, and one of the mockeries of history."

In writing the history of the struggle, the Arabs seldom consider to what extent they are themselves responsible for the situation that was created. It does not occur to them what an effect their attacks had in making the Jews organize themselves for communal defence and political action and establish underground bodies to ensure their safety; they do not take into account the fact that it was their reluctance to reach an agreement that would recognize even the partial right of the Jews that imperilled the Jewish community and compelled it to develop its strength in order to safeguard its survival. Zionism, which started as an ideology, became a necessity of life not only for Diaspora Jewry but also for the Jews of Palestine. Neither Arabs nor Jews generally understand how richly the Arabs deserve to have an enduring monument erected to them in the temple of Zionism.

The late King Abdallah himself was keenly aware that the Arabs' extremism might be disastrous to them. In a letter dated June 5, 1938, he explained that Zionism was built on three pillars: the Balfour Declaration, the desire of European countries to get rid of the Jews, and the Arab extremists, who were not ready for any settlement, and only wept and wailed that the postponement of any solution would lead to Palestine breathing its last (*My Memoirs Completed,* English edition, p. 97; also quoted in King Hussein's autobiography, *Uneasy Lies the Head*).

A leading theme in the Arab version of history is the belief that neither the Palestinians nor the other Arabs, but external factors—the imperialists, Zionism and Israel—were to blame for the situation, which arose quite independently of their behaviour and is therefore devoid of all legitimacy from their point of view. Since this reality was imposed upon them, they can describe it as "robbery" and revolt against it. If only they realized to what extent their acts of omission and commission were responsible for the establishment of the State of Israel, their view of this reality as foreign to them would undoubtedly—if only partially—be undermined. Hence, they have developed a defence mechanism that makes them refuse to recognize the facts and seek refuge in their own interpretation of history. People are sometimes impelled to action or inaction by a guilt complex; Arab behaviour in the conflict is motivated by a "non-guilt complex," which finds expression at least in the way they present the situation and in their efforts to convince themselves.

c) THE RESORT TO WAR

The resort to war is generally described as a defensive measure to protect the Arabs of Palestine and the Arab countries. It was not the Arabs, but the Jews who started the war of 1947-49, it is argued. The acts of violence that broke out on Arab initiative immediately after the UN Partition Resolution, which were meant to demonstrate opposition to the decision, are presented as anonymous acts produced, as it were, by spontaneous generation. Dr. Sayegh writes, for instance:

> "Disturbances erupted in Palestine immediately after the adoption by the General Assembly of the Partition Resolution." (*The Arab-Israel Conflict,* 1956, p. 15).

In *The Arabs and the United Nations,* Dr. Muhammed 'Afīfī, Professor of Education at the University of Ein Shams, refers to

> "The increasing violence between Arabs and Jews that followed the adoption of the partition plan by the General Assembly . . ." (p. 59).

As documentary evidence that it was the Jews who started the war, attention is drawn to "Plan Dalet" (Plan D) of the Haganah General Staff (dealt with, for example, by Dr. Khālidī in his article "The Arab Exodus" and by Sha'bān, p. 34), whose objective was (according to *The History of the War of Independence,* published by the Historical Branch of the Israeli General Staff, p. 123) "control over the territory of the Jewish State and the defence of its borders against an invasion by the Arab armies." Khālidī adds that the Jewish occupation of Tiberias and Haifa before the Arab invasion shows that this plan was carried out. This conclusion is reached by means of a selective memory or selective oblivion in regard to the acts by the Palestinian Arabs which preceded Plan Dalet: the attacks on Kfar Szold, Kfar Etzion, Yehiam, Tirat Zvi and other villages, as well as the attempt to disrupt Jewish transport and communications, which made the plan a necessity.

Since the Arabs did not succeed in preventing partition by force, this aim of theirs is forgotten, and the blame for the war is transferred, by a process of oversimplification, to the Jews. It was they who were supposed to have initiated hostilities. Thus, Dr. Sayegh writes:

> "The Arab-Israeli War, therefore, was initiated and launched by prenatal Israel, when Zionist forces invaded the territory of the would-be Arab State." (*Ibid,* p. 29).

Similarly, Dr. 'Afīfī writes of

> "... the war which the Zionist forces had launched on the Arabs of Palestine." (p. 62).

In an article in the *Egyptian Political Science Review*, Ibrahim writes:

> "When Britain withdrew her forces from several regions of Palestine, anarchy broke out in them, and it was this that led to the intervention of the Arab armies, because the Jews did not cease to swarm in secret into Palestine, to rob and burn houses and villages, and expelled 750,000 Arabs. The neighbouring Arab countries felt themselves compelled to intervene in Palestine with their armies, not only to protect their brethren, but, even more, to defend their future." (January-March 1959, p. 135).

Ṣafwat defines the aim as a punitive action against the Zionist gangs and the halting of their aggression against the Arab population (pp. 55, 94). Since Palestine is regarded as an Arab country, the intervention of the Arab States was only natural, and did not constitute an attack. Sha'bān writes:

> "The whole world remembers that the Arabs did not attack a foreign country but went in to safeguard security in the territory of their Homeland and defend it against the acts of aggression and collective destruction perpetrated by the Zionists in Palestine." (p. 33).[4]

We may well understand that the Arabs do not feel particularly comfortable about this chapter in the history of the conflict, which is marked by the initiation of violence and war, and would therefore like to change it. This inclination is, no doubt, due to a number of factors:

1. These accounts are meant to forestall the counter-argument that if the Arabs appealed to the arbitrament of war they must accept its results.

2. The claim that it was not they who started the war reinforces the self-image and the general tendency to argue that the Arabs are not aggressors. They did not defy the United Nations on their own initiative, it is argued; the resort to arms was an unavoidable reaction, and it was Israel that was the aggressor from the moment of her birth.

3. The claim that the Arabs resorted to war only in self-defence is buttressed by subsequent events. Since the Jews won, the war must have been in their interest from the beginning; hence it was they who attacked and the Arabs acted only in self-defence.

4. The description of the invasion by the Arab States as a defensive

operation mitigates their own self-criticism for not making adequate preparations for war, since the war, it is argued, was forced upon them.

5. This also softens the pain of the defeat, for it is worse to be defeated in a war which you started than in one which was imposed upon you.

After the event, the attitude to the question of whether the Arab States should have sent their armies into battle at all become ambivalent: positive and negative at the same time.

Ṣafwat, writing at the beginning of 1952 (before the deposition of King Fārūq of Egypt), regarded the policy of opening hostilities as a foolish improvisation, for the Arabs set out on the enterprise with foolish enthusiasm and eyes shut, without considering the difficulties (p. 55). The principal mistake was the employment of regular armies instead of fighting the Zionist gangs with Arab irregular bands (p. 99).

This was also the attitude of the Muftī of Jerusalem, al-Ḥajj Amīn al-Husseini, who thought the fighting should have been left to the Palestinians, with the Arab countries playing only a supporting role, and accused them of failing to keep their promises and give adequate aid. His main motive was to prevent the Palestinians and their leadership being pushed aside, as actually happened with the entry of the Arab armies. At the Egyptian arms trials in the middle of 1953, the sending of the Egyptian army into war unprepared was denounced as tantamount to treason, and the motive was declared to be Fārūq's desire for glory and not a general national demand.

This attitude raises the question of whether, when it became clear that the Palestinians were not a match for the Jews, it was possible for the Arab States, from the national point of view, to stand idly by. This question is basic to the dilemma which led to the ambivalent attitude to the resort to war.

Nasser's attitude to this question is also ambivalent. Thus, he told the members of the Legislative Assembly in Gaza:

> "When was it decided here in Egypt to declare war? They decided it a week or ten days before the war, and at that time there was nothing on the border of Palestine but one brigade, which was stationed at El-Arish. There was no ammunition, no supply lines. I was in Gaza and I found the soldiers eating cheese and olives, which were supplied to them from Gaza itself. There were not even emergency rations, and we bought cheese and olives for the soldiers so that they could fight. What kind of army is it which goes to war like that? It would have been better if it had not fought, or if it had left the Palestinian people, after it had been armed, to fight the enemy. But the Palestinian people saw that seven Arab States

had gone to war, and then it was satisfied and felt confident about the results of the war." (June 26, 1962).

In *The Philosophy of the Revolution,* however, he wrote:

"The circumstances made it necessary that all the Arab armies should go to war in Palestine." (Arabic edition, p. 66).

Abdallah Tall also vacillates over this question:

"There was a view that the Arab armies should not make war officially, but should be content with assisting the Palestine Arabs with arms, money and volunteers. We are not in a position to decide which of the two views was right. True, the results of the fighting were so bad that it could not have been worse if the Arab armies had remained deployed on the borders and confined themselves to unofficial military aid." (p. 303).

d) THE SHOCK OF DEFEAT

The defeat of the Arabs in the 1948 war took them by surprise. Many of them had underestimated the strength of the Jewish community and boasted that the job would be an easy one. Most military circles believed, or at least hoped, that the war would be a walkover. At the trials of the members of the old régime in the military court, Ahmad al-'Alā'ilī, speaking of the decision to start hostilities, recalled that Prime Minister Nūqrāshī had told the Chamber of Deputies that the war would be a picnic, a promenade—*"nuzha"* (*al-Ahrām,* June 3, 1951, quoted by Niqūlā al-Durr, p. 94).

In his history of the war in several volumes, 'Ārif al-'Ārif sums up:

"The Arabs thought they would win in less than the twinkling of an eye and that it would take no more than a day or two from the time the Arab armies crossed the border until all the colonies were conquered and the enemy would throw down his arms and cast himself on their mercy." (Vol. VI, p. 655).

It may be assumed that this expectation of an easy victory was influenced by the image of the Jew described in the previous chapter. In an interview with Nāṣir al-Dīn al-Nashāshībī, General Glubb explained:

"The Arab states thought that the Jews of Palestine were the same as the Jews of the Baghdad Bazaar in Iraq or the inhabitants of Wadi Abu Jamīl in Beirut." (*Ākhir Sā'a,* July 1, 1953).

Professor Elie Kedouri writes of "the shock administered by the victory of an inferior group hitherto held in contempt" (in his article, "Religion and Politics: the Diaries of Khalīl Sakākīnī," *St. Anthony Papers,* No. 4, 1958, p. 90).

It is true that there were also warnings against involvement in war with the Jews, whose military achievements during the Mandatory period and their success in the struggle with the Palestinians (who were supported by volunteers and assistants from the neighbouring countries) had no doubt made some impression. Haykal recalls how, after he visited Palestine and saw the strength of the Jews, he decided to warn against Egypt entering the war, and when he told Nuqrāshī of his impressions, the latter assured him that Egypt would not start hostilities (*Ākhir Sā'a,* May 13, 1953). Nevertheless, the debacle came as a shock, and the surprise reinforced the impression of the defeat.

e) EXPLANATIONS FOR THE DEFEAT

The Arabs generally describe the 1948 war as "the disaster" or "the great defeat" (*al-hazīma al-kubrā,"* Nasser, I.L., XI/21, 31). In this war, the Jews, who had been described as "gangs" and regarded as doomed to misery and degradation, were revealed as a dangerous opponent. Derision gave place to hatred.

It is difficult to estimate to what extent the defeat was a collective trauma, which left an enduring mark. For the Palestinian Arabs, it was a confirmation of the power of the Jews. For the others, it was the beginning of a direct knowledge of the Israelis.

In any case, for many it was a great disaster for all the Arabs, and even for the Muslims. Israel is regarded as a wedge in the heart of the "Arab region" at a spot of strategic importance, the gateway to the Middle East and a bridge between the continents. From a historical point of view, the defeat was described as a more grievous disaster than the loss of Spain. It was a material, spiritual and moral blow, a national degradation. The decline of the Arabs and their subjection to foreign rule reached a kind of climax with their defeat by the Jews. It was an emotional and ideological shock, depriving the rulers of their peoples' respect, and undermining their legitimacy. It opened up an era of revolutions, shook the Arabs' faith in their heroic self-image and led to an inter-Arab crisis of confidence.

King Hussein said, for instance, in explaining the results of the defeat:

"Many of us lost our self-confidence and our trust in our capacity to act and restore the rights. We began to be suspicious of one another. The Arab States began to accuse each other in order to evade responsibility." (Amman Radio, May 22, 1963, 14:00 hrs.).

Feverish accusations and denunciations were hurled in every direction. The Arab States and their leaders accused each other of responsibility for the downfall. Accusations were levelled at the Arab League and its Military Council. The Palestinians accused their own leaders and the Arab States, and these, in turn, blamed the Palestinians. A simple and popular way of allotting blame was personification, putting the main responsibility on one individual or another: Abdallah, Fārūq, and so forth. The civilian authorities accused the army and the military blamed the politicians.

'Abd al-Raḥmān 'Azzām, who was Secretary-General of the Arab League and in charge of its activities at the time, said that he demanded an enquiry to determine the political and military responsibility, proposing a German General called Artur Schmidt, of Rommel's staff, for the purpose:

"I do not want to anticipate the conclusions, but I have no doubt that any neutral investigation will demonstrate one obvious truth, that we Arabs entered Palestine stronger in numbers and equipment than the Jews. It is clear to me that the artillery of each Arab army was stronger than the Jewish artillery."

He describes how the Iraqis boasted at the Ālay Conference that they could reach and liberate Haifa, but the proposal was not carried out (*Ākhir Sā'a,* May 27, 1953).

However, we have in our possession the report of an Iraqi parliamentary enquiry committee which was appointed in February 1949 to investigate the 1948 war. This is a secret document which reached Israel and was published as a book under the name of *Behind the Scenes,* translated into Hebrew by S. Segev, Maarachot, 1954. ('Ārif al-'Ārif discusses the appointment of this committee in *The Disaster,* Vol. IV, p. 896.) The report describes the developments on the inter-Arab plane and analyses the reasons for the defeat. The Arab leaders, it says, did not reach agreement about the ultimate aim, which made it impossible to coordinate military operations and allocate objectives. The Arab countries did not throw sufficient forces into the battle. The Palestinians did not bear the burden of the fighting—and so on and so forth.

f) BASIC SOCIAL FACTORS IN THE DOWNFALL

Arab public opinion has devoted much attention to the reasons for the defeat and the lessons to be learnt from it. A large number of books and articles on the subject—the "literature of the disaster"—have appeared. Some of them express painful soul-searching, bitter self-criticism, profound suffering and anxiety, but we also find belief in satanic plots, the attempt to put the blame on a scapegoat, and mere absurdities.

The most interesting works of this kind are those that attribute the downfall to basic factors, fundamental defects in Arab society. There is no space here to sum up these analyses, and I shall have to be content to note a number of main factors that are given: the absence of national cohesion and unity of aims (Zurayk, English edition, p. 35); the failure of the national movement to reach maturity and strike roots in Arab reality; dissensions; a backward mentality; superficiality; absence of ideals and a spirit of self-sacrifice; lack of sincerity in public life and inter-State relations; intrigues; corruption; devotion to narrow interests, hypocritically presented as pure nationalism; lack of dedication; disunity; absence of a basic scientific approach; a tendency to superficial improvisations; a gap between talk and action; self-glorification; trust in dreams and inability to see the reality and evaluate the forces facing the Arabs; a backward way of life; conservatism; and so on, and so forth.

It should be noted that this criticism is, in the main, tendencious, as it aims at stimulating the Arabs to reform and national unity. Sometimes such things are said, not out of conviction of their truth but in order to achieve extrinsic aims or score off rivals, and sometimes they look like declamation for the sake of catharsis, a confession which is mere lip-service, in order to atone for the downfall, obtain absolution for the guilt, and avoid the need to improve the situation.

Nasser has devoted much attention to the defeat of 1948. His explanations are tendencious and cover a broad spectrum of excuses according to the needs of the moment. He lays the blame on the Arab regimes, the treachery of reaction, insincerity, improvisation, inadequate armaments, imperialism, and so forth. He argues that the Arab will was not free—i.e. it was subordinate to foreign influences, and therefore the full strength of the Arabs was not brought into play (November 8, 1960). Factionalism is very often presented as the main reason for the downfall, and appeals are made for unity.

In the light of history, all the defeats, including the Crusader conquest, are regarded as the outcome of disunity and fratricidal discord in the Arab world, while unity is "the armour against which the waves of invaders are broken" (March 20, 1958, I.L., XI/2092). Sometimes, on a higher plane, he trenchantly charges the Arabs themselves with the responsibility:

> 'In ourselves, in the Arab nations, is the reason for the loss of Palestine, and our leaders are the main reason." (December 13, 1953, I.L., I/152-7).

In this address he gave unpreparedness and inactivity as the reasons for the defeat. The leaders were content with speeches:

> "The leadership in their speeches said 'so-called Israel,' and did nothing but speechify about 'so-called Israel.' "

Almost a decade later he said:

> "I believe that the reasons for the disaster of 1948 lay in ourselves more than in the Jews . . . It was the moral aspect that was responsible for our failure in 1948." (Speech to members of the Legislative Assembly in Gaza, June 26, 1962).

Sometimes analyses of basic internal social factors are combined with attempts to externalize the blame. In this way, even if fundamental faults are admitted they are attributed to the operation of external factors. Thus Bahā' al-Dīn explains that the Arabs were unable to prevent Zionism achieving its aims "because of the economic and social backwardness that was imposed on them *(al-mafrūḍ 'alayhā)* (1965, p. 127). In other words, the Arabs are not to blame for their backwardness, which was produced by the outside world. This point of view is very common.

Historical, and even religious, reasons are given. Tall connects the loss of Palestine with "the abolition of the Caliphate" (1964, p. 236).[5]

g) CRITICISM OF THE ARMY AND THE CONDUCT OF HOSTILITIES

The Arabs do not point to any incidental mishap but for which the results of the war would have been different. The struggle of 1948 was too momentous for such an argument, and its results were not determined by any one decisive battle. The closest approach to such an interpretation, perhaps, is the attribution of the defeat to the truce, which, it is contended, the Arabs generously accepted and which stood between them and victory. This explanation is pretty frequent. On the other hand, it is noteworthy that there is little criticism of the way the Arabs fought. As far as I am aware, not a single Arab State has published an official history of the War—naturally, the defeated side has less interest in a detailed description of the conflict. In this connection, ʻAlūsh wrote:

"Many books have attempted to deal with the defeat in Palestine in 1948, but these books, as far as I have read, deal with the problem from the general political point of view. Few books have tried to deal with the military aspect." (p. 16).

Hottinger notes that, in discussing the subject, the Arabs are not apt to mention their military mistakes. He explains that when the Army takes power, it is not prone to assume the responsibility for a military defeat and finds it more convenient to blame the civilian leadership in the previous regimes (p. 249).

The latter tendency is very frequently met with, and the charge no doubt contains an element of truth. Qassem, the Iraqi dictator, explained:

"The Palestine War in 1948 was in the nature of a plot against the Iraqi army, for the Iraqi army was dispersed over a front of 170 kms. The aim was to weaken the army on all fronts and leave it without reserves, which enabled the enemy to strike at it from every side." (Baghdad Radio, December 10, 1962, 13:00 hrs.).

Similarly, Nasser claimed:

"We were not defeated in Palestine in 1948, for the Egyptian army did not fight in 1948." (March 3, 1955, I.L., II/667).

Nasser charged that there was no wholehearted political and military involvement, and the aim was limited. He explained, according to an article by Haykal, that the Arabs only engaged in "semi-military operations," with the aim of diverting internal pressure against the regime, and that that was the reason why the war was a failure (*al-Ahrām,* May 18, 1963).

Each Arab army disclaims responsibility, but other armies are frequently blamed. Even before the war was over, the Arab countries started accusing each other of treachery, of abandoning fronts, holding up aid, failure to cooperate, and the like. General Ismāʻīl Ṣafwat, for instance, says that the Egyptians, by not informing the Jordanians and the Iraqis of the situation, prevented their receiving assistance (*Behind the Curtain,* p. 125).

King Abdallah, who was appointed Supreme Commander, regarded the Egyptians as the principal culprits; they did not cooperate with him, refused to give him information about the position of their forces, although they had appointed him to the supreme command, held up a shipload of ammunition meant for the Legion, and so forth (*My Memoirs Completed,* English edition, p. 24).

The Egyptians, on the other hand, accused the Jordanians of standing by when the Jews attacked the Egyptian forces. The withdrawal of the Jordanians from Lydda and Ramleh exposed the flanks of the Iraqi and Egyptian armies, while Glubb prevented the Iraqis supporting the Egyptians ('Alūba, pp. 145-6, and others).

The self-image has its effect on the way in which the war is described—for example, in grandiloquent comparisons between the small-scale battles of this war and events that have changed the course of world history. The retreat of the Jordanians from Lydda and Ramleh, 'Iṣmat explains, exposed the right flank of the Egyptian army, as the surrender of the Belgians to Germany in World War II compelled the British to withdraw to Dunkirk. However, he adds, with considerable apparent self-satisfaction, the Egyptian forces did not come to such a pass as the British at Dunkirk—thanks, of course to their heroism (p. 120).

To Hottinger's explanation of why there is so little criticism of the way the war was fought, we may add another factor: the effort to save the self-image of the Arabs: heroism, courage, manliness *(muruwwa),* which have been leading themes in their poetry and culture since the days of the Jāhiliyya. Hence, too, the bitterness and pain at this defeat, which became a "catastrophe" and seriously damaged their self-image, especially since they were beaten by such insignificant forces as those of the Jews. It is much better, therefore, to put the blame on others. Indeed, the reluctance to admit that the Arabs were defeated in actual fighting is prominent not only in military circles but even among civilians. 'Ārif al-'Ārif, for instance, enumerates a wide range of faults and reasons for the defeat (in Vol. III, pp. 653ff); where military affairs are concerned, he puts the blame on lack of political-military guidance, inadequate coordination, shortage of equipment, badly prepared equipment, failure to mobilize the potential, the absence of a belligerent atmosphere in the Arab countries on the eve of the war, the shortsightedness of the Arab League, neglect of the main objectives and too much attention to secondary matters, lack of information, and contempt and distrust for the Palestinians. In the main, that is, he blames the political-military leadership, but not the fighters.

Bahā' al-Dīn explains that the people were not short of heroism *(shajā'a),* but only of equipment (*adawāt*—p. 252). Rāfi'ī declares that the army showed courage and fighting spirit, but did not have adequate leadership and arms (1959, p. 348).

Side by side, therefore, with the emphasis on the significance of the defeat and the lessons that should be drawn from it, we find attempts to belittle it and deny that it is of any importance or meaning. The very fact that the Arabs are bent on war makes it necessary, in their own interests, to insist that the defeat was not a precedent. Some, accordingly, describe the 1948 War as a comedy *(mahzala)*—Ṣafwat begins his chapter on the war with the words: "The comedy of Palestine began." Nasser also uses this expression (e.g. in I. L., III/668, March 3, 1955). A somewhat similar phrase is "the theatrical show *(masraḥiyya)* of the Palestine War," (*al-Rushaydāt,* p. 256). (In much the same way, the Six-Day War was at first described as *naksa*—a set-back.)

Internally, the blame is laid mainly on reaction and treachery:

> "Treachery and not weakness was the primary reason for the loss of my country." (*al-Manār,* December 11, 1964, in a series of articles: "Thus My Land was Lost").

This accusation also performs a psychological function by clearing the rest of the Arabs of guilt and preserving the heroic self-image. Furthermore, all Arabs become comrades in distress, for they were all innocent victims of reactionary treachery.

The debate on the allocation of blame has divided the Arabs, but the experience of defeat and the bitterness that accompanied it have been a unifying factor, on both the emotional and conscious planes. Nasser, for example, wrote in *The Philosophy of the Revolution:*

> 'All the Arab peoples entered into the Palestine War with the same degree of enthusiasm. They all shared the same feelings and the same evaluation of the boundaries of their security. They emerged from the war with the same bitterness and disappointment . . . When the siege and the fighting in Palestine were over, and I returned to the Homeland, the entire region had become one in my view." (p. 44, Arabic edition).

Thus the defeat became a factor in the "unity of sorrow and destiny" which the Arabs are in a habit of citing as one of the components of their nationalism.

h) DEFEAT ASCRIBED TO WESTERN PLOTS

To complement the claim that the Arab fighter was not to blame for the defeat, it is repeatedly argued that the Israelis' victory was not achieved thanks to their skill and courage, but owing to the imperialist aid they received. While the Arabs, it is said, suffered from a shortage of armaments, imperialism spared no effort to equip the Israelis. Forseeing the outcome of the conflict, the imperialists pushed the Arabs into battle in order to achieve their hostile objectives. By regarding imperialism as their principal opponent in the war, the Arabs mitigate the acuteness of their self-criticism: true, they were defeated, but by mighty world forces. Thus, Nasser said:

> "We know that the Palestine downfall was not a downfall at all, but a plot of Imperialism against the Arab people with the aim of dividing it and imbuing it with a spirit of defeatism." (July 28, 1959).
>
> "It was not Israel that fought in that battle, but the imperialists, and in the struggle of 1948 we were not masters of our own will." (June 26, 1962).

Niqūlā al-Durr deals heatedly and at length with the question of the blame for the 1948 downfall. It is not true, he declares, that the Arab nation was defeated and that it was weak and unable to resist the aggressors; it is not true that the Arab States were unable to get arms and ammunition; it is not true that the downfall was a result of the failures of the Arab League: "The truth is that the reason for the disaster was the 'Hidden Hand'—namely, Imperialism" (p. 68).

The United Nations, too, was an instrument in the hands of the imperialists, who wanted to bring about the defeat of the Arabs. It betrayed its responsibility. The League of Nations and the UN were the agents of the West in the establishment of Israel. Nasser declared:

> "It was not in any way Israel that was victorious in 1948; the victory was gained by the Security Council, which was Israel's ally; and acted for the consolidation of Israel in this territory and worked for the expulsion of Arab nationalism from this blessed land." (March 3, 1955, I.L., III/666).

Ṣafwat blames the British, who prevented the Arabs training in the use of arms because they expected the war and its results. It was they who pushed Arabs and Jews into war (p. 56). Nasser repeats the argument that the Jews had tanks and the Egyptians had none. The English withheld tanks and artillery from Egypt even after they had been paid for, while the Jews received arms from every quarter (see, e.g., December 13, 1953, October 12, 1960, June 22, 1962, January 9, 1963 and December 24, 1964).

Tall says that the British handed over Haifa, Jaffa, Safad and Tiberias to the Jews, prevented the Arabs consolidating their defences, and gave the Jews freedom of action (1965, pp. 300-1). According to al-Khūlī, they evacuated Jewish areas first and supplied the Jews with arms (p. 16).

It is repeatedly alleged that the truce was imposed in order to prevent an Arab victory and save the Jews. 'Aqqād writes:

> "The Arab armies swamped the Jewish gangs, and then the West saved the Jews through the cease-fire." (p. 29).

Dr. 'Afīfī says that the Arab forces were about to enter Tel Aviv when the Security Council hurriedly intervened (p. 62—similarly al-Khūlī, p. 17, Sha'bān, p. 31, and 'Iṣmat, p. 119). Nasser declared:

> 'The Israeli forces could not have seized as much territory as they did, had not the Arab States alone accepted the limitations of the UN cease-fire decision. For Israel, these decisions were a safe opportunity for the continuation of hostilities." (To Associated Press, October 9, 1959).

Such statements not only belittle the capacity of Israel but also reinforce the self-image of the Arabs as unaggressive, while the Jews are cunning and treacherous.

It seems to have been forgotten in Egypt that in 1949 it was Britain's threat to come to her aid under the terms of the 1936 treaty by taking military measures against Israel that led to the withdrawal of the Israeli forces from Abu Aweigila and El-Arish.

One of the motives for undervaluing Israel's achievements is to give the impression that the results of the war were a mere episode, unconnected with either basic Arab weaknesses or the strength of the Jews, and that its importance has been exaggerated. It is sometimes alleged that the Jews were superior in armaments and military manpower. Walīd al-Khālidī wrote in *al-Anwār,* May 21, 1963, that when the Arab armies started operations on May 15, 1948 they consisted of only six brigades as against twelve Israeli ones. (Actually, the Jews had ten improvised brigades; the Arabs had tanks, armoured cars and artillery, while the Jews had only light weapons. Nor does Khālidī take the local Palestinian fighters into account.)

Al-Durr, on the other hand, even though he regards imperialism as the main factor in the Arab defeat, writes:

> "The strength of the enemy at this decisive period [in May 1948] was inestimably less than the Arab power." (p. 69).

And here is an interesting passage from a speech by Nasser:

> "Today we are in 1955. We are different from the past, and so I say to Israel and those who threaten us in her name that there is an ancient proverb which says that a man does not stop lying and lying until people believe him. Then he lies and lies and lies until he believes himself. So Israel believes that she routed the Egyptian army in 1948 and threatens us today, relying on this vain belief. Today I say to her: The Egyptian Army under the command of 'Abd al-Ḥakīm 'Āmir is no different from the Egyptian Army before, but the methods which led to our defeat in the past have been completely changed and will not be restored." (May 3, 1955, I.L., III/666).

If it is the same army, that implies that there was nothing wrong with the Arab fighters: the fault lay in their leadership.

Nasser and Haykal constantly emphasize the importance of the Egyptian young officers' revolution in 1952 and its influence, not only in Egypt but also in other parts of the Arab world, as the basic cause of the general transformation. For them, the defeat is a point of departure, a means to glorify the present and the future, to show that the Arab world now has a new leadership which can imbue the people with a sense of values and direction. This devoted and vigorous leadership, they argue, will be able to lead the Arabs to victory.

Many of the trends apparent in explanations of the 1948 defeat recur in 1967. The similarity is striking indeed.

i) COMBINED EXPLANATIONS

Some authors summarize the factors that led to the results of the 1948 war. The components of such summaries and the order in which they are placed are of interest. Nasser declared, for example:

> "We lost Palestine without a fight. We lost it through the operations of imperialism, the arbitrary rule and the arms monopolies, and then the Zionist gangs succeeded in stealing Palestine." (October 19, 1960).

'Alūba gives the following reasons: (1) the British and American plot to liquidate Palestine and hand it over to the Jews; (2) the torpidity of the Arabs and their unreadiness for war; (3) treachery through the purchase of defective weapons; (4) the choice of Abdallah as Supreme Commander, which was disastrous not because he meant to betray the Arabs but because power in Transjordan was in the hands of the British and he could not oppose them, even if he wanted to (1964, pp. 144-5).

Haykal gave a comprehensive explanation in 1962 in an article entitled "In Memory of the Fifteenth of May 1948, What is the Road Back to Palestine and When?":

"All the Arab Governments followed the mood that wanted war, but they had no will for war.

"They dreamt of war in the official proclamations issued by their commanders, but on the battlefield itself they avoided war.

"The reason was not a shortage of manpower or arms. The position of our Commands was in striking contrast to the position of the enemy's Command.

"The Arab Governments had more arms than devotion to the objective, while the enemy had more devotion to the objective than arms.

"It is not true that seven Arab armies were thrown into battle, as Israeli propaganda now alleges.

"The army of Yemen was not there at all.

"The army of Saudi Arabia contributed one company of the Royal Guard, whose glorious deeds in battle consisted only of the acts of one officer, who, after raising his voice in prayer to Allah, ventured to slaughter one or two of the inhabitants of the Jewish settlement of Be'erot Yitzhak.

"The Lebanese Army kept itself to itself, with its one battalion on the Lebanese side of the frontier.

"The Syrian army was full of fervour, after its unfortunate experience at Samakh, but it was leaderless.

"There were left, therefore, two armed forces:

"The Hashemite Army forces, including those of Jordan and Iraq, commanded by the British and the powers of treachery.

"The forces of the Egyptian Army, the Supreme Command of which was in the control of ignorance, folly and the arms trade.

"When the position became more serious, and through the circumstances of the fighting the Egyptian forces emerged from the control of the Supreme Command and could fight and achieve substantial results, Hashemite treachery did not allow them to do so: King Abdallah made common cause with Israel, he secretly met with her leaders, and then evacuated Lydda and Ramleh, exposing the flank of the Egyptian Army, while the Iraqi Army sat still, inactive and depressed, under the well known watch-word 'No Orders' . . .

"The cunning of all the Arab Governments was directed more against their people than against their enemy.

"King 'Abd al-'Azīz al-Sa'ūd was prepared, as he put it, to slaughter his eldest son, but he was not prepared, even as a tactical threat, to stop the supply of oil so long as justice had not been done.

"The kings of the Hashemite family were prepared—according to their tradition—to weep and wail, but they were not prepared to change their ways and put an end to their treachery and their ties with the enemy.

"King Fārūq was prepared to permit the Egyptian army to go to Palestine—perhaps because of the will to adventure or the desire to get rid of it, but he was not prepared to allow that army to win.

"The rulers of Lebanon were not prepared for anything at all.

"The Imam of Yemen at the time—like his heir today—was interested only in surrendering to narcotic drugs and the illusions of his imagination.

"Our fears were realized. Nothing else could have been expected: Palestine was lost.

"And then we tried to console ourselves by calling 1948 the year of disaster. This term itself reflected the desire to evade responsibility and blame destiny, while destiny is innocent, but we wanted to continue to evade and escape.

"We placed the responsibility on the strength of the enemy, when the strength of the enemy was only the creature of our imagination.

"I have already said and I say again: more than the enemy succeeded in defeating us on the battlefield, we defeated ourselves.

"Our weakness—rather than the enemy's strength—was the powerful factor in the final result . . . When we talk of the defeat, weakness and surrender of 1948, it would be mistaken and dangerous to attribute the whole affair to the military sphere and limit it to what happened on the battlefield in Palestine. The military operations in Palestine were only a mirror of the social, economic and political situation which existed at the time in the Arab capitals.

"The Arab world was then ruled by reactionary strata, which exploited their peoples and controlled their resources, or most of them." (*al-Ahrām,* May 18, 1962).

j) GOOD OUT OF EVIL

The downfall is described as the first step in a dialectical process, in which it has become the major factor in Arab national and social resurgence. Amīn al-Husseini wrote:

> "Bitter and painful indeed are the sufferings we have endured, but those of us who have vision bless them, because they were the motive force in our awakening and revival." (*al-Ḥayāt,* November 24, 1953).

Dr. Naṣir writes:

> "Every evil assumes a garb of good, and everything that is negative, in Hegel's view, assumes a garb of the positive, for the coming of Israel vigorously aroused the Arab States." (p. 32).

Arab intellectuals regard the "disaster" as a most serious trial which led to the cleansing and purification of the Arabs and the beginning of spiritual reform. Nasser declared, for instance:

> "The Palestine War in 1948 was the spark which was kindled in men's hearts . . . The tragedy of Palestine was a victory for the Arabs, for it lit the fire of Arab nationalism . . . and the tragedy of Palestine was the flame which aroused the Arab conscience in every country." (October 9, 1959).

Abu al-Majd gives a similar explanation (pp. 34-35), concluding: "The defeat became a victory." Ṣafwat also writes on similar lines (p. 97).

The Treaty of Unity signed on April 16, 1963, between Egypt, Syria and Iraq, declared:

> "It was the disaster of Palestine that uncovered the design of the reactionary strata and revealed the shame of the treachery of the anti-national parties, which are foreign agents, and their indifference to the people's aims and aspirations. It was this disaster that demonstrated the weakness and backwardness of the economic and social regimes that reigned in the land then; it was it that liberated the revolutionary energy of the masses of our people and aroused the spirit of revolt against exploiting Imperialism, poverty and backwardness, and pointed clearly to the road to success, the road of unity, liberty and Socialism."[6]

In a lecture at the American University in Beirut on "The Catastrophe and Ideological Consciousness," Dr. Hasan Sa'ab explained that the defeat "was a turning point in our modern history." He regarded it as the stimulus which led to all the great changes in Arab Nationalism: the intellectual shock and the quest for a change in the internal regime, for a better inter-Arab arrangement than the League, for the completion of independence, for a different basis for relations with the new world, and for increased strength in order to change the balance of forces with Israel (*Ideological Consciousness,* pp. 41-2).

This presentation of the 1948 war as so important for the national movement arouses a certain degree of discomfort, for it gives the impression that Arab nationalism did not arise out of the Arabs themselves, but was a reaction to the clash between them and an external factor, Israel, which thus became, as it were, the godfather of the movement. The same spokesmen, therefore, sometimes declare that the war and the "disaster" were not really of great historical importance. Thus, Nasser wrote:

"The argument that the source of the revolution of July 23 is the results of the Palestine War is not correct." (*The Philosophy of the Revolution,* Part I).

The Egyptian National Charter explains that the roots of the military revolution of July 1952 go back to the failure of the revolution of 1919:

"It was these that created the July revolution, and not the defeat of the Egyptian Army in battle."

* * *

The self-image and the general approach prevalent in the Arab countries are not helpful in contributing to a sincere view of history. Their interpretation of history is a mixture of self-criticism with belief in all kinds of demonic forces and externalization of blame; an effort to learn the lessons of the past with superficial statements like those of Professor 'Afīfī, which try to plaster over facts. The self-criticism is sometimes spoiled by a tendency to denounce rivals, which makes it a merely verbal exercise. Behind this mask of evasive explanations, it seems that, despite all the excuses, the defeat has left a strong impression. However, it is natural for defeats to be forgotten and their effects to fade away in the course of time.

Chapter 8
FROM IDEOLOGY TO ATTITUDE

So far, we have dealt mainly with the way the Arabs express their attitude to the conflict. To what extent does the outward expression reflect their actual position? To answer this question, we must try to emerge from the external sphere of ideologies and public statements and penetrate to the inner reality. For the purpose of this analysis, we shall distinguish between several different aspects of the problem:

First: the sincerity of Arab statements and declarations. To what extent do these reflect their real views? How, for example, are we to understand the objective of liquidation? Is it merely a demagogic target, an ostensible goal? Does it reflect emotions, aspirations, abstract desires? Or is it a practical political objective?

Second: the distribution of such ideas. To what extent do the Arab public accept and identify themselves with the concepts which are part of the ideology?

Third: What is the significance of these ideas, even if they are sincerely expressed and accepted by the Arab public? What is the relationship between talk and action, between attitude and policy?

Fourth: What is the force behind the Arab attitude? What is the place of psychological and geopolitical factors?

Finally, we shall survey and sum up the principal trends which can be traced in the Arab attitude.

1. ERRORS IN EVALUATION

Before trying to answer these questions—and we must note that the replies will, to a considerable extent, be estimates—we must bear in mind possible tendencies in ourselves which are liable to distort our evaluations.

Our experiences with landowners among the upper class of the Palestinian Arabs in Mandatory times, who were unable to resist the temptation of high prices and sold their lands to Jews despite nationalist declarations, aroused an attitude of doubt in our minds as to the sincerity of Arab statements—in fact, we tend to assume that insincerity manifested then indicates insincerity today.

Furthermore, if the statements of the Arabs reflect their attitudes, the conflict is shown to be more intense. Since we find it more convenient to regard it as superficial and transitory, we may, therefore, tend to believe that their true attitude is not expressed by their public declarations, or that the declarations only represent the views of a minority; indeed, many Jews tended to attribute Arab antagonism to Jewish settlement to artificial incitement by the "effendis" and to believe that the incitement was confined to them. It was not always realized that although national consciousness was not widespread among the ordinary Arabs, they, too, opposed the outsiders—the Jews—who had arrived from far-off places and were making a success. Sometimes, indeed, their antagonism was mitigated by the benefits derived from the presence of the Jews; the attitude was mixed: satisfaction with the advantages they derived from the strangers, combined with antagonism to the strangers themselves. Sometimes, good relations on the personal level were projected by the Jews onto the public plane and regarded as indicating the true Arab attitude. But we must always distinguish between personal relationships and attitudes on the political and national plane.

Since the pre-State period, the difficulty of evaluating Arab sincerity has not diminished—perhaps it has increased. The emphasis on liquidation—if only on the political plane—has become more emphatic, and it is hard for anyone to grasp that someone else aspires to destroy him: that his destruction has become an ideal, for which his opponent hopes and prays. One's mind revolts against the bare possibility that someone else regards the shedding of one's blood, or one's disappearance, as an ideal and an act of justice. Besides, the more a man is satisfied with himself, the harder it will be for him to conceive that someone else is against him. He is, therefore, liable to close his eyes to such manifestations, to look for signs and indications that the situation is different, grasping at trivialities, even at the cost of self-deception.

On the surface, it might appear that the opposite possibility also exists: that we might exaggerate the significance of Arab denunciations of Israel in order to emphasize the gravity of the threat, either to reinforce the call for a concerted defence effort, or as an aftermath of the traumatic experience of the Nazi holocaust. It appears to me that the two tendencies to error—by minimizing or by exaggerating—are not equal in strength, either in essence or from the historical point of view. Historically, I believe we may generalize that ideas and hopes for a speedy peace and settlement with the Arabs have been more widespread in the Jewish community than the tendency to exaggerate the seriousness of their antagonism.

2. SINCERITY OF ARAB STATEMENTS

Let us examine some of the reasons given for doubting or denying the sincerity of Arab statements about their attitude in the conflict.

a) ARE THE DECLARATIONS PROPAGANDA FOR INTERNAL CONSUMPTION?

This is, no doubt, true of some statements by Arab leaders, but we must realize that the fact does not lessen their importance or give any ground for satisfaction, especially when this kind of pabulum becomes the daily bread of the masses, and the leaders repeat the same formulae hundreds and thousands of times. Even if we assume that the leadership does not believe that the goal is attainable, the fact that they find it necessary to feed their peoples with these calls for liquidation day after day is certainly of considerable significance and importance, not because they believe they can carry them out or intend to put them into practice, but because such declarations are evidence of the aspiration or mood which gives rise to them and is also stimulated by them.

Foreigners, as well as Israelis, have explained away the extreme denunciations of Israel by Arab leaders on the assumption that they cannot keep their power without talking in this way and that their lives would be in danger if they expressed themselves otherwise. It is frequently argued that in this regard the Arab leaders are caught in a vicious circle from which they cannot escape.

This explanation is far from satisfactory. Declarations by leaders that Israel should be liquidated not only express the expectations of their listeners; they also arouse such expectations. Is it really true that Arab leaders only follow in the wake of public opinion, or do they guide it? If they only follow in the footsteps of the crowd, we would see signs of some effort to extricate themselves from this bacchanalia of abuse and calls for Israel's liquidation, or at least to moderate its excesses. Are we to regard the call for the destruction of Israel as a life insurance policy for Arab leaders? If there is a difference in the mood of leaders and led, it is worth noting the maxim annunciated by Professor Robert North, Director of the Institute for the Study of Integration and Conflicts at Stamford University: "In the long run a leadership is seldom less pathological than its constituents" ("The Race between Destruction and Adaptibility," *Bulletin of the Atomic Scientists,* March, 1964, p. 28).

It might be suggested that the Arabs express themselves in extreme terms because they feel that they are caught in a web of circumstance and unable to solve their problems, but this does not seem to be an adequate explanation for their habit of presenting liquidation as the goal and the extreme frequency with which they do so. Nor is it easy to accept the argument that they are being led astray by their own rhetoric; the liquidation of a State is not a rhetorical expression. Experts in semantics are prone to explain the roots of conflicts by linguistic misunderstandings, but such explanations make no contribution to the understanding of this aspect of the Arab-Israel dispute.[1] We cannot assume that there is some semantic distinction between what we and the Arabs understand by the term "liquidation"; it is not merely a matter of hyperbole. Even if we take the statements of the leaders as mere rhetoric designed to win popular support, that would be important testimony to the moods dominant among the Arab public.

Another factor that must be taken into account is that of persistence over a long period of time. One might understand the leaders, as a temporary expedient or tactic, telling the people things which they themselves do not believe; it seems hardly credible that they would continue to make such declarations for a period of twenty years. Furthermore, it is conceivable that the leaders might make such insincere declarations on marginal matters which are not basic to their policy, but not on such a momentous subject as the liquidation of a State, especially as they themselves allot an important place to their policy towards Israel in the framework of Arab nationalism, and insist on her liquidation as a national goal and objective. The call for liquidation cannot be mere demagogy aimed at winning the hearts of the people or diverting their attention. A national ideal is a matter of educating the youth of the nation, and it may be assumed that on these subjects, if on no others, the leadership tends to be sincere.

Some observers have argued that the disappointment of the Arab leaders with their own achievements in the conflict, their feelings of despair, their consciousness that they have not kept their promises and obligations, have pushed them into the use of extreme and bitter expressions. This argument is put forward by, for instance, Joseph Johnson in "Arab vs Israeli: A Persistent Challenge," *Middle East Journal,* Vol. 18, 1 (Winter 1964), pp. 1-13. There may be some truth in this, but it is only partial. If these declarations do not reflect the purposes of the leaders, they are involving themselves in an over-commitment, which may result in the creation of dangerous pressure in the form of a demand that they should meet their obligations. It can hardly be assumed that they are so blind as not to perceive this.

b) IS IT EXTREMISM FOR BARGAINING OR DEFENCE?

Another suggestion is that the Arabs are well aware that they have no hope of liquidating Israel, and that their declarations are an extreme preliminary position in negotiations, in which they would be prepared to compromise for something less than the demands they present at the beginning.

There is some room for the assumption that this suggestion is correct as a description of the *result* rather than of the aim. We may hope so. Where the aim is concerned, it does not seem plausible, when the Arabs repeat over and over again that they are not prepared for any contact with Israel. Furthermore, continual brooding on the possibility of liquidation and discussion of plans for the purpose show that they mean what they say, if only they could implement their aims. Their view is that, despite all the difficulties, the liquidation of Israel is essential. Their historical outlook is that there is no solution but by a drastic surgical operation on a national scale. They do not take the matter lightly; they treat it as a question of destiny, as they frequently say: a war for life or death.

c) IS IT A RITUAL IDEOLOGY?

There is room for another argument: that parts of the Arab ideology, including the objective of liquidation, are ritual in character. According to some writers, an ideology may be operative and influential for a while, but, since it was moulded in certain historical circumstances, it may no longer be in keeping with the circumstances after the passage of time. However, since involvements with the ideology, as an institutionalized doctrine, have been created in the meantime, it cannot be discarded offhand, and it thus becomes an empty ritual, a matter of routine and rhetoric.[2] According to this argument, analogies may be drawn from a field which has been extensively studied in the West; the development of Soviet ideology, which has undergone a process of ritualization.

First of all, Western observers may be exaggerating the degree of ritualism in the Soviet ideology. Secondly—and this is the most important point—this argument ignores several major factors. For the present generation in the Soviet Union, the Marxist-Leninist ideology has been inherited from a doctrine developed half a century ago and more, and insofar as it has ceased to be appropriate to changing circumstances parts of it have become a burden. But the Arab ideology has been created by the present generation. Moreover, it is not a broad outlook on life and a theory of history; it is only a partial ideology, and therefore comes up against reality on a narrower front. If it becomes clear that it is not compatible with reality, namely that liquidation is impractical, the incompatibility may be postponed by merely postponing action. Of course, repeated and accumulated postponements *sine die* would weaken the aim and make it a matter of ritual. But it cannot be assumed that we have already reached this stage. If we accept Erich Fromm's theory of the transition of ideology from the operative to the ritual stage, the Arab ideology cannot be said to have completed the process.

It may also be argued that the clash between ideology and reality does not have to lead directly to ritualization. Incompatibility between ideology and reality may lead, not to ritualization but to radicalization. Movements sometimes become more extreme in their attitudes, to the point of fanaticism, just because reality refutes their ideas.[3]

d) SOMETIMES THE ARABS TALK DIFFERENTLY

Another argument is that Arab leaders or ordinary people, including students, especially when away from home, sometimes express themselves in more moderate terms, even to the extent of accepting Israel's existence. For instance, foreign observers who have had conversations with Nasser say that, when pressed on the subject of Israel, his replies have implied something like an admission that Israel is a fact, and that a solution to the problem had better be left to the future.

It is true that in the attitudes adopted by the Arabs there is sometimes a degree of duality, or duplicity, for which they blame themselves. One may be surprised to find Arab leaders, after expressing themselves with moderation, spouting fire and brimstone next day in public, making speeches full of hatred and emphasizing once again the need for a violent solution and liquidation as the goal.

Nasser himself recalled in his letter to President Kennedy (August 18, 1961) that President Eisenhower told him in 1960 that Arab leaders were in the habit of making forceful statements in public on the Palestine question and then, in discussions with the US Government, trying to soften the impression of their intransigence by assurances that their declarations were meant "for internal comsumption." Nasser expresses his disapproval of this practice, but his own statement confirms its existence, although he uses it as a weapon against his rivals (*al-Ahrām,* September 21, 1962).

Which shall we believe: what the statesmen say in private or their declarations in public? Americans, for instance, are prone to believe that a Senator's private conversation indicates his true intentions, while his speeches to an audience of voters are sometimes the tribute he has to pay in order to keep his seat, a matter of "politics" in the pejorative sense. If in the United States a private statement is an indication of real intentions, the reverse seems to be true, very often, in the Arab countries, where public proclamations are more significant than the soft words whispered to foreign journalists. Even if the masses cannot impose their will on their leaders by democratic processes, the importance of the public declarations lies in the fact that they create commitments and arouse expectations that the leadership will practice what it preaches. We can picture Nasser, or some other Arab leader, in conversation with a foreigner, observing his interlocutor, judging what will make a good impression on him, and expressing himself accordingly. This is not necessarily a matter of deliberate cunning. People like to make a good impression. The Arab leader, smarting under a sense of his country's backwardness, wants to make an impression of modernity, and he is prone to make an effort to gain the goodwill of the man he is talking to, especially as he will feel that talk of liquidation is liable to be repellent.

In analyzing the distinction between the attitude indicated by speeches and that expressed in interviews with foreigners, we must also take into account the fact that Arab leaders possess facilities for a certain measure of duplicity, for they can make sure that statements they make to foreign observers or in appearances abroad will not be reported in the home press, which is under their supervision and control. For example, when the Jordanian Press reported Hussein's visit to the United States in 1959, there was no mention of his statement that there might be a partial solution to the problem of the refugees by their settlement in Arab countries, but it was stated that "he displayed human concern for the fate of the refugees" (*al-Jihād,* March 29, 1959). Such liberties are, indeed, limited by inter-Arab rivalries, for if their statements are not reported by the press of their own country, they may be given publicity by the communications media of the others.

However, closer study indicates that the difference between Arab statements for external consumption and what they say to their own peoples is not so great after all. It is more a matter of style and formulation than of content. Accurate analysis is necessary, for moderate language does not always mean moderate intentions. The use of "indirect, euphemistic expressions" referring to liquidation does not show an attitude of moderation. The linguistic formulae used by the Arabs to specify their objectives in the conflict, which were surveyed in Chapter I, make it possible to understand the same phrase in different senses. A situation may be created in which the Arabs will understand one meaning of the phrase, while others will perceive a different one. The foreigner will imagine that a declaration of the need for a solution according to the principles of justice and the United Nations expresses a pious wish, while the Arabs will interpret it as advocating the rejection of the *fait accompli,* namely, of Israel's existence. There is nothing accidental about these possibilites; they reflect difficulties involved in the objective of liquidation and the Arabs' own uncertainty about its achievement. A foreigner may return from an Arab country and testify that he has never heard anyone mention the liquidation of Israel (I have met such persons), but further on in the conversation he will admit that he has repeatedly heard talk of "the liberation of Palestine."

When Nasser declared, before the Six-Day War, that he was "prepared" to defer the solution of the problem, this did not mean that he recognized Israel's existence and did not hope to succeed one day in liquidating her. The deferment could have been merely tactical, motivated by an awareness that the aim could not be achieved for the time being, accompanied by the hope that it could be in the future. Foreigners are liable to emerge after a meeting with Nasser highly pleased with the results, attributing the "deferment" to their moderate influence. But talk to foreigners about deferment is perfectly compatible with exhortations to his own people about the need for prolonged preparations for the clash with Israel.

It is very doubtful whether any significant conclusions about Arab aims in the dispute can be drawn from statements made abroad, particularly by students. They are influenced by the foreign environment, and even if they are sincere at the time, what really counts is the way they behave and think when they are in their own national environment at home. The attitude in a conflict, as psychologists explain, is not an individual but a collective matter, and it is conditioned by membership in a society. Many Arab students abroad are critical about various features of life in their own countries and the Arab world as a whole, and therefore have reservations about official policy in many spheres. But this does not mean that they are not in agreement with the objective of liquidation, and they themselves often employ indirect expressions. For example, they emphasize that the existence of Israel is a mistake for which the West is partly responsible and which it ought, therefore, help to rectify. We should also take into account the need to discount to some extent the testimony of students and other Arabs abroad, as in the case of political emigrés (see Margaret Mead and Rhoda Metraux's article "The Anthropology of Human Conflict," McNeil volume, p. 123, note). These students are not free from inner conflict and tension, owing to the contrast between the achievements of their host countries and the position in their own, and they may tend to accommodate their modes of expression to the accepted norms in the former.

Courtesy towards an individual Israeli is not evidence of the attitude towards the Israelis as a whole and their State. As Professor Allport says:

> "People who hate groups in the abstract will, in actual conduct, often act fairly and even kindly toward individual members of the group." (*The Nature of Prejudice,* 1958, p. 341).

The Israeli Arabs constitute a separate group, but their statements about the conflict cannot serve as evidence, for reasons already mentioned.

From personal evidence I can testify that sometimes, at the beginning of a conversation with an Arab, one may imagine that his attitude is different from the official one, but as the discussion continues the familiar arguments of the accepted ideology come up, leading to the logical conclusion: the idea of liquidation. For instance, your interlocutor may admit at first that it is not realistic or legitimate to think of liquidating a State, but he will go on to argue that a terrible injustice has been done to the Arabs, that it is inhuman to forget or condone it, and that "the Palestinians must have their rights restored." Sometimes one can sense a struggle between the attitude that is being adopted for the purpose of the discussion with strangers and the emotional identification with the usual Arab position.

Furthermore, when Arabs make statements which appear to contradict the position to which they are nevertheless committed, it is not merely a tactical evasion; the contradictions may express different layers of opinion and consciousness. When they say they do not aim at the liquidation of Israel, they cannot be simply accused of lying: at that particular moment their attention may be focused on "the liberation of Palestine" and "the restoration of the usurped rights." When they emphasize that they are in favour of the settlement of disputes by peaceful means, this does not prevent them demanding and hoping for the liquidation of Israel's sovereignty by an international effort. When they declare that they believe in peaceful coexistence and respect for sovereignty of States, they are sincere, but at that particular moment they are concentrating on the principle and relegating the apparent exception to the backs of their minds. When they admit that the reality of international order does not permit the liquidation of a State, their agreement comes from the logical layer of the analysis, which does not negate the layer of hopes and aspirations that it may, after all, be possible. The coexistence of such concepts indicates, not split consciousness, but the doubts, perplexities and dissonances which are part of their attitude.

In evaluating this phenomenon, we must remember that we Israelis are not always consistent either, and sometimes cling to incompatible ideas. People are apt to notice and censure the contradictions in the ideas of others, while being tolerant or even completely oblivious of the weaknesses in their own.

Even the contradictions that have been revealed by this analysis of the Arab attitude, as well as others which the analysis may not have been penetrating enough to discover, do not constitute a sign of insincerity. The human mind is quite flexible: if a man holds on to one end of the stick, that is no reason why he should not keep hold of the other at the same time. He may believe that Israel is evil and ought to disappear, and at the same time be aware of her praiseworthy features, just as he may recognize that there is some good in Israel without changing his opinion about her and acquiescing in her existence. It is just these inconsistencies, ambivalences and self-criticisms that enable him to cling to his attitude and endow it with sufficient flexibility to contain the facts which are incompatible with it but cannot be denied. It is true that when there are inconsistencies they are generally accompanied by an effort to minimize them, but people cannot be expected to be completely logical. The Polish philosopher Leszek Kolakovski could write an essay "In Praise of Inconsistency" and argue that the contradictions which prevent complete consistency are a characteristic not only of thought but also of reality.[4]

e) LEADERS AND WRITERS

Political leaders are generally suspect of making a tactical use of words, as in the Quranic aphorism: "They say with their mouths what is not in their hearts." The same applies to professional propagandists. But it is difficult to believe that all the books on the conflict are written by hired pamphleteers; indeed, no inconsiderable proportion seems to express conviction. It is difficult to imagine that 'Alūba, an old, highly respected, though perhaps eccentric man, is not speaking from the heart. Similar considerations would apply to Mūsā al-'Alamī, Constantine Zurayk, Bahā' al-Dīn, Dr. Khālidī, Dr. Sa'ab, Dr. Sayegh and many others. In Egypt, authors are under government control and direction, but this does not apply to the professors at the American University of Beirut; nevertheless, there is no substantial difference between their statements on Israel and the attitude in the United Arab Republic. Since, therefore, there are at least some writers whose virulent denunciations of Israel are sincere, it follows that sincere devotion to the attitude in question is at least possible, and perhaps there are others whose writing is not meant to deceive.

Not all the books that vigorously deny Israel's right to exist have been written at the behest of some propaganda machine. For example, 'Alūsh, who adopts this attitude, is critical, to the point of hostility, of all the ruling circles in the Arab countries, including Nasser and the faction of the Ba'th which was in power in Syria at the time when his book was written, and it is difficult to believe that he did not write out of deep conviction.

Books dealing on general lines with the problems of Arab Nationalism (like those of Sharāra, 'Abd al-Dā'im, Bazzāz and others) include chapters or casual references to the conflict, which imply the same attitude. It seems hardly likely that their position is insincere only where the conflict is concerned, for in that case one would have to deny the sincerity of their nationalist principles, of which their attitude to the conflict is an organic part. There is also another phenomenon which may, perhaps, be regarded as instructive: although all these books express an almost identical attitude on the basic question of denying Israel's right to exist, and although books on the subject appear in large numbers and the ground has been so thoroughly covered that there is not much room for novelty or originality, the authors do not copy from each other. Of course they are influenced by previous works, sometimes quoting them as authorities or criticizing them in one regard or another; no doubt there are plagiarisms here and there; but these are much fewer than might have been expected. When I read these works my impression was that each author was digesting the ideas for himself and expressing them in his own personal way—though, apparently, without worrying too much that he might be repeating what had already been written several times without adding anything particularly new. The assumption underlying such writing may be that, even if there is no novelty in content, the author's contribution lies in the particular form in which he expresses these ideas. The fervour of the writing appears to indicate personal conviction.

There is no need to expect complete and sincere identification with every detail of the attitude as presented in this work, which is a synthesis of the ideas of many authors. If all these details had been present in any single book, there would have been no need for all the labour that has been devoted to the task of accumulating them and combining them into a single structure. The key, the central element, the major principle of the attitude, is the politicidal objective, which is liable to predispose the authors to adopt and proclaim various ideas derogatory to the Jews and to Israel. The function of the details of the images and the ideology is to strengthen and justify the aim of liquidation, and they should not be regarded as having independent validity.

It should also be remembered that the stereotyped image economizes effort, as it makes accurate distinctions unnecessary—which may be another reason for the tendency to adopt it.

It is possible that the leadership is more clearheaded than the people and is aware that the Arab image of Israel is not correct in all its details. But this is not a matter of detail. An awareness that Israel is not so vile as she is painted is not necessarily incompatible with the hope for her disappearance. The emphasis here is on the hope, which, indeed, is not always identical with faith.

Even if we accept the argument that the authors of the crude anti-Semitic propaganda literature which describes Israel in the most scurrilous terms do not entirely believe what they say, their writings are significant as evidence of the atmosphere in their institutions or their countries, which impels them to write in this way.[5] If these authors are aware that their allegations are false, but nevertheless utilize them as a means of denigrating Israel, this clearly shows their attitude, on the principle expressed by Nilus, the disseminator of *The Protocols of the Elders of Zion,* that it is not the truth that counts but the results it produces

> "Let us suppose that the Protocols are false, but is it not possible that God should make use of them in order to expose the iniquity that is already approaching? Did not the Ass of Balaam utter prophecy! For the sake of our faith God can transform the bones of a dog into sacred relics: He can also make the announcement of truth come out of the mouth of a liar." (John S. Curtiss: *An Appraisal of the Protocols of Zion,* p. 71).

It may be that the principal motive of the Egyptian leadership is a geopolitical conception which regards Israel as an obstacle to the grandeur of Egypt, since she obstructs territorial continuity with the Arab countries in the Middle East, and her removal is, therefore, a matter of logical calculation of interests. A geopolitical attitude, however, may be cloaked in an ideology, even as a rationalization in which people may come to believe.

f) CONVICTION AND COHERENCE

The sincerity of the ideology could also be investigated from the point of view of its content. On the one hand, can it be satisfying? Does it contain elements which can meet a psychological need for the Arabs? Or does it contain repellent elements, which make it inconceivable that anyone should believe in it?

One might be wrong if one concludes from one's own revulsion at certain ideas that they will also repel someone else. The idea of liquidation and the demonological fantasies may arouse disgust, but this does not mean that Arabs will reject them. If one surveys the Arab argument as a whole, even if one does not accept it, it may be admitted that it contains elements which may be persuasive. The ideological system consists of simple ideas: Palestine was stolen from the Arabs; they are entitled to have it restored even if that means the liquidation of Israel; since Israel was established by robbery, it is an evil State. A man may find depth and satisfaction in this ideology in accordance with the depth of his intellectual inclinations, and thus be perfectly sincere in advocating it. Professors like Zurayk, Sayegh, Khālidī, Sa'ab and Fāris can develop it with a considerable degree of sophistication, and be perfectly sincere in their attitudes. In the system of ideas which we have surveyed, and which in combination make up the Arab attitude, there is also a measure of continuity, consistency and inner logic.

It is not composed of fragmentary concepts. The Arab ideologists and their leaders have taken pains to weave a tissue of a certain completeness and even inner consistency. If the entire system is not perfectly coherent, it is built of parts, or clusters, each of which has a considerable coherence of its own. Even such a degree of coherence facilitates sincere conviction.

True, as we have seen, there are also contradictions and dissonances, but they cannot be said to be so prominent as to undermine the attitude as a whole. The main contradiction involves the possibility of achieving the goal, and it is the chief source of all the perplexities, sometimes arousing doubts as to whether it is practicable.

g) SINCERITY AS A DEVELOPING PROGRESS

Sincerity may be, not a primary datum, but the outcome of development. Let us assume that the Arab leaders express opinions about Israel in which they do not believe at all. The result, then, would be the creation of a gap or dissonance between their words and their opinions or beliefs. Such a gap makes people feel uncomfortable, and they would therefore like to narrow it down. This is the basis of the theory of "cognitive dissonance" evolved by Professor Leon Festinger and others. As the result of this process, the authors of the declarations tend to believe in their own statements. "A propagandist often has a tendency to be persuaded by his own propaganda," writes R.K. White in the article already mentioned (Kelman volume, p. 272), giving empirical proofs of his thesis. Writing and speech influence the writer and the speaker. White adds: "Self-deception is probably a good deal commoner than consciously cynical lying in our society"—and probably in other societies as well. Repetition, too, helps the ideas to penetrate to the consciousness of the propagandist.

Even if the extreme language used by the Arab leaders against Israel is only like a musical score which they perform, or a role which they play, the effort to articulate their ideas is a cause of self-persuasion. Sometimes a person's attitude can be altered by compelling him to declaim ideas which it is desired to impart to him. Hence the maxim "saying is believing" (see Janis and Smith, "Effects of Education and Persuasion on National and International Images," in the Kelman volume, p. 215; Janis and King "The Influence of Role-Playing on Opinion Change," in M. Jahoda and N. Warren [eds.], *Attitudes*).

It cannot be assumed, therefore, that the leaders are merely repeating statements of which they are not convinced. If such arguments are used to obtain popularity among the people, which means that they have considerable persuasive power, it may be assumed that, generally, only statements of which a man himself is convinced are capable of convincing others. Only words that go out from the heart can reach the heart.

Of course, there is the possibility of conscious cynicism and deliberate demagogy, which were prominent characteristics of, for instance, Goebbels and his circle. But this is possible in a limited group; it seems hardly likely that a large number of people dispersed over a number of countries and highly variegated in character—political leaders and authors, intellectuals and ordinary people, religious men and secularists—who do not all live under a totalitarian regime which tells them what to say, should all keep repeating the same attitude without believing in it. It seems more reasonable to assume that they are somewhat innocent than that they are cynical machinators.

There is no contradiction between the tactical exploitation of ideology and belief in it. Tactics and demagogy may coexist with ideology. Although the latter lays down directions for the former, it can also use it as an instrument. Nevertheless, ideology is not merely subordinate to tactics and demagogy: even when the leaders use it as a tactical expedient, it does not follow that they do not believe in it.

The conclusion which emerges is that the attitude which has been depicted here is probably sincere. However, we must examine in what way this sincerity is expressed and what are its limitations. There are grounds for the assumption that it applies mainly to the nucleus of the Arab attitude: namely, the desire that Israel should not survive and the hope that this desire will be realized. The rest—all the justifications, reasons, explanations, arguments, historical accounts and images—are merely interpretative and auxiliary to this nucleus. They are not, therefore, matters of principle: belief in and support for the details may be half-hearted.

2. DISTRIBUTION OF IDEOLOGY AND IMAGES

To what extent is the Arab public identified with the statements issuing from the leaders, the press, radio, television and literature? In other words, how far has the official image presented in the press and other communications media been internalized and become a part of the consciousness of the people?

As we have noted, the ideology and the images embody the cognitive content of the hostility and hatred. As the number of those who had a direct knowledge of the Jews of Palestine declines, hatred of Israel is relegated to the plane of ideas. Side by side with the question of the extent of identification with the images and the goal, therefore, there is another question: How widespread is the hatred of Israel, or, to what extent do the Arabs participate in the conscious and the emotional elements of their attitude to Israel?

We cannot investigate the extent of public identification with the ideology by direct research or field studies,* and therefore we must investigate which factors are liable to influence it, and what indirect evidence there is which can indicate the degree of vitality that these ideas possess in Arab public opinion. It should be emphasized again that such identification need not apply to all the details of the attitude as given in this book, which is an attempt to synthesize many outlooks; what we are concerned with is identification with the principal aspects of the Arab attitude in the conflict, especially, as a minimum, with the view that Israel deserves to disappear.

a) FACTORS INFLUENCING IDENTIFICATION

a) Only a minority of the Arabs feel direct concern and involvement with the question of Palestine. It seems hardly likely that Israel should be the principal preoccupation of a community most of whose members are engaged in the quest for their daily bread. Most of them do not regard what happened in Palestine as a personal disaster; so far as they are concerned, the conflict is an abstract and theoretical matter. It may be assumed, however, that the Six-Day War has swelled the numbers of those directly affected by the conflict—for instance, in Egypt, where the results were more tangible, relatives of casualties and evacuees from the Suez Canal area, while the shock of defeat and the suffering from the economic results were more widespread.

* It should be noted that it is particularly difficult to conduct such a survey of the absorption of anti-Semitic ideas. There may be a disinclination to talk about such subjects. Belief in the Protocols, for instance, may lead to a tendency to regard the subject as an esoteric one, on which silence is mandatory, especially when talking to the Jews.

Propagandists emphasize that Israel is a danger to all Arabs, in order to create a direct personal involvement in the conflict, but it does not seem reasonable that the populace, especially in countries not bordering on Israel, should accept this point of view. The very fact that the ideologists repeatedly emphasize that the conflict ought to be the focus of Arab nationalism testifies to their lack of success in making it so. The Israeli danger appears distant and verbal. The attitudes and images created among the Arabs are not based on personal, direct experience; they are the results of environmental influence and current ideas. It is not surprising if the propaganda is only superficially absorbed; the attitude to Israel is an acquired one, and the identification with the official attitude is passive in character.

Descriptions of attitudes to Israel in the rural sector are not common. In his book *The End of Israel,* Ṣabrī Abu al-Majd describes how he learned about the conflict as a child in an Egyptian village in the mid-thirties by listening to the Sheikh and the *'Umda* (the local headman) reading aloud from the only newspaper that reached the village in a circle which used to gather by the mosque—and then his hatred for Israel grew with his love for the Arabs (pp. 9-12). However, although he describes these feelings of hatred as typical of the village, his description cannot be regarded as proof that this was really so.

The problems that trouble most Arabs are in different categories: for the majority, the conflict comes not far from the end of the list; in fact, some irritation may develop at the repeated and emphatic references to it.

b) However, even if the Arabs have no direct experience of Israel and it does not occupy an important place in the daily life of the individual, it may be assumed that they are generally aware of the official attitude that Israel and Zionism are enemies of Arab nationalism, especially in view of the influence of mass communications media and the prevailing atmosphere of incitement. It may also be assumed that the absence of direct knowledge does not necessarily involve indifference, and that the masses are not only aware of the official attitude but also agree with it. After all, nothing is required of most of them but concurrence in the abstract: acceptance of the images and support for the official attitude are easier for the very reason that they make no difference to daily life, for the success of the influence of propaganda is in inverse ratio to the importance of the subject (see Brown, 1963, note on p. 55).

c) Evidence of the Arab man-in-the-street's indifference to the conflict may be found in the fact that, in contrast to the publicistic material, Arab *belles lettres,* which may be assumed to be more spontaneous and to reflect the general way of thinking more accurately than political writing, pays little attention to the conflict and the Jews. References to the conflict and the portrayal of Jews and Israelis in modern Arabic literature are worth studying, but the fact that the subject is not extensively treated may be noted as a partial and provisional conclusion. Generally, it prefers to deal with the numerous social problems that affect the Arab world. (For example, Najīb Maḥfūẓ, Egypt's greatest living novelist, has not dealt with the conflict in his writings.) There are cases, it is true, where the official attitude is adopted and the Jews and Israel are denounced. In *Anā Aḥyā* ("I Shall Live"), a famous novel by the Lebanese authoress Layla Ba'labakkī, for instance, there are virulent anti-Israeli expressions, such as "Nazi rule," "the dregs of humanity" and "the destruction of this dangerous bacillus," implied praise for a character who "watered the ground with the blood of the bastards,"[5] and so forth. It may be assumed that after the Six-Day War the conflict and the events connected with it will preoccupy novelists more than in the past.

Arabic literary works dealing specifically with the conflict are in a category by themselves.[6] Most of them are by Palestinians, who are directly concerned, and who give it a central place in their work, so that they do not justify clearcut conclusions about the mood of the Arab man in the street.

d) Although most of the Arabs have no direct, personal experience of the conflict, it should be remembered that people do not identify themselves only with their personal views. Only a small part of their opinions are original; they become sure of their personal ideas when they realize that they are not alone. As Kurt Lewin puts it:

> "This dependence of the individual on the group for a determination of what does and what does not constitute 'reality' is less surprising if we remember that the individual's own experience is necessarily limited. In other words, the probability that his judgement will be right is heightened if the individual places greater trust in the experience of the group, whether or not this group experience tallies with his own." (*Resolving Social Conflicts,* p. 57).
>
> "The sentiments of the individual towards a group are determined less by his knowledge about that group than by the sentiments prevalent in the social atmosphere which surrounds him." (*Ibid.,* p. 63).

The social element in attitudes and ideologies is emphasized by modern social psychology. Steven Withey and Daniel Katz explain that people take on a particular ideology because they belong to a particular nation;

it is not the ideology that ties them into the national structure, but their involvement in the national way of life that ties them to the ideology (McNeil volume, p. 70). Faris emphasizes the same point when he says that political attitudes are determined not primarily by the personality of the individuals who constitute the public in question but by membership in a particular reference group. Attitudes are generally created by a social process which affects individuals through the influence of the group. It may be assumed that for many Arabs the accepted attitude towards Israel becomes a part of their conception of Arab nationalism, as if Israel had become a part—though a negative one—of the Arab national ego. This is perceptible in Arab nationalist literature, in which Israel symbolizes the factors that nationalism wishes to overcome. Arabs are, thus, liable to adopt the anti-Israel attitude through their self-identification as nationalists.

Even if individuals in a particular society may have opinions different from those generally accepted, each of them may imagine that he alone takes the exceptional view, while everyone else is faithful to the general outlook. (This phenomenon has been called "pluralistic ignorance"—see Krech, Crutchfield and Ballachy, *Individual in Society,* pp. 269 and 512, and the Kelman volume, pp. 200-1. Its effect on the attitude of the Palestinian refugees has been described in I. and J. Galtung's *A Pilot Project from Gaza,* February 1964, Oslo, p. 22.) As a result, no one dares to express in public an opinion opposed to the general view; everyone supinely supports it only because no one realizes that others have similar reservations to his own. (Hence the importance of Bourguiba's pronouncements, which constituted at the time a breach of Arab pluralistic ignorance.)

e) The fact that the conflict is not expressed in the life of the individual may lead foreign visitors to the Arab countries to get the impression from talks and contacts that it is only of limited reality in the Arab consciousness, as an abstract, rootless superstructure. Such a view may be exaggerated and mistaken. No individual ever lives the ideological life of his group twenty-four hours a day. The conflict exists on the national plane, while the individual grapples with his personal problems and undoubtedly puts them first. Withey and Katz explain in the article quoted that a person's national involvement does not occupy much of his "psychological life space," except under conditions of war. Then his nationalist concepts are embodied in the roles he plays in daily life, for instance in the army or some other form of active participation in the war effort, and the struggle with the opponent takes on a more tangible meaning (McNeil volume, p. 72).

Moreover, the circle with which most Arabs identify themselves is a narrow one; it is certainly not the nation as a whole, as Dr. Hamady explains (p. 95), though it may be assumed that it will steadily expand with the spread of Arab nationalism. However, the superficiality of the individual's attitude to the conflict does not mean that the conflict itself is superficial. Identification could be latent, and be actualized when various factors come to the fore. (The latter are described by Withey and Katz, in the article already quoted, as "arousal factors": an appeal to the public coupled with the brandishing of ideological symbols—national honour, national interest and security, national aims and national strength. And indeed, as we have seen, such factors are to be found in the ideological appeal to the Arab public.)

f) There is also another factor to be taken into account. The conflict belongs to the area of foreign policy, and studies of public opinion—though mainly in developed countries—have shown that interest in this field is limited, and many people show considerable ignorance of foreign affairs, even in the relationship between their own country and others.

'Abd al-'Azīz Fahmī remarked, comparing the citizen's attitude to the conference of non-aligned nations in 1964 and to the food shortage which existed in Egypt at the time:

> "The ordinary citizen generally takes no interest in politics except to the extent that it affects the necessities of daily life, his personal and social interests; and he examines any policy proposed to him by the criteria of his personal needs and affairs." (*Akhbār al-Yawm*—October 3, 1964).

g) If we accept the general view of Orientalists and sociologists that the Arabs generally suffer from frustration, we should note that "frustrated people are more credulous than those who are not frustrated" (Brown, p. 111). They will, therefore, be more prone to accept the image of Israel, which contains a considerable element of prejudice.

h) The question might also be considered from the opposite point of view. There is nothing in the acceptance of the Arab ideology and images to arouse rejection and opposition. On the contrary, the psychological functions which the ideology can fulfil—as a channel for dissatisfaction, resentment and frustration, and a safety valve for aggressive impulses—may help to make it acceptable. The more the images and the attitude fulfil psychological functions, the more active will be the identification.

i) Islam contains the seeds of an anti-Jewish outlook, even if in latent form. The ideology can make use of them, bring them to life, and exploit the emotional attachment to Islam in order to win support.

j) It may be added that the tendency to identification with what is regarded as the accepted view is liable to be particularly strong in an Arab society, which has been accustomed to acquiescence in the fiats of rulers and legislation from above. In such a society, the suggestive power of the official attitude is liable to be particularly strong. On the other hand, the political mobilization of the population is still limited in scope, and this is liable to limit the extent of their identification with political attitudes.

k) The survey of the Arab ideology given in this work is based on an analysis of published works. How widespread is their circulation among the people and to what extent are they read?

Even if we make what is from our point of view the optimistic assumption that these books are published in small editions, we must remember that there is no need for any one person to read them all, and we can hardly expect that anyone would be able to do so. They all present the same basic attitude, so that one or two books would be enough to make the reader familiar with it. The criterion, therefore, should be, not the circulation of each book, but the combined circulation of all the books dealing with the conflict. The circulation of the dailies and weeklies, which also express various parts of the attitude, is undoubtedly very great.

If the price of the works has an effect on their distribution, it is noteworthy that in Egypt they can be bought for a few coppers. The "Nationalism" and "Policy" series cost only a few Egyptian piastres (worth about 2½ cents each) and most of them are printed on cheap paper. *Human Sacrifices in the Talmud,* a 146-page booklet, is sold for 5 Egyptian piastres, Rushdī's *Zionism and Its Fosterchild Israel,* 442 pages, for 80 piastres, *Inside Israel,* 367 pages, for 24 piastres, and Sīdham's doctoral dissertation, *The Arab Refugee Problem,* 235 pages, for 30 piastres, while the annual subscription to the 12 al-Hilāl books, which included 'Alūba's *Palestine and the Conscience of Mankind* and Bahā' al-Dīn's *Judaica,* costs only 1 Egyptian pound (about £1 sterling or less than 2½ dollars). Tall's *The Danger of World Jewry to Islam and Christianity* was issued in a fairly luxurious edition, on excellent paper, with detailed indexes, for 60 piastres.

In Egypt, these books are published with Government support, which is not the case in Lebanon, where most of the publishing firms are private and the prices are therefore much higher. 'Alūsh's *The Journey to Palestine,* 231 pages, costs 4 Lebanese pounds (each worth about 29 cents, or

2s. 5d.) and Niqūlā al-Durr's *Thus Lost and Thus Redeemed,* 316 pages (including index), cost 5 Lebanese pounds. It may be assumed that there is a market for such books, otherwise they would not be printed. This would seem to apply even to such an expensive work as Dabbāgh's *Our Country Palestine,* Part I, 820 pages (including indexes), a geographical work of great scope but no doubt of more limited appeal, which costs 16 Lebanese pounds.

Another possibly significant indication is the fact that several books have been published in parallel both in Egypt and in Lebanon: examples are 'Izzat's *I Was in Israel* and Bītī's *Eliminate Israel.* Since the commercial aspect is important in Lebanon, and books can only be published if readers are willing to pay for them, publication is a sign of demand, and we may also draw conclusions as to the extent of the demand and readership for such works in Egypt.

Another criterion is the number of editions. Tūnisī's translation of *The Protocols of the Elders of Zion,* published by a commercial firm, went into four editions—and obviously the first three had to be sold out before the fourth was printed. Qamḥāwī's 900-page *Disaster and Reconstruction* went into two editions: so did Rushdī's *Zionism and Its Fosterchild Israel,* Darwaza's *The History of the Children of Israel From Their Books* (in Egypt) and the Arabic translation of Israel Cohen's history, *This is Zionism.* This is not conclusive proof of the extent to which such books are read, but it would certainly be optimistic to assume that they are not.

It is true that the percentage of literacy is small in the Arab countries, but even those who cannot read will learn of the viewpoint expressed in such books, which is identical with the Arab attitude, from broadcasts and the influence of the environment. It is only for convenience that the present study is based on the literature, as a concentrated expression of the Arab attitude.

l) There are empirical indications (though not from the Arab countries) that it is the leaders in people's immediate neighbourhood who have the greatest influence on the adoption of images and ideas (see Deutsch and Merritt's article in the Kelman volume, p. 153).[7] This is now the accepted view in the theory of public communications. Professor Elihu Katz, summing up these conclusions (in connection with studies in the United States), emphasizes that opinion leaders are more open to the influence of mass communications media than the people they lead. This may be the circle which reads most of the propaganda literature. As Professor Katz puts it:

"Ideas flow *from* radio and print to the opinion leaders and *from* them to the less active sections of the population." (See his article "Two-step Flow of Communications" in *Human Behavior and International Politics,* ed. Singer, pp. 293 ff, and Krech, Crutchfield and Ballachey, pp. 234-7).

According to Katz's article, it appears that opinion leaders are influenced more by persons than by communications media. It may be assumed that in the Arab countries the individual, the leader, is more influential than the programme or the party.

m) In the Arab world, official statements are generally treated with a certain degree of scepticism, as mere politics *("siyāsa")* and not a true expression of attitudes and opinions. It cannot be assumed that Governments and leaders succeed in playing the role of mediator between events and their images in the minds of their flocks and thus giving them their final interpretation. Among the Arab public there is a considerable degree of doubt as to the sincerity of their rulers, a constant suspicion that the latter are working for their own personal benefit—an attitude which is supported by a long historical memory of corruption by public servants. The Arab leadership has often been caught out in falsehoods, and there seems to be a distrust of statements coming from the mass communications media. Hence, the widespread listening to Israeli broadcasts, which increased particularly during and after the Sinai Campaign, when the gap between the veracity of Arab and Israeli stations was obvious. It may be assumed that there is a certain degree of immunity to incessant propaganda.

This does not necessarily imply reserve as to the leaders' allegations against Israel; the critical attitude may apply more to facts than to opinions, just as those who listen to the Israel radio may accept the facts while rejecting the commentary (there are indications of similar tendencies elsewhere—see Janis and Smith, in the Kelman volume, p. 212).

n) From the intellectual point of view, this ideology is capable of convincing those who want to be convinced, and it contains adequate arguments for the purpose. It is simple in its values and concepts; it may be summed up in a few straightforward syllogisms: "The State of Israel has been established by the robbery and expropriation of the Arabs. The injustice must be rectified and justice meted out. Hence Israel's existence must be abolished." As a chain of simple ideas, this is easy to explain and easy to understand and accept. It has some claims to scientific logic, a historical basis, and completeness. It is also compatible with other ideas about Arab nationalism and its spirit. It constitutes a well-knit ideological system and thus endows the individual ideas with additional importance and significance. Its capacity to carry conviction makes it easier to identify with it. Moreover, the possibility of variations without affecting the basic attitude enables both religious circles and freethinkers to adhere to it each in their own way.

o) A foreign observer, it is true, may find the Arab ideology and imagery about the conflict so artificial, irrational, inflated, melodramatic and uncouth that it is difficult for him to believe that such conceptions should be current in any community. The foreigner's attitude, however, is no guide to the question of the extent to which these views are supported among the Arabs, especially as there are even some foreigners who justify the ideology. Even if the outsider may find its arguments unconvincing, it should be remembered that ideological argumentation is not a matter of rigid truth intended to influence that unbeliever; its main purpose is to convince the convinced, and sometimes the ideas are accepted not so much because of their content as because of their origin and the function they perform.

p) The very fact that most Arabs have no direct knowledge or experience of the Israelis may strengthen the tendency to absorb demonological ideas about them. It is just the paucity of contact with Jews and Israelis that facilitates dehumanization. This applies particularly to the children of the refugees, who had no direct knowledge of the Israelis.

q) It seems unlikely that the vast propaganda effort which the Arab Governments have devoted to the conflict, the incessant repetition, the harping on the subject by all the mass communications media and the instruction in the schools, should fail to produce results. It may reasonably be assumed that the various publicity methods succeed in disseminating and hardening the Arab attitude, which takes root in the consciousness of the people and becomes a psychological and sociological fact by dint of constant repetition.

r) Even if identification with the images and the ideology of liquidation is superficial and ritual, it is difficult to accept the view that they are confined to leaders and propagandists, and that the people are free from them. Such a view is only a relic of the "popularist" approach, which regards the people as basically natural and good, while only the leaders are corrupt and evil. Since the leaders, or at least some of them, are admired by the people, the masses identify themselves with what they say. Nasser, for example, is admired by many Arabs, and it may be assumed that his authority will lead to the acceptance of his views (otherwise a dissonance would arise).

s) It may be argued that the "official public image" does not reflect the totality of the "private images," since the Arab regimes are not democratic. Such an argument confuses democracy with popularity. There have been democratic regimes which were not popular and were overthrown by the votes of the people. On the other hand, the fact that a regime is not democratic—and the argument is no doubt intended to apply to Egypt, which is the leader in the dissemination of the Arab anti-Israel ideology—does not imply that it is not popular; even if some aspects of its policy are criticized, this does not mean that its attitude to the Arab-Israel question is not generally accepted.

t) The fact that ideas contained in the Arab ideology are often repeated by intellectuals and academics is another indication that it is not limited to ruling circles and that the ideas can spread among the people. It is hardly credible that they have been briefed in detail by the authorities and merely repeat their directives.

u) Another indication of the hold of the ideology and the images on the Arab masses is the fact that they like to hear about the conflict. Nasser told the members of the Gaza Legislative Assembly when they visited Cairo:

> "When I used to make speeches about [economic] development in Syria, the people listened to me, but when I talked about Palestine and Arab unification, they went wild with enthusiasm." (June 26, 1962).

Anyone who has listened to Nasser's broadcast speeches has no doubt noted that cries are sometimes heard from the crowd calling on him to talk about Palestine. Even his speech at Bizerta on December 13, 1963 was interrupted by cries of "Palestine." Nasser seemed to be speaking the truth when he said:

> "Wherever I go I hear continual cries and shouts from this good people, I hear cries about Palestine and its liberation." (October 19, 1960).

If these cries are not spontaneous, the question arises: Why should they be organized? Why should anyone devote effort to the purpose? Are these only Palestinian refugees?

The Palestine question was a factor in public opinion even before the 1948 war. The report of the Iraqi Parliamentary Enquiry Committee says that the Arab leaders acted without energy because their main purpose was to meet the mood of the public.

> "The action taken by the Arab states was only a pretence for the purpose of appeasing public opinion." (*Behind the Curtain,* trans. S. Segev, *Maarachot,* 1954, p. 65).
>
> "The participation of some of the Arab States in the deliberations [of the Arab League on Palestine] was aimed merely at appeasing public opinion in their countries." (*Ibid.,* p. 15).

Here is further evidence of public interest in the question.

(The mass enthusiasm which flooded Egypt on the eve of the Six-Day War is also evidence of the widespread emotional attitude towards Israel, which, it may be assumed, was one of the factors that motivated Nasser's actions.)

v) It is true that the Arab leadership utilizes the Palestine question for extreme and demagogic declarations in order to win the sympathy of the people, but this, too, is evidence of mass interest. The argument that this is mere rhetoric and phraseology is self-defeating, for it is only a popular subject that lends itself to demagogic oratory in order to achieve popularity. If the masses were indifferent to the subject, it could not be exploited in this way. The frequently heard argument that Arab public opinion is merely a prey to incitement is an illusion.

w) Arab intellectuals also harp on the theme of the conflict and exploit it to support their pleas for the modernization of their society. They say: Unless we reform our society we shall not achieve our aims in the conflict; hence we need, first of all, a change of values at home, and only then will Palestine be liberated. This is a frequently expressed argument. Qamḥāwī writes, for example:

> "Even if Israel gave up half her territory and funds, we do not want peace, for it is only a deceit and a loss. For any peace the Arab countries may conclude with Israel means the disappearance of one of the main motives for unity and an awakening for a change in the situation and the strengthening of our souls; if we establish ties with Israel, we shall give her time for recovery and time for a new aggression." (1962, vol. II, p. 421).

It may be assumed that for the intellectuals the reform of Arab society is a more important aim than the restoration of Palestine, but they are aware, apparently, that the aspiration of their people to achieve its aims in the conflict, as well as the hostility, bitterness and aggressive emotions connected with it, constitute a force that can impel their people to change their way of life. And we can be sure that, as Arab writers, they know their people and understand what will influence it.

x) In the Arab countries, as in many others, there are protest movements by intellectuals, but there is no sign that these are directed against the rulers' attitude to Israel—here, apparently, they agree with the authorities. We may hope that there are some groups who do not agree with this ideology and particularly with the extreme aim of the destruction of Israel, but so long as they remain in hiding and have not the courage to proclaim their views in public their attitude is a barren one, because it does not directly influence the mood of the people or form part of the "effective public opinion" that is expressed in speech or action. For political life, the acid test of the importance of an idea is the response it arouses among the public. Small islands of moderation, the very existence of which is problematical, do not affect the character of the ocean. There have been a few Arabs who have opposed the official line and called for compromise and peace with Israel, but the question that arises first of all is how many Arabs have even heard of them. It is a mistake to seize on something said by an individual Arab, when neither he nor his statement is known to the general public, and base conclusions on it, especially as such phenomena have become more and more rare in recent years. The existence of moderate Arabs may be gratifying, but they have made no name for themselves and there is no indication that they have any influence. Moderation is not popular today in the Arab countries, where compromise is synonymous with treason. Just because it is radical and drastic, liquidation is likely to enjoy support among the Arab public, which, as Berger testifies, lives in an atmosphere of "political extremism" (p. 331).

b) SUMMING UP

Actually, the question of the image that is current among the people is less important from the practical point of view than may appear at first glance. Research has shown that there is no close causal connection between accepted images and the behaviour of States on the international scene (see Note 4 to Chapter 9). States do not behave in accordance with images; on the contrary, people adapt their images and outlooks to the policy of the State. Nations do not fight because they have an unfavourable image of their opponents; the image is unfavourable because the conflict exists. The importance of the image that is painted in Arab propaganda and ideology, even if it is an artificial one, lies in the fact that it is the leadership which is trying to disseminate it among the people.

There is no simple answer to the question whether the Arab public identifies itself with the ideology and the images it contains; no categorical unqualified yes or no would be adequate. We must avoid two extremes, two superficial assumptions: the one which says that the image painted by the communications media, including the objective of liquidation, is prevalent in the consciousness of all the Arabs; and the second, that this image is of no importance, since it is mere fantasy and empty phraseology. Both these extreme attitudes are undoubtedly mistaken: the truth lies somewhere in between. But where exactly is it? On the basis of the considerations explained in this chapter, my personal guess is that the attitude of the Arab public is closer to the extreme of identification with the outlook described than to the extreme of its rejection.

Let me try to describe the extent of identification according to the categories generally used in studies of attitudes and beliefs by social psychologists (e.g. Krech and Crutchfield's *The Theory and Problems of Social Psychology,* Chapters 5 and 7, or Daniel Katz's article "The Functional Approach to the Study of Attitudes," in the *Public Opinion Quarterly*).

1) The extent of familiarity with the *content* of the opinions, the cognitive aspects of the attitude. It may be assumed that the fact that Israel is regarded as the enemy of Arab nationalism and that Arab nationalism opposes the existence of Israel is widely known among Arabs.

It should be emphasized that such knowledge does not mean complete familiarity with all the details of the ideological structure, but an awareness of its principles: that the Jews took possession of an Arab country and drove out the Arabs, that the Palestinians have the right to return, that Israel is the enemy of Arab nationalism and an ally of imperialism, that the Arabs have set themselves the goal of liquidating her, and so forth.

2) *Intensity,* the degree of devotion to these opinions. Here we are concerned with the degree of conviction or certainty, and the extent to which it is reinforced by emotion.

It appears that the intensity of devotion to the Arab attitude towards Israel is particularly great among those who are directly involved in the conflict, for whom it is a daily experience and preoccupation (refugees, political staff of the Arab League, propaganda personnel and part of the leadership). It may be assumed that in many circles the conviction of the justice of the attitude is less intense, that this applies to most of the Arab world, and that the intensity declines the further off the country concerned is from Israel. In Allport's terms (*The Nature of Prejudice,* Chapter 17), we may say that for the majority the attitude to the conflict is a matter of superficial conformity, while it has functional significance only for a minority. This distinction is connected with the next category.

3) *Centrality,* namely the degree of importance of the attitude or belief, the extent to which it is central in the personality, behaviour or spiritual world of the Arabs. The degree of centrality, Katz tells us, depends on the importance of the function performed by the attitude in the value system connected with the self-concept or the self-image (see his article "The Functional Approach to the Study of Attitudes").

For the self-image of most of the Arabs, the conflict is marginal. The emphatic efforts of Palestinian propagandists, who want to make the conflict the focus of Arab nationalism, and the intensity of their protest at the fact that this is not so, may be taken as evidence of a generally low level of centrality. The conflict is central for the refugees and, no doubt, in certain circles in Syria, but it is not particularly central, it may be assumed, among most Egyptians.

Egyptian interest in the conflict has been political, not popular. It is noteworthy that Nasser, when speaking in Egypt before the Six-Day War, generally devoted no more than a few sentences to the subject, since it was not so interesting to the people as to justify a lengthier treatment. When he spoke in Syria, however, before and after the union, he devoted more attention to it.

4) *Saliency,* the extent to which people can discuss any other subject without being reminded of the conflict; the degree in which they find it a continual stimulus. In most of the Arab world, many subjects can be discussed without bringing up the conflict at all. In Egypt, for instance, saliency has been low, as visitors have testified, but it is higher in Jordan and Syria, and even in Lebanon.

In an article on a tour of the borders of Jordan, for instance, Abdallah al-Imām wrote:

> "Every political discussion in Jordan is, naturally, a talk about the problem of Palestine. People talk about 'the problem' and the meaning here is, of course, 'the problem of Palestine.' The problem has made a strong political impression even on the ordinary man in the street." (*Rūz al-Yūsuf,* July 26, 1965).

When an Egyptian journalist points this out, he is no doubt aware of the contrast with the low degree of saliency attached to the problem in Egypt. Eric Rouleau reports from Damascus:

> "Hostility to the Zionist State is a feeling common to all Syrians. It is practically impossible to mention any subject, political, economic, social or cultural, with-

out the conversation naturally turning, at one moment or another, to the subject of the *'Karitha,'* the catastrophe. Nowhere in the Arab world have I found such extreme sensitivity to an event which entered into history twenty years ago." (*Le Monde,* October 13, 1966).

It may be assumed that the Six-Day War has enhanced the centrality and saliency of the conflict in most of the Arab countries, especially in Egypt.

3. IMPORTANCE OF IDEOLOGY AND IMAGES

a) THE CATHARSIS ARGUMENT

It may be argued that Arab talk about the objective of liquidation and images of the Jews and Israel are mere verbal aggression, which reduces the pressure for actual aggression, and that it is better for people to abuse each other than to break each other's heads. The Arabs, according to this argument, console themselves by attacking Israel with words; by compensating themselves with the pleasures of scurrility, they lessen the need for physical violence. They are well aware that Israel is an inexorable fact, and the plethora of talk about destroying her does not testify to their devotion to the objective and the strength of their convictions; it is merely a compensation for their impotence. Thus, in fact, by their abuse of Israel, the Arabs make it easier for themselves to acquiesce in her existence. It is a similar process of catharsis to what we see in the theatre, when people seem to find relief from their aggressive tendencies by witnessing and identifying themselves with violent action on the stage.

Nasser hinted at the cathartic effect of speeches about Palestine:

"I feel in the depths of my heart that the tragedy which has descended upon all of us in Palestine is merely the result of the complacency that descended on our souls after all the flowery speeches and the mass assemblies. We used to listen to the speeches and afterwards feel placid, and this placidity was the primary and basic reason for the disaster of Palestine." (Address at the Palestine Club in Alexandria, December 13, 1953, I.L., I/153).

However, psychologists tell us (Berkowitz, Chapter 8; Faris, p. 27) that we should not imagine that there is some kind of reservoir of hostility and aggression which can be emptied by means of the catharsis of symbolic aggression. The satisfaction of catharsis is limited in duration. The image of aggression replaces it only for a short time; in the long term, thinking about aggression and the experiences involved in images associated with it lead to the strengthening of aggressive tendencies. Thus, catharsis does not reduce hostility and aggression; on the contrary, the repetition of hostile talk consolidates them. As Faris puts it:

> "The overt expression of hostility increases aggression rather than reducing it." (p. 27).

Even if the ideology and the images have a cathartic effect, that is not the end of their influence, which is a durable one. Allport points out that those nations and tribes that are aggressive within the group are also aggressive outside, while peaceful social units tend to be peaceful in their external relations as well (see his article, "The Role of Expectancy," in *War: Studies from Psychology, Sociology, Anthropology,* eds. Bramson and Goethals).

Moreover, the abuse of Israel is not merely a catharsis, but constitutes what Allport calls "antilocution." Verbal aggression is a prelude to actual aggression:

> "Although most barking (antilocution) does not lead to biting, yet there is never a bite without previous barking." (*The Nature of Prejudice,* p. 56).

b) THE GAP BETWEEN TALK AND ACTION

Another argument is that no importance should be attributed to the talk of the leaders, the ideology and the images because there is a great gap between what the Arabs say and what they do.

It is true that there is a great deal of insincerity in Arab public life: the leaders have a habit of making meaningless declarations to win a reputation for nationalism. They compete with each other in verbal extremism, and then, as Eisenhower said to Nasser, they ask for their statements not not to be understood literally (quoted in Nasser's letter to Kennedy, cited in an earlier chapter). The pronouncements of Arab leaders are often made for exhibitionist or tactical purposes, and have no profound significance. The Arab leaders have frequently been false to each other, pretending friendship while secretly planning subversion and attacks; they have talked about fidelity to Arab unity while trying to injure each other and foment disunity; they have proclaimed action for the general good while working for their private benefit. In Haykal's phrase, they have spoken with "enthusiasm"—which he defined as "talking about what is beyond their reach and shirking action" (*al-Ahrām,* January 17, 1964).

It should be emphasized that not only foreigners are aware of these phenomena: the Arabs themselves are the severest critics of this kind of behaviour.

It is necessary to examine the relationship between ideology and action: the extent to which ideologies shape or influence the behaviour of societies and States. This problem is of practical importance for the purpose of prognosis and policy decisions. In the West particular attention has been paid to the question of the Soviet Union's ideology and its influence on the country's actions. Reshtar, Bell and others, who have discussed the extent to which the Marxist-Communist ideology can be a guide in forecasting the actions of the Soviet Union, have reached the general conclusion that the study of the ideology is essential for the understanding of the regime and its behaviour, but the ideological factor is not a sufficient basis for a forecast. In many cases they found that Russia's behaviour was determined by interests and pragmatic considerations, which may even have been incompatible with the ideology.[8] In a clash between ideology and interest, interest usually comes first; the ideology is not the final determinant. Even where it seems to be merely a matter of translating the ideology into action, which would appear to be a necessary outcome, it would be a mistake to assume uncritically that the ideology is a sufficient cause; even in such cases, there have also been pragmatic factors in the shape of circumstances which were in keeping with the demands of the ideology and led to its implementation.

If this is so in the Soviet Union, where the ideology is an integrated intellectual system, the same trend applies to the behaviour of the Arabs. Nevertheless, the ideology must be studied if we are to grasp their actions.

An ideology is not only a framework for the interpretation of history; it also embodies, as essential elements, aspirations and hopes for a better world, whether it be a new world or only a reformed and improved one.

In order to clarify this relationship between hopes, their embodiment in ideologies and their implementation in practice, we must investigate the process which connects these elements. For the purpose of the discussion, we shall try to split this process into hierarchical levels. Of course, this will be a somewhat crude, schematic description; there is no intention to describe a process of general validity, but to bring out those points which may be relevant to the Arab ideology.

The first level reflects, on the one hand, emotions and, on the other, aspirations or ideals. Among the Arabs, at this level, we find hostility to Israel and the desire for vengeance, and, on the other hand, the aspiration to liquidate Israel, restore the ancient glories and achieve Arab unity and grandeur, and the ideas connected with these aspirations.

On the second level, these feelings and desires are expressed in words (orally or in writing) and an attempt is made to build them into a system, with explanations and justifications. Here is the place of the ideology: the explanation and justification for the objective of liquidation, the denunciation of Zionism, ideas about national ideology, and so forth. Sir Lewis Namier expressed this relationship between aspirations and their verbal expression by saying that ideas are the libretto to the music of emotions (in his essay "Human Nature in Politics," Harper, Torch Books, 1965).

The third level is that of action. There is no automatic transition between one level and the next: reason intervenes, as a censor, to control it. Between the first level and the second, it examines which of the aspirations and ideas are fit to be expressed and thus to become publicly known; between the second and third, it considers which of the acts dictated by the ideology are possible at all. It tries to find out how various factors will react to the ideology; even more, it considers the possible feedback from the acts which follow from the ideological talk and enjoins abstention from those that may produce undesirable results. Such reactions to acts following on the ideology express the influence of the factors that make up the reality; from the viewpoint of the conflict (again in a superficial form) they are: on the one side, the Arab States, their power, intentions, interests and tendencies; on the other side, Israel and her strength, as well as international factors and conditions. From this point of view, the ideology is a reservoir of institutionalized aspirations which pass through the filter of reason before they are carried out in practice.

Actually, the reason which examines the effects of reality starts operating in the first level, that of aspirations, and curbs in advance the creation of ideas and aspirations if they are unrealistic and their translation into ideology and action is liable to lead to undesirable results. The rejected aspirations are suppressed or repressed, thus creating a difference between an abstract desire and one which develops into a mature will and a plan for action. Generally, it appears, the first level is freer from the control of reality and is more open to extravagant illusions. Here is the place for daydreams and unrealistic utopias. The harmful results of ignoring reality in the first level are not immediately apparent. The serious outcome of implementing aspirations without taking the reality into account are particularly prominent in the level of action. It is here, therefore, that reason is generally brought into play.

Among the Arabs, it appears, there is a high degree of autonomy in the first and second levels: thought, aspiration and expression develop in freedom from control by reality. Since the first level is hidden from view, it is the difference between the second and the third that is particularly obvious. The Arabs (like others) are less realistic and deliberate in speech, and more so in action.

True, this failure to take reality into account may be given an ideological cloak, the argument being: The more you demand, the more you will get. It may be that some exaggeration is desirable, but if it is excessive, a wide gap will be created between the ideological aims and the objective possibilities, so that the transition between them will involve hesitations, and demand a drastic leap forward. Thus Haykal writes:

> "Sometimes it appears to me that the Arabs are more afraid to employ their power than the enemy. We have tremendous, unlimited strength at our disposal in the political, economic and military fields, but our hands tremble even before we start to employ it. Why? Because we do not possess a realistic estimate of this strength. Its utilization is, therefore, an adventure into the unknown." (*al-Ahrām,* January 17, 1964).

In other words, according to this description the Arabs "tremble" at the transition from ideas to actions as if before a plunge into the unknown. If their power had been realistically examined from the beginning, they might have been spared these tremors. Haykal himself, however, is not free from this lack of realism. Although he sees the need for a scientific study of the extent of this strength, he knows the results in advance and wants it only to confirm that the strength is "tremendous."

But Haykal is not alone in this respect. All the Arab political literature is full of self-castigation for failure to live in the world of reality and devotion to vain dreams. King Abdallah summed up the lesson of his experience in these words:

> "My conclusion from all this is that Arabs must give up daydreaming and apply themselves to realities." (*My Memoirs Completed,* p. 30).

The Jordanian White Paper is even more severe:

> "If we Arabs do not leave behind the reasons for our weakness, then our living in the world of dreams will almost certainly reduce us to the lowest level or to the disappearance of the nation, which contains all the factors of life." (*Jordan, the Palestine Problem and Arab Relations*, p. 37).

Orientalists and others have noted this gap between the ideal and the act among the Arabs, and analysed this sensitive subject each in his own way. Some have regarded it as a manifestation of the Arab national character. Thus, Dr. Hamady writes:

> "The Arab becomes enthusiastic and proclaims his readiness to act, but when the time for action comes he shies away." (p. 45).

Others have associated this phenomenon with the difference between the literary and the spoken language (Shouby in "The Influence of the Arabic Language on the Psychology of the Arabs"). Morroe Berger says that the difference between the ideal and the real is particularly outstanding among the Arabs. The Arab is fascinated by ideal forms:

> "He clings to them emotionally even while he knows they are contradicted by reality." (p. 179).

Berger quotes Jamīl Ṣalība, who said that the Syrian or Lebanese

> ". . . often imagines things and believes that they really exist because they fit his feelings and dreams whereas actually they remain confined to the world of imagination . . . Feelings are to him the criterion of existence." (p. 180).

He notes, for example, that Islam persisted in describing the office of Caliph as endowed with authority and power, though it had long since been divested of any real strength; in other words, the Islamic ideology about the Caliphate was divorced from reality. A similar situation existed in the juridical sphere: life went one way and law another; Professor Schacht, the noted authority on Islamic law, described the difference as an antinomy which he believed to be inherent in Muhammadan law.

Since ideology among the Arabs is largely autonomous, it is certainly not a reliable guide to their future actions. Anyone who deduced from the ideology of the UAR that Nasser was about to act in any particular way would be making a mistake, and the same applies to other leaders. It is not surprising if many have little respect for the Arab ideology: if it does not appear to influence their actions, it is of little value. Among the staff of Government departments interested in political action, there is a general tendency to ignore the ideological aspect of Arab life.

Since the objective of liquidation belongs to the ideological sphere, it is widely regarded as an abstract aim, having no influence on Arab day-to-day behaviour, far-off and uninteresting, for the Arabs do not actually engage in liquidation but only talk about it, and their preparations have not always been thorough and indicative of a collective iron determination. It is true that the ideology is not always operative as a guide to action; it is more in the nature of ritual or lip-service, a collection of formulae which are repeated without being regarded as binding to action.

But even if the ideology does not indicate political actions, it should not be ignored for that reason.[9] The passion for practicality, the insistence on immediate operative results as the only criterion, is too narrow; the urge for *Realpolitik* is liable to be unrealistic. The importance of the ideology lies in the fact that it reflects Arab emotions and aspirations. If it does not indicate what they are going to do, it describes what they would like to do. It is a summation of the aims that beckon to them from afar, which, even, if they do not mark out the road, determine the general direction of the journey. If it does not embody the policy, it expresses its foundations, its "meta-politics"; it is the matrix of ideas and emotions in which policy is made.[10]

In order to penetrate the mind of the Arab public and examine the factors that impel it to action, it is not enough to investigate their acts and make deductions. Actions are a compromise between impulses and aspirations and, on the other hand, the realities that impose limitations on them. Without understanding the aspirations and wishes which are embodied in the ideology, we shall not properly understand the actions either.

It is true that if circumstances arise which necessitate behaviour incompatible with the ideology, the circumstances will prevail. Lack of ideological consistency will be explained away. People are quite capable of manipulating their ideology if the conditions make it necessary. Reality is more powerful than ideology. On the other hand, the ideology affects the perception of reality.

It should be emphasized that the gap between ideology and reality depends on the reality preventing the realization of the ideology, in this case the liquidation of Israel. The fact that this ideology is not realistic is due, not to its intrinsic character, but to the characteristics of the reality, and an essential factor in this reality is the relative strength of Israel. It follows that the ideology and its practical importance for the objective of liquidation can be evaluated only if we take into account the external factors which prevent its realization. But these factors are not static: fluctuations in their strength and the opponent's acts of omission and commission affect the degree to which this ideology is realistic.

Those who argue that the ideology of the Arabs and the statements of their leaders are mere talk, tactics, and nothing more, and that the gap between what they say and what they do makes their words completely irrelevant, may be reminded that political statements everywhere are characterized by a certain degree of insincerity, cynicism, the use of words for tactical purposes, and semantic manipulation. Since the existence of a certain gap between ideology and action is universal, the difference between various groups lies in the size of the gap. Even among the Arabs, it is not infinite. There is much demagogy among the Arab leaders, but this does not mean that everything they say is demagogy. It is not always easy, it is true, to distinguish between demagogy and self-persuasion, but the difference necessitates a critical approach, and not the wholesale rejection of their statements as meaningless.

4. GEOPOLITICAL AND PSYCHOLOGICAL FACTORS

Professor Jessie Bernard has drawn attention to the prevalent tendency to take an exaggeratedly psychological view of conflicts—as if they existed only in consciousness and feeling and were derived from stereotypes, prejudices, hostilities and fears—and to emphasize the function of irrational factors (see her article in the Singer volume). In the Arab attitude to the conflict there are certainly many psychological aspects, but in addition there is a real issue: the struggle for a territory. The Arab fear of the Israeli threat, as we have already mentioned, was not merely a nightmare; it derived from the success of the Jews in overcoming their difficulties and acquiring most of the territory of Palestine, and from the fear that this was only a beginning, leading to additional gains and territorial expansion.

In this chapter an attempt will be made to go beyond the confines of ideology and attitude, in order to examine which are the factors that sustain them and the conflict itself.

Opinions differ over the importance of the factors that affect the behaviour of nations or, to take a narrower view, which arouse or sustain international conflicts. Some writers tend to emphasize the geopolitical factors and favour the "realistic" view that territory, population or economic resources, as "substantial" factors, constitute the foundation of historical events, including conflicts; the psychological aspects being regarded as only a corollary of these basic factors. Others emphasize the significance of subjective "psychological" factors: national character, historical heritage, ideologies and regimes, arguing that so-called objective factors draw their character and importance from human beings and their modes of thought, for the real problem is the projection of the objective factors in human life. For example, it is argued, there is nothing objective in geography which dictates the existence of a conflict. The geography of France and Britain or France and Germany remains unaltered; all that has changed is the "evaluation" of the geographical facts. Geographical proximity lead to clashes and disputes, but sometimes to cooperation and friendship instead. Against the background of the same geography, the Scandinavian countries have sometimes been rivals and sometimes friends. The factors which influence evaluation, and which on the surface seem to be marginal to the objective factors, are therefore important for the understanding of the position, since they determine the weight which has to be given to the objective factor. Disputes, therefore, depend on the form in which reality is reflected in the ideas of men, or, as the Covenant of UNESCO declared in a famous aphorism: "Wars begin in the minds of men."[11]

This controversy about the place of geopolitical as against psychological factors in history and in disputes may be reflected, for instance, in the way in which the two sides have explained what the Arab-Israel conflict is about and the reasons for its persistence. Among Israelis, the tendency has been to argue that it is not an irreconcilable clash of geopolitical and economic interests, and that Israel's existence does no harm to the Arab States and is no barrier to their development. In particular, they have pointed to the absence of any "real" antagonism between Egypt and Israel. According to the Israeli approach, the Arab talk about the impossibility of compromise or settlement is a flagrant exaggeration. True, Israel interrupts the territorial continuity of the Arab world, but there are states, like Pakistan, which remain viable although their territory is discontinuous—and Israel is prepared to offer transit facilities between Egypt and Jordan. Besides, there are States consisting of islands, which, of course, lack continuous land territories. Nor are Arab fears of Israeli economic domination or competition valid, for in time of peace they could trade as equals. Israelis, therefore, tend to regard the psychological factor as the main one operating among the Arabs: their feeling of hurt pride, the desire for revenge, and the like—and they believe that these factors are ephemeral.

The Arabs, on the other hand, will argue that the psychological aspect, which foreigners, as well as Israelis, regard as a weighty element in their attitude, is not the major factor. Thus, Nasser argued in his letter to Kennedy on August 18, 1961, that the Arab attitude to Israel was not due to an emotionally loaded complex, but to aggression in the past and dangers apparent in the present, which threatened a dark future, imbued with factors of tension and anxiety which might lead to an explosion at any moment. The Palestine problem, he declared, needed no psychological mobilization, since the entire nation lived the problem as an actual fact and not an emotional complex (*al-Ahrām,* September 21, 1962; Speeches in English, 1961, p. 210).

In the same vein, he wrote to the Arab Students' Organization in America:

> "The falsehood of Imperialism and Zionism—which argue that the problem of Palestine is a question of a blow to Arab prestige in the 1948 War—has been exposed." (*Cairo Radio,* June 24, 1964, 13:30 hrs.).

This frequent insistence by the Arabs that the dispute is not based on psychological and emotional factors may be interpreted in two ways. According to the straightforward interpretation, this is a description of the state of affairs as they see it, and their emphasis is meant to refute the opposite view, which they know to be current among foreigners. According to a second, more subtle, view, this insistence points to a suppressed consciousness of the importance of the emotional factor in their attitude. There may be a grain of truth in both interpretations.

Again, the relativity of this confrontation between the two factors is born out by the different approach to the contention that Israel is a danger and a threat to the Arabs. From the Israeli point of view, this is a psychological illusion; for the Arabs, it is a geopolitical and historical fact. Similarly, the Israelis will regard the Arab ideology as a rationalization of the psychological factors, while the Arabs see it as an explanation of the reality.

There are, indeed, grounds for the argument that the Arab emphasis on the conflict as an abstract matter of principle and ideology shows that they feel that the geopolitical aspect is not the main one. The objective observer may also find it difficult to agree with their contention that Israel's existence is a danger to the Arab world, and that coexistence is quite impossible. Again, however, what really counts is not how the position is understood by a foreigner, but how it is understood by the Arabs themselves. An outsider may find it difficult to accept the argument that the dispute is an ideological one: a clash between two national doctrines, as the Arabs describe it. He may admit that Israel's existence may conflict with the conception of Arab grandeur, that the very fact of her establishment is evidence of their weakness, and her continued existence shows their inability to liquidate her. But if Israel obstructs the Arabs' grand design and their ambitions to greatness, which undoubtedly constitute a powerful factor nourished by historical memories and religious claims, this does not mean that the clash is ideological, unless they are making an ideology out of ambition. However, even if this is not an ideological confrontation, the Arabs tend to ideologize it.

The distinction between "objective" geopolitical, tangible factors and "subjective" ideological and emotional ones may be relative. An aspiration for "grandeur" may be regarded as compensation for psychological complexes or megalomania, or it may be presented as a logical geopolitical concept. The same applies to the relation between geopolitical interests and ideological visions. It is often said, for instance, that Russia's historical drive for control of Constantinople and the Straits was due to a real geopolitical interest, but it would be difficult to show that such control was really vital for her survival. It is a fact that Russia continued to exist without achieving this aim, even if it meant some discomfort. Her demand for control of the Straits was not only a vital need; it was derived from her conception of how she ought to live and enhance her security and greatness. States do not merely seek to meet minimal needs for survival, which constitute a geopolitical interest; sometimes, after achieving a certain level of existence and security, they try to raise the level. As Aristotle said, States were created for the sake of life, but they exist for the sake of the good life. Geopolitical interests are influenced by the image of the reality to which States aspire.[12] It is true that this image is not an abstract one, unrelated to the conditions of reality; generally, it depends on the desired reality being regarded as achievable. The horizons of geopolitical interest may expand and contract in accordance with such factors as balance of forces, vitality, demographic pressure, the ambitions of leaders, regimes, ideologies, and so forth.

The same considerations apply here. The liquidation of Israel is not a vital necessity for the Arabs, but their desire to achieve that objective is dictated by their conception of a more perfect national life, for Israel's existence, in their view, is an obstacle to the development of their national identity. So long as they have not lost hope of their capacity to remove this obstacle, they are likely to adhere to their aim.

We can examine this problem of the factors which sustain the Arab attitude against the background of a broader, more general question: what are the factors which motivate nations and impel them to action? In his great book, *Paix et Guerre entre les Nations,* Raymond Aron considers the question of the factors that have impelled States to war and conquest; what lies at the basis of disputes, and what have been the aims of foreign policy. He divides these factors into three groups: a) security, which, in its primary form, means the assurance of survival; b) the quest for power and the expansion of assets; c) the quest for glory. These distinctions may seem to be somewhat ambiguous. The expansion of assets, for example, will usually increase security (though not always—sometimes, indeed, it may have the opposite effect by provoking the enemy) and enhance national glory as well. The distinction between the three factors refers to the dominant motive of a particular operation or plan: the primary goal it is intended to attain.

The three factors certainly exist in the Arab attitude: a) The Arabs declare that Israel is a threat to their security and even to their survival. b) The restoration of Palestine means the enchancement of the assets of Arabism. c) The factor of glory is emphasized in the repeated charge that the establishment and survival of Israel constitute a stain on Arab honour and prestige. The first two factors appear to be more realistic, but it should not be assumed that the third is less capable of motivating attitudes and actions. People have endangered their lives and property for glory; competition for glory has been a major factor in history.

General Ḥasan Muṣṭafā explains this point:

"The Zionist leaders thought in the past that after the establishment of Israel the Arabs would submit to the accomplished fact and would be compelled with the passage of time to acquiesce in its existence among them. But events have shown that they were mistaken. The Arabs regarded the State of Israel as the greatest disaster that has happened to their people. This disaster touched the most vital aspect of their honour and national greatness, and it was one of the major incentives to their resurgence and liberation from imperialism, their revolution against the conditions that reigned in their countries and the deposition of

of Israel becomes a unifying factor. There is undoubtedly some truth in this, but it should be added that their agreement over Israel has been superficial and generally negative, so that the conflict has not made a substantial contribution to unity and cooperation. More decisive have been differences of opinion over problems and interests which they regarded as more concrete and important: the conflict has been of marginal importance in comparison with other matters that preoccupied them. The division of the Arab world into neutralist and Western States, "progressive" or "revolutionary" and "conservative," recent controversies over Yemen and Southern Arabia, were reflected, not so much in emotional attitudes towards Israel, as in their incapacity to agree on joint policies for action against her. Differences of opinion arose both in regard to each important element in the attitude to the conflict and in the operations against Israel. The conflict, thus, not only unites the Arab countries, but also divides them.

There is no doubt that the conflict has been aggravated by Arab divisions, which have led to competition in ostentatious opposition to Israel, at least on the verbal plane. On the other hand, the divisions have led to each country having more than one opponent, and the confrontation with Israel has been diluted by other confrontations. Joint Arab activity against Israel has been entangled in the various and opposed interests of the Arab countries in regard to other matters. We have witnessed the phenomenon of antagonistic collaboration, or the existence of tacit agreement cutting across the formal confrontation between Israel and the opposing Arab coalition. Thus, in many matters one Arab State or another has a joint interest with Israel—which has lessened the possibilities of agreement between them for joint action against her.[14] Leila S. Kadi, whose book *Arab Summit Conferences and the Palestine Problem: 1936-1950, 1964-1966*, is highly critical of the attitude of the Arab States in the conflict, confirms this fact:

> "On the surface, the Arab Governments claim that they are all against Israel, but when it comes to practical decisions, it is difficult to adopt a policy which does not prejudice the narrow interests of one or more of the Arab Governments. Israel ends up by being rarely without the unsolicited support of one Arab Government or another." (p. 193).

The system of inter-Arab relationships is affected by one basic fact: even if they are not all equal, none of them has been strong enough to enforce its views on its rivals; but, on the other hand, even the weakest has been strong enough to hinder, if not to disrupt, any joint Arab action that is opposed to its policy and interests.

Whenever Arab rivalry threatens the position of any particular leader, his main attention will be directed towards the rivalry itself, and the question of Israel is relegated into the background, although his emotional attitude to Israel will remain unchanged. And, since inter-Arab rivalry has been the normal situation, and periods of better relations have been no more than brief truces, the attention of the Arabs has been distracted from their quarrel with Israel for most of the time. Coser quotes (in Proposition 7) Ross, who explains that a society which is ridden by a number of conflicts presents less danger of a violent outbreak than if it were torn by a single conflict. Thus, the rifts among the Arab States arising out of the Arab-Israel conflict in various directions have had a moderating influence on the Arab-Israeli confrontation.

The threat which many of the Arab States pose to each other is concrete and short-term, while the threat posed by Israel, though their emphasis on it has been no mere pretence, has been mainly abstract. It is hard to believe that the Egyptians were really afraid (before the Six-Day War) of Israeli expansion across the Suez Canal. The more distant Arab countries were certainly not troubled by nightmares of Israeli expansion. It was only for Jordan that the threat was more substantial.

The effects of the divisions in the Arab world on the conflict have therefore been mixed: on the one hand, they have exacerbated the attitude; on the other, they have made it more moderate in practice; their divisions have made war more difficult, but—and this is another paradoxical aspect of the conflict—they have also made it harder to arrive at a peace settlement.

The exploitation of the conflict within the framework of inter-Arab rivalry by one factor—in this case the UAR—against the others has begun to make it a nuisance to some of the other countries against whom it has been used. It is no accident that it was Bourguiba, Nasser's rival, who called for a settlement.

The Arab attitude has also been influenced by factors outside the framework of the Arab-Israel confrontation, i.e. by the international set-up and the cold war. In the competition between the Powers, the USSR has won a foothold and influence in the Middle East by establishing relations with most of the Arab countries. Her military aid to many of them and support for the Arab attitude against Israel, even if she has not gone so far as to back the objective of liquidation, have been important factors in providing a substantial basis for their hopes of victory. They have been liable to interpret Soviet support and opposition to Israel not as matters of policy and transitory interest, but as recognition of the justice of their attitude and even of support for their ideas. It is not without reason that they recall that in 1903 Lenin prevented recognition of the Bund Jewish Socialist Party as a nationally representative movement. The Communist and Soviet opposition to Zionism has been consistent, except for a brief period in which Russia supported the 1947 partition decision and recognized Israel on her establishment—an episode which the Arabs can now regard as a thing of the past. The Arab Left can find support for the notion of ideological kinship in the anti-Jewish statements of Marx and Engels. China's agreement to the proposition that Israel is a manifestation of colonialist-imperialist remains, as well as her support for the Palestine Liberation Organization, have also encouraged extremism. The Arabs feel that they are not isolated, but are backed by powerful world forces.

Even if the West has support Israel, its support has been limited and often partial. Its readiness to help Israel has been weaker than the Soviet Union's willingness to work for the Arabs. It has indeed sold Israel arms, but generally with limitations and with apologies to the Arabs, while the USSR has sent the latter generous shipments of weapons. The West's support for Israel, Bahā' al-Dīn explains, is like the support of a father for his bastard son. The Arabs regard Israel's ties with the West as a plot against them, but their view of imperialism as an immoral and treacherous factor leaves room for the hope that in time of trial it will abandon Israel to her fate.

The Arab attitude has an independent character of its own and is not a result of the cold war. It was not the cold war that produced the conflict, and it is not the reason for the Arab attitude, but it has facilitated its persistence and increased its intensity.

a) THE UNITED ARAB REPUBLIC

It could be argued that there is no substantial clash of interests between Egypt and Israel, and that it should therefore have been easy for the Egyptians to agree to a peace settlement, especially as there is a desert between the two countries. But Egypt may regard the existence of Israel as a barrier to her greatness and an obstacle to the mission her leaders have undertaken for the unification of the Arab world. Moreover, since she is overpopulated, while her resources and living room are limited and she must expand her industry, she needs the other Arab countries as markets and sources of income. For Egypt, Arab unity is not only a matter of nationalism and ideology, but also of economic interest, while Israel is like a wedge separating her from the eastern Arab States. The antagonism between the two countries is, therefore, a geopolitical one. Haykal explains:

> "The Egyptian people will not allow an artificial barrier to sever the land link between it and the other countries of the Arab Middle East, especially a foreign and hostile barrier." (June 12, 1964).

Nasser declared:

> "Israel wanted to finally establish the geographical isolation of Egypt from the Arab world." (At Port Said, December 23, 1966).

Such an antagonism did not exist for the "Fiiaraonic," particularist Egypt, whose nationalism was opposed to pan-Arabism and which, therefore, did not show much interest in the Palestine struggle. Egypt's interest, therefore, depends on her general political conceptions. It is no accident that in the same article in which Prince Ḥalīm 'Abbās called for peace with Israel, he spoke of the unity of the Nile Valley, including Sudan, as Egypt's major interest (*Le Messager,* March 18, 1952).

When the Sudanese rejected unity with Egypt, and Egypt leaned toward Arab unity, especially with the Arab countries in Asia, the position was basically transformed.[15] The breakup of the UAR brought out the importance of territorial continuity, for had it not been for Israel Nasser would have been able to despatch his forces to Syria and enforce unity. It is a paradox of history that Israel turned out to be a protection for the eastern Arab countries from imposed unity with Egypt. Historically, there is nothing new about the idea of the conquest of these countries by Egypt. Muhammad Ali's campaigns are not a matter of the distant past.

While Egypt was consolidated as a separate country in the course of many generations, and its population has an Egyptian national consciousness, Syria, Jordan and, to some extent, Iraq as well have no historical distinctiveness or fully formed separate nationalisms, and their consciousness is Arab. Ordinary Egyptians still call themselves Egyptians first and Arabs only afterwards, but the Syrians, Jordanians and Iraqis regard themselves first and foremost as Arabs. In Egypt, interest in Arab unity has been confined mainly to the upper political echelons and has not been a matter of private, personal experience. This fact has an important influence upon the attitude of the people to the conflict, affecting its "non-saliency," which has already been mentioned. Hence, there is some truth in statements that the conflict is not a quarrel between the Egyptian people and Israel. But even if unity, as an interest and an ideology, is still on the political level, a beginning has already been made with the process of bringing it down to the level of popular feeling and understanding, since the educational and propaganda systems have been harnessed to the task. Even if the conflict is not salient in the country's internal life, Nasser frequently explains that a particular measure is required for the war with Israel. He repeatedly declared, for example (e.g. on November 23, 1962), that "the liberation of Yemen is a step towards getting rid of Zionism." This implies that the watchword of getting rid of Zionism may not have been without influence by that time.

Furthermore, the shame of the 1948 defeat may be more serious for Egypt, as the leading Arab country, than for the others, even though she did not have many casualties (a little more than a thousand killed—see my article "On the Arab Losses in 1948," *Maarachot,* No. 166, March 1965; on the other hand, Egyptian losses in the Six-Day War were twelve times as great, according to Nasser's own admission).

Since Nasser, as the country's central personality, has left his impression on its history for a decade and a half, it is important to examine his approach to the conflict. It may be assumed that, in addition to the geopolitical and ideological interest, he also has an emotional approach to the question. The moderation which he has sometimes adopted does not indicate indifference. He himself testifies on the subject in his early work *The Philosophy of the Revolution,* in which he describes his feelings as a youth during the demonstrations on November 2, the anniversary of the Balfour Declaration, and he repeatedly returns to the Palestine problem. His view that the conflict with Israel would be a prolonged one was expressed in his introduction to *This is Zionism,* which appeared in 1954 as the first in the "Chosen For You" indoctrination series issued by the Officers' Regime:

> "The struggle between ourselves and Zionism has not yet been finished; even more, it may not yet have started. We and Zionism have a near tomorrow and a distant tomorrow in which we shall wash away shame, achieve our aspirations and restore our rights." (p. 8).

Even though his references to Israel were generally brief, and he refrained from invectives, a listener to his speeches would gain the impression that he was imbued with a cold hatred. His view of Israel as part of imperialism and one of the factors obstructing Egypt's progress is not simulated, and no doubt grew in intensity after the events of 1956 and, even more, after the defeat of 1967.

The conflict has been frequently used by Egypt in her inter-Arab and even international relations. Her spokesmen have emphasized that she alone can fight Israel, as is shown by the fact that Israel has concentrated her efforts against her as the major enemy—which has been used to back her claim to leadership in the Arab world. She has also used the conflict and the activities connected with it as a means of subversion against her Arab rivals.

b) JORDAN

Jordan's connection with the conflict is more complex than that of any other Arab country, and may be assumed to involve the broadest spectrum of opinion—from extremism to moderation—both in the ruling circles and in various parts of the population. She is also the closest of all the Arab countries to the conflict and more deeply affected by it. The chapter on "Jordan and the Palestine Problem" in the Jordanian White Paper begins as follows:

> "The problem of Palestine is a problem for all the Arabs, both peoples and individuals, but in the Hashemite Kingdom it is the problem of the Jordanian homeland and the Jordanian family and the Jordanian citizen." (p. 28).

Jordan's future is more closely involved with developments in the conflict than that of any other Arab country. The booklet continues:

> "Palestine for the Jordanian Hashemite Kingdom, is, therefore, not merely a political problem; it is not only a question of principles, values and rights, but it is a problem that fills the soul of the Arab citizen of Jordan, arouses his emotions, occupies his thoughts and guides his actions." (p. 29).

For Jordanians the conflict is more "salient" and "central" in everyday life. There are two reasons for this: geographical, since Jordan and Israel were one country at the beginning of the Mandate, and demographic: the large proportion of Palestinians in the Jordanian population. Geographical contiguity can and does operate in two opposite directions: it produces acute rivalry, and at the same time calls for cooperation. Jordan's contiguity to Israel and the length of the borders between them arouse the suspicion that Israeli expansion is likely to be at her expense. On the other hand, it may be assumed that, if the conflict had not taken the form of an all-Arab confrontation, a settlement with Jordan would have been much easier to achieve. Her weakness and the dynasty's concern for its future would have encouraged the quest for a solution. The late King Abdallah, who was mainly interested in the Jordanian framework and had little faith in the Arab League, visualized the possibility of a settlement, if only as a transitory stage, from which his country would have derived economic benefit as well (e.g. by facilities in Haifa Port). In fact, the only negotiations for a settlement between Israel and an Arab ruler have been those with Abdallah.[16]

There are undoubtedly circles in Jordan that realize in the depths of their hearts that Israel is not only an enemy but also a screen against Egyptian domination. Although they are Arab nationalists and believe in Arab unity, they also believe in independence as an ideal and an interest of the regime, and their concept of unity is different from Egypt's. They have no reserves as to the basic Arab attitude towards Israel, but they also want to preserve Jordan's integrity and monarchical regime. They would like Jordan to swallow up Palestine if only that were possible, but the Palestinian nationalists hope that Palestine will swallow Jordan. In this way they are on the same side as Jordan's rivals. The antagonism is categorical. For some of the population of Jordan, the very existence of the conflict casts doubt on the distinctiveness of Jordan, while the spokesmen of the regime, headed by the King, use the conflict as a means for the creation of this distinctiveness, exploiting it and the threat from Israel to mobilize popular support and establish national unity. The conflict also serves to present Jordan as a country with a national mission, as a bastion against the State of Israel and a potential base of operations by other Arabs against her.

Jordan's special conditions affect her policy in day-to-day affairs. The monarchical regime and the country's ties with and dependence on the West have created differences with Egypt, Iraq and Syria; she has been unable to follow their lead in foreign affairs, including their policy in the conflict. The fact that she has had a closer and more extensive experience of the conflict than the other Arab countries leads to a better knowledge of it, and the lesson of the extreme Arab attitudes in Mandatory days, which have been disastrous for the Arabs, may also have influenced her in the direction of moderation.

c) SYRIA

In Syria's deep interest in the conflict the ideological factor undoubtedly plays a prominent role. Syria is the cradle of Arab nationalism, the centre of the Ba'th, the Arab nationalist party which pioneered in pan-Arab nationalist ideology, and a source of radical nationalist and social attitudes. Arab consciousness is strong in Syria, where the Arab-Israel conflict exists on a popular level. She was active on the inter-Arab scene in support of the Palestinians even in Mandatory days. Her ties with Palestine are a matter of history, for Palestine was a part of Syria under Ottoman rule. It is difficult to estimate the force of this historical memory in Syrian consciousness today and the extent to which it is a stimulus, but it may be noted that Anṭūn Sa'da's antagonism to Zionism was based on this aspect of the question (*Al-Za'īm fī Marāḥil al-Mas'ala al-Filasṭīniyya,* Beirut, 1949).

Syria was the centre for the organization of volunteers against the Jews in 1948 and the base for Qāwuqjī's "Liberation Army." It may be noted that Syria was perhaps the only Arab country to recognize such volunteer service in calculating army seniority, as well as the first in which the defeat led to the collapse of the regime.

Syria's attitude in the conflict has also been influenced by the fact that her internal character has not yet solidified; there have been discussions, intrigues and schemes for mergers with Iraq, Jordan or Egypt, both in internal controversies and in competition between Arab States. At the same time, this instability contributed to her involvement in the conflict.

Under the regimes which were interested in the consolidation of the country as an independent unit or in unification with Iraq (Ḥusnī al-Za'īm's rule and part of Shishaklī's), anti-Israel tension abated, but whenever there was a plan for unity with Egypt Israel was regarded as an obstacle and a barrier.

The existence of Israel has not affected everyday life and economic activity in Syria, but the question of water resources and the fear of Israeli expansion have had their effects. It should be remembered that because of the water problem the Syrians did not accept the Mandatory frontier as delimited after World War I. The country's internal instability, as expressed in the numerous revolts and coups, has no doubt aroused fear as to her capacity to confront Israel.

An additional source of tension was the constant disputes and incidents in connection with the demilitarized zones, which added fuel to the flames.

The majority of these areas were not occupied by the Israeli forces in the 1948 war but were evacuated under the Armistice Agreement, and Syria did not recognize Israeli sovereignty over them.

Recent clashes between radical tendencies in Syria have also been reflected in extreme hostility towards Israel. Since the conflict has existed on the popular plane, a stronger obligation to act has been felt, frustration and shame at the absence of achievement have been more intense, and these, in turn, have strengthened the trend to radicalization.

d) LEBANON

Lebanon's association with the conflict reflects the complex and paradoxical character of the country. She is international in contacts and commerce, a crossroads and a Middle East centre for international agencies and commercial companies, so that she must maintain good relations both with her neighbours and with the West. Her political structure, founded on inter-communal equilibrium, makes her sensitive to any change or upset, in case the balance, on which her existence as a State depends, is disturbed. It may be assumed that this fear has intensified in recent years, especially among the Maronite Christians, since the equilibrium has been weakened.

Lebanon's approach to the conflict is complicated by her communal structure. The Muslims are influenced in this respect by their co-religionists in other Arab countries, but they are alive to Lebanon's special character, which is the source of her wealth, and since they are interested in this prosperity continuing, many of them support her special character.

The Christians may recognize in their hearts the kinship between the Jewish island and the Christian island in the Muslim ocean, and they are concerned at the possibility of being swamped by the flood of Muslim Arab nationalism, but they consider that the way to ensure their separate survival is to cooperate with Arab nationalism in order to blunt the impact of pan-Arab feeling. However, they are not by any means uniform. The Greek-Orthodox, who have no centre of their own and are scattered throughout the Arab countries, are more closely integrated with Arab nationalism and have adopted its approach. The Maronites, who have a centre, show a more moderate attitude to Israel. It may be assumed that Christian Lebanon would have been ready to acquiesce in the existence of a Jewish State, if only to get rid of the refugee population, which endangers the communal balance.

On the other hand, Elias Koussa may have been right when he said in 1963:

> "Israel asserts that Lebanon wants, or is capable of wanting, to make peace with Israel. I say: No! The prosperity, wealth and success that reign in Lebanon today are the outcome of the present state of war between the Arab countries and Israel. For had it not been for this state of war, most of the money that flows from Saudi Arabia, Kuweit and Iraq to Lebanon would flow to Israel, to Tel Aviv and Haifa and Jerusalem. Lebanon, therefore, has the strongest motives for opposing the signature of a peace treaty with Israel." (Minutes of the *New Outlook* International Symposium, Hebrew, p. 47).

It is doubtful whether there would be much danger of Arab money flowing to Israel, but in general the conception appears to be correct. As Professor A. J. Mayer, of Harvard University, put it, "Lebanon thrives on disaster": whenever there is unrest, nationalization or revolt in the Arab countries, capital is smuggled into Lebanon. She also benefits from the isolation of Haifa port from its Arab hinterland, for imports to Jordan pass through her territory, and she has profited by the United Nations maintaining the Middle East headquarters of its agencies in Beirut. There is no doubt that Lebanon regards Israel as a potential economic competitor, and if she has no interest in the liquidation of Israel, she is interested in the continuation of the Arab-Israel dispute, so long as it does not erupt into acts of hostility or outbreaks that will shake the stability of the Middle East: she finds the dispute quite useful so long as it remains quiescent.

Lebanon's specific problems are reflected in the details of her approach to the conflict. On the one hand, her international ties make it difficult for her to comply with the rulings of the Arab boycott. She is interested in contacts with the European market, and has reservations about an Arab Common Market. On the other hand, her special character makes her sensitive to the possibility of arousing the suspicion that she is not truly devoted to the Arab attitude; hence, she sometimes displays ostentatious hostility to Israel.

Because of her Western character and her interest in the maintenance of close ties with the West, Lebanon is interested in the latter not spoiling its relations with the Middle East because of its ties with Israel. A pro-Israel attitude by the West may make it more difficult for Lebanon to remain pro-Western; hence she has an interest in the West being anti-Israel, and her representatives often take the lead in denouncing Israel to the West, their education and Western culture enabling them to be more successful than other Arabs in winning the attention of the public there. Lebanon also has contacts with her emigré communities overseas, which can be exploited as a local anti-Israel factor.

Lebanon is not interested in provoking Israel. Her policy is hostility without risks. For two decades, Israel's border with Lebanon was the quietest of them all, and the proceedings of the Israel-Lebanon Mixed Armistice Commission were comparatively regular and effective.

e) INTERACTION OF FACTORS

The "Arab attitude" in the collective sense is the sum of the attitudes of the individuals who constitute the Arab public and those of the units into which it is divided. At first glance, it may seem to exist only in the abstract, as a generalization, but from the point of view of the confrontation between the parties it is the collective attitude that is real, and not the attitudes of private citizens, especially as these are determined by their group affiliations. The "Arab attitude" is a social and political concept, and it is therefore important mainly as the attitude of the Arab States, as expressed by their Governments, for there is a mutual relationship between the "political attitude" and the "public attitude," and it may be assumed that it is the former which is generally decisive, since the political leadership influences the public attitude, though it is also influenced by it. The importance of the public attitude lies in its not being entirely dependent on the Government or the ruler, so that it may make for continuity.

The factors that sustain the Arab attitude are the totality of the factors which are operative among the Arabs in their consciousness and their emotions: ideological factors, feelings and experiences, considerations of interest, geopolitics, and political conceptions—some of them specific to particular Arab countries and some common to all; some are even due to lack of cooperation: namely, the rivalries between the Arab States; some belong to foreign policy and others to internal policy. It is difficult to establish the specific importance of each of these components; the Arab attitude is influenced by the totality of them.

Since this work is concerned with explaining the Arab attitude, it necessarily emphasizes the ideological factor, which is the explanation of the attitude which the Arabs give to themselves, but there is no clear-cut boundary between the ideological factor, which is regarded as subjective, and that of interest, which is considered objective. The ideology can be a sublimation of an emotional impulse and also of interests; while interests, by assuming the cloak of ideology, assume greater force.

5. THE NATURE OF THE ARAB ATTITUDE

a) THE FORMATION OF THE ARAB ATTITUDE

The Arab attitude came into being as a reaction to certain events: Jewish immigration, the War of Independence and the transformation of part of Palestine into a Jewish State. From this point of view, the attitude constitutes the opposition of a national group to the taking of its territory. These events created emotional experiences, particularly since the problem of the refugees and the demand for the "restoration of their rights" arose as a result of the 1948 war.

During the first period after the defeat of 1948, the leitmotif in the Arab attitude was psychological; it was manifested in numerous expressions of affront and the demand for revenge. There were many references to disgrace and humiliation, testifying to the depth of the wound inflicted on the Arabs. With the passage of time, the psychological motivation became less salient, though it undoubtedly persists, and the Arab attitude in the conflict took on the character of an ideological system. It may be assumed that it is harder to maintain an attitude in a conflict by harping on psychological motives, which are particularly apt to fade in intensity; while, when the conflict becomes ideological, and arguments and ideas are put forward in its support, it is institutionalized and becomes more rigid, persistent and stable. This distinction underlies Haykal's injunction that hatred of the United States "ought to become scientific and not just an emotional hatred, for the latter is liable to fade away of itself" (*al-Ahrām,* November 10, 1967).

Direct experience is replaced by ideological indoctrination, which also makes it possible to teach the components of the attitude and hand it down to the next generation, as well as to disseminate it all over the Arab world. Considerable effort has been dedicated to the elaboration of the ideology, not because the Arabs have a consuming appetite for this kind of pursuit, but because they need the ideology in the conflict. It both reflects the attitude and completes it. At the same time, the ideology affects the character of the attitude, which becomes less spontaneous and more deliberate and fanatical, not so much a matter of frenzy as a cold, implacable hatred, endowing it with greater intellectual depth and emotional intensity. The contention that the establishment of Israel was an injustice, and that her survival is therefore unjust, deepens the sense of wrong by making the emotion into a doctrine. The emotional trauma resulting from the experience of defeat provided the impulse for the ideology, but today it is the ideology that creates the emotion.

In some sections of the Arab world, the attitude is also intensified, both intellectually and emotionally, by emphasizing the idea that the establishment of Israel was a manifestation of colonialism, exploiting Arab weakness and inferiority. On the one hand, this idea is offensive, but on the other, it arouses indignation against racialist foreigners and gives the attitude a significance within the framework of world trends towards the liberation of colonial peoples as the Messianic idea of the mid-twentieth century.

b) DIFFERENT STRATA IN THE ARAB ATTITUDE

We have found a considerable measure of consensus between Arab statements on Israel, so that they can be combined to form an ideological structure with a high degree of inner consistency. But there is another feature which is, perhaps, even more important: beneath the pragmatic political attitude, which demands the rectification of the injustice, we can find various strata of political, historical and cultural arguments, which complement it and give it fuller significance and, as it were, a dimension of depth. The Arab attitude is, therefore, built in tiers. The demand for justice to the Palestinians is complemented by a political argument that Zionism is a manifestation of greed and colonialism, and that Israel is an imperialistic base. The charge that Zionism is a racialist movement, prepared to sacrifice Arab for Jewish welfare, can be connected up historically with the conquest of Canaan after the Exodus, while an analogy may be drawn between the permission granted to the Israelites to attack the Canaanites, who had done them no wrong, with the right assumed by the Zionists to settle in Palestine at the expense of the Arabs, who had never persecuted the Jews. The Israelis are accused of doing the same to the Arabs as their forefathers did to the peoples of Canaan. The charge of selfishness levelled against Jewry leads directly to the denigration of Zionism: its cultural and theological expression is the Chosen People idea. The emphasis on the alleged Jewish claim to a monopoly of God creates an association with the monopolistic element in imperialism—and again the circle is closed. The bond between Israel and imperialism is not accidental, but historical and cultural. The antagonism between Arab nationalism and Zionism is presented as not merely a clash between a natural and an artificial nationalism, but as parallel to the antagonism between Islam's universalism, broad outlook and tolerance and its teachings on the equality of man, and the narrow, particularistic, tribal, jealous and selfish attitude of Judaism. Denunciations of Jews and Judaism, even if influenced by Western anti-Semitic literature, contain Islamic elements, the seeds of which are to be found in the Quran.

For the Leftist version of the Arab attitude, the Jewish character is an embodiment of capitalism. Zionism is the agent of colonialism, and Israel the creature of imperialism. Israel embodies capitalism and its developed stage, imperialism, so that hatred and condemnation of both are combined and strengthened. Zionism and Israel are presented as antagonistic to the march of history; therefore, they are evil and condemned to extinction. The peculiar circumstances of Israel, as a State which should never have existed, its artificiality, and the way in which it was established, create insuperable contradictions which will lead to its fall, while the individual Israeli and Jew is characterized by a combination of inner complications and contradictions which will give him no rest. In addition to the complexes of the Jews, which follow from the depravity of the Jewish spirit, the Israeli suffers from complexes produced by his aggression and the displacement of the Arabs in the course of Israel's establishment. The contradictions of Israel and the complexes produced by his aggression and the displacement of the Arabs in the course of Israel's establishment. The contradictions of Israel and the complexes of the Jew can be resolved by the ending of their existence. As there is no room for Israel in the world, so there is no room for the Jews as bearers of Judaism, and they ought to assimilate. The preservation of their religion is the preservation of their depravity. Their failure to assimilate is presented as something evil: racialism, isolationism, arrogance and intrigue. Hence, there are two opposed and incompatible possibilites: either the Jews will disappear or they will dominate the world. These possibilities are also reflected on a smaller scale in regard to Israel: either she will be liquidated or she will dominate the Middle East.

There is no need for all these conceptual elements to be present in the attitude of any particular leader or ideologist. Everyone can choose such parts of the outlook as suit himself and his character, and there is no need for him to be aware of all its details. He can begin with part of the system and halt of his own accord, without going into all its branches and ramifications. There is no need to be absolutely exhaustive in adopting every detail of the outlook, even if such a lack of thoroughness seems lack of consistency.

It is possible to separate the main ideas that have appeared in the Arab attitude into strata, and examine the place in these strata of several leaders and authors whose statements have been surveyed in this work.

a) Political Depravity, the Pragmatic Approach

Israel was established by aggression and the expropriation of the Palestinians. Non-repatriation of the Palestinians means the perpetuation of the wrong done to them. Justice must be done to them and their "rights" restored, even if this means that Israel must disappear. The Arab world will insist on this. Israel is aggressive, and her existence involves dangers to other parts of the Arab world. The Arabs have no antagonism towards Judaism as a faith, or even to the Jews; they only oppose their help to Israel, the agent of imperialism.

These points are to be found in the usual, official political attitude which is expressed by Arab leaders like Nasser, Hussein and others.

b) The Depravity of Zionism—The Ideological Approach

The establishment of Israel by aggression is not a matter of chance; it reflects the nature of Zionism, which concentrates on its own advantage and, therefore, does not hesitate to attack the rights and welfare of others. Zionism is racialist and colonialist—which is reflected in the fact that Israel was established in order to serve imperialist interests, and the Balfour Declaration was issued for that purpose. Israel's ties with the imperialist States which back her are fundamental: the danger of Israeli expansion is due to Israel's Zionist-imperialist greed. Since she is a manifestation of colonialism, her liquidation is equivalent to the "national liberation" of the Palestinians. This attitude is frequently repeated by Sayegh, Sa‘ab, Khālidī, Shukairy and the Arab Left—‘Alūsh.

c) Historical Depravity—The Ethnic Approach

The various features of Zionist depravity are not accidental manifestations of a single act. The Jews are selfish and have always put their own interests first, coveted others' land, and expropriated the Canaanite Arabs, like the Palestinian Arabs. History repeats itself: everywhere they are hated aliens.

The depravity of Zionism and Israel is a historical characteristic.

This concept is favoured by Dr. Naṣr, Aḥmad, Nashāshībī and Sharāra.

d) Cultural and Religious Depravity

Zionism is not a foreign growth in Judaism, but an essential part of it. Zionism is typically Jewish, and Judaism is Zionist. Jewish and Zionist selfishness is derived from a spiritual and theological characteristic of Judaism as a manifestation of the spirit and faith of the Jews, which is expressed in their attitude to the Deity and to the world. Their claim to be the sole sons of God implies the denial of sonship to the rest of humanity, like their denial of the heritage to Ishmael and Esau, and implies the right to inflict any evil on others. This greed and monopolization of the Deity are incompatible with the idea of monotheism, the universality of God and the brotherhood of man. The basis of the depravity, is, therefore, cultural. The scope of the struggle is extended: if the depravity is not only historical, but cultural and religious, then not only Israel, but Judaism as well, must disappear.

These are the concepts of 'Aqqād, Tall, 'Alūba, Darwaza, Wākid, Faruki, Ṭabbāra, Ramāmī and Zu'bī.

In the descriptions of this ecology of opinions, it should be noted that the demarcation lines between the various strata are by no means as sharp as they are schematically presented here. The strata are not sectionalized, and the attribution of an individual to any particular stratum is not exclusive. Since the lower strata provide depth, significance and support for the attitudes expressed in the higher ones, each of those mentioned sometimes draws ideas from the strata below.[17] It may be assumed that, even if the political leadership is generally content to rely on the argumentation of the upper, political and pragmatic stratum, it is familiar with the ideas of the other strata and makes use of them. The views and ideas mentioned by the political leaders are only the top of the iceberg; they are supported by the ideological mass below, which complements them and helps to sustain the emotional attitude towards Israel.

c) AGREEMENT ON THE OBJECTIVE, DIFFERENCES ON METHODS

On the goal, that Israel ought not to exist, there is a large measure of agreement. The belief that Israel was established by aggression and usurpation of Arab territory may be said, according to the evidence at our disposal, to be current among the Arabs, at least among those who write or speak in public.

At the present stage of the conflict, we cannot find any statement by any important circle acquiescing in the existence of Israel as she is.[18] If there is any talk of acquiescence, it is with a truncated and fragmented Israel, whose capacity to survive would be problematical. As we have noted, there may be Arab circles who think differently and are prepared to accept Israel's existence, but do not dare express their views; even the majority of Arab Communists have adopted the Arab nationalist attitude to Israel. But feelings and concealed opinions are not political facts, and cannot be examined without occult powers to penetrate into the secret places of the heart and discover the existence of undercover groups with a favourable attitude to Israel.

There is a break in the homogeneity of the Arab attitude when it comes to a plan of operations, which is a matter of controversy because of differences of opinion and interests.* The aspiration to liquidate Israel is not a blind craze, but takes the realities into account. The confrontation between goal and reality leads to a complex of problems about the possibility of action, which arouse doubt and uncertainty about the practicability of the aim. These problems have a feed-back effect on the goal, leading to the postponement of action and radicalization of the attitude.

d) THE GOAL AND THE PLAN

Israel's survival and consolidation over two decades appear to be incompatible with her liquidation and intensify the problem of how the objective is to be achieved. Thus, the more the conflict continues and Israel stabilizes her position, the more urgent becomes the need for a reply to the question of the plan. As this plan involves a complex series of difficulties, every group concerned with the conflict, when it realizes that the accepted solutions are not practicable, places its trust in a different solution, without realizing that its own answer is not free from doubts and difficulties either. This is a recurrent phenomenon.

* Problems of the Arab programme, as it took shape up to the Six-Day War, are considered in a manuscript work of mine. Here the question is summed up under main headings.

Those who are alive to the difficulty of liquidating Israel by war cling to the possibility of achieving the aim by peaceful means: through the Arab boycott and blockade, as a result of internal collapse, or by an international effort to send back the Jews to the countries from which they came. This point of view, it may be assumed, is becoming rarer.

Others, who have despaired of liquidation by peaceful means, emphasize that war is inevitable and that Israel will be destroyed by violence. "The robbery of Palestine," Shukairy declared shortly before the Six-Day War, "will be annulled only by war" (Palestine Liberation Organization radio, February 2, 1967, 07:30 hrs.). How is this to come about? Since the power of one Arab State is not sufficient, it becomes necessary to combine their efforts. The aspiration for Arab unity is not predicated on the requirements of the Arabs in the conflict. But the road to unity is full of pitfalls, and although everyone proclaims the idea, there is nothing that divides the Arab world so much as the effort to achieve it. It would appear that, in order to increase their power and influence, the Arab States ought to combine and cooperate, in the hope that cooperation, which is tantamount to a partial, functional unity, would bring them closer together and lead to the creation of a supra-national Arab union. But the actual result of inter-Arab rapprochement and solidarity is to confirm the divisions. Furthermore, cooperation arouses internal dissensions and further splits. If a "core country" (to use the term employed by political scientists like Karl Deutsch and Ernest Hass) is necessary to provide the leadership for the union, the dialectical result is that the other States do not wish to be led and denounce the leader. "Independence" and "unity" are popular ideas, but they are not compatible, as Syria found out when she united with Egypt. The UAR, as the leading Arab State, regards unity as its mission, and when it despaired of creating unity by inter-governmental agreement, it tried to bring it about by appealing to the peoples over the heads of their rulers. In self-defence, these rulers regard greater closeness with Egypt as a danger to themselves, and dissensions grow. Thus Arab unity involves a series of self-frustrating antinomies.[19] This, of course, has a direct effect on Arab operations against Israel; the problem of the programme is complicated by the tangle of inter-Arab relations.

The initiation of war by means of a rational decision necessitates confidence in its results, which will depend on preparedness and superiority in strength. Since such preparedness covers many spheres—military, economic, social and political—it will call for a great deal of time; hence, the need for postponement until it is achieved.[20] But postponement, although it may be regarded as a practical policy, may lead to further postponements, so that it becomes institutionalized and the goal becomes nonoperative, as a mere aspiration, postponed to the Greek kalends. The eschatologization of the achievement of the goal means the ritualization of the goal itself.

Those who are in a hurry, because they understand the significance of postponement until full preparedness is achieved and unity established, turn to the idea of guerrilla warfare in the immediate future and pin their hopes to the example of Algeria. Here again, however, when they or others examine the idea, they realize that Algeria is not the same as Israel. There, the people fought inside their own country, while the majority of the Palestinians are outside Israel and the territory she holds, necessitating a violent penetration by a fighting people into its Promised Land. Such an invasion, however, is an act of war, which can be carried out only by armies—bringing them back to the need for a war to be waged by Arab armed forces, which depends on military preparedness, which has not yet been achieved.

Since warfare on the Algerian model is not a practical possibility, the Arabs cherish abstract notions of "a war of national liberation" as an expression of the popular will latent in the Arab masses, a will which is believed to be irresistible. But in order that this will may be realized, the "reactionary" regimes and rulers, which prevent the establishment of popular regimes, must first be swept away. Thus the longing for a magic formula which will bring down the walls of Israel does not shorten the road, but lengthens it, by postulating the need for internal revolutionary changes of regime, especially in Jordan. These regimes fight back; in the actual confrontation they are by no means powerless, or short of arguments in the controversies of inter-Arab rivalry, and they are supported by certain interests among their own people, while the internal situation is quite unsatisfactory in the States known as "progressive."

Events in the sphere of the conflict have been determined and influenced more by inter-Arab relations and their vicissitudes than by the confrontation between the Arab States and Israel. Paradoxically, the problem of the programme of the Arab States against Israel is mainly an inter-Arab problem, and only secondarily an Arab-Israeli one.

Just as the ideology of the conflict has led to a hardening of the Arab attitude, so the problems involved in the programme have led to a process of radicalization. The plan of action against Israel, which was presented as an operation by States, has become an ideal centering on the activities of "fedayeenism" (self-sacrifice) and "pioneers of war," and such ideas as "mobilization of the popular will," "popular war" and "the revolutionary spirit." This radicalization has pushed even circles with more traditional inclinations into approval for such notions. Inter-Arab competition, while diminishing preparedness as a whole, has worked in favour of radicalization. This trend suffers from the limitation that it does not enjoy unanimous support, since it is also directed against several of the Arab regimes, which call a halt from time to time and try to resist and frustrate it.

On the one hand, this development and the rise of the "popular war" idea are due to the exhaustion of the conventional recipes, which have not led to the achievement of the goal. On the other hand, it may be assumed that they are an expression of the present-day climate and the ideas current in China and Vietnam about the latent powers of the masses, which, it is believed, can overcome any technological advantage. It is not a matter of copying the doctrine of Mao Tse Tung; the influence comes from the circumstances.

The Palestinians' despair of action by the Arab States has led them to combine in underground organizations for the main purpose of striking at Israel. In earlier periods, most of the infiltration was motivated by economic drives, but today it is entirely violent in character, aiming at injury and sabotage. Violation of frontiers is a vent for hostility and vengefulness and a means for drawing the Arab States into operations against Israel. Although troublesome, they cannot undermine Israel's existence.

In the meantime (until the Six-Day War), the struggle against Israel was constantly being postponed. This postponement might be regarded as a kind of scaffolding to protect the faith that one day, after all, the aim would be achieved, even if the reality was not promising for the present and the forseeable future; it meant escaping to the future from the disappointing present.

The refutation of ideology by reality does not necessarily lead to acquiescence in the reality, but sometimes even to extremism and fanaticism (see Festinger et al., *When Prophecy Fails*), either as a demonstrative defiance of the frustrating reality, or as self-intoxication in defence against it.

There are grounds for the assumption that, parallel with and as a reaction against radicalization, there has also developed some acquiescence in Israel's existence, even if only in despair and in the absence of any alternative; while, conversely, radicalization has been to some extent a reaction against readiness to accept Israel. This acquiescence, it should be noted, is rather an assumption on the basis of analysis than a fact supported by evidence.

These trends undoubtedly affect the Arab devotion to the objective—which indicates not self-confidence, but, on the contrary, scepticism—, leading to inner debate, doubts as to its practicality, ambiguous statements, and even first indications of despair at the possibility of liquidating Israel and a measure of acquiescence in her existence. Nevertheless, even if the reality prevents the achievement of the objective, it can still be cherished by virtue of the faith that the Arabs will overcome in the end by reason of their numerical advantage, the confidence created by their faith in the justice of their claim, and the inspiration of the belief that, in the long run, God, or history, is on their side.

There is an antipodal difference between acquiescence in Israel's existence due to considerations of principle, including those of international morality, which implies a frontal rejection of the Arab ideology, and doubts and perplexities as to the practicality of the aim. The doubts of the Arabs do not refer to Israel's right to exist but to their capacity to destroy her. The rejection of Israel's right to exist and the belief that she ought to disappear are matters of principle and ideology, while the indications of acquiescence are pragmatic and dictated by a hostile reality. But estimates of capacity are not categorical. Just as there can be no absolute certainty that the Arabs are able to destroy Israel, so there can be no absolute certainty that it cannot be done. Hence, they can continue to cherish their hopes, despite the growing contrary evidence, and at the same time persevere, despite the dissonances, in clinging to the goal while doubting the possibility of its achievement. This situation may also affect the Arabs' sincerity and their identification with the goal, neither of which are complete, though it would be mistaken to regard this ambivalent attitude as an indication of half-heartedness, deceitfulness and mental reservations. The evaluation of the Arab attitude is influenced, therefore, by an evaluation of the extent to which the achievement of the objective can be realistically expected.

e) SUMMING UP

The declarations of the leaders are not a reliable measure of what they intend to do, but their statements have much to teach us about the Arabs and their conduct, as well as expressing their "verbal behaviour." The fact that they repeatedly emphasize the same ideas entitles us to assume that the ideas contain something fundamental to them, something important for the understanding of the Arabs and their attitude, even if we do not always see a direct connection between it and their actions. Even if we say that all this is nothing but phraseology, the fact that they use these phrases and not others is significant. Any attempt to study the Arab side in the conflict or the conflict itself would, therefore, be incomplete without devoting a major part of our attention to their ideology.

It may be argued that we are adopting too cold and rational an approach to the Arabs' image of Israel, their ideology in the conflict, and various manifestations of hatred of Zionism and the Jews. We are attempting to judge and evaluate, it may be said, while Arab ideas, hatred, and aspirations for liquidation are not cold principles; they are only a result of the terrible stimulus of the Arab experience. A territory that was theirs has been taken away from them and a small Jewish community has routed their States, with their armies. The blow is not only due to the numerical relationship; the defeat has undermined their faith in their self-image and brutally trampled upon their romantic view of their nationalism and culture. Hence, it may be argued, we should not go too far in drawing conclusions from this ideology, for it expresses, not true attitudes but angry emotions.

There is some truth in this argument, and no doubt it correctly explains the depth of the Arab trauma, but it would be dangerous to regard it as a justification for an ideology of hate. A single outburst may be accidental; a momentary fury may not be reliable evidence; but a frenzy that persists for twenty years is undoubtedly significant. Even if the Arabs' attitude is a reaction to what they have suffered, the character of the reaction has implications in regard to them and their attitude in the conflict. A community, like an individual, may reasonably be judged not only by its actions but also by the purposes it proclaims, even if they are not capable of being realized. Declarations are also actions.

It is possible not to attribute practical importance to the scurrility and the distorted images, and to console ourselves with the thought that these are only manifestations of weakness and emotional complexes, but the idea that no attention should be paid to falsehood and abuse because "truth" will prevail is over-optimistic, at least for the short run. False and distorted ideas are not devoid of significance, and are capable of impelling people to action. If evil is "banal," as Hannah Arendt believes, that does not render it impotent. Ideologies are not necessarily good and constructive; evil has its own philosophy and spiritual doctrines, which have great power for action when they are cherished. People need not be criminals in their private lives in order to perpetrate the most terrible crimes when they are obsessed by an ideology which they regard as justified and which prescribes such actions. Doctrines that call for destruction have an idealism of their own, which may even lead to supreme personal devotion and self-sacrifice. An ideology which describes the enemy as a monster may provide ideological justification for abandoning all scruples where he is concerned; by dehumanizing him it puts him beyond the reach of mercy.

It should be admitted that there is a considerable element of truth and justice in the ideology of the Arabs; one can understand their feeling that Arab nationalism has suffered an injustice by losing the territory of Israel. Their burning pain is sincere. The Arab indictment against Zionism partly consists of correct charges, though in part it is a distortion.

To understand the Arab attitude, the Israeli must understand what he would do were he an Arab, and what attitude he would adopt towards Israel; he should try to visualize the depths of the Arab conviction of injustice. Let him imagine that he is a Palestinian refugee, who has been uprooted from the neighbourhood where he and his fathers lived, who has been deprived of his property by strangers, and who regards its restitution as a matter of fundamental right and justice. Let him try to evaluate the force of the blow to Arab nationalism inflicted by Israel's existence and consolidation; let him try to see the objective of liquidating Israel as not only an expression of psychological complexes, but a deduction from the geopolitical and national concept of Arab unity. Let him ask himself what he would demand of Israel and what price he would exact for a compromise, when territorial concessions are not of any basic value, for it is not territory that Arab nationalism lacks.

Hence, with all the natural desire of an Israeli to condemn the Arabs for their attitude towards us and their objective of liquidation, we must understand the tragic position that has been created, and the difficulty—which is the nub of the conflict—that the Arab demand for the restoration of the *status quo* means national suicide for Israel. Since Israel's capacity to offer concessions that would not affect her survival has been so limited, the Arabs have regarded acquiescence in her existence as a unilateral concession, another blow at their honour in addition to the blow they have suffered already by the very fact of Israel's establishment, and surrender to a reality the creation of which they regard as an injustice. The main difficulty of the conflict has been that the Arabs have not found the way to present less extreme and categorical demands, regarding any concession as too small if it left Israel in existence, while for Israel any concession was too great if it narrowed and endangered the basis of her survival.

Chapter 9
POSSIBILITIES OF CHANGE

In discussing the possibility of a change in the Arab attitude, Israelis should be on guard against a tendency to exaggerate apparent indications that such a change is on the horizon, such as—to take an outstanding example—some of Bourguiba's statements in the years preceding the Six-Day War. In the past, many Jews believed that the rise of a new Arab leadership—after the decline of the traditional politicians and religious leaders, who were thought to have an interest in opposing Zionism—would lead to a more favourable attitude to Zionist settlement. It was also commonly thought that social progress in the Arab countries—what Erskine Childers called "the erosion of antagonism by social reform" (in his article "Palestine the Broken Triangle")—would make it easier for them to accept Israel, but although a popular socialist leadership gained power in several Arab States before very long, the antagonism to Israel only grew more intense.

It may be readily agreed that changes will come, but it is more difficult to forecast how they will come, and even harder to suggest how to ensure that the development will be in the desired direction.

1. CHANGES OF ATTITUDE ON THE ABSTRACT PLANE

Let us see what we can learn from social psychology about the problem of change of attitude.[1]

First, we shall distinguish between two possible directions of change: a congruent change, which leaves the attitude basically the same while reinforcing existing trends, and—the type in which we are interested—an incongruent change, which involves a reversal of the attitude: for instance, from denunciation to praise. The first type of change is easier to achieve than the second; indeed, such variations in the Arab attitude to Israel as have taken place so far have been mainly of the first type.

An attitude which is institutionalized by ideology is harder to change, since the ideological interpretation is largely impervious to refutatory communications. A kind of closed system is created, suppressing the learning process and producing a degree of blindness.

A "multiplex" attitude, which is many-sided, variegated and rich in details, with its parts constituting a comprehensive system, is harder to change than a simple one. It may be assumed that for most of the Arab public the attitude to the conflict is simple, while it is complex and many-sided for the ideologists. The latter, therefore, display greater resistance to a change.

The more the attitude constitutes a system of closely knit and mutually supporting concepts, the harder it will be to change.

The force of a communication tending to contradict an outlook which has already been formed will appear to be trivial in comparison with that of the general attitude, or it will be interpreted as an exception, which does not refute the rule. It is easier to change a partial conception and a fragmentary image; a comprehensive image is more "impenetrable" (Kelman volume, p. 81).

Dissonances in the attitude, unsound and ambivalent concepts, constitute weaknesses, openings or cracks through which a change may be introduced. Such weaknesses indeed exist in the Arab attitude: conviction of its validity is incomplete and it involves considerable discomfort and perplexity. It consists of a mixture of truth and falsehood, and it is easier to believe in a falsehood which is repeatedly and vigorously confirmed than to halt halfway down the slippery slope of half-truth. Indeed, the idea that Israel is not so bad weakens the categorical force of the death sentence pronounced against her.

According to the theory of cognitive dissonance, the stronger the external forces that impose on a person a mode of behaviour which is not in keeping with his attitude the less is the magnitude of the dissonance, for he regards the difference between his attitude and his behaviour as understandable and feels no need to reconcile them. On the other hand, when the factors which compel a person to act in a way incompatible with his attitude are of minor importance, the dissonance will be great. (See the concise explanation in Krech, Crutchfield and Ballachy, p. 262.) This leads to an important conclusion in regard to the feelings of the Arabs about the dissonance between their attitude and their actions. Since the factors which prevent the achievement of the objective are of considerable weight (e.g. the balance of forces, the strength of Israel, "World Zionism," divisions in the Arab world, the international structure, and the possibility of Big-Power intervention), they will regard the dissonance as trivial, so that the impulse to close the gap will be weak and the capacity to persevere in the attitude will be considerable. (These principles may be of significance in evaluating the attitude of the Arabs who came under Israeli rule as a result of the Six-Day War.)

Another type of dissonance is to be found in the relation between images and realities, in connection with the demonological and scurrilous descriptions of Israel and the Jews. Although these ideas make the attitude more comprehensive, as we have seen, they are not so essential that it is impossible to object to the survival of Israel without them. There is no need to believe in *The Protocols of the Elders of Zion* in order to deny Israel's right to exist. It is possible to stop short, as the publications of the Palestine Liberation Organization's Research Centre do, and be content with denunciations of colonialism in Zionism. It can also be founded on the idea of Israel as a danger to the Arab States and the historical account of the injuries she has done them.

The more an attitude is rooted in the personality the harder it is to change. In this connection, Brown (1963, pp. 55 ff) distinguishes between opinions, attitudes and character traits. He explains that a person's opinion can easily be changed, while his attitudes are more rigid, since they depend upon his character traits. These are rooted in the nuclear personality, as distinguished from the peripheral personality. In other words, we can arrange a person's ideas in order according to the depth of their roots, starting with those that are not an organic part of him and culminating in those that are organically bound up with the structure of his personality.

It would seem unlikely that the attitude of the Arabs is connected with their nuclear personality (if such a thing actually exists). The attitude, with its ideology, is mainly the result of historical circumstances.

The more an attitude meets a person's needs and fulfils functions in his life, the harder it will be to change. So long as the needs exist and the functions are necessary, there will be inner resistance to change; an interest in the preservation of the attitude will be created, and there will be an emotional attachment to it.

It may indeed be assumed that the Arab attitude in the conflict performs psychological functions in externalizing feelings of frustration and dissatisfaction. According to Daniel Katz's classification of the factors in the formation of an attitude, it may be assumed that those functions which he calls the ego defence play an important part among the Arabs. (See his article, mentioned above, and the summary in Janis and Smith's article in the Kelman volume, pp. 206 ff.) These functions are fulfilled by the attitude according to need: for refugees who have not been absorbed in the Arab countries, who live in hardship and suffer from a feeling of exile, the attitude is very important and serves as a source of hope for a transformation of their lives, while for those Arabs who live far from Israel it is only of marginal importance and their readiness for a change or acquiescence would be greater.

Studies conducted in the United States have shown that on matters of foreign policy people's ideas are not fixed; they have more readiness for change and are, as it were, more fickle, than in regard to home affairs (Deutsch and Merritt in the Kelman volume, p. 156). It may be assumed that this is the case in the Arab countries as well. In most of them the conflict appears to be a matter of foreign policy, but in some the presence of the Palestinians makes it also part of home affairs.

So far, we have discussed a change in the attitude as if it were a closed system, considering the extent to which the attitude itself can change as the result of its own specific internal characteristics. As psychologists explain, however, change springs rather from outside the attitude—from the influence of external events—than from within it. People's attitudes change mainly as the result of changes in the social climate in which they live, in the environment and the effect of events and circumstances. Moreover, since attitudes in the conflict are of a group character and are determined within a society, changes in them will depend on changes in the circumstances of the group and its understanding of them. Such changes are comprehensive and have implications for the entire value system of the group.

2. ATTITUDE CHANGES IN HISTORICAL PERSPECTIVE

Our generation has witnessed frequent alterations in images: the roles of friend and foe have been exchanged at a rapid rate. In his study of American images, Harold Isaacs explains:

"Thus in a matter of only a few years, people were called upon to transfer their images of 'Oriental cruelty' from the Chinese to the Japanese and back to the

> Chinese again. In a single generation, the dominant images of the German have moved from the *gemütlich* bourgeois to the booted militarist, to the Nazi mass murderer, and back again to older images of efficient, hard-working people divided between West (friendly) and East (unfriendly or captive). In an even shorter space of time, Americans have been called upon by events to leap from images of the wanton Japanese murderers of Nanking and the Bataan Death March to new images of reformed sinners and earnest democrats, from bloody-handed rapists and sadistic captors to the delicacy of flower arrangements and the color of a kabuki play. In the same period of time, Americans have also been shuttled from the totalitarian monster of Stalin in the purge years to 'Uncle Joe' of the war years and back to the crazed megalomaniac hidden behind the Kremlin walls until he died." (*Scratches on our Minds,* p. 406).

Many other examples may be given from images of other peoples.

There have also been extreme changes in images in the Arab world. Up to the middle of the 50's the Soviet Union and the Communists were regarded as abominable and Communism was identified with atheism, but since then, in some of the Arab countries, Socialism has become an admired ideology and the Soviet Union a friend.

In Egypt the Muslim Brotherhood was admired by the masses as the exponents of the purification of Islam and the return to its sources, and they had close ties with some of the officers in Nasser's entourage, but overnight they became an object of execration by the spokesmen of the regime. King Fārūq's image also changed rapidly in the eyes of the officers, who, according to reports, still supported him about half a year before the 1962 revolution.

Extreme changes in inter-Arab relations have also been reflected in imagery. The UAR's propaganda organs used to shower Hussein with abuse, depicting him as a traitor and son of a family of traitors, a servant of imperialism, an enemy of Arabism, and so forth. This did not, however, prevent his coming to terms with Nasser—followed by another quarrel, another reconciliation, and so on. Similarly with Nasser's relations with Kings Sa'ūd and Fayṣal of Saudi Arabia and President Bourguiba. The same kind of process is frequently repeated: abuse and scurrility are followed by reconciliation and embraces, which, in their turn, are followed by a new outbreak of abuse. One day Nasser is admired in Tunis; the next —as at the end of April 1965—he is denounced at a mass demonstration. One day the mob enthusiastically cheers the leader; next day they mutilate his corpse in the public square.

Changes in American attitudes have not followed internal developments, but reflect changed political circumstances or new events—"spectacular events," in Deutsch and Merritt's term, such as victory in the World War and the establishment of the international line-up in the Cold War.

Changes in inter-Arab relations and the images of each other painted by the Arab States have been caused by political vicissitudes and political decisions. It is true that, over and above the charges of treachery and collaboration with the enemy, the Arabs could appeal to the unifying idea of Arabism, presenting differences and disputes as ephemeral family quarrels of negligible significance in comparison with the mighty tide of cooperation between all Arabs. They could also credit themselves with magnanimity towards the repentant sinner; in fact, after the quarrel was over the rivals generally ignored that it had ever existed and forgot the abuse they had showered on each other, as if they had always been friends. The foreign observer might marvel at these sharp transitions from strident hostility to friendship, suspecting that there was a large degree of hypocrisy in the reconciliations and that the really permanent factor was the hostility, which in turn became latent and overt.

3. FACTORS FOR CHANGE

An alteration in the Arab attitude towards Israel could come about as the result of a change in a number of variables inside the Arab countries themselves. The following are a number of situations which might lead to a change.

a) DEVELOPMENT AND INDUSTRIALIZATION

The atmosphere might change when the Arab countries begin to pay more attention to their own internal affairs. In Egypt, for instance, there is a tendency to engage in external activities in order to win prestige and acquire foreign political assets. Concentration on home affairs may lead to a decline in the interest in the conflict, which is mainly a matter of foreign relations. As a result, there may be a change in the national ethos and scale of values, so that the dispute will lose its importance.

It has been noted, for example, that development and industrialization in the Soviet Union have reduced the need for external tension to ensure internal mobilization (Professor Milton Shulman, *Beyond the Cold War*).

Greater emphasis on home affairs may lead to a tendency to shorten the front of external conflict and reduce the expenditure involved. However, so long as the Arab countries are ruled by military regimes, dominated entirely or partially by the army, the conflict serves the purposes of the regime, which explains the expenditures as required for military consolidation.

Development may lead to greater self-satisfaction and the weakening of aggressive tendencies. This is the kind of peace which reigns today in Western Europe, and which Raymond Aron calls "peace by satisfaction" (*Paix et Guerre,* p. 160). However, development may not only increase satisfaction but also provide the State with more effective means of aggression. When Germany was aggressive, it was not because she was underdeveloped.

The view that increased attention to development will be at the expense of attention to foreign affairs assumes that "attention" is a fixed quantity which is allocated among various spheres of interest. But activity on the foreign scene would not necessarily be at the expense of home affairs; there could be parallel activity in both fields, as we have seen in Egypt in recent years. Moreover, inadequate success in internal economic development (as in Egypt) may lead to a revival of interest in foreign affairs and an attempt to find consolation by externalizing the blame and the manipulation of symbols.

b) THE NEW GENERATION

Before the Six-Day War, it might have been hoped that the new generation would have a different approach. Since the youth had not experienced the shame of subordination to a foreign power or lived through the process of liberation, they might be freer from complexes and adopt a more local, less emotional attitude, concentrating on the improvement of living standards, modernization, and liberation from the burden of tradition. Among the Arab youth, according to complaints from journalists and moralists, there are manifestations known in other societies: nihilism, individualism, indifference to politics and the erosion of values. Such phenomena might weaken devotion to a belligerent aim like the liquidation of Israel. The new generation might be less involved in the "obligation" to destroy Israel and find it easier to accept her as an accomplished fact. During a visit to Lebanon, Muhammad Khaydar of Algeria said:

> "In my opinion, if the Palestine problem is not solved in the next decade, no solution will ever be found, because the next generation is losing its emotional ties with the homeland." (*al-Ḥawādith,* January 11, 1963).

It might be argued, on the other hand, that the difficulties experienced by the intelligentsia, especially the flood of university graduates, in finding their place in the Arab economic structure might create frustrations that would drive them to seek scapegoats and find an external target for their resentments. Another factor which has to be taken into account is the efforts of the regime, which controls education, to foster hatred of Israel among the coming generation. Moreover, radicalization of the attitude against Israel is more widespread among the younger generation.

The Six-Day War has frustrated the expectation that the rise of a new generation might lead to a change. The resentment and humiliation aroused by the debacle will not soon be forgotten or the ardent desire for revenge placated.

c) UNITY AND DISUNITY

Arab union could do away with the complaints and dissatisfaction associated with disunity, and reduce the fear of Israel and her expansion. At the same time, however, it might increase the power of the Arabs and reduce their fear of starting a violent confrontation with Israel. While some countries have turned to war and expansion after their consolidation—e.g. Spain, France and Germany—this tendency was only a possible development, not an inevitable one. However, if the Arabs refuse to acquiesce in Israel's existence today because of their weakness, they might refuse to acquiesce in it after achieving unity by reason of their strength. If union was established—which does not appear likely—as a result of the domination of one element or country, it would no doubt be tempted to fight Israel in order to consolidate its leadership. Furthermore, a major and repeated argument for unity is that it is required for the destruction of Israel—which is another reason why it does not seem likely that an Arab union would suddenly become an ally of the Jewish State.

The paradoxical feature of the situation, as we have noted, is that disunity prevents joint Arab action but also rapprochement with Israel;

it prevents war but also prevents peace, i.e. it maintains the conflict in a position of neither peace nor war.

d) THE LEADERSHIP AND THE IDEOLOGY

A major factor in the process of change is the political leadership. In view of the instrumental nature of the ideology and its development by the leaders, the question of change must be examined not so much from the psychological as from the political viewpoint, for it is the leadership that has created the ideology of the attitude and it could change it. It is more reasonable to expect a change of policy to bring about a change of ideology than to hope for the converse process. The examples mentioned of changes in the images of the Japanese and the Germans were not caused by changes in national character, but by alterations in political circumstances. The leader generally has more influence on the attitude of the people than the people on the attitude of the leader.[2] It is true that, by developing the ideology against Israel and repeatedly proclaiming devotion to it, the Arab leadership has undertaken to uphold it, but the chains are not unbreakable if the leaders change their minds. Today they proclaim that Israel's continued existence is a threat to Arab nationalism, and that the Arab countries cannot achieve prosperity in our neighbourhood, but the leaders are quite capable of developing a new ideology of tolerance, and even of good neighbourliness and cooperation. Even if the Arab attitude, as expressed in the ideology, has roots in the Islamic image of the Jews, and perhaps even deeper ones, the Islamic factor is only a prop for those who want to use it, but it does not impose itself and cannot be assumed to be a barrier to any alteration in the ideology. It can be empirically shown that conservative Islamic factors have sometimes shown greater readiness to acquiesce in Israel's existence. The same applies to the geopolitical argument: it may be used to support opposite conclusions, and in any case it does not compel anyone to employ it either. An ideology is, thus, not a straitjacket; it always leaves room for flexibility, manipulation, interpretation and extenuation. The Arabs' figurative and flexible use of their language and of "indirect expressions" makes it particularly easy to alter the meaning of accepted phrases and conceptions. The ideology of the conflict is of major importance today in moulding the present attitude of the Arabs, but it could be blown away like chaff before the wind at some future date.

The Arab leadership is not free to do as it wishes without limitations, however. One difficulty lies in the fact that as long as the change does not encompass all the Arab States, a retreat by one would be exploited by its rivals to attack it; Arab leaders are vulnerable to each other, for criticism in one Arab country is liable to influence public opinion in another. From the political point of view there is no Arab union, but where inter-Arab abuse is concerned, the Arab world is united in what is almost a single system. Even this aspect, however, should not be exaggerated: no one can point to a single case in which Arab leaders have been deposed only because they were denounced by their rivals on account of their activities in the Arab-Israel conflict.

There are grounds for the assumption that the rigidity and indivisibility of the Arab attitude is an obstacle to change. Since there can be no partial liquidation, such an objective does not permit a gradual, cumulative change; there is no possibility of transition from liquidation to "a little liquidation," and so on, little by little to "no liquidation." A change in the attitude to Israel, therefore, necessitates a "quantum jump," which is undoubtedly more difficult than a gradual alteration—especially as what is required is a comprehensive change, a revaluation of other parts of the Arabs' national ideology which are connected with their attitude in the conflict. We should not, therefore, underestimate the difficulties that would face the Arab leadership in accustoming their people to a change in the attitude towards Israel which they have so far proclaimed, fostered and taught their peoples to cherish.

For the leadership to change its attitude, there is a need for adequate motives, or a significant, "spectacular" event that will make a change necessary. If not, the momentum of the existing situation—even if only for the reason that it exists—is decisive, for a change means creating something new. So far, no clear and sufficiently powerful motivation for a change has been revealed among the Arab leaders. By and large, the conflict has been of service to them, and although its exploitation by rivals has sometimes created a measure of discomfort for one factor or another, that has not been an unbearable burden.

e) THE THIRD RIVAL

A major factor in a change of relations between rivals may be the existence of a third rival. A quarrel between the two rivals and an external factor changes the nature of the previous quarrel, even if the triangle thus created is not equilateral. The dispute between China and the Soviet Union, for example, has moderated the rivalry between the latter and the United States. It is true that the relations between the trio are complex, for each of the three is in conflict at the same time with each of the others, and may be an ally—if only a tacit one—with either of the other two against the third.

The same applies to inter-Arab rivalry. It would not be surprising if, in its heart of hearts, one Arab factor has feelings of *Schadenfreude* when Israel strikes a blow at its rival. The Egyptian leaders, no doubt, were pleased with the blows suffered by Syria after the break-up of the UAR, which they regarded as proof of the magnitude of Syria's crime in breaking away from her Egyptian partner.

It is quite possible to imagine situations in which inter-Arab rivalry reaches such heights that one Arab factor may be prepared to cooperate with Israel against another. This applies even to Syria, which has gone to extremes in hostility towards Israel. Ṣalāḥ al-Bīṭār describes, in the *Protocols of the Unity Conversations* between the Syrians, Iraqis and Egyptians, in the months of March-April 1963, the situation in Syria which led to the break-up of the UAR and the resentment of the Egyptians, how the situation "went so far that some said: With Israel and not with Egypt." (Second Session, Part I, published in book form by *al-Ahrām,* August 1963, p. 72, middle column—this part appeared in *al-Ahrām,* July 1, 1963).

The wealth of possibilities affecting these matters which is latent in the political situation goes beyond anything conceivable by our imagination or understanding. Combinations may arise which cannot be foreseen in advance, or even credited at this stage. In the history of mankind there have been innumerable examples of erroneous evaluation of prospects and inability to foresee the future, especially where peace and war are concerned. However, it is easier, it is true, to envisage the possibility that developments will compel some Arab State or leader to make a partial or temporary arrangement with Israel than that they would reject the accepted attitude to the conflict, though even that is not entirely out of the question.

f) EXHAUSTION AND DISAPPOINTMENT

Another cause of change could be disappointment at failure to achieve the aim in the conflict. Time after time the Arabs have hoped that they were on the point of obtaining their goal through a variety of means: the pressure of the refugees, summit conferences, various organizations, the diversion of the Jordan, a strangulating boycott, an approaching increase in military strength to an adequate level of preparedness. Leaders have not been sparing of declarations that victory was near; authors have written that before very long the goal would be attained. Fu'ad Naṣḥī, for example, concludes his book with these words:

> "I issue this book ten years after the usurpation of Palestine and the establishment of the so-called State of Israel . . . And I am not yet closing it . . . because I hope to write its conclusion next year, and then I will say that the struggle for Palestine has been completed and the Jews have left it never again to return." (*Palestine in the Struggle*, p. 251).

The State of Israel has since completed its second decade.

The Arabs have hoped for a long series of false dawns. It is a melancholy total they have to show in their national balance-sheet of the conflict. Nāṣir al-Dīn al-Naṣhāshībī, in his despair, openly expresses his feelings:

> "I ask myself already when I will return. I ask when my son will return. Am I pessimistic?" (*al-Jumhūriyya*, May 20, 1964).

True, the Arabs have shown an extraordinary capacity to reawaken their hopes. They have fanned the dying flame until it flared up again, repeated the operation when it has died down once more, and so on over and over again. How long can they go on like this?

This development may be regarded as the outcome of exhaustion and disappointment.[3] The continuance of the situation, without the slightest sign on the horizon of a real solution of the conflict, and the solutions proposed by the Arabs appearing to be no more than verbal ostentation, may suggest the possibility—if only as a matter of abstract analysis—of disappointment and despair at the possibility of the liquidation of Israel.

Exhaustion of the Arabs, the active party in the conflict, depends on the life expectancy of irredentist feeling and how long they can sustain their claim for the disappearance of Israel. At first this exhaustion finds expression in the transition from the operative to the ritual stage of the ideology. Intellectual devotion to the ideology weakens, though something is left of the emotional attachment, and the approach becomes pragmatic: acceptance of, and acquiescence in, the reality. Then the attitude enters into the stage of de-ideologization, which is the opposite process to the bolstering of the attitude by ideological means.

By its nature, the conflict is a struggle of attrition, a competition in perseverance and endurance. On the one hand, it has weighed more heavily on Israel than it has on the Arabs—apart from the refugees, whose strength has, no doubt, been sapped even more. On the other hand, the absence of any alternative has given Israel the energy to face the struggle, since it is more important for her to survive than for the Arabs to destroy her. The "balance of vitality" is on Israel's side. This fundamental fact is apparent in the extent of the effort that the parties have invested in order to achieve their aims in the conflict. While Israel spares no labour or energy to safeguard her existence, the exertions of the Arab countries have been half-hearted, and the 1948 war, as Nasser put it, was a "half-war."

While the Arabs have lost hope of a speedy solution, it is also possible that they may refuse to abandon their aim but pursue it with more vigour and activity, in order to cover up and extenuate their disappointment (as in the process already mentioned, "when prophecy fails"). However, there are grounds for the assumption that this is more applicable to the proximate stage. In the long term it is difficult to hold fast to a prophecy that has proved false while closing one's eyes to the reality. There is also the possibility that the radicalization of the Arab attitude, the activities connected with the summit conferences, the United Arab Command, the National Liberation Organization, the Palestinian Army and the Fatah Organization, will in the end have an opposite result. The object of these activities is to arouse the hope that the conflict has entered upon a new, practical stage, as the Arab leaders loudly proclaim. Disappointment with all these efforts may arouse despair, and, as a dialectical result, strengthen tendencies to acquiesce in the situation. Efforts to strike at Israel by infiltration and violence have assumed a symbolic character, with the aim of preserving the spark of hope, rather than doing actual damage. Paradoxically, too, the very idea that time works against the Arabs and therefore they must act "now or never," which lies at the base of the radical approach, contains the seeds of acquiescence in the situation. The Arab national approach to Israel can be eroded. The Arabs justified their demand for her liquidation as a condition for the achievement of unity, but in recent years there has been a decline in the emphasis on unity as a practical goal, and there is talk of the road being a long one. This deferment of the achievement of unity to the distant future is liable to transform it from a practical, operative goal to a ritual, eschatological one—and if unity is not near, there is no urgency in the annihilation of Israel. An obstacle is felt to be troublesome if it stands on the road which one intends to travel.

There is a considerable measure of disappointment in the Arab countries at the failure to achieve national goals; Arab nationalism, according to its own spokesmen, is in a state of crisis. This position affects the fervour of the faith in the ideology and goals of Arab national unity. We may, possibly, see the re-awakening of local nationalist ideologies. It was the ideology of Arab unity that clashed with Israel; when particularistic ideologies arise, the scope of the confrontation with Israel will be reduced, at least insofar as most of the Arab countries are concerned, and they may be able to adopt a more tolerant attitude to her existence. Furthermore, recognition of the heterogeneity of the Arab world may help them to recognize the existence of Israel.

A diminution of ideological ardour may bring the Arabs to a clearer perception of the circumstances in which they live, enabling them to realize the differences, even the incompatibility, between the ideology and other Arab interests and tendencies. These processes involve the enhancement of their self-insight, which, in fact, is beginning to have an effect: they have started to explain to themselves that the "plots" of their external enemies —imperialism and Israel—are not the only obstacles to the achievements of national aims, but that they themselves bear the responsibility for their own dissensions. As Daniel Katz explains, the way to a change in an attitude which is based on ego-defence lies in self-insight. Since the attitude towards Israel contains considerable elements of Arab self-defence, as we have seen by the way in which the Arabs interpret history, greater self-insight may also help to bring about some change in the attitude.

It is also possible that we may witness a decline in radical ardour within some Arab countries once they are disappointed with their achievements and the revolutionary impetus wanes. A decline in radicalism in internal affairs is also liable to help to produce a more moderate approach to external problems.

g) EXTERNAL INFLUENCES

The conflict is not a closed system; it is inevitably influenced by events in the world at large. If the world moves towards anarchy, instability and frequent armed conflict, the Arabs will tend to cling to their attitude, while a better organized and regulated world will inevitably reinforce the *status quo* and diminish the opportunities for changing it by force.

A thaw in the relations between the Powers would reduce the intensity of the competition between them in the Middle East, which is especially liable to be exploited by the Arab side, and thus lead towards pacification. However, as we have noted, although the Cold War intensified the conflict, it did not create it, and the view, sometimes expressed, that the settlement of the Cold War would automatically lead to an Arab-Israeli settlement is exaggerated. Moreover, it is an implied insult to the Arabs, suggesting that their antagonism to Israel is only an unreal reflection of an external conflict.

Developments in the Arab-Israel conflict may also be influenced by the general world political climate. The radicalization of the Arab attitude and the hopes for achievements through a "People's War" on the Chinese and Vietnamese models have been influenced by the atmosphere and trends of thought in East Asia; the success or failure of such movements might be reflected in the atmosphere in the Middle East.

What kind of atmosphere will prevail in the world? In a world which despatches expeditions to outer space, will there not, ultimately, be a change in the scale of earthly values until conflicts over trivial areas of territory will appear frivolous? Some observers, however, indeed, have been so hasty as to prophecy that the development of nuclear armaments has made the nation-state obsolete, that the world will aim at broader unions, and the peoples will be less interested in nationalism and sovereignty. Such prophecies are very far from realization. It seems clear that neither the world's political structure nor its values are about to be transformed in the near future. States will continue to compete and clash, and quarrels and conflicts will arise between them.

Israel's attitude in the conflict and its effect in bringing about a change in the Arab side, as well as the possibility of a resort to violence (i.e. war), is outside the framework of this work. I will only point out this: despite the general character of conflicts, which is marked by reciprocal influence —the actions of one side affecting those of the other—the Arab demand for liquidation leaves Israel with a narrow range of manoeuvre in influencing, appeasing, or making concessions to the other party. The Arab attitude is largely autonomous. The concept of mutual dependence and reciprocal action is appropriate to this conflict on a more abstract level than that of history and practical affairs.[4] The dilemma facing Israel is this: the demand for liquidation cannot be met by any offer of compromise, since there can be no such thing as semi-liquidation; while a moderate attitude towards the rival party, any gesture or concession based on the assumption that liquidation is not his object, may seem to imply the contemptuous view that his demand is not sincere and that he can be bought over for a trifle.

The Arab-Israel conflict is a grave one; the Arab attitude is rigid and is supported by an ideological basis, but this does not imply that the situation is immune to the effects of time and incapable of change.

We should not be discouraged by an admission of the difficulties. The conflict is not plastic; it cannot be moulded to our heart's desire; but it is not so granite-hard that it is impervious to influence. Modesty demands that we should adopt relative concepts and be aware of the limits of our capacity. If we admit the difficulties involved in settling the conflict, we are not underestimating the value of the human intelligence, but only emphasizing its limitations.

We must take an historical view of the situation. Present events, as we see them, make up only a small segment of the great stream of history. There is no finality in the historical process; a solution of the conflict and a peace settlement would not be the millennium. Even a settlement would not mean the dawn of a Golden Age, for nations have quarrelled and made up in turn, and reconciliation may contain, if only in latent form, the seeds of a new conflict.[5] Even if humanity succeeds in preventing large-scale wars, there will still be conflicts and clashes between nations.

The study of the conflict reveals the relativity of the attitudes of the parties. If we consider the course of its development, we shall also perceive the historical relativity of the conflict.

Appendix

THE PROBLEM OF SUBJECTIVITY

To what extent is an Israeli capable of conducting a calm and objective study of the Israel-Arab conflict in general and, in particular, of the Arab attitude? The problem may be split up into a number of questions: To what extent can he resist the influence of prejudices, interests and hopes? To what extent does the threat to his own national survival, which lies at the root of the Arab attitude, permit the Israeli to judge it on its own merits? Can he be clear-sighted enough to correctly evaluate the role of the historical circumstances and their role in its adoption? Can he give an attentive ear to the Arabs' griefs and grievances? Can he appreciate their pain and the depth of their sense of injustice, and evaluate the force of the blow to Arab nationalism involved in the establishment and consolidation of Israel? Can he envisage himself as a Palestinian refugee, uprooted from the soil of his forefathers, who regards its restoration as a matter of elementary right and justice? Can the Israeli withstand the temptation to condemn the Arabs as they are revealed in their objective of liquidation, which he may regard as a sign of callousness and barbarity, and to see the "indirect expressions" as mere hypocrisy, pretence and deceit? If he has inclinations to psychology he is liable to regard the objective of liquidation as a sign of mental sickness and latent destructive tendencies, as a result of the Arabs' failure to adapt themselves to the modern world and assume the responsibility for their own fate.

It is difficult for an Israeli to preserve his equanimity in the face of the flood of scurrility, incitement and demonological slander, and the inability, revealed in the Arab ideology, to arrive at a balanced judgement, achieve a measure of objectivity in understanding our problems and regard the Israelis as mortals, with their vices and virtues. The one-sided approach, the falsehoods and distortions, the anti-Semitic motifs, the exploitation of *The Protocols of the Elders of Zion* in books issued under official Egyptian auspices, the lack of self-criticism, the self-glorification—all these arouse revulsion and make it more difficult for the Israeli to rise above himself to the extent required to achieve a more or less balanced evaluation.

Here I believe I must make a few personal remarks. The writing of any book demands an intellectual effort; this work has also required an emotional one. The reading of the Arab literature of the conflict has often made my blood run cold. These are not the outpourings of the mobs in the bazaars, but the writings and speeches of the foremost Arab authors and public figures. I am not under any illusion that we in Israel are immaculate. It is possible to understand the bitter protest of the Arabs at the loss of a country. One can understand their anger, their hatred of Zionism, and even the reasons for their charge of racialism, but many of them go far beyond the limits of what is reasonable.

In my childhood, my family lived in an Arab neighbourhood in Haifa. From my father I acquired a liking for the beauty of the Arabic, and later I studied Arabic language and literature at the University on Mount Scopus. When I recall the period of the 1948 war, I believe I did not hate the Arabs. Even the death in battle of my brother and other contemporaries did not fill me with resentment. I regarded the war as some kind of historic necessity. I carried out my intelligence duties for years, when it was my task to unearth their secrets, without hatred (again, at least, so I believe). I was frequently concerned lest emotions blur my vision and distort my evaluation.

As I read and studied their writings on the conflict and the speeches of their leaders, I would often be perplexed as to how to take their statements, and shocked at their content and form. I am afraid that such feelings may distort my vision.

With all an author's desire to be regarded as an impartial researcher, to show understanding for the sufferings of the people who are the subjects of the study, to control oneself and avoid an attitude of condemnation, not to disqualify oneself in the eyes of Israelis and others, who are in any case liable to suspect one of being blinded by the conflict and unable to see things as they are—I nevertheless try to overcome the tendency to cover up unpleasant manifestations of the Arab attitude towards Israel. In pursuing the reputation of an objective judge, a man may show so much understanding that he may lean over backwards and justify undesirable manifestations. I would rather give a true description of the lamentable truth than try to be forgiving and congenial.

These considerations involve a distinction between an impartial judgement and the distorting influence of the effort to appear impartial. I will permit myself to quote a passage I wrote a few years ago, which was concerned, it is true, with general phenomena in conflicts, but in the writing of which I was influenced mainly by my personal experience, which was acquired in the course of the Arab-Israel dispute, and by trends in connection with the conflict which I met with among the Jewish public:

> "Sometimes the desire to form a balanced judgement of the conflict, and not to attribute responsibility for the conflict largely to one side, a generally positive aspiration, may prove a pitfall and distort the picture . . . Symmetries in objectives, modes of action, and interrelationships of two sides in the conflict must be examined carefully. It is sometimes the very desire to adopt the stance of a neutral judge that leads the observer to close his eyes to inconvenient patterns of behaviour on the part of one side or the other in the conflict or at least to regard them benignly. Adopting a neutral stand is liable to intoxicate the observer with a euphoria of self-righteousness; he will derive great satisfaction from his rectitude and from his capacity to transcend issues and view them from lofty heights. His awareness of affinity with one side of the conflict may inculcate in him a tendency towards ostentatious neutrality, leading him to tip the scales and do violence to the facts." (Y. Harkabi: *Nuclear War and Nuclear Peace,* Israel Program for Scientific Translations, 1966, p. 270).

The problem of balanced judgement in social, political and historical research presents difficult demands. Such studies will be of little value if they deliberately deal only with subjects in regard to which the researcher can be impartial, unprejudiced, and indifferent to the emotions and values involved. The tendency to limit oneself to minutiae amenable to scientific examination; the worship of a narrow scientism; reluctance to deal with the great problems that confront society and mankind because they present particular difficulties in finding fully scientific substantiation for one's conclusions, or because they involve value judgements—all these are liable to lead to sterility, for the measure of scientific objectivity that can be applied to a particular subject is often in direct proportion to its triviality. The efforts of social and political science must be devoted to tackling not only problems that can be dealt with by scientific methods, but also those important questions which are harder to investigate without a margin of doubt and uncertainty. Generally, it is problems of public importance that are complicated by emotional attitudes and involve value judgements.

Any attempt to analyse the complexes of others should be preceded by an analysis of oneself, sometimes referred to as "preparatory analysis."

Indeed, some (like Erich Fromm) have proposed that a person engaged in the study of an international conflict should first of all undergo a psychoanalytical examination. This I have not done; at the most, I have examined myself by introspection.

In order to try to prevent value assumptions and prejudices distorting one's vision, it is better, as proposed by Gunnar Myrdal,* not to conceal or suppress them, but, on the contrary, to try to bring them to the surface and expose them. The very fact that the researcher questions himself about his own interests and defence mechanisms, which may influence his assumptions and results, is likely to help him to overcome his prejudices. Of course, there can be no complete safeguard, and there is a danger that the exercise may become a matter of ritual and routine, a kind of ostentatious spiritual strip-tease. Nevertheless, such self-questioning may also help by giving the reader an account of the author's concepts and outlooks. The following is an attempt at a summary, by no means exhaustive, of these factors:

Since I belong to the Israeli side, I am liable to be strict with the Arabs and lenient with the Jews.

Since it was the coming of the Jews that aroused the conflict, I may tend to divert my attention from its beginnings and concentrate on the Arab reaction.

The consciousness that we are the cause of the conflict may lead us to seize joyfully on any faults in the Arab attitude: anti-Semitism, brutality, blindness and distortion.

I have taken part in controversies on various aspects of the conflict and criticized the attitudes of Israelis, who have on several occasions expressed viewpoints which seemed to me mistaken. Either through a sense of superiority or out of interest, they sometimes describe Arab antagonism as artificial and superficial, or as due to Arab social backwardness. This may lead me, on the rebound, to overemphasize the profundity of the conflict. Sometimes a man has a perverse impulse to say infuriating things, to oversell, or to denounce too sharply ideas which he rejects.

My choice of the Arab position as a subject of research is by no means

* My attention has been drawn by Prof. S. Herman to Gunnar Myrdal's remarks on this question, which are to be found in Appendix II, Volume II of his monumental work *The American Dilemma.* In fact, Myrdal's advice is quite generally valid. It is applicable to the historian, for example, and is emphasized by Carr in his booklet *What Is History?*

accidental. I regard its study as a matter of not only academic, but also educational and political importance. It may help us to understand the Arabs' motives in the conflict, as well as their methods, or what is called in more high-flown language their operational code.

My choice of this subject for research may lead me to overemphasize its importance and profundity. The labour I have devoted to the task of evolving a consistent system from its ideas may lead me to exaggerate their significance, consistency and hold upon Arab public opinion.

My own tendency is to believe in the importance of ideology, though not as an abstract system but as a dimension of history, and I have been interested for several years in the question of the relationship between ideology and action. Hence I am liable to exaggerate the importance of ideology.

In presenting the Arab attitude I may sometimes try to make it convincing because of the suspicion that it is difficult to participate in the perplexities of another people and penetrate to the depths of its soul, as well as because, as an Israeli, I may tend to belittle and undervalue the ideas it contains. On the other hand, I may—again as an Israeli—subject them to too hostile analysis.

The burden of the conflict certainly tends to distort the conceptions of both sides. Because of the limits of the subject, I have dealt with distortions asymmetrically, but I am far from belittling the dangers of pathological social developments which the conflict may produce on the Israeli side.

As for the central problem in the conflict, I realize that Zionism aspired to take a piece of territory from another people, and was therefore necessarily subject to the perplexities on which I touched in my booklet on the Israeli side in the conflict. I can understand the Arabs' charge that an injustice has been done to Arab nationalism, but I reject their conclusions. Arab nationalism claims that, first of all, the injustice must be rectified by abolishing the State of Israel, on the principle of *fiat justitia ruat coelum,* and only then will it be possible to return to normality. The tragedy of the Arab attitude, as I see it, lies in the fact that it can visualize no rectification of the injustice except by the perpetration of a greater injustice: the destruction of the State of Israel.

I am apprehensive as to the results of the conflict and concerned for the future. So long as it persists, we shall have to live in the shadow of its threats and perils. I am deeply troubled by the thought that it is those that have been affected by a disaster who have failed to foresee it. Among some Jews in Israel, there has always been an inclination—partly due, I believe, to a lack of understanding of the conflict—which I regard as suicidal (*The Attitude of Israel in the Arab-Israel Conflict,* pp. 37-39). My studies of nuclear strategy have aroused the fear that the horrors of the twentieth century may be only the beginning of the horrors yet in store for humanity.

I have identified myself so closely with this work that it has become part of my world outlook. But this also involves a danger. The scientific validity of a study of this kind depends to a considerable extent upon the exclusion of the human factor, so that its truth should be more general and not influenced by or involved with subjective truths.

I have come to regard the conflict as of symbolic significance for human existence. Basically, it is a clash between demands for justice, on the part of both the Arabs and the Jews. Claims that there is a "just solution" which can meet the "just" demands of both sides is only an attempt to plaster over the problems of human reality; any such solution can only be a verbal one. There is not always a "natural justice" which has only to be revealed; there is an arbitrary element in a so-called "just solution." The reality of human life necessarily involves contradictions, for it is a concomitant of the human condition that the very existence of one is liable to be an "injustice" injurious to the other. Beyond these contradictions, men are bound to give priority to the existential aspects of their lives and the effort to safeguard them. In my opinion, this is also the fundamental Israeli attitude today.

In my opinion, we have done too little in Israel to study this conflict, and it ought to be the subject of prolonged and detailed research in an academic framework. There is no comparison, even proportionately, between the efforts devoted in the West to the study of the Cold War and our effort to enquire into the Arab-Israel conflict. The reason, no doubt, lies deep, and is connected with aspects of our national psychology; it is not merely a question of neglect.

It may be argued that the discussion and formulation of our opponent's attitude, of the kind attempted in this work, may induce him to adhere to his position and make it more difficult for him to withdraw, that describing his attitude as serious and extreme may initiate the process of the "self-fulfiling prophecy." and that this study is, therefore, harmful. Such an argument is liable to imply an exaggerated self-esteem, as if there is really a simple and direct connection between our talk and reality, as if our words determine the facts. Moreover, a deliberate policy of refusing to look facts in the face cannot be pursued indefinitely. A knowledge of our opponent's attitude, arguments and complaints need not undermine our confidence in our own road. In principle, I believe that the search for truth and the abandonment of illusions are the way to a cure. Sometimes, moreover, the study and repetition of the opponent's arguments may have a beneficial influence both on him (Kelman volume, p. 224) and on the side which does so. Professor A. Rapoport had good reason for his proposal that each side should give an account of the opponent's arguments to the opponent in question, as a method of settling a conflict (*Fights, Games and Debates,* 1960). Of course, that in itself is not sufficient.

The study of the opponent's attitude and his criticism of us can also serve as a mirror in which we can better see ourselves and draw our own attention to aspects that we are liable to ignore, thus constituting a factor for self-improvement. Even if the opponent's criticism is directed at known faults, the very fact that it comes from the opponent is an irritant which may be transformed into a positive stimulus.

The study of the opponent's attitude and charges, as they are, helps to humanize him. An arbitrary assessment of his demands in order to adapt them to our own wishes—in this case, by describing his attitude as if it does not imply any antagonism to our existence—is as good as degrading him and regarding him as less than human, for we dismiss his words, his literature and the statements of his leaders and assume the right to determine what his purposes and wishes are, even in contradiction to the manner in which he presents them.

I believe there is a danger of dehumanizing the opponent in the conflict, which would also take the form of rejecting the possibility that he, too, may have ideas, ideologies, aspirations and an emotional attachment to the country. Without this realization that he, too, can have aims and ideals which stir his soul as his "truth" I am afraid that we shall not adequately understand his behaviour and it will take us by surprise.

The main conclusion from this work, as I see it, is that we must educate and fortify ourselves to face a conflict that may be a protracted one. This can be done only if we see the situation as it really is, without embellishment, without distortions arising out of our ideologies, our self-assurance, and hopes that are doomed to disappointment. The inspiration of the ideals that have guided us and been our source of strength is not sufficient. We must foster the determination that is founded on a relentless perception of the situation and the difficulties it involves. By the same token, we must spare no effort in order to bring about a settlement to the conflict, while remaining aware of our limitations.

POSTSCRIPT

Over three years have passed since this book was completed in the Hebrew original, and almost three years since the Six-Day War. The fact that the new conditions created by the war have led so far to no basic change in the Arab attitude is a demonstration of its stability as described in the book. Some critics argued that my description of the attitude was too static—that, like everything else in this world, the Arab attitude would change one day. No doubt, reality is more powerful than any system of ideas, and people change their ideologies under pressure of facts. It appears, however, that the conditions which will actually compel the Arabs to agree to acceptance of Israel have not yet been created, and I believe that the account given in this book will help to explain the reason why this is so.

Today, Arab spokesmen try to play down the genocidal and politicidal terms which were employed with particular virulence on the eve of the Six-Day War, but an examination of their attitude does not reveal any substantial change. What Haykal says today differs from what Shukairy said yesterday, at the most, in the elegance of the language used. When Haykal declares that there is no room in the Middle East for Arab nationalism and for Israel as well (*al-Ahrām,* February 21, 1969), the logical conclusion is that Israel must be liquidated.

Arab policy is entangled in the contradiction between the "nays" adopted at the Khartoum Conference—no negotiations with Israel, no peace with Israel, no recognition of Israel and no compromise over the rights of the Palestinians to their homeland (the latter being a euphemistic equivalent for the liquidation of Israel), and the agreement of some of them to the Security Council resolution of November 22, 1967. The attitude expressed at Khartoum was a matter of principle; the acceptance of the Security Council resolution was, at the most, a tactical move. The underlying concept is that, while the utmost which can be demanded of the Arab States is to refrain from initiating hostilities, no such restriction applies to the Palestinians, or to the Arab countries' right to assist them. The Security Council resolution becomes, not a means for the achievement of peace, but only an instrument for weakening Israel. The Arab demand is that Israel should withdraw from the territories she holds in obedience to the resolution, while they should be permitted to persist in their refusal to liquidate the conflict and conclude a peace agreement with Israel.

The Palestinians, on their part, repeatedly proclaim that they do not accept the Security Council resolution and will not recognize any peace settlement. By supporting them, the Arab States endorse their attitude. The Fataḥ leaders declare that their aim is "a pluralistic, secular, democratic Palestinian State," but in statements made for internal consumption they emphasize that it must be an "Arab" State, and there seems to have been a hardening of their policy on this particular point of the "Arabism" of "liberated Palestine." Article 6 of the Palestine National Covenant, as amended at the Cairo Conference of the Palestine Liberation Organization in Cairo on 1-17 July 1968, states:

> "The Jews who were permanently resident in Palestine at the beginning of the Zionist invasion will be recognized as Palestinians"—

implying that those Jews who settled in the country after 1917 would be regarded as foreigners and compelled to leave. This is a much more restrictive formula than that contained in the original text of the same article as adopted at the foundation conference of the PLO, from which it could be understood that Jews who lived in Palestine before 1948 would be recognized as Palestinians. Apparently it was felt that the number of Jews must be reduced in case they might constitute a majority. This is the kind of pluralism in which the PLO believes.

There is nothing new in the attitude to Israel expressed by the Fataḥ and other fedayeen organizations when compared with that described in this book. The only novelty lies in their programme, which I have analysed in my booklet: *Fedayeen Action and Arab Strategy,* Adelphi Paper No. 53, London, The Institute for Strategic Studies, December 1968, to which I refer the reader.

Since the Six-Day War there may have been a decline in the use of anti-Semitic themes, as a result of the Arabs' realization that the extremist character of their public statements has repelled foreign public opinion. The picture, however, is by no means uniform, and the fact that, despite the effort to present the moderate image, there are still some who resort to these themes only shows how strongly entrenched they have become as a part of the Arab attitude. Evidence of this may be seen in the book about the Six-Day War written by Sa'ad Jum'a, then Prime Minister of Jordan (*The Great Plot and the Fateful Struggle,* Beirut, Dar al-Kateb al-Arabi, July 1968), which explains Israel's victory on the basis of the Protocols of the Elders of Zion.

The defeat of 1967 might have been expected to bring about a transvaluation of values and an agonizing reappraisal among the Arab peoples. The intellectuals have pointed to structural weaknesses in Arab society as the basic cause of the debacle, but these are the same weaknesses that they have always called on the Arabs to rectify and which they emphasized after the 1948 defeat.

Nasser in his speech of March 30, 1969, went so far as to declare that the UAR armed forces were not put to the test, since they did not participate in the war, but there is nothing new in this argument either. There are grounds for the impression that the weaknesses denounced by the intellectuals have been intensified as a result of the defeat, for there has been growing disintegration, a deeper distrust of others and of the authorities, and a more flagrant disregard of the truth in Arab public life. It is possible that some circles have arrived at the conclusion that a continuation of the dispute will be to the disadvantage of the Arabs, and that they had better cut their losses and reach a settlement with Israel, but these have not yet given unequivocal public expression to their views.

It is also possible that the Palestinians on the West Bank, now under Israeli rule, would like to see a settlement, since they have a great deal to lose from conflict and war. On the other hand, they would like the Arab States to agree to such a settlement, not only for fear of being stigmatized as traitors if they reach such a settlement on their own but—which is even more serious—to avoid being cut off from their families and relatives who are dispersed in the Arab world. A vicious circle has been created: the West Bank Palestinians cannot make peace because of the Arab States, while the latter are shackled by their obligations to the Palestinians, especially towards the Palestinians living in their own countries, whose attitude to Israel is particularly extreme. Israel's agreement to the 1947 Partition Plan implied recognition of a Palestinian Arab entity, and if it was not embodied in a Palestinian State, the fault lay not with Israel, but with the Arabs. Today, as in the past, the fact that these Palestinians are not prepared to settle for a State in part of Palestine, but demand "the restoration of the entire Homeland," means that in the end it is they who will be the sufferers. Any conflict is a tragedy, but for Israel this one also has a positive side, as a stimulus to greater cohesion and unity, while for the Arabs it means nothing but loss. If they come to realize this fact, they may one day be prepared to put an end to the conflict and start a new era of cooperation and progress.

June 1970

NOTES

INTRODUCTION

1. The distinction of three components in an attitude is to be found in the psychological literature, with minor differences in nomenclature: Krech, Crutchfield and Ballachy, p. 140; Daniel Katz's article; Scott, in the Kelman volume, p. 72 (for detailed references to these and other general works on sociology, etc., see Bibliography III).
2. Another method, followed by Lane in his American investigation (see Bibliography III), is that of "interviews in depth" with a limited number of individuals. In the case of our subject, this would also involve great difficulty, especially as such Arabs could only be contacted outside their national environment. Opinions expressed by Arabs abroad on various aspects of the conflict are discussed in Chapter 8. As a result of the Six-Day War, it is true, there has been a considerable increase in the number of Arabs whose attitudes could be investigated by field studies, but it should be taken into account that their replies would be affected by their present position under Israeli rule.
3. The expression "effective public opinion" is taken from R. Gilpin's *Scientists and Nuclear Policy* (Princeton, 1962).

CHAPTER 1

1. For example, Professor Jessie Barnard explains: "Conflict arises when there are incompatible or mutually exclusive goals or aims or values espoused by human beings" (1957, p. 38). Professor Boulding, former, director of the Center for Research on Conflict Resolution at the University of Michigan, writes: "Conflict may be defined a situation of competition in which parties are *aware* of the incompatibility of potential future positions and in which each party *wishes* to occupy a position that is incompatible with the wishes of the other" (p. 5). Raymond Aron defines conflict as "opposition between groups and individuals for the possession of goods which are in short supply or the attainment of mutually incompatible values" (1957, p. 179).

2. It is noteworthy that an explanation of the conflict which revolves around the idea of the objective is a teleological one—expressing its conscious aim—and should be complemented by a causative explanation of its source, namely, what impelled the adoption of objective.
3. In these statements we can distinguish various shades of severity against Israel. "A settlement in accordance with UN resolutions" refers to resolutions actually adopted, whether on partition or on the refugees' right to repatriation. "A settlement in keeping with the UN Charter" or "the principles of the UN" is a more flexible formula, which allows of two contrary interpretations: one in the spirit of the Arab demand for liquidation, on the grounds that the partition resolution of 1947 was incompatible with the UN Charter; and an opposite interpretation—respect for the integrity of States in accordance with the UN Charter. As for the rights of the Palestinians, "the rights of the Arabs of Palestine" is a less extreme expression from the point of view of the Arab attitude than the "right of the Palestinian Arab people." Formulae of a more emphatic anti-Israel character are "support for the (just) struggle for the restoration of legal rights," sometimes made even more emphatic by the addition of "against Imperialism and Zionism" or "support for the natural right of the Palestinian people to self-determination."
4. Similarly, the Arab League States declared, when they started their war against Israel, that their object was: "to enable them 'the Arabs of Palestine) to defend their lives so that they should achieve the independence and unity of Palestine" (Rushdi, p. 106). In other words, the prevention of the implementation of the partition plan is presented as a purely defensive operation.

   In a like fashion Shukairy called at a press conference for the development of terrorist activities inside Israel in order to "repulse Israeli aggression in its own territory" (PLO Radio, October 25, 1966, 20:00 hrs).
5. As Ahmad put it: "The watchword of Zionism was the redemption of the land of Judea of the restoration of the kingdom of Israel, which meant the liquidation of Muslim rule" *(Israel—the Misled People,* p. 24).
6. These measurements are carried out in semi-automatic "content inquiries" by computer. The Department for the Study of International Conflicts and Integration at the University of Stanford specialized in one of these systems, known as The General Inquirer, which has been developed in the United States. The value of such methods is a matter of controversy. Sometimes, perhaps, the work that has to be invested in such studies is out of all proportion to the results, which might, though not always, be achieved by a general impression. Professor Karl Deutch regards the system as an important departure in political science. See Deutch K.W., "Recent Trends in Research Methods in Political Science" in: *A Design for Political Science: Scope, Objective and Methods,* Monograph 6, American Academy of Political and Social Science (Philadelphia, 1966). Studies of this kind in connection with the Arab-Israel conflict are possible and may yet be carried out one day.
7. Nasser said, for instance: "Egypt is dedicated to the rights of the Palestinian

Arab people. The question does not call for any negotiations. The UN adopted a resolution on Palestine in 1947, just as in 1949 it adopted another resolution on the rights of the Palestinian people" (speaking to the press on November 28, 1955, I.L., VI/1042).

8. Nasser's demands for compliance with UN resolutions were repeated with particular frequency in 1954–55: "Egypt wants to appeal frankly to the Western World in regard to repeated aggression from Israel against the borders of the Arab countries. We want to say that if this aggression does not stop and if Israel is not restored at least to what the UN has decided time after time, there will be a danger of an explosion in the Arab East, from which the Arab East will not lose nearly so much as those who protect Israel and show so much tolerance to her. Ṭhe sufferings and torments of the uprooted sons of Palestine are sufficient in themselves to refute any argument in defence of Israel or in justification of her repeated aggression. For the honour of the UN, the leaders of that body must do something substantial for the implementation of its decisions, which have been trampled by Israel. In saying this, Egypt expressed the feelings of forty million Arabs." (At the al-Azhar Mosque on the second anniversary of the Revolution, July 23, 1954, I.L., II/419–20.)

"I cannot see any speedy solution to this situation unless world public opinion or international pressure compels Israel to evacuate the area she occupied without regard to the partition plan, or according to some condition in any possible situation . . .

"The leaders of Egypt and the Arabs have repeatedly declared that it will be quite impossible to facilitate the paving of the way *(al-tamhīd)* for the making of peace *(Ṣulḥ)* with Israel unless Israel honours the decisions of the Security Council. But Israel has never ceased to provoke the UN and continues her barbaric attacks on the villages at the front, which have angered world public opinion and impelled the American Government to lay the blame on Israel." (Press interview, September 13, 1954, I.L., III/524.)

9. Bourguiba wrote in a letter to Nasser: "You know better than anyone else that it is not a problem of the aim, in connection with which there cannot be any differences of opinion, namely to enable our Palestinian brethren to regain their stolen homeland. What certain circles find it difficult to understand, or have understood imperfectly, either deliberately or unintentionally, is that the problem is how to achieve the aim. Intentionally or unintentionally, they have confused the end with the means, and treated the effect to discover the means as if it were the abondonment of, or indifference to, the aim . . . The purpose of this plan is not acquiescence and the acceptance of a compromise solution *(inṣāf al-ḥulūl)*, as some believe, but to get the problem moving after it has been deadlocked . . .

"I hoped, and time has proved that I was right, that Israel would not agree to accept the United Nations resolutions; thus, unwillingly, she strengthens our position, for the Arab Sates will show the Western States that in their struggle for Palestine they are defending the UN resolutions, which are in accordance with our principles. It is obvious to me, and events have confirmed this, that the Powers will condemn Israel's refusal to comply with the UN decision; the Arabs will indirectly profit from this, and as a result of controversy between Israel and her supporters the foundations on which Zionist colonialism stands will be undermined.

"One of two things will happen: Israel will ultimately accept the decisions of the international organizations—which is a very unlikely possibility—will permit the refugees to return and give up part of the conquered country. In this way, conditions will be changed in favour of the Arabs and new possibilities will be revealed which will lead to the final solution *(al-ḥall al-nihā'ī)*. Another possibility, which is more likely, is that Israel will persist in her refusal, and then it is the Arab position that will be stronger, even if war breaks out between the parties . . .

"I remember that in my address to the Kings and Presidents who assembled in Cairo I said that sometimes the struggle requires that those responsible should endanger their prestige and their past, and bring down the wrath of the masses on their heads, for the sake of a sounder solution, the effectiveness of which will not be visible until some time has passed." *(āl-'Amal,* April 30, 1965, quoted in 'Anbatāwī, *The Palestinian Documents for 1965,* pp. 185–8.)

This explanation was repeated by Bourguiba in a memorandum to the third Summit Conference *(āl-'Amal,* September 14, 1965, *op. cit.,* p. 486; see also: Leila S. Kadi, *Arab Summit Conferences and the Palestine Problem,* p. 174). It is noteworthy that Bourguiba has no compunctions about using the expression "final solution," which has assumed a special significance since the Nazi Holocaust—but perhaps he is not aware of this.

10. This confirmed by the Egyptian Indoctrination Authority in *al-marja' al-Mawaḥḥad lil-Taw'iyya al-Qawmiyya* ("The Standard Source for National Education"), Part II, 1966, pp. 22–24. In directives to army officers on how to explain to the troops the rejection of Bourguiba's proposals, it is emphasized that the step-by-step method may be suitable for the struggle against Imperialism, but not for the categorical Arab-Israel confronatation. Bourguiba's method assumes a recognition, even if only partial, of the accomplished fact; hence it is tantamount to defeatism, which will be injurious to morale. This criticism does not present Bourguiba as a traitor to the cause, but only objects to the effectiveness of his methods. (See my book *How the Arab Attitude Against Israel was Explained in the Egyptian Army* (Hebrew), Israel Defence Forces, General Staff, 1967, pp. 105–8.)
11. Wākid wrote: "The Jews would use the opportunities for emigration had not the Government of Israel enacted laws preventing their doing so" (*Israel in the Balance,* 1959, p. 28). "The journalist Uri Avneri, owner of *Ha'Olam Hazeh,* says that Israel is like a prison which a man who has entered it cannot leave. Worse that, it is like a trap from which a man cannot excape" (p. 75).
12. Khālidī's statement that there is no room for two nationalities sounds like

an echo of the words traditionally ascribed to Muhammad: "There shall not be together two religions in the Arabian Peninsula," which was given as justification for the expulsion of the Jews from the peninsula in the days of ʿUmar ibn al-Khaṭṭab and is mentioned, for instance, by Tall, *The Danger of World Jewry to Islam and Christianity,* p. 52.

13. It is true that ʿAlūsh, who adopts an extremist approach, calls for "a moral attitude towards the Jews," and says that "it should be clear that under no circumstances shall we throw the Jews into the sea" (p. 219), but a few pages later he himself points out the connection between politicide and genocide. He explains that the struggle against Israel will be "a momentous struggle, for the fate of the Arabs depends on it, since the Jew, who has burned all his bridges, in front and behind, to the right and the left, is prepared to do the same as Samson, unless the Arabs kill him before the hair grows on his head" (*Journey to Palestine,* p. 225).
14. ʿAlūsh p. 146, quoted from the Arab Nationalist Movements' book *Maʿa al-Quwmiyya al-ʿArabioyya* ("With Arab Nationalism"), (first edition, published by Ittiḥād Baʿathāt al-Kuwayt, April 1957, pp. 9–10). "Revenge" as a motive and a description of the action aimed at is common in the Arab literature of the conflict; so is the expression *"maʿrakat al-thaʾr"* ("the campaign of vengeance")—see King Hussein's letter to Nasser of November 18, 1965 (al-Hindāwī, p. 148).
15. This aim is by no means a new one. The Jerusalem weekly *al-Shabāb,* edited by Imīl al Ghawrī, published on February 9, 1935, a *feuilleton* called "A Vision of the Night" describing a session of the Palestinian parliament after the expulsion of the Jews and the British and the establishment of an Arab State. The Speaker proposes the appointment of a parliamentary committee to discuss the question of the Zionist settlements—established by the Jews in the neighbourhood of the coast so that they should be under the protection of the British Fleet—which, according to the article, are now deserted, and to provide homes in Tel Aviv for Transjordanian Bedouin who had fought for the liberation of Palestine (Yehoshua Ben Hanania, "The Arabs Describe the State of Israel," *Haboker,* April 15, 1952).
16. Klineberg, *The Human Dimension in International Relations,* p. 86.
17. Denouncing the politicians who were to blame for the loss of Palestine because they did nothing but make numerous speeches, Nasser said: "They used to talk in their speeches about 'so-called Israel' and did nothing but speechify about 'so-called Israel'" (December 13, 1953, I.L., I/156). Colonel Muhammad Ṣafwat begins his book *Israel, the Common Enemy* (1952) with the words: "So-called Israel is no longer 'so-called,' but has become an accomplished fact."
18. Arab statements implying recognition of Israel and her right to continue to exist are very rare, and most of them are hedged round with conditions. Some of them appeared in Egypt at the beginning of the fifties. Press accounts about Israel's readiness to support Egypt in the struggle against the British were

published in *Rūz al-Yūsuf* and *al-Muṣawwar* at the end of 1951. Prince ʿAbbās Ḥalīm wrote in *Le Messager,* Cairo, an article entitled "Le paix avec Israel, que a interêt a l'empècher?" (March 8, 1952), in which he advocated peace with Israel. In reply to various reactions, he published a second article in the same paper (March 15, 1952) called "Illusions et réalités," in which he wrote that, while Israel would have to settle the problem of the refugees, especially by absorbing them, Egypt's main interest was in the Sudan; it was therefore important to work for cooperation with Israel and try to achieve a favourable attitude towards Egypt on the part of Israel and the Jews outside. He was preceded by Ismāʿīl Ṣidqī in 1949. The noted Egyptian author Salāma Mūsā expressed appreciation of the Jews and their contribution to culture and spoke of the need for peace with Israel. (He was imprisoned in 1953 as a result of these statements.)

The attitude of the Arab Communists constitutes another story. Until 1947, the Communist parties in the Middle East (like the others) were hostile to Zionism and supported Arab nationalist demands: cessation of immigration, prohibition of land sales, and the right of the Palestinian Arabs to self-determination. Soviet support for partition led to a change in their attitude: although they had previously opposed it, they now supported it too, and issued declarations favouring the right of the Jews to a State and recognizing them as a nation. In 1948 the Communists opposed the war and even demonstrated against it, describing it as an imperialist plot backed by the Arab bourgeoisie. The change in the Soviet attitude towards Israel, especially in 1954–55, brought about a change in their attitude as well. In the Syrian parliament, Khālid Bakdāsh attacked Israel's right to exist and declared that the Jews are not a nation. The resolutions of the central committee of the Syrian-Lebanese Communist Party on May 7, 1956, denounced the idea of the Jewish National Home (ʿAlūsh, *Journey to Palestine,* pp. 129–46).

Communist support for Israel at one stage is clear from the text of resolutions passed by the Syrian-Lebanese Communist Party (no date given, but apparently at the end of the forties or the beginning of the fifties) quoted at the end of Ibrāhīm al-Ḥilū's book *Communism and Zionism Are Twins.* The main points in the resolutions are: support for the Soviet attitude to partition and the establishment of two independent Palestinian states; the Jews concentrated in Palestine were becoming a nation; opposition to reactionary Zionism; the struggle against the Jews as a strategem of the Arab bourgeoisie to divert attention from the struggle with Imperialism; Zionism as a danger only as an agent of Imperialism; pacification would lead to the deepening of the chasm between the Jewish working masses and the Zionist bourgeoisie. In recent years, mention of the possibility of a settlement with Israel has become even rarer. In *al-Muṣawwar* (August 17, 1961) Fikrī Abāẓa raised the idea of the establishment of a Middle East federation in which Palestine would combine with Israel after the abolition of its religious character (i.e., after it should cease to be a Jewish State—Y.H.): "The Israelis would be citizens in this federation, which would guarantee all minorities their full rights in accordance with international conditions," Abāẓa writes. It is noteworthy that, although these statements did not imply recognition of Israel's right to independence, they were regarded as heresy and Abāẓa was suspended from his paper for a time.

Bashir Ben Yahmad, editor of *Jeune Afrique,* proposed in his paper the establishment of a federation on the pattern of the USA, in which Israel would have a similar status to that of the American States, but would have to repatriate the refugees (January 1965).

19. Quotations from Nasser demanding the implementation of the partition decision have been given above. Declarations that Egypt had no aggressive intentions were repeated at the end of 1955 after the arms deal with Czechoslovakia and in connection with it. It may be assumed that Nasser was particularly anxious at the time to weaken the impression made by the deal. He emphasized that it was not Egypt but Israel that was aggressive, as was proved by Israeli border raids. He made no reference whatsoever to the acceptance of Israel's right to exist.

20. For example, Najīb al-Khūrī Naṣṣār, editor and owner of *al-Karmil,* warned in his book *On Zionism* (1911) about Zionism's intentions to acquire a homeland and the dangers involved, and called for counter-action to prevent the loss of Palestine, "so that we should not become the objects of the curses of our fathers and our descendants because of the loss of the land which our forefathers won with their blood" (p. 64).

'Umar Ṣāliḥ al-Barghūthī wrote, in an article in Kurd Ali's book *Khiṭaṭ al-Sha'm:* ("Regions of Syria") "The aspiration of all the immigrants was to get the Arabs out of the country and acquire it as their property" (Vol. III, 1925, p. 227).

21. Today, Arabs explain away agreement to Jewish immigration as having been due to philanthropic motives at a time when the political intentions had not been grasped. Thus, Ṭarabīn explains Fayṣal's consent to the agreement with Weizmann: "It must be noted that the Arabs at that time regarded Zionism not according to its political imperialistic nature and imagined that its aim was the immigration of a small number of persecuted Jews." (*Lectures on the History of the Palestine Problem,* 1958, p. 64.)

22. The demand for the prohibition of the sale of lands to the Jews was made as an Arab national demand, according to Dr. Gabbay, *A Political Study of Arab-Jewish Conflict: The Arab Refugee Problem* (English edition, Geneva, 1959, p. 27), by the Fifth Arab Congress in 1922.

There was opposition to the Jews even before that. In 1891, Arab notables in Jerusalem presented a petition against Jewish immigration to the authorities in Constantinople. There was opposition to the purchase of land by the Palestine Jewish Colonization Association in Galilee in 1900 (Alsberg, "The Arab Question in the Policy of the Zionist Executive before World War I": in *Shivat Ziyon,* vol. IV, 1955–57, p. 162, and Y. Lunz's article "The Diplomatic

Contacts between the Zionist Movement and the Arab National at the End of World War I" in *Hamizraḥ Heḥadash,* Vol. XII, No. 4, pp. 212–29).

23. In the above-mentioned article in *Le Messager,* March 3, 1952, Prince ʿAbbās Ḥalīm expressed his disbelief in the collapse of Israel.
24. For example, Nasser declared: "Israel has cut all the lines of land communication between Egypt and the Arab countries east of Suez. We believe that Egypt and the Arab countries are entitled to achieve the land communication lines which are essential for their trade, prosperity and defence plans . . . Israel has seized the southern part of Palestine which stretches down to the Gulf of Aqaba, although the UN and the Arab States have not recognized Israel's right to this territory." (At a press conference, September 13, 1954, I.L., III/523.)

CHAPTER 2

1. For ideology as compensation for lack of achievement and realistic planning, see: Brunswik, E.F., "Environmental Control and the Impoverishment of Thought" in: Friedrich, C.J. (ed.), *Totalitarianism* (New York, Universal Library, 1964), p. 174. Festinger, Ricken and Shechter have shown that when the expectations of a group or sect are disappointed, it does not necessarily regard this as a refutation of their doctrines and discard them. Sometimes the contrary is the case: the disappointment leads to more fanatical devotion and propaganda activity (summarized in the Maccoby, Newcomb and Hartley, *Readings in Social Psychology,* 3rd edition, pp. 156f.). Arab activity in regard to the conflict may be partly a reaction to the frustrating reality; this may be part of the explanation of the more extreme manifestations that have followed the Six-Day War.
2. The term "ideology" is not used in this work in the commonly accepted sense. For example, R. Lane, one of the modern students of this subject, applies the word particularly to the system of concepts, attitudes and beliefs which are held by men in connection with political affairs ("latent political ideology"). For the ideological system of the exponents of the ideology he uses the term "forensic ideology," because of its polemical function and the debate and controversy involved (this is the declared ideology). He also makes a distinction between "implied" and "express" ideology, namely: between the ideas in the mind and those that people proclaim. Lane tries to reveal the (latent) ideology through conversations with 15 persons, from which he generalizes about the ideology current in the United States. In this sense, his approach is similar to that of American sociologists who define ideology as a system of beliefs (see his book *Political Ideology*). William Scott, in his article "Empirical Evaluation of Values and Ideologies," in the Singer volume, refers to cultural ideologies as concepts current in the culture of a group. In this sense, every group has an ideology. This is an anthropological conception of

the term. In the present work, ideology is regarded as a political and social, and not as a cultural, manifestation, though it may be influenced by cultural factors.

3. The publishing department of the Egyptian Ministry of Culture and National Guidance, the General Egyptian Institute for Information, Publishing, Distribution and Printing (al-Mu'assasa al-Miṣriyya al-'Āmma lil-Anbā' wa-al-Nashr wa-al-Tawzḥ' wa-al-Ṭibā'a) contains a number of institutions, of which the principal one is the Nationalist Printing and Publishing House *(Dār al-Qawmiyya lil-Ṭibā'a wa-al-Nashr)*. The latter issues a wide variety of publications according to "a plan prepared by 'Abd al-Qādir Ḥātim, Vice-President for Culture and Guidance." (For an article about these companies, their place in the Egyptian political system and their national function see *al-Muṣawwar,* March 12, 1965.) The company issues several series of books for national propaganda and orientation, including many works on the conflict.
4. The allegation that the Jews intended to expand beyond the borders of Palestine was made as early as 1911 by Naṣṣār Najīb al-Khūrī in a book called *Zionism* published in Haifa, on the grounds of articles in the *Jewish Encylopaedia* and verses quoted in it: "Their numbers will increase until Palestine is too small and then they will expand to Lebanon and Trans-Jordan: that is why they add the word Syria to Palestine, and in some cases Turkey and Asia and the East" (pp. 4–5).
5. The expression "vertical expansion" may be taken from 'Izzat's book *I Was in Israel,* in which he describes how the late Moshe Sharett told him: "The only expansion that Israel will carry out is vertical expansion" (p. 49).
6. The argument that the Zionist enterprise is doomed because of its unnatural character was put forward in the twenties by 'Umar Ṣāliḥ al-Barghūthī in an article on the history of Zionism appearing in Kurd Ali's book *Khiṭaṭ al-Sha'm* ("Regions of Syria"): "Even if the Jews have made some progress, I believe that their success is only temporary, although they have been helped by Britain and the Western States, for any movement which is not natural and which is not impelled by a true faith is bound to end in failure" (1925, Vol. III, p. 231).
7. 'Alūsh, who may be regarded as a leftist Palestinian, denounced Shukairy for presenting the conflict as a Palestinian-Israeli, and not an Arab-Israeli, one by emphasizing the claims of the refugees at the UN. 'Alūsh suspected that Shukairy's intention was to prevent the intervention of the Arab States in the conflict. From his own extreme Pan-Arab point of view, Shukairy's claims implied a recognition of the fragmentation of the Arab world into separate States and acquiescence in the frontiers delineated by Imperialism (*Journey to Palestine,* 1964, p. 58).
8. Dr. Hasan Sa'ab wrote: "Our test *(miḥnatunā)* as against Israel is the historic criterion for the possibility that our other aspirations will be fully or freely realized" or whether there will be a national surrender to Israeli superiority and international force. The continued existence of Israel meant "the annul-

ment of any possibility of Arab development or growth." Hence a change in the balance against Israel "is not only a pressing necessity in order to achieve the restoration of the rights of our brethren the Arabs of Palestine but a necessity to enable us to ace according to out rights" and not according to Israel's will (*Ideological Consciousness,* p. 56–57). In other words, the struggle against Israel is a test of Arab freedom of action and independence and the extent to which the Arabs can be their own masters in their territory. Sa'ab also declared that the inability of the Arabs to master Israel raised doubts as to the value of all their national achievements.

ʿAbd al-Dā'im wrote: "Imperialism in the heart (of the Arab countries) has a fundamental support, namely Israel, which makes their independence imaginary and liable to collapse at any moment so long as we do not stand up to this imperialistic danger" (*The Arab Homeland and the Revolution,* p. 254).

Similarly, Nasser says: "The liberation of Palestine, besides being a right, is the true guarantee for the freedom and unification of the entire Arab people" (November 24, 1966).

9. The ideologization of the clash which is involved in a conflict is typical of the role played by intellectuals. Coser, following Marx, Zimmel and Mannheim, emphasizes the function of intellectuals in transforming the clash of interests into a clash of ideologies. The intellectuals brought about the "objectivization" of social movements by changing them from groups representing interests into ideological movements. By abstractification and depersonalization, the opposition involved in the conflict—a struggle not against a particular capitalist but against capitalism—becomes sharper. Thus, the intellectuals brought about the deepening of the struggle by divesting it of the personal motivation and making it a struggle over eternal verities (*The Social Functions of Social Conflict,* p. 116). In his article "The Sociology of Human Conflict" (McNeil volume p. 101), Professor Angel continues the same line of thought, explaining Zimmel's conception of the severity of ideological conflict: "Conflict is intense if it is ideological. Personal goals and ambitions are more easily compromised than impersonal causes."
10. It is noteworthy that Nashāshībī, the whole of whose book is written in a tone of crude belligerence, adds: "[We are] inclined to peace if they are so inclined, but if they are not so inclined, we shall continue to threaten, warn and prepare for the next round" (p. 172). This seems to be lip service to the verse in the Quran: "And if they incline to peace, do than incline to its; and put thy trust in Allah. Lo! He is the Hearer, the Knower" (Surah VIII, The Spoils, v. 61). Nashāshībī seems to assume that Israel, by her very nature, cannot incline to peace.
11. The contention that the use of force is "a convincing argument" is used by both rivals. Thus, Nashāshībī writes: "The enemy understands nothing but the language of force. We must speak to him in this language" (p. 245).

CHAPTER 3

1. Stranger writes: "Projection commonly takes the form of exaggerating in other persons a disapproved characteristic which one does not wish to recognize in oneself" (McNeil volume, p. 55).
2. See Ralph K. White, "Images in the Context of International Conflict," Kelman volume, p. 259.
3. Erikson, E.H., "Wholeness and Totality—A Psychiatric Contribution" in: Friedrich, C.J. (ed.), *Totalitarianism* (New York University Library Edition, 1964), p. 165.
4. See Pruitt's discussion of "contrasting perspective" in his article "Definition of the Situation as a Determinant of International Action" in the Kelman volume, p. 396, and Stagner's article in the McNeil volume, p. 57.
5. Allport calls this "complementary projection," which he defines as "the process of explaining and justifying our own state of mind by reference to imagined intention and behavior of others" (*The Nature of Prejudice*, p. 367).
6. Similarly, Kurt Lewin explains: "Incorrect stereotypes (prejudices) are functionally equivalent to wrong concepts (theories)" (*Resolving Social Conflicts*, p. 62).
7. A comparison of the roles played by the idea of the enemy can also be useful for the understanding of the specific characteristics of nations. It should be noted, however, that this indicator is not included in the Yale plan for comparison between peoples (which places the emphasis on quantitative study). See Merritt, R.L., and Rokkan S., *Comparing Nations: The Use of Quantitative Data in Cross-National Research* (New Haven and London, Yale University Press, 1966).
8. Gibb, Sir Hamilton, Z.R., "Social Reform: Factor X" in: Laqueur, W.Z. (ed.), *The Middle East in Transition* (London, Routledge & Kegan Paul, 1958), p. 8.
9. The urge to believe in plots as an explanation may be due to the tendency to secrecy which S. Hamady ascribes to the Arabs, in her *Temperament and Character of the Arabs*, p. 37.
10. The idea of the "hidden hand" is emphasized in works in which the anti-imperialistic theme is conspicuous. A chapter in Niqūlā al-Durr's *Thus It Was Lost and Thus It Will Return* is headed "The Hidden Hand and Its Helpers" (p. 57). We find the same motif in ʿAlūsh's *The Journey to Palestine* and in works with anti-Semitic tinge centering on the great plot of the Elders of Zion (Zuʿbī and Shamīs, for example).
11. The expression "community of consent" is taken from Deutch, K.W. et al., *Political Community and the North Atlantic Area* (Princeton University Press, 1957).
12. Allport distinguishes between "intropunitive" persons, who tend to blame themselves, and the "extropunitive," who blame others. See his article "The Function of Expectation" in the Bramson and Goethals volume, p. 181.

13. Similarly, White speaks of "diffused hostility that somehow seeks a hate-object" in the Kelman volume, p. 268.
14. S. Hamady writes: "Their [the Arabs'] public-mindedness is not developed and their social consciousness is weak. The allegiance toward the state is shaky and identification with leaders is not strong " (p. 230). "The Arabs so far have demonstrated an incapacity for discipline and abiding unity. They experience collective outbursts of enthusiasm but do not pursue patiently collective endeavours, which are usually embraced halfheartedly" (p. 100).
15. On the need to consider the anthropological aspect of conflicts involving meetings between cultures, see "The Anthropology of Human Conflict," by Margaret Mead and Rhoda Metraux, in the McNeil volume, pp. 116, 122.
16. Shouby's explanation that the Arabic language in itself tempts the Arabs to fanciful exaggeration may be correct, but this is not sufficient to explain the copious use of abusive expressions (see his article listed in Bibliography III).
17. Hayakawa S.I., *Language in Thought and Action* (London, George Allen and Unwin Ltd., Second Ed., 1965), pp. 83–5.
18. Allport calls this "verbal realism" (*The Nature of Prejudice,* p. 182).
19. See the articles "Dār al-Ḥarb," Dār al-Islām" and "Jihād" in *The Encyclopaedia of Islam* and Kadduri, M., "The Islamic Theory of International Relations and its Contemporary Relevance" in: Proctor, J.H. (ed.), *Islam and International Relations* (New York, Praeger, London, Pall Mall, 1955).
20. "Islam must be completely made over before the concept of *jihād* can be eliminated" (D.B. Macdonald in *Shorter Encyclopaedia of Islam,* p. 89a).
21. For example, in the pamphlet issued by the Palestinian Arab Committee in Egypt, *The Jews and Islam in Ancient Days and Today, the Jews and Palestine and the Verses of the Jihād and the Ḥadīths About Them,* 1937. The call for the Jihād is mentioned by al-Jiyār, p. 94.
22. Freud writes: "It is always possible to bind together a considerable number of people in love, so long as there are other people left over to receive the manifestations of their aggressiveness" (*Civilization and Its Discontents,* N.Y., Norton & Co., p. 61).
23. The expression "negative reference group" is Newcomb's; it is quoted by Coser, p. 90. When André Malraux was asked about the purpose of his travels to the Far East he replied: "Cultiver ma différence."
24. Research has shown that there is a correlation between suppressive treatment or neglect of children and a tendency on their part to distorted images (Allport, *The Nature of Prejudice,* p. 285). In the chapter on "The Rearing of Children" (pp. 134 ff.) in Berger's *The Arab World,* there are details which arouse some suspicion as to the possible frequency of these phenomena in the upbringing of children in the Arab countries. Definite conclusions, however, could be drawn only after detailed study.
25. The frequency of manifestations of authoritarianism is discussed by Professor L.H. Melikian, head of the Department of Psychology at the American Uni-

versity in Beirut, in "Authoritarianism and Its Correlates in the Egyptian Culture and the United States," *Journal of Social Issues,* Vol. 15, No. 3, (1959) and "The Dethronement of the Father," *Middle East Forum,* Vol 36, No. 1 (January 1960).

26. Considerable attention is paid to the reason for the Soviet support of partition. ʿAlūsh suggests a number of reasons, such as the weakness of the USSR and Stalin's wish to gain the support of World Zionism, the wish to find an opening in an area that appeared to be an Imperialist preserve, the fact that the prospects of Communism seemed to be better in the industrialized Jewish State than in the agricultural Arab countries, the numerous Jews among the Communist leaders in Eastern Europe, and, finally, Stalin's callous readiness to send entire peoples into exile (pp. 135–6).
27. Coser's explanation might apply partially to neo-colonialism: "Disappearance of the original enemy leads to a search for new enemies so that the group may continue to engage in conflict, thereby maintaining a structure that it would be in danger of losing were there no longer an enemy" (p. 105).
28. The belief in deliberate imperialist plans leads some writers to regard the handing over of Alexandretta to the Turks and Palestine to the Jews as links in a single chain. This is the attitude of Niqūlā al-Durr, cited with approval by ʿAlūsh (p. 70).

CHAPTER 4

1. It should be noted that there is a great difference between the denunciation of Zionism after its victory (which is presented in this chapter) and its denunciation by Barghūthī on the grounds that it cannot succeed, in his article on the subject (written in 1925) in Kurd Ali's book *Khiṭaṭ al-Sha'm* ("Regions of Syria"). He explains that Zionism is "a fantastic idea devoid of truth . . . Their [the Zionists'] call for a return to this country is particularly hard to realize because: 1. their nationalism has been obliterated (from it); 2. they [the Jews] are divided in their tendencies and traditions; 3. the Jews are united by religion but divided by nationality—they have one faith but they are many nations; 4. they have nothing to unite them and they do not act according to a single programme; 5. the Arabs are the masters of the land and constitute a part of a vast Arab ocean" (Vol. IV, pp. 230–1).
2. In his effort to deny the bond of the Jews with the Holy Land, which is expressed in Jewish liturgy, ʿAqqād pours scorn on the prayers of the Jews: "Their emotions towards Palestine in this period were no more than yearnings for ancient glory and the expectation of a time that would be chosen by God without their having any part in bringing it nearer or postponing it in regard to the Divine will, and their prayers, which they used to repeat every day or every week, seeking the favour of God, were mere repetitious verbiage, which is at the most meaningless" (p. 20).

3. One reason for Dr. Sayyid Nawfal's denunciation of Hans Kohn for finding early signs of a national outlook among the Jews (see Chapter 6, Section 4) is, no doubt, that if nationalism started among the Jews, they must, after all, be a nation.
4. Wākid declares, p. 27, that the Zionists are of Mongolian origin and do not belong to the Semitic peoples of Asia; later he identifies them with the Khazars. According to Darwaza, on the other hand, there are Aryan, and not Khazar elements in those known as Ashkenazim. He quotes Balādhurī, who, in his book *The Conquest of the Lands,* says that a "certificate of security," presented by the Arab Commander Ḥabīb ibn-Maslama to the inhabitants of the city of Wasīl, in the country of the Armenians and Khazars, applied to the Jews as well, implying that there were already Jews there at the time of the Caliph 'Uthmān ibn 'Affān (p. 573).

   In the introduction to the Arabic translation of Jacques Tani's *The Fifth Column in Zion,* Political Books, No. 160, Muhammad Sa'īd 'Abd al-Fattāḥ refers to a history of the Zionist Organization called *Unity in Diversity,* by the Russian writer A. L. Kubofitzky, published in 1948, which says on page 377 that the Ashkenazim are descended not from Jacob, but from the Khazars.
5. The emphasis on this point may be an echo of Muslim religious law. Under "Dār al-Ḥarb" Macdonald explains in *The Shorter Encyclopaedia of Islam* (p. 69) that when a Muslim country is conquered by non-Muslims and becomes Dār al-Ḥarb, it is the duty of all Muslims to leave it, and any woman who refuses to accompany her husband is liable to immediate divorce.
6. The idea of the continuity between the ancient Jews and those of today leads 'Iṣmat to compare the change of name from Sarai to Sarah with the case of the late Foreign Minister Moshe Sharett, whose original name was Shertok (p. 21). Such changes of name are presented as a deep-seated Jewish characteristic. The idea may be connected with that of the cunning and rootlessness ascribed to the Jews.
7. On the other hand, there is a forgiving attitude towards cruelties perpetrated by Muslims. Muhammad's behaviour to the Jewish tribes of Medina, and especially to the Qurayẓa, 750 of whose men were executed and their women and children sold into slavery after they had surrendered, is presented in the spirit of Muslim tradition as an act of just retribution for the intrigues of the Jews against Islam (Tall, p. 50).
8. Zionism as an example is presented in as early a work Naṣṣār's *Zionism* (Haifa, 1911, p. 63): "We know that Zionism and its supporters have become strong and wealthy organizations; in order to resist their aims the heart of every Ottoman must be flowing over with nationalism for this purpose, and the land needs leaders as faithful as Herzl, who will give priority to the general over the private interest." (Naṣṣār was still speaking in the name of the Ottomans, and not the Arabs.)

CHAPTER 5

1. The pogrom at Granada in 1066, in which a mob attacked and murdered three or four thousand Jews, was undoubtedly exceptional (see Rosenblatt's "The Jews in Islam"). On the literary incitement that preceded the pogrom, see Moshe Perlman's article "Eleventh Century Andalusian Author on the Jews of Granada."
2. Professor Ben-Sasson writes in a similar vein: "In Islam—Ishmael—bodily injuries and mob violence were not the main phenomena of exile. Religious coercion was limited to a few fanatics, like the al-Muwaḥḥidūn (Almohades) in 12th-century Spain and North Africa, but degradation and social oppression were part of the law of the Islamic state and society, and were particularly marked in those countries where they were not overshadowed by the threat of death" (*Encyclopaedia Hebraica,* Vol. 10, article *"Galut,"* p. 822).
3. A similar explanation, quoting the same verse from the Quran, is given by Ibn Khaldūn, who explains that in the past the Jews were endowed with a colective consciousness *(ʿaṣabiyya),* but they lost it "and degradation was their lot for many generations" (p. 91 in Emanuel Koplewitz's Hebrew translation). The Arabic expression is *rusūkh al-dhall,* which indicates that degradation had become rooted in them.
4. Al-Bayḍāwī explains that this verse means that "the sparing of them in return for the *jizya* was a great mercy." (According to a tradition from Ibn ʿAbbās, when the *jizya* was collected the vassal was struck on the nape of the neck. The *Encyclopaedia of Islam* (new edition, Vol II, p. 562a) explains that apart from Shāfiʿī, commentators and jurists demanded payment by a degrading process, and that it was on the basis of this verse that the degrading signs on the clothing of the unbelievers were instituted.)

   The original meaning of the expression *'an yad,* here translated "readily," was, as Professor Kister shows, "according to their capacity" ("ʿAn Yadin Quran IX/29," *Arabica,* Tome XI, 1964, pp. 272–278). But the accepted interpretation was that the payment must be made by hand, directly, and not through an intermediary.

   The verses referring to the degradation of the Jews were translated into action by those who observed them. Maimonides suffered this degradation and, since he was unaware of the sufferings of the Jews in Europe from the persecutions that accompanied the Crusades, he could not make a balanced judgement and declared that the position of the Jews in the Muslim countries was worse than enywhere else. In *Iggeret Teiman* ("The Epistle of Yemen"), he writes: "The nation of Ishmael injures us greatly and legislates to do us harm and make us hate . . . For never has a nation risen up against Israel to injure us more than it, nor has anyone gone so far in degrading and scorning and hating her as they do" (pp. 54 and 85 in the Halkin edition). Similarly, Rabbi Bahya said, "The sons of Ishmael are worse for Israel than the sons of Esau" (quoted by Halkin, note on p. 94).

In later generations, the picture appeared to be more balanced. Iliyās al-Ayyūbi, in his pamphlet *The Voice of Liberty for the Defence of Jewish Nation* (Alexandria, 1913), wrote: "The Jews in the countries where Islam spread were in a position of degradation and wretchedness according to the formula of the verse which stipulates that they must pay the *jizya* and be brought low." But their position was better than in the Christian countries, as they suffered degradation but not confiscation of property and burning at the stake (pp. 50–1). It should also be noted that this rule of degradation was not always observed and the position of the Jews in general improved.

5. For example, according to a tradition quoted too by Rosenblatt from Balādhurī's *The Conquest of the Lands* (p. 162), Muhammad said: "He that does harm to a protected person [Christian or Jew], I shall be his prosecutor on the Day of Judgment." There are also other examples. As an example of an opprobrious statement, there is Jāḥiẓ's saying (quoted by Rosenblatt—Bayān, I, p. 165): "A Jew cannot talk to an Arab without plotting to kill him."
6. The subject is discussed in H.Z. Hirshberg's paper "The Jews in the Countries of Islam" in *Chapters in the History of the Arabs and Islam* (Hebrew), edited by Hava Lazarus-Yaffe, Tel Aviv, 1967, pp. 262–315; S.D. Goitein, "The Grim Creed" in *The Dinaburg Volume* (Hebrew); Poliakov, *De Mahomet aux Maranes.*

   It should be noted that there has been a lack of balance in the treatment of this subject. Research has concentrated mainly on the positive aspects of the relationships between Jews and Islam (Goitein, *Jews and Arabs,* Rosenthal, *Judaism and Islam,* and others), or on the influence of Judaism on Islam, and has neglected manifestations of opposition and hostility. It may well be that in addition to the fact that it is more pleasant to deal with "positive" subjects, scholars were also influenced by psychological motives to deal with the encouraging aspects. Where Israel is concerned, the discussion of the kinship between Judaism and Islam may have been regarded as a contribution to better relations.
7. This an anti-Jewish work written by Samuel al-Maghribī, a Jew converted to Islam, in the 12th century. It was published recently by Professor M. Perlman in a scientific edition with English translation and notes—see Bibliography. (I am grateful to Professor Ben-Sasson for drawing my attention to this book.) According to Professor Perlman, the book was reissued in Egypt in 1939, but there may be particular significance in the fact that it was reissued there in 1961 in Maktabat al-Jihād al-Kubrā "Library of the Great Jihad" (consolidated list of publications of the Government of the UAR, No. 613). The same publisher also issued another book, which, according to its name, also deals with religious polemics: *Al-Risāla al-Sab'iyya bi-Ibṭāl al-yahūdiyya* ("The Abrogation of Judaism"), by Israel Samuel Ha-Yerushalmi (No. 614 in the same list).
8. Eliahu Sapir, "Hatred for the Jews in Arabic Literature," *Ha-Shiloah,* Vol. VI (1899), pp. 272–9; Joshua Ben Haninah (Jacob Joshua), "Arab Anti-Zionist

Literature," *Ha-Shiloah,* 1925/6, Vol. XLIII, pp. 272–79; "An Anti-Jewish Book in Arabic," *Haaretz,* December 19, 1926; "A Book on Hitler in Arabic," *Davar* (evening edition), February 24, 1935; "The Jews in Arabic Literature," *Moznavim,* Vol. XVIII, 1934/5, pp. 34–8, 305–9, 394–7; Sylvia Haim, "Arabic anti-Semitic Literature" in *Jewish Social Studies,* Vol. 17 (1955), pp. 307–12.

9. For a summary of Ibn Ḥazm's attitude, see Professor Perlman's article (note 1). Ibn Ḥazm wrote about the general, historical and cultural aspects rather than than specifically about the Jews of Granada. Dr. al-Ramādī uses him as an authority (1962, pp. 13ff.).

10. As an indication of foreign influences on Arab anti-Semitism, we may examine the frequency of quotation. My impression is that the author most quoted by Arab writers on this subject is Douglas Reed, who is referred to by Rushdī, p. 43; Tūnisī, p. 43; ʿA'qād, pp. 46, 66; ʿAlūba, p. 160; Abu al-Majd, p. 12; al Hindāwī p. 40; and others. Le Bon is quoted both in order to denigrate the Jewish contribution to civilization and to emphasize the superior merits of the Arabs (Wākid, Tall, Ṭabbāra and others). ʿAlūba mentions other French works: Maria Christina Gustininani Benditi, *Beginnings,* Rome Press, 1951, and the edition of the Protocols published by Bernard Gracia, 1937. Tall refers frequently to Arnold Leese's books and quotes from them. ʿIṣmat and Ḥarb refer to *La Vieille France* edited by Urbain Gotier, which, according to Norman Cohen (p. 165), also contains the text of the Protocols, and to the French newspapers. Yamīn translated from the version in *La Vielle France.* American sources, such as *Common Sense,* are also mentioned, while Tall refers to the *Key to the Mystery,* Missouri, 1938.

11. The statement that there are "numerous" Arabic books which quote or refer to the Protocols is a matter of relativity or taste. No doubt, I have not been able to obtain all the books which deal with the conflict, with the Jews or with Israel; so I cannot testify to the exact number of Arabic works which refer to the Protocols. The list of such works which have been in my possession is to be found in Bibliographical Appendices 2, 3 and 4. The number seems to be so considerable as to indicate a trend. I have classified them into three lists: 1) complete translations; 2) books containing summaries of the Protocols; 3) books referring to or quoting from the Protocols.

12. The story about the books suspiciously disappearing from the market is not limited to the Protocols. Kanafānī notes that Disraeli's *David Alroy* had disappeared ("What is noteworthy is its disappearance from world markets during the past few years"). Apparently he ascribed this phenomenon to Disraeli's emphasis on the "purity of the race," which is supposed to have become embarassing for the Jews (1966, p. 64).

13. The connection between the Protocols and the Nazi Holocaust was known to Dr. Bārūdī, who wrote that they "finally fell into the hands of Hitler's men and were the direct cause *(al-ʿāmil al-mubāshir)* of the brutal assault of Nazism against the Jews" (pp. 6–7).

14. Al-Ḥajj's book is dedicated to the Mufti of Jerusalem and prefaced by a

letter from him. It is a strange work, said to have been composed by a person who penetrated into the Masonic Order and rose to high position, claiming to reveal its secrets and those of the Jews in the style of the Protocols. The book consists of disconnected passages on various subjects, from Herzl to Ahasuerus. An article based on this book, showing its continued influence, was published in *al-Ḥayāt,* September 13, 1967. Other books dealing with masonary are: Muhammad Ali al-Zu'bī, *Al-Māsumiyya Munshi' at Mulk Isrā'īl* ("Masonry the Creator of the Kingdom of Israel"), Part 1, al-'Irafān Publishing House, Beirut, 1956, 157 pp. (not seen by me); Wākid, Luṭfī, Dr. Naṣr, and Nājī; see Bibliography.

15. The charge that the Jews are rent by internecine strife is mentioned in the Quran, referring to Jews joining two groups of Arab tribes that fought each other at Medina: "Yet it is ye who slay each other and drive out a party of your people from their homes, supporting one another against them by sin and transgression" (Sura II, The Cow, v. 85).
16. This idea of an imbalance in the Jewish character, marked by the coexistence of two extremes, is also emphasized by Dr. Muhammad Kāmil Hussein: "Unexampled cruelty and callousness as against pity and sensibility, spirituality and materialism. In the nature of the Jew two streams meet, a positive and a negative, which do not merge. But while in times of stress men usually bring their good qualities to the fore, the Jews reveal their evil qualities" (in his article, "The Most Beautiful of Stories, the Story of the Exodus from Egypt and the Jewish Mentality," *Mutanawwi'at* ["Miscellanies"] Vol. 1, pp. 27–8). Dr. Hussein's analysis of the Jewish character has no connection with the conflict, nor has it any obvious political purpose. He explains that the Exodus was the traumatic event which moulded the Jewish character for generations, for they were within a step of death when they szw Pharaoh and his army pursue them, when, suddenly, they were delivered without any effort on their part, bringing about a kind of psychic cataclysm: a sudden transition from abysmal despair to salvation. Nearness to death, Dr. Hussein says, hardens a man's character, as happened to Dostoyevsky when he faced a firing squad and was suddenly told that he had been pardoned. Lenin underwent a similar experience when he saw his brother executed. It was this traumatic experience, according to Hussein, which forged the Jews into a nation, but it was a nation of an exceptional character, for nations are genèrally moulded by a natural historical process through their ties with their homeland. The Jews, therefore, are like an unnatural plant—grown by hydroponics, and not in the soil.

    The transition from despair to deliverance was made even more crucial by their emotional characteristics, which were the outcome of the events that preceded the Exodus, he continues. When the Egyptians enslaved and persecuted them, they became morose and self-contained. Persecution inbued them with feelings of depression and humiliation eradicating any tendency to self-respect, heroism and revolt, for no rebellion could have any chance of success. On the other hand, it endowed them with an extraordinary capacity for resisting oppression, though through submission. Moses ventured to revolt because he was different from the Jews, having been brought up in the environment of Pharaoh's court. Their state of mind before the miracle of the Red Sea crossing was worsened by a number of factors: their anxiety at the possibility of Egyptian retribution for the silver and gold vessels they had borrowed and failed to return, as well as a feeling of guilt because they had had to abandon the weak and infirm in their hasty flight. This experience created in them the tendency to sacrifice sentiment for the sake of life. Their deliverance inplanted in them the faith that it was their Jewishness which had saved them—hence their devotion to it . . .

The trauma produced in them a latent mental ailment, an attitude of suppressed arrogance, in tolerance and lack of generosity towards others, characteristics which would develop in a situation of affluence which they have not yet achieved. Hence the Jew does not know how to live and let live. (Dr. Naṣr expresses similar views.)

17. The characteristics of the Jews are summed up in the usual way in the article "Jews" in the dictionary compiled by the distinguished Egyptian writer Ahmad Amīn [*Qāmús al-'Adāt wa-al-Taqālīd wa-al-Ta'ābīr al-Miṣriyya* ("The Dictionary of the Egyptian Habits, Traditions and Expressons") hajmat al-Ta'līf wa-al-Mashr, Cairo, 1953 p. 420]. "Distinguished for the preservation of their race, their introverted nature, white skin and blue eyes, distinguished in finance, avaricious, they control America, they corrupt faith and religion." Amīn denigrates the Jews at greater length in his book Fayḍ al-Khātir e.g., in Part 8, pp. 43 and 99. (My attention was drawn to these passages by Dr. Menahem Milson.)
18. Dr. Muhammad Kāmil Hussein also gives the use of the blood of their slaughtered brethren as one of the characteristics of the Jews (op. cit., p. 28).
19. Ṣafwat wrote in 1952 about the Jews in the Arab countries: "They are a very large fifth column and willingly support Israel, helping with information and through connections with prominent personalities to receive information and pass it on regularly" (p. 198).

A resolution passed by the Islamic Conference in Amman in 1966 stated: "The Jews in the Arab countries have not adopted an attitude of respect to the protection awarded to them by Islam over the generations. They have helped World Zionists and Israel by every kind of encouragement in its aggression against the Arabs, and its usurpation of their land and the Muslim holy places in Palestine. The Conference hereby declares that the Jews in the Muslim countries whose ties with Zionism and Israel shall be proved shall be regarded as fighting against the Muslim; they will not be deserving of the protection and defence which the Muslim States prescribe for peaceful members or protected faiths, and it will be the duty of the Muslim Governments to treat them as aggressive comtatants" (Amman Radio, September 22, 1967, 14:15 hrs.).
20. Faris writes: "If we must kill, it becomes easier to the extent that we define

the victim as inhuman. The soldier must be taught to think about the enemy as subhuman, so that he should willingly bring himself to use the dagger against him" (p. 57). Similarly, Jessie Bernard, citing Buchan, states that the negative image of the enemy has the value of making it easier for people to ignore the accepted dictates of morality and kill without pangs of conscience (*The Nature of Conflict,* p. 54).

CHAPTER 6

1. Nasser stigmatized Israel as selfish and always concerned only with her own good as early as 1954: "Israel is so selfish that she thinks that people are always thinking only of her, but actually we have more important concerns" (interview with a journalist, September 13, 1954, IL., III/521). He went on to say that she seized territories not meant for her according to the partition resolution: "Israel has done nothing to satisfy the Arabs. On the contrary, when we tried to settle our disputes with the Western Governments, she tried to make difficulties, without heeding the desire of the Western leaders and the Arab countries to create more stability and what would come in its wake for the benefit of world peace. The Israeli leaders act only for their own good. irrespective of the damage that might be involved for others, including the security of the Western countries whose friends they claim to be. The Israelis argue that they are the only friends of democracy in the Middle East, but their acts refute this. The truth is that Israel is a friend only to herself, and she hesitates between West and East according to what she thinks will get her most benefit from both sides" (ibid., pp. 524–5).
2. The Histadrut is described as a capitalist institution in disguise. In the Egyptian periodical *Talīʿa* May 5, 1966), there is an article called "The Histadrut, a Trade Union Facade for a Capitalist Institution."
3. In Israel there is "a concealed devotion to racism" *(al-iʿtimāq al-Kitmānī lil-ʿunṣuriyya)*. Razūq deals at length with communal tensions *(A Glance at the Israeli Parties)*.
4. S. Hamady seems to imply that ambivalence has deep roots among the Arabs: "In general his [the Arab's] feelings of ambivalence are not accompanied by guilt and anxiety" (p. 84). In other words, the Arabs have a degree of "tolerance for ambivalence." (It should be noted that this is not necessarily identical with what psychologists call "tolerance for ambiguity.")

CHAPTER 7

1. According to Dr. Faruki, the Arabs are the summit of creation and if their greatness and excellence are not obvious at present, they are endowed with the greatest potential for improvement: "That Arabs are the best of men is for

us an article of faith" (1962, p. 3). The Arabs often apply to themselves the Quranic expression *ummat wasaṭ*—the middle, or central people, the people of the middle way.

2. Psychologists testify that situations of anxiety and tension, which are typical on conflicts, lead to a tendency to extreme, polarized, judgements without any light and shade. Stanger gives this tendency in the McNeil volume, p. 56, as an example of intolerance of ambiguity.
3. Von Grunebaum, G.V., "Self-Image and Approach to History" in *Historians of the Middle East* (University of London, 1962). See also Hourani's criticism of this article in the same volume.
4. Tall explains: "After the crimes of the English and the Jews against the Arabs in Palestine multiplied, and after it became clear that the Jewish gangs were making no distinction between combatants and non-combatants, and were not restrained by any consideration of honour or the laws of war, the Arab League decided to send the Arab armies into Palestine to save the Arab people from the barbarism of the Jews and from their terror and treachery" (pp. 302–3).
5. Donmeh (Judeo-Moslem sect derived from the followers of Sabbatai Zevi) are blamed by Tall for the abolition of the Caliphate (p. 233) and by Naṣḥī for the estrangement of Turkey from Islam (p. 38).
6. Dr. Butrus Butrus Ghālī cites the Balfour Declaration and the activities of the Zionists as factors which led to the revival of Egypt's ties with Arabism (his article on the UAR's foreign policy in the *Egyptian Political Science Review,* December 1962, p. 9).

CHAPTER 8

1. Examples of such misunderstandings in the UN Security Council may be found in E.S. Glenn's article "Semantic Difficulties in International Communication" in: Hayakawa, S.I. (ed.), *The Use and Misuse of Language* (Greenwich, Conn., Fawcett Publications, 1962).
2. Fromm says that ideas begin by being helpful and later cease to be so, but his definition is different from the concept used here. According to him, the ideology is from the beginning a ritualist institutionalization of ideas from which people have become alienated. The ideology is a deceptive substitute for the ideas. Thus, for instance, Marx developed ideas, which were later transformed into an ideology. See Fromm E., *May Man Prevail?* (Doubleday, N.Y., 1961), pp. 122–5. Boulding defined three phases in an ideology: 1) people believe; 2) they believe that they believe; 3) they cease to believe (see Boulding K., *The Meaning of the XXth Century* [Harper, New York, 1964], p. 151).
3. Bell D., *The End of Ideology* (Collier, N.Y., 1962), p. 352; Lane R.E., *Political Ideology* (Free Press, N.Y., 1962), p. 356; Festinger L. et al., *When Prophecy Fails* (Minneapolis, 1956).

4. Kolakovsky, L., *Al Hareshut Hanetunah* (Hebrew translation, Sifriat Hapoʿalim, 1964).
5. It is the arguments that are not sincere that are sometimes the most significant. Prof. A. Mazrui of the Makarere University in Uganda says that a book written by a sincere author from one of the African countries in support of the idea of Pan-Africanism is less significant than a book supporting the same idea written by a hypocrite. What a sincere author writes indicates his personal outlook; what the hypocrite writes may indicate the ideas current in his environment. See Silvert, K.H. (ed.), *Discussion at Bellagio: The Political Alternatives of Development* (New York, 1964).
6. There are many collections of poetry by refugees. A novel that may be mentioned is Ḥalīm Barakāt's *Sittat Ayyām,* Beirut, 1961, the story of a Lebanese village near the border during the week before it is taken by the enemy. (In a survey of modern Arab literature in *Daedalus,* Autumn, 1966, this book is regarded as marking the beginning of the Arab political novel.) There is also a virulently anti-Semitic play *Ilāh Isrā'īl* ("The God of Israel"), published by Dār al-Qalam, Cairo (undated), by Ali Ahmad Bākathīr, an Egyptian whose father came from Hadramaut and his mother from Indonesia. It portrays the Jews as enemies of the human race, cunning and covetous, responsible for world wars, aspiring for world domination, and so forth. The author, who has also written other plays, such as *The New Shylock* (symbolizing Israel) and *The Chosen People of God* (a description of internal disintegration in Israel), is discussed in an article, "Bakathir Drama," in: Lewis, B. and Holt, D.M., *Historians of the Middle East,* 1962. There are also *Rijāl fī al-Shams (Men in the Sun),* by Ghassān Kanafānī, Dār al-Talīʿa, Beirut, 1963, 106 pp., and a collection of stories by Kanafānī, *Arḍ al-Burtuqāl al-Ḥazīn (The Land of the Melancholy Orange),* Dār al-Fajr al-Jadīd, Beirut, 1963, 127 pp. Ṣabrī Ḥāfiẓ criticises the literature on the Palestinian disaster because "it has not risen to the universal human level" *(al-Ādāb,* April 1964).
7. On the major functions of primary groups and reference groups in influencing the attitudes of others, see Krech, Crutchfield and Ballachy, pp. 193 ff., and Lane and Sears.
8. Reshtar, J.S., *Problems of Analysing and Predicting Soviet Behavior* (N.Y., Doubleday, 1955); Bell, D., "Ten Theories in Search of Reality: The Prediction of Soviet Behavior," *World Politics,* April 1958, or in *The End of Ideology* (Collier, N.Y., 1962).
9. There is a long tradition of contempt for ideology as a variety of falsehood, a tissue of rationalizations, a superstructure of ideas covering a foundation of interests. The attitude may also be expressed in the rejection of programmes and ideals in the name of action and the practical approach. Behind the acts of men, however, there are ideas of some kind, without which we cannot understand the significance of their actions. History is meaningless if we do not complement the so-called historical facts with a conceptual explanation, for the conceptual aspect is the expression of the aim and the cause of the act.

From this point of view, history is, in Collingwood's well-known phrase, the history of thought and ideology is partially the thought dimension of history.

10. For ideology as an influence on the form and style of thought, see: Leites, N., *The Operational Code of the Politburo* (New York, 1951); Bauer, R.A., Inkeles, A. and Kluckhohn, C., *How the Soviet System Works* (N.Y., Vintage, 1960), pp. 35–9; Friedrich, C.J. and Brzezinski, Z.K., *Totalitarian Dictatorship and Autocracy* (Harvard University Press, 1957), p. 115.
11. A similar explanation of the relationship between geopolitical and psychological factors is given by Klineberg in Chapter I of his book (see Bibliography).
12. Hence, moreover, "vital interests" and "vital living-space" are relative and depend on the personal concepts of leaders. To take a well-known and extreme example, Hitler's ideas on these subjects were different from those of his predecessors and successors. Stanley Hoffman writes: "World politics in this century has proven that geography can be exploited by a policy as much as policies are 'dictated' by geography. What counts in policy-making is how the policy-maker views the environment, and to what use he wants to put it. 'The most stubborn facts are those of the spirit, not those of the physical world' (Jean Gottmann). Therefore the consideration of men's values, beliefs and emotions, of their purposes and ideas, is indispensable" (*Contemporary Theory in International Relations,* p. 173).
13. In the Arab literature of the conflict, Israel is frequently referred to as the heart *(qalb)* of the Arab world. Even if this expression is meant to indicate a powerful emotional attachment to the territory, it also has a geopolitical significance, emphasizing its centrality and vital importance.
14. This is an example of what the French call *ennemis frères*. Even in a fierce and bitter conflict, there are always areas in which the rivals are allies. In the practical world, therefore, a conflict is not a "zero sum game." The area of common interests between Israel and each Arab State is different—which contributes to the difficulty of establishing a common Arab attitude.
15. It is noteworthy that even when Egypt thinks in Egyptian, and not pan-Arab, terms, conscious of her greatness and her mission in the Middle East, she is still liable to regard the liquidation of Israel as a goal. For example, Hussein Mu'a's *Miṣr wa-Risāltuhā*—"Egypt and her Mission," (undated—this is one of the first publications of the Officers' Revolution), to which Nasser wrote a preface and which resembles in appearance the Ikhtarnā Lak series and carries the national coat-of-arms, is an extreme manifestation of nationalism in an Egyptian framework. The writer describes Egypt's historic function in fighting invaders who broke into the Middle East. Egypt, he said, protected Syria, which had belonged to Egypt for 650 years. "Through our country Syria *(Shām)* was delivered from the Crusaders; it was the armies of Egypt that cleared out the plague of the Mongols, and through Egypt, by God's will, Palestine shall be delivered from Israel" (p. 110).
16. The question remains: what were Abdallah's motives? His desire to consolidate his kingdom was an important one. According to a book praising the king's

policy, which was published anonymously in Beirut as by "a great Arab statesman," *Daur al-ḥuluq wal-ʻaql fi maʻrakat al-taḥīr* (*The Function of Morality and Reason in the Liberation Struggle*, pp. 63–4), Abdallah wanted to accept the Peel Commission's Partition proposal as a first step in the containment of the Zionist danger. He wrote to the Arab leaders to warn them against the negative attitude which they had adopted. His attitude was that since the Arabs did not have the strength to resist the Zionist danger once and for all, they had no choice but to agree on a step-by-step policy and act on the principle of "take and demand more." (It may be asked whether this was really his own approach or whether these ideas were influenced by, or an echo of, Bourguiba's policy.) In *My Memoirs Completed*, Abdallah writes: "War and Peace are two things that mankind will continue to experience until the Resurrection, just as season follows season, summer, autumn, winter, and spring—and as day follows night; it is the way of God with His creation" (Arabic, p. 16; English, p. 11). This seems to indicate that he regarded peace as only transitory.

17. For example, Dr. Walīd Qamḥāwī, whose book is full of self-denunciations and who takes the Jews as an example, also criticizes the "Chosen People complex" (Part 1, p. 39, 1962). Again, in denying the value of the kibbutz as a form of social organization, Kiyālī writes "The kibbutz is not a pioneering experiment for the world, or an example for others to follow, but a sign of the arrogance, the discrimination and the isolationism characteristic of the Jewish people, the creation of its genius and the outcome of its special qualities, exactly as is implied by the significance of God's chosen people" (1966, p. 107).
18. ʻAbd al-Qādir's support for the existence of the State of Israel *(Le Conflict Judéo-arabe)* is not of any political significance, for he is an exile and wrote in French. Waṣfī al-Tall charged him with writing for Israeli money (at a press conference on January 7, 1967, according to Amman Radio, same date).
19. Examples of these "antinonies" are:

    Hasty union as against preparations for unification. It seems logical to speed up the process of reunification before the separate personalities of the Arab States take firm shape. On the other hand, a hasty unification of inchoate units would lead to chaos; it may be therefore be better to prepare for unity, to enable the units to take shape in the first place, to make the bricks before trying to build the wall. The trouble is that the delay facilitates the consolidation of local nationalisms, which are liable to oppose unity.

    Equality or leadership? A union headed by a leading State, which controls the operation of the union, is more practical, but repels those who do not want to be led. A union of equals is more attractive, but is not practical.

    Integration or preservation of frameworks? Since the frontiers in the Middle East were demarkated by the imperialists, there is a natural aspiration to wipe them out and bring about a complete merger. On the other hand, the creation of a large body might lead to chaos, while the preservation of the separate frameworks might produce separatist pressures.

    Blocs. It would seem that a merger of two Arab States would mean lessening the total number, namely, an approach to unity. On the other hand, a bloc of States might try to keep separate, thus holding up the next stage of unification. Furthermore, the formation of blocs has always aroused opposition from the other States: the Hashemites opposed the Syrian-Egyptian union, and Egypt opposed the possibility of a union between Syria and Iraq.

20. A key to Nasser's approach may be found in his speech of February 26, 1962, to the members of the Gaza Legislative Council who were visiting Cairo. It contains in concentrated form the themes to which he repeatedly returned on latter occasions:

"Whoever wants to go to war ought to prepare for it. Whoever wishes to achieve his goal ought not to gamble with the future of his country or that of others, and whoever made high sounding words and political bargaining is a traitor to his country, his people and himself. Such a traitor endangers the destiny of his people:

"The commander who is not ready to go into battle usually tries to deceive the people and make them believe that he is ready for the war. The commander who has no confidence in winning the battle tries to deceive the people and make them believe that victory is about to be achieved. Such a commander betrays his country and his nation. Even the Quran appealed to those wishing to go into battle to prepare for it. Hence we ought to get ready, instead of making speeches, entering into political bargaining and drowning the people in a sea of imagination and hopes while we are not ready for a war. Hence, we must be prepared not only in so far as power and strength are concerned, but also morally. Lack of moral considerations was responsible for our 1948 disaster . . .

"When I take a decision I have to be sure that I can impose such a decision on my forces, can obtain the upper hand over Ben-Gurion as well as the people who are backing Ben-Gurion. Otherwise, I would be gambling with the fate of my country and I would be exposing it to another disaster similar to that which occurred in 1948 . . .

"Whoever says that we should go to war without getting ready for it, is a traitor to his country and his people and is a gambler who gambles with the fate of his country and his people. War is not fought by means of high sounding words. War involves the fate of countries and it is a matter of life or death. We ought to have thought in 1947 of what was to happen in 1948 . . .

"We must adhere to the moral values, work, get ready and denounce the wiles of professional politicians. We must unite and sink our differences because we have before us a difficult situation. Anyone who tells you that your situation is easy is deceiving you. The Palestine case is one of the most difficult in the world; it is not a matter of Israel alone, but of Israel and other powers behind her. But God is greater than those who are behind Israel. Se are faithful, and with our faith we can achieve our aim. Naturally, Arab unity is one of the factors in our favour. It is also catastrophic for Israel . . .

"Although we actually lost the 1948 battle it was you who suffered from this loss. The 1948 disaster, however, brought the danger home to the Arab people in all Arab countries, Had not [attention] been drawn to this danger, they would have been lost and Arab nationalism would have been replaced by Zionist nationalism from the Nile to the Euphrates. You were the people who paid for having the attention of Arab countries drawn to the danger. You paid a high price to draw our attention to the menace and to awaken the whole Arab nation. The Arab nation, hence, has a duty to fulfil in the restoration of your rights and the realisation of your goals and aspirations in Palestine.

"Imperialism, Zionism and the reactionary elements will, by all means in their power, try to crush the Arab nation on the ground that Arab unity constitutes the only means of the realisation of our goals in so far as the restoration of Palestine is concerned."

CHAPTER 9

1. Crech, Kruchfield and Ballachy, Chapter 7; Faris's article "Interaction Levels and Intergroup Relations"; Daniel Katz's "The Functional Approach to the Study of Attitudes"; articles by de Sola Pool, Deutsch and Merritt, and Janis and Brewster Smith in the Kellman volume; articles by Morton Deutsch and Bronfenberger in the Fisher volume.
2. Social psychologists and political scientists repeatedly emphasize that public attitudes do not have much influence in international relations; on the contrary, decision-makers have a great influence on public opinion. See Singer, J.D., "Peace Research, Peace Action," *Bulletin of the Atomic Scientists,* January 1963, pp. 13–17.
3. We may apply to this question the central idea of Richardson's theory of "war moods" (for a simple explanation see Boulding, pp. 143–4, or Rappaport, pp. 54–5). Richardson assumed that in the cycle peace—war—peace there is a successive series of situations, which embody an ambivalent attitude, overt and covert, to the rival (the Freudian influence). He presented the following pattern:

Situation Dominant mood	Peace Friendly	Arms Race Friendly	War Hostile	Attrition Hostile
Repressed mood	Friendly	Hostile	Friendly	War weariness

Armistice War weariness	Post-war War weariness	Peace Friendly
Hostile	Friendly	Friendly

This pattern might be appropriate to changes in a conflict situation in which exhaustion develops as a result of mutual attrition.

4. There is room for a comparative study of conflicts and their resolution, ranging from flexible conflicts, in which an action by one party meets with a response by the other and influences the attitude, to conflicts in which the attitudes are rigid. There is also room for a further distinction according to the degree of symmetry between the parties in the flexibility of the reaction to the rival, as well as in regard to the direction—congruent or incongruent—of the change. In the Arab attitude, for example, there is a measure of flexibility in the direction of intensification. Through its actions Israel is, generally, more capable of intensifying Arab fury than reducing it. At any rate, that has been the situation so far.
5. Prof. Robert C. Angell: "Since the equilibrium almost always involves a power differential, conflict remains latent even when there is surface accommodation" (McNeil volume, p. 103).

BIBLIOGRAPHY

The following bibliographical list does not contain all the literature on the Arab attitude in the conflict, but rather the limited literature analysed for the purpose of this research programme. This research is mainly based upon sources written by Arabs, and not on summaries of Arab sources written by non-Arabs. The main bulk of the bibliography is, therefore, in Arabic.

Essays on the Arab-Israeli conflict in Hebrew are scanty, and mainly deal with the descriptive historical aspect, rather than the Arab attitude *per se*. The Hebrew essays mentioned in this work are cited either in the body of the text or in the notes.

I. ARABIC SOURCES

1. al-'Abd, Ibrāhīm, *al-'Unf wa-al-Salām fī Dirāsat al-Istrātijiyya al-Ṣahyūniyya* ("Violence and Peace, A Study of Zionist Strategy"), The Research Centre, The Palestine Liberation Organization, Beirut, March, 1967, 138p.
2. 'Abdallāh, King, *al-Takmila min Mudhakkarāt Ṣāḥib al-Jalāla al-Hāshimiyya al-Malik 'Abdallāh Ibn Ḥusayn* ("A Supplement to His Hashemite Excellency King 'Abdallāh Ibn Ḥusayn's Memoirs"), Amman, 1951, 123p.
3. 'Abd al-Dā'im, 'Abdallāh, *al-Waṭan al-'Arabī wa-al-Thawra* ("The Arab Homeland and The Revolution"), Dār al-Ādāb, Beirut, 1963.
4. 'Abd al-Ḥamīd (Liwā' Arkān al-Ḥarb, Major General) Muḥammad Kamāl, *Ma'rakat Sīnā wa-Qanāt al-Suwīs'* ("The Sinai Campaign and the Suez Canal"), Kutub Qawmiyya, No. 291, Cairo, 23.10.1964, 196p.
5. 'Abd al-Karīm, Aḥmad, *Taḥwīl Majrā Nahr al-Urdunn* ("The Diversion of the Jordan River"), Kutub Qawmiyya, No. 50, Cairo, 16.4.1960, 63p.
6. 'Abd al-Nāṣir [Nasser], Jamāl, a) *Falsafat al-Thawra* ("The Philosophy of the Revolution"), al-Maṭba'a al-'Ilmiyya, 10th. edition, Cairo, undated, 80p.
   b)—*Khuṭab wa-Taṣrīḥāt 1953–1959* ("Speeches and Declarations 1953–1959"), Ikhtarnā Lak, 11 Vol., Cairo, 2157p.
   c)—*al-Taḥwīl al-'Aẓīm* ("The Tremendous Turn"), the opening speech, 26.3.1964, Kutub Qawmiyya, No. 285, Cairo.
7. al-'Ābid, Ibrāhīm, *al-Mābāy al-Ḥizb al-Ḥākim fī Isrā'īl* ("Mapai, the Ruling Party in Israel"), The Research Centre, The Palestine Liberation Organization, Beirut, Nov. 1966, 105p.
8. Abu Ghazāla Bassām, *al-Judhūr al-Irhābiyya li-Ḥizb Ḥīrūt al-Isrā'īlī* ("The Terrorist Origins of the Israeli Herut Party"), The Research Centre, The Palestine Liberation Organization, Beirut, Oct. 1966, 101p.

9. Abu al-Ḥajjāj Yūsuf, Isrā'īl wa-Taḥwīl Nahr al-Urdun ("Israel and the Diversion of the Jordan River"), *al-Majalla al-Miṣriyya lil-'Ulūm al-Siyāsiyya,* No. 44, Nov. 1964, pp. 25–44.

10. Abu al-Majd, Ṣabrī, *Nihāyat Isrā'īl* ("The End of Israel"), with an introduction by Aḥmad Sa'īd, al-Sharika al-'Arabiyya lil-Ṭibā'a wa-al-Nashr, Cairo, 1960, 164p.

11. Abu al-Naṣr, 'Umar, *Nihāyat Isrā'īl* ("The End of Israel"), al-Maktaba al-'Aṣriyya, Sidon-Beirut, 1955, 196p.

12. Aḥmad, Aḥmad Yūsuf, *al-Sh'b al-Ḍalīl, Isrā'īl* ("Israel—the Misled People"), Kutub Qawmiyya, No. 176, Cairo, 1962, 78p.

13. al-'Alamī, Mūsā, *'Ibrat Filasṭīn* ("The Lesson of Palestine"), Dār al-Kashshāf, 2nd ed., Beirut, 1949.

14. 'Alī, Muḥammad 'Alī, *Fī Dākhil Isrā'īl* ("Inside Israel"), Kutub Qawmiyya, No. 222, Cairo, undated, 367p.

15. 'Alī, Muḥammad 'Alī and al-Ḥamṣānī, Ibrāhīm, *Isrā'īl Qā'ida 'Udwāniyya* ("Israel, a Base of Aggression"), From East and West, Cairo, 2.10.1964, 400p.

16. 'Alūba, Muḥammad 'Alī, *Filasṭīn wa-al-Ḍamīr al-Insānī* ("Palestine and the Conscience of Mankind"), Dār al-Hilāl, Cairo, March 1964, 225p.

17. 'Alūsh, Nājī, *al-Masīra Ilā Filasṭīn* ("The Journey to Palestine") Dār al-Ṭalī'a, Beirut, Sept. 1964, 230p.

18. Amān, Ḥilmī 'Abdallāh, *Filasṭīn fī al-Ta'rīkh al-Ḥadīth* ("Palestine in Modern History"), textbook for the 6th grade of elementary schools, Gaza, 1967, 65p.

19. 'Ammār, Shākir, *al-Arab wa-Isrā'īl* ("The Arabs and Israel"), Dār al-Kashshāf, Beirut, 1954, 80p.

20. 'Anbatāwī, Dr. Mundhir Fā'iq, *al-Wathā'iq al-Filasṭīniyya li-'Am 1965* ("The Palestine Documents—1965"), a publication of the Institute For Palestinian Studies, Beirut, 605 p.

21. al-'Aqqād, 'Abbās Maḥmūd, *al-Ṣahyūniyya al-'Ālamiyya* ("World Zionism"), Ikhtarnā Lak, No. 27, Cairo, 1956, 166p.; with an appendix containing *The Protocols of the Elders of Zion* (abridged).

22. al-Ārif, 'Ārif, *al-Nakba, Nakbat Bayt al-Maqdis wa-al-Firdaws al-Mafqūd 1947–1955* ("The Disaster, the Calamity of the Holy Land and the Lost Paradise 1947–1955"), 5 vols., 1133p.; vol. 6 contains lists of soldiers killed; another volume contains photographs, al-Maktaba al-'Aṣriyya lil-Ṭibā'a wa-al-Nashr, Sidon, Beirut.

23. al-'Aryān, Sa'īd and 'Alwān, Ḥasan, *al-Tarbiya al-Dīniyya* ("Religious Education"), UAR Ministry of Education, 2nd part, 4th grade of elementary schools, 7th ed., 1965.

24. 'Awwīs, Dr. Yaḥyā, *Isrā'īl wa-al-Duwal al-Kubrā* ("Israel and the Great Powers"), Ikhtarnā Lak, No. 23, 1956, 158p.

25. 'Azzām, Ṣalāḥ, *al-Ṣahyūniyya Taduqqu Abwāb Ifrīqiyā* ("Zionism Raps on the Doors of Africa"), Ikhtarnā lil-Jundī, No. 44, Cairo 30p.

26. Badūr, Dr. 'Abd al-Fattāḥ, Qaḍiyyatunā al-Muqaddasa Qaḍiyyat Filasṭīn ("Our Holy Cause—Palestine"), *al-Majalla al-Miṣriyya lil-'Ulūm al-Siyāsiyya,* No. 30, Cairo, Sept. 1963, pp. 19–50.

27. Bahā' al-Dīn, Dr. Aḥmad, *Isrā'īliyyāt* ("Judaica"), Kitāb al-Hilāl, No. 158, Cairo, March 1965, 257p.

28. Bākathīr, 'Alī Aḥmad, *Ilāh Isrā'īl* ("The God of Israel"), three plays, Dār al-Qalam, Cairo, undated, 219p.

29. Barānq, Muḥammad Aḥmad and al-Maḥjūb, Muḥammad Yūsuf, *Muḥammad wa-al-Yahūd* ("Muḥammad and the Jews"), Mu'assasat al-Maṭbū'āt al-Ḥadītha, Cairo, undated, 140p.

30. al-Barghūthī, 'Umar Ṣāliḥ, Ta'rīkh al-Ṣahyūniyya wa-'Amaluhā al-Akhīr ("The History of Zionism and Its Latest Venture"), Muḥammad Kurd 'Alī, *Khiṭaṭ al-Sha'm,* part 3, pp. 203–231, Damascus, 1925.
31. Bārūdī, Dr. Riyād, *al-Yahūdiyya al-'Alamiyya* ("International Jewry"), *Dār* al-Thaqāfa, Beirut, undated (printed in the 1950's), 90p.
32. Basīsū, Dr. Sa'dī, *Isrā'īl, Jināya wa-Khiyāna* ("Israel, Crime and Treason"), part 1 (part 2, though published, did not reach me), Kutub Siyāsiyya No. 82, Cairo, 25.10.58, 79p.
33. Basīsū, Dr. Sa'dī, *al-Ṣahyūniyya Naqd wa-Taḥlīl* ("Zionism, Criticism and Analysis"), with introduction by Aḥmad Ḥilmī Bāshā, Jerusalem, 1945, 279 p.; an additional edition, Gaza, 1954.
34. Bayhūm, Muḥammad Jamīl, *Filasṭīn Andalus al-Sharq* ("Palestine—The Middle-Eastern Spain"), Beirut, 1946, 265p.
35. al-Bazzāz, Dr. 'Abd al-Raḥmān, *Buḥūth fī al-Qawmiyya al-'Arabiyya* ("Studies in Arab Nationalism"), Lectures at the Institute For Advanced Arab Studies of the Arab League, 1961–2, Cairo, 1962.
36 al-Bazzāz, 'Abd al-Raḥmān, *Hādhihi Qawmiyyatunā* ("This Is Our Nationality"), 2nd ed. of *ibid.,* Dār al-Qalam, Cairo, 1964, 448p.
37. al-Bīṭār, Dr. Nadīm, *al-Fa''āliyya al-Thawriyya fī al-Nakba* ("The Revolutionary Effectiveness of the Disaster"), Dār al-Ittiḥād, Beirut, 1965, 155p.
38. Bītī, Īlīn, *Azīlu Isrā'īl Hādhā Huwa al-Ḥall* ("Eliminate Israel, This is the Solution"), the English translation, Dār al-'Ilm lil-Malāyīn, Beirut, 1957, 143p.
39. Brūtūkūl Ḥukamā' Ṣahyūn ("The Protocol of the Elders of Zion"), Kutub Siyāsiyya, No. 5, Cairo, 13.4.57, 119p.
40. al-Dabbāgh, Muṣṭafā Murād, *Bilādunā Filastin* ("Our Country Palestine"), part 1, Dār al-Talī'a, Beirut, Jan. 1965, 732p.
41. Darwazah [Darwaza], Muḥammad 'Izzat, *al-Qaḍiyya al-Filasṭīniyya fī Mukhtalaf Marāḥilihā* ("The Palestine Problem Throughout Its Various Phases"), (previous edition published in 1951), Manshūrāt al-Maktaba al-'Aṣriyya, Sidon & Beirut, part 1, introduction dated 1959; 341p.; part 2, 1961, 352p. and 115p.; appendices.
42. Darwazah [Darwaza], Muḥammad 'Izzat, *Ta'rīkh Banī Isrā'īl min Asfārihim* ("The History of the Children of Israel from Their Books"), three parts, Ikhtarnā Lak, No. 83, 85, 87, al-Dār al-Qawmiyya lil-Tibā'a wa-al-Nashr, Cairo, 1960, 581p. (The previous edition was published by Dār al-Nahḍa.)
43. Dasūqī, Ṣalāḥ, *Amrīkā Musta'mara Ṣahyūniyya* ("America: a Zionist Colony"), Majallat al-Būlīs, Cairo, 1957, 81p.
44. Dasūqī, Ṣalāḥ, *Imbarāṭūriyyat Isrā'īl* ("The Israeli Empire"), Majallat al-Būlīs, Cairo, Oct. 1956, 141p.
45. al-Durr, Niqūlā, Hākadhā Dā'at wa-Hākadhā Ta'ūdu: Dawr al-Nafṭ wa-al Madfa' fī Taḥvīr Filasṭīn ("Thus Lost and Thus Redeemed: the Role of Oil and the Cannon in the Liberation of Palestine"), Dār al-Ḥawādith, Beirut, 1963, 314p.
46. Fahmī, Wafīq al-'Aziz, *al-'Udwān al-Thulāthī wa-al-Ḍamīr al-'Ālamī* ("The Threefold Aggression and the World Conscience"), Kutub Qawmiyya, No. 292, 29.10.1964, 197p.
47. Faraj ('Amīd Brigadier General), 'Izz al-Dīn, *Qaḍiyyat Nahr al-Urdun* ("The Problem of the Jordan River"), Ikhtarnā lil-Jundī, No. 53, undated, 66p.
48. Fāris, Ḥabīb, *al-Dhabā'iḥ al-Bashariyya al-Talmūdiyya* ("Human Sacrifices in the Talmud"), Kutub Qawmiyya, No. 184, explanations and notes by Jalāl, 'Abd al-'Ātī, checked by Surūr, 'Abd al-'Azīz, Cairo, 1962, 184p.

49. al-Fārūqī, Dr. Rājī Ismā'īl, *Uṣūl al-Ṣahyūniyya fī al-Dīn al-Yahūdī* ("The Origins of Zionism in the Jewish Religion"), lectures at the Institute For Advanced Arab Studies 1963–1964, Arab League Publications, Cairo, undated, 100p.
50. *Filasṭīn, Dawr al-Khulq wa-al-'Aql fī Ma'rakat al-Taḥrīr* ("Palestine, the Role of Ethics and Logic in the Battle of Liberation"), anonymous author, presented as a 'prominent Arab statesman', Dār al-Abḥāth wa-al-Nashr, Beirut, March 1967, 152p.
51. Ford [Fūrd], see: *al-Ṣahyūnī al-'Ālamī*
52. al-Fuqī, Ahmad Ḥāmid, see: *al-Ṣahyūniyya Sāfira, Muqarrarāt al-Yahūd*
53. al-Ghādirī, Nuhād, *al-Kitāb al-Aswad fī Ḥaqīqat 'Abd al-Nāṣir wa-Mawqifihi min al-Waḥda wa-al-Ishtirākiyya wa-Qaḍiyyat Filasṭīn* ("The Black Book of the Truth About 'Abd al-Nāṣir and His Attitudes Towards Arab Union, Socialism and the Palestine Problem"), Maṭābi' al-Jumhūriyya, undated—1962, Damascus, 165p.
54. Ḥabībī, Salwā, *al-Ṣuḥuf al-Isrā'īliyya* ("The Israeli Press"), Research Centre, The Palestine Liberation Organization, Beirut, Nov. 1966, 45p.
55. Hādhihi Hiya al-Ṣahyūniyya, see: al-Lajna al-Thaqāfiyya bi-Hay'at al-Taḥrīr.
56. Ḥafiẓ, Ḥamdī, Ādwā' 'Alā Siyāsat Amrīkā wa-Īrān wa-Isrā'īl, Anābīb al-Batrūl al-'Arabiyya wa-al-Mu'āmarāt al-Isti'māriyya ("Light on American, Iranian and Israeli Policy, Arab Petroleum Lines and Imperialist Conspiracies"), *al-Majalla al-Miṣriyya lil-'Ulūm al-Siyāsiyya,* No. 44, Nov. 1964, pp. 97–118.
57. al-Ḥājj, Yūsuf, *Fī Sabīl al-Ḥaqq, Haykal Sulaymān aw al-Waṭan al-Qawmī al-Yahūdī* ("For the Sake of the Truth, Solomon's Temple or the Jewish National Home"), Beirut, 1934, 236p.
58. Ḥamād, Khayrī, *al-Taṭawwurāt al-Akhīra fī Qadiyyat Filasṭīn* ("The Latest Developments in the Palestine Problem"), Kutub Qawmiyya, No. 280, Cairo, 31.5.1964. (The book has an appendix covering 1965, which indicates later printing.) 451p.
59. Ḥamdān, Ḥamdān, *Isrā'īl . . . wa-Taḥwīl al-Urdun* ("Israel and The Diversion of the Jordan River"), Dār Dimashq lil-Ṭibā'a wa-al-Nashr, Damascus, undated, 94p.
60. Ḥamdān, Muḥammad Miṣbāḥ, *al-Isti'mār wa-al-Ṣahyūniyya al-'Ālamiyya* ("Imperialism and International Zionism"), introduction by Muḥammad 'Alī al-Zu'bī, al-Maktaba al-'Aṣriyya, Sidon, Beirut, 1967, 293 p.
61. Harb, Īmīl al-Khūrī, *Mu'āmarat al-Yahūd 'Alā al-Masīḥiyya* ("The Conspiracy of the Jews Against Christianity"), Dār al-'Ilm lil-Malāyīn, Beirut, Nov. 1947, 84 p.
62. Ḥasan, Muḥammad Muṣṭafā, *Lan Tamurra Isrā'īl* ("Israel Will Never Pass"), Kutub Siyāsiyya No. 172, Cairo, 14.8.60, 60 p.
63. Ḥātim, Dr. Muḥammad 'Abd al-Qādir, al-Qawmiyya al-'Arabiyya Wāqi' wa-Madhhab ("The Arab Nationality: Reality and Ideology"), *Majallat al-'Ulūm al-Siyāsiyya,* No. 4, Jan.–March 1909, pp. 5–16. Published also in pamphlet form.
64. al-Hay'āt al-'Arabiyya al-'Ulyā ("The Arab Higher Committee"), Mīthāq al-Ḥaraka al-Waṭaniyya al-Filasṭīniyya ("The Covenant of the Palestine National Movement"), undated, Beirut.
65. Haykal, Dr. Yūsuf, *al-Qaḍiyya al-Filasṭīniyya, Taḥlīl wa-Naqd* ("The Palestine Problem, Analysis and Criticism"), Jaffa, 1937, 280 p.
66. Ḥijāzī, 'Arafāt, *Filasṭīn Arḍ al-Thawrāt* ("Palestine, the Land of Revolt"), Silsilat al-Taw'iya al-Filasṭīniyya, undated, 102 p.
67. Ḥijāzī, 'Arafāt, *al-Ṣahyūniyya, Nash'atuhā wa-Qiyāduhā wa-Munaẓẓamātuhā al-Sirriyya* ("Zionism, its Growth, Leadership and Secret Organizations"), Silsilat al-Taw'iya al-Filasṭīniyya, undated, 98 p.
68. al-Ḥilū, Ibrāhīm, *al-Shuyū'iyya wa-al-Ṣahyūniyya Taw'amān* ("Communism and Zionism Are Twins") Manshūrāt Maktab Ḥusayn al-Nūrī, Damascus, undated, 173p.

69. al-Hindāwī, Dhūqān, *al-Qaḍiyya al-Filasṭīniyya,* lil-Ṣaff al-Thālith al-Thānawī al-Adabī ("The Palestine Problem," a textbook, 3rd grade of secondary schools (humanities) al-Mamlaka al-Urduniyya al-Hāshimiyya, Wizārat al-Tarbiya wa-al-Ta'līm, 1964,148p.

70. al-Ḥusayn [Hussein], Jalālat al-Malik (His Majesty The King), *al-Risālatān al-Malakiyyatām li-Siyādat Ra'īs al-Jumhūriyya al-'Arabiyya al-Muttaḥida* ("Two Royal Dispatches to His Excellency the President of the United Arab Republic"), 1965, 24 p.

71. al-Ḥusaynī [Husseini], Muḥammad Amīn, *Ḥaqā'iq Qaḍiyyat Filasṭīn* ("The Truths of the Palestine Problem"), Cairo, 1954, 220 p.

72. Ibrāhīm, al-Sayyid Muḥammad, Bariṭāniyā Awwal min Du'ā li-Qiyām Isrā'īl ("Britain, the First Advocate for the Existence of Israel"), *al-Majalla al-Miṣriyya lil-'Ulūm al-Siyāsiyya,* No. 4, Cairo, Jan.–March 1959, pp. 131–136.

73. Idārat al-Tawjīh al-Ma'nawī ("The Education Directorate of the UAR Armed Forces), pamphlets on planning lessons:
a) *Kayfa Nuḥarrir Filasṭīn* ("How We Shall Liberate Palestine")
b) *Isrā'īl wa-Ahdāfuhā* ("Israel and Her Aims"), April 1965
c) *Qaḍiyyat Filasṭīn wa-Miyāhunā al-'Arabiyya* ("The Problem of Palestine and Our Arab Waters")
d) *Isrā'īl wa-al-Isti'mār* ("Israel and Imperialism")
e) *al-Tassallul al-Isrā'īlī wa-Wasā'il al-Qaḍā' 'Alayhā* ("The Israeli Infiltration and the Means of Her Annihilation")
f) *Qaḍiyyat Filasṭīn* ("The Palestine Problem"), see: al-Khūlī, Ḥasan Ṣabrī
g) *al-Marji' al-Muwaḥḥad lil-Taw'iya al-Qawmiyya* ("The Standard Authorized Textbook for the Improvement of the National Consciousness"), first vol., 1965, 389 p. and 288 p., sec. vol., 1966, 316 p.
h) *al-Murshid lil-Taw'iya al-Qawmiyya* ("The Book of Instruction for the Improvement of the National Consciousness"), 1966, 204 p.

74. al-Imām, ('Amīd Brigadier General), *al-Sulḥ ma'a Isrā'īl* ("Reconciliation With Israel"), Kitāb lil-Jami', Dār al-Jumhūriyya, 2nd edition, Cairo, 1954, 198 p.

75. 'Iṣmat, 'Abd al-Raḥmān Sāmī, *al-Ṣahyūniyya wa-al-Māsūniyya* ("Zionism and Freemasonry"), 2nd ed., Alexandria, 1950, 132p. (The last leaf of the volume in my possession is missing.)

76. Īzūlī, 'Abd al-'Azīz, *'Izat Kārithat Filasṭīn al-'Arabiyya* ("The Lesson of the Arab Palestine Disaster"), Maṭābi' Ibn Zaydūn, Damascus, undated, 226 p.

77. 'Izzat, Ibrāhīm, *Anā 'Ā'id min Isrā'īl* ("I Have Returned from Israel"), Manshūrāt Dār Maktabat al-Ḥayāt, Beirut, 1958, 126 p.

78. Īzzat, Ibrāhīm, *Kuntu fī Isrā'īl* ("I Was in Israel"), introduction by Iḥsān 'Abd al-Quddūs, al-Maktab al-Tijārī, Beirut, 1957, 129p. (Published also in an Egyptian edition.)

79. al-Jammāl, Dr. Aḥmad 'Abd al-Qādir, *Min Mushkilāt al-Sharq al-Awsaṭ* ("Some Middle-Eastern Problems"), al-Maktaba al-Anjlū-Miṣriyya, Cairo, 1955, 634 p.

80. al-Jiyār, 'Abd al-Ghaffār, *Filasṭīn lil-'Arab* ("Palestine for The Arabs"), Dār al-Kitāb al-'Arabī, Cairo, 1947, 109 p.

81. Jūrjī, Farīd 'Abdallāh, *Isrā'īl al-Zā'ifa* ("The Spurious Israel"), Kutub Qawmiyya, No. 296, Cairo, 22.1.1965, 147p.

82. Ka'dān, Bashīr and Shālātī, Shafīq, *Hā'ulā' al-Ṣahā'ina* ("These Zionists"), Damascus, 1946, 298 p.

83. Kafūrī, M., *al-Ṣahyūniyya, Nash'atuhā wa-Atharuhā al-Ijtimā'ī* ("Zionism, Its Growth and Its Social Effects"), Egypt, 1946, 72 p.

84. Kāmil, Jalāl, *Filasṭīn wa-Tajmī' al-Quwwa al-'Arabiyya* ("Palestine and the Assemblage of the Arab Power"), Ikhtarnā lil-Jundī, No. 58, Cairo, 1964, 85 p.

85. Kanafāni, Ghassān, *Adab al-Muqāwama fi Filasṭīn al-Muḥtalla 1948–1966* ("The Literature of the Resistance in Occupied Palestine, 1948–1966"), Manshūrāt Dār al-Adāb, Beirut, 1966, 144 p.
86. Kanafānī, Ghassān, *Rijāl Fī al-Shams* ("Men in the Sun", a collection of short stories about the life of Arab refugees), Dār al-Ṭalī'a, Beirut, 1963, 106 p.
87. Kanafānī, Ghassān, al-Shakhṣiyya al-Yahūdiyya fī al-Riwāya al-Ṣahyūniyya al-Mu'-'āṣira ("The Jewish Personality in the Contemporary Zionist Short Story"), *al-Ādāb*, March 1963, pp. 50–53.
88. Kayyālī, 'Abd al-Wahhāb, *al-Kībūtz aw al-Mazāri' al-Jamā'iyya fī Isrā'īl* ("The Kibbutz, or the Collective Farms in Israel"), The Research Centre, The Palestine Liberation Organization, Beirut, Sept. 1966, 130 p.
89. Kayyālī, 'Abd al-Wahhāb, *al-Maṭāmi' al-Sahyūniyya al-Tawassu'iyya* ("Zionist Expansionist Aspirations"), The Research Centre, The Palestine Liberation Organization, Beirut, July 1966, 136 p.
90. al-Khūlī, Ḥasan Ṣabrī, *Qaḍiyyat Filasṭīn* ("The Palestine Problem"), a lecture by the personal representative of the President of the UAR, published by the Education Directorate of the UAR Armed Forces, 1966 (?), 63 p.
91. al-Kīlānī, Mūsā Zayd, *Sanawāt al-Ightiṣāb, Isrā'īl 1948–1965* ("The Years of Robbery, Israel 1948–1965"), introduction by Dr. Qadrī Tūqān, al-Dār al-Urduniyya lil-Nashr wa-al-Tawzī', Amman, 1965, 140 p.
92. al-Lajna al-Filasṭīniyya al-'Arabiyya bi-Misr (The Arab—Palestine Committee in Egypt), *al-Yahūd wa-al-Islām Qadīmā wa-Ḥadīthā; al-Yahūd wa-Filasṭīn wa-Āyāt al-Jihād wa-al-Aḥādīth 'Anhu* ("The Jews and Islam in Ancient and Modern Times; The Jews and Palestine, the Quran Verses and the Traditions of the Jihad"), Cairo, 1937, 31 p.
93. al-Lajna al-Thaqāfiyya bi-Hay'at al-Taḥrīr (The Education Committee of the Liberation Organization), (I. Cohen), *Hādhihi al-Ṣahyūniyya* ("This is Zionism"), introduction by Nasser, Ikhtarnā Lak, No. 1, Cairo, March 1954, 151 p.
94. al-Lajna al-Thaqāfiyya bi-Hay'at al-Taḥrīr (The Education Committee of the Liberation Organization) *Zu'amā' al-'Iṣābāt al-Isti'māriyya* ("The Leaders of the Imperialist Gangs"), introduction by Nasser, Ikhtarnā Lak, No. 2, Cairo, April 1954, 222 p.
95. Luṭfī, Tawfīq, *Naḥnu wa-Isā'īl, Dirāsa Taḥlīliyya* ("We and Israel, an Analytic Study"), including a play, *'Adhārā Ṣahyūn* ("The Virgins of Zion"), Dār al-Udabā', Cairo, undated, 146 p.
96. Maḥfuẓ, (al-'Amīd, Brigadier General) Muḥammad Jamāl al-Dīn, *Quwwātunā al-Musallaḥa Fī Muwājahat Taḥaddiyāt al-Marḥala al-Qādima* ("Our Armed Forces Facing the Challenges of the Next Stage"), the Education Directorate of the UAR Armed Forces, July 1965, 158p.
97. Maḥlāwī Fatḥī 'Uthmān, *Ra's Ḥarba Ḍidd al-Qawmiyya al-'Arabiyya* ("A Spearhead Against Arab Nationalism"), *Majallat al-'Ulūm al-Siyāsiyya,* No. 4, Jan.–March 1959, pp.115–118.
98. al-Mamlaka al-Urduniyya al-Hāshimiyya, Wizārat al-Khārijiyya (The Hashemite Kingdom of Jordan, the Ministry of Foreign Affairs), *al-Urdun wa-al-Qaḍiyya al-Filasṭīniyya wa-al-'Ulāqāt al-'Arabiyya* ("Jordan, the Palestine Problem and Inter-Arab Relations"—The Jordanian White Paper), 1962, 37p.
99. al-Mārik, Fahd, *Kayfa Nantaṣiru 'Alā Isā'īl* ("How We Shall Overcome Israel"), Beirut, 1966, 384p.
100. Muḥammad, Dr. Muḥammad 'Iwaḍ, *al-Isti'mār wa-al-Madhāhib al-Isti'māriyya* lil-Ṣaff al-Thālith al-Thānawī ("Imperialism and Its Methods", a textbook for the 3rd grade of secondary schools), Syrian Ministry of Education 1966, 140p.

101. *Munaẓẓamat al-Taḥrīr al-Filasṭīniyya wa-Jumhūriyyat al-Ṣīn al-Sha'biyya* ("The Palestine Liberation Organization and The People's Republic of China"), PLO publication, undated, 81p.
102. Munaẓẓamat al-Taḥrīr al-Filasṭīniyya (The Palestine Liberation Organization, PLO), *al-Mīthāq, al-Niẓām al-Siyāsī, Qarārāt al-Mu'tamar al-Waṭa-nī* ("The Covenant, The Political Organization and The Resolutions of The National Convention"), Jerusalem, 1964.
103. Muṣṭafā, (Za'īm al-Rukn, Brigadier, Staff) Ḥasan, *Isrāīl wa-al-Qunbula al-Dharriyya* ("Israel and the Atomic Bomb"), Dār al-Ṭalī'a, Beirut, 1961, 232p.
104. Muṣṭafā, ('Amīd al-Rukn, Lt.-General, Staff) Ḥasan, *al-Musā'adat al-'Askariyya al-Almāniyya li-Isrā'īl* ("German Military Aid To Israel"), Dār al-Ṭalī'a, Beirut, Oct. 1965, 176p.
105. Muṭlaq, Rafīq Ḥabīb, *al-Ḥayāt al-Siyāsiyya Fī Isrā'īl* ("The Political Life in Israel"), The Research Centre, The Palestine Liberation Organization, Beirut, Nov. 1966, 106p.
106. Muṭlaq, Rafīq Ḥabīb, ed. see: *al-Yawmiyyāt al-Filasṭīniyya* ("The Palestine Yearbook"), 1965.
107. al-Nābulsī, Fayṣal 'Abd al-Laṭīf, *al-Takattul al-Raj'ī wa-Awdat Filasṭīn* ("The Reactionary Alliance and the Return to Palestine"), Kutub Qawmiyya, No. 224, selected radio and TV pieces, Cairo, undated, 67p.
108. Nājī, S., *al-Mufsidūn fī al-Arḍ,aw Jarā'im al-Yahūd al-Siyāsiyya wa-al-Ijtimā'iyya 'Ibra al-Ta'rīkh* ("The Corruptors of the Earth or the Political and Social Crimes of the Jews Throughout History"), Maṭba'at al-Inshā'), Damascus, 1965, 470p.
109. Na'nā'a, Maḥmūd, *al-Ṣahyūniyya fī al-Sittīnāt, al-Fātikān wa-al-Yahūd* ("Zionism in the Sixties, the Vatican and the Jews"), From West and East, Dār al-Qawmiyya lil-Ṭibā'a wa-al-Nashr, Cairo, 4.10.1964, 313p.
110. al-Nashāshībī, Nāṣir al-Dīn, *Tadhkarat 'Awda* ("Return Ticket"), al-Maktab al-Tijārī, Beirut, July 1962, 346p.
111. al-Nashāshībī, Nāṣir al-Dīn, *al-Waḥda wa-Qaḍiyyat Filasṭīn* ("Arab Unity and the Palestine Problem"), Kutub Qawmiyya, No. 109, 15.5.1961, 64p.
112. Naṣḥī, Fu'ād, *Filasṭīn fī al-Ma'ra-ka* ("Palestine in the Struggle"), Maṭba'at al-Taḥrīr, Cairo, 1958, 155p.
113. Nasim, Māhir, *al-Shuyū'iyya wa-al-Ṣahyūniyya* ("Communism and Zionism"), al-Maktaba al-Dawliyya, No. 1, Dār al-Ma'ārif, Cairo, 1959, 191p.
114. Naṣr, Dr. Muḥammad 'Abd al-Mu'izz, *al-Ṣahyūniyya fī al-Majāl al-Dawlī* ("Zionism in International Affairs") Ikhtarna Lak, No. 32, 1957, 160p.
115. Naṣṣār, Najīb al-Khūrī, *al-Ṣahyūniyya, Ta'rīkhuhā, Gharaduhā, Ahammiyyatuhā* ("Zionism, Its History, Purpose and Significance"), Maṭba'at al-Karmil, Haifa, 1911, 69p.
116. Nawfal, Dr. Sayyid, *Dawr al-Jumhūriyya al-'Arabiyya al-Muttaḥida fī Ibrāz al-Kiyān al-Filasṭīnī* ("The Role of the UAR in Promoting the Palestinian Entity"), *ibid,* No. 39, June 1964, pp. 65–76.
117. Nawfal, Dr. Sayyid, al-Kiyān al-Filasṭīnī ("The Palestinian Entity"), No. 32, Nov. 1963, pp. 27–38.
118. Nawfal, Dr, Sayyid, Ṣirā' al-Qawmiyya al-'Arabiyya ma'a al-Isti'mār wa-al-Ṣahyūniyya ("The Struggle of Arab Nationalism against Imperialism and Zionism"), *al-Majalla al-Miṣriyya lil-'Ulūm al-Siyāsiyya,* No. 13, April 1962, pp. 73–87.
119. Naẓīf, 'Alī Muḥammad, *A'wān Isrā'īl fī Miṣr* ("Collaborators with Israel in Egypt"), Dār al-Ma'ārif, Cairo, 1955, 139p.

120. al-Qāḍī, Layla, *al-Histadrūt* ("The Histadrut"), The Research Centre, The Palestine Liberation Organization, Beirut, March 1967, 93p.

121. Qamḥāwī, Dr. Walīd, *al-Nakba wa-al-Binā' fī al-Waṭan al-'Arabī* ("Disaster and Reconstruction in the Arab Homeland"), 2nd ed. 1st vol., 353p.; 2nd vol., 471p.; Dār al-'Ilm lil-Malāyīn, Beirut, 1962, (1st ed. 1956).

122. al-Qāsim, Anīs, *al-I'dād al-Thawrī li-Ma'rakat al-Taḥrīr* ("Revolutionary Preparation for the Battle of Liberation"), The Research Centre, The Palestine Liberation Organization, Beirut, Feb. 1967, 360p.

123. al-Qāsim, Anīs, *Min al-Tīh Ilā al-Quds* ("From the Desert to Jerusalem"), Libya, 1965, 243p.

124. al-Qāsim, Anīs, *Naḥnu wa-al-Fātīkān wa-Isrāīl* ("We, the Vatican and Israel"), The Research Centre, The Palestine Liberation Organization, Beirut, June 1966, 215p.

125. *al-Qawmiyya al-'Arabiyya wa-al-Isti'mār* ("Arab Nationalism and Imperialism"), an anthology, Ikhtarnā Lak, No. 32, Cairo, 1957, 158p.

126. al-Quṣrī, ('Amīd, Brigadier-General) Muḥammad Fā'iz, *Filasṭīn Ma'sāt Al-alam al-'Ārabī* ("Palestine, the Tragedy of the Arab World"), (part I, a play on the death of a Syrian officer in 1948; part 2, a political and military analysis of the war) al-Maktaba al-Ta'-āwuniyya, Damascus, 1959, 320p.

127. al-Quṣrī ('Amīd, Brigadier General), Muḥammad Fā'iz, *Ḥarb Filasṭīn 'Ām 1948* ("The Palestine War, 1948"), part 1, *al-Ṣirā' al-Siyāsī Bayna al-Ṣahyūniyya wa-al-'Arab* ("The Political Struggle Between Zionism and the Arabs"), Dār al-Ma'rifa, Cairo 1961, 218p.

128. al-Quṣrī ('Āmīd, Brigadier General), Muḥammad Fā'iz, *ibid.* part 2, *Marḥalat al-Niḍāl wa-al-Jihād* ("The Stage of Struggle and Jihad"), Damascus, 1962, 321p.

129. al-Rāfi'ī, 'Abd al-Raḥmān, *Thawrat 26 Yūlyū 1952, Ta'rīkhunā al-Qawmī fi Sab' Sanawāt* ("The Revolution of July 26, 1952, Our National History of the Last Seven Years"), Maktabat al-Nahḍa al-Miṣriyya, Cairo, 1959.

130. al-Ramādī, Dr. Jamāl, *al-Isrā'īliyyun wa-al-Mu'āmara* al-Kubrā ("The Israelis and the Great Conspiracy"), Kutub Qawmiyya, No. 148, Cairo, 1962, 76p.

131. al-Ramlī, Fatḥī, *al-Ṣahyūniyya, A'lā Marāḥil al-Isti'mār* ("Zionism, the Most Advanced Phase of Imperialism"), Wikālat al-Ṣaḥāfa al-Ifrīqiyya, Cairo, Aug. 1956, 255p.

132. Rashīd, 'Alī Hāshim, *Aghānī al-'Awda* ("The Songs of Return"), Dār Mamfīs lil-Ṭibā'a, Cairo (introduction is dated June 1960), 200p.

133. Razūq, As'ad, *Nazra fī Aḥtāb Isrā'īl* ("A Glance At The Israeli Parties"), The Research Centre, The Palestine Liberation Organization, Beirut, Dec. 1966, 103p.

134. Rif'at ('Aqīd, Colonel), Ibrāhīm, *Hāulā A'dā'uka* ("These Are Your Enemies"), Ikhtarnā lil-Jundī, No. 25, Cairo, 44p.

135. al-Rushaydāt, Shafīq, *Filasṭīn, Ta'rīkhā wa-'Ibratā wa-Maṣīrā* ("Palestine, Its History, Its Lesson and Its Destiny"), Dār al-Nashr al-Mutthida lil-Ta'līf wa-al-Tarjama, Beirut, 1961, 408p.

136. Rushdī, 'Umar, *al-Ṣahyūniyya wa-Rabībatuhā Isrā'īl* ("Zionism and Its Fosterchild Israel"), 2nd ed. Maktabat al-Nahḍa al-Miṣriyya, Cairo, 1965, 437p.

137. Sa'b [Sa'ab] Dr. Ḥasan, *al-Wa'ī al-'Aqā'idī* ("Ideological Consciousness") Dār al-'Ilm lil-Malāyīn, Beirut, 1959.

138. Sa'd, Ṣādiq, *Filasṭīn fī Mukhālib al-Isti'mār* ("Palestine in the Claws of Imperialism"), Cairo, 1964, 118p.

139. al-Safarī, 'Īsā, *Filasṭīn al-'Arabiyya bayna al-Intidāb wa-al-Ṣahyūniyya* ("Arab Palestine Between the Mandate and Zionism"), includes: book 1: 1917–1936, 260p.; book 2: The 1936 Revolt, 192p. Maktabat Filasṭīn al-Jadīda, Jaffa, 1937.

140. Ṣafwat (Qā'imqām Arkan al-Ḥarb, Colonel) Muḥammad *Isra'īl al-'Adū al-Mushtarak* ("Israel, the Common Enemy"), introduction dated Feb. 1952, Maktabat al-Nahḍa al-Miṣriyya, 1952, 223p. (Possibly republished in 1956, since it appears in a list of publications of the Egyptian Ministry of Education of that year.)

141. *al Ṣahyūrī al-'Ālamī* ("The International Zionist"), translated from English, introduction by Shamīs, 'Abd al-Mun'im, Kutub Siyāsiyya, No. 76, Cairo, 30.8.1958, 122p.

142. *al-Ṣahyūniyya Sāfira, Muqarrarāt al-Yahūd* ("Zionism Unveiled, the Resolutions of the Jews"), introduction by al-Fuqī, Sayyid Aḥmad Ḥāmid, Maṭba'at al-Sunna al-Muḥammadiyya, Cairo, 1951, 232p. (*The Products of the Elders of Zion,* according to al-Khūrī, Anṭūn's version.)

143. Ṣā'igh [Sayegh], Anīs, *Filasṭīn wa-al-Qawmiyya al-'Arabiyya* ("Palestine and Arab Nationalism"), The Research Centre, The Palestine Liberation Organization, Beirut, Oct. 1966, 119p.

144. a) Sā'igh [Sayegh], Dr. Fā'iz, *al-Ma'had al-Afrū-Āsyawī fī Tal-Abīb* ("The Afro-Asian Institute in Tel-Aviv"), The Research Centre, The Palestine Liberation Organization, Beirut, Jan. 1967.
b)—*Hafna min Dubāb, Baḥth fī Mufahīm al-Būrqibiyya wa-Shi ārātihā* ("A Handful of Fog, a Study in the Conceptual Structure of Bourgibism and Its Slogans"), The Research Centre, The Palestine Liberation Organization, Beirut, May 1965, July 1966, 28p.

145. Ṣāliḥ, (al-Liwā', Major General) Ḥāmid Aḥmad, *Baynanā wa-Bayna Isrā'īl* ("Between US and Israel"), Niḍāluna, No. 10, the Education Directorate of the UAR Armed Forces, April 1964, 42p.

146. Ṣaliḥ, (al-Liwā', Major-General) Ḥāmid Aḥmad, *Ma'rakat Būr Sa'īd* ("The Battle of Port Said"), the Publication Directorate of the UAR Armed Forces, Cairo, 23.12.1964, 122p.

147. Sayyid Aḥmad, Hāmid Ismā'īl, *al-Isti'mar al-Sahyūnī fī Asiyā wa-Ifrīqiyā* ("Zionist Imperialism in Asia and Africa"), Kutub Siyasiyya, No. 331, Cairo, undated, 100p.

148. Sha'bān, Muḥammad Ḥusayn, *Ibn Jūryūn. . . al-Kadhdhāb* ("Ben-Gurion . . . the Liar"), Kutub Qawmiyya, No. 233, Cairo, 1963, 59p.

149. al-Shā'ib, Fu'ād, ed., *al-Ma'rifa* ("Knowledge"), Issue No. 48, an anthology on "The Palestine Problem and the Struggle Against World Zionism", March 1966, 456p.

150. Shamīs, 'Abd al-Mun'im, *Asrār al-Ṣahyūniyya* ("The Secrets of Zionism"), Kutub Siyāsiyya, No. 1, 1957, 105p.

151. Shamīs, 'Abd al-Mun'im, *Mandūb al-Urdun fī Isrā'īl* ("The Representative of Jordan In Israel"), Kutub Siyāsiyya, No. 111, 14.6.1959, 71p.

152. Sharaf, Ṭah Aḥmad, *Isrā'īl min Ṣun'al-Isti'mār* ("Israel—The Creation of Imperialism"), Ikhtarnā Lak, No. 38, Cairo, 1957, 200p.

153. Sharāra, 'Abd al-Laṭīf, *Fī al-Qawmiyya al-'Arabiyya* ("On Arab Nationalism"), Manshūrāt 'Unaydāt, Beirut, 1957.

154. Sharāra, 'Abd al-Laṭīf, *al-Ṣahyūniyya, Jarimat al-'Aṣr al-Kubrā* ("Zionism, the Greatest Crime of the Age"), Dār al-Makshūf, Beirut, 1964, 273p.

155. al-Sharqāwī, Maḥmūd, *al-Tasallul al-Isārilī fī Ifrīqiya* ("The Israeli Infiltration Into Africa"), Nidaluna, No. 11, the Education Directorate of the UAR Armed Forces, July, 1964, 79p.

156. Shīdl, Dr. Frāns Jūzf (transliterated from Ar.), *Usṭūrat Isrā'īl* ("The Myth of Israel"), translated by al-Qabbānī, 'Ādil and 'Abd al-Qādir, Aḥmad, Kutub Siyāsiyya, No. 263, Cairo, 164p.

157. Shukrī, Ṣalāḥ al-Dīn, *Filasṭīn wa-Mu'tamar al-Qimma al-'Arabī* ("Palestine and the Arab Summit Conference"), introduction by Ḥasūna, 'Abd al-Khāliq, Maktab al-

Ṣaḥāfa lil-Sharq al-'Arabī, Damascus, 1964, 256p.; published also in an Egyptian edition, Kutub Siyāsiyya, No. 40, the new series.

158. a) al-Shuqayrī, Aḥmad, *Min al-Quds Ilā Wāshinṭūn* ("From Jerusalem to Washington", the author's meditations on his way to Washington to establish the Arab Office there), Maṭba'at al-Sardajī, Acre, 1937, 92p.

b)—*Qaḍāyā 'Arabiyya,* ("Arab Problems", speeches at the UN), translated by Ḥammād, Khayrī, al-Maktab al-Tijārī, Beirut, Feb. 1961, 276p.

c)—*Difā'unā'an Filasṭīn wa-al-Jazā'ir* ("Our Defence of Palestine and Algeria", speeches at the UN, 1960), translated by Ḥammād, Khayrī, al-Maktab al-Tijārī, Beirut, Jan. 1962, 209p.

d)—*Mawāqif Ḥāsima wa-Qawmiyya fī Qaḍiyyat Filasṭīn* ("Uncompromising and National Attitudes on the Palestine Problem"), The Palestine Liberation Organization, Dār al-Qalam, Cairo, undated, 80p.

159. Sīdham, Dr. Idwārd, *Mushkilat al-Lāji'īn al-'Arab* ("The Arab Refugee Problem"), Maṭba'at al-Waḥda, Cairo, July 1961, 442p.; an additional edition, with foreword by Nawfal, Dr. Sayyid, Kutub Qawmiyya, No. 265, selected radio and TV pieces, Cairo. undated, 235p.

160. Skūt [Scott] (Lt.. Col.) Jūn Krīj, *al-Ḥukūma al-Sirriyya fi Baritāniyā* ("The Secret Government in Britain"), translated from English, Dār al-Naṣr, Cairo, 1957, 108p. (see also Bibliographic appendix.)

161. Ṭabbāra, 'Afīf 'Abd al-Fattāḥ, *al-Yahūd fī al-Qur'ān* ("The Jews in the Quran"), Dār al-'Ilm lil-Malāyīn, Beirut, 1966, 239p.

162. Ṭah, Riyāḍ, *Filasṭīn al-Yawm Lā Ghadā* ("Palestine Today, Not Tomorrow"), Beirut (?), 1963, 98p.

163. Ṭā'i', Aḥmad Faraj, *Ṣafahāt Maṭwiyya 'an Filasṭīn* ("Forgotten Pages About Palestine"), The Arab Socialist Union, Dār Maṭābi' al-Sha'b (UAR), undated, 210p.

164. Talḥūq, Wadī', *al-Sabiyya al-Jadīda fī Filasṭīn* ("The New Crusade in Palestine") Maṭba'at al-Niḍāl, Damascus, 1948, 163p.

165. al-Tall, 'Abdallāh, *Filasṭīn wa-Ba'th al-Qawmiyya al-'Arabiyya* ("Palestine and the Revival of Arab Nationalism"), Kutub Qawmiyya, No. 29, Cairo, 3.11.1959, 45p.

166. al-Tall, 'Abdallāh, *Kārithat Filasṭīn* ("The Palestine Disaster"), Maṭba'at Miṣr, Cairo, 1959, 446p.

167. al-Tall, 'Abdallāh, *Khaṭr al-Yahūdiyya al-'Ālamiyya 'Alā al-Islām wa-al-Masihiyya* ("The Danger of World Jewry to Islam and Christianity"), Dār al-Qalam, Cairo, 1964, 414p. and index.

168. Tanī, Jāq, *al-Tābúr al-Khāmis li-Sahyún, Akhṭar Taqrīrāt 'An al-Ṣahyúniyya al-'Alamiyya* ("The Fifth Column in Zion, the Most Dangerous Resolutions of World Zionism"), translated from English, Kutub Siyāsiyya, No. 160, 2nd ed. 22.4.60, 78p.

169. Ṭarabin, Aḥmad, *Muḥāḍarāt fī Ta'rīkh Qaḍiyyat Filasṭīn Mundhu Nash'at al-Ḥaraka al-Ṣahyūniyya Ḥatta Nushūb al-Thawra al-Kubrā* ("Lectures on the Palestine Problem from the Beginning of the Zionist Movement until the Outbreak of the Great Revolt"), Institute For Advanced Arab Studies, the Arab League, 1959, 276p.

170. Tārū, Jīrūm and Jān [Tharaud, Jerome and Jean], *Sha'b Isrā'īl 'Indamā Yaḥkuma* ("The Israeli People When in Power"), translation Kutub Siyāsiyya, no. 30, Cairo, 28.9.1957, 76p., earlier translation by Yamin, Antun titled: *Idhā Malaka Isrā'īl* ("If Israel Ruled"). (see also: bibliographical addendum, a.)

171. al-Tūnisī, Muḥammad Khalīfa, *al-Khaṭr al-Yahūdī, Brūtūkālāt Hukamā' Ṣahyūn* ("The Jewish Danger, *the Protocols of the Elders of Zion"*) introduction: 'Aqqād, 'Abbās Maḥmūd, 3rd, ed., Maktabat Dār al-'Urūba, Cairo, 1961, 249p.

172. al-Tūnisī, Muḥammad Khalīfa, *ibid.* 4th ed., Dār al-Kitāb al-'Arabī, Beirut, undated, 233p. *Al-Anwār* of March 8, 1970, listed this work as a bestseller; this possibly indicates the issue of a fifth edition.

173. Wākīd, Muḥammad 'Aṭiyya, *Isrā'īl fī al-Mizān* ("Israel in the Balance"), Kutub Siyāsiyya, No. 103, Cairo, 12.4.1959, 78p.

174. Wākid, Muḥammad 'Aṭiyya, *Isrā'īl Wakr al-Isti'mār* ("Israel, the Den of Imperialism"), Kutub Siyāsiyya, No. 107, Cairo, 16.5. 1959, 62 p.

175. Wizārat al-Thaqāfa wa-al-Irshād (The Ministry of Education and Guidance), *Filasṭīn wa-al-Ghazū al-Tatarī al-Jadīd* ("Palestine and the New Tartar Invasion"), al-Silsila al-Siyāsiyya, No. 4, Baghdad 1964, 116 p.

176. Yamīn, al-Khūrī Anṭūn, *Mu'āmarat al-Yahūdiyya 'Alā al-Shu'ūb* ("The Conspiracy of Judaism Against the Nations"), a translation from the French of the *Protocols of the Elders of Zion* (see bibliographical addendum, b.)

177. al-Yawimyyāt al-Filasṭīniyya-1965 ("The Palestinian Year-Book") The Research Centre, The Palestine Liberation Organization, part 1:413 p.; Part 2:368 p., ed. Muṭlaq, Rafīq Ḥabīb, Beirut, Sept.–Dec. 1966.

178. Yūsuf (Naqīb, Captain), Nūr al-Dīn Muḥammad, *Isrā'īl Ṣanī'at al-Isti'mār* ("Israel, The Product of Imperialism"), Niḍāluna, No. 12, published by the Education Directorate of the Armed UAR Forces, Aug. 1964, 62p.

179. Zu'aytar, Akram, *al-Qaḍiyya al-Filasṭīniyya* ("The Palestine Problem"), Dār al-Ma'ārif, Cairo, 1955, 301 p.

180. al-Zu'bī, Muḥammad 'Ali, *Isrā'īl, Bint Bariṭāniyā al-Bikr* ("Israel, Britain's Firstborn Daughter"), al-Maktaba al-Sharqiyya, Cairo, undated, 191 p.

181. Zurayk [Zurayq], Constantine [Kunsṭanṭīn], *Ma'nā al-Nakba* ("The Meaning of Disaster"), Dār al-'Ilm lil-Malāyīn, Beirut, 1948, 87 p.

182. Zurayk [Zurayq], Constantine [Kunsṭanṭīn], *Ma'nā al-Nakba Mujaddad* ("The Meaning of Disaster Revised"), Dār al-'Ilm lil-Malāyīn, Beirut, 1967, 124p.

II. ENGLISH AND FRENCH SOURCES

1. King Abdallah, *My Memoirs Completed,* trans. H.W. Glidden, American Council of Learned Studies (Washington D.C., 1954).

2. Abdel-Kader, A.R. *Le conflit judéo-arabe, juifs et arabes face à l'avenir* (Paris, Francois Maspero, 1961).

3. Abdul Rahman, Asad, *United States and West German Aid to Israel,* tr. by L.S. Kadi, Facts and Figures Series, No. 6, Research Center, Palestine Liberation Organization (Beirut, October 1966).

4. Abi-Mershid, Walid, *Israel Withdrawal from Sinai,* The Institute for Palestine Studies, No. 1 (Beirut, 1966).

5. Afifi, Muhamed el-Hadi, *The Arabs and the United Nations* (London, Longmans, 1964).

6. Alami, Musa, "The Lesson of Palestine", *Middle East Journal,* Vol. 3 (Autumn 1949), pp. 373–405.

7. Berger, Morroe, *The Arab World* (London, Weidenfield & Nicolson, 1962).

8. Childers, E.B., "Palestine: the broken triangle," *Journal of International Affairs,* Vol 19, No. 1 (1965), pp. 87–100.

9. Childers E.B., *The Road to Suez* (London, Macgibbon & Kee, 1962).

10. Cohn Norman, *Warrant for Genocide, The myth of the Jewish world conspiracy and the Protocols of Zion* (London, Eyre & Spottiswoode, 1967).
11. Curtis, J.S., *An Appraisal of the Protocols of Zion* (Columbia University Press, 1942).
12. Darwazah, Alhakam, *A Short Survey of the Palestine Problem,* Facts & Figures Series, No. 7, Research Center, Palestine Liberation Organization (Beirut, November, 1966).
13. al-Faruki, Ismail Ragi A., *On Arabism, Urubah and Religion: A study of the fundamental Ideas of Arabism and of Islam as its Highest Moment of Consciousness* (Amsterdam, Djambatan, 1962).
14. Gabbay, R.E., *A Political Study of Arab Jewish Conflict: The Arab Refugee Problem* (Geneva, Librairie Droz, 1959).
15. Goitein, S.D., *Jews and Arabs, their Contact through Ages* (New York, Schocken, 1955, 1964).
16. Hadawi, Sami, "Israel's Sham Peace Offers", *Middle East Forum,* Feb.–Mar., 1964, pp. 27–29.
17. Hadawi, Sami, *United Nations Resolutions on Palestine 1947–1965.* Institute for Palestine Studies, No. 2 (Beirut, no date).
18. Haim, Sylvia, "Arabic Antisemitic Literature", *Jewish Social Studies,* Vol 17 (1955), pp. 307–312.
19. Haim, Sylvia, *Arab Nationalism: An Anthology* (University of California, 1962).
20. Hamady, S., *Temperament and Character of the Arabs* (New York, Twayne Publishers, 1960).
21. Hottinger, A., *The Arabs* (London, Thames and Hudson, 1963).
22. Iskandar, Marwan, *The Arab Boycott of Israel,* Palestine Monographs No. 6, Research Center, Palestine Liberation Organization (Beirut, November 1966).
23. Johnson, J.E., "Arab vs. Israeli: A Persistent Challenge", *Middle East Journal,* Vol. 18 (Winter 1964), pp. 1–13.
24. Jabara, Abdeen, M., *The Armistice in International Law and the Egyptian Search of Israel bound Cargo etc.,* Palestine Monographs, No. 2, Research Center, Palestine Liberation Organization (Beirut, June 1966).
25. Kadi, Leila S., *Arab Summit Conferences and the Palestine Problem: 1936–1950,* 1964–1966, Palestine Books No. 4, Research Center, Palestine Liberation Organization (Beirut 1966).
26. Karanjia, R.K., *The Arab Dawn* (Bombay, 1958B).
27. Kedouri, E., "Religion and Politics, The Diaries of Khalil Sakakini", *St. Antony Papers,* No. 4, Middle East Affairs, No. 1 (London, 1958).
28. al Khalidi, Walid, "Reappraisal, An Examination of Western Attitudes to the Palestine Problem", *Middle East Forum* (Summer 1958), pp. 18–22, 29.
"Why Did the Palestinians Leave?" *Middle East Forum* (July 1959), pp. 21–24, 35–37.
"The Fall of Haifa", *Middle East Forum* (December 1959), pp. 22–32.
Plan Dalet, the Zionist Master Plan for the Conquest of Palestine", *Middle East Forum* (November 1961), pp. 22–28.
29. Mandel, N., "Attempts at an Arab Zionist Entente: 1913–1914", *Middle East Studies,* Vol. 1, No. 3 (April 1965), pp. 238–267.
30. Mahamad, Fadhil Zaky, *Congress and Foreign Policy; A Case Study of the U.S. Congress in Shaping the American Stand towards Palestine,* Ministry of Culture and Guidance (Baghdad 1965).
31. Oron Y. (Ed.), *The Middle East Record,* Vols. 1–2, 1960–1961, Shiloah Research Center, Tel-Aviv.

32. Parkes, James, *Antisemitism* (London, Vallentine Mitchell, 1963).
33. Perlman, M., "Eleventh Century Andalusian Author on the Jews of Granada", *American Academy for Jewish Research,* Vol. 18 (1948–1949), pp. 269–290.
34. Perlman, M. (Trans. & Ed.) *Ifham el-Yahud,* American Academy for Jewish Research, Vol. 32 (1964).
35. Poliakov, L., *De Mohomiet aux Marranes* (Paris, Calman Lévy, 1961).
36. al Razzaz, Munif, *The Evolution of the Meaning of Nationalism* (N.Y., Doubleday, 1963).
37. Rosenblatt, Samuel, "The Jews in Islam" in: Pinson, K.S. (Ed.) *Essays on Antisemitism,* 2 Ed. (New York, Jewish Social Studies, 1946). pp. 111–120.
38. Rousan, Mahmoud, *Palestine and the Internationalization of Jerusalem,* Ministry of Culture and Guidance (Baghdad, 1965).
39. Sa'ab, Hasan, *Zionism and Racism,* Palestine Essays No. 2, Research Center, Palestine Liberation Organization (Beirut, December 1965).
40. Sayegh, Fayez E., *Understanding of the Arab Mind,* The Organization of the Arab Students in the United States, June 1953.
"The Encounter of Two Ideologies—Zionism and Arabism" in: *The Arab Nation, Paths Obstacles and Fulfilment* (Washington, The M.E. Institute, 1961), pp. 73–91.
The United Nations and the Palestine Question, April 1947—April 1965, Facts and Figures Series No. 2, Research Center, Palestine Liberation Organization (Beirut, May 1965).
Zionist Colonialism in Palestine, Palestine Monograph No. 1, Research Center, Palestine Liberation Organization (Beirut, September 1965).
Discrimination in Education against the Arabs in Israel, Facts and Figures Series No. 3, Research Center, Palestine Liberation Organization Beirut, September 1966).
41. Shouby, Eli, "The Influence of the Arabic Language on the Psychology of the Arabs", *Middle East Journal,* Vol. 5 (Summer 1951), pp. 284–302.
42. Shukairy, Ahmad, *Liberation not Negotiation,* Palestine Books No. 3, Research Center, Palestine Liberation Organization (Beirut, 1966).
43. Smith, W.C., *Islam in Modern History* (Princeton University Press, 1957).
44. Tannous, Izzat, *Tension and Peace in the Middle East,* The Palestine Arab Refugee Office (New York, May 1957).
45. Tibawi, A.L., "Visions of the Return, The Palestinian Refugees in Arabic Poetry and Art", *Middle East Journal,* Vol. 17 (Late Autumn 1963), pp. 507–526.
46. Vajda, G., "Juifs et musulmans selon le hadith", *Journal Asiatique,* 1937, pp. 57–127.
47. Zurayk, Constantine, *The Meaning of Disaster* (trans, by R.B. Winder), Khayat (Beirut, 1956).

III. GENERAL REFERENCE WORKS

1. Allport, G.W., The Nature of Prejudice (New York, Doubleday Anchor, 1958).
2. Aron, R., *Paix et Guerre entre les Nations* (Paris, Calman Lévy, 1962).
3. Aron, R., "Conflict and War from the Viewpoint of Historical Sociology" in: *The Nature of Conflict* (Paris, Unesco, 1957), pp. 177–203.
4. Berkowitz, L., *Aggression: A Social Psychological Approach* (McGraw Hill, 1962).
5. Bernard, J., "The Sociological Study of Conflict" in: *The Nature of Conflict* (Paris, Unesco, 1957), pp. 64–73, 100–102.
6. Boulding, K.E., *Conflict and Defense: A General Theory* (Harper & Bros., 1962; or Harper Torch Books, 1963).

7. Bramson, L. and Goethals, G.W. (Eds.), *War: Studies from Psychology, Sociology, Anthropology* (Basic Books, 1964).
8. Brown, J.A.C., *Techniques of Persuasion* (Penguin, 1963).
9. Coser, L., *The Social Functions of Social Conflict* (Free Press, 1956: Collier Macmillan, 1964).
10. Dollard, J. et al., *Frustration and Aggression* (New Haven, Yale University Press, 1939, 1961).
11. Faris, R.E.L., "Interaction Levels and Intergroup Relations" in: Sherif, M. (Ed.), *Intergroup Relations and Leadership* (New York, Wiley, 1962), pp. 24–45.
12. Fisher, R. (Ed.) *International Conflict and Behavioral Sciences: The Craegville Papers* (Basic Books, 1964).
13. Hoffmann, S.H., *Contemporary Theory in International Relations* (Prentice Hall Inc., 1960).
14. Isaacs, H.R., *Scratches on Our Minds: American Images of China and India* (New York, John Day, 1958).
15. Jahoda, M. & Warren, N. (Eds.), *Attitudes* (Penguin Modern Psychological Readings, 1966).
16. Katz, D., "The Functional Approach to the Study of Attitudes", *Public Opinion Quarterly*, Vol. 24 (1960), pp. 163–204.
17. Kelman, H.C. (Ed.), *International Behavior: A Social-Psychological Analysis* (Holt, Rinehart and Winston, 1965).
18. Klineberg, O., *The Human Dimension in International Relations* (Holt, Rinehart and Winston, 1964).
19. Krech, D., Crutchfield, R.S., *The Theory and Problems of Social Psychology* (McGraw Hill, 1948).
20. Krech, D., Crutchfield, R.S. & Ballachy, E.L., *Individual in Society* (McGraw Hill, Kogakusha, 1962).
21. Lane, R.E., *Political Ideology: Why the American Common Man Believers What He Does* (New York, Free Press, 1962).
22. Lane, R.E. & Sears, D.O., *Public Opinion* (Englewood Cliffs, Prentice Hall, Inc., 1964).
23. Lewin, K., *Resolving Social Conflict* (New York, Harper, 1948).
24. Maccoby, E., Newcomb, T.M. & Hartley, E.L. (Eds.), *Readings in Social Psychology*, 3rd Edition (Holt, Rinehart & Winston, 1958).
25. McNeil, E.B. (Ed.), *The Nature of Human Conflict* (Englewood Cliffs, Prentice Hall Inc., 1965).
26. Rapoport, A., *Fights, Games and Debates* (Ann Arbor, The University of Michigan Press, 1960).
27. Schelling, T.C., *The Strategy of Conflict* (Cambridge, Harvard University Press, 1960).
28. Singer, J.D. (Ed.), *Human Behavior and International Politics* (Chicago, Rand MacNally, 1965).
29. Sperrazzo, G. (Ed.), *Psychology and International Relations* (Georgetown University Press, 1965).
30. Waltz, K., *Man, the State and War* (New York, Columbia University Press, 1959).
31. Wright, Quincy et al. (Eds.), *Preventing World War III: Some Proposals* (New York, Simon & Schuster, 1962).

IV. BIBLIOGRAPHICAL APPENDIX

Translations of the Protocols of the Elders of Zion

1. Yamīn, al-Khūrī Anṭūn, *Mu'āmarat al-Yahūdiyya 'Alā al Shu'ūb au Maḍābit al-Jalsāt al-Sirriyya li-Ḥukamā' Isrā'il* (The Conspiracy of Judaism against the Nations, or the Protocols of the Secret Meetings of the Elders of Israel) 288p. No date, probably second half of twenties. Translated from the French version of "La Vieille France."
2. Zurayk, Frederick, *Ahdāf al-Ṣahyūniyya* (The Goals of Zionism) printed by Jamiyyat al-Tamaddun al-Islāmī (described by Mrs. Silvia Haim).
3. al-Tunisī, Muhammad Khalīfa, *al-Khaṭr al-Yahūdī, Brūtūkūlāt Hukamā' Sahyūn* (The Jewish Danger, the Protocols of the Elders of Zion). Translated from Briton's English edition. First Edition, Dār al-Kitāb al-'Arabī, Cairo 1951, 180 pp. A long introduction Second edition as the first.

   Third edition, Dār al-'Urūba, Cairo 1961, 249 pp. An Introduction by 'Abbās Mahmūd al-'Aqqād, his article from the newspaper "al-Asās" of 23.11.51. The translator's introduction dated 16.3.61 was enlarged.

   Fourth edition, Dar al-Kitābal-'Arabī Beirut, undated, 223 pp. including Introductions as in the third edition.

   The Lebanese newspaper *al-Anwār* of March 8, 1970 placed this book as first in the list of nonfiction best-sellers. It seems that it refers to a new edition or new reprint.
4. *al-Ṣahyūniyya Sāfira, Muqarrāt al-Yahūd* (Zionism Unveiled, the Resolutions of the Jews"), Introduction dated August 1951 signed by al-Fuqi, Ahmad Ḥāmid, Cairo, 232 pp. Yamīn's version.
5. *Brūtūkūl Ḥukamā' Sahyūn* (The Protocol of the Elders of Zion), Kutub Siyāsiyya, No. 5, Cairo 13.4.57, 119p.
6. Nasim, Māhir, *al-Shuyú 'iyya wa-al Ṣahyuniyya* ("Communism and Zionism"), al-Maktaba al-Dawliyya, No. 1, Dār al-Ma'ārif, Cairo 1959, 191p. Text like that of Kutab Siyāsiyya.
7. Abū al-Rus, Iliya, *al-Yahudiyya al-'Alāmiyya wa-harbuha al-Mustmirr 'ala al-Masiḥiyya,* Beirut 1964 pp. 191–273 includes Tūnisi's version.
8. Nuwaihiḍ, 'Ajjaj, Brūtūkūlāt Hukama' Sahy (Protocols of Elders of Zion). Two Volumes, No. 1, 309 pp.; No. 2, 303 pp. Beirut 1967. Translated from the Briton's Marsden version. Nuwaihiḍ was Director of the Arabic department of the broadcasting station in Jerusalem 1940–1944.
9. Shauqī 'abd al-Nāṣir (President Nasser's brother), *Brūtūkūlāt Hukamma' Ṣahyun wa-ta'alīm al-Talmūd* ("Protocols of the Elders of Zion and the Precepts of the Talmud"), al-Tiba'a al-Thaniyya, no date (but as *al-Nahar* of 9.5.68 announced the publication of this book it seems that the date is 1968), 232 pp.

INDEX OF NAMES